The Sunwoman in the Wilderness

The Religious Beliefs and Practices of George Rapp's Harmony Society

The Asbury Theological Seminary Series in Pietist/Wesleyan Studies

Alice T. Ott

EMETH PRESS
www.emethpress.com

The Sunwoman in the Wilderness:
The Religious Beliefs and Practices of
George Rapp's Harmony Society

Copyright © 2014 Alice T. Ott
Printed in the United States of America on acid-free paper

All rights reserved. No part of this book may be reproduced, or stored in a retrieval system or transmitted in any form or by any means, electronic, mechanical, photocopying, recording, scanning or otherwise, except as permitted by the 1976 United States Copyright Act, or with the prior written permission of Emeth Press. Requests for permission should be ad- dressed to: Emeth Press, P. O. Box 23961, Lexington, KY 40523-3961. http://www.emethpress.com.

Library of Congress Cataloging-in-Publication Data

Ott, Alice T.
  The Sunwoman in the Wilderness : the religious beliefs and practices of George Rapp's Harmony Society / Alice T. Ott.
       pages cm. -- (Asbury Theological Seminary Series in Pietist/Wesleyan Studies)
  Includes bibliographical references.
  ISBN 978-1-60947-072-2 (alk. paper)
  1. Rapp, George, 1757-1847--Religion. 2. Harmony Society--Doctrines. I. Title.
  HX656.H2O88 2013
  230'.99--dc23
                           2013045752

The photo on the front cover is courtesy of PHMC: Old Economy Village.

Contents

List of Figures / ix

Acknowledgements / xi

1. Introduction / 1

    Interpretations of Rapp and the Harmony Society / 3
    What is Pietism? / 11
    Primary Sources relating to Rapp
       and the Harmony Society / 15
    Chapter Overview / 18
    Relationship with the American Historical
       and Religious Context / 20

2. Separation from Babel (1785-1800) / 29

    Rapp's Separatist Movement in Context / 29
    Early Life and Conversion of Johann Georg Rapp / 41
    Separation from the Lutheran Church / 45
    Formation of the Rapp's Separatist Movement / 48
    Early Religious Beliefs and Practices
       of the Separatist Movement / 51

3. Beholding the Godhead (1790-1800) / 67

    George Rapp's Pastoral Letters (1791-1802) / 67
    Influence of Tersteegen's Mysticism within Württemberg
       Pietism and on Rapp's Separatist Movement / 70
    George Rapp's Steps to the Mystical Union with God / 81

4. The Flight of the Sunwoman (1800-1805) / 95

    From Conventicles to Church / 96
    Johann Georg Rapp as Prophet / 98

    Reasons for Emigration / 103
    Prior and Contemporary Pietist Interpretations
       of the Sunwoman and Her Flight / 106
    Rappite Interpretation of the Sunwoman
       and Her Flight / 116
    Immigration to America / 126

5. Church in the Wilderness (1805-1825) / 129

    History of the Harmony Society (1805-1825) / 130
    Communalism and the Harmony Society / 132
    Revival of 1807-1808 and the Adoption of Celibacy / 143
    The Church in the Wilderness / 154

6. Labyrinths, Grottoes, and Decorative Art (1805-1830) / 175

    Harmonist Material Culture / 176
    Mystical-Theosophical Beliefs: The Sophia Lintel / 178
    Striving for Sanctification: The Labyrinth and Grotto / 195
    Millennial Beliefs: The Golden Rose Lintel / 207

7. Learning in the School of the Holy Spirit (1830-1847) / 215

    George Rapp's Sermons / 217
    Two Trajectories in Rapp's Theology / 220
    Core Reformation Doctrines / 222
    Churchly Pietist Emphases / 230
    "Anabaptist" Ecclesiology / 241

8. The Quest for "Deeper Knowledge" (1825-1847) / 253

    Allegorical Scriptural Hermeneutic / 255
    Cabbalistic and Theosophical Descriptions
       of God and Man / 262
    Alchemistical Practice and Language / 279

9. Yearning for the Eschaton (1824-1847) / 295

    History of the Harmony Society in the
       Economy Era (1824-1847) / 299
    Rapp's Eschatological Presuppositions
       and Approach / 303
    The Progression of Eschatological Events
       in Rapp's Theology / 315

10. Conclusion / 335
Biblical-Eschatological and Mystical-Spiritual
   Trajectories / 337
Boehmist Influence / 344
Importance of the German Religious
   and Historical Background / 346
Sectarian Spirit / 347

Appendicies
A. Manuscript Collections of George Rapp's
    Pastoral Letters / 349
B. Poems by Gottfried Arnold Included in the 1820
    and 1827 *Gesangbücher* / 351
C. Comparison of Rapp Sermon and Arnold's
    Divine Sophia / 353
D. Bible Texts Given for Sermons Transcribed
    in 1838 Sermon Book / 355
E. Comparison of Rapp Sermon and
    Oetinger's *Lehrtafel* / 357
F. Rapp's Interpretation of the Trumpet and
    Bowl Judgments (1824) / 361

Bibliography / 363

List of Figures

1. Primary Sources with Theological Content / 17
2. Photograph of J. W. Petersen's *Das Geheimniß des in der letzten Zeit gebährenden Apocalyptischen Weibes* / 108
3. Photograph of Sophia Lintel, Harmony, Pennsylvania / 180
4. Photograph of Reconstructed Labyrinth, New Harmony, Indiana / 197
5. Photograph of Grotto, Economy, Pennsylvania / 204
6. Photograph of Grotto Interior Economy, Pennsylvania / 206
7. Photograph of Golden Rose Lintel, New Harmony, Indiana / 208
8. Outline of Eschatological Events / 317

Acknowledgements

This volume is a revised and updated version of my PhD doctoral dissertation, which was accepted by Trinity Evangelical Divinity School, Deerfield Illinois in October 2007. The extensive research that this volume required would not have been possible without the helpful assistance of a number of individuals and organizations. I am grateful to the Pennsylvania Historical and Museum Commission for financial assistance during my tenure in 2005-2006 as Scholar in Residence at Old Economy Village, site of the Harmony Society archives. Many thanks go to Sarah Buffington, Curator II at Old Economy Village, for her tireless help in locating and retrieving manuscripts for my use, and to Mary Ann Landis, Site Administrator, for her willingness to interact on my research. Hermann Ehmer of the Landeskirchliches Archiv in Stuttgart graciously read and provided helpful feedback on several chapters of the volume, as did Steven O'Malley of Asbury Theological Seminary during the dissertation phase and later as editor of this volume. My doctoral mentor, Douglas Sweeney, spent numerous hours reading and discussing with me aspects of my research. My research benefited from his insightful comments, as well as those of the other members of the dissertation committee, John Woodbridge and Jeff Bach. Last but not least, I am grateful to my husband, Craig Ott, for his love and constant encouragement during the time of my research and writing.

Alice T. Ott
Deerfield, Illinois

1

Introduction

The eighteenth and the first half of the nineteenth centuries were marked by a unique phenomenon in American religious history: the formation of utopian communes. Some of these were secular in character, formed with the desire to create a perfect world order through economic cooperation.[1] The longest lasting and most successful, however, were the religiously motivated communes. Of these, the Harmony Society formed by George Rapp is among the best-known.

Johann Georg Rapp was born 1757 in the village of Iptingen in the duchy of Württemberg, Germany. Though raised and confirmed in the Lutheran Church, it was only through contact with churchly and radical Pietists that Rapp, a weaver by trade, experienced a spiritual conversion in 1782.[2] He officially broke away from the established church three years later, "because I needed nothing else since I had found Jesus."[3] Like other radical Pietists, Rapp criticized sharply the state Lutheran church and its rites. The pastors were hypocritical, were ignorant of the deeper meaning of the Bible. The Lord's Supper was a travesty, for it was distributed to those who were not "born again." Rapp lambasted it as "idol worship," other Separatists as *Schmierkäs* and *Streichpflaster*, two terms that emphasized the superficial nature of the Lord's Supper.[4] Likewise, baptism as practiced by the Luthe-

---

[1] Muncy divides utopian settlements in the nineteenth century into three types: (1) sectarian or religiously motivated; (2) reform communities, which were secular and idealistic; and (3) purely economic cooperatives. Raymond Lee Muncy, *Sex and Marriage in Utopian Communities. 19th Century America* (Bloomington, Ind.: Indiana University Press, 1973), 3.

[2] See definitions of churchly and radical Pietism below under "What is Pietism?" p. 12f.

[3] Karl Arndt, *George Rapp's Separatists, 1700-1803. A Documentary History* (Worcester, Mass.: Harmony Society Press, 1980), 73.

[4] Arndt, *Doc. Hist. 1700-1803*, 79, 82 and 118. These terms are literally translated as "spreadable cheese" and as "a bandage spread (on the skin)."

ran church was not only meaningless, but impious unless the person had previously experienced the new birth. Rapp's separation from the established Church was marked by his rejection of its worship services, sacraments, clergy and, to a certain extent, its theology.

Within just a few years Rapp became the most important Separatist leader in Württemberg, with a following numbering anywhere from 3,000 (Fritz) to 12,000 persons (Arndt), and with contacts to groups outside the duchy.[5] The social and political situation certainly contributed to this phenomenon, as did the relative tolerance of the government to separatistic groups.[6] The situation changed considerably at the turn of the century. The ducal government developed more absolutist designs and a hard line was taken against the Separatists. Rightly fearing persecution, Rapp, in the summer of 1803, sold his entire property in Iptingen and made plans to immigrate to America along with a group of approximately 700 followers. This separatist group, which in America took the name Harmony Society, flourished economically and spiritually in each of the group's three locations: in Harmony, Pennsylvania (1804-1814), New Harmony, Indiana (1814-1824) and Economy, Pennsylvania (1824-1905).

Rapp gave a theological justification for emigration to America. The group understood itself to be the Sunwoman of Rev 12:6, who fled into the wilderness of America to await the imminent return of Christ, expected to occur in their lifetime. They modeled their communal living on the ideals found in Acts 2 and 4, thus exhibiting a form of primitivism popular among radical Pietists.[7] The members eagerly read their Luther or Berleburg

---

[5] Fritz, *Radikaler Pietismus in Württemberg* (Epfendorf/Neckar: Bibliotheca academica Verlag, 2003), 58-59 and 134. Karl Arndt, *George Rapp's Harmony Society 1785-1847*, rev. ed. (Teaneck, N.J.: Fairleigh Dickinson University Press, 1972), 61. Fritz's estimate is to be preferred.

[6] The military engagement in the Seven Years War resulted in crisis situations politically and economically, as did the steady rise in population. The suffering peasants increasingly turned for comfort to the heart religion of Pietism and ideals of millenarianism. Karl J. R. Arndt, "George Rapp's Harmony Society," in *America's Communal Utopias*, ed. Donald E. Pitzer (Chapel Hill, N.C.: University of North Carolina Press, 1997), 57-87, here 57.

[7] Littell applied the typology of literary primitivism ("myth of the glorious past") to the "radical Christian dissent" of the Anabaptists, Gottfried Arnold, Radical Pietists and others. The author will be using the following definition of primitivism: "The New Testament church was the normative, indeed the Golden Age of Christianity . . . They [the sectarians] saw their own movement as a recovery of a spiritual power and life style that had been lost following the apostolic age. The vision of the distant past provided, in short, the program for the future: a Restitution of the true church." Littell, "Radical Pietism," 166. Hughes and Allen likewise stress the prevalence of primitivism/restorationism in American culture and its connection to millennialism. Richard T. Hughes and Crawford Leonard Allen, *Illusions of Innocence: Protestant Primitivism in America, 1630-1875* (Chicago: University of Chicago Press, 1988), 2-3 and Richard T. Hughes, *The American Quest for the Primitive Church* (Urbana, Ill.: University of Illinois Press, 1988), 12-14.

Bibles and other devotional material, in order to attain a holy, righteous life.[8] The quietistic mysticism of Gerhard Tersteegen with its emphasis on self-denial and submission to God's will was central to their striving for sanctification. Further, the group appropriated a fair measure of Boehmist-inspired doctrine in their cosmogony and anthropology, and to a lesser degree in their Sophialogy. A thorough examination of the religious history and beliefs of George Rapp and the Harmony Society reveals, however, that the Harmonists were not most significantly defined by their Boehmist cosmogony and anthropology as some scholars claim. A sizable core of orthodox Lutheran beliefs remained intact. Rather, two broad categories or trajectories of divergent influences helped to shape Rapp's mature theology, as reflected in his sermons preached in the last two decades of his life (ca. 1830-1847). The first trajectory is biblical-eschatological, and includes core Reformation doctrine, churchly Pietist emphases, "Anabaptist" ecclesiology, and millennialism; the second trajectory is mystical-spiritual, found in an allegorical biblical hermeneutic, Quietistic mysticism, Sophialogy, theosophical, and cabbalistic emphases.

The religious emphases within the two trajectories were not strictly original with the Harmonists. Rather, they were found in differing blends repeatedly among radical Pietists and Separatists in Rapp's homeland of Württemberg. Although the eclectic elements which made up the religious beliefs and practices of George Rapp's Separatist movement and of the Harmony Society under his leadership (1785-1847) were not strictly speaking original to them, their unique mixture of orthodox Lutheran and churchly and radical Pietist emphases found in Württemberg was distinctive. To understand properly Harmonist religious beliefs, they must be examined primarily against the formative backdrop of the Pietist context in Württemberg and, only to a lesser degree, of the religious scene in the United States. This explains the heavy preponderance of German-language research on Pietism, which undergirds this volume.

Interpretations of Rapp and the Harmony Society

When one approaches the topic of the religious beliefs and practices of George Rapp and the Harmony Society, one is struck by the paucity of modern comprehensive studies. Scholarship on the Harmony Society consists for the most part merely of sections in books dealing with multiple Christian sects. The focus is generally on its social structure rather than on its

---

[8]The Berleburg Bible is an eight volume, revised Luther translation of the Bible, published in Berleburg, Germany (1726-42), with commentary influenced by the Philadelphian movement.

religious beliefs.⁹ The few theological treatments are likewise brief and not comprehensive.¹⁰ Ehmer dedicated a short section of his article on Rapp to his theology.¹¹ Durnbaugh and Littell each published articles in which they discuss the whole span of radical Pietist communes in America in little more than twenty pages.¹² Eberhard Fritz's monograph includes a lengthy section on Rapp as the primary Separatist leader in Württemberg during the third chronological era of Fritz's proposed five periods or phases.¹³ His social historical account, however, does not treat the theological beliefs of the group, either in this monograph or in his numerous articles, in anything but a cursory manner.

Karl Arndt, the chief historian of the Harmony Society, wrote two monographs and several articles on the group. He also published eight volumes of its documentary history. The monographs are primarily narrative history, depicting the group from its inception to its demise (1785-1905) in a detailed and thorough fashion. His volumes of documentary history are likewise an invaluable contribution for scholars studying the group. Arndt spent literally thousands of hours collecting manuscripts and deciphering and translating the Gothic German handwriting, a difficult task due to the non-standard, Swabian dialect and the often obscure, mystically-tinged language which was employed. His theological interpretation of the Society's beliefs uses the prevailing theological paradigm of Boehmism, which will be discussed more fully below.¹⁴ Although Arndt claims to aim for neutrality in

---

⁹Examples are Raymond Lee Muncy, *Sex and Marriage in Utopian Communities: 19th Century America* (Bloomington, Ind.: Indiana University Press, 1973); Robert P. Sutton, *Communal Utopias and the American Experience: Religious Communities, 1732-2000* (Westport: Praeger, 2003); and Hermann Schempp, *Gemeinschaftssiedlungen auf religiöser und weltanschaulicher Grundlage* (Tübingen: Mohr, 1969).

¹⁰Gladys Inez Seagle's dissertation, "The Rappite Revolt against Lutheranism, 1804-1904" (Ph.D. diss., New York University, 1963), does deal somewhat more comprehensively with Harmonist religious beliefs (one chapter is devoted to this topic). Her work, therefore, does not adequately discuss the full-spectrum of Rappist religious beliefs. Their eschatology and primitivism, for instance, are only briefly examined. She did not utilize Rapp's sermons and other theological sources at all.

¹¹Hermann Ehmer, "Johann Georg Rapp (1757-1847)," in *Kirchengeschichte Württembergs in Porträts: Pietismus und Erweckungsbewegung* (Holzgerlingen: Hänssler Verlag, 2001), 219-243.

¹² Donald F. Durnbaugh, "Radikaler Pietismus als Grundlage deutschamerikanischer kommunaler Siedlungen," *Pietismus und Neuzeit* 16 (1990): 112-131 and Littell, "Radical Pietism," 164-183.

¹³Fritz, *Radikaler Pietismus*, 122f.

¹⁴Boehmism refers to the distinctive teachings of the theosophist, Jakob Boehme (1575-1624), a shoemaker and visionary-mystic in Görlitz, Schlesien. He strongly criticized the orthodox Lutheran church, which he called "Babel," although he remained a member of that confession throughout his life. In his theosophy he attempted to describe the secret of the self-movements within the Godhead. God was an eternally-conceiving power. Alongside the divine Trinity of Father, Son and Holy

his account, to let the documents speak for themselves, his documentary histories are laced with negative commentary.[15] He speaks of Rapp's "moral inconsistency" and his "fanaticism and greed." Rapp was not a "warm-hearted Christian," rather his mind was "clouded by religious mysticism" and "chilled by Swabian avarice."[16]

In spite of their contribution, the documentary histories omit a large number of theologically significant texts. The eight volumes, which in total number over seven thousand pages, include hundreds of pages documenting the Society's economic endeavors and legal battles with disgruntled former members. Arndt chose, however, to omit certain key theological documents. Only nineteen of the thirty-eight pastoral letters written between 1791 and 1802 by Rapp to members of the Separatist group in Württemberg are included. These letters, according to Ehmer, provide an especially valuable window to Rapp's theology, since they were not written for publication, but for the internal edification of the group.[17] Gladys Seagle considers Rapp's sixty-page pamphlet, *Thoughts on the Destiny of Man*, published in 1824, to be "the most definitive statement of Rappist belief." She finds there evidence of continuity with Lutheran teaching, although typical Boehmist thought (e.g. androgynous nature of God and Adam) is "strangely absent."[18] Yet Arndt included only a small, two-page excerpt of the pamphlet. The few hymns written by Rapp and Harmony Society members which are included in the documentary histories tend to reflect Boehmist themes. However, the topical divisions of the *Harmonisches Gesangbuch* from 1820 evidence many orthodox Lutheran doctrines as well.[19] Finally, Arndt included only five of the 170 sermons in the 1838 sermon book and none of Rapp's sermon notes, because he claimed they are written in a mystical

---

Spirit, a fourth Being, the heavenly Sophia took her place as a personification of the divine wisdom. Based primarily on passages in the book of Proverbs, Sophia incorporated the feminine principle in God, so that God in effect was androgynous, as was Adam before the Fall. The Gnostic "myth" of an androgynous Adam became central to Boehme's theosophy. Ehmer, "Rapp," 225. Cf. Andrew Weeks, *Boehme. An Intellectual Biography of the Seventeenth-Century Philosopher and Mystic* (Albany, NY: State University of New York Press, 1991).

[15]"Gerade weil der Haß gegen Rapps Führung von außen gesehen so glühend war wie die Liebe zu ihm im Innersten der Gesellschaft, wollen wir uns in dieser Geschichte auf Dokumente stützen." Karl J. R. Arndt, *Harmony on the Connoquenessing 1803-1815. A Documentary History* (Worcester, Mass.: Harmony Society Press, 1980), xxxiv.

[16]Arndt, *Doc. Hist. 1803-1815*, 303, 173 and xiii.

[17]Ehmer, "Rapp," 225.

[18]Seagle, "Rappist Revolt," 2 and 134.

[19]There are sections on the incarnation of Christ, His passion and death, His resurrection, faith, spiritual battle and victory, love of Christ, devotional songs, etc. Richard D. Wetzel, *Frontier Musicians on the Connoquenessing, Wabash, and Ohio: A History of the Music and Musicians of George Rapp's Harmony Society, 1805-1906* (Athens, Ohio: Ohio University Press, 1976), 47-48.

style of language difficult to understand.[20] These sermons, however, would enable the researcher to ascertain the main tenets of Harmonist religious beliefs. Most scholars have relied on Arndt's documentary histories for their primary sources of the Harmony Society. Therefore, it is understandable that his emphases have been perpetuated.

The historiography concerning George Rapp reflects the prevailing view that the sources of his theology are to be located primarily in the works of Jakob Boehme. Emanuel Hirsch, in his *Geschichte der neuern evangelischen Theologie*, made a sharp divide between the churchly Pietism rooted in Spener, and radical Pietism, which he viewed as a *schwärmerisch* (fanatical) side movement of the Pietistic era with a different genealogy than churchly Pietism. Radical Pietism, according to Hirsch, had its roots in the writings of Jakob Boehme, whose influence was to be found "with amazing regularity" in their works and which gave to the movement its homogeneous character.[21] This approach was picked up several years later by Chauncey D. Ensign in his 1955 dissertation, "Radical German Pietism," which claimed Boehmism as a "unifying principle" in radical Pietism.[22]

Most likely following the lead of Emanuel Hirsch, Karl Arndt, as we have seen, likewise stresses Boehmist influence on Rapp and the Harmony Society. This is not to say that he entirely ignores other sources of Rapp's theology. In his monograph, *George Rapp's Harmony Society*, he points to the influence of the Berleburg Bible.[23] In his article with the same title he lists, besides Boehme, a number of other sources of influence.[24] Nevertheless, when making summary statements in the volumes of the documentary histories, stress on Boehmist influence predominates. For instance, Arndt refers to the faith of the Harmonists as "this Boehmist, biblical faith" (*diesen [Jacob!] boehmisch-biblischen Glaube*) and of the "strong influence of Jacob Boehme on Rapp's preaching."[25]

Other contemporary scholars have likewise stressed the Boehmist connection. The American historian of the Church of the Brethren, Donald Durnbaugh, in an article on radical Pietist communes in America (1990), concludes that Boehme's influence on the Harmonists, though not the only influence (earlier mystics and Boehme's interpreters are likewise listed)

---

[20] Karl J. R. Arndt, *George Rapp's Years of Glory. Economy on the Ohio 1834-1847. George Rapp's Third Harmony. A Documentary History* (New York: Peter Lang, 1987), 1028.

[21] Emanuel Hirsch, *Geschichte der neuern evangelischen Theologie*, vol. 2 (Gütersloh: C. Bertelsmann, 1951), 208-255, here 208-209.

[22] Chauncey D. Ensign, "Radical German Pietism (c. 1675-c. 1760)" (Ph.D. diss., Boston University, 1955), 16.

[23] Arndt, *Harmony Society*, 416-419.

[24] Arndt mentions Johann Valentin Andreae's *Christianopolis*, Johann Herder, Johann Tauler, Emanuel Swedenborg and Christoph Schütz. Arndt, "Harmony Society," 60-61.

[25] Arndt, *Doc. Hist, 1803-1815*, xxxix and Arndt, *Doc. Hist, 1700-1803*, 242.

was nevertheless primary.[26] A. Gregg Roeber in his chapter on Pietism in North America in the multi-volume set *Geschichte des Pietismus* (1995) likewise notes the Boehmist connection. He not only states that the Harmonists were strongly influenced by Boehme; he mentions no other source of influence.[27] Hermann Ehmer (2001) references Hirsch's *Geschichte* when pointing to the influence of Boehme's mysticism, Sophia-speculation, and concept of the new birth on Rapp's writings.[28] Finally, Eberhard Fritz (2003) asserts that of the Separatist works used by Rapp's disciples, the works of Boehme are of first importance, for "the interaction with the theosophical thought of Boehme was of fundamental importance to Württemberg Separatism."[29] Though most scholars are careful to nuance their views and allow for other sources of influence on Rapp's theology, it is apparent that Boehmist influence is primarily stressed.

Not all scholars have accepted Hirsch's theological interpretation of radical Pietism as centered in Boehmism. Franklin Littell points rather to the radical eschatology of Pietist sectarians.[30] Ernest Stoeffler admits that Boehmism is important in radical Pietism. Nevertheless, he qualifies this assertion: "It would seem, however, that by focusing almost exclusively upon Boehmism, E. Hirsch tends to over-state the Boehmist influence...."[31] Professor Hans Schneider likewise questions whether Boehmism truly is the dominant, integrating factor of radical Pietism.[32]

One negative result of overemphasizing Boehmism, whether among the Harmonists or other radical Pietist groups, is that other important sources of influence on their religion tend to fade into the background. This is a

---

[26]Durnbaugh, "Radikaler Pietismus," 113.

[27]"Ursprünglich aus dem Württembergischen kommend und nochmals von Vorstellungen Jakob Böhmes geprägt, verkörperte die in New Harmony (Indiana) und in Pennsylvanien entstehende Gemeinschaft diese antiweltliche, antileibliche pietistische Strömung." A. Gregg Roeber, "Der Pietismus in Nordamerika im 18. Jahrhundert," in *Geschichte des Pietismus*, vol. 2, *Der Pietismus im achtzehnten Jahrhundert*, ed. Martin Brecht and Klaus Deppermann (Gottingen: Vandenhoeck & Rupprecht, 1995), 666-699, here 698.

[28]Ehmer, "Rapp," 222-226.

[29]"An erster Stelle stehen die Werke von Jakob Böhme. Die Auseinandersetzung mit den theosophischen Gedanken Böhmes gehörte zum Grundanliegen des württembergischen Separatismus." Fritz, *Radikaler Pietismus*, 271.

[30]Franklin Littell, "Radical Pietism in American History," in *Continental Pietism and Early American Christianity*, ed. F. Ernest Stoeffler (Grand Rapids, Mich.: Eerdmans, 1976), 167.

[31]F. Ernest Stoeffler, *German Pietism during the Eighteenth Century* (Leiden: E. J. Brill, 1973), 169, n. 2.

[32]"Ist der Einfluß Boehmes wirklich *die* dominierende und integrierende Kraft, die dem radikalen Pietismus seine gewisse Geschlossenheit verleiht oder ist hier nicht eine stärkere Vielfalt von Traditionen zu berücksichtigen?" Hans Schneider, "Der radikale Pietismus in der neueren Forschung," *Pietismus und Neuzeit* 8 (1982): 15-42 and 9 (1983): 117-151.

grave danger, as the risk of a skewed interpretation is large. Rapp and the Harmony Society were influenced by a broad number of eclectic sources, of which Boehmist influence was but one. This is not to say that other radical Pietist groups were not most significantly influenced by Jacob Boehme,[33] nor that Boehmist influence on the Harmony Society was negligible, merely that it has been often overstressed. The contribution of the theosophical philosopher from Görlitz on the Harmonists was limited for the most part to their cosmological, anthropological and Sophialogical beliefs, although these aspects admittedly impacted tangentially several other elements of their religious beliefs. Boehmist beliefs, though important, were but a few aspects of the distinctive blend of orthodox Lutheran and (often heterodox) radical Pietist emphases that made up the Harmonist religion.[34] The Harmony Society's defining beliefs were not found exclusively or primarily in the cosmogony of Jakob Boehme, but in core Reformation doctrine and in other distinctive emphases of churchly and radical Pietism. The roots of Harmonist eschatology, which were so central to their religious beliefs, were not Boehmist. Rather, their pedigree was linked to a Württemberg tradition of millenarianism, which claimed Johann Albrecht Bengel (and to a lesser degree Philipp Jakob Spener) as its founding father, and which continued to develop among Bengel's Pietist followers in the following decades.[35] Harmonist views of sanctification were strongly shaped by a Tersteegian brand of quietistic mysticism, which was popular in Pietist circles in Württemberg. Rapp depended primarily on Friedrich Christoph Oetinger's use of cabbalistic concepts to describe the Godhead, not Boehme. Harmonist Sophialogy was influenced as strongly by Gottfried Arnold as it was by the Görlitz theosophist.[36]

American scholars have tended to neglect the religious and historical background of Harmonist beliefs in radical and churchly Pietism in Württemberg. Karl Arndt, the chief historian of the group, failed to link

---

[33] Jeff Bach in *Voices of the Turtledoves: The Sacred World of Ephrata* (University Park, Pa.: Pennsylvania State University Press, 2003), and Joachim Trautwein in *Die Theosophie Michael Hahns und ihre Quellen* (Stuttgart: Calwer Verlag, 1969), have both cogently argued for the prominent role of Boehme on the radical Pietists they studied, the Ephrata Cloister and Michael Hahn.

[34] Schneider, in his historiographical survey, notes that the roots of radical Pietism in the Reformation churchly tradition have largely been ignored. Rather scholarship has focused on establishing the heterodox elements of the movement. "Die bisherige Forschung hat sich zumeist um den Nachweis heterodoxer Einflüsse im Radikalpietismus bemüht, dem Nachweis einer reformatorisch-kirchlichen Erbmasse aber weit weniger Beachtung geschenkt." Schneider, "Der radikale Pietismus in der neueren Forschung," 141.

[35] The influence of Spener on Bengel is discussed in chapter nine.

[36] Arnold's Sophia doctrine was dependent in many ways on Boehme. His link between Sophia and the Beloved of the Song of Solomon, however, was distinctive to his interpretation, and not found in Boehme. This emphasis was found in Harmonist Sophialogy.

Rapp's Separatist movement in Württemberg to radical Pietism in his discussion of their religious beliefs.[37] Although he rightly contended, for instance, that Rapp's views of celibacy were drawn from the interpretation of Rev 14:4 found in the Berleburg Bible commentary, he neglected to connect this practice to churchly and radical Pietists in their homeland, who likewise promoted celibacy (e.g., *Hahnsche Gemeinschaft*), and with whom Rapp had contact prior to his immigration to Pennsylvania.[38]

Arthur Versluis, a professor at Michigan State University, roots Harmonist religion in "Western esotericism – in particular, Christian theosophy and alchemy," with no mention of Pietism.[39] His methodology is based on examining an (incomplete) list of 360 books owned by the Harmony Society in 1829 for titles which reveal esoteric, theosophical and alchemistical content.[40] This approach is suspect for two reasons: (1) It is false to assume that because a book was owned by the Harmonists they agreed with any or all of its content. This must first be established by examining primary sources. Primary sources reveal, for instance, that the Harmonists owned and read Swedenborg, but rejected his anti-Trinitarian stance.[41] Versluis

---

[37] Arndt, *Harmony Society*, 15-49 and 416-419. The author describes the religion of the Harmonists with no mention of Pietism. However, in volume one of his documentary history, *George Rapp's Separatists*, xxiii, he does acknowledge: "From the point of view of church history, Rapp's Harmony Society is the still unrecognized highest development of Swabian Pietism." In spite of this statement, Arndt fails to connect adequately the religious beliefs of the Harmonists to the German Pietist movement.

[38] "Kolb, der Hüter des geistlichen Erbes und Herausgeber der Schriften [Michael] Hahns, hielt, wie die übrigen leitenden Brüder, an die Ehelosigkeit fest." Gustav Adolf Benrath, "Die Erweckung innerhalb der deutschen Landeskirchen, 1815-1888," in *Geschichte des Pietismus*, vol. 3, *Der Pietismus im neunzehnten und zwanzigsten Jahrhundert* (Göttingen: Vandenhoeck & Ruprecht, 2000), 232.

[39] Arthur Versluis, "Western Esotericism and the Harmony Society," http://www.esoteric.msu.edu/Versluis.html, [Accessed September 17, 2013], 20.

[40] It is possible to establish some of the books that were in the Harmony Society library in 1829, the year that Romelius Langenbacher made a (partial) list of German books owned. This list is proven to be incomplete, however, through the simple fact that the correspondence of the Society includes orders for books that are not included in the list. For instance on Feb. 9, 1820, the Harmony Society ordered ninety different titles from a bookseller in Philadelphia. A comparison with the 1829 list reveals that only forty-one of these books are in the 1829 list. While it is possible that some of the books were sold or given away, it is unlikely that more than half of the books, which the Society had specifically ordered, were disposed of in this manner. Likewise, Harmonists included verses from Gottfried Arnold hymns in their paraphrases of passages from the Song of Solomon, although this volume is not included in the list. Therefore, though the 1829 list is a valuable source for determining some of the books that Rapp and the Harmonists were acquainted with, it should not be viewed as exhaustive.

[41] Cf. Frederick Rapp's remark to the Swedenborgian Samuel Worcester, Dec. 19, 1822. "We are tolerably well acquainted with the writings of Swedenborg, they

himself admits Rapp's own treatise, *Thoughts on the Destiny of Man*, includes "relatively little trace of all of Rapp's esoteric studies."[42] (2) The 1829 list of books owned includes many more Lutheran or Pietist Bible commentaries, sermon collections, hymnbooks and devotional literature than esoteric volumes. Yet Versluis fails to mention these sources of influence. An article by De Cunzo, O'Malley et. al. on the religious significance of Rapp's garden at Economy likewise claimed that the Harmonists possessed a "secret, hermetic, cabbalistic" world view such as that reflected in the painting *Turris Antonia*.[43] Once again, no mention is made of their religious and historical roots in radical Württemberg Pietism. On the contrary, German scholars are usually careful to place George Rapp and the Harmonists against a Pietist backdrop.[44]

Many studies of the Harmony Society have pointed to the authoritarian style of Rapp's leadership. Arndt refers to it as "uncompromising" and as "despotism."[45] Littell writes more sympathetically of Rapp "exercising great patriarchal authority," although the freedom of individual members remained.[46] Neither of these scholars, however, has made the connection to the German historical background. Hartmut Lehmann in *Pietismus und weltliche Ordnung in Württemberg* (1969) has stressed that a distinctive feature of Württemberg Pietism was the prominent role that local leaders or patriarchs played. These patriarchs frequently claimed unconditional authority in religious issues.[47] Set in this historical context, the authoritarian style of "Father Rapp," as he was known to his followers, makes more sense. Likewise, an interest in scientific experiments (alchemy), which Rapp personally pursued for several years, was not uncommon among German

---

contain many usefull things, yet most of his readers understand him in a too sensual manner." The Harmonists were strict Trinitarians, and though Frederick Rapp diplomatically referred to Swedenborg as one of many "Witnesses of truth," they nevertheless rejected many or most Swedenborgian tenets. Arndt, *Doc. Hist. 1820-1824*, 511-515; cf. 401-404.

[42] Versluis, "Western Esotericism and the Harmony Society," 29.

[43] Lu Ann De Cunzo, Therese O'Malley, Michael J. Lewis, George E. Thomas, and Christa Wilmanns-Wells, "Father Rapp's Garden at Economy: Harmony Society Culture in Microcosm," in *Landscape Archaeology : Reading and Interpreting the American Historical Landscape*, ed. Rebecca Yamin and Karen Bescherer Metheny (Knoxville: University of Tennessee Press, 1996), 107, 109.

[44] Examples are the monograph, *Radikaler Pietismus in Württemberg* (2003), and articles by Eberhard Fritz on Rapp's Separatist movement prior to emigration.

[45] Arndt, "Harmony Society," 78-79. Cf. Fritz, *Radikaler Pietismus*, 145f.

[46] Littell, "Radical Pietism," 178.

[47] Hartmut Lehmann, *Pietismus und weltliche Ordnung in Württemberg vom 17. bis zum 20. Jahrhundert* (Stuttgart: W. Kohlhammer, 1969), 15. In a personal conversation on November 2, 2006, Lehmann suggested that Rapp's leadership might reflect the authoritarian stance that Lutheran pastors adopted toward their congregations.

churchly and radical Pietists, as recent studies have shown.[48] Arndt draws the theological link to the works of the Swiss Renaissance physician and alchemist Paracelsus, but not to the historical roots of alchemistical activity in Pietism.[49] These typical elements of radical German Pietist belief appear less exotic and bizarre and more understandable only when understood in context. The historical connections between Harmonist religious beliefs and their backdrop in the German setting, and to a lesser degree in the American, are crucial. One of the goals of this volume is to clarify the roots and nature of Rapp's theology, and to contribute to the broader discussion of the interrelationship between churchly and radical Pietism.

What is Pietism?

The definition of Pietism has been the object of much scholarly debate in the last four or five decades. While all modern descriptions of Pietism note the obvious parallels between the reform movements in Germany (Pietism), England (Puritanism) and the Netherlands (*Nadere Reformatie*) at the beginning of the seventeenth century, scholars are divided in how these parallels are to be interpreted. Are the English and Dutch phenomena to be viewed as "preparatory forces" (Martin Schmidt) or as "forerunners" (Hans Beyreuther) of German Pietism? Was Puritanism the "cradle of Pietism" as Heppe and Goeters contended?[50] Or should the English and Dutch expressions be considered Pietism in the true sense of the word? Scholars have proposed differing solutions to this terminological and ideological problem.

F. Ernest Stoeffler begins the first volume of his two volume history of Pietism with English Puritanism, before moving to the Reformed phenomenon in the Netherlands, and finally to the Lutheran reform movement, which had its roots in Johann Arndt and not in Spener.[51] In spite of this ecclesiastically and geographically inclusive definition, Stoeffler was careful to

---

[48]"Von Böhme und der Kabbala war der weitere Rückgriff auf die Alchemie, die *Physica sacra* und das Forschen im Buch der Natur neben dem der Schrift nicht weit. Dabei wird von der Annahme ausgegangen, aus den Prozessen der Chemie lasse sich etwas für die Metaphysik und das Verstehen der Bibel lernen, Chemie und Theologie seien nicht zwei Dinge, sondern eines." Therefore, alchemy was practiced by the Württemberg Bengel student Oetinger and the Separatists, Johann Samuel Carl and Freiherr von Leiningen. Martin Brecht, "Der württembergische Pietismus," in *Geschichte des Pietismus*, vol. 2, *Der Pietismus im achtzehnten Jahrhundert*, ed. Martin Brecht and Klaus Deppermann (Göttingen: Vandenhoeck & Ruprecht, 1995), 275, cf. 238 and 283. Cf. W. R. Ward, *Early Evangelicalism. A Global Intellectual History, 1670-1789* (Cambridge: Cambridge University Press, 2006), 6-23.

[49]Arndt, *Harmony Society*, 531-533.

[50]Cf. Martin Brecht's discussion in the "Introduction," *Geschichte des Pietismus*, vol. 1, ed. Martin Brecht (Göttingen: Vandenhoeck & Rupprecht, 1993), 3-10, here 5.

[51]Schneider notes that Arndt's following in the seventeenth century cannot be compared to the distinctive movement that Spener initiated. Schneider, "Radikaler Pietismus," 131.

maintain Pietism's integrity as a historical movement of experiential Christians within the Reformation churches of the seventeenth and eighteenth centuries, albeit with continuing influence up to the present.[52] According to Martin Brecht in the introduction to volume one of the four volume *Geschichte des Pietismus*, there are "important reasons" to have an early and broad definition of Pietism, one that includes the English and Dutch expressions.[53] In contrast to Stoeffler, however, the four volume set extends its depiction of Pietism to include the revival movements of the nineteenth and twentieth century. Temporal inclusiveness is matched with confessional breadth – besides Lutheran and Reformed expressions of Pietism, the Catholic revival movement in Allgäu, and the evangelical and fundamentalist movements in the United States are included.

Johannes Wallmann argues that such a broad and inclusive definition of Pietism uses said label as a typological term for a certain form of piety. The term thus loses its usefulness in depicting an identifiable historical epoch. With such usage, Pietism becomes essentially a history of Protestantism in the last three centuries. Wallmann's solution is to suggest a broad (beginning with Arndt, ca. 1600) and narrow (beginning with Spener and Johann Jacob Schütz, ca. 1675) definition of Pietism. Puritanism and the *Nadere Reformatie* belong to the broad, but not the narrow definition of Pietism, which was Lutheran in its origin.[54]

In this volume, the term Pietism will be used in its narrow sense to depict the renewal movement within the German Lutheran church, which began with Spener and Schütz in the last quarter of the seventeenth century.[55] The movement was characterized by the formation of conventicles (*collegia pietatis*), in which "born again" children of God gathered for spiritual nurture. The Bible and devotional literature were studied in these conventicles as a means to attain a sanctified and holy life, a *praxis pietatis*. A strong sense of camaraderie developed between the conventicle members. Calling each other brothers and sisters, the members were conscious both of being a part of a distinct movement and of their status as redeemed, a form of elitism that led to conflict with non-Pietist neighbors.

---

[52] F. Ernest Stoeffler, *Rise of Evangelical Pietism* (Leiden: Brill, 1965), 8.

[53] Brecht, "Introduction," 3-4.

[54] Johannes Wallmann, *Der Pietismus* (Göttingen: Vandenhoeck & Ruprecht, 1990); Johannes Wallmann, "Pietismus – ein Epochenbegriff oder ein typologischer Begriff?" *Pietismus und Neuzeit* 30 (2004): 191-224; and Johannes Wallmann, " Kirchliche und radikaler Pietismus. Zu einer kirchengeschichtlichen Grundunterscheidung," *Der radikale Pietismus. Perspectiven der Forschung*, eds. Wolfgang Breul, Marcus Meier and Lothar Vogel (Göttingen: Vandenhoeck & Ruprecht, 2010), 19-43.

[55] Andreas Deppermann in his very influential book, *Johann Jakob Schütz und die Anfänge des Pietismus* (Tübingen: Mohr Siebeck, 2002) argues convincingly that Schütz's form of radical Pietism in Frankfurt predated and significantly influenced Spener.

Most members of the Pietist movement remained faithful church-goers, that is, they were churchly Pietists. This did not preclude their frequent direct or indirect criticism of the failings of the institutional church. Nevertheless, in spite of their criticism, churchly Pietists valued the sacraments and means of grace sufficiently to remain true to their Lutheran or Reformed upbringing. Churchly Pietists, thus, were those members of the Pietist movement who retained membership within the Lutheran or Reformed Church, yet sought spiritual nurture within Pietist *ecclesiolae*.

Within the Pietist movement a smaller, radical wing existed. Since the 1960s scholarly convention has assigned the title of "radical Pietism" to this wing of the movement in a manner parallel to the term "Radical Reformation" used by Reformation historians.[56] Traditionally, church historians have defined radical Pietism by the heterodox views its proponents held and by its vigorous criticism of the church, which resulted in separation.[57] Hans Schneider, however, notes that not all those who separated from the church held heterodox views (e.g. Jean de Labadie). Some Pietists who remained within the church or returned to it, however, did espouse heterodox views (e.g. Gottfried Arnold, Michael Hahn, Friedrich Christoph Oetinger). Personal biographies reveal that some persons moved between churchly and radical Pietism once or more during their lifetime. In fact, the formation of *ecclesiolae in ecclesia* often bore within itself the first step toward separation from the church. The boundaries between the two branches of the one movement were thus fluid and porous.[58]

The term Separatist refers to a person who withdrew from the institutional church for reasons of religious belief.[59] A Separatist normally but not

---

[56]Wallmann, "Kirchliche und radikaler Pietismus," 19. Martin Brecht in "Der radikale Pietismus – die Problematik einer historischen Kategorie" *Der radikale Pietismus. Perspectiven der Forschung*, eds. Wolfgang Breul, Marcus Meier and Lothar Vogel (Göttingen: Vandenhoeck & Ruprecht, 2010), 11-18, here 12, notes that the term "radical Pietism" is not sharply defined and difficult since the adjective "radical" has more than one meaning.

[57]Schneider, "Radikaler Pietismus," 134.

[58]Ibid., 134-136. The porous-ness between the two branches of Pietism is further developed in several articles in the 2010 volume, *Der radikale Pietismus. Perspectiven der Forschung*, eds. Wolfgang Breul, Marcus Meier and Lothar Vogel (Göttingen: Vandenhoeck & Ruprecht, 2010), e.g. Veronica Albrecht-Birkner and Udo Sträter, "Die radikale Phase des frühen August Hermann Francke," 57-84 and Dietrich Meyer, "Die Herrnhuter Brüdergemeine als Brücke zwischen radikalem und kirchlichem Pietismus," 129-146.

[59]Eberhard Fritz defines a Separatist as a person who for religious reasons intentionally refused attendance at the Lord's Supper. This initial refusal was the basis for other acts of rejection – baptism of children, military service, swearing the oath of allegiance, school attendance, etc. Eberhard Fritz, "Kirch seye eben ein steinen Hauß, Gott wohne nicht darinn. Verhörprotokolle als Quellen zur Geschichte des radikalem Pietismus in Württemberg," *Blätter für württembergische Kirchengeschichte* 102 (2002): 69-108, here 69-70.

always upheld certain typical heterodox views. A radical Pietist can be defined both social-historically and theologically.[60] Members of the radical wing usually (but not always) separated from the church, thus exhibiting a dissenting or sectarian type of behavior. They likewise generally upheld a number of typical heterodox teachings. These often included a Boehmist cosmogony, teaching on the dual nature of Adam and Christ, microcosm/macrocosm speculation, Sophia mysticism, millennial teaching, a spiritualist ecclesiology and view of the sacraments, and dabbling in cabbalism and alchemy.[61]

Württemberg Pietism refers to one branch of the Pietist movement which grew up in the duchy of that name after 1680.[62] Over time Württemberg Pietism developed its own special flavor, distinct from other branches of the movement. The eschatological system of the revered Johann Albrecht Bengel led to a general and fervent belief among Württemberg Pietists in a literal thousand year millennium on or over this earth. Besides millennialism (which included the setting of dates for the return of Christ), Württemberg Pietism was characterized by biblicism and mystical and theosophical speculation.[63]

---

[60]Radical Pietism has been defined theologically by some scholars (Hirsch, Ensign, Durnbaugh) as characterized primarily by the teachings of the theosophist Jakob Boehme (see discussion above). Franklin Littell, on the other hand, finds the "controlling factor" to be radical eschatology, which included a "normative use of the early church" (primitivism). Franklin Littell, "Radical Pietism in American History," in *Continental Pietism and Early American Christianity*, ed. F. Ernst Stoeffler (Grand Rapids, Mich.: Eerdmans, 1976), 167. A sociological definition is proposed by Eberhard Fritz in *Radikaler Pietismus in Württemberg: Religiöse Ideale im Konflikt mit gesellschaftlichen Realitäten* (Epfendorf: Bibliotheca Academica, 2003), 14 as "aktive Ablehnung der verfassten protestantischen Kirche durch Menschen, die dies äußerlich durch die Verweigerung des Abendmahls-Sakraments zum Ausdruck bringen." Goertz points out that exclusively theological definitions are not able to grasp the phenomenon of radical Pietism sufficiently. "Weiterhelfen dagegen könnte eine Deutung, die den Pietismus als Reformbewegung betrachtet und sozialgeschichtlich relevante Aspekte mit theologischen verbindet." Hans-Jürgen Goertz, *Religiöse Bewegungen in der Fruhen Neuzeit* (Munich: R. Oldenbourg, 1993), 103. Like Goertz, the author finds it helpful to define radical Pietism in both theological (radical eschatology, primitivism, mystical spiritualism) and sociological terms (separation, sectarianism).

[61]Hans Schneider notes that radical Pietism in the eighteenth century was almost exclusively characterized by Philadelphian beliefs, which gave considerable unity to the movement. Hans Schneider, "Der radikaler Pietismus im 17. Jahrhundert," in *Geschichte des Pietismus*, Vol. 1 (Göttingen: Vandenhoeck & Ruprecht, 1990), 406.

[62]Studies on German Pietism are normally divided into five branches: Spener, Halle Pietism, Zinzendorf, Württemberg Pietism, and radical Pietism.

[63]Cf. F. Ernest Stoeffler, *German Pietism during the Eighteenth Century* (Leiden: Brill, 1973), 88-130 and Martin Brecht, "Der württembergische Pietismus" in

Primary Sources relating to Rapp and the Harmony Society

Several early histories and descriptions of the Harmony Society were written in the nineteenth century, and may be considered primary sources. These accounts were frequently unabashedly biased (either positively or negatively) and therefore must be utilized critically. Early travelers, such as F. Cuming (1810), John Melish (1811), Robert Owen (1825) and Traugott Bromme (1839), who published descriptions of the Society, were clearly impressed with the economic achievements of the Harmonists and therefore cast the Society in a rosy light.[64] Their accounts provide some invaluable, eye-witness information about Harmonist settlements, manufacturing and agriculture. The Harmonists, however, were quite secretive about their religious beliefs and shared only the briefest outlines of their religion with outsiders. Therefore, these travelers' descriptions are of limited value for ascertaining Harmonist religious beliefs.

Aaron Williams published in 1866 a volume entitled *The Harmony Society*, which consisted of a series of articles reformatted as a book. One section of the book had appeared as a reply to a "slanderous" piece against the Harmonists published in the *Atlantic Monthly*, a piece that had done "very great injustice to that worthy Society."[65] The remainder of the book had been published as a series of articles in the *Pittsburgh Commercial*. Prior to publication, each article had been submitted for inspection and approval by the current trustees of the Harmony Society, a fact documented on the frontispiece of the volume. After a fire, Williams and his family had resided with the Harmonists at Economy for a lengthy period of time and learned to appreciate the group. His account was based on original documents and oral interviews with existing members and is therefore quite valuable as a historical source. Nevertheless, his positive bias requires the modern researcher to approach the work with caution. As a Doctor of Divinity and pastor in a neighboring town, Williams was keenly interested in Harmonist religious beliefs. His volume included quite extensive sections on their religion, written sympathetically and in accordance with Harmonist self-understanding. Williams depicted accurately those aspects of the Harmonist religious beliefs which the Society was willing to share with him. These

---

Geschichte des Pietismus, Vol. 2 (Göttingen: Vandenhoeck & Ruprecht, 1995), 225-295.

[64]Fortescue Cuming, *Sketches of a Tour to the Western Country* (Pittsburgh: Cramer, Spear and Eichbaum, 1810); John Melish, *Travels through the United States of America* (Philedelphia: T&G Palmer, 1812); Robert Owen, *Threading My Way. An Autobiography* (New York: A. M. Kelley, 1874); and Traugott Bromme, *Nordamerika's Bewohner, Schönheiten und Naturschätze* (Stuttgart: J. Scheible, 1839).

[65]Aaron Williams, *The Harmony Society at Economy, Penna.* (Pittsburgh: W.S. Haven, 1866), 24.

included a very detailed description of their cosmogony and anthropology, thus giving the appearance that these were their most important doctrines. Other controversial tenets, such as universalism (*die Wiederbringung aller Dinge*), Sophia doctrine, Melchizedekan priesthood, and the role of the Harmony Society in the millennium, were not referred to at all. Nor was the quietistic doctrine of self-denial for the purpose of achieving the mystical union with Christ. Finally, Williams' depiction of Harmonist religious beliefs was written twenty years after Rapp's death. He received his information from Rapp's successors and not from the founder of the Society. This source is thus less relevant for Harmonist religious beliefs during Rapp's lifetime.

In 1833, one year after withdrawing from the Harmony Society, twenty-five year old Jonathan Wagner published in Württemberg a treatise entitled *Geschichte u. Verhältnisse der Harmoniegesellschaft*. His purpose was to correct falsely positive reports published in American newspapers and to prove that Harmonists were held captive in such "ignorance and slavish tyranny as history had scarcely known."[66] His pamphlet was clearly negatively biased and based on the bitter exaggerations of a disgruntled former member. Nevertheless, in spite of these serious reservations, the pamphlet does provide insight into the 1832 secession of one-third of all Harmonists (including Wagner) and into Rapp's millennial speculations in the late 1820s, which Wagner had experienced first-hand. Viktor Rauscher, a pastor in Rapp's hometown of Iptingen, published in 1885 a lengthy article on Rapp and the Harmonists.[67] The author had easy access to the church council records in Iptingen and environs. He depicted Rapp's Separatist movement prior to emigration in a surprisingly accurate and magnanimous fashion. However, for his account of the Harmony Society in America, he relied on the biased, negative accounts of Jonathan Wagner and the article penned by Hermann Markworth in 1882, and therefore presented a skewed interpretation.[68]

A wide variety of relevant sources with theological content are extant in the Harmony Society archives and in Arndt's volumes of documentary history. Church consistory minutes and visitation reports give valuable insight into the growth of Rapp's Separatist movement in Württemberg.[69] Two ear-

---

[66] Jonathan Wagner, *Geschichte u. Verhältnisse der Harmoniegesellschaft* (Vaihingen an der Enz: Deininger, 1833), 4-5.

[67] Viktor Rauscher, "Des Separatisten G. Rapp Leben und Treiben," *Theologische Studien aus Württemberg* 6 (1885): 253-313.

[68] Hermann Markworth, "Die Rappischen Kolonien," *Beilage zur Sonntagsmorgen*, (Cincinnati: Heinrich Haacke & Co, July 16, 1882).

[69] See the following articles for the use of consistory minutes as primary sources: Fritz, "Kirch seye," 75-77; Eberhard Fritz, "Die Konsolidierung des württembergischen Pietismus im frühen 19. Jahrhundert. Eine Befragung von 1821 als als Dokument einer Übergangszeit." *Blätter für württembergische Kirchengeschichte*, 108-109 (2008-2009): 363-392; Beate Popkin, "Der Kirchenkonvent in Württemberg," *Blätter für württembergische Kirchengeschichte* 96 (1996), 98-118; and Norbert Haag, "Bücher auf dem Lande. Zum Genese des

ly statements of faith written in Württemberg, as well as several later declarations reveal important elements of their religious beliefs. Prior to emigration (1791-1802), Rapp wrote numerous letters to his disciples, of which thirty-seven have been preserved. The 1838 sermon book, as well as 1680 of Rapp's sermon notes, are extant. In 1824, the Harmonist leader wrote a philosophical treatise, entitled *Thoughts on the Destiny of Man*. Some letters of Rapp and other Harmonist leaders touch on theological topics. The early manuscript hymnbooks, the *Harmonisches Gesangbuch* published in 1820 and 1827, and the books of hymns and poems, *Eine kleine Sammlung* (1824) and *Feurige Kohlen* (1826), provide insight into Harmonist religious beliefs. At least one later worship service liturgy exists (1834). The contents of the Harmony Society library are a relevant indication of potential influence. Material sources include religious symbols as architectural details, church architecture, cemetery layout, alchemistical materials and garden structures such as labyrinths and grottoes.

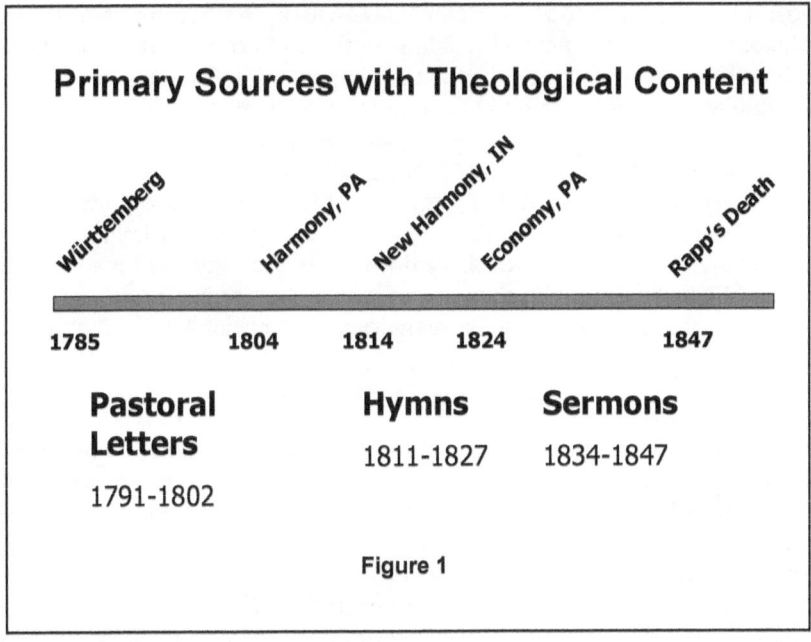

Figure 1

The lengthy list above attests that sources with theological content are quite numerous. Nevertheless, no one type of source is available for the entire time frame of Rapp's leadership of his Separatist movement in Germany and of the Harmony Society, 1785-1847 (see figure 1). Church consistory records, Rapp's pastoral letters and several brief declarations of faith are

---

Ulmer Pietismus," *Blätter für württembergische Kirchengeschichte* 89 (1989): 48-98 here 78.

available for the Württemberg era (1785-1805). Virtually no primary sources with theological value are available from the first settlement at Harmony, Penn. (1805-1814). Manuscript and printed hymnody is plenteous for the New Harmony decade (1814-1824). Sermons are extant primarily from the last two decades of Rapp's lifetime (ca. 1830-1847). The lack of one type of source for the entire period makes it difficult, if not impossible, for the researcher to make definitive statements about the development and progression of the group's religious beliefs. Due to the numerous sermons from the Economy era, it is possible to draw significant conclusions about Rapp's mature theology.

The majority of the sources reflecting Harmonist religious beliefs have been written by George Rapp (pastoral letters, sermons, hymns). However, there are some primary sources available which were written by other Harmonist leaders and laypeople. For example, a large corpus of religious hymns exists, written by both named and unnamed Harmony Society members. Letters of several Harmonist leaders reflect religious beliefs, notably those of Frederick Rapp and Romelius Langenbacher. These sources are valuable as a reflection of the religious notions of ordinary Harmonists, as well as the extent to which they actually appropriated Rapp's views. It is possible at times to discover convergence and divergence between Rapp's beliefs and those of Harmony Society members (e.g. the degree to which Rapp's promotion of celibacy was actually adopted).

The vast majority of primary sources utilized are in the German language. Frequent quotes from the manuscript and printed primary sources are included in the text, since these documents are otherwise inaccessible to most English readers. In those cases where the German wording is crucial or a quotation is short, the German original is included in the footnote.

Chapter Overview

In the ensuing chapters, a roughly chronological religious history of Rapp's Separatist movement and the Harmony Society from the inception of the former until Rapp's death in 1847 unfolds. Both a chronological and thematic approach is employed in the central chapters. Narrative accounts prevail in the descriptions of the life of Rapp, the conflict with church and state in Württemberg, the historical context of radical and churchly Pietist beliefs and in the description of the formation and development of their religious Society on American soil (chapters 2, 4, 5 and 9). In the remaining sections an analytical, thematic approach predominates in which Harmony Society primary sources with theological content are analyzed, compared and interpreted. Certain key theological themes and religious practices are most appropriately discussed at specific junctures of the chronological narrative. For instance, the pastoral letters written by Rapp to his followers prior to emigration concern two main themes – quietistic mysticism and their early millennial speculation. Therefore, these themes are elaborated upon in the third and fourth chapters dealing with the Württemberg era.

Careful attention will be given to the historical context in which these theological texts arose. Often that context is the radical and churchly Pietism that George Rapp experienced and appropriated while still in Württemberg, Germany. Although the American religious and historical context will not be ignored, due to the community's insulated position in American society the German background is of greater importance.

Chapter two portrays the development of Rapp's Separatist movement in Württemberg from 1785-1800. The life of Johann Georg Rapp is placed against its historical, socio-economic and religious setting. Rapp's roots in churchly Pietism are depicted, then the formation of his Separatist movement and finally, early Separatist religious beliefs and practices. In chapter three, Rapp's pastoral letters to members of his movement, which provide insight into his pastoral care, are utilized. The influence of Gerhard Tersteegen's quietistic mysticism on Rapp's Separatists is demonstrated. Followers were encouraged to follow the path of self-denial in order to reach the mystical union with God. In chapter four, Rapp's concept of the Sunwoman in the wilderness (Rev 12:6), which was central to Harmonist self-understanding, is compared and contrasted with other past and contemporary theologians.

The analysis of Rapp's pastoral letters and hymns in chapters three and four brings up the important issue of influences on his theology. It is often difficult or impossible to pinpoint definitively the sources of Rapp's religious beliefs. Rapp virtually never gave credit to the sources he employed, even when quoting extensively from other authors.[70] Evidence of influence is often serendipitous –when verbatim or conceptual borrowing is recognized through broad reading of sources with which Rapp was acquainted. Only tentative statements about the sources of Harmonist religious beliefs are made unless influence or dependency can be firmly established. Firm evidence of influence is when: (1) Rapp borrowed verbatim from another source (e.g. Gottfried Arnold, Oetinger, Bengel, and Jung-Stilling), or; (2) Rapp paraphrased concepts from another author, and clear evidence exists that Rapp or the Harmony Society owned the volume in question (e.g. Tersteegen, Boehme, Gichtel, Christoph Schütz).[71]

In the fifth chapter, the formation of the Harmony Society is discussed. This came about after emigration to Pennsylvania through the adoption of communalism and the Articles of Association in 1805. The Harmonist church in the wilderness was divided into conventicles by sex and gender. Besides the traditional Christian holidays, confession, the love feast, Harmony Fest and Harvest Home were celebrated once a year. The theological basis for Rapp's patriarchal leadership and for the adoption of celibacy is

---

[70]The author has discovered only one instance when Rapp gave credit to the source (Bengel) that he used in his sermon (MG-437/Box22/Folder 82B/A-3).

[71]The incomplete 1829 list of books owned by the Society is a valuable source for determining some of the books with which Rapp was acquainted, as are book orders by the Harmony Society.

unpacked. An explication of the nature of Harmonist worship and hymnody completes the chapter.

Chapter six describes the role of religious beliefs in the material culture of the Harmony Society. Although the community adopted a dissenting style of architecture, a few religious symbols were displayed as architectural details on their buildings. These symbols reflect distinctive radical Pietist teachings to which the Society held. Mystical-spiritual beliefs were depicted in the Sophia lintel at Harmony. A striving for sanctification was underscored through the labyrinths and corresponding grottoes at each of the three successive Harmonist settlements. The golden rose symbol on the brick church at New Harmony affirmed the distinctive millennial hope of the Harmonists.

Rapp's sermons form the basis for the analysis in chapters seven, eight and nine. In chapter seven aspects of Rapp's biblical-eschatological trajectory are discussed. These include his "core Reformation doctrine," namely a high view of Scripture, orthodox formulations of the Trinity, the deity of Christ, the atonement, and justification by faith. Churchly Pietist emphases (regeneration, perfectionism and the priesthood of all believers) and an "Anabaptist" ecclesiology (primitivism, believer's church, believer's baptism, shunning) likewise form part of the biblical-eschatological trajectory. In the following chapter the elements of Harmonist doctrine that reflect a mystical-spiritual orientation come under examination. These include an allegorical, biblical hermeneutic, cabbalistic conceptions of the Godhead, a theosophical cosmogony and anthropology, and transmutation and spiritual alchemy. Chapter nine includes a thorough discussion of later Harmonist eschatological beliefs. Rapp's presuppositions and approach to biblical eschatology are first unpacked. A timeline of eschatological events is drawn from Rapp's apocalyptic sermons. Examples of Harmonist application of the Book of Revelation to the interpretation of current events are given. Rapp's dating of the return of Christ is unfolded, along with the universalist doctrine (*die Wiederbringung aller Dinge*) so popular among Württemberg Pietists. A sectarian spirit is reflected in the doctrine of the unique role and mission of the Harmony Society in the *eschaton*. The chapter concludes with the Harmonist expectation to meet Christ at his Second Advent in Palestine. In chapter ten, conclusions are drawn.

Relationship with the American Historical and Religious Context

The Harmony Society has been dubbed by Bryan Wilson as an introversionist sect. By that Wilson means that the Harmonists insulated themselves from the surrounding culture physically, socially and through the use of the

German language.[72] In contrast to conversionist sects, the Harmonists undertook little evangelism. They were only open to accepting new members who had emigrated from Germany and, in particular, Württemberg. The term "introversionist," however, is not completely accurate. Unlike some introversionist sects, the Harmonists influenced the American historical context in a number of significant ways. They contributed to the settling of the Western frontier, to the formation of other communal societies, and to local economic growth. Members of the Harmony Society provided valuable public service and brought influence to bear on the political arena. American conceptions of freedom and democracy impacted the Harmony Society in return.

The Harmony Society played a significant role in the settling of the Western frontier. It established three flourishing towns, two in western Pennsylvania and one in pre-statehood Indiana. Frederick Rapp, the adopted son of the Harmonist leader, served as a representative at the Constitutional Convention of the State of Indiana in 1816. As a member of the committee on the militia, Frederick Rapp successfully represented the pacifist position of the Harmonists and ensured that Article VII in the Indiana Constitution allowed conscientious objectors to pay a fine in lieu of military service. He also supported the strong statement against slavery which was adopted into the state's first constitution.[73] Further, Frederick was named by the Indiana Legislature in 1820 as one of the commissioners to select a site for the capital city, Indianapolis, and to plan and lay out the town. The following year Frederick helped to organize the banking system of the new state. This public service corresponded to George Rapp's conviction, which he expressed in a letter to Frederick while at the Constitutional Convention, "our religious principles oblige us at every opportunity to do good to others and to advance the wellbeing of mankind."[74]

The success of the Harmony Society as a utopian community led directly to the formation of other communes in the first half of the nineteenth century. In 1812 John Melish published a description of the Harmony Society in his *Travels through the United States of America*, which spread the fame of the Rappite community. In the volume Melish expressed the opinion that the Harmony Society "will, in all probability, be a model for other societies."[75] His prediction proved to be accurate.[76] The Harmonist commune

---

[72] Bryan R. Wilson, "An Analysis of Sect Development," in *Patterns of Sectarianism: Organisation and Ideology in Social and Religious Movements*, ed. B. R. Wilson (London: Heinemann, 1967), 22-45, here especially 26-27, n. 1. Cf. Wilson, *Social Dimensions*, 120.

[73] F. Rapp officiated as the director of the Vincennes Bank as well as of the Farmers Bank of Harmony. Donald E. Pitzer and Josephine M. Elliott. *New Harmony's First Utopians, 1814-1824*. 2d ed. (Historic New Harmony, Ind.: University of Southern Indiana Press, 2002), 241-242.

[74] Arndt, "George Rapp's Harmony Society," 165-179, here 169.

[75] Arndt, *Doc. Hist. 1803-1815*, 462.

was the model and inspiration for Robert Owen, who purchased New Harmony in 1824, as well as for the community in Korntal, Württemberg (1819) founded by Pietists and Separatists.[77] Interestingly, former Harmonists were often dissatisfied with Rapp's leadership but not with the concept of a communal society. Former Harmonists were thus key members in the founding of a number of other utopian communes.[78]

The frugal and hard-working Harmonists quickly achieved economic prowess and wealth at each of their settlements. Their unique and innovative combination of agricultural and manufacturing endeavors was highly successful. Not only did they produce everyday items for their own use, but for sale in Harmonist stores at their successive settlements, and in such cities as Vincennes, Indiana and New Orleans. The Society was among the first in America to raise silk worms and produce prize-winning silk textiles. They produced high-quality woolen items from imported merino sheep. The wealth of the Society was such as to allow them to provide a financial loan to the State of Indiana in 1823.

The Harmony Society achieved considerable influence not just economically, but within the local political arena as well. The Society subscribed to numerous English and German language newspapers. They kept abreast of current affairs and developed their own political opinions.[79] Harmonist males applied for and received American citizenship. They exercised their right to vote, albeit in a block, most likely under George Rapp's direction. Due to this fact, it is not surprising that those who aspired to public office or supported particular candidates curried the favor of the Harmony Society.[80] The block vote of the Harmonists was able to swing elections and did so on occasion.[81] Key Harmonists Romelius Langenbacher, Philipp Bentel, and Conrad Feucht served on the Economy Township election committee for the incumbent John Quincy Adams in the 1828 presidential election.[82] All of these activities are inconsistent with an entirely introversionist sect.

---

[76]George and Frederick Rapp frequently received letters requesting information on how to form a communal society, e.g. from Swedenborgian Samuel Worcester. Arndt, *Doc. Hist. 1820-1824*, 401-404.

[77]It also influenced George Flower and the Quaker Morris Birkbeck, who founded an English settlement near New Harmony, but in Illinois. Arndt, *Rapp's Harmony Society*, 197-198.

[78]Communes founded by former Harmonists: Blooming Grove (1804), Teutonia (1827), New Philadelphia Society (1833), and the Bethel and Aurora colonies (1844 and 1855).

[79]For instance, the Harmonists became passionate opponents of Jacksonian Democracy. They lobbied for tariffs high enough to protect their own and other American manufactured products.

[80]William B. Clarke in a September, 1828 letter sought to win support from the Harmonists for his preferred Congressional and County Commissioner candidates.

[81]The block vote led to the defeat of J. S. Stevenson in the Pennsylvania 1828 Congressional election. Arndt, *Doc. Hist. 1826-1834*, 357-359.

[82]Arndt, *George Rapp's Harmony Society*, 263, 379, 400-402, 409-415.

The communal experiment of George Rapp and the Harmony Society had considerable influence on British and European intelligentsia and social reformers, and therefore on intellectual trends. Melish's description of the Harmony Society stood in sharp contrast to the slums generated by the Industrial Revolution in the large cities of England and the United States. His complete chapter on the Harmonists was reprinted in 1815 in the English journal, *The Philanthropist*. These two publications caught the imagination of social reformers, who were interested in a new social structure that would meet the needs of the working class. The Scot Robert Owen had already instituted a social experiment to better the plight of the working class at his cotton factory in New Lanark, near Glasgow. Through these publications he became aware of the Harmonists and later bought New Harmony from its founders to attempt his own, short-lived communal experiment.

The Harmonist settlements became a center of what Eberhard Fritz refers to as "social tourism."[83] English and German intellectuals made the current Harmonist town a stopping point on their international travels.[84] The predominantly positive reports of these influential visitors furthered the international reputation of the Harmony Society in the first half of the nineteenth century. The broad renown of the group was furthered when British poet, Lord Byron (1788-1824), included four stanzas on Rapp's institution of celibacy in his satiric poem "Don Juan," which he wrote between 1818 and 1819.

The most important contribution of the Harmony Society to European intellectual history, however, was the influence that this radical Pietist communal society had on Friedrich Engels and Karl Marx. In October 1844, Engels penned an article on the communal settlements of North America and England. He viewed the settlements of the Harmonists, the Shakers, and the Zoarites as the most impressive, primarily due to their economic success. E. Fritz summarized Engels' argument that the "union of workers and an introduction of community of goods among the working class was an appropriate model to bring about social reform and to eliminate crass social differences."[85] Engels' article has been viewed as a crucial text of the early Communist movement. Insights gained from the Harmony Society and other successful American communes thus flowed directly into the *Communist Manifesto*, published in 1848, and indirectly into the broader stream of European intellectual history.[86]

---

[83]This section is largely dependent on Eberhard Fritz's chapters on the influence of the Harmonists on European intellectual history in *Radikaler Pietismus*, 363-393, here 364.

[84] Economy hosted Prince Bernhard of Saxon-Weimar-Eisenach, the German politician and economist Friedrich List, and the poet Nicholas Lenau, among many others.

[85]Fritz, *Radikaler Pietismus*, 371.

[86]Ibid., 372.

Not only did the Harmony Society impact the American historical context in a number of significant ways. In spite of their (partial) attempt to maintain a German island, insulated from the surrounding American culture, members of the Society were nevertheless influenced by it. The most significant influence occurred gradually and was most prominent among the children of the original immigrants. Unlike their parents, who had not known democracy in their homeland of Württemberg, the younger generation grew up observing a greater level of personal freedom in the culture around them than they experienced within the Harmony Society. It is a struggle for all sectarian groups to win the second generation to the community's values with the same degree of fervor that the founding members exhibited. This situation for the Harmonists was further exacerbated by the stark contrast between Rapp's old-world, authoritarian leadership and the surrounding democratic context. Not surprisingly, a considerable number of the younger (and older) generation chose to leave the Society for this reason.[87]

This volume offers a religious history of the Harmony Society. Therefore, the question of the degree to which Harmonist religion influenced and was influenced by the American religious context is an important one. As mentioned previously, the Harmonists were quite secretive about their religious beliefs to outsiders. Though the Society was quite well-known in its time, it was a small group which maintained a linguistic barrier to the surrounding culture during Rapp's lifetime. Thus, with the exception of its direct influence upon the formation of utopian communes within the United States, the Harmony Society's effect upon the broader flow of American religious history must be seen as relatively negligible.

Was the Harmony Society influenced by the trends within the American religious context? That is a harder question, one which the sources do not allow us to answer conclusively. Many key aspects of their religion were likewise to be found among the general American population in the first half of the nineteenth century. Immigrant groups such as the Harmonists, Zoarites, and Amana Society formed utopian communes on American soil. But this phenomenon was likewise found among indigenous American groups: the Shakers, the Oneida community, and the transcendentalist community at Brook Farm. Nevertheless, George Rapp and his key followers had decided upon this social structure prior to emigration. Therefore, although the Harmonists influenced other Americans to form communal societies, their decision for this social structure pre-dated the American context.

The same conclusion must be drawn concerning Harmonist millennial beliefs. Although George Rapp continued to fine-tune and update his eschatological speculations, the main outlines of Harmonist millennial beliefs

---

[87] Wagner, *Geschichte der Harmoniegesellschaft*, 9 and 14 points to the dissatisfaction of the young people, and the contrast between American democracy and the governance of the Harmony Society.

were developed before crossing the Atlantic. Millennialism had a long tradition within Pietist circles in Württemberg, extending back to Philipp Jakob Spener and then to Johann Albrecht Bengel in the 1740s, and brought to a fever-pitch after the French Revolution. The 1829 list of books owned by the Harmony Society demonstrates that the Harmonists continued to buy German books on eschatology and most likely to be influenced by millennial trends within Germany. There is much less evidence that they were privy to or influenced by English language millennial thought.[88] Further, the Harmonist concept of primitivism, of attempting to reinstitute the golden age of the apostolic church, was explicated in their statement of faith long before emigration and not first adopted in the United States.

Although Harmonist interaction with the American religious context was relatively minor, a religious history of the group is nevertheless of importance. Admittedly, the Harmonists adopted communal, millennial, perfectionistic and primitivistic convictions prior to emigration. There existed, however, significant parallelism between religious trends in the United States, the British Isles, and on the Continent during this era. For several decades, American and European historians have been aware that colonial religious history must be positioned within a transatlantic frame of reference.[89] The macroanalysis provided by Atlantic history allows broader trends to be realized and exciting new research questions to be posed.[90] A

---

[88]George Rapp did not read English or speak it well, but through translators at least on one occasion he discussed millennial trends with visitors from England. Arndt, *Doc. Hist. 1834-1847*, 474-475.

[89]In 1972, Sydney E. Ahlstrom proposed that, "religious history as a field of study must be placed . . . theoretically within the larger frame of world history." Sydney E. Ahlstrom, *A Religious History of the American People* (New Haven: Yale University Press, 1972), xivf. Jon Butler's 1985 article "The Future of American Religious History: Prospectus, Agenda, Transatlantic *Problematique*," *William and Mary Quarterly*, 3d Ser., 42 (1985): 167-183 called historians to examine American lay religious practice in the context of its European antecedents. Patricia Bonomi in *Under the Cope of Heaven: Religion, Society and Politics in Colonial America* (New York: Oxford University Press, 1986) like cogently argued for a transatlantic approach. W. R. Ward's *The Protestant Evangelical Awakening* (Cambridge: Cambridge University Press, 1992) demonstrated the transatlantic connections between religion and international politics in the series of "awakenings" on the Continent, in England and in the New World. Cf. Susan O'Brien, "A Transatlantic Community of Saints. The Great Awakening and the First Evangelical Network, 1735-1755," *American Historical Review* 91 (1986), 811-832 and Michael J. Crawford, *Seasons of Grace. Colonial New England's Revival Tradition in its British Context* (New York: Oxford University Press, 1991).

[90] Research topics include imperial exploration, settlement and colonial development on the four continents that frame the Atlantic, colonial merchants and trade routes and economic development, African slave trade, etc. Most recently Alison Games in a forum in *William and Mary Quarterly* questioned whether the Atlantic world was too small and too arbitrary a unit of analysis to be useful any longer. Alison Games, "Beyond the Atlantic: English Globetrotters and Transoceanic

transatlantic approach with regard to religious history involves noting the European roots of much of American religion, as well as the transformation and maturation of the transported religious tradition in the New World.[91]

Therefore, a study of Harmonist beliefs allows the American religious historian to note the convergence of important religious trends on both sides of the Atlantic. The Harmonists typified and exemplified many features of religious life found in nineteenth century America. For example, during the end of the eighteenth and the first half of the nineteenth century, millennial speculation was rampant among splinter groups not just in Germany, but in England and in the United States as well (e.g. Millerites and Seventh-Day Adventists). Primitivism was found not just among the Harmonists during this era. Thomas Campbell, who emigrated from Ireland to western Pennsylvania in 1807, summoned Christians of every denomination to restore the purity of the New Testament Church, to mention but one example. A striving for holiness, for perfectionism, was found not just among churchly and radical Pietists in Germany, but among followers of John Wesley in England and America. Democracy and religious freedom in America allowed utopian communes to flourish here in numbers unseen either on the Continent or in the British Isles. Nevertheless, fledgling communes were found among Pietists and Separatists in Germany and socially-minded Britons during the first half of the nineteenth century.

Forty years ago, German-American scholar F. Ernest Stoeffler issued a call for recognition of the role of Germans and other ethnic and racial minorities in the development of the American religious culture. He stated that the importance of the Anglo-Saxon, Puritan tradition, which had become a part of our national mythology, was overemphasized and "based partly on fact and partly on fancy." Other traditions, particularly German Pietism, should "rightfully share in the glory and the shame of what happened in our history." Too long had the story of American religious life been told from the perspective of the dominant linguistic group.[92] Stoeffler's call has not fallen on deaf ears. Charles Cohen in a 1997 article was able to declare that there is now a "post-Puritan paradigm of American religious history." Scholars are now recognizing that pluralism rather than Puritanism

---

Connections," *William and Mary Quarterly*, 3d ser., 63 (October 2006): 675-742. Cf. Peter A. Coclanis, "Atlantic World or Atlantic/World?" *William and Mary Quarterly*, 3d ser., 63 (October 2006): 725-742.

[91] Hermann Wellenreuther, "Die atlantische Welt des 18. Jahrhunderts. Überlegungen zur Bedeutung des Atlantiks für die Welt der Frommen im Britischen Weltreich," in *Transatlantische Religionsgeschichte. 18. bis 20. Jahrhundert*, ed. Hartmut Lehmann (Göttingen: Wallstein, 2006), 9-30, here 10-12. Cf. A. Gregg Roeber, "The Problem of the Eighteenth Century in Transatlantic Religious History," in *In Search of Peace and Prosperity. New German Settlements in Eighteenth-Century Europe and America*, ed. Hartmut Lehmann, Hermann Wellenreuther and Renate Wilson (University Park, Pa.,: Pennsylvania State University Press, 2000), 115-138.

[92] F. Ernest Stoeffler, ed. *Continental Pietism and Early American Christianity* (Grand Rapids: Eerdmans, 1976), 10-11.

more accurately defines early American history.⁹³ Jon Butler echoes Stoeffler when he notes that: "Pietism with its distinctive emphasis on a 'new birth' and individual spiritual vitality, not only reshaped German Christianity, but reshaped much of Western Protestantism as well, including late eighteenth-century Anglo-American Protestantism."⁹⁴ In the last decade, the influence of German Pietism on American religion has been emphasized in a number of important studies.⁹⁵ Although the Harmony Society was but a small Germanic group, it contributed to the settling of America and caught the imagination of many in a fashion disproportional to its size. It formed part of the rich, pluralistic, and diverse tapestry of American religious history. The religion of the Harmony Society paralleled key transatlantic trends found in the British Isles, in the United States and on the Continent. Therefore, a closer look at the religious beliefs of the Harmony Society is both warranted and profitable.

---

⁹³Charles L. Cohen, "The Post-Puritan Paradigm of Early American Religious History," *William and Mary Quarterly*, 3d ser., 54 (October 1997): 695-722. Cf. James D. Bratt, "A New Narrative for American Religious History?" *Fides et Historia* 23 (1991): 19-30 and William R. Hutchinson, "From Unity to Multiplicity: American Religion(s) as a Concern for the Historian," *Amerikastudien* 38 (1993): 343-350.

⁹⁴Jon Butler, "The Spiritual Importance of the Eighteenth Century," in *In Search of Peace and Prosperity: New German Settlements in Eighteenth-Century Europe and America*, ed. Hartmut Lehmann, Hermann Wellenreuther, and Renate Wilson (University Park, Pa.: Pennsylvania State University Press, 2000), 101-114.

⁹⁵ Examples are: Hans-Jürgen Grabbe, ed. *Halle Pietism, Colonial North America, and the Young United States* (Kempten: Franz Steiner Verlag, 2008); Jonathan Strom, ed. *Pietism and Community in Europe and North America, 1650-1850* (Leiden: Brill, 2010); Jonathan Strom, Hartmut Lehmann and James Van Horn Melton, eds. *Pietism in Germany and North America 1680-1820* (Burlington, VT.: Ashgate, 2009); and J. Steven O'Malley, *Early German-American Evangelicalism: Pietist Sources on Discipleship and Sanctification* (Lanham, Md.: Scarecrow Press, 1995).

2

Separation from Babel (1785-1800)

Tucked in the south-west corner of Germany between France and Switzerland lay in the eighteenth century the small duchy of Württemberg. Before the climactic changes following the French Revolution, the territorial lands of the dukes of Württemberg consisted of clustered but partially disconnected territory, interspersed with free imperial cities (e.g. Reutlingen, Ulm) and land pockets belonging to other duchies and principalities.

Rapp's Separatist Movement in Context

Political and Historical Context

Württemberg, along with the margraviate Baden, and the archbishopric dioceses of Constance and Augsburg, belonged to the Swabian *Kreis*, one of ten regional administrative districts of the Holy Roman Empire. The post-1648 imperial constitution regulated the relationships between the empire (*Reich*), the regions (*Kreise*) and the individual territorial states (such as Württemberg) by a "complex system of checks and balances."[1] The Swabian *Kreis* has been often regarded by scholars as being the best functioning of the ten *Kreise*. It was nevertheless frequently wrought with internal divisions, between Protestants and Catholics for instance, as well as conflicts with the emperor and the nearby Austrian authorities. These conflicts resulted in a series of different coalitions both within and without the *Kreis*, which were formed to achieve the prevailing political aims of Württemberg at the end of the eighteenth century—protection of its current territory, territorial expansion, and achieving the enhanced status of kingdom.[2]

The French Revolution and the ensuing Napoleonic wars (1789-1815) had a profound effect on all of western and central Europe. These massive,

---

[1]Peter H. Wilson, *War, State and Society in Württemberg, 1677-1793* (Cambridge: Cambridge University Press, 1995), 8. For the best comprehensive history of Württemberg see the five-volume set published in behalf of the *Kommission für geschichtliche Landeskunde in Baden-Württemberg*. Relevant here are Meinrad Schaab, Hansmartin Schwarzmaier, and Michael Klein, *Handbuch der Baden-Württembergischen Geschichte*, vol. 2, *Die Territorien im Alten Reich* (Stuttgart: Klett-Cotta, 1995); and Hansmartin Schwarzmaier, Michael Klein, et al. *Handbuch der Baden-Württembergischen Geschichte*, vol. 3, *Vom Ende des Alten Reiches bis zum Ende der Monarchien* (Stuttgart: Klett-Cotta, 1992).

[2]Wilson, *War, State and Society*, 8-9.

transformative events ultimately resulted in the map of Europe being redrawn and the Holy Roman Empire being formally dissolved (August 6, 1806). The duchy of Württemberg was likewise rocked by these tumultuous events. Württemberg's small size, its lack of military strength, and its unfortunate geographical location between France and Austria placed it in an extremely vulnerable position. It was repeatedly economically ravished by enemy invasion and coalition troop movements through its territories. Therefore, to secure its position and to protect its political interests, the duchy felt it necessary to join coalitions and even change alliances several times during the Napoleonic conflict. The relationship between France and Württemberg at the dawn of the nineteenth century alternated between ally and enemy several times within this time frame.

In March 1793, after the execution of Louis XVI, the Holy Roman Empire declared war on France. Württemberg as an imperial coalition member was required to send seven thousand troops to the front.[3] After Prussia withdrew from the coalition, the French took advantage of the weakened imperial strength. Under General Moreau, the French invaded their near neighbor Württemberg and occupied Stuttgart (July 18, 1796). To the chagrin of the Empire, Württemberg withdrew from the imperial coalition and made a separate peace with France the following month (August 7, 1796). Austria responded by invading the duchy. In October 1797, the peace of Campo Formio reestablished relationships between the Austria and the duchy.

In spite of the armistice with France, the French invaded Württemberg again in March, 1799. The duchy responded by changing alliances and joining the second imperial coalition against France. Fear of a full-scale French invasion of their territory, however, remained rampant and reached its climax in the spring and summer of 1800. General Moreau crossed the Rhine and French troops occupied and, on Napoleon's command, destroyed the Württemberg fortress of Hohentwiel (May 1, 1800). Shortly thereafter, Duke Friedrich left the territory with his family to seek refuge in Prussian Erlangen, an event which only increased the fear and rampant apocalyptic speculation in many circles. Some friends and relatives of Separatists became convinced by these disastrous events of the truthfulness of the radical Pietist message.[4] The Luneville peace treaty of February 9, 1801 ended the conflict between the two antagonists, Württemberg and France. As a condition for peace Württemberg relinquished its land holdings west on the Rhine. It was compensated with land parcels contiguous to its own territory

---

[3]During the coalition war of Austria, Prussia, and the Swabian *Kreis* against the Republic of France, Württemberg troops bravely participated in the storming of the Weißenburg line on Oct. 13, 1793. Heinrich Hermelink, *Geschichte der evangelischen Kirche in Württemberg von der Reformation bis zur Gegenwart* (Stuttgart/Tübingen: Rainer Wunderlich Verlag, 1949), 278.

[4]Eberhard Fritz, *Radikaler Pietismus in Württemberg: Religiöse Ideale im Konflikt mit gesellschaftlichen Realitäten* (Epfendorf: Bibliotheca Academica, 2003), 155.

east of the Rhine, made available through the secularization (1803) of church-held properties and the assimilation of the free imperial cities and smaller, secularly-held principalities in 1806 (*Mediatisierung*). Württemberg doubled its territory in the process.[5] Duke Friedrich on February 25, 1803 was elevated to Elector (*Kurfürst*) by Napoleon. The new territories were administered separately as New-Württemberg from 1803-1806. On January 2, 1806, old Württemberg and New-Württemberg were combined to form a united kingdom.[6] In exchange, Württemberg entered the Rhine coalition (*Rheinbund*) and was obligated in 1806 to war on the side of France against Prussia, in 1809 against Austria, and in 1812 against Russia. In 1813 at the battle of Leipzig, however, the Württemberg general Count Normann changed alliance and joined forces with the coalition against Napoleon. The same year the Württemberg troops fought with Austria, Prussia and Russia against their former ally, Napoleon.[7]

The dismal plight of the common people of Württemberg worsened through the military conflicts of the eighteenth century.[8] Unfortunately, the dukes of Württemberg in this era were frequently insensitive to the needs of the populace and thereby added to its suffering. Duke Eberhard Ludwig (1717-1733) regarded the French court of Louis XIV as his model. The pleasure-driven duke placed the day-by-day governing of the duchy in the hands of his mistress, Wilhelmine von Grävenitz, who was universally disliked by the citizens. Through excessive taxation, the ruling house acquired sufficient wealth, at the expense of the impoverished villagers, to build a lavish new court in Ludwigsburg (eight miles north of Stuttgart). Within several decades, the court at Ludwigsburg, which was modeled upon Versailles, became one of the most luxurious and magnificent in Europe.[9] Eberhard Ludwig's successor, Karl Alexander (1733-1737), was scarcely an improvement. His Roman Catholic faith was deeply resented by the predomi-

---

[5]Napoleon followed a policy of rewarding the middle-sized territories (such as Württemberg) as the expense of the smallest principalities in order to have a buffer against the superpowers, Austria and Prussia. Württemberg was also favored due to family ties of the ducal house with the Czars of Russia. Hermelink, *Geschichte der evangelischen Kirche*, 280.

[6]At the time that Württemberg was elevated to a kingdom (January 1806), all church lands and properties were absorbed into and administered by the state treasury. Clergy salaries were paid by the state. Hermelink, *Geschichte der evangelischen Kirche*, 281.

[7]Georg Leibbrandt, *Die Auswanderung aus Schwaben nach Rußland 1816-1823* (Stuttgart: Ausland und Heimat Verlag, 1928), 9, n. 2.

[8]Württemberg had not recovered economically from the devastations by the wars during Louis XIV's reign, particularly the Pfalz war of succession (1685–1697). During the year 1693, the duchy was destroyed to such an extent that its economic standing had not yet recovered by the middle of the eighteenth century. Hermann Ehmer, "Württemberg," in *TRE*, vol. 36, ed. Gerhard Müller (New York: W. de Gruyter, 2004), 343-368, here 344.

[9]Leibbrandt, *Auswanderung aus Schwaben nach Rußland*, 10, n. 2.

nantly Protestant population of the duchy. His financial advisor, the Jew Süss Oppenheimer, was both unscrupulous and rapacious. Not surprisingly, Oppenheimer was executed soon after Karl Alexander's death.[10]

The early reign of Duke Karl Eugen (1737-1793) was similarly marked by an opulent court, massive castle building and the renovation of existing palatial structures. Peasants were burdened with increased taxation and involuntary servitude for long periods to labor on his building projects. It is thus not surprising that luxury and an opulent lifestyle were decried as heinous vices by Pietist preachers in this era. On his fiftieth birthday, however, Karl Eugen publicly regretted his former policies. Most likely influenced by his second wife, Franziska von Hohenheim, whose family was sympathetic to radical Pietist teachings, Karl Eugen pursued later in life a relatively conciliatory approach to religious dissidents. He encouraged the church and local governmental authorities to avoid confrontation with Separatists and to intervene only when absolutely necessary. This conciliatory policy toward dissidents enabled a nearly unhindered rise and spread of Rapp's Separatist movement.[11]

Friedrich II (duke 1797-1803; elector 1803-1806; king 1806-1816) reversed, however, the conciliatory approach of Karl Eugen. He responded to the challenges engendered by the French Revolution and the Napoleonic wars, as well as to his own persistent struggles with the provincial diet (*Landtag*), by enforcing a policy of monarchial absolutism. Friedrich's policies had a strongly despotic character, more so than those of "less efficient rulers of the *Ancien Regime*." They likewise greatly affected the lives of the common people in significant ways.[12] Friedrich's pursuit of a luxurious, "representative court" burdened the lower classes with excessive taxes. In September, 1801 he issued a command that those who rejected the Lutheran religion of the land would no longer be treated as subjects of the duchy and would be forced to emigrate.[13] Two years later, the Elector issued an intolerant Separatist decree, which included virtually no concessions for those who believed differently.[14] On December 30, 1805, he dissolved the

---

[10]F. Ernest Stoeffler, *German Pietism during the Eighteenth Century* (Leiden: E. J. Brill, 1973), 89.

[11]Stoeffler, *German Pietism*, 89 and Fritz, *Radikaler Pietismus*, 123. From 1787 to 1800 George Rapp experienced only eight relatively mild punishments– five fines for keeping his children from school attendance, two fines for cutting wood on the Sabbath, and an announced two day incarceration in the prison tower, which he did not serve since all the Separatists in Iptingen demanded the same punishment for themselves. Ibid., 133.

[12]Hartmut Lehmann, "Neupietismus und Säkularisierung. Beobachtungen zum sozialen Umfeld und politischen Hintergrund von Erweckungsbewegung und Gemeinschaftsbewegung," *Pietismus und Neuzeit* 15 (1989): 40-58.

[13]Fritz, *Radikaler Pietismus*, 152. Cf. HStAS A 213 Bü 3100.

[14]The decree against Separatists from Dec. 27, 1803 commanded that "Versammlungen von ungehorsamen Separatisten 'durch polizeiliche Gewalt, die auf Kosten der Separatisten selbst auszuüben ist, zu zerstören, jene Renitenz,

provincial constitution. The following year King Friedrich withdrew the right of citizens to emigrate from Württemberg. In 1809, he forcibly introduced, in some locations with military troops, a new "rationalistic" liturgy for the Lutheran Church, in which all mention of the devil was removed. Pietists responded by becoming increasingly convinced that the end of the age was at hand. Many concluded that the Lutheran Church was beyond repair, and therefore separated from it.

Socio-Economic Context

The rise of Rapp's Separatist movement in the 1780s and 1790s took place in decades characterized by what Eberhard Fritz refers to as "critical [social] symptoms or manifestations." Fritz argues that these "critical symptoms" (krisenhafte Erscheinungen) increased the willingness of villagers in Württemberg to buck the traditional social (village) and religious (church) system and separate from the Lutheran Church.[15] Fritz specifically elaborates the dissolution of the traditional village structure as a crucial element allowing the rise of the Separatist movement. Two other factors likewise influenced the rise of Rapp's Separatist movement: the increase in poverty experienced by villagers in the eighteenth century, and the impressive level of literacy among the lower classes.[16]

The rapid growth in village population in Württemberg throughout the eighteenth century outpaced the social and economic resources of many communities and swelled the ranks of the impoverished.[17] A very large number of legitimate (and illegitimate) children were born to village folk in this century. Although high child mortality rates (only approximately one-half of children born reached the marriageable age of twenty) held sway throughout the century, the great number of births resulted in a burgeoning population rate.[18] In most villages the land holdings of the tenant farmers were of necessity split into smaller and smaller portions to accommodate the increased population. Even in good years many farmers could barely produce enough surplus to feed their families until the next harvest. Bad harvests were common, since the production rate of one of the chief crops,

---

Verachtung und Injurie gegen Gesetz und Obrigkeit zu untersuchen und die angemessenen Strafen zu diktieren.'" Gerhard Schäfer, *Zu erbauen und zu erhalten das rechte Heil der Kirche: Eine Geschichte der Evangelischen Landeskirche in Württemberg* (Stuttgart: J. F. Steinkopf, 1984), 212.

[15]Fritz, *Radikaler Pietismus*, 122.

[16]Fritz discusses these other social elements in other sections of his volume, *Radikaler Pietismus*.

[17]Paul Sauer, "Not und Armut in den Dörfern des Mittleren Neckarraumes in vorindustriellen Zeit," *Zeitschrift für württembergische Landesgeschichte* 41 (1982): 131-149, here 137 and 142.

[18]Sauer estimates that between 1700 and 1799 approximately 40 children were born each year per 1000 inhabitants. In 1978, by contrast, only 10 births per 1000 were registered in Baden-Württemberg. Sauer, "Not und Armut," 140-141.

grapes, was particularly sensitive to excessive rainfall. It became increasingly difficult for tenant farmers to pay the numerous tithes and taxes on the land (paid mostly in natural produce) to its noble, secular or religious owner. Villagers were required yearly to provide a certain number of days of statute labor (*Frondienst*) to their lord for building projects or other services. Particularly loathsome were the hunting expeditions that the nobility held with little or no concern for the damaged crops and ruined harvests of the tenant farmers.[19] The invasions of Württemberg and the movement of troops through its territories during times of military conflict furthered the sorry plight of the lower classes. The soldiers of General Moreau, who invaded Württemberg several times in the 1790s, plundered the houses, confiscated money and natural produce and damaged crops.[20]

In an attempt to limit the number of impoverished families in a village, communities in the eighteenth to mid-nineteenth century frequently enforced two very drastic and hated policies. Poor persons were refused not only citizenship and the right to relocate geographically, but even the right to marry. Not surprisingly, the number of illegitimate children was quite high during this period.[21] In spite of love for their homeland, many villagers in Württemberg were impelled to immigrate for economic reasons to America or elsewhere to make a better life for themselves and their families. Those who remained were often required to combine farming with a trade (weaving, barrel making, etc.) in order to make an adequate living.[22]

The rise in population did not just result in increased poverty in the villages. It likewise threatened the traditional village social structure. Sabean and Findeisen's research indicates that suddenly in the 1780s marriages between persons of different social and economic classes virtually ceased in the villages of Württemberg. This fact was just one sign that the village structure, which had served as the "basis of social solidarity," was greatly shaken and no longer functioned as it had previously.[23] Findeisen, therefore, speaks of the radical Pietism of the late eighteenth century as a "crisis cult," which arose in response to social and economic stressors. The disintegration of traditional, local village unity and solidarity increased the wil-

---

[19]Sauer, "Not und Armut," 134-135.
[20]Leibbrandt, *Auswanderung aus Schwaben*, 23-24.
[21]Sauer, "Not und Armut," 145-147.
[22]"Die meisten Handwerker betreiben nebenher auch Ackerbau. Überhaupt ist es eine Eigentümlichkeit Württembergs, daß der Unterschied zwischen Stadt und Land, industrieller und landwirtschaftlicher Bevölkerung nicht in dem Maße wie anderwärts sich bemerkbar machte." Leibbrandt, *Auswanderung aus Schwaben*, 19. Interestingly, the economic success of the Harmony Society was based on the combination of agriculture with manufacture, something practiced in the villages of Württemberg by Rapp and many of his followers.
[23]Fritz, *Radikaler Pietismus*, 122.

lingness of individuals to engage in the social protest involved in forming or joining dissident religious groups.[24]

One other social factor was influential in the rise of radical Pietism in general and Rapp's Separatist movement in particular—the reading of devotional literature. Eberhard Fritz notes that the reading of radical Pietist books served as the chief transmitter (*Leitmedium*) of Separatist and mystical-spiritual thought in the villages of Württemberg.[25] This, of course, presupposed a considerable level of literacy among potential and actual members of the Separatist movement, who were usually from the lower and lower-middle classes (farmers and craftsmen), and not the so-called educated classes. The fact that leaders as well as some members of Separatist conventicles were able to read and comprehend the convoluted thought patterns of theosophist Jakob Boehme and the mystical language of Johannes Tauler, attests to the level of literacy acquired by the lower classes in this era. The basic village school education was further developed and refined by participation in the "reading culture" cultivated in the Pietist and Separatist conventicles. Books were not only eagerly read, but borrowed from neighbors or bought by villagers, as property inventories prepared upon death indicate. With the beginning of an extended period of peace in 1715, the lower classes in the villages of Württemberg were often enough above subsistence level to afford occasionally to buy books, and they did so. Hans Medick's microhistorical study of the country village Laichingen (*Schwabisch Alb*) demonstrates that in the second half of the eighteenth century, village inhabitants possessed on the average more books than the population of the university town of Tübingen.[26]

Religious Context

The Pietism that existed in Württemberg and elsewhere in Germany between 1780 and 1815, although retaining continuity with the earlier Spenerian and Halle forms of the phenomenon, was nevertheless sufficiently different to warrant the title "Neo-Pietism."[27] In contrast to the earlier Pietism,

---

[24]Hans-Volkmar Findeisen, "Pietismus in Fellbach 1750-1820 zwischen sozialem Protest und bürgerlicher Anpassung" (Ph.D. diss., University of Tübingen, 1985), 265.

[25]Fritz, *Radikaler Pietismus*, 274.

[26]Ibid., 265-266 and 271. Petra Schad, in *Buchbesitz im Herzogtum Württemberg im 18. Jahrhundert am Beispiel der Amtsstadt Wildberg und des Dorfes Blsslngen/Enz* (Stuttgart: Thorbecke Verlag, 2002), 141-153, correlates socio-economic status and ownership of books for a town (Wildberg) and village (Bissingen) in Württemberg in the eighteenth century. Households with below average income (categories a and b) often owned as many books as households with above-average income (categories A and B).

[27]Horst Weigelt, in "Der Pietismus im Überrgang vom 18. zum 19. Jahrhundert," in *Geschichte des Pietismus*, vol. 2. *Der Pietismus im achtzehnten Jahrhundert*, ed. Martin Brecht and Klaus Deppermann (Göttingen: Vandenhoeck & Ruprecht, 1995),

which developed in opposition to the perceived "deadness" of Lutheran and Reformed Orthodoxy,[28] Neo-Pietism had an entirely different foe--rationalist, Enlightenment thought and Neology.[29] The few remnants of Lu-

---

700, 744-745, does not use the term "Neo-Pietism" for the Pietism between 1780-1815/1819. Rather he speaks of "transitional Pietism" (*Übergangspietismus*), which reacted to Enlightenment theology, opposed the French Revolution, and was influenced by the individualism of the *Sturm und Drang*. This transitional Pietism was followed by the revival movement after 1815 in Germany. Groth likewise speaks of the Pietism between 1780-1820 as the "Übergangsphase vom alten Pietismus des 18. Jahrhunderts zur Erweckungsbewgung des 19. Jahrhunderts." Friedhelm Groth, *Die "Wiederbringung aller Dinge" im württembergischen Pietismus* (Göttingen: Vandenheock & Ruprecht, 1984), 30. Martin Brecht in "Der Spätpietismus—ein vergessenes oder vernachlässigtes Kapitel der protestantischen Kirchengeschichte," *Pietismus und Neuzeit* 10 (1984): 124-151 uses the term "late Pietism" for this phenonomenon. He later suggests the label "postenlightenment Pietism" (*nachaufklärerischer Pietismus*) in place of *Spätpietismus*. Martin Brecht, *Ausgewählte Aufsätze*, vol. 2, *Pietismus* (Stuttgart: Calwer Verlag, 1997), 557. Stoeffler, in *German Pietism*, 236-242, uses the term "Neo-Pietism" for what Weigelt and Groth define as "transitional Pietism," and Brecht as "late Pietism." The author will be using Stoeffler's terminology, since that term emphasizes the newness and distinctive character of late, anti-Enlightenment Pietism.

[28]A simplistic interpretation of Pietism as a response to "dead orthodoxy" has been rejected by contemporary scholars. This view was first proposed by Friedrich August Gotttreu Tholuck (1799-1877) in *Vorgeschichte des Rationalismus*, vol. 2, *Das kirchliche Leben des siebzehnten Jahrhunderts bis in die Anfänge der Aufklärung* (Berlin: Wiegandt und Grieben, 1861). A more nuanced view of the relationship between Lutheran orthodoxy and Pietism and of the reform efforts within Lutheran orthodoxy was first advanced in the 1920s by Hans Leube, *Die Reformidee in der deutschen lutherischen Kirche zur Zeit der Orthodoxie* (Leipzig: Dörffling & Francke, 1924). More recently Johannes Wallmann, "Pietismus und Orthodoxie: Überlegungen und Fragen zur Pietismusforschung," in *Geist und Geschichte der Reformation*, ed. Hanns Rückett (Berlin: de Gruyter,1966); Sabine Holtz, *Theologie und Alltag. Lehre und Leben in den Predigten der Tübinger Theologen 1550-1750* (Tübingen: J.C. Mohr, 1993), and Martin Brecht, "Das Aufkommen der neuen Frömmigkeitsbewegung in Deutschland," in *Geschichte des Pietismus*, vol. 2, *Das 17. und frühe 18. Jahrhundert*, ed. Martin Brecht (Göttingen: Vandenhoeck & Ruprecht, 1993), 113-203, have successfully laid to rest inaccurate stereotypes of "dead" Lutheran orthodoxy.

[29]Neology refers to a German theological development in the second half of the eighteenth century that "shifted the criterion of the validity of religious insights from revelation to reason" and "virtually transformed man's interest in eternal salvation into mere desire for temporal happiness." Stoeffler, *German Pietism*, 239. It should be noted that Neologism and Enlightenment theology in Germany were not monolithic structures. For example, there were considerable differences between the more theologically conservative stance of transitional theologian Siegmund Jacob Baumgarten (1706-1757) and of the Neologist Johann Salomo Semler (1725-1791), and the radical biblical criticism of Gotthold Ephraim Lessing (1729-1781) and Hermann Samuel Reimarus (1694-1768). See W. R. Ward, *Christianity under the Ancien Regime 1648-1789* (Cambridge: Cambridge University Press, 1999), 171-181;

theran Orthodoxy, which persisted until the end of the eighteenth century, actually joined forces with their former adversaries, the (Neo-)Pietists, against this common, new enemy.[30] Unlike Spenerian and Halle Pietism, which adopted some elements of the rationalist agenda, Neo-Pietism reacted decidedly against the encroachments of Enlightenment thought in theology and in the church.[31] Neo-Pietists of the churchly and radical persuasions, in contrast to the Neologians and rationalists, continued to emphasize the need for salvation, the deity of Christ, the doctrine of substitutionary atonement and the trust-worthiness of the Biblical record.[32] Rapp likewise reflected the Neo-Pietist, anti-Enlightenment stance. His position was stated most clearly in one later sermon, although evidence of this sentiment was found scattered throughout his writings. In the late sermon Rapp declared that "Voltaire and his kind" had "laid the foundation for the great decline" in the Christian religion. These men falsely interpreted the Bible by using "philosophical rules." By applying these rules, "enlightened" theologians concluded that "Jesus was but a good man," and that "Christ's work of redemption was merely allegorical," since man was saved from sin by living morally. "Therefore the sacrifice of atonement and the divine revelation of God is obliterated. This then completely annihilates the Christian

---

Henning Graf Reventlow, Walter Sparn and John Woodbridge, eds., *Historische Kritik und biblischer Kanon in der deutschen Aufklärung* (Wiesbaden: Harrossowitz, 1988); and Ellen Judy Wilson, "Aufklärung," in *Encyclopedia of the Enlightenment*, ed. Peter Hanns Reill (New York: Facts on File, 1996), 22-23.

[30]Stoeffler lists J. B. E. Carpzov (1720-1803), J. M. Gooze (b. 1717) and J. F. S. Seiler (1733-1807) as belonging to late Lutheran Orthodoxy. Stoeffler, *German Pietism*, 241, n. 2.

[31]The relationship between Pietism and the Enlightenment has been hotly contested by scholars. Some, particularly earlier, scholars have argued that Pietism directly paved the way for the Enlightenment. Key examples include Friedrich Lauchert, "Pietism," in *The Catholic Encyclopedia*, vol. 12, ed. Charles G. Herbermann, et al. (New York: Appleton, 1911), 80-82; Emanuel Hirsch, *Geschichte der neuern Evangelischen Theologie*, vol. 2 (Gütersloh: Bertelsmann, 1951); and Hans Frei, *The Eclipse of the Biblical Narrative* (New Haven: Yale University Press, 1974), 38-40. Subsequent scholars have usually noted the complex relationship between the two movements. See Mark Noll, "Pietism," in *Evangelical Dictionary of Theology*, 2d ed., ed. Walter A. Elwell (Grand Rapids, Mich.: Baker, 2001), 855-858; Carl Mirbt, "Pietism," in *The New Schaff-Herzog Encyclopedia of Religious Knowledge*, vol. 9, ed. Samuel Macauley Jackson and George William Gilmore (Grand Rapids, Mich.: Baker, 1951), 53-67; and Ellen Judy Wilson, "Pietism," in *Encyclopedia of the Enlightenment*, ed. Peter Hanns Reill (New York: Facts on File, 1996), 328. For points of contact between the Enlightenment and Pietism in Württemberg see Dieter Narr, "Berührung von Aufklärung und Pietismus in Württemberg des 18. Jahrhunderts," *Blätter für württembergische Kirchengeschichte* 66/67 (1966-1967): 264-277.

[32]Weigelt, "Pietismus im Überrgang," 744.

religion at its foundation and leads to complete atheism," Rapp proclaimed.[33]

Churchly Pietists in Württemberg at the end of the eighteenth and beginning of the nineteenth centuries were adamant in their opposition to two "rationalist" changes in Lutheran worship, embodied in the new hymnbook of 1791 and the revised liturgy of 1809.[34] In the new hymnbook, only twenty-nine Luther hymns remained unchanged. Other hymns were partially altered, at times to the point of becoming unrecognizable. But the majority of hymns, which had been sung for three hundred years in church, school and home, were replaced with decidedly rationalistic hymns.[35] The opposition to use of the hymnbook was so great that its usage needed to be enforced, in Kirchentellinsfurt (1800) with military troops. A similar situation occurred less than two decades later when a new worship liturgy was introduced. Traditional prayers were replaced with ones reflecting a more "modern" spirit. The greatest opposition arose, however, over the baptismal liturgy. The concept of original sin was virtually eliminated, being replaced by a statement affirming the "noble powers of good" slumbering within the child's soul. Further, the "renunciation of the devil and all his works" was replaced with a weak formula against superstition and the lack of faith. Both churchly Pietists and traditional Lutherans were concerned that without the formula renouncing Satan, the sacrament of baptism had lost its validity. Many Pietists, who till this time had maintained a tenuous relationship to the established church, became convinced through these innovations to separate. For radical Pietists, the innovations further confirmed their conviction of the bleak spiritual state of the Lutheran Church. Because

---

[33]MG-437/ Box 22/ Folder 82B/ Gr E-7. Cf. Statements by Rapp in his 1824 philosophical treatise: "The erroneous doctrines and nonsense, propagated against the christian religion and its founder; the abominable calumnies of the present age . . . the haters of Christ, *the sceptics and despisers of the bible*, have all to be put to flight;" and "Therefore is the principle of modern philosophy thoroughly false, which declares practical reason self-sufficient, without either bible or any other divine revelation." George Rapp, *Thoughts on the Destiny of Man particularly with Reference to the Present Times* (Harmony, Ind.: [s.n.], 1824), 14 and 20.

[34]For the significance of the introduction of the new hymnbook and liturgy see: Hermelink, *Geschichte der evangelischen*, 287-296; Hartmut Lehmann, "Der politische Widerstand gegen die Einführunng des neuen Gesangbuches von 1791 in Württemberg," *Blätter für württembergische Kirchengeschichte*, 66/67 (1966-1967): 247-263; Gerhard Schäfer, "Zum württembergischen Gesangbuch vom Jahr 1791," *Zeitschrift für württembergische Landesgeschichte* 41 (1982): 400-413; and Eberhard Fritz, "Entstehung von pietistischen Privatversammlungen und Widerstand gegen die Liturgie von 1809," *Blätter für württembergische Kirchengeschichte* 91 (1991): 173-188.

[35]Schäfer, *Zu Erbauen*, 192-194, argues that the 1791 hymnbook was not rationalistic. This contrasts with Hermann Ehmer, Heinrich Frommer, Rainer Jooß and Jörg Thierfelder, eds., *Gott und die Welt in Württemberg* (Stuttgart: Calwer, 2000), 131-132, who emphasize the rationalistic elements and particularly that Pietist contemporaries viewed the hymnbook as rationalistic.

King Friedrich was the nominal head of the church and the liturgy revision was ordered by him, it was binding as law and enforced in spite of massive opposition.[36]

Churchly and radical Pietists in Württemberg were initially hesitant or even positive in their response to the French Revolution. Some theological students at Tübingen and pious members of the lower class were enamored by the ideals of freedom and equality that the Revolution embodied. Many farmers and craftsmen initially interpreted the Revolution and ensuing war to be more a struggle against despotism than a war of one nation against a foreign enemy.[37] However, after the storming of the Tuileries, the execution of Louis XVI in 1793, and the Reign of Terror, most members of the Pietist movement became decided opponents of the French Revolution. The Revolution was thought to reflect in great measure the "spirit of radical Enlightenment," which Neo-Pietists adamantly deplored and resisted.[38]

Millennial speculation among Pietists received abundant new fodder in the wake of the tumultuous events surrounding the French Revolution and led directly to the spectacular growth in the Separatist movement from the 1790s to circa 1815.[39] Hartmut Lehman estimates that at the end of the eighteenth century one quarter of all Protestants in Germany, whether from the lower or middle classes, adhered to some variant of millenarianism.[40] The end of the *Ancien Regime* and the bloody Napoleonic wars could only be a sign that the end was imminent and the Anti-Christ would soon appear.

---

[36]Ehmer, *Gott und die Welt*, 131-132, and Leibrandt, *Auswanderung*, 34-36. From 1734 to 1797 Catholic dukes were nominal heads of the Württemberg Landeskirche, though they turned over the direction of the church to a *Kirchenrat*. Eberhard Fritz, "Christian Gottlob Pregizer und die 'Pregizianer.' Zur Genese einer pietischen Gruppierung im frühen 19. Jahrhundert." In Norbert Haag et al., ed. *Tradition und Fortschritt. Württembergische Kirchengeschichte im Wandel* (Epfendorf/Neckar: Bibliotheca Academica, 2008): 239-268, here 243, n. 21. With the addition of non-Protestant territory to the kingdom of Württemberg in the Napoleonic era, it was no longer possible for the king as head of the Lutheran Church to not tolerate other confessions. Ibid., "Das Ende des langen 18. Jahrhunderts. Erfahrungen des frühen Pietismus als Voraussetzung für die Selbstorganization und Institutionalisierung des württembergischen Pietismus im frühen 19. Jahrhundert." In Christian Soboth and Udo Sträter, eds. *"Aus Gottes Wort und eigner Erfahrung gezieget." Erfahrung – Glauben, Erkennen und Gestalten im Pietismus*, ed. Halle: Verlag der Franckeschen Stiftung, 2012: 879-892, here 879.

[37]Leibbrandt, *Auswanderung*, 8-9.

[38]Weigelt, "Pietismus im Übergang," 744.

[39]Oliver's book, *Prophets and Millennialists*, demonstrates how the French Revolution stimulated prophetical interest in England. W. H. Oliver, *Prophets and Millennialists. The Uses of Biblical Prophecy in England from the 1790s to the 1840s* (Auckland: Auckland University Press, 1978).

[40]Hartmut Lehmann, "Pietistic Millenarianism in Late Eighteenth-Century Germany," in *The Transformation of Political Culture. England and Germany in the Late Eighteenth Century*, ed. Eckhart Hellmuth (London: German Historical Institute, 1990), 327-338, here 331.

Württemberg Pietist Christian Armbruster in *Die sieben letzten Posaunen* (1814) declared that the first of the seven trumpets in the book of Revelation (Rev 8:6) was blown in 1787 [sic] at the beginning of the French Revolution and that three of the trumpet judgments would be specifically upon France in the imminent cataclysm. God would not allow Napoleon ultimately to be victorious, because of France's rationalistic, anti-Christian agenda, particularly the replacement of the "time of the Lord Christ," the Christian week, with the ten day cycle and calendar.[41] Some Württemberg Pietists claimed that Napoleon was the Anti-Christ or "Apollyon" (with the "N" of negation set before it) of Rev 9:11.[42]

A small group of radical Pietists in Württemberg came to a different conclusion. Centered in the two villages of Nordheim and Horrheim, these radicals likewise observed the political events surrounding the French Revolution in the light of biblical prophecy, particularly the Book of Revelation. They concluded that Napoleon was not the Anti-Christ, rather a Messiah figure chosen by God to inaugurate the coming kingdom of God. Christoph Greulich, an early leader of this persuasion in Nordheim, was convinced that Napoleon was the instrument of God who would overcome the forces of the Anti-Christ depicted in Revelation. The Horrheim Separatists appropriated and elaborated Greulich's views. The Horrheim church visitation protocol of 1805-1806 reported that the local Separatists venerated Napoleon as their "brother," the "chosen of God," the "son of God," the "risen Christ," and the "promised king of Israel."[43] George Rapp corresponded with Christoph Greulich prior to his immigration to the United States in 1803. Rapp, unlike the Nordheim and Horrheim Separatists, however, espoused a moderate view of the role of Napoleon in the upcoming eschatological events. For the Separatist leader, Bonaparte was sent by God to help persecuted, true believers.[44]

Neo-Pietists were distinguished from earlier Pietists not only in their anti-Enlightenment stance and their response to the French Revolution. These later Pietists were likewise characterized by a stronger emphasis on individuality and subjective experience, reflections of the contemporary *Sturm und Drang* and Romantic movements.[45] The *Sturm und Drang*:

> ... was in essence a protest of the younger generation against the hegemony of the prevailing rationalism. The emphasis was upon man's inner experience, upon the legitimacy and significance of feeling, upon the freedom of

---

[41] Christian Armbruster, *Die sieben letzten Posaunen oder Wehen, wann sie anfangen und aufhören und von den 70 Danielischen Wochen und 42 prophetischen Monaten* (Ulm: [s.n.], 1814), 16-17 and 20.

[42] W. Claus, *Württembergische Väter. Von Brastberger bis Dann. Bilder aus dem christlichen Leben Württemberg*, vol. 2 (Stuttgart/Calw: Verlag der Vereinssbuchhandlung, 1905), 286.

[43] Fritz, *Radikaler Pietismus*, 187-188, 191.

[44] Ibid., 186 and 188.

[45] Weigelt, "Pietismus im Übergang," 700 and 745.

the individual to express himself vis-à-vis accepted artistic, attitudinal, intellectual, or behavioral norms. It made room for the irrational aspects of man's experience and for his elemental needs.[46]

The movement, which first arose in the writings of Friedrich Gottlieb Klopstock, reached its fullest religious expression in the writings of Johann Gottfried Herder.[47] Neo-Pietists rejected rationalism and particularly Neologism because of the latter's rejection of revelation in favor of reason as the ultimate source of religious authority. They found support for their experience-oriented piety in the representatives of the *Sturm und Drang* and Romantic movements, which were both likewise empiricist in nature. They parted company with both intellectual movements, however, when their representatives emphasized human experience alone to the neglect of Scriptural revelation.[48] Hymns written by average members of the Harmony Society and preserved in their manuscript and printed hymnals reflect these intellectual and cultural trends.

Early Life and Conversion of Johann Georg Rapp

Johann Georg Rapp was born on November 1, 1757 in Iptingen as the second of five children to Johann Adam (1720-1771) and Rosine Rapp. Ancestors of the Rapps had been residents in this northwest corner of Württemberg, first in Nussdorf, then in Iptingen, for generations. The Rapp family was quite poor and belonged to the lower class in the village. Johann Adam had inherited large debts from his father. His wife, Rosine, was the poor daughter of a citizen in Mönsheim and thus unable to improve the family fortune through dowry. In years with poor harvests, the Rapps most likely went hungry at times.[49]

Later church records indicate that Johann Georg was an intelligent pupil at school, although given to melancholy and stubbornness.[50] These two characteristics perhaps explain his later propensity for mystical piety (melancholy) and his aggressive leadership qualities (stubbornness). Johann Georg lost his father at the young age of thirteen (May 16, 1771), and inherited the

---

[46]Stoeffler, *German Pietism*, 240.
[47]Karl Arndt has demonstrated the influence of Herder on George Rapp in Karl J. R. Arndt, "Herder and the Harmony Society," *Germanic* Review 16, no. 2 (April 1941): 108-113.
[48]Stoeffler, *German Pietism*, 240-241.
[49]For this section on Rapp's early life the author utilized Karl J. R. Arndt, *George Rapp's Harmony Society 1785-1847*, rev. ed. (Teaneck, N.J.: Fairleigh Dickinson University Press, 1972), 15-22 and Eberhard Fritz, "Johann Georg Rapp (1757-1847) und die Separatisten in Iptingen. Mit einer Edition der relevanten Iptinger Kirchenkonventsprotokolle," *Blätter für Württembergische Kirchengeschichte* 95 (1995): 129-203, here 141-144.
[50]1785 Iptingen annual church report. Arndt, *Doc. Hist. 1700-1803*, 75-76.

latter's debt. The following spring, on April 26, 1772, the youth was confirmed by the pietistically-inclined Pastor Friedrich Christian Göz in the Lutheran church in Iptingen. At the same time, Johann Georg left the village school in order to learn the craft of a linen weaver.

Eberhard Fritz suggests that after the death of Johann Adam Rapp, Georg's father, Pastor Göz served as a sort of surrogate father and role model for the orphaned youth.[51] In any case, Johann Georg attended as a teenager the churchly Pietist conventicle led by Pastor Göz, prior to the latter's death in 1779.[52] Conventicles were a significant, even defining aspect of the Pietist landscape in Württemberg ever since Spener's visit to the duchy in the 1680s. Therefore, a few words about their development are in order. Although conventicles were established in the cities and larger towns at the beginning of the eighteenth century, it was not until mid-century that this typical form of piety spread to many of the villages of Württemberg.[53] The Pietist decree of 1743 assured the legality of churchly Pietist (though not separatistic) conventicles in the duchy, thereby contributing to their spread throughout the land.[54] Some of the conventicles in the villages after 1750 were led by pietistically-oriented pastors (such as Göz). With the increasing influence of Enlightenment theology on the new generation of pastors and theologians, however, the number of pastors sympathetic to the *collegia pietatis* had sharply declined.[55] By default, the leadership of conventicles passed to gifted laymen and from the church building or pastor's home to the *Stube* (living room) of a farmer or craftsman.

This development can likewise be observed in George Rapp's hometown of Iptingen. The conventicle was founded by Pastor Wilhelm Christian Gmelin (1684-1746) soon after beginning his ministry in Iptingen in 1739. By 1742 the group had grown to twenty or thirty members who met in the pastor's home to sing, pray, read from the Bible and review the sermon.[56] After

---

[51]Fritz, "Rapp und die Separatisten in Iptingen," 142.

[52]Arndt, *Doc. Hist. 1700-1803*, 164. Fritz questions whether the statement of Rapp's attendance at Pastor Göz's conventicle in the 1790 Iptingen annual church report is accurate, since Rapp makes no mention of it in his conversion account. The author does not consider the absence from the conversion account to be adequate grounds to dismiss this clear statement in the church record.

[53]Fritz, "Rapp und die Separatisten in Iptingen," 133.

[54]Arndt, *Doc. Hist. 1700-1803*, 20-35, contains a transcription of the 1743 Rescript. The decree allowed conventicles led by the pastor or schoolteacher, though not at night or during Sunday worship. Laymen might only lead the meetings when the pastor was hindered from attending. The number of participants was limited. Visitors from other localities were not allowed to attend.

[55]Claus, *Väter 2*, 272. Cf. Christian Dietrich and Ferdinand Brockes, *Die Privat-Erbauungsgemeinschaften innerhalb der evangelischen Kirchen Deutschlands* (Stuttgart: Buchhandlung des Deutschen Philadelphiavereins, 1903), 220 and Stoeffler, *German Pietism*, 74.

[56]Fritz, "Rapp und die Separatisten in Iptingen," 138-140. Gmelin himself had prior to this time espoused separatist leanings in two tracts, been suspended from

the death of Gmelin, the leadership of the Iptingen conventicle passed to laymen, most likely because the new pastor, Wilhelm Christian Faber (1726-1761), was not inclined to lead it.[57] The following pastor, Friedrich Christian Göz (1761-1779), however, was a convinced Pietist. He took over the leadership of the group, which met in the parsonage. It was in this churchly Pietist conventicle that Johann Georg Rapp in his teenage years received his introduction to the Pietist form of doctrine and spirituality. Thus, even prior to his journeyman travels and later conversion, Rapp was acquainted with and had roots in the churchly Pietist movement in Württemberg.

Sometime after 1777 but before 1780 Johann Georg left Iptingen for several years to earn his living as a journeyman linen weaver.[58] By his own admission, he lived as the "most badly-behaved person" imaginable during his wanderings. His life during this period was morally evil (*übel*); he was a "slave to sin" (*Sünden-Knecht*).[59] By 1780, he returned to Iptingen. His behavior upon arrival was such that Göz's successor, Pastor Andreas Genter, recommended his abstention from the Eucharist until his morals had improved.[60] Although Rapp soon began to receive the Lord's Supper again, he was plagued daily with a strong sense of "inner unrest." In a written statement that Rapp submitted to the Iptingen church council (*Kirchenkonvent*) in 1785, he described his spiritual journey from "inner unrest" to conversion and finally to separation from the Lutheran Church.[61]

Rapp's long inward struggle to achieve conversion occurred in three stages spread out over several years (1780 to 1782). His experience thus

---

ministry (1708) and exiled from the duchy. Though reinstated to the ministry of the Lutheran Church in 1717, his rigorous Communion discipline in his next two churches (Ochsenbach and Iptingen) suggest continuing sympathy with Separatist thought, which according to Fritz, could be the root of Rapp's radical Pietism.

[57]Fritz notes Faber's "critical attitude" toward the Pietist meeting in his 1760 comments in the *Visitationsprotokoll*. Fritz, "Rapp und die Separatisten in Iptingen," 140.

[58]Fritz notes that a journeymanship was not required as a linen weaver, but that he may have wandered and worked for several years to relieve the financial situation of his family. Fritz, "Rapp und die Separatisten in Iptingen," 143.

[59]Arndt, *Doc. Hist. 1700-1803*, 67 and 71.

[60]Ibid., 67.

[61]Local church councils or *Kirchenkonvente* were established in 1644 throughout Württemberg. They consisted of the pastor, the secular superintendent (*Ortsvorsteher*), and several committee members chosen by the former. The board met once weekly to discuss issues of church discipline, charitable giving, and school administration. Schäfer, *Zu Erbauen*, 104-105. Cf. Helga Schnabel-Schüle, "Calvinistische Kirchenzucht in Württemberg? Zur Theorie und Praxis der württembergischen Kirchenkonvente," *Zeitschrift für württembergische Landesgeschichte* 52 (1993): 169-223, and Eberhard Fritz, "Die Kirche im Dorf. Studien und Beobachtungen zur kirchlichen Situation in der ländlichen Gemeinde des Herzogtums Württemberg," *Zeitschrift für Württembergische Landesgeschichte* 52 (1993): 155-178, especially 165-166.

reflected, so he said, Job 33:29-30: "Behold, God does all these things, twice, three times, with a man, to bring back his soul from the pit, that he may see the light of life."[62] In 1780 he first had "such a strong conviction to surrender [him]self to Jesus," a conviction that did not bear fruit because he "loved the world too much." In 1781, Rapp's spiritual unrest became even stronger. Yet he "did not remain faithful." Finally in 1782:

> [T]he Lord again had compassion on me, the world became very bitter to me, for the call of the Father was too strong for me. Then the love of Jesus became so precious to me because for the third time [cf. Job 33:29-30] he had shown me his mercy and had sought me. As is usually the case with beginners who want to start with being pious themselves, for an entire quarter year I took much pain to achieve this, until I was oppressed and heavy-laden. One day I was completely still. Then the spirit of Jesus worked on me more strongly than I have ever before experienced, and the verse of Jesus was brought close to my heart, Revelation 3: "Behold, I stand at the door and knock; if any man hear my voice," etc. Then I felt so small that I did not care to open my eyes. It was then that I saw that salvation is in Christ Jesus alone.[63]

Rapp's long spiritual struggle to achieve conversion was reminiscent of the *Busskampf* (repentance struggle) prior to the *Durchbruch* (radical conversion) that characterized the spirituality of Halle Pietism. His final submission in 1782 likewise included a heart-felt recognition that justification was by faith alone in Christ and not by works (Luther's Reformation discovery).

Soon after he had experienced conversion, Johann Georg Rapp began to attend the churchly Pietist conventicle, whose leadership, after the death of Pastor Göz, had passed into the hands of laymen. It met in the house of the farmer, Johannes Weber, and was visited by approximately twenty-five persons of both sexes. The group read and discussed texts from the Bible or from other Pietist devotional literature.[64] As was common in that era, Rapp likewise attended conventicles in other neighboring villages. Prior to his separation from the Lutheran Church in 1785, Rapp had not only visited the conventicle in Lomersheim, but had been asked to teach it.[65] He most likely met his future wife, Christina Benzinger, while visiting the Pietist conventicle in the neighboring village, Friolzheim. The two were married on February 4, 1783. Christina Benzinger came from a much more prosperous family than did Georg Rapp. She brought three times as much wealth into the marriage as her bridegroom, with the result that the couple no longer

---

[62]Arndt, *Doc. Hist. 1700-1803*, 71.

[63]Ibid. Karl Arndt's translation into English, used here, is found in: Arndt, *Rapp's Harmony Society*, 18.

[64]Examples of literature used are Brastberger and Steinhofer's commentary on Hebrews. Fritz, "Rapp und die Separatisten in Iptingen," 142-143.

[65]Testimony of Christian Hörnle, June 5, 1787, Qu. 73. Arndt, *Doc. Hist. 1700-1803*, 117.

belonged to the poorest in the village.[66] After their wedding, they continued to visit the meetings at Weber's house as a couple. It is thus apparent that George Rapp's spiritual roots were found in churchly Pietism, before he became a Separatist.

Separation from the Lutheran Church

After Johann Georg and Christina Benzinger were married, the couple celebrated in 1783 the Eucharist two last times in the Lutheran Church in Iptingen. Their two children, Johannes (b. December 22, 1783) and Rosine (b. February 10, 1785), both received the sacrament of baptism there, although at the time of the birth of Rosine the couple had already separated from the Lutheran Church.[67] The decisive event of separation took place at the latest by early 1785.

Georg Rapp on more than one occasion between 1785 and 1787 was summoned to appear before the Iptingen church council to give an account of, among other things, why he had separated from the Lutheran Church. On those occasions Rapp explicated the reasons for his separation. He emphasized that it was not due to spiritual pride that he and wife had turned their backs on the church.[68] Rather, after his radical conversion experience, Rapp became convinced that he no longer needed the "means of grace" (*Gnadenmittel*) that the Church administered. "Because I have found Jesus" and "because Jesus as the Word of Life has shined brightly in my heart," he stated in 1785, "I don't need anything else."[69] He had received "a different and better light" than that found in the established church, and therefore no longer needed the public observance of the Eucharist.[70] He not only did not need the Lutheran Church, attending worship and receiving Communion there would actually hinder his new-found faith. The "various [rationalistic?] opinions about the Word of God" served more to "enervate than edify" his Christian life. "This is the reason, why I have separated from the church, because I lose more [spiritual] power than I receive from it." Therefore, he would follow his conscience and remain absent from public worship. Rapp felt that it would be a mortal sin (*eine Sünde zum Todt*) to ignore his conscience and attend the Lutheran Church.[71] He was convinced that separation was the correct decision for him, though not for all people. As proof,

---

[66]Fritz, *Radikaler Pietismus*, 128. Cf. Fritz, "Rapp und die Separatisten in Iptingen," 144.

[67]Fritz, "Rapp und die Separatisten in Iptingen," 144.

[68]"dieses hab ich aber nicht gethan aus Eigen sinn oder Hochmuth, wie man es mir ausdeutet, und viele liebloße urtheil über mich ergehen." Arndt, *Doc. Hist. 1700-1803*, 72.

[69]Ibid., 71.

[70]"Er habe eben ein anders u: bessres Licht bekommen u: brauche jetzo den offentlichen Gebrauch des heil. Abendmals in der Kirche nicht mehr." Ibid., 68.

[71]Ibid., 72.

Rapp explained that since separation his former spiritual unrest had been calmed, and he had experienced the "authentic peace of God."[72]

Rapp and his wife did not need the Lutheran Church because, in their opinion, in its present state the church was woefully inadequate. Within the established church lay persons did not have the apostolic freedom to speak the prophetic word impressed upon them by the Holy Spirit (1 Cor 14:27-32). Since the Apostle Paul exhorted believers not to curb the Spirit, it was necessary for Separatists to leave the established church and form their own fellowship groups, where the Spirit could have full sway.[73] The contemporary Lutheran Church was in the opinion of Rapp and the members of the Separatist movement no longer in the position "to call itself a Christian church." Instead it was identified with Babel/Babylon of Revelation 18. True believers, "those who are one mind and spirit with God should remain together, and the rest are Babel. In Babel a fire has been ignited, and he who does not go out of Babel will be burnt with it," Rapp warned the Iptingen church council in 1785.[74]

The established church was identified with Babel for several reasons. In the first place, the majority of the church members "called themselves Christians, but lived like heathens. Therefore a true Separatist could never enter the church."[75] Similarly, the celebration of the Eucharist was consistently abused by inadequate Communion discipline. Since unregenerate persons regularly attended the sacrament, it was time to "go out of Babel." The sacrament had become nothing but "idol worship."[76] Second, the Lutheran pastors were no longer authentic servants of God. The clergy was more concerned with their status in society (*Herrenstand*) and the accumulation of wealth, than in living a humble, consistent Christian life.[77] They did not preach the true Word of God. What they presented to the congregation was not "deep" enough. Their sermons lacked spiritual power and did not paint the path to salvation "narrow" enough. Although the clergy was theologically trained, their studies had proven to be a waste of money. A Separatist without money could learn more from the Holy Spirit.[78]

It was not long before the couple came into conflict with Weber, the leader of the churchly Pietist conventicle in Iptingen. Rapp explained to the church visitation committee on May 18, 1787 the reason for leaving this group meeting:

> They used to also go previously to Jacob Weber in the *Stunde*, but believe that it is no longer necessary. Weber taught, and when they said to him: He must also lay aside vanity, if he wants to teach, for he is a rich man . . . he

---

[72]Ibid., 76.
[73]Ibid., 274.
[74]Ibid., 110.
[75]Ibid., 105.
[76]Ibid., 76 and 79.
[77]Ibid., 91 and 107.
[78]Ibid., 105.

wasn't in agreement with that, for he did not want to humble himself. But no one can cast out the devil, if he still has him [the devil] within himself. Finally, Weber wrote a letter to him: he may no longer come to him [for the conventicle].[79]

Rapp very undiplomatically accused the conventicle leader of greed and hypocrisy, of being unfit to teach. A church report from 1792 stated however that Rapp's split from the Iptingen conventicle was caused by doctrinal reasons. Although Rapp had "achieved a good knowledge of the Scriptures," he began to "mix in doctrines that he had picked up elsewhere." For this reason the separation took place.[80] It is very possible that both of these reports are true–that Rapp was sharing disconcerting Separatist teachings in the meeting. The final break came, however, when he insulted the group leader.

The connection between Rapp and churchly Pietist conventicles continued in other locations even after his separation from the Church. In 1787 Rapp affirmed to the church visitation committee that the Wiernsheim conventicle had asked him to teach there several times and that he had complied. He had likewise been asked to teach the Pietist groups in Friolzheim (his wife's birthplace), in Illingen and in Heimsheim. In Lomersheim, Rapp, upon being asked, explained a hymn from the Ebersdorfer hymnbook and exegeted a passage from the Book of Hebrews.[81] The pastor from the Remstaler village of Strümpfelbach sent a written complaint to the Iptingen authorities, stating that Rapp (wrongly) deported himself as a teacher in the very large Pietist meetings there. The conventicle in Strümpfelbach became more radical and separatistic through Rapp's influence.[82]

The fact that Rapp visited churchly Pietist conventicles even after he had separated from the Church points to the degree of fellowship between churchly and radical Pietists. Churchly Pietists in this era apparently had few qualms about inviting Separatists to teach in their meetings. It was through teaching in Pietist (as opposed to Separatist) conventicles that Rapp won a large following for his convictions. Rapp's continuing connection to conventicles of the Pietist movement confirms Hans Schneider's contention that the boundaries between churchly and radical Pietism were fluid and that the personal histories of individuals likewise reflected mobility between the two branches of the one movement.[83]

---

[79]Ibid., 110.

[80]Fritz, "Rapp und die Separatisten in Iptingen," 194-195.

[81]Arndt, *Doc. Hist. 1700-1803*, 110, 117.

[82]Fritz, *Radikaler Pietismus*, 149 and "Rapp und die Separatisten in Iptingen," 172.

[83]Hans Schneider, "Der radikale Pietismus in der neueren Forschung," *Pietismus und Neuzeit* 9 (1983): 117-151, here 131-133.

Formation of the Rapp's Separatist Movement

After expulsion from the meeting at Weber's house, Rapp and his wife kept to themselves for approximately a year and concentrated on discovering and deepening their own Christian convictions.[84] After this time the Rapps began meeting (again?) with Christian Hörnle, Michael Conzelmann and their wives every other day for Bible study, thus forming the beginning of a Separatist conventicle in Iptingen.

In 1787 Rapp's small group edification meeting experienced a large increase in attendance. In that year:

> Fourteen people left the old conventicle (*Stund*) [at Weber's house] and asked him [Rapp], if he would lead a *Stund* in his house and would receive them into it, because they perceived that he and his wife strive to lead a Christian walk. This request went against his grain, but he [Rapp] finally agreed to it.[85]

This sudden growth of the Separatist conventicle proved the death knell for the Pietist small group. By 1791, Weber's meeting had virtually ceased to exist. In contrast, in 1795 the Separatist conventicle had twenty-nine members. Later the Iptingen pastor Andreas Genter (1731-1802) reckoned that fifty to sixty Separatists or approximately 5% of the population were to be found in the village.[86]

The conventicle was visited not just by folk from Iptingen. In 1788, Separatist Johann Georg Walz reported that people would walk ten to twelve hours to attend the meetings. An Iptingen church report in 1792 confirmed this fact:

> Outsiders, who come here to the Separatist meeting, are from every end and place in the land [Württemberg] ... from Wiernsheim, Lomersheim, Illingen, Großglattbach, also from Aurich near Vaihingen, Ensingen, from Calw, from Nufringen, from Gärtringen, Ehningen, Walddorf, Schorndorf, Strümpfelbach ...[87]

The meetings would often be very large when visitors were present or when a love feast was celebrated. Not infrequently seventy to eighty persons were crammed into Rapp's modest house.[88] Members of both sexes and old and young were all together. Because visitors often traveled a day's

---

[84]Letter from J. F. Flattich to W. F. Trautwein, Jan. 7, 1788. Johann Friedrich Flattich, *Briefe*, ed. Hermann Ehmer and Christoph Duncker (Stuttgart: Calwer Verlag, 1997), 254. This is confirmed by the Iptingen church report from 1785: "Dieses neuseparatistische Ehepaar hält sich seit der Visitation ruhig, macht sich keinen Anhang, bleibt aus der privatversammlung, unterläßt auch das Conventiculum mit Christian Hörnle und Conzelmann." Arndt, *Doc. Hist. 1700-1803*, 77.

[85]Flattich, *Briefe*, 254.
[86]Fritz, "Rapp und die Separatisten in Iptingen," 148.
[87]Ibid., 168 and 172.
[88]Fritz, *Radikaler Pietismus*, 133.

journey to the meeting, food was shared and overnight accommodations provided. A benevolent fund was established for needy brethren. The visitors desired not just fellowship with believers of similar persuasion, but also to hear Rapp preach. Therefore, the Separatist leader usually taught the meeting. "Räpple [diminutive nickname for Rapp] explains a chapter out of the New, also the Old Testament, wherever he receives insight, but especially out of the Revelation of John," a member reported in 1788.[89] Schoolmaster Kolb visited the Iptingen conventicle at the dawn of the nineteenth century and described the impact that Rapp's teaching had on him: "I also came once in the meeting of the Separatist Rapp, and heard him speak with majestic words about the Revelation of John, so that I was very drawn toward his strong, fiery spirit."[90] Even Pastor Genter of Iptingen, who was hostile toward Rapp, could not deny the power of his preaching.[91]

The Iptingen Separatist conventicle at its peak in the 1790s was in many ways atypical of similar meetings in other villages. It was much larger than most groups and therefore no longer a small intimate group in which each member had ample opportunity to contribute to the conversation. Although discussion of the Biblical passage or radical Pietist text took place after the teaching session, Rapp's more formalized message was the central focus.[92] Findeisen's contention that George Rapp and Michael Hahn introduced the practice of having exposition of Scripture or a more formal teaching session in the conventicle is certainly correct.[93] The Separatist conventicle in Iptingen (circa 1790) was not only larger than most but it was not divided by age, sex and marital status as some of the Pietist and Separatist conventicles were (for example in Kornwestheim and Fellbach).[94] It was likewise regularly visited by Separatists from other villages. Nevertheless it was led by Rapp or another layman and held in private homes (occasionally in open

---

[89]May 14, 1788 Interrogation of Johann Georg Walz. Fritz, "Rapp und die Separatisten in Iptingen," 167.

[90]"Ich kam auch einmal in eine Versammlung von der Separatisten Rapp, und hörte denselben mit majestätischen Worten über die heil.Offenbarung reden, so daß ich von diesem starken, feurigen Geist sehr angezogen wurde." Claus, *Väter 2*, 288.

[91]LKA A 26/473,2. Cf. Fritz, "Rapp und die Separatisten in Iptingen," 146.

[92]June 5, 1787 Interrogation of Johannes Hörnle. "Qu 104: Wer aber das Wort führe und lehre? R: Alle, wer einen Aufschluss bekomme. Meist aber der Rapp." Arndt, *Doc. Hist. 1700-1803*, 122.

[93]Findeisen, *Pietismus in Fellbach*, 129.

[94]Cf. Martin Brecht, "Hahn und der Pietismus im mittlerem Neckarraum," 419-420 (Pietist conventicles in Kornwestheim) and Findeisen, *Pietismus in Fellbach*, 128-130 (Pietist/Separatist conventicles). The separation of genders was not required by the 1743 Pietist rescript, which viewed the conventicles as a variant of the household devotional meeting (*Hausandacht*). Rather it was a Pietist innovation based on their view of the role of women. Eberhard Gutekunst, "Das Pietistenrescript von 1743," *Blätter für Württembergische Kirchengeschichte* 94 (1994): 9-26, here 24.

fields). Singing was an important element.⁹⁵ Unlike the dirge-like tunes often used in the Lutheran Church, Separatists in Rapp's movement sang joyful songs, often to the accompaniment of the zither. Hymns were frequently sung to popular secular melodies. For example, the Separatists in Strümpfelbach sang the well-loved Paul Gerhardt hymn, *Befiehl du deine Wege*, to the tune of "I loved only Ismene."⁹⁶

The Separatist conventicle in Iptingen was but one of dozens of similar fellowship groups in villages throughout Württemberg. One can speak of a network of conventicles scattered throughout the duchy, many of which were loosely or more tightly under the umbrella of Rapp's leadership. Some of the Separatist conventicles in other villages arose in a similar manner to the one in Iptingen. That is, conventicles were originally visited by members of the churchly Pietist movement, folk who still regularly attended the Lutheran Church. Through Rapp's itinerant preaching in the various villages, many of the former Pietist groups gradually radicalized and included more and more Separatists. The number of Separatists likewise grew exponentially during the tumultuous years of the Napoleonic wars. In time a large number of the conventicles became entirely separatistic in character and looked to Rapp for spiritual leadership.⁹⁷ He complied by regularly visiting the groups in other villages and by maintaining written contact through pastoral letters. Rapp's Separatist movement was thus born. It consisted of numerous conventicles or fellowship groups scattered throughout the duchy, though most numerous in the northwest corner around Iptingen and in the Rems River valley. Members of the network were connected through family and friendship ties, which were maintained by the reciprocal visiting of conventicle meetings and occasional area-wide gatherings for love feasts or merely for fellowship and to hear George Rapp preach.

Rapp's separation from the Lutheran Church and the rise of his Separatist movement did not go unnoticed by the church and secular authorities. It has already been noted that during the later reign of Duke Karl Eugen (d. 1793) a relatively conciliatory policy toward Separatists was pursued, thus allowing Rapp's movement to arise almost unhindered. Rapp and the other Separatists were frequently summoned to appear before the Iptingen church council or the combined civil and religious affairs office in Maulbronn to account for illegal attendance at *Separatist* conventicles, the holding of conventicles during Lutheran worship services, a violation in the size

---

⁹⁵Cf. Grutschnig-Kieser's helpful discussion of the role of singing in Pietism. Konstanze Grutschnig-Kieser, *Der "Geistliche Würtz-Kräuter und Blumen-Garten" des Christoph Schütz. Ein radikalpietistisches „Universal-Gesang-Buch"* (Göttingen: Vandenhoeck & Ruprecht, 2006), 12-17.

⁹⁶Fritz, *Radikaler Pietismus*, 149.

⁹⁷ The radicalization and transformation of originally churchly Pietist conventicles into Separatist ones has been documented for the villages of Fellbach and Strümpfelbach. Findeisen, "Pietismus in Fellbach," 133f. Cf. Fritz, *Radikaler Pietismus*, 149 and idem, "Rapp und die Separatisten in Iptingen," 172.

of the groups, the visiting of conventicles in other villages (*Auslaufen*), all violations of the 1743 Pietist *Reskript*, regulating such matters.[98] However, from 1787 to 1800 George Rapp experienced only eight relatively mild punishments--five fines for keeping his children from attending school, two fines for cutting wood on the Sabbath, which were infractions against ecclesiastical law (*Kirchenordnung*). Rapp was sentenced to a two day incarceration in the prison tower, which he didn't serve because all the Separatists in Iptingen demanded the same punishment for themselves.[99] Nevertheless, the Separatists considered the fines and frequent summonings to account for their beliefs as a form of religious persecution. After 1800, during the reign of Friedrich II, harassment of Separatists increased both in intensity and frequency.

The conflict between the Separatists and the church and civil authorities centered on the rejection by the former of certain aspects of the religious, cultural, and political life. The Separatists not only withdrew their membership from the Lutheran Church, they specifically rejected the Lutheran celebration of the Eucharist, baptism and confirmation. The village schools were affiliated with the Church, and therefore, Separatist children did not attend in most cases. Separatists refused to swear the oath of allegiance to the reigning duke or king or to have their young men serve in the military. These central points of conflict were the focus of two nearly identical declarations of faith, which the Separatists, at the request of the government, drew up and submitted to the Württemberg legislature in 1798 and 1799. These documents form the basis for the discussion of early Separatist beliefs in the section below, although reference to church council minutes will also be included.

Early Religious Beliefs and Practices of the Separatist Movement

The Lomersheimer (March 1, 1798) and the Ölbronner (November, 1799) Declarations of Faith were not statements of faith in the traditional sense of the word.[100] They did not discuss typical doctrines such as the nature of God, soteriology or eschatology. Rather the declarations of faith were apologetic writings, which focused on those areas of conflict that had arisen between the church and civil authorities and members of their movement. The declarations were most likely formulated by George Rapp, although signed by other Separatists as well. They expressed in cautious but clear

---

[98] A transcription of the 1743 Pietist *Reskript* is in Arndt, *Doc. Hist. 1700-1803*, 20-35.

[99] Fritz, *Radikaler Pietismus*, 133.

[100] A similar statement of faith was prepared by the Separatists in neighboring Baden, which was also influenced by the Rapp movement. Walter Alfred Sick, *Die Conventikel des Separatismus in Baden* (Schönau-Schwarzwald: A. Müller, 1936), 29 and 45.

terms their views of the church, baptism, Eucharist, school attendance, swearing of oaths and military service. The Separatists supported their written convictions through an appeal to Scripture and in some cases to the practices of the primitive church.

From Spiritualist to "Anabaptist" Ecclesiology

In the first years after his separation from the Lutheran Church (ca. 1785-1790), George Rapp espoused a spiritualist ecclesiology. This type of ecclesiology was a direct descendent of the mystical-spiritualism of the sixteenth and seventeenth centuries, although it expressed itself differently due to the changed church-historical context of the eighteenth century. According to this view, "All attempts to reform the church within were an attempt to mend Babylon (*Babelsflickerei*)—not only futile but also dangerous for one's own Christian existence."[101] The preaching of the Word in the confessional churches was not adequately Spirit-filled, nor were the outward sacraments necessary for salvation. True Christianity was inward and spiritual (John 4:24), all outward forms were not just irrelevant, but superfluous. Therefore, the vast majority of radical Pietists held that it was impious to form any "sect" or church. The true church was invisible and true Christians were scattered throughout all confessions and religions.[102] This spiritualist ecclesiology was propagated by the radical Pietist members of the German Philadelphian movement, the authors of the Berleburg Bible commentary, Hochmann von Hochenau (Church of the Spirit), Gerhard Tersteegen, and by George Rapp in the first years after his conversion (1780s).

Rapp propounded a spiritualist ecclesiology in 1787 when he explained to the church council in Iptingen that attendance at public worship was unnecessary. "The outward church is irrelevant," he stated. True worship was "doing what pleases God and that to which the Spirit says 'Amen.'"[103] Two years earlier in 1785 the Iptingen church council asked the Separatist leader why he abstained from attending worship, since the church was "the spiritual mother of all spiritual children." Quoting Gal 4:26, Rapp responded that he did not recognize a spiritual mother on earth. The "heavenly Jerusalem that is above" was the only spiritual mother.[104] His spiritualist understanding of the church meant that outward forms were irrelevant. Worship

---

[101]Hans Schneider, "Understanding the Church: Issues of Pietist Ecclesiology," in *Pietism and Community*, ed. Jonathan Strom (Leiden: Brill, 2010): 15-35, here 26. Radical Pietist spiritualist ecclesiology contrasts with the churchly Pietist approach of Spener, who upheld the definition of the church in Article 7 of the Augsburg Confession: the church was "the assembly of believers among whom the Gospel is preached in its purity and the holy sacraments are administered according to the Gospel." Ibid., 18 and 23.

[102]Schneider, "Pietist Ecclesiology," 28.

[103]Arndt, *Doc. Hist. 1700-1803*, 105.

[104]Ibid., 75.

was "in spirit and in truth," not in any one location or in any one manner. As Rapp stated, true worship was pleasing God in one's daily actions; it was not dependent on outward buildings or public worship.

After 1790 there was a radical paradigm shift in Rapp's conception of the church. The Separatist leader no longer rejected outward forms and practices in favor of inward, spiritual worship. Instead he proposed in the Lomersheimer and the Ölbronner statements of faith a visible church of "true believers" that emulated the primitive Jerusalem church. The two documents began with a declaration that the Separatist movement was an attempt to restore as much as possible the "ancient Christian religion of the first Christians," which had been in decline for centuries. The true Christian church was founded upon the "model of the holy apostles and fathers of the primitive church." It included the freedom to speak a prophetic word within their meetings when imparted by the Holy Spirit (1 Cor 14:27-32). In the manner of the first Christians, the church would gather in houses, be united in heart and spirit (Acts 4:32), and encourage one another to grow in faith and good works (Heb 10:24-25). These "apostolic principles" were found in the Bible and therefore could be defended by the Separatists "against all attacks of the prevailing [Lutheran] religion and of the sovereign state." It could certainly not be detrimental to the state, they argued, that the Separatists did not attend Lutheran worship, since they continued to uphold the truths of the "Law and the Gospel."[105] Like other radical Pietists, members of Rapp's Separatist movement eagerly read Gottfried Arnold's glowing description of the early church, found in the latter's *Ketzer-Geschichte* (1699) and *Die erste Liebe* (1696).[106] The Separatist goal was to emulate as much as possible the practices of the primitive church. Interestingly, the Lomersheimer declaration stated the intention of the Separatist movement in 1798 to "form their own church" (*Gemeine*). The wording was weakened in the 1799 Ölbronner statement, most likely for political reasons, to merely read, "form their own fellowship" (*Gemeinschaft*).[107] Thus, as early as the spring of 1798, the Separatist movement aimed to be more than a mere clustering of conventicles scattered throughout the villages of Württemberg. It desired to be a unified movement of house churches that semi-regularly met for larger events, such as love feasts. Rapp's disciples promoted the formation of a voluntaristic Separatist church (*Gemeine*), formed of "true believers."

Thus the Rappite movement had moved from a spiritualist ecclesiology to the second main radical Pietist ecclesiology represented by the "Schwar-

---

[105]Ibid., 273-279 and 295-300.

[106]Many Separatists from Rottenacker used Arnold's *Ketzer-Geschichte* as a textbook for "homeschooling" their children. It is likely that some from Rapp's movement likewise used Arnold as a textbook. Fritz, *Radikaler Pietismus*, 317 and 321.

[107]Arndt, *Doc. Hist. 1700-1803*, 273-275 and 295.

zenau Neutäufer" (New Baptists), an "Anabaptist" view.[108] The original leaders of the Schwarzenau Brethren were radical Pietists. Through association with Anabaptist Mennonites, through their reading of the New Testament and of Gottfried Arnold's glowing accounts of the primitive Jerusalem church in his historical works, the Brethren under Alexander Mack's leadership took "a decided step away from spiritualist individualism toward the establishment of a community in concrete form."[109] While retaining some radical Pietist tenets, the Brethren adopted "such basic Mennonite principles as a gathered church, a disciplined church [use of the ban], obedience to Scripture, discipleship and outward ordinances [baptism, Lord's Supper] as necessary expressions of inward convictions."[110] George Rapp's Separatists likewise made the decisive move from a spiritualist ecclesiology to one that advocated a visible community of believers. Like the Schwarzenau Brethren, they also came to reject infant baptism, the swearing of oaths and military service. A radicalization of the founders of the Schwarzenauer Neutäufer has been traced by Marcus Meier to the apocalyptic atmosphere in the years 1704-1706, which resulted in a "desire for a gathering of true believers in a transconfessional fellowship."[111] A similar fever-pitched apocalypticism surrounded the epoch of the French Revolution (1789-1815), and could explain the decisive paradigm shift in Rapp's ecclesiology from a spiritualist to an "Anabaptist" form.

Certainly the use of the term "Anabaptist" is somewhat problematic since there was and is no one "Anabaptism." Rather, from the days of the Radical Reformation onward, there was a wide variety of (ana-)baptistic groups from a number of distinct geographical areas—Switzerland, South-Germany and Austria, and the Netherlands. Each of these movements "drew upon differing theological traditions, vocabularies and motifs."[112] Some like Hans Denck and David Joris held spiritualist views. Melchior Hoffmann, Menno Simons and Dirk Philips taught that Christ did not acquire his hu-

---

[108]Schneider, "Pietist Ecclesiology," 26 refers to this as a "biblicist-legalistic" ecclesiology; on page 31 as "the conception of the older Anabaptism in the context of Radical Pietism." Schneider includes a third radical Pietist ecclesiology represented by the Community of True Inspiration, in which a visible community was formed under the direction of Holy Spirit through the mouth of prophets. Ibid., 29-30.

[109]Ibid., 33.

[110]Dale R. Stoffer, "Anabaptized Pietism: The Schwarzenau Brethren," in *The Dilemma of Anabaptist Piety*, ed. Stephen L. Longenecker (Bridgewater, Va.: Forum for Religious Studies, 1997), 35-45, here 38. Stoffer lists four radical Pietist tenets that the Brethren retained: (1) the importance of a sanctified life for the regenerated;(2) the "balance between inward and outward;" (3) "the early church provides the truest and purest example of biblical Christianity;" and (4) all "sects of Christianity have fallen away from the purity of the early church." Ibid.

[111]Marcus Meier, *Die Schwarzenauer Neutäufer. Genese einer Gemeindebildung zwischen Pietismus und Täufertum* (Göttingen: Vandenhoeck & Ruprecht, 2008), 76.

[112]Thomas N. Finger, *A Contemporary Anabaptist Theology* (Downer's Grove, Ill.: Inter-Varsity Press, 2004), 12.

man flesh from Mary, but brought "celestial flesh" from heaven. The Hutterites stressed the importance of communal living. The lack of one authority recognized by all groups has made the characterization of Anabaptism problematic from the sixteenth century until the present day.[113] Nevertheless, despite the inherent difficulty with the term, the label "Anabaptist" ecclesiology is a useful and appropriate one for Rapp's ecclesial beliefs. It has already been noted that the concept and practice of a visible community of believers was unusual within radical Pietism.[114] Prior interpretations of Rapp's Separatist movement and the Harmony Society have falsely assumed that it espoused a spiritualist ecclesiology throughout its history. This misrepresentation exists since scholars have not analyzed all theological texts for the Rappite movement.

The question arises whether Rapp's Separatists adopted an "Anabaptist" ecclesiology through personal contact with Anabaptists in Württemberg, through reading Anabaptist literature, or through another avenue. To answer that question it is first necessary to unpack more generally the relationship between Anabaptism and Pietism in the German territories, and particularly in Württemberg. The writers of anti-Pietist tracts and edicts (circa 1700) from Württemberg, the Palatinate, and Switzerland were convinced that Pietism embodied Anabaptist principles.[115] Likewise two earlier scholars of Pietism, Max Goebel and Albrecht Ritschl insisted on a close relationship between Pietism and Anabaptism. In his three volume work (1849-1860), Goebel argued that "Pietism in all its various expressions was the moderate or weakened form" of sixteenth century Anabaptism.[116] Ritschl in his monumental *History of Pietism* (1880-1886) agreed with Goebel's conclusions. Nevertheless, despite the similarity between the two movements, neither scholar maintained a direct relationship of Anabaptism upon Pietism. Unlike these earlier approaches, twentieth century scholars have shown little interest in the Anabaptist-Pietist relationship. They have stressed that Anabaptists were not tolerated in the Holy Roman Empire

---

[113]Stayer, "Täufer I," *TRE*, 597.

[114]Many scholars generalize and assume all radical Pietists had a spiritualist ecclesiology. Cf. statement by Dale Stoffer: "Of course, the Radical Pietists rejected the need for the outward observance of both baptism and communion, advocating instead spiritual baptism and spiritual communion with Christ." Stoffer, "Anabaptized Pietism," 41. Trautwein only utilized early statements of Rapp in Württemberg, and assumed that he upheld a spiritualist ecclesiology throughout his lifetime: "Ein Mann wie Rapp ging hier den spiritualistischen Weg zu Ende." Joachim Trautwein, *Die Theosophie Michael Hahns und ihre Quellen* (Stuttgart: Calwer Verlag, 1969), 243, n. 8.

[115]Meier, *Die Schwarzenauer Neutäufer*, 13. Colberg's *Platonisch-Hermetische Christenthum* claimed that there were 57 points of similarity between the two movements; Schelwig's *Wigandiana* claimed 19 points of similar doctrine.

[116]Hans Schneider, "The Attitude of Pietists toward Anabaptism," in *The Dilemma of Anabaptist Piety*, ed. Stephen L. Longenecker (Bridgewater, Va.: Forum for Religious Studies, 1997), 47-55, here 47-48.

after the Thirty Years War except in several regions in Germany, which did not include Württemberg. Therefore, German Pietists in Württemberg and elsewhere in the seventeenth and eighteenth centuries had virtually no opportunity to become personally acquainted with Mennonites or other Anabaptists or to read their writings.[117]

Only recently have scholars readdressed the issue. Johannes Wallmann has pointed out that strict boundaries between radical Pietism and groups outside the church, such as the Anabaptists, is problematical. The transconfessional nature of radical Pietism led to a willingness to utilize devotional literature from different traditions, including Anabaptism.[118] Clearly the illegal status of Anabaptism after the Thirty Years War reduced the number of Mennonites in Württemberg to a very small number.[119] Nevertheless, since 1650 Swiss Mennonites immigrated to areas of the Palatinate that bordered Württemberg. Furthermore, on some estates in Württemberg belonging to the *Reichsritterschaft*, that is, members of the lower nobility who held property independent of the territorial lords of Württemberg, Anabaptists were welcomed in the eighteenth century.[120] Marcus Meier in *Die Schwarzenauer Neutäufer* (2008) demonstrates that some radical Pietists in Württemberg, as well as in the Palatinate and Hessen, had knowledge of Anabaptist writings and personal contact with Mennonites.[121] Interestingly, the three areas in Württemberg where the strongest concentrations of Anabaptists were found before the Thirty Years War were likewise the same areas where radical Pietism and Separatism were strongest in the late eighteenth century (Klosteramt Maulbronn, the Rems river valley, and the Göppinger region). This fact caused Friedrich Fritz to postulate that a residual memory of Anabaptism remained among the common people in those areas, thus preparing the ground for the reception of the church-critical views of Rapp's Separatist movement.[122] Although there is no documentary evidence, it is possible that Rapp personally knew or was directly influenced by Mennonites living very near his hometown of Iptingen on the es-

---

[117]Ibid., 49.

[118]Johannes Wallmann, *Der Pietismus* (Göttingen: Vandenhoeck & Ruprecht, 1990), 80.

[119]Only the Lutheran, Reformed and Catholic religions had legal status. Friedrich Fritz, "Die Wiedertäufer und der württembergische Pietismus," *Blätter für württembergische Kirchengeschichte* 43 (1939): 81-109, here 83. Cf. Claus-Peter Clasen, *Die Wiedertaüfer im Herzogtum Württemberg und in benachbarten Herrschaften. Ausbreitung, Geisteswelt und Soziologie* (Stuttgart: W. Kohlhammer Verlag, 1965), 42-47.

[120]Fritz, "Die Wiedertäufer und der württembergische Pietismus," 84.

[121]Meier, *Die Schwarzenauer Neutäufer*, 77. Johann Kipping, one of the first eight baptized Schwarzenauer Neutäufer, read Menno Simons' *Fundamentum* in June 1706 at Schloss Schaubeck, near Ludwigsburg in Württemberg. Württemberg radical Pietists Polycarp Bauer and Christian Gottfried Schmoller were also influenced in their views of baptism by reading Anabaptist writings. Ibid., 64-66.

[122]Fritz, "Die Wiedertäufer und der württembergische Pietismus," 107-108.

tates of Lerchenhof and Friedrichshof.[123] Another port of entry for an "Anabaptist" ecclesiology for Rapp's disciples in Württemberg was their reading of the New Testament in conjunction with Gottfried Arnold's *Die erste Liebe* and *Kirchen und Ketzer Geschichte*.[124] Through these sources they came to similar convictions as the Schwarzenau Brethren.

Baptism

The most consistent of Rapp's Separatists rejected child baptism for a number of reasons. In the first place, they argued that child baptism was not to be found in the Gospels or in the rest of Scripture.[125] Nor was it the practice of the early church fathers to administer the sacrament generally to all people, even to those who were [still] evil.[126] In 1785, Rapp expressed doubt whether baptism as it was practiced in the Lutheran Church was pleasing to God for this very reason--it was generally administered to all.[127] A second reason why the Separatists rejected child baptism was because most Lutherans wrongly mistook the sacrament of baptism for regeneration. The Separatists argued that "outward baptism does not contribute to salvation." As proof they noted that children, who had been outwardly baptized, continued to exhibit the same "wild and unrefined nature" that they possessed prior to the administration of the sacrament.[128] In spite of these arguments, the Lomersheimer declaration provided some leeway to Separatist parents to allow their infants to be baptized in the Lutheran Church. Since child baptism was neither expressly commanded nor forbidden in Scripture, the principle in 1 Cor 7:14, "being sanctified by the believing partner," could be applied, in this case to the relationship between parent and child.[129]

---

[123]Ibid., 107. Fritz specifically notes the adoption of Mennonite-style beards by the men of the Rappite movement through contact with Anabaptists. The Lerchenhof and Friedrichshof belonged to the *reichsritterschaftlich* lords of Rippur, and were therefore outside the jurisdiction of Württemberg. Ibid., 84.

[124]Gottfried Arnold defended the Anabaptists against the charge that they were heretics in his *Ketzer-Geschichte*. Due to his spiritualist stance, however, Arnold reproached them for forming a new sect, since he rejected all organized and institutional forms of Christianity in favor of an invisible church of the Spirit. Schneider, "Attitude of Pietists," 54-55. The Schwarzenau Brethren mentioned Arnold's *Die erste Liebe* as an influence on their rejection of infant baptism in favor of believers' baptism. Ibid., 51.

[125]Response of Johann Georg Walz from Iptingen in the Seubert-Krippendorf-Dürrmenz report March-May, 1803. Arndt, *Doc. Hist. 1700-1803*, 343. Cf. ibid., 275.

[126]Arndt, *Doc. Hist. 1700-1803*, 275.

[127]Ibid., 108.

[128]Ibid., 108 and 453.

[129]Ibid., 275. This approach accords with Meier's second and largest group of radical Pietists, who had mystical spiritual tendencies yet allowed water baptism as an outward sign (e.g. Arnold, Grubmann, Hochmann, Horch). The first group stood in the tradition of the Quakers and rejected entirely water baptism (e.g. Dippel,

Ideally, if one baptized at all, one should not baptize children, but adults who of their own free will had repented and experienced regeneration. Only in such a case could baptism be considered a "seal of Christianity."[130] The Lomersheimer and Ölbronner declarations appropriated some of the arguments of the Anabaptists in suggesting that believers' baptism was vastly preferable to child baptism. They argued that the image employed in Rom 6:3-4 of being buried with Christ in baptism and then arising to new life was only appropriate if the person had previously experienced conversion. Interestingly, there exists one report of re-baptism of Separatist adults by Johann Georg Rapp during the early years of the movement. In a letter written January 17, 1843 to George Rapp, former Separatist David Gloss reflected back on the day, when he along with three other key members of Rapp's movement, was re-baptized. "I was . . . with you, the young Hörnle, Michael Esterle and the old Jacob Dürr, [when we went] over the . . . [?] to the Nagold River, where you baptized all of us. And then we went back to your [Rapp's] house. When we arrived we held the first love feast."[131]

If Gloss is referring to the first official love feast celebrated at Rapp's house in Iptingen, that event took place in 1790.[132] The re-baptism by Rapp of the four leading Separatists took place in the Nagold River and therefore was some form of baptism by immersion.[133] Baptism by immersion likewise reflected the image of death and resurrection (Rom 6:3-4) to which the statements of faith appealed. Eberhard Fritz is correct in noting that the re-baptism of adults was unusual and virtually unknown among Separatists, since most upheld a spiritualist ecclesiology.[134] The occurrence of re-baptism within Rapp's Separatist movement indicates that early spiritualist notions of baptism (1785-1790) had been replaced with "Anabaptist" and outward conceptions of the sacrament. Several later Rapp sermons (ca. 1830s), which will be discussed in chapter seven, suggest that adult baptism by immersion continued to be an option for members of the Harmony Society.

Some of the Separatists within Rapp's movement did have their babies baptized in the Lutheran Church, often due to social pressure rather than

---

Seebach). The third group were influenced by Anabaptist principles and argued for the importance of water baptism. Meier, *Die Schwarzenauer Neutäufer*, 140.

[130]Arndt, *Doc. Hist. 1700-1803*, 275.

[131]Karl J. R. Arndt, *George Rapp's Years of Glory. Economy on the Ohio, 1834-1847. George Rapp's Third Harmony. A Documentary History* (New York: Peter Lang, 1987), 646.

[132]Fritz, *Radikaler Pietismus*, 143.

[133]The verb used for baptism in this text (*traufen* = to drip or trickle) may suggest pouring or sprinkling while standing in the Nagold River.

[134]Fritz, *Radikaler Pietismus*, 142. He suggests that Karl Arndt might have wrongly transcribed the letter from Gloss. Ibid., n. 96. The author has checked the original letter in the archives and Arndt's transcription is correct. Therefore, although unusual, this event certainly occurred. (Gloss would not lie to Rapp, since the latter was present and would know the difference.)

religious conviction. Johann Georg Walz from Iptingen admitted in 1803 that he "had his child baptized to avoid gossip and defamation (*Nachrede*), since in and of itself baptism was unnecessary."[135] Other radical Pietists of the Separatist movement baptized their infants themselves to avoid having them forcibly baptized in the Lutheran Church. For if the baby was baptized by the father immediately after the birth, the established church was by necessity forced to recognize this act as a legitimate baptism. To repeat the procedure within the church would be to commit an illegal act of "re-baptism." Approximately fifty cases of Separatist "lay baptism" (*Selbsttaufe*) were recorded in the church records for the decades at the end of the eighteenth and the beginning of the nineteenth centuries.[136] Since most Separatists rejected the very concept of pedobaptism, these lay baptisms of infants should be understood as (successful) attempts to outfox the religious authorities and prevent a church baptism. Separatist Johann Friedrich Kocher admitted this maneuver explicitly. When asked why he baptized his son himself he replied, "because his child would otherwise be baptized in the church. Therefore with his [lay] baptism he anticipated [and prevented] the public baptism."[137]

In the place of child baptism, the Lomersheimer declaration espoused child dedication as the correct biblical procedure. "Therefore it would be better not to baptize children, until they themselves desire to become Christians in true form, but they should be blessed by proven men according to Mark 10:13-16," the declaration read.[138] One early description of a child dedication was found in the church minutes for May 18, 1787. The male child of Johannes Hörnle was blessed in the following fashion:

> They laid the child on the table and all of them from the greatest to the smallest, each of them prayed for the child, either especially loud or on their knees, however the Spirit led each of them, that God would receive him into His covenant and allow him to grow up in His grace. When the prayer session was over, Hörnle stood up and said: It had been revealed to him, the child should be named Joseph.[139]

The child dedication of Joseph Hörnle was not adequate, however, to prevent the child from being forcibly baptized against the parent's will in the Lutheran Church on June 8, 1787.[140] It is not unlikely that child dedication took the place of child baptism in the Harmony Society, when the social

---

[135]Seubert-Krippendorf-Dürrmenz report, March-May, 1803. Arndt, *Doc. Hist. 1700-1803*, 343. It should be noted that the spiritualist Berleburg Bibel commentary likely contributed to a rejection of baptism by the Lutheran church by members of Rapp's movement. Fritz, "Die Wiedertäufer und der württembergische Pietismus," 105-106.
[136]Fritz, *Radikaler Pietismus*, 299.
[137]Fritz, "Rapp und die Separatisten in Iptingen," 183. Cf. ibid., 184
[138]Arndt, *Doc. Hist. 1700-1803*, 275.
[139]Ibid., 119.
[140]Fritz, "Rapp und die Separatisten in Iptingen," 170.

and religious pressure exerted by the state Lutheran church was removed. However, no explicit documentary evidence exists to support this supposition.

Eucharist

Rapp and his Separatist followers rejected the Eucharist as celebrated in the Lutheran Church primarily because it was administered widely to unregenerate persons. As early as 1782 and the climax of his conversion experience Rapp had begun to reinterpret the Lord's Supper (*Abendmahl*) in a spiritualist manner. In the description of his conversion and the reasons for separation which he submitted to the Iptingen church council in 1785 Rapp stated that the Bible passage, Rev 3:20, was strongly impressed upon his heart earlier in 1782. He who heard Christ's voice and opened the door of his life would experience that Christ entered "to hold the Lord's Supper (*Abendmahl*)" with him. Luther's 1545 translation of the Bible that Rapp used translated the verse in question with *Abendmahl*, which in German refers to the Eucharistic celebration and not just fellowship around an ordinary meal.[141] Rapp took Luther's translation literally and came to believe that the true Eucharist was inward and spiritual. On April 15, 1785, Rapp used Rev 3:20 as his biblical proof text against the outward Eucharist to the Iptingen church council as the notes by the local pastor, Andreas Genter, in the council minutes indicated.[142] Later in 1787, the Separatist leader declared to the church authorities that at that time the Separatists did not celebrate the Lord's Supper "outwardly, but rather inwardly, through the outpouring of the Spirit. This is food for the soul but not the body that they eat."[143] "No one could live without the inward partaking" of the Eucharist. Rapp went on to qualify his spiritualist understanding of the sacrament. "[T]he outward Eucharist could also be valid, when worthy guests were present, according to 1 Cor 11," he declared.[144]

In 1790, Rapp's Separatists celebrated their first love feast (*Liebesmahl*) followed by a Eucharistic celebration with "worthy" members of their movement. This is once again evidence that a radical paradigm shift from a spiritualist to an "Anabaptist" conception had occurred in their ecclesial understanding. Each member would usually only celebrate the Eucharist once yearly. It was a conviction of the Separatists that an annual observance of the Lord's Supper was adequate and the more frequent (monthly or bimonthly) observance an abuse practiced by the Lutheran Church.[145] Al-

---

[141] http://www.luther-bibel-1545.de/ [Accessed January 13, 2007]. The Greek word δειπνήσω merely connotes "to eat or dine."

[142] Arndt, *Doc. Hist. 1700-1803*, 68.

[143] Ibid., 106.

[144] Ibid., 108.

[145] "wann aber das Abenmal gar wenig, oder selten gehalten würde, so wäre ich der erste mit Christi Glider oft, und viel darzu zu gehen, zum Gedächtniß." Ibid., 72.

though an individual Separatist would only celebrate Communion annually, it was necessary to hold a number of Eucharistic celebrations to accommodate all of the Separatists. Villages with large Separatist groups (Gündelbach, Knittlingen, Ölbronn) would hold their own individual celebrations. Rapp divided the remaining members from other villages into three groups, in order that the number of attendees would fit into his house in Iptingen.[146]

The Lomersheimer and Ölbronner declarations contained a fairly detailed description of how the love feast (*Liebesmahl*) and Eucharist were celebrated. The celebration intentionally approximated the practice of the primitive church.

> First we inform our brotherhoods that at this or that time the *agape* will be held. At the place where the brothers have met an address and admonition is given by a brother who has first been elected by the entire congregation. Then there is confession, secret and public, according to circumstances. When all disagreements have been settled and unity has been renewed, and after each has this feeling toward the other and complete peace and unity reigns in our midst, then we flow together in the innermost harmony of love and honesty. We pray and also sing a song of praise, then each presents the gift he has brought and out of it a meal is prepared which is eaten in common while we are mindful of the genial presence of our Lord Jesus Christ. . . . And when the conversation is ended and the meal finished it becomes still. Then after a short address bread and wine are brought and blessed and a brother distributes it. "Mark well, do this in memory of me," thus the external testifies to the internal and this at a time of harmony. We have never parted from each other without blessing.[147]

Prior to the love feast itself, the members of the community underwent a period of public and private confession. A brother who had been elected by the congregation (*Gemeine*) introduced the meeting with a message of exhortation. The declaration did not explain which sort of "circumstances" warranted public rather than private confession. Perhaps moral failings or inter-personal conflicts that were widely known required that all within the group became cognizant of the ensuing repentance and reconciliation. In any case, the goal of the confession session was to eliminate all resentments and conflicts that existed between individuals in the fellowship, so that "complete peace and unity" and the "innermost harmony of love and honesty" could flow between them. Only when unity and harmony reigned between hearts could the external celebration of the sacrament correspond to the internal spiritual state.

---

[146]"Das heil. Abendmahl werde in ihren Versammlungen etwa des Jahres einmal für diejenige, welche sich dazu melden, gehalten. Johann Georg Rapp theile dise, weil es in seinem Hause an Raum fehle, in 3 Classen ein." Seubert-Krippendorf-Dürrmenz report March-May, 1803. Ibid., 340. Cf. Pastoral letter #3, Ibid., 254f.

[147]Ibid., 276. The author has used Arndt's translation in Arndt, *Rapp's Harmony Society*, 37. For a helpful background to the practice of the Eucharist in the Lutheran Church see Fritz, *Radikaler Pietismus*, 301-310.

After a time of prayer and singing, the actual love feast took place. Fashioned after the *agape* meals of the New Testament, the love feast was a common meal to which all participants contributed food. The conversation and fellowship around the table took place in the awareness that the "friendship of the Lord Jesus Christ" was likewise also being experienced. The love feast was followed by the Eucharistic celebration itself. After a time of silence, Rapp or the brother officiating addressed the congregation with a short message. Then the leader "read aloud the biblical formula (*Einsegnungsworte*) [in 1 Cor 11] and administered the elements, in that he presented the plate with bread to each person and also allowed the glass with wine to be circulated."[148]

Confirmation

Rapp's Separatists rejected not just the sacraments of baptism and the Eucharist as practiced in the Lutheran church, but confirmation as well. The reasons they gave in the Lomersheimer declaration were both religious and practical. In the confirmation ceremony, the young people renounced the devil and swore, using the name of God, to live consistently as Christians. The Separatists understood this to be an offense against the first commandment, of taking the Lord's name in vain. Many of the young people would be tempted to merely "swear with their mouth" and not with their heart. It was sinful to promise faithfulness to Christ lightly, and then be unable to keep that promise (Math 21:28f). On a practical level, the Separatists rejected confirmation because of the social customs that surrounded the ceremony. It was customary to give the confirmand new clothes and possibly a party to celebrate the event. These customs were a burden for impoverished parents, distracted the recipient from the true meaning of the ceremony, and increased pride and haughtiness.[149]

School Attendance

The Separatists rejected sending their children to the village schools. They agreed with the government that children needed to be educated and that the public schools were good and useful for other (non-Separatist) citizens. Nevertheless, in the Lomersheimer declaration they argued that it was preferable to follow the admonition of Gen 6:6-7 and teach their own children. The main reason given in the declaration for Separatists withholding their children from school was their conviction that school attendance would corrupt their offspring. Through excessive contact and acquaintance with non-Separatist children, their sons and daughters would lose their

---

[148]Arndt, *Doc. Hist, 1700-1803*, 340.
[149]Ibid., 277.

"simple disposition" and take on the worldly characteristics of the other pupils.[150]

In confrontation with the church and civil authorities over school attendance, Separatist parents gave other, at times less diplomatic, reasons. George Rapp declared that the corruption that was found in the church had also crept into the school. It was "against his principles" and "God had shown him" that he must teach his two children. "The church and the school were not from God but from the devil." These two institutions were thus closely linked in the mind of the Separatist leader, since Lutheran religious instruction occupied a central role in the curriculum.[151] To separate from the church meant to withdraw from the public school. Michael Conzelmann refused to send his daughter to school—it was "against God's will and his own conviction," he told the representatives of the civil government in May, 1793. Johannes Hörnle's adamant refusal to send his son Joseph to school was because "they baptized his child against his will, and therefore he would not send him to school."[152] These and other Separatists were willing to pay fines repeatedly rather than pollute their children with the worldly influences present in the local village schools.

Swearing of Oaths and Military Service

When a new duke initiated his reign in Württemberg, it was decreed that all adult residents of the duchy swear an oath of fealty and obedience to him. Likewise the sons of citizens swore fealty when they reached the age of adulthood.[153] In the Lomersheimer declaration of faith, the Separatists defended their rejection of the oath of fealty on religious grounds. Swearing oaths was an offense against Christ's direct command in the Sermon on the Mount (Matt 5:33-37) and in Jas 5:12. Although they intended to be good and loyal citizens of the land, their consciences would not allow them to swear fealty.[154] Some Separatists were willing to shake hands in place of swearing the fealty oath.

In 1794 Duke Ludwig Eugen due to the military conflicts following the onset of the French Revolution attempted (with modest success) to institute a general military draft system.[155] Each community was required to provide

---

[150] Ibid., 276.

[151] Fritz, "Rapp und die Separatisten in Iptingen," 174, 176, 178 and 181. The school ordinance of 1729 in Württemberg placed religious instruction at the core of the curriculum. In 1795 other more secular subjects were added to the curriculum: natural sciences, church and secular history and agricultural studies, as well as the memorization of hymns from the 1791 "rationalist" hymnbook. Fritz, *Radikaler Pietismus*, 318-319.

[152] Fritz, "Rapp und die Separatisten in Iptingen," 179.

[153] Fritz, *Radikaler Pietismus*, 345-347.

[154] Arndt, *Doc. Hist, 1700-1803*, 277-278.

[155] Hermann Ehmer in personal correspondence to the author noted (April, 2007) that initially all citizens, not just Separatists, rejected the military draft.

a certain number of men between seventeen and thirty years of age to serve in the military. Wealthier draftees were able to pay for substitutes rather than become soldiers themselves. Therefore, the burden of the draft fell upon the lower classes. The son of a leading Iptingen Separatist, Christian Hörnle, was drafted in 1794. Along with ten other Separatists from Iptingen, Großglattbach, Lomersheim, Ölbronn and Großvillars, Hörnle appealed directly to Duke Ludwig Eugen and received permission to provide a substitute soldier.[156] This possibility was gradually extended to other Separatist conscientious objectors. Two Separatist draftees from Fellbach, who were unable to raise the necessary funds to provide a substitute, however, fled their village and sought refuge for a time in the radical Pietist nest, Ihinger Hof.[157]

In the Lomersheimer and Ölbronner declarations the section on military service did not, for political reasons, argue biblically or from the standpoint of conscientious objection. Rather they argued that Separatist men were unfit to be soldiers. "For a good soldier must have a liberal-minded and fiery nature and possess authority. In such matters our brethren can no longer be trained, because their disposition is proven to be exactly the opposite."[158] Through their "repentance struggles," Separatists had withdrawn themselves from the "vain mode of life of the glories of the world." It would cause great damage to "their inner peace" or possibly even rob them of the "noble status of regeneration," if they were forced to bear arms. They were willing, however, to pay the substitute fees or even to suffer persecution to avoid military service. Nevertheless, the document assured the government that, although the Separatists rejected military service, they would continue to be obedient and loyal citizens of the land. Better times were coming, when man "would learn war no more" (Isa 2:4).[159]

Although the two declarations of faith did not argue biblically against war, other documents prove that the Separatists were pacifists for religious and not merely pragmatic reasons. Like the Anabaptists before them, they based their arguments against war and the bearing of arms on the Sermon on the Mount. Separatists in Fellbach argued against the military thus: "It is written in Mathew 5: Blessed are the peacemakers, for they will be called the children of God. Further: Love your enemies, bless those who curse you, do good to those who hate you, pray for those who insult and persecute you." Furthermore, "it was against their conscience to go to war and to shoot and kill the enemy, whom one should love."[160] Jakob Becker from Ölbronn in 1804 stated that he had withheld his children from school "because the church sanctioned and promoted the shedding of blood, because it [the church] acknowledged the practice of war as legitimate. Such teach-

---

[156] Fritz, *Radikaler Pietismus*, 354-357.
[157] Findeisen, *Pietismus in Fellbach*, 210-211.
[158] Arndt, *Doc. Hist. 1700-1803*, 278.
[159] Ibid.
[160] Findeisen, *Pietismus in Fellbach*, 212.

ing is false and the teaching of the Anti-Christ."[161] Finally, Separatists in Strümpfelbach were pacifists not only because of the commands in the Sermon on the Mount. To participate in war would be to hinder God's judgment upon the nations. The minutes of the church council (*Kirchenkonvent*) recorded that "[t]hey consider it a sin to work against God's judgments upon France and Germany."[162]

The Lomersheimer and Ölbronner declarations of faith reveal that Rapp's Separatist movement moved from a spiritualist ecclesiology to an "Anabaptist" one. Members of the movement came to believe that an outward, visible church of true believers was necessary. Separatists rejected child baptism, the Eucharist and confirmation in the Lutheran church. By the 1790s the only recorded act of re-baptism took place, and annual love feasts were organized. They used "Anabaptist" arguments to reject the swearing of oaths and military service.

---

[161] Fritz, *Radikaler Pietismus*, 358.
[162] Ibid., 355.

3

Beholding the Godhead
(1790-1800)

By the 1790s George Rapp had become the undisputed leader of the Separatist movement in Württemberg. Some Pietist and a large number of Separatist conventicle groups scattered throughout the villages of the duchy looked to Rapp for spiritual leadership. Rapp provided this leadership by visiting the various villages on a semi-regular basis and teaching in their conventicles. His widely-spread followers likewise frequently trekked up to ten or twelve hours to attend the Separatist conventicle in Rapp's hometown of Iptingen.[1] But another means existed by which Rapp provided spiritual counsel for his scattered followers--through the writing of pastoral letters.

George Rapp's Pastoral Letters (1791-1802)

George Rapp's pastoral letters were written in response to penned enquiries from his followers. That is, for the most part, they were written to a specific person to meet a specific need. None of the original correspondence from his disciples, which formed the basis for Rapp's written replies, remains extant. Therefore, the scanty historical details that survived the process of transcription and editing are in most cases difficult to understand and interpret. The extant letters are not the originals written in Rapp's hand, rather they are copies, transcribed and preserved for spiritual edification by members of his movement. Names and places were frequently masked to enable the letters to be read more generally as circular corres-

---

[1]Eberhard Fritz, "Johann Georg Rapp (1757-1847) und die Separatisten in Iptingen. Mit einer Edition der relevanten Iptinger Kirchenkonventsprotokolle," *Blätter für Württembergische Kirchengeschichte* 95 (1995): 129-203, here 168 and 172.

pondence in the various conventicles. The circular nature of the pastoral letters is clearly evident in one particular case. Although the letter was addressed to "a dear brother," several lines later Rapp changed to the plural address "brethren," indicating that his exposition of 1 Kings 11, in this case, was intended for a wider audience than the one individual disciple.[2] Most likely, the surviving pastoral letters are but a fraction of the actual letters written by Rapp in this twelve-year period. Only one or two of the letter recipients can be positively identified.[3]

Rapp's pastoral letters provide a valuable window not just into his early teaching, but also into his soul. We find a leader who was easily and deeply moved by the troubles and suffering that his followers were experiencing, and who was able to comfort and encourage effectively.[4] Rapp's pastoral concern and spiritual fervency was evidenced in the way that he prayed for his followers in his pastoral letters:

> My desire, dear brethren, is that the name of the Lord Jesus would be held up high among you, in order that you may acquire much love for Him, to follow uprightly His commandments, that you, by becoming aware of the power of the Holy Spirit, may become rich in the knowledge of God the Father and of Jesus Christ. For in that [knowledge] there is eternal life—you could not acquire anything greater.[5]

It was likewise demonstrated in the manner in which he signed his letters. He was "their willing servant and brother in Christ," "their brother with inclinations of true love for them," or "bound in true love," and "their poor brother."[6] Rapp reminded his followers that he was still a "poor miserable sinner." Therefore, they should look to the "Lord Jesus for their example" and not to Rapp.[7] Besides spiritual advice and counsel, six of Rapp's extant pastoral letters contain expositions of biblical passages that he sent in response to requests from followers.[8]

Karl Arndt in his volume of documentary history, *George Rapp's Separatists*, published eighteen of Rapp's pastoral letters, which he found in an old composition book, as well as an individual unbound pastoral letter dated

---

[2]Karl J. R. Arndt, *George Rapp's Separatists, 1700-1803. A Documentary History*, (Worcester, Mass.: Harmony Society Press, 1980), 245.

[3]Eberhard Fritz, *Radikaler Pietismus in Württemberg: Religiöse Ideale im Konflikt mit gesellschaftlichen Realitäten* (Epfendorf: Bibliotheca Academica, 2003), 276.

[4]Two examples are Composition book, letter #1 (Arndt, *Doc. Hist. 1700-1803*, 233) and 1-5005, Box 16, Folder 1, Viehmeyer Collection, Letter # 20. Fritz notes that Rapp in this period was a "pastorally oriented, organizationally-gifted Separatist leader", who only later became authoritarian. Eberhard Fritz, "Johann Christoph Blumhardt und die Anhänger des Johann Georg Rapp in Iptingen." *Blätter für Württembergische Kirchengeschichte*, 106 (2006): 27-37, here 30.

[5]MG-185, 1-5005, Box 16, Folder 1, Collection #2, Letter #27.

[6]Arndt, *Doc. Hist. 1700-1803*, 234, 246, 267, 268 and 272.

[7]MG-185, 1-5005, Box 16, Folder 1, Viehmeyer Collection, Letter # 20.

[8]Composition Book letters #2, 4, 5, 9, 14, 15 and 16.

June 6, 1794.⁹ Two other bound volumes of manuscript pastoral letters were discovered in 2005 while the author was working in the Harmony Society archives. These contained some of the letters found in the composition book that Arndt utilized, but nineteen previously unknown letters as well. The discovery of the nineteen previously unpublished pastoral letters is a great find, which significantly adds to our understanding of Rapp's theology while still in Württemberg.

In total, thirty-seven of Rapp's pastoral letters are extant in three manuscript collections. The earliest dated letter is from 1791, the latest is from August 13, 1802. The three manuscript collections will be referred to as the Composition book, the Viehmeyer collection, and Collection #2. The Viehmeyer collection contains thirteen letters not included in the Composition book; Collection #2 contains six new letters. A comparison of the three manuscript collections is included in Appendix A.

The Viehmeyer collection is so entitled because the inner cover of the bound booklet was signed first by "Joh. Michael Viehmeyer of Rohrbrun," then by "Ludwig Hagmaier [sic] of Neuenbürg," two loyal disciples of George Rapp.¹⁰ Of the three bound manuscript collections, the Viehmeyer collection is clearly the oldest. The inner cover is dated June 24, 1798, most likely the date when the two men began to transcribe collected pastoral letters. This collection contains more orthographical and grammatical irregularities than the Composition book, which is probably the youngest of the three. The Viehmeyer collection likewise includes a number of historical details and personal names that are eliminated or disguised by the abbreviation N.N. (*nomen nescio*) in Collection #2, thus indicating that it is most likely older than this collection. For example, letter #26 in the Viehmeyer collection, written September 8, 1801, includes three and a half lines of text that are replaced with a long dash in Collection #2. These crucial lines make reference to Christina Muntz, wife of the wealthy farmer, Johann Georg Muntz, who had "written a very accusatory letter." This historical detail is significant because it shows that conflict and disagreement with the Separatist leader were present in Württemberg, prior to the abolition of private

---

⁹Arndt incorrectly states that his first volume of documentary history, *George Rapp's Separatists*, contains twenty-nine pastoral letters. Arndt, *Doc. Hist. 1700-1803*, 233. Perhaps Arndt was swayed by the statement at the beginning of the Composition book: "Abschrift von *29* Briefen welche unser Vater Georg Rapp in Deutschland von 1793 biss 1802 [1799 is written over with 1802] an verschieden seiner damaligen Brueder und Schwestern geschrieben." The composition book which claimed to contain twenty-nine letters, in actuality only included eighteen letters. Arndt rearranged the order of the pastoral letters included in the composition book, although he retained the composition book's number of 1-18. The following is Arndt's order: 1, 2, 3, 4, 6, 5, 7, 8, 14, 9, 10, 11, 15, 16, 17, 12, 13, 18.

¹⁰Viehmeyer was born 1775, emigrated in 1805 and remained loyal to George Rapp until his death in 1854, as did Hagmayer who died in Economy in 1849. Arndt suggests that letter #8 was written to Viehmeyer. Arndt, *Doc. Hist. 1700-1803*, 267. Letter #18 was written to Hagmayer. Ibid., 321.

property on American soil, which most severely affected wealthier persons. Interestingly, the Muntz family (father, mother and seven children) did emigrate from Heutensbach and join the Harmony Society. They withdrew, however, in 1806 after only a brief sojourn in the communal settlement. Johann Georg Muntz was later listed as a plaintiff in a law suit against George Rapp to recover funds paid into the common treasury. The case was dropped, however, in 1807. Thus this brief reference in the Viehmeyer collection letter demonstrates that the Muntz family's conflict with Rapp had deep roots--it existed prior to emigration and the institution of communalism. In the same letter, the Viehmeyer copy includes the names of two early dissidents who left the Harmony Society in 1806 because they disagreed with Rapp's asceticism: David Gloss and J. Georg Wild.[11] These names were disguised with N.N. in Collection #2. Furthermore, the newly discovered letters in both the Viehmeyer Collection and Collection #2 contain valuable historical information concerning the development of the Separatist movement from a cluster of conventicles in widely spread villages to an organized sectarian church.[12]

All three pastoral letter collections contain copies of six different expositions of Biblical passages by Rapp that he sent in response to requests from followers.[13] However, there are no letters with Scriptural exegesis in the newly discovered nineteen letters of the Viehmeyer collection and Collection #2. Nevertheless, these previously unknown letters are quite significant theologically. For example, Letter #6 in Collection #2 provides one of the clearest explanations of Rapp's view of the need for conversion and of soteriology in general. Furthermore, the newly discovered letters round out considerably the description of Rapp's mystical piety, which he appropriated from the Reformed mystic, Gerhard Tersteegen. Although mystical piety of the Tersteegian brand is likewise found in the Composition book collection, the newly discovered letters increase our knowledge of it greatly, as the quotations in the following section demonstrate. It is to the subject of Tersteegian mysticism and its influence upon the Rappites that we now turn in the pastoral letters of George Rapp.

Influence of Tersteegen's Mysticism within Württember Pietism and on Rapp's Separatist Movement

The influence of Jacob Boehme and to a lesser degree of Gottfried Arnold on radical Pietism has long been acknowledged by scholars. Peter Erb, howev-

---

[11]MG-185, 1-5005, Box 16, Folder 1, Viehmeyer Collection and Collection #2, Letter # 26.

[12]Examples: MG-185, 1-5005, Box 16, Folder 1, Viehmeyer Collection, #20 and #23; ibid., Collection #2, #31.

[13]Composition Book letters #2, 4, 5, 9, 14, 15 and 16.

er, correctly notes that the influence on radical Pietism of the Reformed Pietist mystic, Gerhard Tersteegen, has not been given adequate attention:

> Within that diverse body of spirituality known as Radical Pietism, no writer was of greater significance for colonial Pennsylvania religious life than Gerhard Tersteegen (1697-1769), yet students of German-American religion have consistently avoided a careful analysis of his work and influence. . . . Such scholarly shortcomings have resulted in numerous misrepresentations of German spiritual traditions in the eighteenth century.[14]

Although Erb is referring specifically to radical Pietism in colonial Pennsylvania, a similar contention could be made for later radical Pietism in some parts of Germany (Rhineland and Württemberg).[15]

One scholar who has argued for the importance and influence of Tersteegen's brand of Reformed, quietistic mysticism on radical Pietism is F. Ernest Stoeffler. He contends that three streams of mystical piety converged in radical Pietism: (1) the mystical trends of Johann Arndt (*Wahres Christentum*) and his followers in the Lutheran tradition; (2) Boehmist theosophical mysticism; and (3) the Quietism of men like Miguel de Molinos, as well as older mystics (Theresa of Jesus, John of the Cross), who in turn influenced the seventeenth- century female mystic, Mme. de la Mothe Guyon. Tersteegen not only relied on this third tradition when developing his own brand of pietistically-inspired Quietism. He also edited and published the works of Mme. Guyon and other French Quietists, thus making their thought available to German separatistic and churchly Pietists.[16] Steven O'Malley reminds us that Tersteegen's theological orientation combined motifs not just from French Catholic mysticism, but also from the Cocceius tradition of covenant theology, German Reformed Pietism, and older Rhineland mysticism.[17]

---

[14]Peter C. Erb, "Gerhard Tersteegen, Christopher Saur, and Pennsylvania Sectarians," *Brethren Life and Thought* 20 (Summer 1975): 153-157, here 153. Cf. J. Steven O'Malley, "The Influence of Gerhard Tersteegen in the Documents of Early German-American Evangelicalism." In *Pietism, Revivalism and Modernity, 1650-1850*, ed. Fred van Lieburg (Newcastle upon Tyne: Cambridge Scholars Publishing, 2008), 232-255, here 243f on the frequent reprints of Tersteegen in colonial America.

[15]Ulrich Bister documents the publication of Tersteegen's works in colonial America, particularly those printed by Christoph Saur I and his son of the same name for the Reformed radical Pietists who emigrated from the Rhineland and Wittgensteiner land. Ulrich Bister, "Gerhard Tersteegen – Die Rezeption seiner Schriften in Nordamerika und sein dortiger Freundeskreis," in *Gerhard Tersteegen Evangelischer Mystik inmitten der Aufklärung*, ed. Manfred Kock and Jürgen Thiesbonenkamp (Cologne: Rheinland Verlag, 1997), 123-134, here 126-131. Cf. F. Ernest Stoeffler, *Mysticism in the Devotional Literature of Colonial Pennsylvania* (Allentown, Pa.: Pennsylvania German Folklore Society, 1949), 91-113.

[16]F. Ernest Stoeffler, *German Pietism during the Eighteenth Century* (Leiden: E. J. Brill, 1973), 172.

[17]J. Steven O'Malley, *Early German-American Evangelicalism: Pietist Sources on Discipleship and Sanctification* (Lanham, Md.: Scarecrow Press, 1995), 144-158.

Life and Work of Gerhard Tersteegen

Before proceeding with a discussion of the influence of Tersteegen on Württemberg Pietism and on the Rappites, it is expedient to describe briefly his life and work. Gerhard Tersteegen (1697-1769) was a mystic of the Reformed confession, an author of religious works, a revival preacher and a spiritual guide to hundreds. Born in Moers in the lower Rhineland, as a youth he experienced a severe and lengthy period of spiritual crisis (1713-1724) after coming into contact with Pietist believers, a crisis characterized by increasing "darkness." His spiritual father, Wilhelm Hoffmann (1685-1746), was a convert and an avid admirer of the radical Pietist Hochmann von Hochenau and his mystical-spiritualist views. Hoffmann introduced Tersteegen to mystical spirituality, particularly to the French and Spanish Quietist tradition.[18] This quietistic tradition helped Tersteegen to understand and overcome his crisis of faith. His spiritual crisis came to its culmination in 1724, when he wrote a letter to Jesus in his own blood, in which he completely submitted his will to Christ. "Not my will, but your will be done! Command, rule over and reign in me!" After 1724 he served as a spiritual mentor (*Seelenführer*) to many. Through personal conversation and in correspondence Tersteegen sought to encourage spiritual growth in those "truth-loving" souls who turned to him. Beginning in 1727, he was the spiritual leader of a small spiritual commune (six brothers and two sisters), often referred to as the "Pilgerhütte," for which Tersteegen wrote a semi-monastic rule (*Einige wichtige Verhaltens-Regeln an eine beysammen wohnende Brüder-Gesellschaft*).[19] His most influential written work was his collection of hymns and poems entitled *Geistliches Blumengärtlein*, which went through numerous editions beginning in 1729.

Tersteegen mined the works of Tauler, Thomas à Kempis, Pseudo-Macarius, Brother Lawrence, et al. for his mystical piety, which he viewed as consistent with biblical, spiritual discipleship. He differed from the French Catholic quietists not only in his rejection of works righteousness, but in his active evangelistic and revivalist zeal. Ibid., 147-148 and 156-157.

[18]W. R. Ward, *The Protestant Evangelical Awakening* (Cambridge: Cambridge University Press, 1992), 232-237. "Quietism (Lat. *quies, quietus*, passivity) in the broadest sense is the doctrine which declares that man's highest perfection consists in a sort of psychical self-annihilation and a consequent absorption of the soul into the Divine Essence even during the present life. In the state of "quietude" the mind is wholly inactive; it no longer thinks or wills on its own account, but remains passive while God acts within it. . . ." "Quietism finally, in the strictest acceptation of the term, is the doctrine put forth and defended in the seventeenth century by Molinos and Petrucci. Out of their teaching developed the less radical form known as Semiquietism, whose principle advocates were Fénelon and Madame Guyon." Edward A. Pace, "Quietism," in *The Catholic Encyclopedia*, vol. 12 (New York: Appleton, 1911), 608-610, here 608.

[19]Wolfram Janzen, "Gerhard Tersteegen," in *Biographisch-Bibliographisches Kirchenlexikon Online*, Band 11 (1996) Spalten 674-695. http://www.bautz.de/bbkl. [Accessed December 14, 2006]. Cf. Ward, *Evangelical Awakening*, 236.

Tersteegen's famous hymn *Gott ist gegenwärtig* (God is present with us) has been viewed by a number of scholars as epitomizing the Reformed mystic's beliefs.[20] The God who was with us as Immanuel was a God of love, not a God of wrathful vengeance. According to Tersteegen, it was not possible to experience the presence of God, however, without prior reconciliation through the grace of God in Jesus Christ, a Pietist conversion.[21] Experiencing the presence of God was the goal of the spiritual life. Achieving this goal was facilitated by physically and mentally withdrawing from the world in order to concentrate fully on God. "Tersteegen called unrelentingly to solitude and self-denial – two fundamental words for the spiritual piety, which he represented. In the presence of God, the ego (*das Ich*) must die, the love of self must disappear, the will must be weakened, reason must be brought to silence."[22]

By becoming indifferent to the outward stimuli of the world's values and activities, by remaining untouched by either joy or sorrow, it was possible to achieve a state of quietness and passive resignation (*Gelassenheit*). God was not exterior to the human person, rather He was to be found by "sinking into the ground of one's soul," which was likewise the experience of "sinking into the ocean of God's love."[23] Union with God was a gift that one might seek by practicing incessant inward prayer, but it could not be earned. Finally the path to the spiritual union with God included much physical and especially spiritual suffering or "darkness," as Tersteegen called it.[24]

The degree to which Tersteegen was dependent upon the French and Spanish Quietists has been a matter of much debate by scholars.[25] The brief

---

[20]See Cornelis Pieter van Andel, "Gerhard Tersteegen," in *Orthodoxie und Pietismus*, ed. Martin Greschat (Stuttgart: Kohlhammer, 1982), 331-346, here 334; and Hansgünter Ludewig, *Gebet und Gotteserfahrung bei Gerhard Tersteegen* (Göttingen: Vandenhoeck & Ruprecht, 1986), which uses this hymn as the basis of his description of Tersteegen's spirituality.

[21]This reflects the conviction found in Question 1 of the Heidelberg Catechism: "What is your only comfort in life and death? Answer: That I, with body and soul, both in life and death, am not my own, but belong unto my Savior Jesus Christ; who with His precious blood has fully satisfied for all my sins, and delivered me from all the power of the devil; and so preserves me . . ." *Doctrinal Standards of the Christian Reformed Church consisting of the Belgic Confession, the Heidelberg Confession and the Canons of Dort* (Grand Rapids: Christian Reformed Church, 1962), 22.

[22]Van Andel, "Gerhard Tersteegen," 335.

[23]"Ich will, anstatt an mich zu denken, Ins Meer der Liebe mich ersenken." Gerhard Tersteegen, *Geistliches Blumengärtlein inniger Seelen nebst der Frommen Lotterie* [hereafter *GBG*] (Stuttgart: Steinkopf, 1868), III, #93, 375.

[24]Van Andel, "Gerhard Tersteegen," 335.

[25]Ludewig, *Gebet und Gotteserfahrung*, 19-58 contains an extremely helpful historiographical analysis of older and contemporary interpretations of Tersteegen's work. He notes that with Nigg, Löschhorn, Zeller and della Croce after ca. 1960 a new phase of interpretation began in which the emphasis shifted to

survey of Tersteegen's thought above indicates that he combined within his thought and person both Quietist and Pietist emphases. Stoeffler correctly notes:

> It is not even necessary to debate the related question as to whether Tersteegen should be regarded as a mystic or a Pietist. On the basis of his writings one must conclude that he was obviously both. . . .[H]e combined the insights of Reformed Pietism with those of French Quietism, and came out both as a mystic and a Pietist, depending on what aspect of his theology one wishes to emphasize.[26]

Tersteegen aspired to follow a "middle course between a mystic and a member of the Reformed church."[27] Like other Reformed Pietists, Tersteegen stressed the necessity of a personal experience of religious conversion. Salvation was based upon the objective saving work of Christ on the cross, "a theologumenon not emphasized to the same degree by the [Catholic] Quietists." Finally Tersteegen attempted to be "thoroughly biblical in his theology."[28] Tersteegen clearly adopted typical quietistic vocabulary and conceptions (*Stille, Einkehr, Verleugnung, Vernichtigung, Gelassenheit*) and understood the life of faith in passive terms.[29] Nevertheless, Tersteegen remained a Reformed Pietist, who understood the steps to the mystical union with God not to be a "self-executed way into God's presence," but "the earnest attempt of a person who has already been regenerated by divine grace to integrate his own will with that of God."[30]

After the death of Tersteegen in 1769, the spiritual heritage of this "Protestant saint" was carried on by his groups of friends and disciples in the Mülheim area under the leadership of Johann Engelbert Evertsen (1722-1807). These circles of friends arranged to have Tersteegen's remaining works published. Due to these efforts, Tersteegen continued to exert influence on churchly Pietism, particularly in the Rhineland and Württemberg, but also on free church groups such as the Mennonites,

---

religious experience rather than dogmatic systems. This resulted in a lessening of the dichotomy between Protestant faith and (Catholic) quietistic mysticism.

[26]Stoeffler, *German Pietism*, 197.

[27]Ward, *Evangelical Awakening*, 232-233.

[28]Stoeffler, *German Pietism*, 198-199. Cf. O'Malley, *Early German-American Evangelicalism*, 144-148; and Gustav Adolf Benrath notes (p. 311) in "Tersteegen's Begriff der Mystik und der mystischen Theologie," in *Der radikale Pietismus. Perspectiven der Forschung*, eds. Wolfgang Breul, Marcus Meier and Lothar Vogel (Göttingen: Vandenhoeck & Ruprecht, 2010), 303-325, that Tersteegen's view of mystical theology is built on the scriptural foundation of the necessity of Christ's death for sin and man's conversion.

[29]Steven O'Malley in personal correspondence (January, 2007) to the author noted that these quietistic terms were found in the Rhineland mystics, extending back to Tauler and Meister Eckhart. Tersteegen adopted this vocabulary to translate the French and Spanish quietists into German.

[30]Stoeffler, *German Pietism*, 199-200.

Quakers and Baptists and on radical Pietists in Germany, America and Russia.[31]

Influence of Tersteegen in Württemberg

Johann Ludwig Fricker (1729-1766), a Württemberg Pietist with theosophical leanings, may have been one source of the reception of Tersteegian thought in the duchy. Fricker came into contact with the mystical piety of Tersteegen while visiting the latter's fellowship groups on the lower Rhine. Fricker's devotional book, *Weisheit im Staube,* became quite popular among Württemberg Pietists. In this work, "Fricker's chief emphasis seems to be contained in the following statement, in which one finds overtones of Tersteegen: 'Learn diligently to differentiate between the voice of God and of your Savior in your heart and all other stirrings within you.'" The Christian was advised not to live by the law, but rather in inward "unbroken fellowship with God," a Tersteegian emphasis.[32]

Unfortunately, the reception of Tersteegian thought in Württemberg has not been systematically explored.[33] Only incidental indications of the latter's popularity are available. Findeisen's examination of the books owned by Pietist households in the Württemberg village of Fellbach is one such case. He notes that in the period between 1781 and the 1840s, books by Tersteegen (30 individual books) were the fourth most popular after those by three Württemberg Pietist authors: Michael Hahn (138 individual books), F. C. Oetinger (70) and the Pietist hymn-writer, P. F. Hiller (55). [34] Similarly, an inventory of the books owned by the Württemberg Separatist

---

[31]Janzen, *Biographisch-Bibliographisches Kirchenlexikon.* J. Steven O'Malley has documented the influence of Tersteegen on John Wesley and on German-American evangelicals in two articles: O'Malley, "The Influence of Gerhard Tersteegen"; and Ibid., "Pietistic Influence on John Wesley: Wesley and Gerhard Tersteegen," *Wesleyan Theological Journal* 31 (Fall 1996): 48-70.

[32] Stoeffler, *German Pietism,* 119. Martin Brecht, "Der württembergische Pietismus," in *Geschichte des Pietismus,* Vol. 2 (Göttingen: Vandenhoeck & Ruprecht, 1995), 279, likewise notes that the chief topic of *Weisheit im Staube* is the "perception of God," although he makes no link to Tersteegen.

[33]The reception of Tersteegen's hymns in radical Pietist hymnbooks as well as in those of the Lutheran and Reformed churches has been explored recently in Christian Bunners, "Gerhard Tersteegen's Lieder im Gesangbuch. Ein Rezeptionsgeschichtlicher Beitrag," in *Gerhard Tersteegen – Evangelischer Mystik inmitten der Aufklärung,* ed. Manfred Kock and Jürgen Thiesbonenkamp (Cologne: Rheinland Verlag, 1997), 77-100.

[34]Findeisen notes that particularly in the first two decades of the nineteenth century works by the three mentioned Württemberg Pietists *and Tersteegen* grew strongly in popularity at the expense of other Pietist writers such as Johann Arndt. Hans-Volkmar Findeisen, "Pietismus in Fellbach 1750-1820 zwischen sozialem Protest und bürgerlicher Anpassung" (Ph.D. diss., University of Tübingen, 1985), 169-170. In the 1790s many Fellbach Pietists became members of Rapp's Separatist movement.

Johannes Barth (1747-1797) from Neuhausen reveals that besides works by Boehme, Gichtel, Gottfried Arnold and other churchly and radical Pietist authors, he also owned three different volumes by Tersteegen, as well as the latter's translation of Mme. Guyon.[35]

Influence of Tersteegen on George Rapp

Michael Hahn was both an acquaintance of George Rapp and after circa 1787 a fellow (and later a rival) leader within the radical Pietist/Separatist movement in Württemberg.[36] Hahn claimed in a letter to the Fellbacher Pietist, David Maile, that "he himself [Hahn] was also a great lover of the pure mysticism of Tersteegen."[37] Hahn in his ethical writings appropriated nearly word for word passages from Tersteegen, as well as other German mystics.[38] This is significant for two reasons. First, it establishes the importance of Tersteegen within at least this radical branch of Württemberg Pietism to which both Hahn and Rapp belonged. Second, Rapp himself claimed to the church consistory in Iptingen on May 18, 1787 to have visited Hahn in 1785 and to have received spiritual insights and comfort from him.[39] In the consistory minutes (written in the third person), Rapp first emphasized that he had developed his religious convictions under the influence of the Holy Spirit alone and without human sources. He then mentioned one notable exception.

> Except two years ago [1785], when he [Rapp] visited the brothers in Tübingen and became ill, a young person by the name of Michael Hahn from Altdorf opened up the way to him, that he might progress through steps and levels of purification. He [Rapp] had had constant unrest in his heart. He also discovered [these steps], and through them came to experience rest.[40]

It is not unlikely that the insights that Rapp received from Hahn related to the quietistic mysticism of Tersteegen, which the latter revered.[41] This

---

[35]Fritz, *Radikaler Pietismus*, 270, n. 45.

[36]Joachim Trautwein, *Die Theosophie Michael Hahns und ihre Quellen* (Stuttgart: Calwer Verlag, 1969), 251.

[37]Michael Hahn, *Send-Briefe über einzelne Capitel aus dem alten und neuen Testament und Antworten auf Fragen über Herzenserfahrungen. Nebst einem Anhang von Briefen über das Hohe Lied Salomo und einigen Liedern* (Tubingen: L.F. Fues, 1830), 698. Quoted in Findeisen, "Pietismus in Fellbach," 240.

[38] Trautwein, *Die Theosophie Michael Hahns*, 267-269.

[39]Eberhard Fritz suggests that Rapp may have met Michael Hahn in the fall of 1779, that is, earlier than 1785, at the Ihinger Hof, a center for radical Pietist activity in Württemberg, when Hahn was resident there. Hahn may have influenced Rapp to separate from the Lutheran church. Fritz, *Radikaler Pietismus*, 69-70 and 126-129.

[40]Arndt, *Doc. Hist. 1700-1803*, 105.

[41]Trautwein, *Die Theosophie Hahns*, 73-74, notes the contact between Hahn and Rapp without suggesting to what the "steps of purification" referred. Apart from Tersteegian mysticism, the only other reasonable possibilities are either that Hahn shared a Boehmist, alchemistically-tinged conception of purification with Rapp, one

likelihood is strengthened by the fact that Rapp in the written explanation of his separation from the church (April 17, 1785) noted that at about the time of his separation (1785), he again experienced a period of spiritual unrest. This point in time coincides with the "unrest in heart" that Rapp experienced prior to receiving insight from Michael Hahn, likewise in 1785. It is therefore probably one and the same occurrence. Rapp described the spiritual unrest and its resolution thus:

> Since that time I have not come to church again ... But because the Lord saw my weakness this light [of conversion] was again darkened. This caused me much sorrow and misery for my friend had departed and was looking through the gate [allusion to Song Sol 5:4-8], for the suffering and sadness which follows separation filled me with horror, and I could not comprehend it. From that time on, however, the Lord let me know full well that in eternity nothing counts but being small and pure, and he showed me that he remains truly in no man unless he has tested him through thousands of trials. And this I certainly had to experience until I finally surrendered my will to God so that my will became his will, and his will my will.[42]

In this text Rapp did not mention Hahn. This however, is not an insurmountable difficulty. We have already seen that Rapp emphasized that his religious convictions were chiefly developed without human influence. The "steps of purification" that Hahn shared with Rapp could well be the Tersteegian teaching that man must first "be tested through thousands of trials" in order to be purified.[43] These trials served to break the human will and make it subservient to the will of God, likewise a central focus of the Reformed mystic. This text informs us that Rapp's long years of spiritual unrest (1780-1785) were finally resolved by adopting a form of mystical piety, probably from Tersteegen.

---

in which the soul was progressively purified in the fires of the forge, just as precious metals were repeatedly fired and purified, or that he shared another distinctive blend of Tersteegian mysticism and Boehmist theosophy. See Trautwein, ibid., 267-269, in which he argues that although Hahn in his ethical writings appropriated nearly word for word passages from Tersteegen and the German mystics, nevertheless Hahn's central, driving interest in *Gnosis* and theosophy was quite different from Tersteegen's emphasis. It should be noted that Trautwein's interest is in Hahn's theosophy, and therefore he may be underemphasizing the influence of Tersteegen. Tersteegen likewise used the image of purification by fire through suffering (as did the Rappites) albeit without a concurrent notion of an alchemistical forge. Tersteegen was likely dependent on the biblical image in Isa. 48:10 and elsewhere. Examples in *GBG* include: "So schmelzt das Feuer weg die tiefste Eigenheit, So führt ein Jammerthal zur wahren Heiligkeit," Tersteegen, *GBG*, I, #221, 40. Cf. ibid., #239, 43 and #393, 70. For the Harmonist view of purification by fire see *Harmonisches Gesangbuch* (Allentown, Pa.: Heinrich Ebner, 1820), #270 and 271, 203-204.

[42] Arndt, *Doc. Hist. 1700-1803*, 73. Karl Arndt's translation.

[43] It could also stem from contact with other mystical authors, such as Tauler.

Furthermore, the discussion of Rapp's steps to the union with God which follows will make clear that Rapp's own teaching concerning "levels of purification" or "levels of sanctification" in his pastoral letters came within the context of a Tersteegian brand of pietistic Quietism.[44] According to Rapp's pastoral letters, purification occurred through suffering and trials. The purpose of purification was to annihilate the self-will in order to experience the peace that the beatific vision provided. Whether Rapp received these insights from Hahn or not cannot be stated with certitude. Rapp's statement to the Iptingen consistory was unfortunately too short and generalized to make a definitive link between Hahn's spiritual input and Rapp's appropriation of Tersteegian mysticism. It is however a tantalizing possibility.

We have already noted that Rapp did not give credit to theological sources that influenced his thought. Therefore, it is possible to establish the influence of Tersteegen on Rapp (and the Rappites) during the Württemberg era primarily through a qualitative analysis of Rapp's pastoral letters written prior to emigration (1791-1802). These letters demonstrate with certainty that Rapp had read Tersteegen's writings while still in Germany. His pastoral letters frequently used both the language and concepts of Tersteegen's brand of spirituality, as will be demonstrated below.

Influence of Tersteegen on the Harmonists

Direct evidence of Tersteegen's influence is available for the period after immigration to the United States and, to a lesser degree, before immigration. Prior to the Harmony Society's publication of their own hymnals in 1820 and 1827, the Harmonist colony depended on other printed hymn collections for their musical and worship needs. Of these, Tersteegen's hymnbook, *Geistliches Blumen-Gärtlein* [hereafter *GBG*], was among the most popular, along with the *Davidisches Psalterspiel*,[45] a radical Pietist hymnbook first published in 1718 for the Inspired church in Schaffhausen, Germany, and the hymnbook of the Lutheran Church in Württemberg (*Württembergisches Gesangbuch*).[46] The early and continuing importance of Tersteegen's *GBG* is evidenced by the multiple copies of six different editions of this hymnbook extant in the Harmony Society archives at Old Econ-

---

[44]Arndt, *Doc. Hist. 1700-1803*, 267f; MG-185, 1-5005, Box 16, Folder 1, Viehmayer collection, # 24 and #27; and MG-185, 1-5005, Box 16, Folder 1, Collection #2, # 6.

[45]See Bunners, "Gerhard Tersteegens Lieder," 80-84 and Hedwig T. Durnbaugh, "Ephrata, Amana, Harmonie: Drei christliche kommunistische Gemeinschaften in Amerika. Beispiele kirchlicher Identität im Kirchenlied," *Bulletin der Internationalen Arbeitsgemeinschaft für Hymnologie* 24 (1996): 203-218. The 1753 edition of the *Davidisches Psalterspiel* contained seven hymns by Tersteegen; the 1791 Saur edition had fourteen.

[46]Richard D. Wetzel, *Frontier Musicians on the Connoquennessing, Wabash and Ohio. A History of the Music and Musicians of George Rapp's Harmony Society (1805-1906)* (Athens: Ohio University Press, 1976), 37.

omy Village, namely the 1756, 1766, 1769, 1779, 1786, 1794, and 1834 editions.[47] Many of these volumes were owned by individual Rappites while still in Germany and brought with them to America.[48] The German mystic was held in such high esteem by Harmonist David Lenz, that he inscribed in his personal copy of the Tersteegen hymnbook the following words: "Long live Tersteegen and his spirit direct us to the Word of God-- Hallelujah."[49] Similarly, many Harmonists copied into the inner covers of their Bibles or hymnbooks Tersteegen's confession of faith (*Erklärung*), which he wrote shortly before his death and which was included in later editions of the *GBG*. Some Harmonists composed their own personal confessions, inspired by the great mystic's example.[50] Through the regular singing of Tersteegen's hymns and the reading of his religious poetry included in the *GBG*, the Rappites absorbed Tersteegen's brand of mysticism, both before and after emigration. Acquaintance with Tersteegen's works was not limited to his popular volume of hymns and poems. The 1829 list of German books owned by the Harmony Society included thirteen books by Tersteegen (five different titles), as well as six copies of three French quietistic works that Tersteegen translated into German.[51]

It is therefore not surprising that when the Harmonists produced their own hymnbooks in 1820 and 1827 topics were included that reflected Tersteegen's influence. In the register of the 1820 hymnbook, there are twelve hymns that reflect the topic of annihilation or denial of the self and of the world (*Verleugnung seiner selbst und der Welt*), a Tersteegian emphasis. Of these hymns, some contain themes distinctly reminiscent of those found in the *GBG*: denial of the world, the self and the senses resulting in achieving a state of inner peace (#63, #64, #308); the experience of darkness when God is absent (#288); and God as the ocean who fills our nothingness (*Nichts*)

---

[47]Wetzel, *Frontier Musicians*, 69, n. 1 and n. 38. Wetzel notes that *GBG* fell into disuse after the publication of the Harmonist hymnbooks. The author's comparison of the *GBG* hymns with the Harmonist hymnbooks supports this contention--none of Tersteegen's 111 hymns were included in either the 1820 or 1827 Harmonist hymnbooks.

[48]For example, David Lenz's signed copy of the *GBG* includes on the inner leaf that he spent 48 X [Kreuzer--a German unit of currency] for the volume, that is, he bought it while still in Württemberg. The fact that most of the extant copies are early editions suggests that they were owned by Rappites prior to emigration.

[49]Wetzel, *Frontier Musicians*, 38.

[50]Ibid., 37.

[51]The following Tersteegen works were included in the 1829 list of books owned: 5 copies *Auserlesene Lebens-Beschreibungen Heiliger Seelen*, 2 copies *Geistliches Blumen Gärtlein*, 2 copies *Weg der Wahrheit*, 2 copies *Geistliche Brosamen*, 2 copies *Geistliche und erbauliche Briefe*, 3 copies *Der Frau L. M. Guyon Beschäftigungen*, 1 copy Mme. Guyon's *Die heilige Liebe Gottes* and 2 copies of Jean de Bernieres-Louvigny's *Das verborgene Leben mit Christo in Gott*. Karl J. R. Arndt, *George Rapp's Successors and Material Heirs 1847- 1916* (Teaneck, N.J.: Fairleigh Dickinson University Press, 1971), 415-428.

and the sun who illuminates the path of truth (#288).[52] One hymn speaks of the *Pilgerhütte*, the name of the commune founded by Tersteegen.[53] The 1827 hymnbook likewise contained a section on the denial of self-will (*Verleugnung seiner selbst und der Welt*) as well as on bearing one's cross or suffering (*Kreuz und Leiden*). One hymn in the former section prayed in successive verses that the heart would be dispossessed of its self-hood (*Eigenheit*), that reason and one's own cleverness would be abolished, that one's own will would be completely broken, and that the heart would be emptied of all its selfishness. Only when one's self-will was abolished could the heart be still in the will of Jesus. "O heart, depart, and sink oneself in Jesus," the hymn ends.[54] The emphases listed above are distinctly mystical and quietistic and probably Tersteegian. It must be noted that some of the hymns in the above sections of both hymnbooks, however, do not display these distinctively Tersteegian language and conceptions.

Furthermore, it is important to remember that while still in Württemberg the Rappites read other mystical writers besides Tersteegen, most notably Johannes Tauler.[55] As mentioned above, the 1829 list of books owned by the Harmony Society included (besides a copy of Tauler's sermons) German translations of the French Quietists by Tersteegen. An unnamed Harmonist in 1822 was well enough acquainted with the founder of Quietism, the Spanish priest de Molinos, to draw a picture of him and write a poem in his honor on the back cover of his personal manuscript hymnbook.[56] Although even average Harmonists were by the 1820s familiar with the French and Spanish Quietists, it is nevertheless probable that the port of entry for quietistic mysticism *while still in Württemberg* came directly through Tersteegen's own writings, particularly through the usage of his *GBG* both before and after emigration, and not through his translations of other Quietist writings. Unfortunately, the sources do not allow us to determine exactly when the Rappites and later the Harmonists became acquainted with the French and Spanish Quietists.

---

[52]1820 *Gesangbuch*, 43-45 (#60-65), 199 (#265), 203 (#270), 204 (#271), 218 (#288), 235 (#308), 248 (#324).

[53]1820 *Gesangbuch*, 43 (#65).

[54]*Harmonisches Gesangbuch* (Oekonomie, Pa.: Harmony Society Publications, 1827), 95-96 (#122).

[55]The 1787 annual Iptingen church minutes reported that Johannes Widmann, a member of Rapp's Separatist movement, owned a copy of Tauler's sermons. Arndt, *Doc. Hist. 1700-1803*, 142. The Maulbronn-Dürrmenz-Knittlingen report of 1803 noted that the Rappites in their meetings occasionally read from Johannes Tauler. Ibid., 339-340. A description of the 1832 Harmonist Easter celebration included a copy of a Tauler dialogue, *Die Kette*. University of Southern Indiana archives, MSS #311, Box 46, Folder 14.

[56]D. Michael de Molinos, sacerdos, "Was andre weist im Wort von Fried u. Ruh gepriesen, hat dieser mit der That bis in den Tod erwiesen, doch schloss die böse Welt den Friedensbothen ein, die Unruh will ja nicht, durch Ruh vertrieben seyn. Apr 15. 1822". OEV, MS hymnbook pM 10.1.

George Rapp's Steps to the Mystical Union with God

George Rapp's quietistic mysticism was prominent in his pastoral letters written between 1791 and 1802. His steps to the mystical union with God presupposed a prior, foundational experience of conversion. Only then were the later stages toward a mystical union with God possible: annihilation of self-will, passive resignation, purification through suffering and the beatific vision. In this section parallels between Rapp's mystical theology and Tersteegen's *GBG* will be demonstrated, primarily in the footnotes. The focus is upon this Tersteegen work because the *GBG* was well known to many members of the movement both before and after emigration. Not only similarities but also differences between Rapp's portrayal of his mystical piety and Tersteegen's *GBG* will be noted.

Repentance and Conversion

Like Tersteegen before him, Rapp believed that a personal experience of conversion was requisite to progress toward the mystical union with God.[57] In a pastoral letter written on April 12, 1798, Rapp made the necessity of conversion abundantly clear. The Separatist leader addressed the recipient of the letter as a "dear friend" rather than a "brother," the term reserved for regenerated Pietists or Separatists. The man had read some of Johann Arndt's works (*Wahres Christentum*?) and had been partially "enlightened" by them, but had not yet come to a full conversion (*Durchbruch*). Therefore, George Rapp explained in some detail the state of this friend's soul and the path he ought to pursue.

> You are separated from God and his light by a complete birth. Your spirit, soul and body are equally corrupted. With your intellect you may no longer be helped and your good works are useless. For this reason God must and will annihilate all your selfish things little by little through repentance and return to Him, leaving nothing out. On the contrary, he will allow you to become thoroughly poor in your own understanding, so that you will be prepared for faith. It stands written, Therefore since we have been justified through faith, we have peace with God through our Lord Jesus Christ. Thus you now dare to surrender yourself completely to God. . . . God sent his Son for your salvation, not that you on your own can become pious or holy enough, rather that you believe in Him. For only pure and undefiled desires, united with love, can be called "living faith." And this faith purifies the heart

---

[57] Stoeffler, *German Pietism*, 198. See O'Malley, "Influence of Gerhard Tersteegen," for an analysis of Tersteegen's Pentecost, 1753 "revivalist" sermon, which called listeners to conversion and an ongoing life of progressive sanctification.

through the blood of Christ, so that you may no longer tolerate and produce wrong deeds, just as your Lord Jesus did not.[58]

In this passage Rapp emphasized a number of central orthodox Lutheran doctrines, albeit partially in language atypical of orthodox theologians. He explained that the recipient of the letter was totally corrupted by sin in every aspect of his being (spirit, soul and body) and therefore separated from God (original sin/total depravity). Man's own efforts to save himself through his intellect or his good works were useless, for, as Rapp reminded the reader, one could never become "pious or holy enough" on one's own (rejection of works righteousness).[59] God must destroy the bonds of self and sin. Salvation and the ensuing peace with God were made possible alone through the shed blood of Christ on the cross (doctrine of atonement). He then quoted Rom 5:1 to underscore the Lutheran doctrine of justification by faith. The atoning work of Christ, which "purifies the heart" from sin, could only be appropriated by the individual through faith alone.

Not only did Rapp display good orthodox Lutheran theology (in unconventional language) in this text, but some typical Pietist concerns as well. He stressed that everyone needed to experience regeneration through a conversion experience, a central dogma of Pietist theology. It was not adequate merely to be baptized in the Lutheran church and verbally affirm the doctrines of the Augsburg Confession. The will must be entirely surrendered to God. Only through "much repentance and change of heart does one reach forgiveness and grace (*Begnadigung*)," Rapp claimed in another section of this letter.[60] Conversion, however, must be a "complete birth."[61] It was insufficient to be saved by grace and then proceed to live a lukewarm Christian life. Rapp viewed true salvation as one composite whole, embracing both regeneration and progressive sanctification. "Living faith" that saves was found only in the person who had become a "new creation" (2 Cor 5:17), thus displaying "pure and undefiled desires, united with love." Such a person would "no longer tolerate and produce wrong deeds," rather he would follow the example of Jesus and produce works worthy of salvation. In this text, Rapp reflected the typical Pietist criticism of the "dead faith" so prevalent in the contemporary Lutheran Church. That ecclesial body's strong focus on justification by faith (*Christus für uns*) had resulted in many cases in a morally weak religion. The Pietist reform movement

---

[58]MG-185, 1-5005, Box 16, Folder 1, Collection #2, Letter # 6.

[59]Cf. Pastoral Letter #13, Arndt, *Doc. Hist. 1700-1803*, 311: "denn du weißest wohl, daß du zu deiner Seeligkeit kein Haarbreit beygetragen hast noch kanst u. nichts thun magst, als dich halten als ein Armer der kein Vermögen mehr hat sich selber zu helfen."

[60]MG-185, 1-5005, Box 16, Folder 1, Collection #2, Letter # 6.

[61]Occasionally the Separatist leader described growth in sanctification as plural births (rather than a "complete birth"), possibly reflecting or adapting the Boehmist notion of the cycle of births within the Godhead. MG-185, 1-5005, Box 16, Folder 1, Viehmeyer Collection, Letter # 19, #23 and #24.

claimed that it was inadequate merely to have "Christ for us." He must likewise be "in us" (*Christus in uns*).⁶² Christ's presence in the believer through the Holy Spirit enabled and empowered the Christian to live a God-pleasing life.

In this same letter, Rapp claimed that there were levels in sanctification through which one must progress.⁶³ These levels in progressive holiness paralleled the steps on the path to the mystical union with God. We have already seen that the first essential step was repentance and conversion. The ultimate goal was the experience of the divine presence, the beatific vision, the mystical union with God. The in-between steps toward this goal, which can be subsumed under the broad topics of the annihilation of the self-will and purification through suffering, as well as the mystical union itself, should not be understood to be strictly chronological. Rather than resembling a straight line, the remaining steps were more like a spiral that circled back on itself while making forward progress. Backward progress was not excluded as the phenomenon of the mystical union was not a permanent but an occasional experience toward which one must strive incessantly. Neither Rapp nor Tersteegen was interested in establishing a strict taxonomy of steps to the mystical union with God. Like other Protestant mystics, Tersteegen did not feel constrained by the traditional Christian tripartite path to the mystical union—purgation, illumination, and union.⁶⁴ In its place both Rapp and Tersteegen employed other medieval mystical language, "turning from self" (*Abkehr*) and "entering into God" (*Einkehr*) in the mystical union.⁶⁵

Annihilation of the Self-Will

Tersteegen had recognized that even his best attempts to live morally were laced with a subtle egoism. Therefore, the self and all worldly plea-

---

⁶²The long-enduring *Christus für uns/Christus in uns* debate between orthodox and Pietist theologians in the eighteenth century typified the fundamental difference between these two branches of Christianity.

⁶³"so wann du deiner wohl selbst wahr, daß du die Heiligung Stuffen weise anziehest . . . " MG-185, 1-5005, Box 16, Folder 1, Collection #2, Letter # 6. Steven O'Malley suggests that the levels of sanctification may reflect the *scala paradisis* of Reformed Pietism found in F. A. Lampe and Gerhard Tersteegen. Personal correspondence, January 2007.

⁶⁴This stands in sharp contrast to traditional medieval mysticism of the Roman Catholic tradition. Protestant mystics either redefined or multiplied the steps to the mystical union. Evelyn Underhill expanded the number of steps to five rungs on the mystical ladder, other Protestant mystics to seven. According to Stoeffler, the "milder form of mysticism found in German Pietism," in contrast to the great Catholic mystics, had four elements: (1) removal of impediments to spiritual growth; (2) meditation; (3) fixation of affections on God; and (4) experiential knowledge and enjoyment of God. Stoeffler, *Mysticism*, 10-11, 104f.

⁶⁵See section on the mystical union below, and particularly footnote 105.

sures were viewed by the Reformed mystic as evil. They needed to be cut off radically, because they hindered a relationship with God. Everything that was important to a person--honor and reputation, money, property, house and home, friends and relatives, needed to be denied in order to gain the greatest good, God Himself.[66] Pietist writers, especially Tersteegen, used a drastic term to describe this action of turning away (*Abkehr*) from the world and self-will--annihilation (*Vernichtigung*).[67] Tersteegen himself described what annihilation of the self signified, "This word *Vernichtigung* means nothing else but the complete destruction of the old man [Rom 6:6] through dispossession."[68]

Rapp appropriated Tersteegen's quietistic emphasis on the annihilation of the self. In fact, he stated in one pastoral letter that the denial of oneself was a main tenet of their belief.[69] Self-denial and annihilation of self-will would remain a central doctrine throughout Rapp's leadership of the Separatist movement and of the Harmony Society. In a pastoral letter written October 9, 1799, the Separatist leader encouraged a disciple to allow God "to annihilate you, with all your many selfish desires." He then asked the rhetorical question, "Would the soul lose anything of precious value through being annihilated? No, nothing! When conquered, the soul will be led to the entirety of God (*Allheit*) and be completely swallowed up in it," that is, experience the mystical union.[70] In another undated pastoral letter, Rapp likewise affirmed that God and not man's effort was responsible for the annihilation of the self.

> Blessed are those, who achieve and continue to walk in the inner paths of the Spirit, until God has destroyed their entire self. This annihilation brings forth the true poverty, where self-choice no longer remains for the person. He

---

[66] Van Andel, "Tersteegen," 335.

[67] Langen notes that, "Von den einzelnen Vertretern hat Tersteegen diese Terminologie [for the *Abkehr von der Welt*] am stärksten entwickelt." August Langen, *Der Wortschatz des Deutschen Pietismus*, 2d ed. (Tübingen: Max Niemeyer, 1968), 139f. Examples of Tersteegen's use of the term *Vernichtigung* in the *GBG*: "Vernichte, Herr, die Eigenheit, Zerstör das Meine gar; Dein Leben der Abhänglichkeit Werd in mir offenbar." Tersteegen, *GBG*, III, #55, 303. "alles aber muß sich endigen in Vernichtigung seiner selbst und leydentlicher Überlaßung an Gott." Tersteegen, *Br.* II, 402, quoted in Langen, *Wortschatz*, 147.

[68] Tersteegen, vLE 238 (II, 6, n. 8). Quoted in Ludewig, *Gebet und Gotteserfahrung*, 143.

[69] "denn die Verleugnung unserer selbst ist bey uns ein Hauptpunkt." Arndt, *Doc. Hist. 1700-1803*, 284.

[70] "biß Er dich vernichtiget, mit all deinem vielen Eigenen, denn wer seine Seel ein mal verliert vom Edlem? Nichts! bezwungen, der wird zur allheit ein geführt, u: davon ganz verschlungen." MG-185, 1-5005, Box 16, Folder 1, Viehmeyer Collection, Letter # 23. The contrast between the *Nichtigkeit* of man and the *Allheit* of God is a central concept in Tersteegen. Ludewig, *Gebet und Gotteserfahrung*, 138-140.

must in faith grasp God's unlimited mercy, which our Savior has purchased for humanity. Let us walk in these paths.[71]

Although Rapp here claimed that the annihilation "destroyed the entire self," the passage above and other pastoral letters affirmed that only the negative forces of egoism (*Ichheit*) were actually eliminated.[72] What needed to be destroyed were self-love (*Aigenliebe*), self-centeredness (*Eigenheit*) and self-will.[73] There in the midst of self-love and selfish egoism, Satan the adversary held sway, keeping both the individual soul and entire Separatist conventicles in bondage. In order to be prepared for the "golden era" of the Lamb, the *Eigenheit* must be radically cut off.[74]

Likewise, for the Christian committed to achieving the *unio mystica* there could be no room for self-will, "self-choice no longer remains."[75] Rapp used two unique images to describe the annihilation of the self-will that are otherwise not common either in Pietism or in Tersteegen (although the second of these is found in Tauler): the will becoming thin and becoming poor (in spirit).[76] "In this state of poverty, a man is inwardly gathered into the One. Then the will is thin and all powers of the soul depend upon Him, and he then falls into the eternal mercy of God the Father...."[77] By stating that the will was "thin," Rapp affirmed that although the individual voluntative faculty did not completely cease to exist in the state of annihilation, it

---

[71]"selig sind aber die, so es erlangen, und darinn fort gehen, biß Gott all ihr eigen vernichtet hat, diese vernichtigung bringt erst die rechte Armuth, wo dem Menschen keine aigene Wahl mehr hat übrig bleibt, und sich im Glauben in Gottes unendlicher Barmhertzigkeit fassen muß, die unser Erlöser der Menschheit erworben und auf diesen Wegen lasset uns Wandlen." MG-185, 1-5005, Box 16, Folder 1, Viehmeyer Collection, Letter # 21.

[72]The term *Ichheit* is an unusual word form, not found in modern German dictionaries. It was not, however, an original word with Rapp. It is found in Johannes Scheffler's (Johannis Angeli Silesi) *Wandersmann* (first publ. 1704) on pages 38, 114, 123, 124 (=egoitas). Langen, *Wortschatz*, 412. *Ichheit* was likewise found in Quirinius Kühlmann's *Kühlpsalter* of 1684, 186. Langen, *Wortschatz*, 413. It is unknown if Rapp had read these mystical works prior to this time or at all.

[73]*Eigenliebe* and *Eigenheit* were common concepts in Pietism and two of the many word formations from *Eigen* and *Selbst*. "Die Zusammensetzungen mit 'Eigen-' und 'Selbst-' und eine Anzahl sinnverwandter Ausdrücke sind bedingt durch die pietistische Grundforderung der Entpersönlichung als einer notwendigen Vorstufe für den 'Einfluß' Gottes in die Seele und das Sichverlieren im Göttlichen. Alle Hinwendungen zum Ich, jedes Beharren in der Eigenheit hindern die *Unio* und werden so fast immer negativ bewertet." Lange, *Wortschatz*, 112.

[74]MG-185, 1-5005, Box 16, Folder 1, Viehmeyer Collection, Letter # 20.

[75]MG-185, 1-5005, Box 16, Folder 1, Viehmeyer Collection, Letter # 21.

[76]This assertion is based on an examination of Langen's *Wortschatz*. See Stoeffler, *Mysticism*, 22: "His [Tauler's] great theme was spiritual poverty."

[77]MG-185, 1-5005, Box 16, Folder 1, Viehmeyer Collection, Letter # 20. The concept of the soul being "gathered" by God is very common in Tersteegen: *GBG*, 196f, 221, 326, 354, 459, 509, 550; and *Br.* I, 84 and 201f; and *Br.* II, 166. Langen, *Wortschatz*, 150-151.

was nevertheless completely submitted to the will of God. For Rapp, like Tersteegen, the annihilation of the self-will did not have ontological ramifications; rather the annihilation affected a psycho-spiritual experience or state.[78] The self-will did not only become thin, the submissive will likewise functioned in a state of self-elected poverty. Pastoral letter #21 quoted above declared that those whose will became truly "poor" were "blessed," an allusion to the Beatitudes (Matt 5:3), where the "poor in spirit" inherit the kingdom of God.

For both Tersteegen and Rapp, the annihilation of the self-will transposed the individual into a state of consciousness receptive to apprehending the numinous presence of God. In this state the human personality was freed both of positive and negative emotions and even of mental conceptions.[79] According to one Rapp pastoral letter, in the process of annihilation, one's emotions ceased, making the way free for faith.[80] Later in the same letter, the Separatist leader declared that mental images were likewise eliminated:

> You forfeit all your [mental] images (*Bilder*) and opinions, your hunger and desires... all your unnecessary scruples fall away, and your sole activity will be to concede yourself to God with all your inward and outward encounters, and thus you will enjoy the peace of God.[81]

Gelassenheit (Passive Resignation)

The annihilation of the self-will resulted in the human personality being enabled to react extremely passively to the vagaries of everyday life. All events were believed to be firmly in the hands of a providential God. Therefore, the goal was not just to accept one's lot in life stoically, but actually to

---

[78] Hansgünter Ludewig correctly notes that the annihilation of the self (*Vernichtigung des Ichs*) for Tersteegen did not signify a change in the ontological nature of man, in his *Sein*, but only in his consciousness of himself (*Bewusstsein*) as burdened with egoism. Ludewig, *Gebet und Gotteserfahrung*, 138f.

[79] Concerning Tersteegen's call to be emotionless and without mental conceptions (*bildlos*): "Die Seele soll sich vom Kreatürlichen scheiden, soll unberührt bleiben von Freude oder Trauer, Furcht oder Hoffnung, kurzum, sie muß für alle äußerlichen Dinge gefühllos werden, sogar für die Bilder, die unsere religiöse Vorstellungswelt kennzeichnen. In der Seele entsteht dadurch ein Zustand von Stille und Gelassenheit: je passiver man sich verhält, um so besser. Es ist nichts nützlicher, als bildlos, werklos, formlos im Schoß des Vaters zu liegen: Nichts haben, als nur Gott in allen, Nichts wollen, als nur Ihm gefallen, Nichts können in dir selber mehr, Nichts sein: dies ist die höchste Lehr." Van Andel, "Tersteegen," 335. Cf. Ludewig, *Gebet und Gotteserfahrung*, 182f.

[80] MG-185, 1-5005, Box 16, Folder 1, Viehmeyer Collection, Letter # 22.

[81] "alle deiner bilder u: Meynungen einbüssest, u: deinen Hunger u: verlangen... da fallen deine unNöthige bedencklichkeiten ab, u: dein thun wird seyn, dich Gott zulassen, in allen deinen begegnissen Jnnerlich u: Äusserlich, u: also geniessest du nun den Frieden Gottes." MG-185, 1-5005, Box 16, Folder 1, Viehmeyer Collection, Letter # 22.

be emotionless and indifferent to whatever came one's way.⁸² The Rappites and later the Harmonists thus sought to achieve a passive, quietistic mental and spiritual state while pursuing an activist lifestyle. Frederick Rapp in a letter he wrote on February 15, 1804 to his adopted father, George, who had already left for America, described the mental and spiritual process of annihilating his self-will and submitting to God's will, whether that meant remaining in Germany or immigrating to the United States.

> With all my strength I wrestled to submit to God's will. Inwardly I always felt contented, but not without. My passions in the end accumulated to such a degree that the marrow in my bones was affected, and I became ill. . . . I was [then] able to reach into the deepest ground [of the soul] . . . Amidst weeping and hot tears . . . I commended myself and all to the secret will and counsel of God which He had since eternity considered for us, and then I could firmly believe that what He had planned for us would surely come about. Thus I became one with His will and rested in it, and *it did not matter to me whether He would leave us here or lead us out* [author's emphasis].⁸³

George Rapp used more radical terms to describe the state of passive resignation to God's will. In a pastoral letter he boldly stated: "He who reaches the level, still here in this world, that he leaves the choice concerning himself to God, he is as cheerful in hell as in heaven."⁸⁴

The state of quietistic, passive resignation that Frederick and George Rapp described above was referred to in Pietist circles by the term *Gelassenheit*. First coined by medieval mystics, the term was taken over by Luther, as well as by Pietists such as Gottfried Arnold, Francke and Tersteegen.⁸⁵ For Tersteegen (and Rapp), *Gelassenheit* referred to "letting go of the ego (*Ich*) in the realm of the will. It signifies that stance, in which the self-

---

⁸²Tersteegen likewise proposed passive indifference to life in the following passages: "Wo du bist und wie dirs gehet, Bald geniedrigt, bald erhöhet, Bald in Freuden, bald in Pein, Bald geschmähet, bald geehret: Bleib gleichgiltig, ungestört, innig nur mit Gott gemein." Tersteegen, *GBG*, I, #218, 39. "O edle Freiheit, da der Wille abgeschieden Von allem, was nicht Gott, steht innig willenlos, von Angst und Treiben frei, erhaben lebt im Frieden, Da nichts ihn rührt noch stört in seines Vaters Schoos." Ibid., I, #250, 45. "Ohn eigne Wahl und Widerstreben, In alles seinen Willen geben, Stets ja sagen, und nimmer nein, So wird man frei von allen Pein. Vergnügt und still nach Gottes Winken Muß unser Wille stracks ersinken, Und ohne Forschen heißen gut, Was Gottes Wille will und thut." Ibid., I, #481, 86.

⁸³Arndt, *Doc. Hist. 1700-1803*, 417-418.

⁸⁴"wer den Grad erreichen mag, noch hier in diesem Welt, daß Er Gott die wahl über sich läßt, der ist in der Hölle so vergnügt als im Himmel." MG-185, 1-5005, Box 16, Folder 1, Viehmeyer Collection, Letter # 23.

⁸⁵Lange, *Wortschatz*, 221-222. O'Malley notes that *Gelassenheit* was prominent especially in Meister Eckhart and Tauler. J. Steven O'Malley, *Early German-American Evangelicalism. Pietist Sources on Discipleship and Sanctification* (Lanham, Md.: Scarecrow Press, 1995), 115, n. 32.

will dies and desires nothing more."[86] This state of passive resignation, though difficult to achieve and maintain, bestowed upon the believer a deep sensation of peace. Rapp described it as experiencing the "kingdom of God within you."[87] Tersteegen likewise wrote in extravagant terms of the peace and joy that *Gelassenheit* brought to the soul.[88]

Suffering and Darkness

For Tersteegen and Rapp the path toward the mystical union with God was lined with pain and suffering. Tersteegen used the concept of darkness primarily to symbolize the suffering that resulted from spiritual remoteness from God. He first used this term to describe his own personal spiritual crisis that culminated in 1724 with the letter of submission to Jesus written in his blood. Just as light was a symbol of the Godhead, so darkness and "dark faith" symbolized distance from God, both to the medieval mystics and to some Pietists like Tersteegen. This temporary period of darkness (in Tersteegen) or dryness (more common in other Pietist writers) was understood to be allowed by God to test one's faith and to further the annihilation of the self.[89]

In his pastoral letters Rapp frequently comforted his followers who were on "dark paths of faith," experiencing a "dark night of faith" or in the midst of "dark faith."[90] He reminded one disciple that although "dark faith" was wearisome, it was not dangerous. Rather it was a normal experience for "all sincere souls," who follow the inner path of the spirit.[91] One should not be surprised when spiritual darkness occurred.

> Therefore, dear brother, do not allow it to seem at all unusual, when through inner poverty and privation all your perceived lights are removed from you

---

[86] For the importance of *Gelassenheit* in Tersteegen see Ludewig, *Gebet und Gotteserfahrung*, 173-175, here 174.

[87] MG-185, 1-5005, Box 16, Folder 1, Collection #2, Letter # 6.

[88] See Ludewig, *Gebet und Gotteserfahrung*, 176-180 for examples.

[89] "Dunkler Glauben: Der hier gesammelte Wortschatz der Pietisten, der den Zustand der Gottesferne umschreibt, wird in zweifacher Bedeutung gebraucht. Er bezeichnet einmal den Zustand der Unbekehrten vor dem Durchbruch, zweitens später auftretende vorübergehende Perioden der 'Dunkelheit,' 'Dürre' und 'Trockenheit,' die Gott als Prüfung zuläßt. . . So wie das Licht für die Gottheit, ist Dunkelheit Ursymbol für die Gottesferne, schon in der ma. mystik und ebenso im Pietismus." Langen, *Wortschatz*, 127. The concept of „dark faith" is likewise found in Tersteegen, *GBG*, I, #510, 91: "Wenn Trost und Licht und Kraft erkalten Und man nur Elend wird gewahr. So fühl ich, was ich bin und kann, So lern ich recht mich Gott ergeben Im Geist und *dunklen Glauben* leben Auf jener schönen Kreuzesbahn," and in the title to ibid., I, #570, 106: "Dunkle Glaubens-Überlassung."

[90] MG-185, 1-5005, Box 16, Folder 1, Collection #2, Letter # 22: "Dunkler Glaubens-Weg;" ibid., Letter #30: "durch den duncklen Glauben gehen;" and ibid., Viehmeyer Collection, Letter # 24: "in übung der Dunklen Glaubens Nacht."

[91] MG-185, 1-5005, Box 16, Folder 1, Collection #2, Letter # 22.

in accordance with poverty of the spirit. God dwells in darkness, and you are learning with me and the other brothers to persevere in dark faith (*duncklen Glauben*).[92]

Not only was "dark faith" a normal experience for the sincere believer, it occurred in accordance with God's will. Rapp reassured one letter recipient that the adverse situation that the disciple was presently facing would not affect his salvation, which had already been secured "according to the eternal providence and plan of God."[93] God would bestow upon the believer the inclination and strength to hold fast to God in all trials.[94]

Tersteegen most often used the concept of darkness to refer to periods of spiritual alienation. Rapp likewise used the term in this fashion, as seen in the longer quote above. "Paths of inner darkness" were common for the soul intent upon reaching the beatific vision.[95] The Holy Spirit would frequently lead the believer into a spiritual desert to teach him true submission and humility.[96] However, Rapp also broadened the concept to include other forms of suffering, notably physical sickness. The Separatist leader encouraged his followers who were suffering poor health to endure patiently the "cross" that was laid upon them. He exhorted them to "persevere in all trials, willingly and unconquerable, with God's help."[97] Physical forms of suffering were also viewed by Tersteegen as promoting sanctification. However, most likely due to his own periods of spiritual crisis, the Reformed mystic emphasized spiritual suffering more than physical forms.

In a number of pastoral letters, Rapp emphasized the purpose of trials, suffering and spiritual darkness in the life of the believer. First and foremost, periods of spiritual or physical suffering served to purify the soul. "God keeps us under the dear cross until we are purified."[98] The Spirit of Jesus would accomplish its purpose "until you are purified, should even your purification last until Judgment Day."[99] Trials and suffering were essential; through them "God annihilates all your self-centeredness (*Eigenheit*), from which you may not be freed in any other way."[100] The Christian was led into the "very narrow [wine?]press" of suffering, in order that "all the powers of the soul might be brought very low and made humble."[101] By

---

[92]"darum lieber Bruder laß dir es doch gar nicht seltsam vorkomen, wan dir durch Jnnerliche Armuth u: Mangel dir alle deine Erkenntliche Lichter benommen werden nach Armuth deß Geistes, Gott wohnet im duncklen, u: du lernest mit mir u: noch Andern Brüdern im *duncklen Glauben* aus harren." MG-185, 1-5005, Box 16, Folder 1, Viehmeyer Collection, Letter # 23.
[93]MG-185, 1-5005, Box 16, Folder 1, Collection #2, Letter # 22.
[94]Ibid., Letter # 6, and ibd. Viehmeyer Collection, Letter # 23.
[95]Ibid., Viehmeyer Collection, Letter # 22.
[96]Ibid., Collection #2, Letter # 1.
[97]Ibid., Collection #2 Letter # 6.
[98]Ibid., Viehmeyer Collection, Letter # 24.
[99]Ibid., Collection #2, Letter # 6.
[100]Ibid., Collection #2, Letter # 22.
[101]Ibid., Collection #2, Letter # 1.

"dying in life" (*das sterbende Leben*), the soul was prepared for the first resurrection and to be present at the wedding feast of the Lamb.[102] Suffering was thus essential, in both Rapp's and Tersteegen's view, to purify the believer from sin, self and the world in preparation for the mystical union with God.[103] Due to its importance for growth in sanctification, Rapp prayed in a pastoral letter not to be released from suffering. Rather in his body he desired to complete the suffering of Christ (Col 1:24). "O Lord, you once suffered and redeemed the world. Therefore, you should no longer suffer, rather I desire to suffer in your place, therefore do not spare me, just as your Father also did not spare you."[104]

Mystical Union with God

Repentance and conversion initiated the spiral path of progressive sanctification. The experience of the mystical union with God was its culmination and goal. The in-between steps of annihilation of the self-will and purification through suffering served to turn the soul away from the world (*Abkehr*). The reverse side of *Abkehr*, the withdrawal from and renunciation of the world and self, was *Einkehr*, which described "entering into" and experiencing communion with God. Although use of the concept of *Einkehr* extended back to the early and medieval Christian mystics, it was appropriated by Pietists like Rapp and particularly Tersteegen to connote the pivotal practice of turning inward and personally experiencing the divine.[105]

For Tersteegen and Rapp, as well as Tauler, *Einkehr* into God and the *unio mystica* took place within the ground of the individual soul and not in some numinous location outside of oneself. Tersteegen encouraged a follower: "Enter child-like into God in the *ground of your soul*."[106] Similarly,

---

[102]Ibid., Collection #2, Letter # 22.

[103]Tersteegen likewise viewed physical and spiritual suffering as effecting purification, humility and progressive sanctification in life. "Durch äußere Widrigkeiten, Durch innres Kreuz und Leiden Wirst du gebeugt und rein: Laß, wie ein Thon, dich wenden In deines Schöpfers Händen; Sie bilden dich recht fein." Tersteegen, *GBG*, I, #187, 34. "O höchste Leidensprob, für Gottgesinnte Herzen! So schmelzt das Feuer weg die tiefste Eigenheit, So führt ein Jammerthal zur wahren Heiligkeit," ibid., #221, 40.

[104]MG-185, 1-5005, Box 16, Folder 1, Collection #2, Letter # 1.

[105]Langen notes that the concept of *Einkehr* was found almost exclusively in Pietist material in Tersteegen: "In unserem Material fast ausschließlich bei Tersteegen belegt. Br. I, 339: 'Nur thue ich noch hinzu, daß alle dergleichen Regungen und Versuchungen uns nicht so sehr müssen hindern in der Einkehr, sondern daß sie uns vielmehr zu einer lauteren und mehr geistlichen Art der Einkehr führen und helfen sollen.'. . . Ders., *GBG* 573: 'Der Phantasie und Sinnen Reich, durch süße Einkehr stets entweich.' " Langen, *Wortschatz*, 155.

[106]"Einkehren: in sich (in Gott): Tersteegen, Br. I, 306: 'kehre kindlich in Gott ein, im Grunde deiner Seele!' – Ders. *GBG* 101: 'O Seel! entsink dem eignen Willen, Kehr in dich ein, und laß dich stillen: Im Seelengrund ist Gott uns nah.' " Langen,

Rapp in a pastoral letter exhorted the letter-recipient first to surrender his will completely to God, then to "grasp yourself in the deepest root of your inner core . . . in faith that God is sufficient for you in time and eternity." Rapp reiterated the necessity of *Abkehr* from self prior to *Einkehr* within the ground of the soul.

> If you follow this path . . . and conquer your entire will, emotions and evil inclinations, and submit yourself to God at all times, then an open door into the inner ground (*Jnneren Grund*) will be given to you, to enter into (*einzukehren*) your soul. . . there stillness will be too loud for you . . . in activity you will be at rest. This is what Christ calls the kingdom of God within you.[107]

Annihilation of the self-will was the necessary prerequisite. The image of open door which Rapp employed, most likely was an allusion to Rev 3:20: "If anyone hears my voice and opens the door, I [Christ] will come in and eat with him and he with me" (*NIV*). A passive, submissive will was able to experience freely deep, intimate communion with Christ within the soul. The goal was not oblivion or a pantheistic absorption into the Godhead, rather soul-satisfying *koinonia* with the object of one's heart's desire, Christ Himself.

For George Rapp, the experience of the mystical union with God was by its very nature ineffable, something that "you may little understand but greatly admire."[108] Nevertheless, in several pastoral letters he attempted to describe the indescribable with two images: falling or sinking into the Godhead and beholding the Godhead. We have noted above that Tersteegen frequently used the images of "sinking into God" and "sinking into the ocean of God's love."[109] This image was likewise found in Tauler and in a Rapp pastoral letter dated October 10, 1794: "Therefore be still and remain by yourselves, in order that you might learn to sink deeper into the ground of God, into the still nothingness, where you find everything."[110] In another

---

Wortschatz, 154. Langen demonstrates that ground (*Grund*) is a metaphor for God himself, for the soul, and for the process of the mystical union itself. Ibid., 162. Among Pietists, Tersteegen is the most important representative of the view that the mystical union takes place in the ground of the soul. "Wieder ist Tersteegen der wichtigste Vertreter dieser Sinngebung. – Tersteegen, *GBG* 20: 'Gedenk nicht mehr an dich, und laß dich Gott im Grund, Demüthig, liebreich, sanft; merk, wenn er dich will stillen: So findst du dich in Gott, und Gott in dir zur Stund.' Ebd. 242: 'Tief im Grund, da ist es schön! Da kann man mit Augen sehn, Wie des Herren Glorie-Glanz Dieses Haus erfüllet ganz. Innig, außer Ort und Zeit ist der Ort zu deinem Throne; ach den Grund, mein König, rein, komm, und ewig drinnen wohne.' " Ibid., 167. However, the concept of the mystical union in the ground of the soul was likewise found in Tauler, who also influenced Rapp's theology. Stoeffler, *Mysticism*, 22-23.

[107] MG-185, 1-5005, Box 16, Folder 1, Collection #2, Letter # 6.

[108] MG-185, 1-5005, Box 16, Folder 1, Viehmeyer Collection, Letter # 22.

[109] Similar images were found in later Harmonist hymns in the 1820 and 1827 hymnbooks. 1820 *Gesangbuch*, #288, 218 (God as the ocean that fills our nothingness) and 1827 *Gesangbuch*, #122, 95-96 (sinking into Jesus).

[110] Arndt, *Doc. Hist. 1700-1803*, 255. Cf. Stoeffler, *Mysticism*, 22.

letter Rapp slightly adapted Tersteegen's and Tauler's concept of sinking into the ocean of the Godhead to *falling* into "God himself" in the ground of the soul.

> For the closer you come to your inner ground, you will become too heavy for yourself, so that you will gladly allow yourself to fall into the formed ground of the Godhead, which is called our sense and understanding, the nothingness. There your sacrifice will be ignited by the holy fire of God, without your effort or deed. There all your powers will become passive and quiet (*gelassen*), and burn in the love of God. The passive ashes fall to the earth, and the spirit ascends in the smoke of prayers to the Ancient One.[111]

The mystical union took place within the ground of the soul, which was likewise the ground of the Godhead. When the burdens of self became too heavy for the soul, the seeking believer would gladly let go of self and passively fall into the Godhead. This ultimate submission to God was equivalent for Rapp to presenting oneself as a burnt offering, pleasing to God and ignited without human effort (cf. Elijah's sacrifice on Mount Carmel). The soul would then burn with the love of God.

In another pastoral letter, Rapp encouraged a brother not to cease from seeking the mystical union until he reached the beatific vision and could behold the Godhead.

> But now compose yourself in good eagerness, and do not slack off, until your inner eye beholds the inward ground in the light of the Godhead. Then your disposition will not be covered with fog or thickened. For through the constant contemplation of the complete perfection of the Godhead ... we behold heavenly and spiritual things, for our pleasure and to be drawn perfectly there.[112]

The concept of "beholding the Godhead" or the *visio Dei* was found in medieval mystics Tauler and Meister Eckhart, besides others.[113] Separatists of the Rapp movement were known to have read Tauler at their conventicle meetings while still in Württemberg. For that reason, the source of this mystical image in Rapp's theology should be sought in Tauler. According to Rapp, seeing God was spiritually satisfying and pleasurable in its own right.

---

[111] MG-185, 1-5005, Box 16, Folder 1, Viehmeyer Collection, Letter # 20. In Letter #3, Arndt, *Doc. Hist. 1700-1803*, 255, Rapp used the term sinking (*ersinken*) rather than falling.

[112] MG-185, 1-5005, Box 16, Folder 1, Collection #2, Letter # 1. Cf. Letter #3, Arndt, *Doc. Hist. 1700-1803*, 255, where Rapp likewise used the concept of beholding the perfection of the Godhead within the inner being.

[113] Johannes Tauler's 39th sermon: "When our Lord has thus well prepared man ... then the Lord comes and brings him to the third degree [mystical union] and in that the Lord truly takes the cloak from his eyes and discovers the truth to him. And then the bright light of the sun rises for him and lights him out of all his distress; it seems to man quite as if he had been quickened on his deathbed. In this experience the Lord leads man quite beyond himself into himself." Translated and quoted in Stoeffler, *Mysticism*, 5. Cf. Ibid., 22.

It likewise had the effect of opening the inner eye of the soul by casting all fog of sin away. One then could behold "heavenly and spiritual things," that is, one became privy not just to God Himself, but to enriching spiritual insights as well. As a result of the beatific vision, the soul was inwardly renewed. The believer enjoyed a deep sense of peace with God, which would not be disturbed by the demands of the Law of Moses. For one would no longer intentionally sin.[114]

This survey of Rapp's steps to the mystical union with God reveals that the Separatist leader's mystical piety was largely dependent upon that of the Pietist Reformed mystic, Gerhard Tersteegen, and to a lesser degree on Tauler. Although Rapp did not give credit to his theological sources, the similarities of language and content between the Tersteegen's *GBG* and Rapp's pastoral letters indicates that the latter was greatly influenced by the works of the Rhineland mystic. Both Tersteegen and Rapp expressed a similar conception of the prior need for conversion before setting off on the path to the mystical union with God. Nevertheless, neither of the two was interested in developing an exact taxonomy of the steps to apprehending the divine. Both used the distinctive quietistic term "annihilation" in a similar fashion to describe the radical nature of abolishing self-love, self-centeredness and self-will (*Abkehr* from the world and self). The annihilation did not have ontological, rather psycho-spiritual ramifications. It resulted for both Tersteegen and Rapp in the seeking believer achieving a state of passive resignation (*Gelassenheit*), in which he/she reacted to the vagaries of life with indifference and extreme passivity. In this state the soul experienced a deep sense of peace. Tersteegen and Rapp both viewed "dark faith," that is, providentially-allowed spiritual and physical suffering, as a means that God employed to purify the believer from the bondage of self. The union with God took place within the inner ground of the soul for both spiritual leaders. This mystical union did not signify a pantheistic absorption into the Godhead, rather intimate fellowship (*Einkehr*) with the object of one's desire, God Himself. These very significant similarities between Tersteegen's and Rapp's mystical piety cannot be accidental. Rapp had clearly read and appropriated Tersteegen's brand of quietistic mysticism if not by the time of his separation from the Lutheran Church (ca. 1785) then certainly prior to the writing his pastoral letters between 1791 and 1802. Tersteegen's works were quite popular in Württemberg among churchly and radical Pietists and it is known that at least some Rappites owned the *GBG* prior to emigration. The influence of Tersteegen on the Harmonists after emigration is well-documented.

In spite of the significant similarities between the mystical piety of Tersteegen and Rapp, there are several differences both in emphasis and in con-

---

[114]"u: also geniessest du nun den Frieden Gottes, u: das Gesez Mosis mag dich nicht mehr beunruhigen, weil du dem sehr Feind wirst, welches dir deinen Frieden stöhret, u: sündigest also nicht mehr, aus der Försaz." MG-185, 1-5005, Box 16, Folder 1, Viehmeyer Collection, Letter # 22.

tent. Tersteegen emphasized the darkness of spiritual suffering more than physical distress, whereas both are equally present in Rapp. Tersteegen's focus on the "ocean of God's love" was largely absent in the pastoral letters of the Separatist leader. Lastly, although the Tersteegian concept of annihilation of the self-will and absolute submission to God's will remained a central aspect of the Harmonist doctrine of sanctification, after emigration the image for the mystical union deviated from Tersteegen's conception. In Harmonist hymnody (circa 1820 onward) and in Rapp's later sermons the mystical union usually was not described as "falling into God" or "beholding the Godhead." Rather, it was depicted in semi-erotic language as union with the heavenly Sophia or Christ the Bridegroom.

Rapp was dependent not only on the quietistic mysticism of Tersteegen. The Separatist and later Harmonist leader likewise adopted elements from other mystical sources. Possibly while still in Württemberg, though definitively after emigration to the United States, Rapp and his followers were acquainted with French and Spanish Quietists in German translation. Furthermore, there is documentary evidence of significant acquaintance with the works of Johannes Tauler by members of the Separatist movement. Rapp likely adopted the concept of "spiritual poverty" and of "beholding the Godhead" (*visio Dei*) from Tauler. "Sinking into God" was found both in Tersteegen and Tauler, as was the concept of the mystical union taking place in the "ground of the soul." August Langen in his *Dictionary of German Pietism* notes that, *among Pietists*, Tersteegen most thoroughly and nearly exclusively developed the terminology of *Abkehr* and *Einkehr*. However, this language was likewise previously found in the writings of Tauler. In summary, Rapp's early theology, reflected in his pastoral letters written before emigration, absorbed and assimilated significant elements from Tersteegen, and, to a lesser degree, from Tauler.

4

The Flight of the Sunwoman (1800-1805)

At the dawn of the nineteenth century the Separatist movement in Württemberg experienced accelerated growth. The number of Rapp's followers increased dramatically. New Separatist groups under Rapp's umbrella of leadership arose in several villages previously unreached by his movement.[1] Since 1799, in connection with the Napoleonic conflict, the region had been repeatedly threatened by French invasion. These threats to the public safety encouraged widespread chiliastic speculation among portions of the population. Some came to understand the ensuing crisis as supporting Rapp's radical Pietist claim that the end of the world was at hand. They thus gathered in Separatist conventicles to prepare for the *eschaton*. This rapid increase of members was attributed by the civil and religious affairs office of Maulbronn-Dürrmenz in 1802 to the apocalyptic fervor that gripped the duchy of Württemberg at this time. Rapp, they reported, was winning followers by preaching that the "Kingdom of God was imminent" and that believers would experience "complete freedom" in the millennial age.[2]

---

[1]Fritz notes the spread of the Rappite movement to Roßwag, Heimerdingen and Eltingen. Fritz provides a good overview of the "high point and crisis" of the Rapp movement ca. 1800. Eberhard Fritz, *Radikaler Pietismus in Württemberg* (Epfendorf/Neckar: Bibliotheca academica, 2003), 152-157, here 155.

[2]Karl J. R. Arndt, *George Rapp's Separatists, 1700-1803. A Documentary History* (Worcester, Mass.: Harmony Society Press, 1980), 325.

From Conventicles to Church

By the spring of 1803 the civil government and religious authorities of Maulbronn-Dürrmenz-Knittlingen recognized that the Separatist movement had in effect become an organized church by appropriating the rights and practices of such a body. First, they argued, the Separatists did not recognize the episcopal authority of the head of the church, the Elector.[3] Rapp's unquestioned role as leader of the movement had consolidated thoroughly by this time. The report claimed that Rapp in effect "had been elected bishop of the Separatists."[4] "The priestly acts, which he [Rapp] performs, belong to the privileges (*Rechte*) of the holy, Christian Church."[5] Second, the Separatist church upheld its own judicial system and church discipline. If difficulties arose between Separatists that could not be resolved locally or if it was necessary to excommunicate a member, the issue would be reported to and decided by Rapp and a group of elders. Third, the Separatists were no longer content merely to hold mid-week or Sunday afternoon conventicles. Religious meetings were held simultaneous to the worship services of the Lutheran Church, both on Sundays and holidays, which constituted an infraction against the Pietist rescript of 1743. Rapp himself preached at these services by providing an "explanation of a chapter of the Bible," thus usurping a right that belonged exclusively to ordained clergy.[6] Fourth, the Separatists either appropriated (Eucharist) or bypassed (baptism) the sacraments of the Lutheran Church. A Eucharistic celebration, with an accompanying love feast, was held once a year for the members. Due to the large number of Separatists, Rapp divided the people into three smaller groups for the Lord's Supper and officiated at the service. Separatists baptized their own babies to prevent them from being baptized (forcibly) in the Lutheran Church. Finally, the Separatist church assumed diaconal duties. A benevolent fund was established from the financial contributions collected at the various meetings. After the costs for ordinary operating expenses (lights, paper, etc.) were paid, the remainder of the money was distributed to meet the needs of impoverished members.[7] The Maulbronn-Dürrmenz-Knittlingen report was indeed correct, when it claimed that the Separatist movement had by 1803 become a Separatist church.

The development of Rapp's movement from a cluster of autonomous Separatist conventicles or fellowship groups (*Gemeinschaften*) in a large number of villages scattered throughout the duchy to an organized church

---

[3]In the Lutheran Church in Württemberg the duke (till 1803), elector (1803-1806) or the king (after 1806) was head of the church and proprietor of ultimate ecclesiastical authority, which was exercised on his behalf by the church consistory in Stuttgart.
[4]Arndt, *Doc. Hist., 1700-1803*, 332-352, here 337.
[5]Ibid., 339.
[6]Ibid., 339-340.
[7]Ibid., 340-342.

(*Gemeine*) was a gradual one. The dated pastoral letters that Rapp wrote to his followers reflect this gradual change. As late as October 9, 1799, Rapp spoke of "brotherhood groups" (*Bruderschaften*) in the plural and not of a singular *Gemeine*, that is, a fully formed Separatist church.[8] Likewise in late January, 1800 he reported, "Our fellowship groups (*Gemeinschaften*) are very united and content and experiencing peace."[9] A year and a half later, however, in September, 1801, Rapp used the singular term "church" rather than the plural *Gemeinschaften*. He declared that God was indeed at work in the *Gemeinde* (alternate form of Rapp's more common term *Gemeine*). More and more "lovers of the inner paths of the Spirit" were being won. "All things were rushing toward the goal."[10]

In a later undated letter, Rapp revealed a much more developed "Anabaptist" ecclesiology than was to be found in the other pastoral letters. He employed the term "Brethren Church" (*Brüder Gemeine*) for his Separatist church, making clear that it was a formed entity. In the letter he stated that just as Christ made the Father visible, so also the *Brüder Gemeine* made Christ visible to the world. The rule of the primitive, apostolic church of Christ was being reinstituted in order that "all would be of one soul and mind," an allusion to Acts 4:32. Because many believers were incapable of achieving this unity without assistance, Christ in his "eternal providence" had chosen "a capable brother" to lead the church. Those who were unwilling to submit to this brother's (i.e. Rapp's) leadership proved that they were "bastards and not children of the proper marriage."[11] This unpublished pastoral letter is significant for several reasons. First, it reveals that by 1802 or 1803 the cluster of *Gemeinschaften* had become a unified, organized *Gemeine*. Second, the letter displays the most developed ecclesiology of any letter prior to emigration. Third, the roots of Rapp's authoritarian, patriarchal style of leadership were developed in Württemberg and not first in the United States. There is thus more continuity in his leadership style than many scholars have previously realized. Rapp was certainly authoritarian, but was he a "prophet"?

---

[8] Pastoral Letter #23, Viehmayer Collection, MG-185, 1-5005, Box 16, Folder 1.

[9] Arndt, *Doc. Hist. 1700-1803*, 308.

[10] Pastoral Letter #26, Viehmayer Collection, MG-185, 1-5005, Box 16, Folder 1. However, as early as March, 1798 in the Lomersheimer Declaration of Faith the Separatists declared their intention to form their own church (*Gemeine*). Arndt, *Doc. Hist., 1700-1803*, 274.

[11] Although this pastoral letter is undated, it was the last letter in a roughly chronological collection of letters, thus indicating that it was probably written shortly before emigration (1802-1803). Internal evidence (fully developed ecclesiology, authoritarian stance) confirms the late dating of the letter. Pastoral Letter #26, Viehmayer Collection, MG-185, 1-5005, Box 16, Folder 1.

Johann Georg Rapp as Prophet

A decade earlier, in the summer of 1791, an important confrontation occurred between Johann Georg Rapp and two men, Special Superintendent Klemm and the Maulbronn civil affairs officer Seubert. Several months before this event, Rapp had been threatened in the decree of February 8, 1791 with expulsion from the duchy if he did not stop spreading his teachings.[12] Rapp and the Separatists refused to discontinue meeting together. In the course of the ensuing interrogation with the representatives of the Dürrmenz Diocese, the Separatist leader responded to elements of this decree. At one point in the examination, he self-assuredly declared: "Why am I to blame that people from all localities of the land press upon me? If they could hear something good from your clergymen, they would not run to Iptingen to poor little Rapp in the twill jacket (*armen Räpple im Zwilchkittel*)."[13] Later in the conversation, Seubert interrupted Rapp's pronouncement that God's judgment would soon envelop the Lutheran church, stating that he should hold his tongue (*Maul halten*). "He was no prophet and did not have the vocation to be one. Yes! he [Rapp] replied obstinately: I am a prophet and called to be one."[14]

This final statement of Rapp's, that he was a prophet and called to be one, has been embraced by scholars as a useful paradigm to reveal Rapp's self-understanding. Rauscher's early account of Rapp's life and work (1885) included the anecdote in full.[15] Karl Arndt introduced his volume, *George Rapp's Harmony Society* (1965), and his article of the same name (1997) with this bold statement. He likewise named chapter three of his monograph, "The Prophet of Iptingen."[16] Eberhard Fritz, in the section of his article entitled "The 'Prophet' of Iptingen," likewise affirms that Rapp's statement (I am a prophet and called to be one) "can be understood as programmatic for his self-understanding."[17] Similarly, in a 2001 article Hermann Ehmer reports this anecdote and then attests: "This consciousness of his calling would be the foundation for the life of Rapp and his followers for the following decades."[18]

While all of these scholars attest to the importance of this anecdote for Rapp's self-understanding, none have explained in what sense Rapp un-

---

[12]Arndt, *Doc. Hist. 1700-1803*, 181.

[13]Ibid., 184. Karl Arndt's translation.

[14]Ibid., 186.

[15]Viktor Rauscher, "Des Separatisten G. Rapp Leben und Treiben," *Theologische Studien aus Württemberg* 6 (1885): 253-313, here 272.

[16]Arndt, *Rapp's Harmony Society*, 15 and Karl J. R. Arndt, "George Rapp's Harmony Society," in *America's Communal Utopias*, ed. Donald E. Pitzer (Chapel Hill, N.C.: University of North Carolina Press, 1997), 57-87, here 15.

[17]Fritz, "Rapp und die Separatisten in Iptingen," 151.

[18]Hermann Ehmer, "Johann Georg Rapp (1757-1847)" in *Kirchengeschichte Württembergs in Porträts: Pietismus und Erweckungsbewegung* (Holzgerlingen: Hänssler Verlag, 2001), 219-243, here 224.

derstood himself to be a prophet. What *did* the term connote for Rapp, in what sense was he a "prophet"? A few preliminary remarks are necessary. In the first place, it should be noted that the civil affairs magistrate Seubert suggested the term "prophet," which Rapp then applied to his own person. Rapp did not introduce the term himself into the conversation. Second, the term "prophet" was not one that he used regularly with regard to himself.[19] His preferred label for his ministry role was "teacher," a term he used quite frequently for himself in his later sermons.[20] Third, the term "prophet," particularly when applied to post-biblical religious figures, can be problematical and easily misunderstood, since the term has a wide range of connotations.

Most definitions of prophecy are based upon the activity of the Old Testament prophets or other figures who founded world religions.[21] In such cases a prophet is: ". . . a charismatic messenger of the divine will, and of that which is right and true according to the Godhead, as well as of future events. After the prophet has received a message through a vision or audible voice, he is impelled by the Godhead to proclaim that which was revealed to him."[22] Definitions of the modern religious phenomenon of prophecy are frequently based on an analogy with the ancient Hebrew and founding prophets. Ever since the evolution of Hebrew prophecy into a written and later canonical tradition, however, "the book replaced the living religious specialist as the primary agent of revelational mediation."[23] Therefore, post-biblical Christian prophecy usually intersects with the canonical tradition in some fashion.

The following categories of modern Christian prophecy may serve as a backdrop against which to compare and contrast Rapp's role as prophet: 1) prophets who founded new sects and whose writings were revered as sacred canon; 2) mystics who received supernatural religious knowledge

---

[19]Visitor Ferdinand Ernst in his travel account stated on July 18, 1819 that: "Each Sunday he speaks here to the people and is reported occasionally to call himself a prophet of God." Karl J. R. Arndt, *A Documentary History of the Indiana Decade of the Harmony Society, 1814-1819*, vol. 1 (Indianapolis: Indiana Historical Society, 1975), 746. Former Harmonist, Jonathan Wagner, in *Geschichte u. Verhältnisse der Harmoniegesellschaft* (Vaihingen an der Enz: Deininger, 1833), 9, 16, 18, 23, stated that Rapp did call himself a prophet. A 1804 poem, which included the term "prophet" for Rapp, was not written by the Separatist leader. MG-185, 1-5005, Box 16, Folder 1, Viehmayer Collection.

[20]MG-185/Box 1-4997/# 8/ Folder 20/Sermon # 1, Dec. 25, 1837 morning; MG-185/Box 1-4997/# 8/ Folder 20/Sermon # 1, Oct 14, 1838 afternoon; and MG-437/Box 22/Folder 82B/D-59.

[21] Gerald T. Sheppard and William E. Herbrechtsmeier, "Prophecy," in *Encyclopedia of Religion*, 2d ed., ed. Lindsay Jones (Detroit: Thomson Gale, 2005), 7424.

[22]Wassilios Klein, "Propheten/Prophetie," in *Theologische Realenzyklopädie*, vol. 27, ed. Gerhard Müller (New York: Walter de Gruyter, 1997), 473.

[23]Sheppard, "Prophecy," 7427.

through an immediate perception of the divine; 3) inspired exegetes of the existing biblical, canonical tradition; 4) ecstatics who received insight primarily into God's will for their personal lives; and 5) social and religious critics of contemporary institutional organizations and policies. These categories of prophets are in a descending order, from those claiming revelation equivalent to the biblical Scriptures to mere social critics.

Joseph Smith, the founder of the (Mormon) Church of the Latter-Day Saints is a prime example of founding prophet of a new sect. He claimed to receive direct revelation from Jesus Christ and the angel Moroni, the words of which have been preserved in the *Book of Mormon* and revered by his followers on a par with Scripture.[24] Prophets within the Inspired movement in Germany were limited to a small number of recognized religious specialists. In an ecstatic state they prophesied, using the biblical formula "Thus saith the Lord." The verbal statements of these prophets were written down verbatim by listeners, preserved and revered at a level approaching that of Scripture.[25] Unlike these, George Rapp never claimed religious revelation on the par with Scripture. He never spoke with "Thus saith the Lord," nor were his verbal statements or writings revered by his followers on a level with the Bible. He was not a prophet like Joseph Smith or the Inspired.

Unlike Jacob Boehme, Johann Georg Rapp never claimed to have extended mystical experiences or visions through which he became privy to esoteric or theosophical knowledge. Boehme, on the other hand, had several periods of week-long visions. The insights accrued through these visions were ineffable. Nevertheless, Boehme attempted to convey in words what he saw and experienced in his *Aurora* and other writings. Boehme's writings were not of equal authority with Scripture. Rapp was likewise not a prophet in this sense.

It has already been noted in the section on ecclesiology that the Separatists, like modern Pentecostal and charismatic Christians, believed in the validity of the prophetic word for the present era. Within their meetings they gave free rein to the Spirit and spoke (ecstatically?) as the Spirit led them. In this sense, not just Rapp but also other members of the Separatist movement received prophetic insights. Often the "revelations" that the Separatists claimed from God belonged to the category of personal insights into the divine will. Thus Johannes Hörnle claimed that God "revealed" to

---

[24]Ibid., 7428. Cf. Richard L. Bushman, *Joseph Smith and the Beginnings of Mormonism* (Urbana, Ill.: University of Illinois Press, 1984), 93-128, and especially 140-142 for the role of Joseph Smith as a modern prophet, and the authoritative role of his prophecies and of the Book of Mormon.

[25]Hans Schneider, "Der radikale Pietismus im 18. Jahrhundert," in *Geschichte des Pietismus*, Vol. 2, *Der Pietismus im achtzehnten Jahrhundert*, ed. Martin Brecht and Klaus Deppermann (Gottingen: Vandenhoeck & Rupprecht, 1995), 107-197, here 146-147. Cf. Hillel Schwartz, *The French Prophets. The History of a Millenarian Group in Eighteenth-Century England* (Berkeley, Calif.: University of California Press, 1980), 30 and 181f.

him that his son should be named Joseph. Others claimed that God disclosed whether or not they should baptize an infant, send their children to school or immigrate to the United States. Rapp's charismatic and prophetic leadership of his movement, however, was more than just personal determination of the will of God.

Rapp was likewise more than just a social and religious critic of existing injustices and institutions. He did at times adopt the posture of an Old Testament prophet and proclaim God's coming wrath to church and civil authorities. But he was by no means the only member of his movement to adopt such a stance. Johann Georg Walz declared to the church council that the Lutheran church was Babel.[26] Christian Hörnle called the Eucharist "idol worship," *Schmier-Käs* and *Streichpflaster* and declared that the Lutheran church was not the true church.[27]

Rapp did, however, understand himself to be an inspired exegete or interpreter of the biblical tradition and it is in this sense that he may be called a prophet.[28] He was convinced that the divine mysteries that had been "hidden for long ages past" were "now revealed and made known" (Rom 16:25) in these last days before the return of Christ. The Book of Revelation was the third testament that revealed the intent of the Old and New Testaments. Rapp had been given wisdom by God to interpret properly certain Scripture passages, particularly apocalyptic, prophetic passages whose surface meaning was obtuse or unclear.[29] Like other contemporary churchly and radical Pietists, Johann Georg Rapp decoded the symbolic images and events found in the Book of Revelation and other prophetic passages and equated them with contemporary events. He was thus a "teacher" who had been specially anointed by the Holy Spirit to reveal biblical mysteries that had remained hidden until that time.[30] This is the meaning of prophet that is found in an early poem written by an unknown Separatist or Harmonist. "For God then has given true wisdom to him [Rapp], that he may open up life buried in death, as he has done for me and you and many others. Therefore, this is my conclusion: Rapp is a man of God. Yes, he is the prophet who God has awakened for us."[31]

The question of what Rapp meant when he claimed that he was a prophet and called to be one is important. To leave that question unanswered is

---

[26] Fritz, "Rapp und die Separatisten in Iptingen," 167.

[27] Ibid., 163. Arndt, *Doc. Hist. 1700-1803*, 79 and 91.

[28] See Sheppard, "Prophecy," 7427.

[29] In a later sermon, Rapp claimed that the Harmony church (rather than he alone) had received insight from the Holy Spirit to open up the mysteries in Scripture, particularly those in the Book of Revelation. MG-185, Box 1-5004/15, Folder 5, O-116.

[30] MG-185/Box 1-4997/# 8/ Folder 20/Sermon # 1, Dec. 25, 1837 morning.

[31] MG-185, 1-5005, Box 16, Folder 1, #1. This poem was copied into the Viehmeyer collection of pastoral letters and dated Dec. 25, 1804. The date however is incorrect, since the poem mentions the departure of David Gloss from the Harmony Society, an event that took place in 1805.

to pave the way for either misunderstandings or a radicalization of his stance. In spite of his radical Pietist beliefs and sectarian inclinations, Rapp was a biblicist who upheld a strong view of Scripture. He never claimed extra-Biblical revelation on par with Scripture or esoteric visions as Boehme did. On the other hand, he did believe that he was uniquely called by God to lead the Separatist movement and later the Harmony Society. He was a teacher-prophet who believed he had been given exceptional insight and wisdom by God into the mysteries hidden in the biblical record. By 1802-1803 Rapp's authoritarian stance was developed to the point that he expected submission to his leadership by members of the *Gemeine*.

Increasing Conflict with Secular and Religious Authorities

The rapid growth of Rapp's movement did not go unnoticed by the secular and church authorities. Duke Friedrich II, who came to rule in 1797, changed his policy from the conciliatory approach of his predecessor to one that took a hard line against members of the Separatist movement. In September 1801 he issued a command that those who rejected the Lutheran religion of the land would no longer be treated as subjects of the duchy and would be forced to emigrate.[32] Although this law was not actually put into practice, its very drafting pointed to the increasing absolutist designs and religious intolerance of the ducal government. With increasing frequency, the Separatists were charged fines for refusing to send their children to school, for baptizing their infants themselves, and for disregarding the stipulations in the 1743 Pietist *Reskript*.[33]

In November 1802 the combined civil and religious affairs office of Maulbronn and Dürrmenz, "due to the strong increase of the Separatists," prepared and sent an extensive report on the Rapp movement to Duke Friedrich. In it, they complained that the fines and punishments placed upon the Separatists had been ineffective. They argued that such a "quickly growing sect" must of necessity be a cause of concern for the government, and asked for help in dealing with the Separatist problem. The former relatively conciliatory policy of the government had in their opinion merely been taken advantage of by the Separatists.[34] Shortly thereafter the conflict between the Rapp movement and the secular and church authorities came to a climax. In February 1803, Rapp preached to three gatherings of Separatists near the village of Knittlingen. Each of the meetings was attended by

---

[32]Fritz, *Radikaler Pietismus*, 152. Cf. HStAS A 213 Bü 3100. The Peace of Augsburg (1555) and the Peace of Westphalia (1648) established a legal basis for the banishment of those not professing the approved religious confession(s).

[33] See examples in Fritz' published edition of the Iptinger Kirchenkonventprotokolle. Eberhard Fritz, "Johann Georg Rapp (1757-1847) und die Separatisten in Iptingen," *Blätter für Württembergische Kirchengeschichte* 95 (1995): 129-203, here 179-185.

[34]Arndt, *Doc. Hist. 1700-1803*, 321-325.

several hundred people. On one occasion so many followers were present that the doors and windows of the house were removed to accommodate more listeners. Rapp's preaching to such large crowds occurred in blatant disregard of the provisions in the Pietist *Reskript*. His civil disobedience was exacerbated in the minds of the authorities by the fact that three years prior a revolutionary leader, Johann Konrad Schwarz, has instigated a minor rebellion in the village of Knittlingen with his republican ideas.[35] Dean Krippendorf, therefore, in his report to the Stuttgart consistory branded Rapp as a troublemaker (*Unruh-Stifter*) and associated him specifically with both Schwarz and the radicals of the Peasants' War of the sixteenth century.[36] Rapp and some of his followers were then ordered to appear at lengthy hearings in Maulbronn, Iptingen and Knittlingen that lasted from March 14-May 23, 1803.

Advisors of Friedrich II, who had recently been promoted from duke to Elector (*Kurfürst*), prepared a lengthy document questioning whether the Separatists should be granted any concessions such as the Waldensians and Roman Catholics enjoyed in the land, or whether "strict measures, including police control" should be applied.[37] On December 27, 1803 Friedrich II issued a decree concerning the Separatists that included none of the possible concessions. The Separatists were not granted the status of a religious body, and their meetings continued to be limited to twenty-five attendees under the supervision of a Lutheran pastor.[38] George Rapp had anticipated such a decree. In the summer of 1803, six months prior to its issuance, Rapp sold his property in Iptingen in two parcels. Accompanied by his son Johannes, Dr. P. F. C. Haller and Christoph Müller, George Rapp left for America to find a safe haven for his flock, where their religion could be practiced in freedom.

Reasons for Emigration

Emigration had long been viewed by members of the Rapp movement as a viable option, if the situation in Württemberg became untenable for the practice of their religious beliefs. Citizens of the duchy had long been aware of enticing emigration goals both within Europe and in the New World. William Penn had visited Germany twice, the second time in 1677 after he had helped form the Quaker colony of New Jersey and drawn up its constitution, which included religious toleration. Shortly after the establishment of the colony of Pennsylvania as a haven for persecuted religious dissidents in 1682, a Frankfurter *Landkompanie* was formed to purchase land in Penn's

---

[35]See Fritz, *Radikaler Pietismus*, 153-154 and Karl J. R. Arndt, *George Rapp's Harmony Society, 1785-1847*, rev. ed. (Teaneck, N. J.: Fairleigh Dickinson University Press, 1972), 47-48.
[36]Arndt, *Doc. Hist. 1700-1803*, 329-330.
[37]Ibid., 368-398.
[38]Ibid., 404-412.

Woods. Throughout the eighteenth century the propaganda of ship agents and the enthusiastic reports of recent emigrants added to the emigration fever in the relatively impoverished land of Württemberg. Repeatedly the ducal government issued warnings to citizens to beware of unscrupulous agents (*Seelenhändler*), and to use caution before deciding to emigrate.[39] During the interrogation after the Knittlingen affair (March-May 1803), members of Rapp's movement expressed their willingness to emigrate rather than discontinue their Separatist meetings.[40] The speed with which Rapp departed after the Knittlingen affair and the large number of Rappites that promptly emigrated suggests that Rapp and his followers had previously discussed emigration and considered it a viable option for some time.

Those of the Rapp movement desiring to emigrate were questioned by the civil authorities in the spring of 1804 concerning their reasons for leaving the country. They consistently gave religious reasons, often the lack of religious freedom. The legal review of the electoral government reported their findings on February 21-22, 1804:

> In general it appears that is it religious fanaticism that has induced these people [Rappites] to emigrate. Irrespective of the fact that the most gracious circular decree regarding the Separatists recently issued by your Highness the Elector embodied much more tolerance than all previous ordinances ... nevertheless the Separatists are not satisfied. They demand *to practice their religion completely unrestricted, and desire to seek this freedom elsewhere, since they cannot receive it in this land* [author's emphasis].[41]

The following month (March 1804), Elector Friedrich II's (intolerant) 1803 decree was given as the "main reason for their present emigration" by members of Rapp's movement to the electoral government.[42] The officials concluded, "They are in the habit of giving a religious twist to everything,

---

[39] Decrees warning against emigration were issued in 1700, 1709, 1717, 1720, 1750, 1753 etc. Ibid., 3, 5, 11, 14, 19, 35, 49.

[40] Ibid., 349-350.

[41] "Im allgemeinen erhellt hieraus, daß es religieuse Schwärmerey ist, welche diese Leute zum Auswandern veranlaßt. Ungeachtet das von Euer Churfürstlichen Durchlaucht vor kurzem gnädigst erlaßene Circularrescript in Separatisten-Sachen weit mehr Toleranz enthält, als alle bisherigen Verordnungen in diesem Fach ... so sind dannoch auch die Separatisten damit nicht zufrieden, verlangen eine ganz ungebundene Religions Übung und wollen, weil sie diese im Land nicht erhalten können, sie anderwärts suchen." Arndt, *Doc. Hist. 1700-1803*, 413.

[42] Ibid., 432-433. This statement in the March 1804 document contradicts Hippel's contention that "die Behörden dazu neigten, denjenigen Faktoren das größte Gewicht zu beizumessen, welche das eigene Land entlasteten und fremden Zuständen, Personen und Institutionen die Verantwortung für die geradezu als peinlich und ehrenrührig empfundene Tatsache des Wegzugs zuzuschieben." Wolfgang von Hippel, *Auswanderung aus Südwestdeutschland: Studien zur württembergischen Auswanderung und Auswanderungspolitik im 18. und 19. Jahrhundert* (Stuttgart: Klett-Cotta, 1984), 59.

therefore also this emigration is for them God's plan (*Gottes Sache*). It is God, who leads them out, and they may not be disobedient to his prompting."[43]

The fact that Rappites stressed religious reasons for their emigration should be taken seriously and not immediately relativized or dismissed.[44] Nevertheless, Wolfgang von Hippel in *Auswanderung aus Südwestdeutschland* correctly notes that "objective reasons and subjective motivations" were frequently mixed. Often there were economic reasons that motivated folk to leave Württemberg (push-factor) and drew them to another country (pull-factor), even when ostensibly religious motivations were stated. Socio-economic and political motivations for emigration in the 1790s and early 1800s were manifold. They included an increase in population resulting in smaller land apportionment, a decrease in occupational opportunities, poverty, poor harvests, rising taxes, and the effects of the Napoleonic wars (military service, quartering of soldiers, destruction of crops).[45] Hippel's tabulation of the reasons given by 2571 emigrants leaving Württemberg between March and June, 1804 (the same time frame in which a large number of Rappites emigrated) reveals that two-thirds of them left for economic reasons (lack of food or work, debt, high taxes). Seventeen percent were "pulled" by the hope of a better future. However, thirteen percent gave separatism as the reason for their emigration.[46] Since approximately 350 adult Rappites (equal to circa thirteen percent of all 2571 emigrants) left Württemberg during these months, it is likely that most or all of Rapp's followers were part of the thirteen percent that gave religious reasons for emigration, although economic factors likely also contributed to their decision.[47] Their emigration hymns, which will be discussed below, likewise testify to the Separatists' religious motivations for leaving their homeland.

---

[43]Arndt, *Doc Hist 1700-1803*, 414. These same sentiments were repeated in the 1804 Iptingen annual church report. Ibid., 452.

[44]Hartmut Lehmann and Georg Leibbrandt both stress the importance of religious motivation for Pietist and Separatist emigrants. Hartmut Lehmann, *Pietismus und weltliche Ordnung in Württemberg vom 17. bis zum 20. Jahrhundert* (Stuttgart: Kohlhammer, 1969), 155f., and Georg Leibbrandt, *Die Auswanderung aus Schwaben nach Rußland 1816-1823* (Stuttgart: Ausland und Heimat Verlag, 1928), 28f.

[45]Hippel, *Auswanderung*, 59-65.

[46]Ibid., 63-66.

[47]The ship *Aurora* brought 300 Harmonists (or ca. 75 adults) to America, arriving on July 4, 1804. Passenger lists for the ships *Atlantic* and *Margaret* arriving in Philadelphia on Sept. 17 and 19, 1804 include 269 adults. Most but not all became Harmonists. These adults would have given reasons for emigration to the electoral government between March and June, 1804. Karl J. R. Arndt, *Harmony on the Connoquenessing 1803-1815. A Documentary History* (Worcester, Mass.: Harmony Society Press, 1980), 30-38.

Prior and Contemporary Pietist Interpretations of the Sunwoman and Her Flight

Not only did the Rappites emigrate primarily for religious reasons, they likewise also gave a theological justification for this momentous decision.[48] They understood their community to be the eschatological Sunwoman of Revelation 12, and their emigration as the Sunwoman's flight into the wilderness of America in order to avoid the imminent judgment upon Babel, the false European Christendom. The identification of their Separatist movement and later of the Harmony Society with this apocalyptic figure is very significant. It cembodied on one hand their firm conviction that the end of the age was at hand. It likewise affirmed their belief that they as true "Children of God," would be preserved and prepared in their place of refuge to play a significant role in Christ's millennial kingdom on earth. The concept of the Sunwoman thus typified their eschatological hope and their self-understanding.

The identification of their community with the Sunwoman of Revelation 12,[49] while bearing some distinctive features, was not without precedent among prior and contemporary Pietists. The fact that the Rappite equation of their movement with the Sunwoman was not entirely unique has not been noted or developed by most historians of the Harmony Society. Karl Arndt, when discussing this aspect of their self-understanding, fails to note that a belief in the contemporary fulfillment of this prophecy was not uncommon among Pietists.[50] This omission by Arndt casts the Separatist

---

[48]Arndt argues, "Only such a religious panic, born of the horror of Revelation could have brought people to sever the bonds that tied them to the lands of their fathers.... Here it was not economic adversity or the promise of great material gain in America that called.... They came here [America] to welcome Christ and to take part in a mysterious transfiguration of fallen man. . . ." Arndt, *Rapp's Harmony Society*, 56.

[49]Rev 12:1-6 and 13-14 (*NIV*): "A great and wondrous sign appeared in heaven: a woman clothed with the sun, with the moon under her feet and a crown of twelve stars on her head. ²She was pregnant and cried out in pain as she was about to give birth. ³Then another sign appeared in heaven: an enormous red dragon with seven heads and ten horns and seven crowns on his heads. ⁴His tail swept a third of the stars out of the sky and flung them to the earth. The dragon stood in front of the woman who was about to give birth, so that he might devour her child the moment it was born. ⁵She gave birth to a son, a male child, who will rule all the nations with an iron scepter. And her child was snatched up to God and to his throne. ⁶The woman fled into the desert to a place prepared for her by God, where she might be taken care of for 1,260 days.... ¹³When the dragon saw that he had been hurled to the earth, he pursued the woman who had given birth to the male child. ¹⁴The woman was given the two wings of a great eagle, so that she might fly to the place prepared for her in the desert, where she would be taken care of for a time, times and half a time, out of the serpent's reach."

movement in a falsely innovative and an unnecessarily extreme light. Some Pietists other than the Rappites (though certainly not all) likewise interpreted Revelation 12 in a similar fashion. Before discussing the Rappite theological justification for emigration, other prior and contemporary interpretations of this Bible passage will be examined in order to set the historical-theological context. The relevant interpretations can be divided into allegorical, historicist, futurist and contemporary-futurist interpretations. [51]

Allegorical Interpretation

Although Jacob Boehme was not a Pietist in the narrow sense, it is appropriate to examine his interpretation of the Sunwoman due to his influence on the later burgeoning radical (and churchly) Pietist movements. Unlike later Pietists, Boehme interpreted the Sunwoman of Revelation 12 in an exclusively allegorical fashion. The German theosophist in his exposition of Genesis, *Mysterium Magnum* (1623), equated Joseph with the Sunwoman. The former's avoidance of adulterous contact with Potiphar's wife in Gen 39:7-10 qualified Joseph, like other regenerated "children of God," to be a "mighty type" of the apocalyptic woman. Like Joseph, the Sunwoman stood upon the moon, which Boehme interpreted to be a type of that "earthly whore," Potiphar's wife/Eve. Not only was Joseph a type of the Sunwoman, but, due to his "chaste and divine purity," also of the son that the woman in Revelation 12 brought forth.[52] In contrast to later Pietists, Boehme did not propose an ecclesiological interpretation of the apocalyptic woman. The individual soul was in view and not a believing community. Nor did he interpret the Sunwoman in an eschatological fashion, as a key element in that string of events leading to the culmination of the present age.[53] Clearly, the Rappites did not turn to Boehme for their interpretation of the Sunwoman.

---

[50]Arndt fails to mention precedents in his article, his documentary history or his monograph. Karl J. R. Arndt, "George Rapp's Harmony Society," in *America's Communal Utopias*, ed. Donald E. Pitzer (Chapel Hill, N.C.: University of North Carolina Press, 1997), 57-87, here 62; Arndt, *Doc. Hist. 1700-1803*, 357-360; and Arndt, *Rapp's Harmony Society*, 58. On the other hand, Ehmer in his article does mention that the Separatists who immigrated to Russia in 1817 likewise had an eschatological motivation. Hermann Ehmer, "Johann Georg Rapp (1757-1847)," in *Kirchengeschichte Württembergs in Porträts*, ed. Siegfried Hermle (Holzgerlingen: Hänssler Verlag, 2001), 218-243, here 227.

[51]Hildegard Gollinger, *Das 'Große Zeichen von Apokalypse 12* (Würzburg-Echter: KBW Verlag, 1971) provides an analysis of contemporary interpretations of Rev 12. They include an equation of the Sunwoman with: (1) Mary; (2) Mary and the church; (3) the people of Israel; (4) OT and NT people of God; (5) the empirical church; and (6) the heavenly eschatological church.

[52]Jacob Boehme, *Mysterium Magnum: Part 2 or an Exposition of the first book of Moses called Genesis*, trans. John Sparrow (Kila, Mont.: Kessinger, 1990), 765.

[53]Boehme, in this two part treatise (written 1620) in response to Paul Kaym's millennialist tract, made abundantly clear that he rejected the concept of a physical, literal millennium on earth, of seven ages of the world (§28, 29, 30), of two

Figure 2

From J. W. Petersen's *Das Geheimniß des in der letzten Zeit gebährenden Apocalyptischen Weibes* (1708)

(1) Woman standing upon the moon; (2) Birth travail; (3) Dragon standing before woman to devour son of the Sunwoman; (4) Christ leads Sunwoman into wilderness; (5) Battle between Michael and dragon; (6) Male son with iron rod; (7) Sunwoman protected from dragon in the wilderness.

---

resurrections (§32, 52, 53), of the setting of dates for the end (§59) and of a physical understanding of either Babel or Zion (§66). Reason and Scripture argue against these views. Jacob Böhme, *Informatorium Novissimorum oder Unterricht von den Letzten Zeiten an Paul Kaym in zwei Theilen* ([s.l.]: [s.n.], 1730), 399-440.

Boehme, however, was among the first to equate the whore Babylon or Babel in Revelation 17 and 18 not with the Roman Catholic Church alone, but with false European Christendom in general. The unregenerate souls within his own Lutheran confession were likewise included within Babel, for it was not limited to any one confession. Babel on the macrocosmic level was found within all confessions; on the microcosmic level it was present within the individual soul. "That is not Zion, but Babel, those who confess God with their mouths, but in their hearts are attached to the great Babylonian whore, to the Dragon of one's own arrogance, greed and lust, and who present themselves as if they were virgins."[54] For Boehme (in contrast to the Rappites), "going out of Babel" (Rev 18:4) referred exclusively to leaving the spiritual realm ruled by Satan. It did not denote physically leaving the established church (separation) or Germany (emigration).

Historicist Interpretations

Luther and Lutheran orthodox theologians after him proposed a historicist interpretation of much of the Book of Revelation. "Adherents to this theory consider Revelation as a symbolic presentation of the total of church history culminating in the second advent."[55] This approach was picked up by some churchly and a few radical Pietists. Radical Pietist Heinrich Horch in his *Mystische und Profetische Bibel* (1712) interpreted Revelation 12 historically. The Sunwoman was the Christian Church at the time of Constantine; her male offspring Constantine himself, a type of Christ in his future kingdom. The 1260 days of the Sunwoman in the wilderness referred to the number of years that the kingdom of the Anti-Christ would reign over the historical Church.[56]

Churchly Pietist Johann Albrecht Bengel likewise had a predominantly historicist interpretation of Revelation 12. In his *Sechzig Reden* (1747) Bengel stated: "In this twelfth chapter [of Revelation] we primarily have a history of the church and the world, to some extent from the first era of the Christian Church, but especially of the last nine centuries."[57] According to Bengel, the Sunwoman was principally embodied in the historic Moravian Brethren Church, because this ecclesial body was especially characterized by purity of faith, practice and polity. The 1260 prophetic days of the Sun-

---

[54] Boehme, *Letzten Zeiten*, §4, 401.

[55] John F. Walvoord, *The Revelation of Jesus Christ* (Chicago: Moody Press, 1966), 18.

[56] Heinrich Horch, *Mystische und profetische Bibel, Das ist die gantze Heil. Schrifft, Altes und Neues Testasmants, auffs neue nach dem Grund verbessert, Sampt Erklärung der fürnemsten Sinnbilder und Weissagungen, Sonderlich des H. Lieds Salomons und der Offenbarung J. C. wie auch denen fürnehmsten Lehren, bevoraus die sich in diese letzen Zeiten schicken* (Marburg: Joh. Kürtzner, 1712), ad. loc. Rev. 12.

[57] Johann Albrecht Bengel, *Sechzig erbauliche Reden über die Offenbarung Johannis oder vielmehr Jesu Christi, sammt eine Nachlese gleichen Inhalts*, 3d ed., (Stuttgart: [s.n.], 1835), 354.

woman in the wilderness started in A.D. 940 in Bohemia. After the Thirty Years War Germany became the place of refuge for the Sunwoman and would continue to be until the onset of the first of two millenniums in 1836. One aspect of the chapter would be fulfilled in the future. The male son of the Sunwoman, Christ, would first rule the nations with an iron rod at his Second Coming.[58]

Futurist Interpretations

Radical Pietists of the Philadelphian movement, in keeping with their strong millennialism, abandoned a historicist interpretation of much of Revelation in favor of a futurist one. For the head of the English Philadelphians, Jane Leade (1624-1704), the Sunwoman of Rev. 12 was a future, pure, chaste virgin church. At the present time, members of this Philadelphian Church were hidden among all confessions and nations. Prior to the return of Christ, which was expected to occur imminently, the church of the Sunwoman would come out of her wilderness into visibility.[59] German Philadelphian Johann Wilhelm Petersen adapted Leade's interpretation. In his two hundred page treatise on Revelation 12 (1708) he identified the Sunwoman exclusively with the converted Jewish nation.

> By this woman, no one other than the Jewish church or the Jewish people may be understood, who in the end times Christ will give birth to in the Spirit and they will be converted to the Lord. All the prophets are full of this [message] and testify clearly to their conversion in the last days.[60]

The identification of the Sunwoman with the converted Jewish nation in the *eschaton* solved, according to Petersen, the dilemma that the latter conversion of the Jews, so prominent in the Old Testament prophets, was otherwise not to be found in John's Revelation. Several decades later (1726-1742), the Philadelphian influenced *Berleburg Bible* commentary interpreted the Sunwoman in a similar fashion, although with one important

---

[58]Bengel, *Sechzig Reden*, 337-338, 349, 360. Cf. Johann Albrecht Bengel, *Erklärte Offenbarung Johannis: Oder vielmehr Jesu Christ: aus dem revidirten Grund-Text übersetzt durch die prophetischen Zahlen ausgeschlossen und allen, die auf das Werk und Wort des Herrn achten, und dem, was vor der Thür ist, würdiglich entgegen zu kommen begehren, vor Augen geleget* (Stuttgart: Fr. Brodhag, 1834), 373-422.

[59]Online copies of Jane Leade's writings, in this case, *Revelations of Revelations* (1683) and *Sixty Propositions* (1697) were accessed at:
http://www.passtheword.org/Jane-Lead/revelatn.html and
http://www.passtheword.org/Jane-Lead/60-propositions.html [accessed Nov. 15, 2006].

[60]Johann Wilhelm Petersen, *Das Geheimniß des in der letzten Zeit gebährenden Apocalyptischen Weibes, Mit welchen eine Neue Kirchen-Zeit angehet, und welches das Grosse Zeichen im Himmel ist, das bisher von den wenigsten erkannt, itzo aber durch den aufschliessenden Geiste Gottes aus den Schrifften der Propheten und Apostel, und absonderlich aus der Heil. Offenbarung am XII c. nach dem wahrhafftigen Sinn eröffnet ist* (Frankfurt: Samuel Heyl and Joh. Gottfried Liebezeit, 1708), 40.

difference. While Petersen identified the Sunwoman exclusively with the converted Jewish nation, the *Berleburg Bible* interpreted the eschatological church as formed primarily from Jewish converts, although heathen converts were also present.[61] Neither Petersen's futurist interpretation nor that in the *Berleburg Bible* allowed for an equation of a church or group existing at that time with the Sunwoman of Revelation 12. Clearly the Jews had not yet been converted *en masse* to Christ.

Contemporary-Futurist Interpretations

On the other hand, some radical Pietist individuals and groups equated the Sunwoman primarily with Gentile Christians and were convinced that they were living in the penultimate era, shortly before the inauguration of the end. These two presuppositions allowed certain persons to identify the Sunwoman either specifically with their own group or more generally with true "children of God" scattered among many sects or confessions (*Partheyen*) and nations. These individuals and groups usually combined a contemporary and futurist interpretation of the Sunwoman with a call to emigrate out of Babel (Rev 18:4) and into God's appointed place of refuge, the "wilderness."

The earliest known proponents of this view were Johann Jacob Zimmermann and his disciple, Johannes Kelpius. Zimmermann (1642-1693) was a Lutheran pastor in the Württemberg town of Bietigheim (that is, until dismissal by the church consistory in 1684), as well as a renowned astronomer and mathematician. The great comets of 1680 and 1681, which Zimmermann had been requested by the duke of Württemberg to observe, further fueled Zimmermann's eschatological speculation, which had already been developing during the past decade due to his close relationship to the chiliast, Ludwig Brunnquell. In his 1681 work, *Cometoscopia*, Zimmermann argued that the west to east movement of the 1680 comet was indicative of the direction of God's judgment, which would first strike Europe and then Asia. America, on the other hand, would be spared, and thus was an ideal goal for immigration. In his most important theological work, *Muthmaßliche Zeit-Bestimmung* (1684), Zimmermann warned that God would send an oriental army, most likely the Turks, to destroy the European Babel.[62] In this work, in his treatise published the following year (*Untersuchung eines Bedenkens*) and before the consistory, Zimmermann made abundantly clear that Babel was not exclusively the Church of Rome, since the Roman Catho-

---

[61]Johann Heinrich Haug, ed., *Die Heilige Schrift Altes und Neues Testaments, nach dem Grund-Text aufs Neue übersehen und übersetzet. Nebst einiger Erklärung des buchstälichen Sinnes wie auch der fürnehmsten Fürbildern und Weissagungen von Christo und seinem Reich, und zugleich einigen Lehren, die auf den Zustand der Kirchen in unseren letzten Zeiten gerichtet sind* (Berleburg: [s.n.], 1726-1742), 338.

[62]Martin Brecht, "Chiliasmus in Württemberg in 17. Jahrhundert," *Pietismus und Neuzeit* 14 (1988): 25-49, here 40-45.

lic Church was a particular church.⁶³ Babel was to be found within all confessions (including the Lutheran), and must be avoided by regenerate souls, both spiritually and physically.

Zimmermann held to a historicist interpretation of the Sunwoman in his *Muthmaßliche Zeit-Bestimmung* (1684). The apocalyptic woman had been nourished in the wilderness for 1260 days, which he understood to be common years. He expected the end of her historic sojourn to take place in the middle of the constellational conjunction in 1692 or 1693, the year the astronomer/theologian reckoned for the outpouring of wrath upon the European Babel.⁶⁴ It is possible, however, that he later changed to a contemporary-futurist view of this Bible passage. The community that he intended to form in America, but died before reaching, was referred to by contemporaries as the Society of the Woman in the Wilderness. Furthermore, Zimmermann ended his *Muthmaßliche Zeit-Bestimmung* with a strong call for the "children of God" to go out of Babel, that is, to emigrate from Germany, in order to avoid the coming wrath.

> The Spirit moves us and all born-again children to go out of Babel ... Rev. 18:5. O how the time of revenge hastens. Now, the seventh angel on the wings of the heavens steps forward to pour out his bowl [of wrath] and cries: It is done! Rev. 16:17. He who can hasten, let him make haste, that he may still be rescued. For when the pouring out [of wrath] has occurred, Babylon with all her heathen cities must fall, and be saturated with the cup of God's wrath. Therefore, let them flee, and let each of us enter into his land.⁶⁵

After Zimmermann's death in Rotterdam prior to embarking for America, his disciple, Johannes Kelpius, was chosen in 1694 to lead the small band

---

⁶³ Johann Jacob Zimmermann, "Untersuchung eines Bedenkens, ob die Evangelischen Kirche mit Recht babel sey und antichristlich zu schelten und davon auszugehen seye? Sonderlich wegen der Symbolischen Bücher," in Philipp Jakob Spener, *Theologische Bedencken* I (Halle, 1712), 341-352. Cf. Friedrich Fritz, "Konventikel in Württemberg von der Reformationszeit bis zum Edikt von 1743," *Blätter für württembergische Kirchengeschichte* 50 (1950): 65-121, here 109.

⁶⁴Johann Jacob Zimmermann, *Muthmaßliche Zeit-Bestimmung gewiß gewärtiger, beedes Göttlicher Gerichten uber das Europeische Babel und Anti-Christenthum ietzigen Seculi, als auch hierauff erfolgenden Herrlichen Auffgangs des Reichs Christi auf Erden, So Aus Veranlassung bißheriger Cometen Erschein- und Beschreibungen Jedoch nicht bloßhin nach Astrologischen Sätzen sondern vielmehr nach heiliger Schrifft Anleitung ausgearbeitet Ambrosius Sehmann, von Caminiez* (Frankfurt: [s.n.], 1684), 112-114.

⁶⁵"Uns und allen Wiedergebornen Kindern gebeut der Geist aus Babel aus zu gehen ... Apoc. 18 v. 5. O! Wie eylet die Zeit der Rache herzu! Iezt tritt der siebende Engel auff den Fittigen des Himmels, daß er seine Schale will ausgiessen, und schreyen: Factum est! Apoc. 16 v. 17. Wer nun eylen kann, der eyle, daß er noch möge errettet werden. Wann aber die Ausgiessung geschehen ist, so muß Babylon mit allen Heyden-Städten fallen, und mit dem Kelch des Zornes Gottes geträncket werden. Darumb lasset sie fahren, und lasset uns ein jeglicher in sein Land ziehen." Zimmermann, *Muthmaßliche Zeit-Bestimmung*, 124-125.

of forty emigrants. On the ridge overlooking the Wissahickon Creek near Germantown, Pennsylvania, the group formed an ascetic, semi-monastic commune, which used rough huts and caves for their domicile. Although their preferred name for the community was the "Contented of the God-loving Soul," the common designation "Society of the Woman in the Wilderness" was also very appropriate. Kelpius' letters abound with references and images from the twelfth chapter of Revelation.

Kelpius had a multifaceted interpretation of both the Sunwoman and the wilderness. On one level the Sunwoman was present within the apostolic church, albeit only in an imperfect fashion.[66] Throughout the history of the church and in the present age, she was hidden as the faithful, believing remnant within all churches and sects. At the imminent end of the age, she would come up out of the barren wilderness of false Christendom "leaning on her Beloved [Christ] as the perfected, eschatological church."[67] Yet in another sense, the Sunwoman was epitomized in the small band of mystics on the Wissahickon Creek, who had fled into the wilderness to escape the evils of Babylon. They had providentially been lifted up by "powerful eagle wings" (Rev 12:14), "borne and conducted wonderfully" by God to this "desert place" in America and preserved "from the arrows of destruction."[68] Kelpius claimed that "the Lord hides *us* from the dragon, that watches so carefully for the birth, in order to devour it" (Rev 12: 4).[69]

Likewise, Kelpius in his correspondence wrote of a three-fold wilderness: the barren wilderness, the fruitful wilderness, and the wilderness of the elect. The barren or corporeal wilderness described the dismal state into which the church and the individual soul had fallen since the time of the primitive church. The fruitful wilderness was the place of spiritual growth and maturity, where the Lord "purifies and proves" the regenerated, individual soul in the "furnace of affliction."[70] The wilderness of the elect was available to but a few "peculiarly chosen Vessels of Honor and Glory."[71] Kelpius and his community understood themselves to be those "elect vessels" within the wilderness of the elect in Pennsylvania. Ernest Lashlee correctly notes:

---

[66]Johannes Kelpius, *The Diarium of Magister Johannes Kelpius*, annotations by Julius Friedrich Sachse, vol. 27, Narrative and Critical History (Lancaster, Pa.: Pennsylvania-German Society, 1917), 68, 71-72.

[67]Kelpius, *Diarium*, 51-52.

[68]Letter of Johann Gottfried Seelig, one of the leaders of the Kelpius community to H. J. Deichmann. Kelpius, *Diarium*, 45.

[69]Ibid., 29.

[70]Ibid., 30 and 86-89. See Ernest L. Lashlee, "Johannes Kelpius and His Woman in the Wilderness. A Chapter in the History of Colonial Pennsylvania Religious Thought," in *Glaube Geist Geschichte. Festschrift für Ernst Benz* (Leiden: Brill, 1967), 327-338, here 337, note 1.

[71]Kelpius, *Diarium*, 89.

The wilderness into which the woman of Revelation 12 fled, in which she is being nourished, and from which she will soon fly heavenward . . . is none other than Pennsylvania. It was here in Penn's Woods, Kelpius believed, that the true Christian, setting aside all engagements and trimming his lamp, should, like the wise virgins, await his bridegroom and prepare for the heavenly wedding feast. Indeed, it was this hope that attracted Kelpius and his little band to the New World.[72]

Thus, on one level, members of Kelpius' Society of the Woman in the Wilderness did understand their group to be an embodiment of the apocalyptic Sunwoman of Revelation 12. A similar interpretation would be proposed by radical elements of the Pietist movement in Württemberg and elsewhere in the first decades of the nineteenth century.

A half century after Bengel's *Erklärte Offenbarung*, Johann Heinrich Jung-Stilling adapted in his commentary on the book of Revelation, *Siegesgeschichte* (1799), Bengel's historicist interpretation of the Sunwoman with relatively few changes.[73] Six years later however, in 1805, Jung-Stilling adjusted his interpretation in a lengthy addendum to the *Siegesgeschichte*. Although he continued to uphold his Bengelian approach to Rev. 12, he added a future interpretation to the historicist one. The historical Moravian Brethren Church of the past and present was likewise a model for the future Sunwoman, an eschatological church formed of the converted nation of Israel and regenerated Christians from all confessions and sects (Separatists, Quakers, and Inspired etc.). In the near future but prior to 1836, the Sunwoman would flee to her appointed place of refuge, where she would be protected from God's wrath poured out upon the nations.[74] Jung-Stilling refrained in his *Nachtrag* from definitively identifying the place of refuge, which he called "*Solyma*" [Jerusalem]. In his earlier eschatological novel, *Das Heimweh*, however, he stated that Russia would "play a great role" as a preliminary place of refuge (*Bergungsort*), prior to the final destination of Palestine.[75] Jung-Stilling's commentary, addendum to the commentary and novel, *Heimweh*, caused a furor among Württemberg Pietists.

So did Johann Jakob Friedrich's *Glaubens- und Hoffnungsblicke*, published in 1800 (several years prior to the Rappite emigration). Like Jung-Stilling, Friedrich built his interpretation of the eschatological events he expected to take place between 1800 and at the latest 1836 on Bengel's sys-

---

[72]Lashlee, "Kelpius," 337.

[73]Johann Heinrich Jung-Stilling, *Die Siegesgeschichte der Christlichen Religion in einer gemeinnützigen Erklärung der Offenbarung Johannis* (Nürnberg: [s.n.], 1799), 283-324.

[74]Ibid., *Erster Nachtrag zur Siegesgeschichte der Christlichen Religion in einer gemeinnützigen Erklärung der Offenbarung Johannis* (Nürnberg: Raw, 1805), 149-163.

[75]Ibid., *Das Heimweh. Vollständige, ungekürzte Ausgabe nach der Erstausgabe von 1794-1796*, ed. and introduced by Martina Maria Sam (Dornach, Switzerland: Verlag am Goetheanum, 1994), xxxvii, 334f, 612f.

tem.⁷⁶ During these first decades of the nineteenth century, chapters 10-11 and 13-20:3 of Revelation would be fulfilled. The Sunwoman of Revelation 12 had for Friedrich its fulfillment both in the history of the Church and in the end times. Unlike Bengel, who understood the Sunwoman's place of refuge directly prior to the culmination of the age to be in Germany and even Württemberg, Friedrich strongly argued that Palestine was the place of refuge for the Sunwoman from the coming tribulation. "It is here in this land [of Canaan], that the woman clothed with the sun, the moon under her feet and surrounded by the twelve tribes of Israel, will make her appearance in new radiance."⁷⁷ Palestine was preferable as a place of refuge for the Sunwoman because this location was supported by Scripture, unlike other suggestions (America or Asiatic Russia). As soon as the Lord opened the door and the Ottoman Empire allowed emigration, the Sunwoman, that is, the "true children of God," should flee to Palestine to escape the coming bowls of wrath.⁷⁸

Fellow Württemberger Michael Hahn, a contemporary and acquaintance of George Rapp, however, disagreed with Bengel's historicist interpretation of the Sunwoman.⁷⁹ In his opinion, Revelation 12 was not fulfilled chiefly in the past, but was being fulfilled now in the penultimate age. He identified the Sunwoman thus, "The woman clothed with the sun is firstly nothing else but the true Spirit-congregation (*Geistesgemeine*) of Jesus, formed from all nations; but she is also to be understood as each soul that lives in God."⁸⁰ Although the great tribulation was near, exactly when it would begin was unknown. When advising his followers considering emigration in the famine years of 1816 and 1817, he reminded them that one could not determine in advance when "the true congregation of the Lord will flee into the wilderness." The flight of the Sunwoman would take place when the Anti-Christ arrived in the European Babel. At that time some but not all members of the Sunwoman would emigrate. In Hahn's opinion the correct goal of emigration was Palestine and not America.

> See, my friends, at that time the exodus, the true emigration will forthwith begin, in my opinion toward the Bridegroom, namely to that location, from

---

⁷⁶Friedrich included Bengel's description of the millennium at the end of his volume.

⁷⁷"Hier im diesem Land ist es, wo das Weib mit der Sonne bekleidet, den Mond unter ihren Füssen, und mit dem zwölf Stämme Israels umgeben, in ihrem neuen Glanze auftritt." Johann Jakob Friedrich, *Glaubens- und Hoffnung-Blick des Volks Gottes in der anti-christlichen Zeit aus den göttlichen Weissagungen gezogen* ([s.l.]: [s.n.], 1801), 5. Cf. Friedrich Fritz, "Johann Jakob Friedrich. Ein Kapitel vom Glauben an einer Bergungsort und an das Tausendjähriges Reich," *Blätter für württembergische Kirchengeschichte* 41 (1937): 140-197, here 153.

⁷⁸Friedrich, *Glaubens- und Hoffnungsblicke*, 160-161.

⁷⁹Johann Michael Hahn, *Briefe und Lieder über die heilige Offenbarung Jesu Christi*, vol. 5. (Tübingen: L.F. Fues, 1820), 183.

⁸⁰Hahn, *Schriften*, vol. 5, 807.

which he originated according to the Scriptures. Therefore, do not go to Astrachen [a city in Siberia] or America, but to Palestine, because there the Bridegroom will return.[81]

Hahn cautioned his followers not to emigrate rashly, before the proper time. Hahn's views concerning the Sunwoman were written after the emigration of the Rappites. They have nevertheless been included in this survey because they represent a culmination of opinions and trends prominent among Separatists and Pietists in Württemberg from the 1790s onward.

In conclusion, it is apparent that a wide variety of interpretations of the Sunwoman and her flight were present among radical and churchly Pietists in the eighteenth and early nineteenth century. Bengel's historicist interpretation of Revelation 12 held great sway among Württembergers and non-Württembergers alike (Jung-Stilling was not from the duchy). Nevertheless, particularly in times of eschatological fervor (the late seventeenth and the late eighteenth centuries), Revelation 12 was often reinterpreted in a contemporary/futurist fashion. At such times millennialists believed that the dawn of the new age was at hand. The Sunwoman was interpreted ecclesiologically as the invisible or visible church of the redeemed in the present or near future. This interpretation did not preclude a focus on the individual soul or on identifying the Sunwoman with one's own group, when such group was believed to embody the spirit of the Sunwoman in an exemplary manner (Society of the Woman in the Wilderness). The flight of the Sunwoman was frequently associated with the call to go out of Babylon/Babel in Rev. 18:4. For radical Württemberg Pietists at the beginning of the nineteenth century, leaving Babel referred to physical separation from the apostate (Lutheran) church and/or emigration from Germany and into the wilderness.

Rappite Interpretation of the Sunwoman and Her Flight

The Legal Review of the electoral government, written February 21-22, 1804, included an interesting note. It stated that in the following month of March 1804, several hundred Separatist families of the Rapp movement would gather near Knittlingen, the village where in 1803 very large Separatist meetings had been held. From there the group of emigrants would proceed on their way toward the Rhine and ultimately America, marching

---

[81]"Sehet, Freunde, zu jener Zeit geht alsdann der Zug, die wahre Auswanderung an, die meines Erachtens dem Bräutigam entgegengeht, nämlich an den Ort, von welchem er nach der Schrift herkommt. Gehet also nicht nach Astrachen oder Amerika, sondern nach Palästina, weil allda der Bräutigam ankommen wird!" Johann Michael Hahn, *Briefe über die Apostel-Geschichte, den Brief an die Galater und Judä ; Briefe und Lieder über die Epistel Petri und Jakobi*, vol. 2 (Tübingen : L.F. Fues, 1820), 207-211, here 211.

to the tune of music (*mit klingendem Spiel*).⁸² Rapp's followers both before and after emigration were fond of singing, music and of processions, so this statement rings true as being fully in keeping with their preferred practice.⁸³ Likewise, later Separatists who joined the mass migration to Russia from Württemberg during and after the famine years of 1816-1817 wrote and sang emigration songs, some of which were similar to those of the Rappites.⁸⁴ Finally, four emigration hymns, written by anonymous members of the Rapp movement, have been preserved. In one of them reference was made to making music while they marched. "Bring your flutes, drums, violins. . . . Let the music be heard and the march. Now we want to march joyfully, and beat the drums at the same time . . . Sing with it new songs, praise God."⁸⁵ Therefore, it is very likely that the 1804 Legal Review was correct: the Separatists of the Rapp movement truly did sing and make music as they proceeded on their way to the "promised land" of America. The Separatists did not sneak from their homes with downcast faces and spirits, rather they proceeded with music and fanfare.

The Rappite emigration songs are valuable source material. The four preserved hymns reflect the early understanding and identification of the Rappite movement with the Sunwoman of Revelation 12 from the standpoint of ordinary members and not the leadership (George or Frederick Rapp). When combined with early correspondence from the emigration years (1804-1806) and George Rapp's pastoral letters to his followers in Württemberg (1791-1802), it is possible to form a relatively complete picture of the Rappite understanding of Sunwoman and her flight. Several later "Sunwoman" sermons by Rapp (ca. 1830s-1840s) will be drawn upon only sparingly and clearly identified as such, when necessary to round out the picture. Using these sources, first the Rappite concept of "leaving Babel," then their understanding of the Sunwoman, and finally of her flight into the wilderness will be examined.

---

⁸²Arndt, *Doc. Hist. 1700-1803*, 413. In personal correspondence to the author (April, 2007), Hermann Ehmer noted that the phrase *mit klingendem Spiel* was used for the marching music of military troops.

⁸³Fritz, *Radikaler Pietismus*, 278.

⁸⁴The Rappite emigration hymns, with their theme of going out of Babel, were similar to those of other "wild" Separatists, as opposed to more moderate elements. Cf. Eberhard Zwink and Joachim Trautwein, "Geistliche Gedichte und Gesänge für die nach Osten eilenden Zioniden, 1817," *Blätter für württembergische Kirchengeschichte* 94 (1994): 47-90, here 51, n. 9 for an example of a hymn by a "wild" Separatist.

⁸⁵". . .bringet her eure Flöten, Paucken, Geigen . . . laßt indes die Musig hören, u. den Marsch. Nun so wollen wir marschieren, freuden voll u. dabei die Paucken rühren . . .singet dazu neue Lieder, lobet Gott." Arndt, *Doc. Hist. 1700-1803*, 444-445.

Babel or Babylon

In the survey of Pietist interpretations of Revelation 12 above, it has already been noted that the concept of the Sunwoman was frequently combined with that of "going out of Babel" (Rev 18:4). With whom or what did the followers of Rapp identify Babel/Babylon? Unlike Luther and Spener before them but similarly to other radical Pietists, the Rappites identified Babel with false Christendom within all confessions and not exclusively with the Roman Catholic Church. According to several of the emigration hymns, the false Christianity of Babel was characterized by "hypocrisy" and "mere [outward] appearance." It was subordinated to the Devil, rather than having Jesus as Commander.[86] Babel referred to superficial, exterior religion, which "loves only the surface and shell, and paints its own God in pictures, church building, altar, and confessional."[87] Not only was Babel superficial religion. Hidden under the pious outward appearance, it was filled with lust and sin, a regular "Sodom and Gomorrah."[88]

In an undated pastoral letter written prior to emigration (between 1791 and 1802), George Rapp expounded on Revelation 18 and the concept of Babel. Babel, for the Separatist leader, was apostate Christendom led by "false clerics with their worship services lacking in Spirit" (*die falsche Clerisey mit ihren geistlosen Gottesdiensten*). The unregenerate clergy had "made all the peoples drunk with the wine of their false teaching" (Rev 17:2; 18:3), their "argumentative spirit" (*ihr disputier Geist*) and their "spirit of rationalism" (*Vernunfts Geist*). Through outward ceremonies, "the *true* light of the pure *truth* of inward worship in Spirit and *truth* has been darkened." The clergy had become "fat and rich," while treating the "Word and Gospel" as merely a craft to be plied.[89]

The apostate city, Babylon the Great, had in the past "killed the servants of Christ and persecuted the true church," and it continued to persecute members of the Rapp movement in the present.[90] One emigration hymn expressed it thus:

> You [Babel] have persecuted the righteous, with you there was no mercy for them.... As often as this people gathered together [in conventicles], to bring to God prayer as an offering, you, world, acted against them, with blatant curses and scorn, with flogging and prison sentences ... which you inflicted on God's children; you grieve them and their God.[91]

Therefore, according to Rapp, "[b]ecause in our land [Germany or Württemberg], Babel still mightily rules and tolerance is unknown, the

---

[86]Ibid., 422.
[87]Ibid.
[88]Ibid.
[89]Ibid., 284.
[90]Ibid.
[91]Ibid., 421. Prison sentences were rare for Separatists prior to 1805. The author has found no evidence that Separatists were flogged.

people still sit by the waters of Babylon and inwardly cry [Ps. 137:1], when we think about our [lack of] freedom. . . ."⁹² For Rapp, the judgment upon Babel/Babylon for its apostasy and persecution of true believers would primarily affect Europe in general and Germany in particular. "A complete restructuring of the city of Babylon is near at hand, which will especially affect the entire continent of Europe," due to its great pride and arrogance.⁹³

In two pastoral letters, Rapp stated that the Fall of Babylon had actually already begun with the secularization of church properties in the lands belonging to the Habsburg dynasty by Emperor Joseph II (reign 1780-1790). Joseph's fundamental conviction regarding the supremacy of the state over the church had as a corollary the state's right to appropriate and administer ecclesiastical property. The funds of all churches, religious houses, and endowments within his empire were thus gathered by law into one great fund called the *Religionsfonds* and then distributed to meet the requirements of public worship.⁹⁴ Rapp believed that these actions by Joseph II, which limited the power of apostate Christendom, initiated the fulfillment of the biblical prophecy concerning the Fall of Babylon in Revelation 17 and 18.

> It is thus now evident, so that we can observe it with open eyes, how the prophecy has been and is being fulfilled. Emperor Joseph was the first, to begin to eat the flesh of the whore [Babylon] [Rev. 17:16] and to gather to himself the income of church properties. He has revealed a completely new era, which will increase and spread from year to year and will not abate, until once again the Kingdom of God and his Christ exists.⁹⁵

The limiting of the Church's power was only the beginning of the complete destruction of Babylon. Next "all angels and good spirits" would be removed from its midst and in their place the devil and his legion would reign in the centers of established religion.⁹⁶ All religions, even the Christian religion, would be destroyed to clear the way for a completely new be-

---

⁹²"da in unserem Lande, Babel noch gewaltig Herscht u: Niemand von keiner Toleranz nichts wissen will und wie Leute noch an den Wassern zu Babel sitzen, u: Jnnerlich weinnen, wenn wir an unsern Freyheit gedencken . . ." Pastoral Letter #30, Viehmayer Collection, MG-185, 1-5005, Box 16, Folder 1.

⁹³Arndt, *Doc. Hist. 1700-1803*, 284.

⁹⁴Hermann Franz, "Joseph II," in *Catholic Encyclopedia*, vol. 8, ed. Charles G. Herbermann, et al. (New York: Appleton, 1910), 508-511.

⁹⁵"so ists nun offenbahr, daß wirs mit hellen Augen sehen könen, wie die Weisagung in die Erfüllung geht u. schon gegangen ist. – Kayser Joseph ist der erste gewesen, der Huren Fleisch hat angefangen zu fressen u. die Einkünfte der Kirchen Güter an sich gezogen, u. eine ganz andere Zeit geoffenbahret, welche sich jezt von Jahr zu Jahr vermehrt u. verbreitet, u. wird nicht nachlassen, biß die Reiche wieder Gottes u. seines Christus seyn." Arndt, *Doc. Hist. 1700-1803*, 282. Cf. Pastoral Letter #30, Viehmayer Collection, MG-185, 1-5005, Box 16, Folder 1.

⁹⁶Arndt, *Doc. Hist. 1700-1803*, 283.

ginning. The final annihilation of Babylon/Babel would occur in an inferno of fire (*scharfes Feuer*) (Rev 18:8), and "nothing would remain."[97]

The complete, imminent destruction of Babel was a central theme in the four preserved Rappite emigration hymns. "Tremble, world . . . be silent, for the end of your existence is already near, for your sins have long been brought before God. The Judge of Babel has been awakened."[98] A second hymn expressed a similar thought: "Now God's wrath will awaken. Pay attention, your Babel will soon crash . . .it is now over."[99] Europe would be completely destroyed in the inferno. But the hymns combined a second element with that of the destruction of Babel. Before the imminent annihilation took place, Rapp's Separatists would successfully "go out of Babylon" (Rev 18:4) and "flee into the wilderness" (Rev 12: 6) and thus avoid the coming destruction of Europe. In the hymns an element of near malicious gloating is present that their persecutors would now receive their due punishment. "Now, farewell, you Württemberger, your judgment in the gloomy fire-dungeon does not reach us, but it will entirely destroy you."[100] The Rapp Separatists as the Sunwoman would be safe in the pastoral landscape of America from the ensuing judgment.

> Up and away, in America
> The sheep's pasture is still to be
> There the Sunwoman is to flee
> That she be removed at the time of evil
> Then judgment will break out to avenge.
>
> Auf auf in America
> Soll noch die Schafweid seyn
> Dahin soll fliehn das Sonnen Weib
> Daß sie entrückt zur bösen Zeit
> Dann wirds Gericht einbrechen
> Zu rächen. [101]

Frederick Rapp declared in a letter written on February 25, 1804 to his adopted father, George Rapp, then in America, that when the latter's follow-

---

[97]Pastoral Letter #24, Viehmeyer Collection, MG-185, 1-5005, Box 16, Folder 1. A *scharfes Feuer* refers to a very hot fire. It is a term from the potter's shed. Comment by Hermann Ehmer, April, 2007.

[98]"Erzittre Welt. . . verstumm, denn deines Daseins Ende, ist nahe schon denn deine Sünde, ist längstens vor Gott dargebracht, und Babels Richter aufgewacht." Arndt, *Doc. Hist. 1700-1803*, 421.

[99]"Nun wird Gottes Grimm erwachen, mercket nur Eure Babel wird bald krachen .. nun ists aus." Ibid., 443.

[100]"Nun Adieu ihr Würtemberger, eur Gericht in dem finstern Feuer Kercker, trifft uns nicht aber euch wirds ganz zerstöhren . . ." Ibid., 442.

[101]Karl Arndt's translation. Ibid., 357 and 446.

ers had left Germany, the son of the Sunwoman, who ruled with an iron rod, would begin to destroy Babel.[102]

"Going out of Babel" for the Rappites in 1804 referred primarily to emigration from Germany. In Rapp's pastoral letter expositing Revelation 18, however, which was written before emigration became a pressing issue, leaving Babel meant separation from the apostate Lutheran Church. According to Rapp, those who did not separate from the church would be hindered in their spiritual development.[103] Thus, like the interpretation of other prior and contemporary radical Pietists, leaving Babel for Rapp's Separatists had a dual meaning: separation and emigration.

Sunwoman of Revelation 12

Explicit and implicit allusions in the emigration hymns make clear that Rapp's Separatists understood their group to be the eschatological Sunwoman of Revelation 12. The hymn verse quoted above, "Up and away, in America," identified their group explicitly with the Sunwoman, who was fleeing to America. Other implicit allusions to Revelation 12 are likewise found in the hymn. All but one of the sixteen verses begins with the word *auf*, translated above as "up and away." The image of ascending and soaring (*schwingen*) on the wings of an eagle, as the Sunwoman did in Rev 12:14 on her flight to the wilderness, is thus alluded to in each verse and not just the fourteenth, where it is explicitly stated. "Up, eagle and soar toward the sun. . ."[104] A second emigration hymn alluded to the battle between Satan and the Sunwoman in Rev 12:17.[105]

For a thorough understanding of the Rappite conception of the Sunwoman it is necessary, however, to turn to Rapp's "Sunwoman" sermons, written in the last two decades of his life (1830s-1840s). The Harmony Society continued to identify their group with the Sunwoman in the wilderness. The later sermons may well include more mature reflections on the eschatological figure or a greater "sectarian spirit" than were present at the time of emigration. These possibilities must be borne in mind. However, due to the paucity of other early sources, these sermons are helpful and necessary to present a well-rounded depiction of the Sunwoman.

---

[102]"wir sehen schon den Tag den der Herr machen wird zu unserer Freude wir sehen aber auch schon daß die Hirten Knaben hinter uns stehen, und wo wir es verlassen, anfangen, und mit Babel den garaus machen werden, zur Ehre unsres Herr Jesu . . . ." The *Hirten-Knabe* is a reference to the son of the Sunwoman, who will pasture the nations with an iron rod. Ibid., 419.

[103]". . . die meiste schon lange am rechten Ziel gehindert hat, daß man nicht ganz aus Babel gegangen ist. Denn so lang man sich nicht verläßt, so ist man in sich selbst in der Creatur u. muß Angst, Noth, Kummer u. Elend tragen vor sein eigen Leben, welches man Subtiler oder gröber liebt, u. nach dem Ausgang viel oder wenig Babels Plagen tragen." Ibid., 283.

[104]Ibid., 445-448.

[105]Ibid., 449.

122 The Sunwoman in the Wilderness

For Rapp, the Sunwoman of Revelation 12 was the true eschatological church. Like Michael Hahn, Rapp rejected a historicist interpretation of this chapter. The Sunwoman was to be found only at the culmination of the age and not in the annals of church history.[106] She was an elite and separated church and characterized by increasing holiness and purity. "The church which Revelation presents under the image of the Sunwoman, will reach, just as the Scripture promises, the highest level of illumination and holiness, which is possible for mankind in mortal bodies, and [be] rich in wisdom, knowledge and divine, miraculous power."[107]

Like the apostolic church, the Sunwoman would be privy to many and varied spiritual gifts.[108] Rapp acknowledged that other Christians would achieve salvation and be present as guests at the wedding feast of the Lamb. However, the Sunwoman of Revelation 12 was in a "special manner" the "bride of Christ" and not just a guest, having "a higher level of preference."[109] Rapp claimed that the Separatist movement which became the Harmony Society was this Sunwoman, the elect bride of Christ.

The identification of Rapp's Separatist movement with the Sunwoman was made by the Separatist leader himself prior to his leaving for America in the summer of 1803. It was then communicated to his followers and later reflected in the emigration songs they wrote and sang in 1804. How and when did Rapp come to identify his movement with the Sunwoman and the correct location of her flight in America? Two later "Sunwoman" sermons provide valuable clues to these questions. In both of these sermons Rapp associated the hidden mysteries found in Revelation 10, in one case with the identification of the Sunwoman and in the other case with the goal of her flight.

Rapp claimed that all events in the penultimate age were to be found in the book of Revelation. "Jesus gave to John the [book of] Revelation, and John gave it to us. In this last or farewell Scripture *all things* are laid and contained."[110] He was convinced that the identification of the Sunwoman with his movement was therefore likewise found in Revelation, specifically in the "mystery of the seven thunders," which were sealed up until the end of the age (Rev 10:4).

> Who is the woman in labor? [Rev 12:2] . . . Here we find the mystery of the seven thunders. That this glorious picture of the *Sunwoman* signifies a civil, religious society and that she will lay the foundation for the kingdom of God is plain as day. . . . Therefore, the millennium is the great nursery (*Pflanz-*

---

[106] MG-185/Box 15/Folder 5/A-25.
[107] MG-185/1-5004/Box 15/Folder 6/Q-104.
[108] MG-437 / Box 22/ Folder 82B/ Gr A-1.
[109] MG-437 / Box 22/ Folder 82B/ Gr B-27.
[110] "Die ofenb: die Jesus dem Joh: gegeben, u Joh: uns gegeben, in dieser valet schrift ist alles gelegen, u enthalten." MG-185/Box 15/Folder 5/A-25.

schule) of the great eternity, just as the *Harmony Society* is for the millennium, and the Israelite religion was previously for Christianity.[111]

The Sunwoman was the "civil and religious" Harmony Society, which would play a significant role in preparing the world for the millennium. Rapp had come to this understanding by properly decoding the "mystery of the seven thunders" in Revelation 10.

Proper Location of the Wilderness

In a second Sunwoman sermon Rapp claimed that in 1802 he perceived that the angel of Revelation 10, who spoke with the "voices of seven thunders," had placed one of his feet on the earth and the other in America, thus indicating the proper goal of emigration.[112] The angel "indicated what the prophesies concerning the church [meant], as well as those concerning the establishment of the kingdom of God, all the way until the return of the Lord himself."[113] Rapp was claiming supernatural insight into eschatological events predicted in the Book of Revelation. The prophecy "concerning the church (*Gemeine*)" could well refer to the identification of the Separatist movement, which Rapp by this time called a *Gemeine*, with the Sunwoman of Revelation 12. Just as the "mystery of the seven thunders" (Rev 10:4), discussed above, included the identification of the Separatists with the Sunwoman, so also the placement of the angel's foot on the continent of North America (Rev 10:2) indicated the proper eschatological goal for the flight of the Sunwoman. Thus, by becoming privy to the "mystery of the seven thunders," Rapp achieved a correct understanding of the Sunwoman by 1803 at the latest and to the proper goal of emigration in 1802, a year before he left Iptingen to prepare the way for the exodus of his followers.

Jonathan Wagner in his early history of the Harmony Society (1833) confirmed that America was divinely revealed to Rapp as the appointed refuge for the Separatists. "God had given him [Rapp] a sign from heaven that he should immigrate to America, because this was the place, where the people of God should be gathered."[114] Although Wagner's history is very biased and must be used with care, his statement corroborates Rapp's claims in the two Sunwoman sermons referenced above. Unlike J. J. Friedrich, who argued in 1800 that Palestine was the correct refuge for the Sunwoman, and Jung-Stilling, who favored Russia, Rapp was convinced that America was the proper goal for emigration.

America and specifically Pennsylvania were mentioned as the goal of the Sunwoman in the Rappite emigration hymns. One hymn exhorted Rapp's

---

[111] MG-185/1-5004/Box 15/Folder 6/Q-24.

[112] Rev 10:2 speaks of the "mighty angel" planting "his right foot on the sea and his left foot on the land." (NIV translation).

[113] MG-185/Box 15/Folder 5/A-25.

[114] Jonathan Wagner, *Geschichte u. Verhältnisse der Harmoniegesellschaft* (Vaihingen an der Enz: Deininger, 1833), 7.

Separatists to "sing to the Lord new songs because He was establishing His kingdom in America."[115] In some hymn verses, America was the "promised land" to which they are fleeing, in others "Silva" or Pennsylvania was given this accolade.[116] America was their new "Fatherland," a place "full of hope," where "God himself would rule them" and they could "rest in peace."[117] The hymns repeatedly called the emigrants to be strong and courageous, not to allow the difficulties of the journey to weaken their faith in God. The sharp contrast between Württemberg and America was underscored, with God Himself leading them to their destination.

> Here only war and discord prevails, there is peace without end
> The unity of the brethren, who will be more than ever united
> In that land, because the Lord will lead us there
> By his Son, who will rule us inwardly
> Yea, He Himself takes us by the hand, and leads us to our rest.[118]

Like Kelpius before them, the Rappites had a multi-faceted concept of the wilderness to which they fleeing. On one hand, it was a place of refuge and rest, where the emigrants would soon experience a "better time" and would not be oppressed by persecution.[119] The wilderness was a place of refuge from the dragon Satan (Rev 12:14) and from the coming conflagration, which would envelop Babel/Babylon. The wilderness was described positively, in one case as a verdant "meadow for grazing sheep" (*Schafweid*), because there spiritual growth would take place.[120] Frederick Rapp in a letter dated February 25, 1804 described prior to emigration the wilderness of America as "a pleasant field where our spirit can develop fully and completely and true brotherly love can be revealed in complete measure, where the influence of the worldly spirit (*Weltgeist*) and many temptations will be considerably milder."[121]

In such a favorable environment where negative spiritual influences were reduced, Rapp's Separatists would be able more easily to prepare themselves for the wedding feast of the Lamb. Rapp explained in a later sermon:

> For this reason, the Woman lives in the wilderness, because there in the meantime she is in her correct location, where she may worship in Spirit and truth inwardly and may outwardly patiently await [the Second Coming of Christ], where she will be properly nourished with the Bread of Life, without being hindered by the Dragon and his beast. In this state of wilderness, it is

---

[115] Arndt, *Doc. Hist. 1700-1803*, 442.
[116] Ibid., 442, 448.
[117] Ibid., 447-449.
[118] Ibid., 449.
[119] Ibid., 448.
[120] Ibid., 446.
[121] Ibid., 419.

said of her, "those that wait upon the Lord will renew their strength" [Isa 40:31].[122]

The wilderness was thus a place of protection and of spiritual preparation.

In conclusion, this discussion of the Rappite conception of the Sunwoman and her flight has revealed considerable continuity with prior and contemporary Pietist interpretations of Revelation 12. Like other radical Pietists, the Rappites interpreted Babel as apostate Christendom within all confessions and not just the Roman Church. They raised the same complaints about Babel (unregenerate clergy; superficial, Spirit-less worship) as Boehme, Gottfried Arnold, and Zimmermann before them. Like Zimmermann and others, Rapp's followers viewed Babel as centered in Europe and particularly in Germany. The call to leave Babel/Babylon could mean both separation from the apostate church and emigration from Germany for Rapp and Zimmermann. The latter two as well as Michael Hahn and Kelpius all associated the flight of the Sunwoman with going out of Babel. Like other radical and churchly Pietists at the beginning of the nineteenth century, Rapp's followers rejected the Bengelian interpretation that the place of refuge for the Sunwoman was in Germany or even Württemberg. Palestine was not an emigration option in 1804 due to the policies of the Ottoman Empire. Rapp's Separatists settled in the wilderness in America. Like Kelpius, the Rappites understood the wilderness to be both a refuge and a place of spiritual preparation for the coming millennium. Finally, George Rapp rejected a historicist interpretation of Revelation 12 as did contemporary and acquaintance Michael Hahn.

In spite of considerable continuity with prior and contemporary Pietists, Rapp's conception of the Sunwoman and her flight had several distinctives. First, he was willing to identify his own group with the eschatological Sunwoman. Although Kelpius and possibly Zimmermann likewise risked such a bold interpretation, most prior and contemporary Pietists were content to identify the Sunwoman with a historic church or the eschatological church hidden within all confessions and not with any one visible body. Further, Rapp's identification of his group with the Sunwoman and the location of the wilderness were based on his own supernatural decoding of the hidden mysteries of the book of Revelation.[123] He had likewise identified the beginning of the Fall of Babylon with the secularization policies of Emperor Joseph II. Admittedly, this approach had a long tradition in Württemberg. J. J. Friedrich as the pastor in Winzerhausen (1795-1810) and the first pastor of Korntal (after 1824) held "newspaper meetings" in which current events were compared with the book of Revelation. Württemberg Pietist Christian Armbruster in *Die sieben letzten Posaunen* (1814) made specific connections between the tumultuous events surrounding the French Revolution

---

[122]MG-185/1-5004/Box 15/Folder 6/R-26.
[123]See the discussion of Rapp's "prophetic" gift on page 104f.

and the trumpet judgments in John's Apocalypse.[124] Nevertheless, the conclusions that Rapp drew from his biblicist approach combined with supernatural insights were uncommon. No group other than the Society of the Woman in the Wilderness had dared to identify exclusively their own group with the Sunwoman of Revelation 12. However, since Kelpius's group of mystics on the Wissahickon River had made this identification of their group with the Sunwoman one hundred years prior, the path was paved for other very devout (sectarian) Christians to follow suit.

Immigration to America

George Rapp and his Separatists had been considering immigration to America for some time. The French colony of Louisiana was, prior to its annexation to the United States in 1803, the group's original immigration goal.[125] But, by the time Rapp and the three members of his reconnaissance team left for the New World to find a suitable haven for the Rappites, the goal had been readjusted to the Mid-Atlantic states. Rapp and his team consisting of his son Johannes, Dr. P. F. C. Haller and Christoph Müller disembarked the ship *Canton* in the harbor of Philadelphia on October 7, 1803. In a letter he wrote several days later to Frederick Reichert Rapp, his representative in Württemberg, the Separatist leader bemoaned that "the journey had been very difficult for him." Frederick should not talk anyone against his or her will into attempting such a "horribly long and dangerous journey." He then bubbled over in praise for America. It was a rich land, full of natural resources. Any man who was willing to work would prosper greatly here. Rapp was very amazed by the friendliness of the people. Most importantly, here was the religious freedom they had been searching for: "Man can think and believe what he wants." Rapp's conclusion was that "I will never again return to Germany."[126]

Within days the team began to make enquiries and scouting expeditions to purchase suitable land in Virginia, Pennsylvania or Ohio. The team found favorable land near Sandy Creek of the Muskigum River in Ohio, which they desired to buy, but were hindered from purchasing due to insufficient funds. In the meanwhile, on July 4, 1804 the first contingent of three hun-

---

[124]Two copies of this book were in the Harmony Society library in 1829. Christian Armbruster, *Die sieben letzten Posaunen oder Wehen, wann sie anfangen und aufhören und von den 70 Danielischen Wochen und 42 prophetischen Monaten* (Ulm: [s.n.], 1814), 16-17.

[125]Arndt claims that Rapp had corresponded with the French government about moving his group to Louisiana. Arndt, *Rapp's Harmony Society*, 636, n. 2. While this claim is reasonable, to my knowledge there is no hard documentary evidence to prove it. Arndt may be confusing Rapp with the Napoleon- admirer Christoph Greulich, who did write to Napoleon. The February 1804 Legal Review of the Electoral government, however, did claim that Rapp's Separatists "probably intended" to immigrate to Louisiana. Arndt, *Doc. Hist. 1700-1803*, 413-414.

[126]Ibid., 366-367.

dred of Rapp's Separatists arrived in Baltimore on the ship *Aurora*. On September 14 of that year Frederick Rapp disembarked from the *Atlantic* with 257 Separatists. Several days later an undesignated number of Rappites arrived in Philadelphia on the *Margaret*. It was not until December 22, 1804, however, that "George Rapp and Society" purchased a large plot of ground on the Connoquenessing Creek, near Zelionople, Pennsylvania.[127] The "holy experiment" was about to begin.

---

[127] Arndt, *Rapp's Harmony Society*, 49-71.

5

Church in the Wilderness
(1805-1825)

On December 22, 1804 George Rapp "and Society" paid their first installment on a plot of land located on the Connoquenessing Creek near Zelienople, Pennsylvania. Shortly thereafter thirty-one Rappite families moved to the location to help clear the land and build their first town of Harmony, where they resided until 1814. The remaining Rappites spent the winter at Busch Hill near Philadelphia or elsewhere, waiting until the first rough log cabins had been built and they could join their comrades. The vanguard of workers suffered greatly that first winter of 1804-1805. Years later in 1829 George Rapp reminisced about the early deprivations: "I cannot tell you about the suffering the first year. We had nothing to eat and had to live in log huts in which we would not have put swine back in Württemberg.... Although the winter was bleak our brotherhood gave us strength." He concluded: "I believe we were a braver band than any regiment of soldiers, albeit we are peaceful people."[1] Despite the fact that the majority of Rappites were not yet present, the Harmony Society was officially founded during that first winter on February 15, 1805.

The Harmony Society as the Sunwoman of Revelation 12 had arrived at the "American wilderness." This chapter portrays key aspects of the early religious beliefs and practices adopted by the Harmonist "church in the wilderness." It begins with a brief history of the first two decades of the Harmony Society during which the community first resided at Harmony, Pennsylvania, then at New Harmony, Indiana. The ideological foundation of the communal society was laid in these years. The practice of "community of goods" reflected the Harmonist understanding of the ideal observance of the primitive Jerusalem church depicted in Acts 2 and 4. Celibacy was instituted after a "fresh revival of religion" swept through the newly-founded community in 1807-1808. Rapp's theological rationale for these two central

---

[1]Remarks by George Rapp, Feb. 15, 1829. OEV, Daniel Reibel's file.

Harmonist practices is the topic of the next two sections of the chapter. Worship practices including their distinctive hymnody and the celebration of Harmonist-specific and other Christian holidays within the Harmonist settlement will then be examined. The chapter closes with a discussion of Rapp's patriarchal leadership style.

History of the Harmony Society (1805-1825)

February 15, 1805 was viewed by Harmonists as the official founding date of the Harmony Society. According to a later recollection of Romelius Langenbacher, it was a solemn day for the new community. First a love feast was held for those present. Then the "covenant" (*Bund*) between the brethren was renewed by the signing of the Articles of Association, which formally established the Harmony Society.[2] The Articles contained three commitments from the new members: (1) to "deliver up and renounce" all privately owned property; (2) to submit to the rules of the congregation and to obey their appointed leaders; and (3) "never to demand a reward. . . for work or services rendered" should they withdraw from the Society.[3] According to the 1805 Articles withdrawing members were entitled to a refund of their original donation to the common treasury, but not for work rendered.[4] In exchange Rapp and his Society promised to provide religious and school instruction and all necessities of life for as long as the members and their families should live. The Articles of Association thus laid the foundation for a communal, economic system involving the abolishment of private property.

The deprivations and suffering that the new community experienced the first winter of 1804-1805 continued for several years. "Every beginning is difficult, and the *Harmonie* experienced that fully," Romelius Langenbacher recalled.[5] Nevertheless the industrious Germans in 1805 speedily established the soon thriving village of Harmony, Pennsylvania. In that year they built forty-six log houses, a large barn, a grist mill and race, began work on a hotel, and cleared and planted over 200 acres of land.[6] In the following sev-

---

[2]Harmony Fest 1839 verso, Library Box 26.

[3]Karl J. R. Arndt, *Harmony on the Connoquenessing, 1803-1815. A Documentary History* (Worcester, Mass.: Harmony Society Press, 1980), 89.

[4]This right was withdrawn in 1818 when the Harmonists publicly burned the records of individual contributions. Rather than a refund a voluntary donation was given to withdrawing members. Arndt states that the clause for refunds was only added in 1808 when Pennsylvania legislature insisted on its inclusion in order to ratify the incorporation of the Society. It was completely removed in 1836. Karl J. R. Arndt, "George Rapp's Harmony Society," in *America's Communal Utopias*, ed. Donald E. Pitzer (Chapel Hill, N.C.: University of North Carolina Press, 1997), 57-87, here 63 and 84-85, note 3.

[5]Karl J. R. Arndt, *George Rapp's Harmony Society 1785-1847*, rev. ed. (Teaneck, N.J.: Fairleigh Dickinson University Press, 1972), 76.

[6]Arndt, *Rapp's Harmony Society*, 76-77.

eral years large quantities of land were progressively brought under the plow. By 1809, the Society was producing tens of thousands of bushels of corn, wheat, rye, potatoes, and other crops. In the same period, they laid the foundation for the production and manufacture of salable goods, which were the key to their economic success--an oil mill, blue-dyers shop, tannery, sawmill, brewery, hemp mill, fulling mill, as well as a wool-manufacturing factory with a wool-carding machine, two spinning jennies and twenty weaver's looms. A store was established in 1807 where neighboring residents could purchase necessary supplies at competitive prices.[7] Rapp's adopted son, Frederick, assumed the role of the Society's business manager. His economic acumen and organizational skill contributed greatly to the increasing financial prowess of the Harmony Society.

The hard work and deprivations of the early years had the positive effect of fostering a strong communal sentiment among the original immigrants, binding them together into a cohesive group. In the early years Rapp's small room and courtyard in Harmony were the gathering point each evening for communal members desiring to talk or pray with their spiritual leader before retiring for the night.[8] Religious fervor ran high, and in 1807-1808 a revival broke out within the Harmony Society, which directly led to the institution of the practice of celibacy. Their brick church, completed in 1808, was the locus for two Sunday and one midweek service. In 1809 Rapp's disciples began affectionately to address their spiritual leader as "Father." Besides religious activities, education of children and cultural pursuits were pursued.

The plot of land on the Connoquenessing Creek was inadequate for a number of reasons. The creek was shallow and not navigable much of the year. The soil in Butler County was not particularly fertile. More damning for the Württemberg vinedressers among them was the fact that the climate there was unfavorable for the cultivation of grapes. Furthermore, the location did not allow for the expansion Rapp expected and desired. The Harmonist leader fully anticipated that the Harmony Society would receive a large influx of Separatists from their homeland of Württemberg in the coming years.[9] Therefore on January 6, 1806 Rapp and 200 signers addressed a petition to Thomas Jefferson, then president of the United States, in which they requested to purchase "thirty thousand acres of [government] land ... in the western Country" of Ohio or Indiana.[10] The Harmonist petition was defeated by one vote in the House of Representatives on February 18, 1806.[11]

By 1814, George Rapp decided that it was time for his community to move westward. They purchased 30,000 acres of land in the Indiana Terri-

---

[7]Ibid., 106-107.
[8]Ibid., 79-80.
[9]Ibid., 133-134.
[10]Arndt, *Doc. Hist. 1803-1815*, 137-141, here 138.
[11]Arndt, *Rapp's Harmony Society*, 90.

tory on the banks of the navigable Wabash River. In the summer of 1814 Johannes Langenbacher led an advance group of Harmonists to their Indiana property to lay the foundations for a new village in the wilderness. Malaria which bred in the swampy lowlands and humid climate near the Wabash promptly struck the advance party, bringing work to a standstill. In the next two years 120 Harmonists died at the new settlement until the swamps could be drained and living conditions improved. After the sickness subsided work on the village of New Harmony progressed quickly. By 1818 the Rapp family resided in a large brick house, described "as the best in Indiana."[12] An impressive brick cruciform church with elegant Georgian porticos was built in 1822. To further fellowship between the members, four large communal dormitories (*Brüderhäuser* 1 to 4) were constructed at New Harmony. The *Bruderhäuser* constituted a communal experiment that was found neither at their previous (Harmony) nor subsequent (Economy) settlements. The communal dormitories did not extinguish or replace the nuclear family with a surrogate family. Rather the familial and mixed-gender nature of the small Harmonist households at Harmony and Economy was merely multiplied and enlarged in the dormitories.[13] The Harmonists quickly became an economic force. They were soon able to sell not just their agricultural surplus but other manufactured goods such as rope, shoes, leather goods, pottery, whiskey, and woolen, linen and cotton cloth in twenty-two states and ten foreign countries.[14] The Harmony Society made a significant contribution to the formation of the state of Indiana in 1816. Frederick Rapp served as a delegate to the first constitutional convention of the state of Indiana. The Harmonists would reside but ten years (1814-1824) at New Harmony, before establishing their third and final settlement of Economy, once again in Pennsylvania.

Communalism and the Harmony Society

Article one of the 1805 Articles of Association laid the foundation for abolition of personal property and community of goods. In this article the signers pledged to:

> ... deliver up, renounce, and transfer all our estate and property consisting of cash, land, cattle, or whatever else it may be, to George Rapp and his Society in Harmony, Butler County, Pennsylvania, as a free gift or donation, for the benefit and use of the congregation there, and bind ourselves on our part, as

---

[12]Karl J. R. Arndt, "George Rapp's Harmony Society," in *America's Communal Utopias*, ed. Donald E. Pitzer (Chapel Hill, N.C.: University of North Carolina Press, 1997), 57-87, here 66-67.

[13]The author's research indicates that *Bruderhaus* Nr. 2, established in 1822, was inhabited by the male and female members of at least the following five families: the Johannes Herrmann, Wilhelm Hinger, Adam Jung, David Kant and Penotus Zundel families.

[14]Arndt, "Rapp's Harmony Society," 66-68.

well as on the part of our heirs and descendants, to make free renunciation thereof, and to leave the same at the disposal of the superintendents of the congregation, as if we never had nor possessed the same [allusion to Acts 4:32-35].[15]

Some recent scholars have claimed that the institution of communalism by the Harmonists was a late idea formed after immigration or adopted primarily for economic reasons. Karl Arndt, the leading historian of the Harmony Society, claimed in 1994 that a lesser form of communalism, mutual assistance without abolition of private property, was planned for Pennsylvania by Rapp's followers until *after immigration*. Then in January and February 1805, Rapp "fanatically" pushed the idea of community of goods on his followers. The only evidence that Arndt provides that community of goods was a late idea was the initial purchase of land by eighteen different Harmonists in Butler County, the site of the first Harmonist settlement, in late 1804.[16] Arndt failed to note that these eighteen persons were charged by Frederick Rapp (December 31, 1804-January 14, 1805) for the land purchased by them, presumably with communal funds.[17] The eighteen purchasers likewise promptly turned the property and proceeds over to the Harmony Society. The purchase of land by individual Harmonists could be explained simply by the fact that the Harmony Society was not legally incorporated at that time. It by no means proves that the abolition of private property was not intended. Interestingly, in his earlier monograph, *George Rapp's Harmony Society* (1972), Arndt argued exactly the opposite of his 1994 statement, namely that "the communist system was in operation before December 1, 1804." As proof he referenced convincingly the extant document listing contributions by Harmonists to the common treasury on that date.[18] Eberhard Fritz in *Radikaler Pietismus* (2003) claims that al-

---

[15]Arndt, *Doc. Hist. 1803-1815*, 89.

[16]Arndt gives no documentary evidence that Rapp pushed the concept of community of goods in Jan.-Feb. 1805. Karl J. R. Arndt, *George Rapp's Disciples, Pioneers and Heirs. A Register of the Harmonists in America*, ed. Donald E. Pitzer and Leigh Ann Chamness (Evansville, Ind.: University of Southern Indiana Press, 1994), 16 and 232, Note 10: "Land was held by the following individual Harmonists: Mathäus Klein 25 acres; Jacob Beker 50 acres; Friederich Braun 20 acres; Georg Rükkenbrod 108 acres; Johannes Hoernle 108 acres; Georg Böhringer 30 acres cleared and 25 acres "bush land"; Johannes Ehman 108 acres; Jacob Eheman 108 acres; Johannes Bamesberger 108 acres; Georg Wagner 108 acres; Michael Rukenbrod 108 acres; Jacob Benzenhöfer 1 acres; Frederich Velte 40 acres and one city lot; Josua Vayhinger 50 acres; Frederich Kurz one city lot and 20 acres; Christoph Lang one city lot and 20 acres; Jacob Scholle 15 acres cleared land and 93 acres "bush land"; Georg Velte 15 acres cleared and 93 acres "bush land.""

[17]Arndt, *Doc. Hist. 1803-1815*, 60-77. Arndt mentions a "final reckoning" of debits and credits on January 14, 1805, but fails to explain that they were *charged* for the land. Arndt, "George Rapp's Harmony Society," 64.

[18]Arndt, *Rapp's Harmony Society*, 70. Arndt later in 1980 emended the date to Dec. 1, 1805. (The last two digits of the year are missing.) Arndt, *Doc. Hist. 1803-*

though Rapp provided a religious rationale for communalism (the practice of the primitive Jerusalem church), the "communistic lifestyle did not spring from a voluntary decision . . . but was dictated by economic necessity."[19] In this section it is argued that community of goods was neither a late innovation developed after immigration nor was it adopted for merely economic reasons. Rapp's pastoral letters and Harmonist narrative histories indicate that the practice of communalism was discussed in Separatist circles in Württemberg and planned upon by some but not all members. Harmonist sources unequivocally claim that communalism was adopted for religious and not economic reasons. However, it cannot be denied that the sharing of finances and labor significantly contributed to the financial prosperity of the Harmony Society.

Concept of Communalism among Separatists in Württemberg

Separatists in Württemberg in the last decades of the eighteenth century, both those affiliated with Rapp and others, viewed the primitive Christian church in Jerusalem as described in Acts 2 and 4 as the ideal model to emulate. Not just "oneness in heart and mind" within the Christian fellowship, but the "holding of possessions in common" was the goal they sought after (Acts 2:44-45 and 4:32-35). Both the Lomersheimer (1798) and Öhlbronner (1799) Declarations of Faith discussed in chapter two expressed the desire to reinstate "the apostolic principles of the first Christian church."[20] These declarations were discussed by members of Rapp's Separatist movement prior to their submission to the government. The Öhlbronner declaration was likewise signed by approximately fifty members of the Rappite movement. Therefore by at least 1798, many members of the movement were aware of and in agreement with the goal of reinstituting apostolic Christianity. Many must have been aware that in Rapp's thinking this included community of goods.

Members of Rapp's movement as well as other unaffiliated Separatists desired to form their own communal settlement within Württemberg, such

---

1815, 126f. Arndt's argument hinges on the correct dating of this document. Internal evidence makes the date Dec. 1, 1805 impossible. A letter from George to Frederick Rapp on August 13, 1805, indicates that David Gloss had already left the Harmony Society and moved to Columbiana County, Ohio, where on Nov. 20, 1805 he purchased land (records of the County Court House in Lisbon, Ohio). The record of contributions lists David Gloss and his donation to the common treasury. Therefore, the year must be Dec. 1, 1804 as Arndt originally argued and not Dec. 1, 1805. The separate sheets belonging to the document were however later additions.

[19] Eberhard Fritz, *Radikaler Pietismus in Württemberg: Religiöse Ideale im Konflikt mit gesellschaftlichen Realitäten* (Epfendorf: Bibliotheca Academica, 2003), 342.

[20] Karl J. R. Arndt, *George Rapp's Separatists, 1700-1803. A Documentary History* (Worcester, Mass.: Harmony Society Press, 1980), 272f and 294f.

as the Herrnhuter had.²¹ However, at the end of the eighteenth century this was not an option. Several decades later this would be feasible, however, as the founding of Korntal (1819) and Wilhelmsdorf (1824) by churchly and radical Pietists indicate. In the meanwhile, Rapp's followers sought to practice a lesser form of communalism. They formed a benevolent fund to meet the needs of impoverished co-religionists. They practiced hospitality by sharing food and lodging with fellow Separatists from other locations. To enable Rapp to concentrate more fully on his itinerant preaching ministry, Rappites helped to bring in his crops.²² Furthermore, Frederick Rapp gathered into a common purse and administered some of the monies earned from the sale of property by Separatists intent upon emigrating in 1804.²³ Other Separatists who remained in the duchy after the emigration of the Rappites likewise attempted to put the apostolic ideal into practice. Separatists in Ulm in 1806 communally worked a farm together although it remained privately owned.²⁴ Later Separatist immigrants to the Caucasus from Esslingen in 1817 wrote a statement declaring their intention to institute community of goods.²⁵

The contemporary source of the primitivist ideal in Württemberg was an 1100 folio page volume by Gottfried Arnold, *Die erste Liebe*, first published in Frankfurt in 1696.²⁶ This work was widely regarded and influenti-

---

[21] Diary of Philipp Mathäus Hahn: "Den 21 September [17]89. Heute früh kamen elf Separatisten zu mir. Wir redeten miteinander von den Gebrechen der äußeren Kirche und von einer anzurichtenden besonderen Gemeine, daß ein Fürst erlauben solte, daß die Separatisten in einem Ort seines Lands sich anbauen und beysamen wohnen dürften, worinn sie Religionsfreiheit hätten und unter keinem Pfarrer und Consistorio stehen dörften wie die Herrenhuter in den preusischen Landen." Martin Brecht and Rudolf F. Paulus, *Philipp Matthäus Hahn. Die Echterdinger Tagebücher 1780-1790* (Berlin: Walter De Gruyter, 1983), 463. Cf. Letter by Harmonist Romelius Langenbacher, July 24, 1847 in which he stated that the Rappites considered buying and forming a settlement in Württemberg. Due to the infeasibility of this endeavor they immigrated to America. Arndt, *Rapp's Disciples*, 7.

[22] Arndt, *Doc. Hist., 1700-1803*, 332-352, particularly 336-337, 339-341.

[23] Letter of Frederick Rapp to George Rapp (in America), March 27, 1804. F. Rapp reported that Christian Hörnle entrusted to him the travel money for his daughter. Later in the letter he stated that he "had much money in his hands [although his own property had not yet sold], and nevertheless gave no account of one cent (*Kreuzer*)." This is an allusion to Acts 4:34-35, "those who owned lands or houses sold them, brought the money from the sales and put it at the apostles' feet," thus surrendering the necessity of the apostles to give an account of how it was distributed. Arndt, *Doc. Hist., 1700-1803*, 437-439.

[24] Fritz, *Radikaler Pietismus*, 342-343.

[25] Georg Leibbrandt, *Die Auswanderung aus Schwaben nach Rußland 1816-1823* (Stuttgart: Ausland und Heimat Verlag, 1928), 118.

[26] Fritz, *Radikaler Pietismus*, 342 and Leibbrandt, *Auswanderung*, 47. Erich Seeberg points out that mystic Antoinette Bourignon and thesophist Johann Georg Gichtel likewise propagated communalistic views since they were convinced that the decline of the church began when community of goods as practiced by the

al in churchly and particularly in radical Pietist circles.[27] In *Die erste Liebe* Arnold depicted the primitive church as normative for Christianity of all ages. The early church was characterized by a heart-felt "first love" for Christ and the brethren. Even before the Constantinian era, however, decline had begun to set in, because the church had left its first love (Rev. 2:4). Both the normative character of primitive Christianity and the dismal state of the post-Constantinian church rang true to radical Pietists and were appropriated by them into their belief system.

In book three of *Die erste Liebe* Arnold quoted numerous patristic authors in his discussion of the duties of the early Christians for one another. The hearts of the early Christians, in Arnold's depiction, were tightly knit together in true brotherly love. It was as if only one heart, soul and spirit beat in the breasts of those in whom the Spirit reigned, such was the unity between them (Acts 4:32).[28] This spiritual fellowship "of heavenly goods" was the basis and foundation for the holding in common of temporal goods. The early Christians believed that because "we live as brothers from common [spiritual] goods" and "because we have mingled together so to speak our hearts and souls and have them in common, we have no scruples about holding our [earthly] goods in common."[29] Thus Gottfried Arnold taught that community of temporal goods was the logical consequence of the har-

---

primitive church was abandoned. However, their propagation of the primitive ideal did not have the influence that Arnold's *Erste Liebe* had. Erich Seeberg, *Gottfried Arnold. Die Wissenschaft und die Mystik seiner Zeit* (Darmstadt: Wissenschaftliche Buchgesellschaft, 1964), 346 and 366-367. Although Karl Arndt, *Doc. Hist. 1803-1815*, xxxiii and Donald E. Pitzer and Josephine M. Elliott, *New Harmony's First Utopians, 1814-1824*, 2d ed. (Historic New Harmony, Ind.: University of Southern Indiana Press, 2002), 230 claimed that Rapp became convinced of communalism through reading Valentin Andreae's *Christianopolis* (1619), there is no evidence that he had read this work (unlike the works of Arnold). Rapp was not seeking to found a utopian Christian city, but to renew communalism as practiced in the primitive church.

[27]Hans Schneider points to its reception by Spener, Francke, the Philadelphian movement, Hochmann von Hochenau, the Inspired, Zinzendorf and during the revival movement in Württemberg. Hans Schneider, ed., *Gottfried Arnold. Die Erste Liebe* (Leipzig: Evangelische Verlagsanstalt, 2002), 200-205. Cf. Martin Schmidt, "Das Frühchristentum in der evangelisch-lutherischen Überlieferung für das Verständnis und die Autorität der altkirchlichen Tradition," *Oecumenica* 6 (1971-1972): 88-110.

[28]Gottfried Arnold, *Die erste Liebe, das ist, Wahre Abbildung der ersten Christen nach ihrem lebendigen Glauben und heiligen Leben, aus der ältesten und bewährtesten Kirchen-Scribenten eigenen Zeugnissen, Exempeln und Reden, nach der Wahrheit der ersten einigen christlichen Religion, allen Liebhabern der historischen Wahrheit, und sonderlich der Antiquität, als in einer nützlichen Kirchen-Historie, treulich und unparteyisch entworfen: worinnen zugleich des Hn. William Cave Erstes Christenthum nach Nothdurft erläutert wird*, 5th. ed. (Leipzig: Samuel Benjamin Walthern, 1732), 3, 3, §1, §2, §8, 390-393.

[29]Arnold, *Erste Liebe*, 3, 3, §7, §9, 447-448.

mony of spirit that reigned among Christians of the primitive church. According to Arnold, the practice of communalism was not only applicable for the early church, but for the contemporary church as well.[30]

George Rapp likewise believed that the primitive church was the model which "true children of God" should emulate and that communalism was the ideal form of social government. A Harmonist narrative history, written in February 1839 probably by Romelius Langenbacher, described how Rapp *prior to emigration* came to uphold the early church as normative and communalism as the goal.

> Then a man [Rapp] was awakened to the old religion of Christ, now in ruins, which was practiced by the first Christians and introduced in Jerusalem by the apostles. But through the great persecutions by the heathens the Christians were dispersed and driven from their homes and properties. Nevertheless in remembrance of them, the Evangelist Luke wrote in Acts 2 and 4, where we can clearly read it: "And they had all things in common and no one said something was his own." In this manner more people were also awakened, and were in agreement with the aforementioned man [Rapp]. They *began a communal life (gemeinschaftliches Leben)*, but were seized and persecuted by the general, so-called church, so that they were forced to seek refuge in North America, which happened in 1804-1807. On February 15, 1805 the covenant was renewed, a love feast held and a basis for communalism (*Gemeinschaftliche Basse*) made, which has been maintained until now and will be maintained until the end of days.[31]

This narrative history is interesting for several reasons. In the first place, it claimed that Rapp and later more (*mehrere*) of his disciples were "awakened" to the communal ideal of Acts 2 and 4. This awakening took place *while still in Württemberg* and almost certainly through the reception of Arnold's *Die erste Liebe*. Second, some, though not all, of Rapp's followers became convinced of the viability and importance of communalism before emigration. For this to occur, Rapp would have had to propagate his discovery among his followers. This presumably occurred both in private conversations and in conventicle meetings. Third, while still in Württemberg members of Rapp's Separatist movement formed a "communal life" (albeit without the abolition of private property). For both Gottfried Arnold and Rapp's Separatists oneness of heart and mind constituted a common spiritual life and the basis for holding temporal property in common. Because Rapp's followers experienced this unity, and shared material goods and services with one another, it was possible for Langenbacher to state that they "lived communally" prior to emigration. Fourth, the signing of the Articles of Association in 1805, which established the Harmony Society, was

---

[30]Ibid., 3, 3, §5, 445.

[31]This Harmonist history was not signed but appears to be in Langenbacher's handwriting. It was written for the 1839 Harmony Fest. It was found by the author written on the reverse side of an 1839 manuscript Harmony Fest hymn. 1839 Harmony Fest Hymn, verso, OEV, Library Box 26.

only a *renewal* of the communal bond that had likewise existed in Germany. The same term *gemeinschaftlich* (communal) was used for the lesser form of spiritual communalism in Württemberg and the full, temporal form in America. Finally, according to Langenbacher the experience of Rapp's Separatists paralleled that of the early Christians. Both groups were persecuted and forced to flee from their homes. Both groups held all things in common.

Several of Rapp's pastoral letters written to his followers during the Württemberg era portrayed the conventicles of his movement as reflecting the communal spirit of Acts 2 and 4. In one undated letter, the Separatist leader wrote that "the brotherhood was well contented in *harmony* and love." The goal of their fellowship was to emulate the primitive church:

> Where the hearts, spirits and minds flow into one [allusion to Acts 4:32], there is truly the Godhead visible. There the precious balm, with which the Holy Spirit anointed the head of Aaron flows . . . From this the entire community becomes cheerful and happy. That we may all be participants of this, may God through Jesus Christ help us. Amen.[32]

In a pastoral letter written in 1800 Rapp repeated the notion that God was "made visible in the true fellowship of brothers." The experience of "hearts and minds flowing together in unity" was only interrupted when self-centeredness (*Eigenheit*) entered in. "We are restless until we admit our guilt. Then our love flows again with that of the brethren into oneness."[33]

Rapp claimed in a late (ca. 1802) pastoral letter that he had been ordained by God to help the congregation (*Gemeine*), "in order that all might have one mind and spirit according to the rule of the church of Christ, to the glory of the Lord."[34] These statements contain once again allusions to the "oneness of heart and mind" in Acts 4:32. The rule of the church was the idealized model practiced by the Jerusalem Christians, which Rapp attempted to initiate even prior to emigration. Although the formation of a communal settlement in Württemberg was not an option for Rapp's Separatists, members of his movement sought to put into practice the apostolic ideal of unity of spirit.

Furthermore, the decision to establish a communal society in America which abolished private property was decided upon by Rapp and some of his followers prior to emigration. A narrative history of the Harmony Socie-

---

[32]"da wo die Herzen, Geister u. Gemüther in eins fliessen, ist wahrhaftig die Gottheit sichtbar, da fließt der köstliche Balsam, der heilige Geist vom Haupt Aaron herab in seinen Bart, ja gar ins ganze Kleid, u. wird davon eine ganze Gesellschaft lustig u. fröhlich, u. daß wir alle Theilnehmer deß seyn mögen, dazu helfe uns Gott durch Jesum Christum – Amen." Arndt, *Doc. Hist. 1700-1803*, 285.

[33]Ibid., 306.

[34]"damit alle also in einen Sinn u: Geist nach der Regul der Gemeine Christi, zur Ehre ihres Herrn. . . " Pastoral Letter #31, Collection # 2, MG-185, 1-5005, Box 16, Folder 1, #2.

ty written by Romelius Langenbacher on July 24, 1847 specifically emphasized this point.

> At this period [in Württemberg] no association or community of property had been established, each family in its native town enjoyed its estate separately. . . . The idea *entertained in Germany by Mr. Rapp and a majority of his people* [my emphasis], of establishing a community of property, was now called into existence, and on the 15 February 1805, an association was created after the manner and form of the first church, as recorded in the Acts of the Apostles, Chapters 2 and 4. Each one having funds left, after defraying the expenses of a long journey, deposited the same into one common fund, out of which the land was paid, and the title taken in the name of George Rapp and Associates.[35]

Langenbacher had personally experienced the events he reported.[36] In this narrative, he presented the Harmonist interpretation of its own history. He thus confirmed that communalism was not a late innovation, decided upon after immigration due to economic necessity. It had long been discussed among Rapp's Separatists in Germany as the declarations of faith and Rapp's pastoral letters indicate. Nevertheless, at the time of the founding of the Harmony Society, some, particularly more wealthy Separatists, balked at the concept of a common treasury. David Gloss and a number of other former Rappites purchased land in Columbiana County, Ohio and left the Harmony Society in 1805 and 1806, although they had originally joined the community. Dr. Haller, who had accompanied George Rapp to America in 1803, never joined the Harmony Society, but formed his own settlement, Blooming Grove, in Lycoming County, Pennsylvania.[37] The deep hurt that early Harmonists felt at the departure of fellow Separatists from their Society was clearly expressed in a poem by an unnamed Harmonist (circa 1805). From the perspective of this poet, "greed and covetousness" was the cause for former Separatists seeking to "buy land here, a house there" and "tear apart souls that had been bound together."[38] Clearly the communal ideal had not been adopted by all Rappites.

---

[35]Quoted in Arndt, *Rapp's Disciples*, 7. Cf. Aaron Williams, *The Harmony Society, at Economy, Penn'a*. (Pittsburgh: W. S. Haven, 1866), 48: "They came, however, most of them at least, with the intention of adopting the community system."

[36]Admittedly, Romelius Langenbacher (1793-1868) would have been a lad during most of these early events. However, he was a member of a convinced Rappite family, arrived in America in 1804 and would have been privy to any information he did not personally experience through his parents or older family members. He served on the Board of Elders during Rapp's lifetime. After the latter's death, he was appointed head trustee of the Harmony Society (1847-1868). Thus in his letters and writings, Langenbacher presented the Harmonist interpretation of its own history.

[37]Arndt, *Rapp's Harmony Society*, 68.

[38]"Was ist die Ursach dann, Von diesem auswärts laufen, Daß einer sich will da Andre dort was kaufen. Ein Land ein Haus und noch dergleichen Haabsuchts gutter, Und reißt aus Geiz entzwey Verbundenen Gemüther." Viehmeyer Collection, MG-

Finally, Harmonist sources unequivocally contend that community of goods was adopted in the United States for religious and not economic reasons. This testimony must be taken seriously. Langenbacher in his narrative history quoted above claimed that communalism was adopted in imitation of the primitive church, that is, from religious motivations. In a letter written by Frederick Rapp on March 7, 1822 he stated: "[O]ur Society is based entirely upon religious principles, and everything is arranged according to the model of the first church after Acts of the Apostles in the 2d and 4th chapters. No one possesses the least as his own."[39] The religious principles upon which the Harmony Society was formed extended to their communistic form of government.

Theological Rationale for Communalism

It has been sufficiently demonstrated that the communal system that the Harmony Society adopted was intended to emulate the community of goods practiced by the early church in Jerusalem and reported in Acts 2 and 4.[40] This fact was likewise reflected in the choice of the name "Harmony" for their society. Rapp in one pastoral letter quoted above linked harmony with love.[41] In a November 1822 letter, Romelius Langenbacher combined "true harmony" with unity.[42] The term itself then embodied the concept of love and unity that ideally should characterize the relationships between true children of God. Therefore, although the word "harmony" is not found in the Bible, the Rappites equated it with the "oneness of heart and mind" found in Acts 4:32.[43] The term "harmony" for the Rappites was a form of shorthand for the whole complex of attitudes and practices found in Acts 2

185, 1-5005, Box 16, Folder 1, #1. This historically valuable poem was found transcribed at the end of the Viehmeyer collection of pastoral letters. The date of the poem was given as Dec. 25, 1804. The date may be incorrect since David Gloss, who is mentioned by name, possibly may not have left the Harmony Society until spring or summer 1805, although definitely before August 15, 1805. (See footnote 18 above.) The poem was written by a devoted Harmonist, who was attempting to come to grips with the departure of David Gloss and others from the Harmony Society.

[39]Karl J. R. Arndt, *A Documentary History of the Indiana Decade of the Harmony Society, 1820-1824* (Indianapolis: Indiana Historical Society, 1978), 363. Cf. ibid., 465, 488-489, 512.

[40]The desire to reinstitute the practices of the primitive church was likewise reflected in their rejection of child baptism and swearing of oaths and in the celebration of the love feast (see chapter 2).

[41]Arndt, *Doc. Hist. 1700-1803*, 285.

[42]Arndt, *Doc. Hist. 1820-1824*, 488.

[43]Viktor Rauscher, "Des Separatisten G. Rapp Leben und Treiben," *Theologische Studien aus Württemberg* VI (1885), 295 first linked the name Harmony with Acts 4:32. Cf. Herman Ehmer, "Johann Georg Rapp (1757-1847)," in *Kirchengeschichte Württembergs in Porträts: Pietismus und Erweckungsbewegung* (Holzgerlingen: Hänssler Verlag, 2001), 229.

and 4—true brotherly love, unity of heart and mind, sharing of "heavenly goods," and the community of temporal goods.⁴⁴ The term was truly "programmatic" for the new communal society.⁴⁵

Rapp and the Harmonists were convinced of the spiritual benefits that unity of heart and mind and community of goods provided for their membership. The Harmonists used two synonymous terms to describe the complex of ideas (unity of heart and mind and sharing of temporal goods) found in Acts 2 and 4--the brotherly spirit (*Bruder Geist*) and the communal spirit (*Gemein* or *Gemeinschaftlicher Geist*). In a letter to his adopted son Frederick (August 15, 1824) George Rapp wrote that the communal fellowship of other "honest, beautiful souls" within the Harmony Society was essential, "because we cannot become what we should alone and by ourselves, rather of necessity only through others."⁴⁶ Two leading Harmonists expressed a similar conception. "That which God cannot accomplish inwardly, that the brotherly spirit does from the outside and does not allow us to become rotten or unfruitful. Rather there are always men there who can salt the others, so that no spiritual rottenness can occur."⁴⁷

Another Rapp letter stated that the communal spirit "replaces and restores all deficiencies; it gives and brings about perfection."⁴⁸ In fact, the Harmonists asserted that "without living in community, no true religion of Christ can exist." The conflicts and passions ignited by persons holding temporal goods privately warred against spiritual growth. The "*mein und*

---

⁴⁴The term "Harmony," which was later adopted by the Esslinger Separatists prior to immigration to the Caucasus in 1817, contained all these elements. In their written declaration (*Sendschreiben*) the Esslinger Separatists stated that they were "united in true love and in the fellowship of the Spirit to a 'harmony.'" They then quoted Acts 4:32f., followed by this statement. "Therefore we are compelled by the Holy Spirit, to unite in true love to a 'harmony' and to hold all things in common [community of goods]." Since this written declaration followed the formation of the Harmony Society, it is not unlikely that they were influenced by the Harmonists. Even if that were the case, it does not negate the fact that both groups of Württemberg Separatists used the term "harmony" in a similar fashion to connote the practices and attitudes of the Jerusalem church, which included a communalistic form of government. Leibbrandt, *Auswanderung*, 118-119.

⁴⁵Eberhard Fritz, "Johann Christoph Blumhardt und die Anhänger des Johann Georg Rapp in Iptingen." *Blätter für Württembergische Kirchengeschichte* 106 (2006): 27-37, here 32-33. Fritz notes that it was likewise programmatic for the Separatists who immigrated to the Caucasus in 1817 (see note 44 above).

⁴⁶Karl J. R. Arndt, *Harmony on the Wabash in Transition, 1824-1826. A Documentary History* (Worcester, Mass.: Harmony Society Press, 1982), 115.

⁴⁷"was Gott im Inwendigen nicht ausrichten kan, das thut der Bruder Geist von außen und lässet uns nicht faul noch unfruchtbar werden, sondern es sind immer Männer da, die die andre einsalzen können, daß keine geistige Faulheit statt finden kann." August 14, 1824. John Reichert and Romelius Langenbacher to Gottlieb Musse. Arndt, *Doc. Hist. 1824-1826*, 112-113.

⁴⁸Ibid., 206.

dein" (mine and yours) mentality was inimical to sanctification.[49] On the other hand, nothing could "be compared with the enjoyment of the brotherly spirit, for all else perishes, but the bond of friendship with the children of God remains and becomes more perfect than ever."[50] Joy and peace, the experience of the kingdom of God on earth were found in the unity of hearts, minds and temporal goods.

The practice of communalism was likewise praised by George Rapp in a number of later sermons. Not only was the abolition of private property the solution for Christianity in his day, but it would be the form of government in the millennial kingdom. Therefore, the Harmonists were encouraged to remain faithful to the communal lifestyle for there alone true happiness could be found. Rapp described communalism as the "active unity" of many persons into one whole.

> The solution of Christendom is no one for himself alone, [but] each for all. For unity and a union of the strength of many for the assistance of the whole, for the prosperity of all, this is the place of the innermost consciousness, and all outward needs declare it to us daily. For only a union of our strength delivers the proof that true happiness is nowhere else to be found except in active unity. He who desires to try it will find the testimony in his conscience, that particularly the imminent Kingdom of God, which will be erected on our earth, consists alone only in the blessed happiness of all, which is dependent upon the efforts of all. Even among those with the greatest differences of character, the most sublime unity nevertheless reaches its best purpose.[51]

Communal values were thus given a theological basis in a number of Rapp's sermons. In fact, when in 1838 the Harmony Society prepared a list of the seven main principles of their Society, community of goods (*Güttergemeinschaft*) was listed first.[52]

This discussion of communalism has demonstrated that community of goods was not a new idea, but long held by some, most likely leading members of Rapp's Separatist movement while still *in Germany*. It was not a late

---

[49]Ibid., 845-846.

[50]Ibid., 582-583.

[51]"Deß Christenthums Lorsung ist Niemand für sich allein, jeder für alle: Den Einh:[eit] u Vereinig: der Kräfte von mehrerin der beyhülfe eines ganzen, zum Wohlstand aller, diß ist der P:[unkt] deß jnnersten bewußtseyn, u alle äußere bedürfniße es uns Tägl: sagen; Denn nur verEinigung unserer kräften, liefern den beweiß, den das wahre glück wird sonst nirgens gefunden als in der Thätigen Einh: Wer es probieren will, wird er das Zeugniß in seinem Gewißen finden: den sonderl: das bevorstehende reich Gottes das auf unserer [Symbol =Erde] soll errichtet werden, besteht nur allein in der Glückseeligk: aller; darin das bestreben aller abhängt, auch bey der grösesten zerschiedenh: der Character, darin die erhabenste Einh: dennoch ihren besten Zweck erreicht." MG-185/1-5004/Box 15/Folder 6/R-144.

[52]Karl J. R. Arndt, *George Rapp's Years of Glory. Economy on the Ohio, 1834-1847. George Rapp's Third Harmony. A Documentary History* (New York: Peter Lang, 1987), 327.

innovation decided upon after emigration, and then "fanatically" pushed by Rapp, nor was it merely due to economic necessity. Rather communalism was adopted for religious reasons—to emulate the primitive church in Jerusalem, to further spiritual growth and because it would be the form of government in Christ's millennial kingdom. Another key tenet of the Harmony Society was likewise adopted by some Rappites prior to emigration—celibacy.

Revival of 1807-1808 and the Adoption of Celibacy

The practice of celibacy had a long tradition among radical Pietists. Prominent promoters such as Johann Georg Gichtel (Jakob Boehme's editor and interpreter), Gottfried Arnold and Hochmann von Hochenau assured that the legitimacy of sexual activity both within and without marriage was hotly discussed in Pietist circles in Württemberg.[53]

Practice of Celibacy in Württemberg

One such discussion on the issue of celibacy took place at a disputation that was held in Ludwigsburg in September of 1773. The well-known Württemberg pastor and churchly Pietist, Philipp Matthäus Hahn, represented the *contra* position. He reported in his journal (Sept. 29, 1773) that he opposed the view that "celibacy was a higher and more perfect thing than the conjugal union, [and] that only 144,000 persons were ordained to be like Christ in this state." He likewise rejected the following radical Pietist arguments:

> ... we are beasts when we participate in fleshly cohabitation, since such could not take place in the Spirit, but only in the flesh. The conjugal union is of course a means to increase the Kingdom of God and Jesus, although impure in and of itself. Therefore, Jesus word concerning eunuchs [Matt 19:12] has not been understood by many.[54]

This anecdote has been quoted since it succinctly portrays the objections to sexual activity that some Separatists upheld. It likewise indicates that the issue of celibacy was prominent enough in Württemberg at the end

---

[53] Andreas Gestrich, "Ehe, Familie, Kinder im Pietismus. Der 'gezählmte Teufel,'" in *Geschichte des Pietismus*, vol. 4, *Glaubenswelt und Lebenswelten*, ed. Hartmut Lehmann (Göttingen: Vandenhoeck & Ruprecht, 1995), 498-521. Cf. Wolfgang Breul, and Christian Soboth, eds. *"Der Herr wird seine Herrlichkeit an uns offenbahren." Liebe, Ehe und Sexualität im Pietismus* (Halle: Verlag der Franckeschen Stiftung, 2011); and Wolfgang Breul, " *Ehe und Sexualität im radikalen Pietismus.*" In *Der radikale Pietismus. Perspektiven der Forschung*. Wolfgang Breul, Marcus Meier and Lothar Vogel, eds. (Göttingen: Vandenhoeck & Ruprecht, 2010), 403-418.

[54] Brecht, *Kornwestheimer Tagebücher*, 193.

of the eighteenth century to be discussed at a disputation by Lutheran and Pietist pastors.

Celibacy, while practiced sporadically by Separatists at the beginning of the eighteenth century, did not become common among radical Pietists in the duchy until 1758. At that time, Christoph Unold, a tailor from Memmingen, propagated celibacy among the Separatists in Gochsen. Later in the 1770s and 1780s visitors to Ihinger Hof, a center of radical Pietist thought in Württemberg, debated the meaning of sexuality for "true children of God." Michael Hahn and Johann Georg Rapp visited on more than one occasion Ihinger Hof. Both radical Pietist leaders came to the conviction that the celibate state was superior to the married, most likely through discussions held at Ihinger Hof.[55] By the 1780s some young Separatists chose to refrain from marriage. Others who were already married abstained from sexual intercourse, usually with the agreement of their spouse.[56]

Most likely shortly after the birth of their second child in February 1786, Rapp and his wife Christina decided to live a life of sexual abstinence--the couple bore no more children. The majority of Rapp's married followers remained sexually active and continued to have babies while in Württemberg. Some, however, followed the example of their leader and pursued the higher goal of chastity. Presumably, in private conversations, if not in conventicle meetings, Rapp propagated while still in Württemberg the spiritual desirability of living a sexually ascetic life.[57] The supplement to the 1791 visitation report of the Dürrmenz Diocese supports this supposition. It reported "that the Separatists considered conjugal duty to be a mortal sin (*eine Todt Sünde*)."[58] That same year (July 2, 1791), a report of the Iptingen church consistory speculated that Johannes Hörnle, whose son Joseph had been forcibly baptized, was abstaining from sexual intercourse since no children had been conceived in his marriage for three years.[59] Thus years prior to the adoption of celibacy in 1807 by the Harmony Society, sexual

---

[55] Fritz, *Radikaler Pietismus*, 334f.

[56] In 1791 a Separatist shoemaker in Hemmingen, Jakob Velm, refused to have sexual relations with his wife, against her will. He was sentenced by the local courts to four weeks in prison. Velm established himself as a Separatist leader loosely affiliated with Rapp. Fritz, *Radikaler Pietismus*, 147.

[57] Fritz, *Radikaler Pietismus*, 129 and 334-336. Cf. Joachim Trautwein, *Die Theosophie Michael Hahns und ihre Quellen* (Stuttgart: Calwer Verlag, 1969), 220, n. 26.

[58] Arndt, *Doc. Hist. 1700-1803*, 188. This same thought (that sexual intercourse was defilement even within marriage) was expressed by several Separatists to Philipp Matthäus Hahn on September 21, 1789. Brecht, *Echterdinger Tagebücher*, 463-464.

[59] The consistory assumed Hörnle was abstaining from sexual intercourse because he didn't want to produce another child that might be baptized forcibly. Eberhard Fritz, "Johann Georg Rapp (1757-1847) und die Separatisten in Iptingen. Mit einer Edition der relevanten Iptinger Kirchenkonventsprotokolle," *Blätter für Württembergische Kirchengeschichte* 95 (1995): 129-203, here 170.

asceticism was a religious value upheld by Rapp and some committed members of his movement. It was likewise practiced by non-Rappite Separatists.

The Revival of 1807-1808 and the Adoption of Celibacy

Approximately two years after the establishment of the Harmony Society in 1805, the newly founded Society was rocked by what Harmonists later called a "fresh revival of religion." Several descriptions of this revival are extant, consisting of later reminiscences by participating Harmonists. A talk by George Rapp to young, new members of the Society on February 15, 1829 described this crucial juncture in the history of their community.[60] In written statements from December 16, 1859 and April 2, 1860, leading Harmonist Romelius Langenbacher remembered the life-changing nature of this event. In 1865 Aaron Williams interviewed surviving Harmonists who had experienced the renewal of religious fervor that gripped the commune. His history of the Society received the written approval of the current Harmonist trustees, and thus is a reliable reflection of their reminiscences.

Williams described the revival in 1807-1808 as similar to that which gave rise to the Separatist movement.[61] This statement provides an important clue as to the nature of the religious revival. New members to the Separatist movement in Württemberg were gained either directly through a conversion experience or indirectly through the proselytizing of already regenerate, churchly Pietists. In the Harmonist revival of 1807, it is likely that some, particularly children of members, experienced conversion for the first time. The descriptions, however, indicate that for most participants the revival involved not a salvation experience but rather a deepening of religious fervor. The use of the term "revival" in this section is dictated by the fact that Harmonists themselves used the term for the event, although admittedly it refers less to a conversionist movement, as to a deepening of religious enthusiasm. Romelius Langenbacher recalled that the political events and military battles taking place in Europe were viewed as signs of Christ's imminent return. The congregation was therefore moved to examine "whether one was suited to hold dear the appearance of the Lord."[62] The expectation of the imminent return of Christ to set up his millennial kingdom provided powerful motivation for a celibate lifestyle for the Harmonists. The revival progressed from a deeper understanding of Christ's

---

[60]This talk by Rapp was written down more or less verbatim by a listener. The original copy was found under the attic floor of the Economy store in the 1980s and translated into English. The author was not able to locate the German original, which had been misplaced.

[61]Williams, *Harmony Society*, 56-57.

[62]Letter from Romelius Langenbacher to Christina Barbara Benzenhöfer, Dec. 16, 1859. Quoted in Arndt, *Rapp's Disciples*, 12.

commands to a strong conviction of sin followed by a desire to live more fully a life of self-denial.

> It was realized that the true imitation of Christ demanded more than natural man suspected or believed. This realization led to a confession of sins, to regret and repentance, and to a more serious conviction to lead a pure life. This had a strong effect on young and old and convinced us that we should live a life of self-denial and discipline, as it is written: those who have women as if they have none.[63]

Aaron Williams described the event similarly: "Deep convictions of sin were experienced, and a general sense of worldliness and backsliding. They acknowledged to each other their consciousness of want of conformity to the spirit of primitive Christianity, which they aimed to restore among other things."[64]

Both Aaron Williams' account and George Rapp's own statement (quoted below) indicate that the decision to institute celibacy in the Harmony Society was not imposed from above, that is by George Rapp, but was rather an outgrowth of the religious enthusiasm engendered by the revival of 1807-1808. In a talk to the young men and women who had just signed the Articles of Association and became members of the Society at the Harmony Fest, 1829, George Rapp described how celibacy had come to be instituted among them. During the revival:

> The young people came to me and stated that they were worried about the propensities of the flesh and that the ultimate in perfect unions was one where such propensities were put aside. I could only agree but asked them if all were capable of attaining such a state. They assured me that they were and we discussed it at our meeting. At first not all members refrained from marriage but as the Society grows in understanding more and more do so, so that now there are only a few of us who give in to this evil.[65]

Aaron Williams stated that the Harmonists themselves "fixed upon the indulgences of the married state, as generally practiced, as not being consistent with that purity of heart and isolation from the world which they desired to cultivate." Only when they had already come to this realization did Rapp "encourage and strongly advocate the growing ascetic spirit" by preaching on relevant passages of Scripture (Matt 19:10-12 and 22: 30; 1 Cor 7:7, 8, and 25-27, 29; 1 Thess 4:3-5; Rev 14:4). Rapp then argued that celibacy was "applicable to all periods of the church," but especially neces-

---

[63]Arndt, *Rapp's Harmony Society*, 97.
[64]Williams, *Harmony Society*, 56.
[65]Talk by G. Rapp to the young signers of the Articles, Harmony Fest, 1829. This document was found translated in the files of former curator Daniel Reibel at Old Economy Village, Pa. Nordhoff in 1874 visited Economy and was assured by older members who had heard the revival described by their parents, that the determination to refrain from marriage originated among the young people, thus corroborating Rapp's 1829 statement. Charles Nordhoff, *The Communistic Societies of the United States* (New York: Hilary House, 1875), 72-73.

sary in this penultimate age before the imminent return of Christ. The spiritual leader therefore urged its adoption, although the decision was initiated from the membership (particularly the young people), discussed in a general meeting, and made by "mutual agreement."[66]

These statements by Rapp and Williams contradict a prevailing opinion that has persisted nearly as long as celibacy had within the Harmony Society, that is, that Rapp despotically imposed and enforced celibacy upon a largely unwilling congregation. This view, which was first espoused by early opponents of the Harmony Society, has been picked up by many contemporary scholars.[67] Harmonist sources, however, have always insisted that celibacy was adopted by mutual agreement, was voluntary and was pursued for religious and not economic reasons. Aaron Williams was assured directly by the Harmonists that:

> Whatever may be thought of the propriety or impropriety of this arrangement [celibacy], it was undoubtedly a purely voluntary sacrifice, which they were led to make, not from any pressure of authority on the part of Rapp (as has been alleged), nor from a desire the more speedily to enrich themselves by checking the further increase of population, but from strong religious conviction.[68]

In an 1819 letter to John S. Wiestling, Society business manager Frederick Rapp corrected the misconception that the "begetting of children or sexual intercourse of married people is forbidden in the *Harmonie* [Society]." This was "false and a lie and an erroneous statement which has been spread among the public for the last twelve to fifteen years," he wrote. Frederick went on to declare:

> The *Harmonie* Society consists only of people who live the religion of Jesus practically and who pursue sanctification. Among these there are some of both sexes who have so advanced in sanctification and who by means of the power of the gospel of Jesus Christ and His vicarious atonement have been so ennobled in their virtue, that they *of their own free will* have given up car-

---

[66] Williams, *Harmony Society*, 56-57.

[67] Early proponents of the view that celibacy was imposed by Rapp on the Harmony Society: Jonathan Wagner, *Geschichte u. Verhältnisse der Harmoniegesellschaft* (Vaihingen an der Enz: Deininger, 1833), 7-8; Hermann Markworth, "Die Rappischen Kolonien." *Beilage zur Sonntagsmorgen*. Cincinnati: Heinrich Haacke & Co, July 16, 1882; and Rauscher, "Separatisten G. Rapp," 295. Later proponents include: Hermann Schempp, *Gemeinschaftssiedlungen auf religiöser und weltanschaulicher Grundlage* (Tübingen: Mohr, 1969), 44 (celibacy not religiously motivated); and Fritz, *Radikaler Pietismus*, 336-337 (celibacy imposed by Rapp). The following scholars note the religious and voluntary nature of the practice of celibacy: Ehmer, "Johann Georg Rapp," 232; and Arndt, *Rapp's Harmony Society*, 97f. and idem, "Rapp's Harmony Society," 65f.

[68] Williams, *Harmony Society*, 30. Traugott Bromme's description of the Harmonists (1839) wrongly stated that celibacy was instituted for economic reasons – the prevention of pregnancies would enable both men and women to put in a full work day. Arndt, *Doc. Hist. 1834-1847*, 433.

nal intercourse and devote themselves fully to prepare for Christ and His Kingdom.[69]

In that same letter Frederick Rapp provided evidence that celibacy was not adopted by all married folk after the 1807 revival. He wrote that in 1819 there were between eighty and one hundred pupils in the Harmonist school aged six to twelve years old, all being children born after the official adoption of celibacy.[70] Karl Arndt's research indicates that at the first Harmonist settlement at Harmony, Pennsylvania (1805-1814) 262 children were born, at New Harmony, Indiana (1814-1824) sixty-nine and at their third settlement, Economy, Pennsylvania only twenty-five children were born between 1825 and 1830.[71] These figures indicate that the adoption of celibacy was truly voluntary. Not all chose to follow the higher path of sexual abstinence. George Rapp was the first to agree that not all had been given the gift of celibacy. The figures likewise indicate that gradually over time more and more Harmonists either adopted celibacy or left the Society due to disagreement over this or other issues. The burden of celibacy was lessened for married couples and families by the fact that families continued to live together in the same house, albeit the men on the upper floor and the women on the ground floor. It should be noted that while the adoption of celibacy was voluntary for married Harmonist members, unspoken (or spoken?) social and religious pressure was brought to bear upon those who indulged their "fleshy lusts." It was hard to buck the religious norms and live comfortably in the Harmony Society while regularly producing the evidence of one's "lust," babies.[72] Yet some married couples continued to do just that, as the figures above indicate.

Even more pressure was brought to bear upon single persons who desired to marry. Prior to the adoption of celibacy, between January 27, 1805 and January 25, 1807, George Rapp performed ten weddings between Harmonist young people. In the midst of the revival and probably after the adoption of celibacy (November 15, 1807) Rapp married his own son, Johannes, to fellow Harmonist Johanna Diem.[73] On August 31, 1808, the couple gave birth to Rapp's beloved granddaughter, Gertrude. Only seven more weddings are listed on the *Verzeichniss der Copulationen*, number twelve being ten years later in September 1817 and the remaining six undated.[74] Harmonist young people who desired to marry after 1807 usually left the Society. Two Harmonist young adults, Conrad Feucht and Hildegard

---

[69] Karl J. R. Arndt, *A Documentary History of the Indiana Decade of the Harmony Society, 1814-1819* (Indianapolis: Indiana Historical Society, 1975), 775.

[70] Ibid.

[71] Arndt, *Rapp's Harmony Society*, 418.

[72] Ibid., 358. Celibacy was never a requirement explicitly stated in the constitution or bylaws of the Harmony Society.

[73] 1807 is given as the year in which celibacy was introduced into the Harmony Society.

[74] Arndt, *Doc. Hist. 1803-1815*, 270-272.

Mutschler, ran away and thus withdrew from the Harmony Society to marry on June 29, 1829. They were readmitted into the Society as a married couple by 1832, and proceeded to enlarge their family by two more sons, born in 1834 and 1837.[75] However this was an exceptional case. Hildegard had served as Rapp's laboratory assistant and was personally close to the patriarchal leader. Feucht became the Society's doctor after his return. In contrast, most young people who ran away and married were not readmitted into the Society.

The revival of 1807-1808 was one of only two seasons of exceptional religious fervor within the Harmony Society that were bequeathed the title "revival" by the Harmonists themselves.[76] This revival of religion took place at the same time or shortly after revivals inaugurating the so-called Second Great Awakening swept through both the English and German speaking populations of Pennsylvania. At the end of the Revolutionary War (1781-1783) the first of several revivals among the Presbyterian Scots-Irish population in nearby Washington County, Pennsylvania broke out under the auspices of John McMillan, Thaddeus Dod and Joseph Smith (not of Mormon fame). Within several years after the great camp meeting revival at Cane Ridge, Kentucky in 1800, the religious excitement had spread along the Ohio River to western Pennsylvania. In 1802 and 1803 camp meetings were held and the excitement continued unabated until 1805, the year the Harmony Society was founded. Thomas Campbell (1763-1854) settled after his arrival from Ireland in 1807 likewise in Washington County, where camp-meeting revivals of the Stone-Campbell movement led to the formation of Christian Association of Washington County in 1809. Shakers were actively evangelizing nearby in southern Ohio in 1805.[77]

Nor was the German population in Pennsylvania immune to the new wave of revivalism. Jacob Albright (1759-1808) adopted the revivalist techniques of the Methodists and evangelized among Lutheran, Reformed and Anabaptist Germans of the mid-Atlantic area starting in 1796. His converts formed what came to be called the Evangelical Association, to which Albright was elected bishop in 1807.[78] Philip William Otterbein (1726-1813), a German Reformed minister in Baltimore, likewise evangelized among the mid-Atlantic German population. Although Otterbein remained a pastor in

---

[75]Arndt, *Rapp's Disciples*, 86-87.

[76]The second revival took place in 1844-1845, and was awakened by Rapp's preaching on the necessity of the Harmony Society to immigrate to Palestine to meet Christ at his Second Coming. Arndt, *Doc. Hist. 1834-1847*, 1073.

[77]Catherine C. Cleveland, *The Great Revival in the West 1797-1805* (Gloucester, Mass.: Peter Smith, 1959), 81-86; Iain H. Murray, *Revival and Revivalism. The Making and Marring of American Evangelicalism 1750-1858* (Edinburgh: Banner of Truth, 1994), 46-56; Winthrop S. Hudson, *Religion in America*, 2d ed. (New York: Scribner's Sons, 1973), 125-126.

[78]Terry M. Heisey, ed. *Evangelical from the Beginning. A History of the Evangelical Congregational Church and its Predecessors – The Evangelical Association and the United Evangelical Church* (Lexington, Ky.: Emeth Press, 2006), 27-32.

good standing within the German Reformed Church, he, along with Mennonite Martin Boehm, founded the United Brethren in Christ in 1800. This was originally a loosely-organized, and unitive revivalist movement, which, along with the Evangelical Association, reaped considerable evangelistic fruit among the so-called "bush meeting Deutsch," or adherents of German revivalist groups.[79]

It is unknown whether and to what extent the revival fever in the surrounding environs precipitated the Harmonist revival of 1807. It is known that Rapp upon arrival in America visited and was assisted by Philipp William Otterbein. The congregation of the latter assisted the Harmonists, who arrived on the ship *Aurora* in the harbor of Baltimore on July 4, 1804. A second group of Harmonists, who arrived in Philadelphia in July and September 1804, were permitted to camp on land north of Philadelphia (Busch Hill) surrounded by German settlers of the United Brethren persuasion. Rapp likewise preached to German gatherings and congregations in Ohio and Pennsylvania prior to the formation of the Harmony Society.[80] It is therefore likely that both Rapp and his followers became aware of the winds of revivalism sweeping through Pennsylvania in the first years of the nineteenth century. Unfortunately the primary source documents are silent on the question of whether Rapp, recognizing the need for a fresh movement of the Spirit in his congregation, borrowed and applied revivalist techniques within the Harmony Society in 1807.

Theological Rationale for Celibacy

It has already been noted that the Harmonists adopted celibacy for religious and not economic reasons. In this section the religious and theological reasons that Rapp and the Harmonists employed to support the practice of celibacy will be examined. Regrettably the sermons that Rapp preached in the 1807 revival in favor of sexual abstinence were not preserved. However, a number of later sermons (1830s-1840s) and several hymns (ca. 1820) pertain to the topic directly and give valuable insight into their theological rationale for the practice of celibacy. These sources allow us to examine the degree of dependency of the Harmonist view of celibacy on the the teachings of theosophist Jacob Boehme.

Boehme's view of marriage and sexuality included paradoxical elements. He did not reject marriage per se; he himself married and fathered four

---

[79]Stephen L. Longenecker, *Piety and Tolerance. Pennsylvania German Religion, 1700-1850* (Metuchen, N.J.: Scarecrow Press, 1994), 105-140; and J. Steven O'Malley, *John Seybert and the Evangelical Heritage* (Lexington, Ky.: Emeth Press, 2008), 71 and 75f..

[80]Arndt, *Doc. Hist. 1803-1815*, 4-6 and idem, *Rapp's Harmony Society*, 69. Cf. George Rapp's talk to young signers of the Articles of Association, 1829: "We had no money and were in a hurry to bring the rest over so I [Rapp] preached sermons to the German churches around Lancaster for money while we looked."

sons. Nevertheless, in his opinion the ideal marriage was one in which God-fearing partners, on the one hand, propagated children without giving in to "devilish-animalistic desires," and, on the other hand, pursued the goal of complete sexual abstinence.[81] Boehme's critique of marriage was later appropriated and propagated by Gichtel, Gottfried Arnold and Hochmann von Hochenau.[82] Gichtel, in particular, radicalized Boehme's views, claiming that any form of marriage and sexuality reflected faithlessness to the virgin Sophia (or Wisdom).[83]

Scholars have long underscored the influence of Boehme's conception of the androgynous nature and the dual fall of Adam on the adoption by radical Pietists of a celibate lifestyle. Fritz Tanner in his monograph *Die Ehe im Pietismus* (1952) and Andreas Gestrich in an article in the fourth volume of *Geschichte des Pietismus* (2004) both point to the reception of a Boehmist conception of creation and the fall as the most significant factor influencing radical Pietists' negative evaluation of marriage and sexuality.[84] Karl Arndt argued that both Boehmist conceptions *and* the interpretation of Rev 14:4 in the Berleburg Bible were the theological rationale undergirding the practice of celibacy in the Harmony Society. Eberhard Fritz reflected Arndt's views, although he shifted the focus primarily upon Boehmist influence.[85] Primary sources reveal that Rapp and the Harmonists employed at times Boehme's cosmogony and anthropology in support of celibacy. Nevertheless, their preferred rationale involved sanctification (growth in purity and love for Christ) and eschatology (being worthy to participate in Christ's millennial kingdom) rather than cosmogony.

On November 11, 1838 Rapp preached a sermon on Revelation 14 in which he argued that celibacy "must also take place here [on earth] and not first in heaven." Committed Christians such as the Harmonists should "completely reintroduce the first fruits of Paradise and the dignity which Adam lost."[86] Rapp was referring to Adam's state before the first of two falls, in which: "Through his will . . . he lost his inward holiness and was

---

[81]Aira Vosa, "Die Ehe bei Jakob Böhme und Johann Georg Gichtel," in *"Der Herr wird seine Herrlichkeit an uns offenbahren." Liebe, Ehe und Sexualität im Pietismus*, eds. Wolfgang Breul and Christian Soboth (Halle: Verlag der Franckeschen Stiftung, 2011), 81-88, here 83-84.

[82]Wolfgang Breul, *"Ehe und Sexualität im radikalen Pietismus,"* in *Der radikale Pietismus. Perspectiven der Forschung*, eds. Wolfgang Breul, Marcus Meier and Lothar Vogel (Göttingen: Vandenhoeck & Ruprecht, 2010), 403-418.

[83]Vosa, "Die Ehe bei Jakob Böhme," 87.

[84]Fritz Tanner, *Die Ehe im Pietismus* (Zurich: Zwingli Verlag, 1952), 7-89; Gestrich, "Ehe, Familie," 498-504.

[85]Fritz, *Radikaler Pietismus*, 334-335; and Arndt, *Rapp's Harmony Society*, 95-98 and 416-419.

[86]1838 sermon book. November 11, 1838. MG-185/Box 1-4997/Box # 8/ Folder 20.

overcome by the lust-spirit of the world. . . . Then the lust arose to reproduce himself in a bestial manner (*nach Thierischer Art fortzupflanzen*)."[87]

The androgynous and virginal state of Adam prior to the awakening of his lust to copulate like the beasts of the field (his first fall), was the state that the Harmonists were called to emulate. When Adam fell, his female element, the chaste virgin Sophia, could no longer tolerate the defilement and fled from him. By avoiding the pollution of sexual intercourse, the celibate Harmonist was in the position to experience the mystical union with Sophia/Christ, and become in a spiritual sense androgynous (again).[88] Thus when practiced in this life, celibacy enabled a partial, spiritual renewal of the paradisiacal, Edenic state that God had intended for the human race. These arguments for celibacy clearly reflect Boehmist influence. But they account for only a portion of Rapp's rationale for sexual asceticism.

Rapp likewise argued that sexual abstinence greatly promoted growth in sanctification. The Christian life involved imitating the life of Christ. Jesus did not marry while on this earth, rather he practiced self-denial against sensuality, and so should the Harmonists.[89] In a sermon on 1 Corinthians 7, George Rapp applied to his congregation Paul's admonition that those who have wives should live as if they had none (1 Cor 7:29). The Harmonist leader argued that it should be as if their marriage partners were dead and gone. All self-will and fleshly desires must be submitted to God. Only by living celibately would they be freed to concern themselves exclusively with the "things of the kingdom of God." By seeking to "please the Lord," one was enabled to "forget the lower things" of the flesh. As a result:

> [T]he love for their Bridegroom grows, because except for Him they have nothing else. Such pure souls are untroubled in all circumstances. . . . They seek with ardent desire the pure love of the Lord, who is the Spirit. This yearning desire draws their disposition away from all other things. This is what it means to live in light, in the presence (*Auge*) of the Lord.[90]

Denying one's baser desires and being sexually chaste served the higher purpose of growing in sanctification and experiencing more deeply the love of God. Therefore, a hymn written by the Rossdann conventicle or company as they were called in the Harmony Society (single women aged twenty-eight to thirty-four years), called upon the sisters and the rest of the community to "never waste your power of youth in despicable lusts," but with the "courage of a hero and a Christian to subdue passion." They would re-

---

[87]MG-185, Box 1-5004, Box 15, Folder 6, Q-39. A fuller discussion of the Boehmist influence on the Harmonists will be found in chapter eight.

[88]MG-185, Box 1-5004, Box 15, Folder 6, P-208.

[89]1838 sermon book. November 11, 1838. MG-185/Box 1-4997/Box # 8/ Folder 20.

[90]MG-185, Box 1-5004, Box 15, Folder 6, P-198.

ceive their due reward in the *eschaton* – their name written in the Book of Life and the victor's crown.[91]

The Harmonists believed that they were living at the brink of the end time. With Christ's Second Advent soon approaching, now more than ever it was important to be watchful and actively prepare oneself for the millennium. Through denying oneself sexually, chaste persons became "worthy for their imminent marriage" with Christ at the wedding feast of the Lamb.[92] The Harmonists believed that now in the present, before the inbreaking of the *eschaton* it was necessary to put into practice the Biblical pattern for the millennial age.

A hymn written by the Epplin company (married and widowed women aged late forties to mid-sixties) reminded the community of the Bible word that in the millennium people would be as the angels of God and neither marry or be given in marriage (Matt 22:30). Therefore, celibacy should also be put into practice in the present. This state was clearly better than the married state, the sisters argued. "There is love, purer friendship without the burden of earth, effective action with happier concord, harmony, everywhere truth, everywhere goodness and beauty, more than all this earth can give."[93] It is noteworthy that average Harmonists and not just Rapp were writing hymns supporting the practice of celibacy. Furthermore, the Harmonists in their sexual abstinence sought to be numbered among the 144,000, who would "stand with the Lamb on Mount Zion," because they had "not defiled themselves with women" (Rev 14:4).[94]

The Harmonists were being prepared in the present age to be a kingdom of priests in the millennial kingdom. Rapp explained in a sermon that within the priesthood formed of all those who had experienced the new birth, there were different levels of rank based on the "measure of the gift of Christ's grace." In the Old Testament, priests were required to have the highest level of purity among the people. "The necessary perfection of the body [in the Old Testament priesthood] was an image of holiness and an example to the church of Christ, which ought not to escape us."[95] Rapp went on to say that the Harmony congregation reflected this holiness and had made it their foundation stone. Their practice of celibacy had advanced them to the highest level of priesthood for the millennial kingdom. Not surprisingly, celibacy

---

[91]*Eine kleine Sammlung* # 30: "Nie verschwinde deine Jugendkraft in schnöden Lüsten! Mit dem Muth des Helden und des Christen, bandage die Leidenschaft.... Im Lebensbuch flammt ihr Nam, Kronen schimmern ihnen."

[92]MG-185, Box 1-5004, Box 15, Folder 6, P-198.

[93]*Eine kleine Sammlung* # 50: "In jener Welt sagt die Schrifft, wird manweder freien, noch sich freien lassen: sondern die menschen warden seyn, wie die Engel Gottes. Da ist Liebe, reinere Freundschafft; ohne die Bürden der Erde; würcksame Thätigkeit mit Glücklicher Eintracht; harmonisch, überall wahrheit, überall Güte und Schönheit, mehr all diese Erde geben kann."

[94]Williams, *Harmony Society*, 57.

[95] MG-437, Box 22, Folder 82B, A-22. See Arndt, *Doc. Hist. 1834-1847*, 443-445.

was one of the Society's seven most important principles according to an 1838 formulation.⁹⁶

Another Rapp sermon reminded his hearers that they were the congregation of the Sunwoman of Revelation 12. Just as Christ in his first birth was born from the *virgin* Mary, so in Christ's second birth as the male son of the Sunwoman, the church of the end times, he was born from a perpetual virgin. The virginal character of the eschatological church or the Sunwoman of Revelation 12 enabled it to endue believers with the power of chastity and celibacy.

> Therefore, the church, even after the birth of the male son [of the Sunwoman] had already been accomplished, continued to remain a virgin. Just as Christ alone was born from a virgin church (*Gemeine*), so it was also truly appropriate that the church, as a mother from whom [the male son] was born, also remained a virgin and was thus equipped with the spirit of the purest and all-powerful love... This pure virgin spirit within us endures all attacks of demands, and is not captivated by evil assaults, rather love devours them itself.⁹⁷

Rapp thus utilized the self-conception of the Harmony Society as the Sunwoman in the Wilderness in his theological rationale for celibacy. The Harmony congregation as the eschatological church was being purified by the Holy Spirit to become "modestly chaste" (*züchtig keusch*) and "without blame" (*ohne Tadel*).⁹⁸ These examples from Rapp sermons and Harmonist hymns demonstrate that the Harmonist rationale for the practice of celibacy went beyond Boehmist cosmogony to include growth in sanctification and preparation for the *eschaton*.

The Church in the Wilderness

The brick meeting-house erected at Harmony, measuring seventy feet by fifty-five feet, was the first Harmonist church built for the communal worship of their God.⁹⁹ Harmonist church architecture reflected the "typically dissenting" style employed by Puritans, Quakers, Moravians and German sectarians in the eighteenth century rather than an "established church" style. Dissenting structures were markedly different from established churches.

---

⁹⁶Arndt, *Doc. Hist. 1834-1847*, 327.

⁹⁷"Deßweg blieb sie die Gem: auch nach der geburt als der Männl:[iche] Sohn schon geb: war, jmmer noch Jungfrau blieb. Gleichwie also Christus allein aus ein Jungfernelichen gem: geboren wurde, so war es auch wirckl: schickl: da die gem: als Mutter aus der geb: auch Jungf: blieb u so ausgerüstet mit dem g: der allerreinsten u allmächtigen Liebe. . .dieser reine Jungf[rau]l: G: hält in uns alle anfälle der anfoderung:[en] aus, u läßt sich von bösen angreifen nicht hinreisen sondern die Liebe verschlingt sie selbst." OEV, MG-185, 1-5004, Box 15, Folder 6, P-278.

⁹⁸OEV, MG-185, 1-5004, Box 15, Folder 6, P-278.

⁹⁹Arndt, *Doc. Hist. 1803-1815*, 454.

They were rectangular rather than cruciform and were designed as essentially auditory structures, designed for the preaching and hearing of the sermon and the prayers. They avoided all the Renaissance motifs in carving that often characterized Georgian established churches. Any ornamentation was thought to be contrary to the simplicity and spirituality of evangelical worship. . . . The exteriors of the meetinghouses were just as devoid of ornamentation as the interiors; they looked like modest country houses built of good brick.[100]

The "dissenting church" commitment to upholding the first commandment resulted in a style that avoided the use of symbols in stained glass and in wood and stone carvings.[101] The Harmonists built four churches at their three successive settlements that followed the dissenting pattern of architecture–simple brick or frame buildings with plain glass windows and little ornamentation.[102] A German visitor, Ferdinand Ernst, visited New Harmony in 1819 and remarked on the lack of altar and decoration in the church.[103] In all of the Harmonist churches the men were seated on one side of the room on benches and the women on the other. At Economy, the women even entered the church through a different door than the men. On a raised platform on the inner side wall, Rapp preached to his congregation, while seated behind a table, rather than at a pulpit.[104]

---

[100]R. Kevin Seastoltz, *A Sense of the Sacred: Theological Foundations of Sacred Architecture and Art* (New York: Continuum, 2005), 186.

[101]Ibid., 187.

[102]The first church at New Harmony (1816) had a rectangular frame structure. The Harmony church, the second New Harmony as well as the Economy church were of brick. In 1822, shortly before the Harmonists sold New Harmony to Robert Owen and formed their third settlement at Economy, Penn., the Society began to erect a second larger and more elaborate church that embodied one "established church" element--a cruciform shape. After their move to Economy in 1824, however, they returned to a simple rectangular church structure. Cf. Pitzer, *New Harmony's First Utopians*, 274 and 280f. Michael J. Lewis correctly indicates that Harmonist architecture most closely reflected the dissenting tradition of the Moravian Brethren rather than that of the Amish, Seventh Day Brethren or other German sectarian groups. This influence is most strongly seen in the Economy Feast Hall and in the communal dormitories (*Bruderhäuser*) at New Harmony. Michael J. Lewis, "Harmonist Architecture: Its Sources and Meaning." Paper presented at the Fifteenth Annual Historic Communal Studies Conference, Winston-Salem, North Carolina, Oct. 6-9, 1988, 62-66. The Harmonists had contact with the Moravians most likely in Germany and with certitude in Pennsylvania. The dissenting Moravian style of architecture was likewise adopted by the founders of Korntal for their church (*Betsaal*), built in 1819.

[103]Report of Ferdinand Ernst, German visitor to New Harmony, 1819: "In the church I found neither an altar nor other decorations. On an elevation of about 3 feet there was a seat for Rapp, beside this a desk, on which lay a Bible. Each Sunday he speaks here to the people..." Arndt, *Doc. Hist. 1814-1819*, 746.

[104]Ibid.

Worship

The Lord's Day was kept holy by members of the Harmony Society. Not only was unnecessary work avoided, but the community met for worship both on Sunday morning and in the late afternoon, each service lasting an hour to an hour and a half.[105] In 1809 Robert Stubbs reported that the Harmonists were called to attend worship by the ringing of the bell in the church cupola.[106] William Owen, son of Robert Owen, noted during his visit in 1824 that "a psalm tune played on a keyed bugle and a French horn," which had a "fine effect," summoned the community to worship.[107]

Romelius Langenbacher in a letter to the Royal District office in Schorndorf, Württemberg on November 1, 1822 declared that, "it is our congregation's purpose and main concern to arrange our divine service exactly according to the directions which the word of God commands."[108] The order and nature of Harmonist worship was described by a number of visitors to the communal settlement. Like the church building itself, Harmonist worship services were, with the exception of holiday services, plain and simple, more reflective of dissenting than established church practice. The services included the basic elements of singing, prayer and a sermon. Unlike some dissenting groups, however, the Harmonists regularly used instrumental music both in their worship services and for impromptu music-making and planned concerts. This was a reflection of their Lutheran heritage. At the time of John Melish's visit in 1811 the Harmony Society already had a small orchestra consisting of three violins, a bass, a clarinet, a flute and two French horns, which was utilized for their religious services.[109] In the next decades the orchestra would continue to grow in size and sophistication. The community sang from hymnbooks to instrumental accompaniment either congregationally "with one accord," or antiphonally. The separate seating of men and women on opposite sides of the room was conducive to effective antiphonal singing. Melish exclaimed that during worship, "so simply, yet so sweetly, did they sing."[110]

Like other Pietists, Rapp and the Harmonists prayed extemporaneously in their worship services, following the leading of the Spirit, rather than using written prayers.[111] This aversion to pre-formulated prayers led Har-

---

[105] Arndt, *Doc. Hist. 1803-1815*, 461.
[106] Ibid., 358.
[107] Arndt, *Doc. Hist. 1824-1826*, 320.
[108] Arndt, *Doc. Hist. 1820-1824*, 492.
[109] Richard D. Wetzel, *Frontier Musicians on the Connoquenessing, Wabash, and Ohio: A History of the Music and Musicians of George Rapp's Harmony Society, 1805-1906* (Athens, Ohio: Ohio University Press, 1976), 19-20.
[110] Arndt, *Doc. Hist. 1803-1815*, 457.
[111] Spener's and Francke's aversion to pre-formulated prayers was picked up by most members of the Pietist movement. Johannes Wallmann, "Frömmigkeit und Gebet," in *Geschichte des Pietismus*, vol. 4, *Glaubenswelt und Lebenswelten*, ed. Hartmut Lehmann (Göttingen: Vandenhoeck & Ruprecht, 1995): 80-101, here 89-94.

monists to cut out carefully the collection of prayers from their volumes of the *Württembergisches Gesangbuch*.[112] One visitor noted that the community knelt down on the floor to pray. Another remarked that, "[i]n praying the Harmonists do not rise up nor kneel down, but bend their bodies forward, almost to their knees."[113] Although Rapp prepared his sermons (1680 sermon notes from Rapp are extant), he preached freely and "with great animation." William Owen noted in his journal that Rapp "spoke in an easy, familiar manner, apparently without preparation and with great fluency.... On the whole as a sermon it was good and practical, with comparatively little fanaticisms about it."[114] When Rapp was absent or indisposed, either Frederick Rapp preached or the community met to discuss a religious subject.

The Sunday evening and Wednesday evening services contained the same elements as the morning worship, with one important exception. After (and perhaps during) Rapp's teaching on Wednesday evening, a time of discussion followed in which members who felt led by the Spirit contributed to the conversation about the biblical passage. For example, concerning the religious service on Wednesday April 16, 1823 Rapp reported: "At night there was a meeting and *we spoke* about the text Jeremiah chapter 31."[115] This format was a reflection of the large group conventicle meetings (*Erbauungsstunde* or *Stunde*) with more formalized teaching followed by discussion, which Rapp taught and led in Württemberg. The Wednesday night meetings in the Harmony Society not only had the same title, *Stunden* or edification meetings, as those the Rappites had experienced in Württemberg, but the same format as well.[116] Despite the element of discussion which Rapp emphasized above, a formalized Bible teaching by the Harmonist leader was central to the Wednesday night meeting, as evidenced by an entire year's worth of Wednesday "sermons" found in the 1838 sermon book.[117]

Another type of religious service was reported by a visitor to the Harmony Society. John Melish described a children's meeting held in August 1811 prior to the twelve o'clock worship service.[118] Members of the Society

---

[112] Wetzel, *Frontier Musicians*, 38.

[113] Arndt, *Doc. Hist. 1814-1819*, 515, and idem. *Doc. Hist. 1803-1815*, 457.

[114] Arndt, *Doc. Hist. 1824-1826*, 320.

[115] Arndt, *Doc. Hist. 1820-1824*, 566.

[116] Cf. Letter of Jacob Henrici to R. L. Baker, Nov. 18, 1844, which makes a distinction between *Stunden* and companies. Arndt, *Doc. Hist. 1834-1847*, 797. Cf. Love Feast Records, MG-185, p. 4: "1852 Aug[ust] 4 [=Wednesday] keine Stunde noch Comp:[anie] diese Woche."

[117] The 1838 Sermon Book is the only extant collection of Rapp sermons for an entire year. It contains 170 messages preached by Rapp from Christmas, 1837 to Dec. 31, 1838. MG-185/Box 1-4997/Box # 8/ Folder 20.

[118] The times given by visitors for the Sunday worship services vary. John Melish, who visited the Harmony Society in August 1811, stated that morning worship was at twelve noon. William Owen reported that in December 1824 worship was at

met with the children in the schoolroom for approximately two hours starting at nine o'clock AM. There the youngsters were "examined," presumably for their knowledge of Christian doctrine. They likewise had the opportunity "to exhibit different specimens of their performances." Melish did not further define what he meant by the "different specimens of performances." It presumably referred to singing, the recitation of poems and musical performances by the children.[119] If so, Melish's report described a sort of "Sunday school program" held for the whole community. It is unknown whether the children regularly received Christian instruction on Sundays in addition to the worship services, or whether such was adequately covered in the daily school curriculum.[120]

Companies

Conventicles were a significant, even defining aspect of the Pietist landscape in Württemberg ever since Spener's visit to the duchy in the 1680s. Rapp and members of the Separatist movement had met prior to emigration in fellowship groups or conventicles in which the Bible and other devotional literature were studied (see chapter two). It is therefore not surprising that by 1820 at the latest, Rapp divided his community into approximately fifty small group conventicles or companies as they were called in the Harmony Society.[121] The companies within the Harmony Society were not formed to expedite the Society's economic pursuits (Arndt), nor were they for the purpose of "prose and poetry competition" (Pitzer).[122] Rather, the

---

eleven o'clock. This discrepancy could be because the Harmonists arose earlier in the winter to take advantage of natural light. They could have also temporarily or permanently changed the worship time between 1811 and 1824. Arndt, *Doc. Hist. 1824-1826*, 320 and idem, *Doc. Hist. 1803-1815*, 461.

[119]Ibid.

[120]Harmonist school curriculum largely followed the pattern found in the Württemberg school system, where religious instruction occupied a central role. Donald E. Pitzer, "Progressive Education in Harmonist New Harmony: 1814-1824," *Contemporary Education* 58, no. 2 (Winter 1987): 67-74, here 70. Pitzer's claim that Harmonist education was based on J. V. Andreae's *Christianopolis* is unfounded. There is no proof that Rapp or the Harmonists were aware of this work.

[121]The first conclusive mention of the companies is found during the New Harmony era (1814-1824). In a letter from Oct. 5, 1820 and again on Nov. 21, Johannes Langenbacher sent greetings to "his company." Arndt, *Doc. Hist. 1820-1824*, 113. It is, however, probable that the companies were instituted long before 1820, possibly shortly after the revival of 1807. See Alice T. Ott, "Community in 'Companies': The Conventicles of George Rapp's Harmony Society compared to those in Württemberg Pietism and the Brüderunität," in *Pietism and Community in Europe and North America, 1650-1850*, ed. Jonathan Strom (Leiden: Brill, 2010), 249-277 for a thorough discussion of Harmonist companies.

[122]". . . [F]or the efficient management of the Society had divided the members into working units of companies." Arndt, *Rapp's Harmony Society*, 199. "While at New Harmony, Rapp divided the entire congregation into five categories according

companies were small groups established for spiritual edification and fellowship. They were a continuation on American soil of the conventicles that the disciples of Rapp had known and loved while still in Württemberg.

Members of the companies met together once or twice a week primarily to effect spiritual advancement and growth in sanctification. This chief purpose and goal was achieved in a number of ways within the Harmonist companies: through Bible exposition and teaching, group discussion, exhortation of one another, mnemonic aids, and the communal singing and writing of hymns. George Rapp himself met with the individual companies "as often as possible, for religious conference or freer social conversation."[123] Male company leaders (and presumably female ones as well) provided a Bible discussion when Rapp was not present. Notes from one such Bible discussion, from the *"Privatversammlung"* [company] led by "S" [unknown leader] in 1832, are extant. Psalm 121:4-8, Jer 31:33 and 2 Tim 4:6 formed the basis for the teaching and ensuing discussion.[124] Discussion by the members present was a key element of the company meetings. Rapp on more than one occasion mentioned the "discussions within the companies."[125] The conversation focused not only on the biblical text, but on its application for the individual life. Within the intimate circle of the company, members "watch[ed] fraternally over each other's conduct," as Williams expressed it.[126] They exhorted each other and received correction in turn.

A discussion or repetition of a sermon was another method employed in the company meetings. This was a method that even Rapp used on occasion when he visited a company. On Nov. 17, 1844 he expressed his frustration with the company members for not being able to repeat the sermon they had heard just that morning. "Even when you today understood my sermon and were inspired by it in your spiritual part, yet it has also been lost again, just like it was in the old days, for you can't bind it, because you have so little born again salt, for otherwise you could also *repeat it in the company.*"[127]

One unique method that the Harmonist companies used to solve the problem of "spiritual forgetfulness" was to summarize the company teaching in one pithy sentence or proverb. These summary statements were written and collected and served in effect as both a pedagogical tool and a mnemonic aid to assist the Harmonist in retaining spiritual truths and insights. In an introduction to the notes from "S's" company teaching, reference to this practice is made:

---

to age and sex for the *purpose of prose and poetry competition* [my emphasis]." Pitzer, *New Harmony's First Utopians*, 243.

[123] Williams, *Harmony Society*, 41-42.

[124] University of Southern Indiana Archives, MSS# 311, Box 46, Folder 14.

[125] MG-185/1-5004/Box 15/Folder 6/P-62 and MG-437/Box 22/ Folder 83. Nov. 17, 1844.

[126] Williams, *Harmony Society*, 41-42.

[127] MG-437/Box 22/ Folder 83. Nov. 17, 1844.

On the 2...th of March, 1832 in the *Privatversammlung* [company] of S, Christianity or the teaching concerning it was discussed and *summarized in two short sentences* [my emphasis] or with few words: "Man, let yourself fall," and "Take your support or rest in faith in the Almighty God." This short statement is very necessary and absolutely indispensable for our pilgrim's path through this entire life.[128]

This text indicates that after the group Bible discussion, the main teaching of the meeting was formulated in this case into two pithy statements, which could easily be remembered. An entire collection of fifty-one of these "short statements" was included in the 1838 sermon book.[129]

One final method for furthering spiritual growth within the companies was the communal writing (and singing) of hymns and poems. Many of the company-composed hymns were written for the Harmony Fest celebration. Of those written, approximately 150 of the best compositions were included in the printed hymnbooks and some were set to music and sung on the Society's anniversary. Likewise in the New Harmony era, the male and female companies were either assigned or chose various passages from the Song of Solomon and the Psalms. They then wrote in their company meetings paraphrases and poems based on those texts, which are preserved in a number of manuscript hymnbooks with the appropriate company name. This discussion of the purpose and methods of the companies demonstrates beyond a doubt that the companies were conventicles formed to further spiritual maturity. They likewise served to provide fellowship and friendship for the members. The theological basis for the religious activities pursued by average Harmonists in their companies was the strongly held belief in the priesthood of all believers.

It is possible to ascertain the composition of the companies during the New Harmony era, since the 1821-1823 Articles of Association were signed in companies.[130] Unlike the former practice whereby all Society members signed one copy of the Articles of Association, fifty copies of the document were made in 1821-1823 and each copy was signed by the individual mem-

---

[128] "Den 2...te Merz 1832 wurde in der Privatversamlung vom S: das Christenthum, oder die Lehre davon in 2 kurzen Säzen, oder mit wenig Worten gesagt ud: zusammen gefasst: Mensch laß dich fallen, ud: nimm eine Fassung im Glauben zu Gott dem Allmächtigen. Dieser kurze Saz ist sehr nötig ud: ganz unentbehrlich vor unsern Pilgerus-Lauf durch das ganze Leben hindurch." USI, MSS# 311, Box 46, Folder 14.

[129] Memorandum Book, 1827-1828 contains similar proverbs, but they are not specifically identified as being from the company meetings. The topics which are reflected in these pithy statements provide the researcher with valuable information as to the type of topics discussed in the company meetings. See Ott, "Community in Companies," for an analysis of the pithy statements.

[130] In December 1835 former Harmonist, Adam Schule, testified under oath in the court case Schreiber vs. Rapp that: "There was Articles at Wabash. [New Harmony was on the Wabash River]. The people divided into companies, and signed in companies." Arndt, *Doc. Hist. 1834-1847*, 151.

bers of one company. What can be learned about the composition of the Harmonist companies from the 1821-1823 Articles? (1) The companies were divided strictly by gender, being either all male or all female. (2) The average size of a Harmonist company was ten to fifteen members. (3) People in the same company were roughly the same age, except when family ties meant that a parent or older sibling was included in a group of younger members. According to a letter by George Rapp, "people who are fairly similar in their opinions and disposition meet together" [in companies].[131] (4) The same marital status however was not *the* decisive factor for inclusion in one or another company. People over forty years of age in 1821 were usually married, at least on paper, and those under forty single. The Harmony Society was virtually a celibate community by this era. (5) Members of the same company did not practice the same occupation, contrary to the contention of Karl Arndt, that the companies were work units. Nor were company members from the same village. (6) Company members did not all live together in the communal dormitory experiment of the New Harmony era–the Community Houses Nr. 1 to 4.[132] (7) Company leaders were generally the same age or slightly older than the mean age of the members, even for companies with youthful members (aged 20-23). Leaders were loyal, faithful members of the Society, most of whom were part of the original emigration (1804-1807). In some cases two persons shared the leadership.[133]

Hymnody

Prior to the printing of distinctive Harmonist hymnbooks in 1820-1827, the Harmonists used Tersteegen's *Geistliches Blumen-Gärtlein*, the *Davidic Psalterspiel* and the *Württembergisches Gesangbuch* for their worship needs (see chapter three). These printed psalters and hymnbooks remained in use during the Society's formative years, and were purchased in quantity until 1815.[134] As early as 1811 however, members of the Harmony Society began

---

[131]Letter written on Oct. 10, 1824 from George to Frederick Rapp. Arndt, *Doc. Hist. 1824-1826*, 208.

[132]All of the seventeen women living in *Bruderhaus* Nr. 1 who were old enough to be in companies (aged 19-64 in 1821) actually were in groups. Ten different companies were represented. Cf. Ott, "Community in 'Companies.'"

[133]Of the twenty-four male companies that signed the 1821-1823 Articles, leaders can be definitively established for only eleven of them. The heads of thirteen out of twenty-five female companies can be ascertained. Leaders of companies were listed in manuscript hymnbooks pM 10.3 and pM 12.2 (which date from the relevant years 1821-1823) for group compositions of hymns.

[134]Richard D. Wetzel, "The Hymnody of George Rapp's Harmony Society," *Hymn* 23 (January 1972): 19-29, here 23. Cf. Alice T. Ott, "Singing to the Lord a New Song: Hymnody and Liturgy in George Rapp's Harmony Society, 1805-1847," in *The Pietist Impulse in Christianity*, ed. Christian T. Collins Winn, et al. (Eugene, Org.: Pickwick Publications, 2011), 233-244.

to collect Harmonist written poems and hymns in personally produced, handwritten hymnbooks. The title pages of many of these manuscript hymnbooks not only gave the owner's name, but were decorated with German folkloric *Fraktur* writing and drawings. Over sixty manuscript hymnbooks are extant in the Harmony Society archives. These handwritten hymnbooks contained poems and hymns written specially for Harmonist feast days and Christian holidays in the first decades of the Society's existence. For instance, hymnbook pM 4.7 included hymns for the 1817 celebrations of Christmas, Easter and the Harmony Fest; pM 12.3 odes and arias used for special holidays in 1822. A number of other manuscript hymnbooks incorporated paraphrases and poems on the Book of Psalms and the Song of Solomon written by small group male and female companies.[135] Thus, although these manuscript hymnbooks were later superseded by printed hymnals, they provide a valuable window into the early worship practices and beliefs of the Harmony Society.

The expanding collection of Harmonist written hymns ultimately became unmanageable in manuscript form. In 1820 the Harmony Society had their first hymnbook published by an Allentown, Pennsylvania printer, Heinrich Ebner. The hymnbook contains 196 hymns in the main section with fifty-eight more in the supplement. In 1822 a second supplement with 117 hymns was added to the hymnbook, published this time by Johann Herman of Lancaster, Ohio. The majority of hymns were written by Harmonists, including George Rapp, although some, as the title indicated, were written either by "other authors" or "adapted from other authors."[136] The prologue to the 1820 *Gesangbuch* noted that "everything that is presented in books and songs in sound words for exhortation and edification is material that man may use to profess the name of the Lord." The prologue then mentioned two exceptional and distinctive types of "edificatory material" that were added to the Harmonist hymnbook. First, besides more traditional hymns for holidays and worship services, "songs about various inward and outward states and experiences of the soul" were incorporated.[137] For example, topical divisions in the 1820 hymnbook related to the experience of regeneration ("repentance," "faith," "conversion of the heart"), the Tersteegian conception of self-denial ("denial of self and the world"), the experience of communion with God and Christ ("longing for God," "love of Christ," "peace and rest of the soul"), and sanctification ("spiritual battle and victory," "following Christ") were included. These hymns reflected the Pietist emphasis on heart-felt experiential religion.

---

[135]Examples are pM10.1, pM10.3, pM12.2, and pM12.3.

[136]Wetzel notes that five hymns were taken from Petrus Wulffing's *Ronsdorffs Silberne Trompeten* (#310, 312, 313, 316 and 323). Wetzel, *Frontier Musicians*, 53-54. The author discovered that three hymns were Gottfried Arnold hymns. See chapter six.

[137]". . . mancherley Seelen-Zustände und Erfahrungen, sowohl innerlich als äußerlich." 1820 *Gesangbuch*, iii-iv.

Second, according to the prologue a large number of the hymns were specifically chosen "to train the youth" of the community by "occupying their minds and thoughts" with edifying material. "Besides morality and religion, the observation of nature" was a legitimate topic for the edification of the youth, because truth was found in both the spiritual and natural realms.[138] This explains the relatively large number of "nature hymns" included both in the main section and the supplements. Hymns praising the beauty of spring (*Der Apfel-Baum prangt schön und weiß*, #224; *Der Frühing ist ein Paradiß*, #289), summer (*Der junge Sommer weicht*, #215), autumn (*Trübe aus westlichem Duft*, # 191), and winter (*Schmückt das Fest mit Wintergrün*, #190) found their place in the 1820 Harmonist hymnbook. Seven hymns on virtue as well as morning and evening songs were added to edify the youthful and older members of the communal settlement.[139] Some of these hymns were largely secular; others combined nature motifs with religious content.

The 1820 *Gesangbuch* included sections with Harmonist-composed hymns for the traditional Christian holidays (Christmas, Good Friday and Easter) and for specifically Harmonist feast days (Harmony Fest and love feast). Other worship hymns were written in praise of God or Christ.[140] However, the majority of hymns in the 1820 hymnbook clearly reflected distinctive doctrines and beliefs, which the Harmony Society espoused. It has already been noted that a considerable number of hymns dealt with the inward and outward states of the soul, thereby displaying Harmonist spirituality. The practice of communalism, described as being enabled through the "brotherly spirit" (*Bruder-Geist*) to live "in the holy bond of unity" and "from a common treasury," was lauded in several hymns.[141] At least one

---

[138]1820 *Gesangbuch*, iv. Wetzel interprets the inclusion of nature hymns and hymns stressing morality as evidence of Enlightenment influence on the Harmonists. Wetzel, "Hymnody," 24. Cf. ibid., *Frontier Musicians*, 44. This statement must be qualified. The nature hymns more closely reflect emphases of the Romantic movement. The Harmonists as Neo-Pietists rejected Neologism and Enlightenment theology. Virtue and morality did not win favor with God, but were the necessary concomitant of saving faith. 1820 *Gesangbuch*, Hymn #53, verse 2 specifically rejects human synergism in salvation: "Ach umsonst ist Kampf und Ringen, wohlgefällig Dir zu seyn; wollen, können und vollbringen, würckst Du in uns ganz allein."

[139]Virtue hymns: #147-152 and #287. Morning hymns: #200 (Wann der heitre Morgen grüßet), #204 (Willkommen frühe Morgen-Sonn), #263 (Wie der Morgenstern uns lächelt). Evening hymns: #85 (Still und hehr ist's wo der Abend dunkelt), #178 (Als mir der Abend graute) and # 220 (Schwärmt ihr muntre Abendwinde). 1820 *Gesangbuch*.

[140]Examples: 1820 *Gesangbuch*, #116 (Preiß sey Dir! Herr der ew'gen Güte!), #315 (Jesus Christus ist der Tempel-Bauer), # 361 (Herr Jesu Himmels Fürst), #362 (Anbetung dir du Welt Regent), and #363 (Herr nach deinem Wohlgefallen). Wetzel's statement that there is an absence of Christology in Harmonist hymns is overstated. Wetzel, "Hymnody," 24.

[141]1820 *Gesangbuch*, #84, #87 and #194.

hymn exhorted the Harmonists to remain chaste and celibate, although the "fire" of lust threatened to overwhelm them. Following verses reminded the Harmonists that "flesh decays and dissolves," and could not be compared to the "riches of love" experienced in union with Christ. "This bond of marriage [with Christ] continues even when the entire world passes away."[142] A relatively large number of hymns extolled Sophia, the feminine personification of Wisdom, who was highly revered by the Harmonists.[143] Several of the topical divisions reflected aspects of Harmonist eschatological beliefs— the "kingdom of God," "hope of Zion," "Zion's Lament," the "return of Christ for judgment," and "heaven and the heavenly Jerusalem." For instance, hymn #297 reflected Harmonist eschatology. It called upon the Lord to inaugurate speedily the end times with judgment for "brazen sinners" and redemption for "his little flock" (*dein Völklein*). A later verse proclaimed their yearning for the culmination: "We have now in our time, Lord, recognized your ways. We wait despite heavy suffering until you call us into the Fatherland [heaven]. The world has cast us out. It cannot understand your Word, Lord. O, remember your kingdom-comrades, and let us soon see your face!"[144]

The 1820 hymnbook ultimately proved inadequate for Harmonist needs. In 1824 the Harmony Society printed a collection of Harmonist written poems and hymns on their newly-acquired printing press. *Eine kleine Sammlung* consists of eighty-four texts printed explicitly by the Society to gain proficiency in the art of printing. Two years later in 1826 a second collection of Harmonist texts were published in *Feurige Kohlen der Aufsteigenden Liebesflammen im Lustspiel der Weisheit* (*Firey Coals of the Ascending Flames of Love in the Enjoyment of Wisdom*). The vast majority of the hymns and poems included in *Eine kleine Sammlung* and *Feurige Kohlen* lacked lasting value. The work of average Harmonists, the poems and hymns frequently lacked meter and rhyme and, therefore, could neither be read nor sung easily. They were likewise generally inferior not just poetically, but conceptually and theologically to the hymns chosen to be included in the Society's best and most extensive hymnbook, published in 1827. Nevertheless, like the manuscript hymnbooks, these volumes provide insight not only into early Harmonist worship (some dated odes and arias for holidays are included), but to the religious musings of average Harmonists as well.

The 1827 *Gesangbuch* was the final hymnbook published for the Harmony Society, and the one that continued in use until the dissolution of the Society in 1905. The new hymnbook included all but fifty of the hymns in the 1820 edition. However, the hymnal was greatly expanded— approximately 290 texts and more than sixty tunes were added. A relatively

---

[142] 1820 *Gesangbuch*, #114.
[143] Examples: 1820 *Gesangbuch*, #97, #100, #106, #113, #152, #161, #269, #280, #281 and #344. See chapter six for a thorough discussion of Harmonist Sophialogy.
[144] 1820 *Gesangbuch*, #297.

large number of hymns from other sources were added to the 1827 *Gesangbuch*—of these the largest number (forty-three) came from the hymnbook of the Ephrata Cloister House Fathers.[145] Fourteen were borrowed from Gottfried Arnold's *Lob und Liebes-Sprüche* and *Neue Göttliche Liebes-Funcken*.[146] Although the number of hymns in the 1827 hymnbook was greatly expanded in comparison to the 1820 edition, the topical divisions and contents of the two hymnals were quite similar with one notable exception—a new section of praise and thanksgiving hymns was added to the 1827 edition with seventeen hymns that had not previously been included.[147] The similarity of the two editions of the Harmonist hymnbook was underscored by the fact that the same prologue with the same set goals was used for both the 1820 and 1827 hymnbooks.

Feast Days

The Harmony Society, despite its emphasis on restoring the primitive, apostolic church, nevertheless celebrated the traditional Christian holidays with some fanfare. By at least the New Harmony era (1814-1824), considerable effort was exerted to make the worship services celebrated on Christmas, Good Friday, Easter, Pentecost, and the Ascension of Christ (*Christi Himmelfahrt*) meaningful and memorable. Largely unnamed Harmonists wrote new hymns to be sung on such occasions. Orchestra leader, Dr. Christoph Müller (ca. 1811-1832), arranged scores for the different musical instruments, practiced with the vocalists, choirs and instrumentalists, as well as composed hymns himself. Wetzel's comment that "by 1819 the Harmonist orchestra [on the Indiana frontier] was one of the most prominent musical organizations outside of the cities of the eastern seaboard" is certainly correct.[148] Musical instruction was available to all Harmonists, and members were encouraged to harness their poetic and musi-

---

[145]Cf. Wetzel, *Frontier Musicians*, 62 and 64-65 (for a list of the borrowed hymns from Ephrata).

[146]See chapter six for a list of the fourteen borrowed Arnold hymns, discovered by the author.

[147]Wetzel states that the 1827 hymnbook reveals a "decrease in humanistic emphasis" since two topical divisions, "On the high nobility of man" and "On man's misery and corruption" were eliminated. Wetzel, *Frontier Musicians*, 62. Wetzel fails to notice that the vast majority of the hymns (nine from twelve) from these topical divisions were included in the 1827 hymnbook under different categories. Neither of the two hymnbooks should be considered humanistic. The "high nobility of man" was rooted in Christ's incarnation, which enabled regenerate man to bring forth the fruits worthy of salvation (1820 hymnbook, #118) and thus to have the image of God in man renewed (ibid., #117). Man's corruption refers to the disastrous effects of original sin. Neither of these are humanistic emphases. Wetzel states that the addition of the praise and thanksgiving hymns indicates "more evidence upon Christ and a Trinitarian theology," likewise an untenable claim. Ibid.

[148]Wetzel, *Frontier Musicians*, 20.

cal talents both for personal recreation and in service of God and the community. This is seen clearly in the elaborate arias, liturgies and worship services planned each year for the Christian holidays and for Harmonist-specific celebrations (Harmony Fest, Harvest Fest, and Love Feast). The examples of Harmonist celebrations of Christian holidays, included below, demonstrate considerable continuity with the Lutheran tradition from which most of the members had sprung.

For the Easter celebration in 1824, the Harmonists prepared an elaborate "passion meditation" (*Passions-Betrachtung*), which alternated congregational song (*Gesang*) with poems, fugues, choir and vocal pieces and recitative texts from the Gospels chanted to music. The *Betrachtung*, which was printed and later included in *Eine kleine Sammlung*, began with the following poem:

> I wander to the grave, where my Redeemer rests,
> And bring my gift for his shed blood.
> Instead of noble splendors, will I, O Man of pain,
> Consecrate to you my heart and life.
> Receive graciously my sacrifice.[149]

It then told the story of Christ's burial and resurrection in song, chant and poem interspersed with first-person applications of the Gospel story ("I consecrate my heart and life to you," "I enclose you in my heart," "My undying desire is alone for Him") and exhortations ("Fear the Most-High, the Father of all things"). Toward the end of the meditation two vocal groups sung antiphonally the traditional Easter greeting – The Lord is risen; the Lord is risen indeed.

Eine kleine Sammlung contains a second liturgy, "The installation of the eternal King Jesus upon Mt. Zion," presumably for Ascension Day, 1824. The text of Psalm 2 was adapted and set to music for three separate choirs and soloists singing the parts of God the Father, the Messiah and David.[150] A program printed on the Harmonist printing press for the Pentecost celebrations on June 7, 1829 is extant. Unfortunately, the order of worship for the Sunday morning service was not included. Two secular march pieces, however, were played by the orchestra in the morning and in the afternoon, possibly for processions to or at different locations (Feast Hall, church or cemetery). The evening program was a full-length concert, which mixed

---

[149]"Ich walle zu dem Grabe, wo mein Erlöser ruht; Und bringe meine Gabe, Für sein vergoßnes blut: Statt edler Specereyen, will ich o Schmerzens-Mann, Dir Herz und Leben weihen, Nimm hold mein Opfer an." *Eine kleine Sammlung Harmonischer Lieder als die erste Probe der anfangenden Druckerey anzusehen* (Harmonie, Ind: Harmony Society Publications, 1824), #28. This liturgy was printed on March 23, 1824, three weeks before Easter on April 18th that year, and therefore was likely used in the 1824 celebration.

[150]*Eine kleine Sammlung*, #53. Printed May 15, 1824.

orchestra and choral pieces, secular (Beethoven's Minuet Nr. 114) and sacred music (Cantata: Come Holy Spirit).[151]

Besides the traditional Christian holidays, the Society celebrated three Harmonist-specific annual festivals: the Harmony Fest, the Harvest Fest and the Love Feast. The Harmony Fest was celebrated each year on February 15, the anniversary of the founding of the Harmony Society in 1805. The only description of the Harmony Fest (1832) by an insider was penned by Romelius Langenbacher on the reverse side of a manuscript hymn. The 1832 Harmony Fest celebration began before dawn streaked the sky. The community and musicians were called together, possibly by the playing of wind instruments from the church tower, as they had been in the previous year.[152] They proceeded to Father Rapp's house and serenaded the venerable patriarch with a song written specially for the occasion, a song consecrating the day to Christ, their King, from the first light of dawn onward.

> Hallelujah to the great King, the Prince of God, the Bridegroom,
> You fathers, be submissive to Him, honor the precious sacrificial Lamb,
> This day is consecrated to Him, early before the first light of dawn,
> Before the sun scatters the night, before we soon celebrate the love feast,
> Sing in rounds, lively and beautiful, let our procession sing festively with violins.[153]

Later around nine AM, the community gathered in the church where Father Rapp preached on or explained (*erklärt*) Psalm 66, which the describer of the celebration found "corresponded completely to our situation."[154] Then a second hymn written specially for the 1832 Harmony Fest was sung.[155] A communal meal was held in the upper floor of the love feast hall at noon. Each table was decorated with wreaths of flowers (*Blumen Gränzen*) and, according to the description, was "filled with God's bless-

---

[151] Wetzel, *Frontier Musicians*, 81. See Plate 8 of the Pentecost program, ibid., after 108.

[152] "Today the 26th Harmonie Festival was celebrated. In the morning at 6 o'clock the wind instruments announced the festival from the church tower." Notation of J. C. Mueller regarding Harmony Fest, 1831. Quoted in Wetzel, *Frontier Musicians*, 84.

[153] "Halleluja dem großen König, dem Fürsten Gottes, Bräutigam, Ihr Vätter seyd ihm unterthänig, verehret das Theure Opferlam, auch dieser Tag sey ihm geweiht, früh vor dem ersten Morgenstrahl, der Sonne die die Nacht zerstreuet, vor unsrem nahen Liebes-Mahl. Sänget in Reigen Munter u. Schön, Festlich zu Geigen unser Gespänn." Library Box 26, Harmony Fest hymn 1832, Rechto. The love feast referred to in the hymn was not the Eucharistic celebration, which was celebrated once a year in October, but a reference to the communal meal.

[154] "Vormittags wurde vom Vatter der 66 Psalm erklärt, der so ganz mit unserm Verhältniß über einstimmte." The situation that was referred to was the secession of one third of the Harmonists, who followed the charlatan Count Leon and left the Harmony Society on March 6, 1832. The Harmony Fest was celebrated in 1832 on May 9, due to the secession. Library Box 26, Harmony Fest hymn 1832, Verso.

[155] Library Box 26, Harmony Fest hymn 1832, Verso.

ing."[156] This most likely refers both to the physical blessing of food and the spiritual blessings of fellowship around the table. At or after the meal, the following question was discussed: why did God in both the old and new covenants feast his people not just with spiritual but with physical food. It was explained (by Rapp?) that outward hunger must first be satisfied before the other spiritual senses can be. God provided for both our physical and spiritual well-being, therefore one ought to thank him and submit one's life to him.[157] Thus even the communal meal was an opportunity for the inculcation of religious beliefs. The description of the 1832 Harmony Fest did not include the afternoon and evening's events. These can be reconstructed with some probability from William Owen's description in his journal entry for Feb. 17, 1825. Owen noted that at the 1825 Harmony Fest, the Harmonists spent the afternoon together. This was followed by another procession and serenade at Rapp's house. "Before breaking up at five o'clock, they marched out of the church in closed ranks preceded by their music, all singing. They halted before Mr. Rapp's house and sang a piece of music and dispersed."[158] At six PM the Harmonists re-gathered, supped together and then celebrated until nine PM.

The Harmony Fest was an all-day celebration. At the Fest the communal values upon which the Society was founded were remembered and reinforced in a number of ways—through the writing and singing of songs extolling their brotherhood, through retelling the story of their Society, and through Rapp's Harmony Fest sermons. Days and weeks before the Harmony Fest both individual members and groups (companies) wrote laudatory songs praising their communal lifestyle and the personification of their group, the female figure *Harmonie*. The one or two best hymns each year were put to music and performed by singers and orchestra on the day of the festival. The act of communally or individually composing hymns praising their brotherhood, and the hymns themselves, served to recommit members to a communal lifestyle and to underscore their religious distinctives and bonds of friendship. Over 150 "Harmony" hymns are preserved in manuscript form or in their printed hymnbooks - *Eine kleine Sammlung* (1824), *Feurige Kohlen* (1826), and the 1820 and 1827 *Gesangbücher*. One of the best-loved was a hymn traditionally assigned to George Rapp, "*Harmonie, du Bruder-Stadt*" (Harmony, city of brotherhood).[159]

---

[156]". . . nach 12 Uhr gieng es zum Mittagsmahl, alle Tafel waren mit Blumen Gränzen geschmückt u. mit Göttlichen Seegen angefüllt." Library Box 26, Harmony Fest hymn 1832, Verso.

[157]Ibid.

[158]Journal of William Owens, Feb. 17, 1825. Quoted in Wetzel, *Frontier Musicians*, 30.

[159]"There are no records to substantiate that he [Rapp] wrote the text 'Harmonie, du Bruderstadt,' but it is generally ascribed to him." Wetzel, *Frontier Musicians*, 45. It was included in the 1820 *Gesangbuch*, #91, and therefore was written prior to that year. It was also included in the 1827 *Gesangbuch*, #163.

The Harmony Fest celebration likewise (at least in some years) included a retelling of their founding narrative.[160] All but one of the ten or more extant accounts were written by George Rapp and included in a Harmony Fest sermon. These narrative accounts told the story of how God had guided and directed their group from Württemberg to the United States and, from there, would ultimately lead them to Palestine to meet Christ at his Second Advent.[161] The narrative histories thus underscored the role of providence in the founding and development of their Society. Furthermore, Rapp in his Harmony Fest sermons extolled the practice of communalism, the importance of love and unity between the brethren and other distinctive religious beliefs.[162] At least in some years a memorial service, held at the cemetery, formed part of the Harmony Fest activities.[163]

The date for the Harvest Fest (*Ernte Fest*) was flexible, generally celebrated mid-week in late July or August, after the bulk of hay, grain and fruit had been harvested.[164] It was likewise an all-day affair and included both religious and secular elements. A worship service with hymns and sermon by George Rapp was held in the morning. Rapp's 1834 Harvest Fest sermon provides insight into the religious aspects of the festival. The Harmonist leader began the sermon with the reminder:

> Today is a day of thanksgiving for the harvest that has been successfully brought in. God has nourished all things, blessed all things, made all things glad ... A harvest that has been so blessed deserves as much as anything else that man thanks God publicly for it. ... It was not our work alone that did this, rather rain must fall at the proper time, frost and heat must alternate suitably. ... So it was in this year 1834. It was as if God desired to make it

---

[160] The surviving documentary evidence for the Harmony Fest is incomplete, therefore it is impossible to state with certitude that a retelling of Harmonist history occurred every year.

[161] Examples of narrative histories written for the Harmony Fest: George Rapp's talk, Harmony Fest, 1829, Daniel Reibel's file; MG-185, 1-5004, Box 15, Folder 6, Q-93; 1839 Harmony Fest Hymn, verso, Library Box 26; MG-437, Box 22, Folder 82B, A-22; MG-437, Box 22, Folder 82B, D-17; and MG-185, 1-5004, Box 15, Folder 6, P-129.

[162] Harmony Fest sermons: Communalism (MG-185/1-5004/Box 15/Folder 6/R-144; MG-185, 1-5004, Box 15, Folder 5, O-122); Harmonie/Sophia (MG-185, Box 15, Folder 5, N-130; MG-437, Box 22, Folder 82B, E-10; MG-185, Box 15, Folder 5, C-23; MG-437, Box 22, Folder 82B, D-29 and D-93); Celibacy (MG-437, Box 22, Folder 82B, A-22); Priesthood in millennium (1839 Harmony Fest hymn/sermon, OEV, Library Box 26; MG-437, Box 22, Folder 82B, D-75; MG-185/Box 15/Folder 5/C-23; MG-185/1-5004/Box 15/Folder 5/O-122; MG-437/Box 22/Folder 82B/A-22).

[163] A hymn included in some manuscript hymnbooks entitled "How blessed are they that die [in the Lord]," was designated as a "cemetery song for the 1818 Harmony Fest." Wetzel, *Frontier Musicians*, 31.

[164] In 1828, the festival was held in mid-July and in 1831 on Wednesday, August 24. Wetzel, *Frontier Musicians*, 79 and 86. In 1852, it was celebrated on Thursday August 12; in 1853 on Thursday July 28 and in 1854 on Thursday, August 24. Love Feast Records, 1851-1865, MG-185, Microfilm roll #316.

completely obvious, that without Him the worker works in vain, that everything is dependent on His blessing.... Our harvest today proclaims that God brings all things that He desires to fruition.... That a good harvest came about despite frost and ice is a reminder and pledge that God always brings about that which He desires.[165]

A hymn written specially for the 1834 Fest similarly proclaimed: "You [Lord] maintain the earth and provide it with rain.... O Lord... you create and give to us all types of grain... You have prepared the soil of the field and watered the furrows of the plows."[166] The Harvest Fest was an opportunity for the Society to thank God for the abundance of crops and to reaffirm their dependency on his gracious provision. Similar to the Harmony Fest, a communal meal was held at noon. In the evening at least in some years a concert was held with both secular and religious music. For example, at the evening Harvest Fest concert in 1831, the orchestra presented a new piece by W. C. Peters, the "March of Pittsburgh."[167]

The third Harmonist-specific festival was the Love Feast (*Liebesmahl*), held once annually in October. Prior to the love feast itself, members were called upon to resolve all conflicts and disagreements between themselves, so that they might receive the Eucharist worthily (Matt 5:23-24). Likewise, those burdened by sin and a guilty conscience were urged to confess their transgressions privately to George Rapp prior to the celebration of the Lord's Supper. Rapp and his Harmonists believed that:

> Without confession of sins no man can attain full righteousness... All sinners must properly go to the priesthood and that [duty] is performed by people who have learned the art of discernment from their own experience through regeneration and who are called spiritual guides (*Seelenführer*). All tendencies [within the person confessing] toward blessedness or damnation are confirmed humanly [by the confessor].[168]

Thus, the Harmonist practice of confession was similar to the Lutheran practice of auricular confession.[169] Although they believed it was possible to be fully forgiven by God for sins without confession to a "priest" (Rapp),

---

[165] MG-185, 1-5004, Box 15, Folder 6, S-28.
[166] 1834 Harvest Fest hymn, OEV, Library Box 26.
[167] Wetzel, *Frontier Musicians*, 86.
[168] Shaker Questions and Answers. MG-437, Box22, Folder 113.
[169] Luther protested the medieval penitential practice with its works of satisfaction and human synergism. In his view the whole of life should be characterized by penitence and repentance. Jürgen Werbick, "Penance, sacrament," in *Dictionary of the Reformation,* ed. Klaus Ganzer and Bruno Steimer, trans. Brian McNeil (New York: Crossroad, 2002), 239. Further, Luther rejected the technical status of penance as a sacrament, although he personally valued confession. "Sacrament or not, confession certainly was a means of grace, of which Luther could say: 'I would long since have been overcome and strangled by the devil if [private] confession had not sustained me.'" Jaroslav Pelikan, *Reformation of Church and Dogma (1300-1700)* (Chicago: University of Chicago Press, 1984), 179.

Harmonists took more seriously than many Protestants the necessity of auricular confession. "Full righteousness," a salved conscience and protection from temptation were only experienced when the Biblical injunction to "confess your sins to one another" (Jas 5:16) was put into practice.

Unlike the simple *agapes* celebrated in homes by the Separatists in Württemberg, the Love Feasts held at Economy, Pennsylvania (the third Harmonist settlement) were elaborate affairs celebrated in the Love Feast Hall, a large second-story room built specially for this occasion and other communal meals.[170] Nevertheless, the elements of the event remained the same as in Württemberg: prior confession, a communal meal and then the Eucharist itself. Like other feast days celebrated by the Harmony Society, the Love Feast at least from the New Harmony days onward included orchestral music, specially written hymns and liturgies. A program of the order of worship for the 1834 Love Feast was printed for the community and still exists. Congregational singing was alternated with choir pieces, recitative chanting and vocal soloists. The format and content of the liturgy were remarkably similar to that used by the established Lutheran Church in Württemberg, which the Separatists turned Harmonists had so emphatically rejected but several decades before. The worship service began with all the vocalists singing Rev 5:13, "Holy is the Lamb who was slain," the first of eight Bible verses set to music or chanted.[171] The liturgy then praised Christ, the "precious Lamb," who sacrificed his "flesh and blood for our sins on the cross." It was Christ's "great, yea immeasurable love" that led him to give "himself and his salvation to us in bread and wine." Next, presumably after the recitative chant of John 6:35, "I am the bread that came down from heaven," the bread was distributed. After the wine was circulated, the Aaronic blessing (Num 6:24-26) was chanted. The service ended with an individual singing or proclaiming, "Praise be the name of the Lord," to which the congregation replied, "Forever, Hallelujah!"[172]

This Love Feast liturgy decidedly reflected the Lutheran tradition in which the Harmonists had their roots. Rapp's love feast sermons likewise stressed Christ's salvific atonement on the cross for the sins of mankind. Nevertheless, in partial contrast to the Lutheran tradition, the Eucharist was not only a means of grace, but a means by which the very life of Christ was inwardly imparted to both the individual soul and the congregation (*Gemeine*) by the Holy Spirit.[173]

---

[170] Adjacent to this building was a wine cellar and a large communal kitchen used to prepare the communal meals. Charles Nordhoff, *The Communistic Societies of the United States* (New York: Hilary House, 1875), 87.

[171] The other Bible verses or allusions to verses are John 6:56, 6:68, 6:35f, 12:13, Gen 28:17, Matt 28:20b and Num 6:24-26. Arndt, *Doc. Hist. 1834-1847*, 31.

[172] Ibid.

[173] MG-185, Box 15, Folder 5, Gr C-36. Cf. MG-437, Box 22, Folder 82b, D-61 and MG-185, 1-5004, Box 15, Folder 6, P-20.

Patriarchal Leadership

One final aspect of the Harmonist "church in the wilderness" deserves attention—the governance of the Harmony Society. In the 1805 Articles of Association, members of the Society pledged not only "to submit to the laws and regulations of the congregation," but "to show due and ready obedience toward those who are chosen and appointed by the congregation as superintendents."[174] Until his death on June 24, 1834, Frederick Rapp served as business manager or secular leader of the Society. George Rapp was the undisputed spiritual leader throughout his lifetime (d. August 7, 1847). Foremen (at times also called superintendents) were appointed to oversee the various manufacturing and agricultural pursuits and placed under Frederick Rapp's authority.[175] In addition to the foremen, a council or synod of elders was elected by the male members of the Society to assist in temporal affairs, to decide if new members should be accepted or old members disciplined or expelled from the Society, and to help settle disputes between members.[176] The council of elders thus assisted the two Rapps (Frederick and George) in the day-to-day business and personnel management of the Society, while issues of more spiritual import remained the sole responsibility of George Rapp. In 1823, the synod of elders consisted of seven brethren; in 1832 it was expanded to twelve regular members, who were elected annually.[177] Issues of grave importance (adoption of celibacy, prohibition of tobacco, etc.) were brought to the entire congregation, where the vote of the majority was decisive.[178]

After 1809 members of the Harmony Society began to address their spiritual leader as "Father Rapp." This title corresponded to the Harmonist leader's self-understanding. In sermons and letters a theological justification was given for Rapp's stern but affectionate, authoritarian and patriar-

---

[174]Translation of Article two in Arndt, *Rapp's Harmony Society*, 72. Cf. idem, *Doc. Hist. 1803-1815*, 82.

[175]German visitor to New Harmony (July 1819), Ferdinand Ernst, confused the "court of the brethren" or elders with the superintendents of the "blacksmiths, shoemakers, saddlers, and carpenters." Arndt, *Doc. Hist. 1814-1819*, 746. Cf. idem, *Doc. Hist. 1826-1834*, 705f and idem, *Doc. Hist. 1834-1847*, 1078. George Rapp assumed both secular and temporal leadership of the Society after Frederick Rapp died in 1834.

[176]Arndt, *Doc. Hist. 1826-1834*, 705f.

[177]Arndt, *Doc. Hist. 1820-1824*, 569-570 and idem, *Doc. Hist. 1826-1834*, 705f. The elders elected on February 21, 1832 were Johannes Schnabel, Friedrich Nachtrieb, Johannes Stahl, Romelius Langenbacher, Adam Nachtrieb, Georg Forstner, Matheus Scholle, Ludwig Schreiber, Johannes Schreiber, Georg Beisser, Friederich Eckensperger and Joseph Hörnle. This is the only list of elders during Rapp's lifetime. Cf. idem, *Doc. Hist. 1834-1847, 1078* for elders elected after Rapp's death.

[178]Letter of Frederick Rapp (December 19, 1822): "principle points have to be governed by a Majority of Votes." Arndt, *Doc. Hist. 1820-1824*, 514.

chal manner of leadership. This form of leadership was found in the Scriptures as "the government of the patriarchal ages."[179] Just as communalism was based on the example of the primitive Jerusalem church, so Rapp's authoritarian style was justified as being the practice of the patriarchs of ancient Israel. This patriarchal government would be renewed in the physical millennial kingdom centered on Jerusalem. According to a Rapp sermon, the Harmony congregation would be well-prepared and suited to participate in the millennium. Their "training" in the "school of the Holy Spirit" in this age would put them in good stead in the millennium, where likewise a "mild patriarchal government (*Vatter regierung*) [would exist] for the blessed, for the happiest and most obedient disciples with their tender child-like disposition."[180] Frederick Rapp in a letter to Samuel Worcester (December 19, 1822) confirmed the same notion: "We also believe for Certain that the nigh approaching Kingdom of Jesus Christ will be governed and conducted in the same manner," that is, with patriarchal leadership. According to his adopted son, Rapp was uniquely gifted to fulfill this role, since the spiritual leader was "sincerely, fully and warmly addicted to the Religion of Jesus Christ, possessing weight and Spirit enough to animate others, and a nice feeling to discern right and wrong, and to give assent and Superiority to truth."

Strict obedience to the rules of the Society and to Rapp and elected elders was required of the membership in the Articles of Association. In another 1822 letter Frederick Rapp admitted that such obedience, though necessary for the Society to function properly, was "very hard for people, who have not the Kingdom of God for their Chief object."[181] The difficulty of submitting to the patriarchal leadership of Rapp and the board of elders resulted in numerous withdrawals from the Society by members throughout the years. The convinced Harmonists who remained, however, valued the stern but fatherly demeanor of Rapp and their leaders. They pledged in a hymn printed in the 1820 *Gesangbuch*: "We are willing to obey. Long live our "fathers," for the protection of righteousness, for the punishment of the transgressor. Under their protection we defy depravity and the Enemy. And we love our fathers as children."[182] The unequal relationship between "father" and "children" was underscored both in this hymn and in the Rapp sermon quoted above.

The authoritarian stance of Rapp toward his followers paralleled that of other "patriarchs" within the various branches of the Pietist *Gemeinschaft* movement in Württemberg in the first half of the nineteenth century. Like Rapp, the patriarchs of the Bengelian *Alt-Pietisten*, the Pregizerianer and the *Hahnsche Gemeinschaften* owed their exalted position to their "charismatic leadership, their degree of sanctification and their ability to correctly in-

---

[179]Arndt, *Doc. Hist. 1826-1834*, 273-274.

[180]"die milde Vatter regierung für die seelige, mit dem zarten Kinder sinne für die Glücklichste u folgsamste Lehrlinge." MG-437, Box 22, Folder 82B, B-60.

[181]Arndt, *Doc. Hist. 1820-1824*, 465.

[182]1820 *Gesangbuch*, #194.

terpret the Bible."[183] The local and regional Pietist patriarchs in Württemberg claimed absolute authority in religious questions. Their advice and counsel was sought by their followers for personal decisions as well.[184] Against such a background, Rapp's authoritarian, patriarchal leadership appears less unique and more understandable. After all, the Harmonist leader and his original disciples had spent the first half of their lives under a non-democratic, absolutist government. Both Lutheran ministers and Pietist patriarchs exerted a considerable degree of authority over their flocks. Rapp's "old world" authoritarian style seemed overbearing particularly to second-generation Harmonists, raised in the democratic American context. Rapp declared to Lewis von Schweinitz, the great-grandson of Zinzendorf who visited Economy in 1831 that although "obedience alone made the success of such enterprises [the Harmony Society] possible," "obedience . . . in America does not outlast the second generation."[185]

---

[183] Manfred Jakubowski-Tiessen, "Eigenkultur und Traditionsbildung," in *Geschichte des Pietismus*, vol. 4, *Glaubenswelt und Lebenswelten*. ed. Hartmut Lehmann (Göttingen: Vandenhoeck & Ruprecht, 1995): 195-210, here 199.

[184] Hartmut Lehmann, *Pietismus und weltliche Ordnung in Württemberg vom 17. bis zum 20. Jahrhundert* (Stuttgart: W. Kohlhammer, 1969), 15-16 and 19.

[185] Arndt, *Doc. Hist. 1826-1834*, 581.

6

Labyrinths, Grottoes, and Decorative Art (1805-1830)

On August 20, 1811, two visitors, John Melish and Dr. Isaac Cleaver of Philadelphia, arrived at the prosperous little town of Harmony. During their visit at the communal settlement the two visitors received an exhaustive tour of the community. No branch of manufacturing or area of the town was left unviewed. Melish, in his published travel journal, described in some detail a unique and unusual element just outside the Harmonist town.[1] On the opposite side of the creek, reached by a wooden bridge decorated with blooming flower boxes, was a meadow with an intricate maze or labyrinth.[2] The labyrinth was formed of "various hedge rows" and "flower gardens" and, according to Melish, was "most elegant." The spiritual leader of the community, George Rapp, accompanied them into the labyrinth, and then, as it were, disappeared. "[W]e soon observed him over the hedge-rows, taking his seat before the house," the "little temple, emblematical of Harmony, in the middle" of the maze. Melish himself finally found his way "with difficulty" to the center, "but the doctor, whom I left on purpose, could not find it, and Mr. Rapp had to point it out to him." Melish stated that "[t]he garden

---

[1]John Melish, *Travels in the United States of America*, Philadelphia, 1812. Chapter nine recounts his visit to Harmony, Pennsylvania. This section is included in Karl J. R. Arndt, *Harmony on the Connoquenessing, 1803-1815. A Documentary History* (Worcester, Mass.: Harmony Society Press, 1980), 451f.

[2]Harmonist labyrinths are actually hedge mazes, although the Harmonists referred to them as "labyrinths." The distinction between labyrinth and maze will be explained later in this chapter.

and temple are emblematical," that is, they had symbolic religious significance.[3]

The anecdote is of interest on a number of levels. Melish's account provides the earliest description of a Harmonist labyrinth, which the Society went on to establish at all three of their successive settlements: Harmony, Pennsylvania, New Harmony, Indiana, and Economy, Pennsylvania. Prior to publishing, Melish submitted his report to Rapp's adopted son and the business manager of the Society, Frederick Rapp, for correction and revision. Thus, this eyewitness account has a "greater ring of authenticity" than many other travelers' description of the Harmony Society.[4] George Rapp's ability to amble easily through the maze to its center, while the visitors either did not succeed or only did so with difficulty is an enlightening commentary on the Harmonist self-understanding. As chosen "children of God," they had the proper blueprint to follow the straight and narrow path to heavenly bliss. Outsiders were at a great disadvantage in this regard, particularly those who were blinded by worldly wisdom (the learned doctor).

Finally, the Melish account underscored twice that the gardens and the labyrinth with its central temple (or grotto, as the Harmonists called it) had emblematic or symbolic religious significance. The labyrinth and grotto were not merely elegant elements of an aristocratically-inspired pleasure garden, such as were found both on the Continent and in America at this time. Rather these elements reflected certain core beliefs to which George Rapp and his Harmony Society subscribed. They were aspects of the Harmonist material culture, which, along with several architectural details and statuary art, proclaimed in stone and hedge key religious convictions.

Harmonist Material Culture

Material culture has been defined as "the totality of artifacts in a culture, the vast universe of objects used by humankind to cope with the physical world, to facilitate social intercourse, to delight our fancy, and to create symbols of meaning."[5] It has long been known that material structures and artifacts reflect not just the world-view but in some cases the religious beliefs of the group that erected or created them. Kevin Seastolz notes in his 2005 volume, *The Sense of the Sacred*, that religion as the "preeminent cultural institution" is primarily communicated and transmitted "through symbols, rituals, myths, stones, and metaphors rather than through doc-

---

[3] Arndt, *Doc. Hist. 1803-1815*, 457.

[4] Karl J. R. Arndt, *George Rapp's Harmony Society 1785-1847*, rev. ed. (Teaneck, N.J.: Fairleigh Dickinson University Press, 1972), 109.

[5] Definition of Melvin Herskovits paraphrased in: Thomas J. Schlereth, "Material Culture Studies and Social History Research," *Journal of Social History* 16 (1983): 111-143, here 112. Cf. Ann Smart Martin, "Material Things and Cultural Meanings: Notes on the Study of Early American Material Culture," *William and Mary Journal*, 3d. ser., 53-1 (Jan. 1996): 5-12.

trinal statements and creeds."⁶ He proceeds in the remainder of the work to discuss how "stones," that is, sacred architecture and art, reflect the theological and religious beliefs of the creators of those aspects of material culture. The interpretation of material culture can be fraught with difficulties, however, when the producers of the culture do not explicate the meaning. In such cases a comparison with other, similar cultural groups is necessary.

What elements of the Harmonist material culture unequivocally reflected religious beliefs? First, the labyrinths at all three sites with the corresponding grottos in the center had religious significance. Melish's two-fold affirmation of this fact certainly rested on his personal conversations with Frederick Rapp and therefore is reliable. Second, skilled masons carved three different stone lintels depicting religious symbols above the doorways of residential houses at Harmony, Pennsylvania–of these the Sophia lintel will be discussed. Finally, the "golden rose" symbol above the north door of the second New Harmony church was specifically related to a passage in Luther's 1545 German Bible translation – Micah 4:8.

This chapter will be organized around the above-mentioned elements of Harmonist material culture, each of which reflected one or more of their core religious beliefs. Mystical or theosophical knowledge, particularly the doctrine of Sophia, was communicated by the Sophia lintel. A striving for sanctification, the concern for righteous, celibate, "harmonious" living was reinforced upon the members of the Society by walking the labyrinth and visiting the grotto. The golden rose symbol reminded the Harmonists of the nature and imminence of the coming millennium. Sophialogy or the doctrine of Sophia belongs to what this volume is labeling the mystical-spiritual trajectory of Rapp's mature theology, the millennial beliefs to the biblical-eschatological trajectory. These two trajectories will be explicated in chapters seven to nine. The following primary sources will be utilized to unpack the religious significance of these elements: (1) travelers' descriptions of the three settlements; (2) the religio-philosophic treatise of George Rapp, *Thoughts on the Destiny of Man* (1824); (3) Harmonist hymnody; and (4) George Rapp's sermons.

In the past, a fair amount of speculation has been brought to bear on the interpretation of the Harmonist labyrinth, grotto and Sophia lintel.⁷ This is in large measure the result of interpreting elements of the material culture without sufficiently taking into account all relevant Harmonist primary source documents. Scholarly interpretations of Harmonist material culture have frequently been dependent upon published (not archival) and English

---

⁶R. Kevin Seastoltz, *A Sense of the Sacred: Theological Foundations of Sacred Architecture and Art* (New York: Continuum, 2005), 2.

⁷One extreme example is Lawrence Thurman's interpretation of the Harmonist grotto as an alchemistical shrine. Lawrence Thurman, "An American Alchemist," *Rosicrucian Digest* 32 (March 1954): 101. This is contrary to Harmonist self-interpretations of the grotto, as reliably reflected in Melish's and other travelers' accounts.

language sources.[8] This has frequently resulted in skewed interpretations. Therefore, in this chapter, the world of Harmonist religious thought as mediated by their German language hymnody and sermons will be employed to uncover valuable insights into the meaning of elements of their material culture. In those cases, such as the labyrinth, grotto and golden rose lintel, where clear documentary evidence is available for an "insider" Harmonist understanding of the element, that will be used. With regard to the religious meaning of the Sophia stone lintel, however, it is necessary to reference standard works and articles on the history of depicting Wisdom/Sophia to argue for a common and appropriate interpretation of its meaning. Only the symbolic meaning of those elements of a structure will be discussed for which documentary evidence exists.[9] For each element of material culture which come under scrutiny in this chapter, first the religious element will be described, then its significance will be established, and finally it will be demonstrated how that meaning is reflected in Harmonist religious beliefs, particularly in their hymns and in Rapp's sermons.

Mystical-Theosophical Beliefs: The Sophia Lintel

On the south-east corner of Main and Mercer streets, at the "Diamond" shaped center of the town of Harmony, a unique stone lintel was incorporated into the doorway of a brick Harmonist residence. The town had first consisted of approximately fifty log cabins, but by 1811 the public buildings had been completed, and brick homes were erected to replace the log

---

[8]Lu Ann De Cunzo, Therese O'Malley, Michael J. Lewis, George E. Thomas, and Christa Wilmanns-Wells, "Father Rapp's Garden at Economy: Harmony Society Culture in Microcosm," in *Landscape Archaeology: Reading and Interpreting the American historical Landscape,* ed. Rebecca Yamin and Karen Bescherer Metheny (Knoxville: University of Tennessee Press, 1996), 91-117; Lilan Laishley, "The Harmonist Labyrinths," *Caerdroia* 32 (2001): 8-20, and Michael J. Lewis, "Harmonist Architecture: Its Sources and Meaning," Paper presented at the Fifteenth Annual Historic Communal Studies Conference, Winston-Salem, North Carolina, Oct. 6-9, 1988, 51-84 all utilize primarily published and English sources, which have led to a skewed interpretation. Both Lewis and De Cunzo reference one Harmonist hymnbook, *Feurige Kohlen.* De Cunzo et al. incorrectly claimed that the hymns were written by George Rapp (they were written by other Harmonists). Although the translations were accurate, the hymns did not support the claim that "Harmony" was the "agent of the congregation's salvation" (p. 109). Contrary to their claim, Hymn #209 does not refer to Harmony at all. De Cunzo, "Rapp's Garden," 109.

[9]The pamphlet, "The Grotto at Old Economy," (Ambridge, Pa.: Harmony Press, 1959), presses the symbolic significance of every possible element of the interior grotto decoration beyond documentary evidence. While the interpretation may be correct, the primary sources do not allow for such detailed elaboration. Some of the so-called symbols could simply reflect contemporary artistic tastes.

ones.[10] One of the earliest brick homes (1811) received an elaborate stone lintel, with an angel-like figure adorning the center keystone. The face of the figure is as large as the stylized triangular robe below it, thus filling the central upper half of the design. Wings with seven individual feathers that extend nearly horizontally frame each side of the face. What appear to be minuscule hands are folded under the chin of the figure in a bowtie-like fashion.[11] The face of the figure is androgynous, that is, neither distinctly male nor female. The ring of hair, however, that surrounds the face is plaited in a feminine fashion. Both Michael Lewis and Charles Stotz point to the distinctly Germanic quality of the Sophia lintel. Although later the Harmonists were to adopt increasingly the American Georgian style, the Sophia and other stone lintels at Harmony were at the beginning of this process of architectural assimilation. With their "heavily carved moldings," "strong rustification" and "sculpted grotesque figures," the lintels and porticos at Harmony "reflected an indigenous German heritage of a vernacular classicism, dating back to German Renaissance architecture of the sixteenth and seventeenth centuries."[12] Stotz likewise sees a "distinctly German flavor" in the "elaborately carved stone ornament, which has a robust vigor and a rich, decorative quality."[13] The planning if not the carving of the stone lintels has been traditionally assigned to Frederick Rapp, an accomplished stone mason and theologically astute person.[14]

The stone lintel at Harmony with the face and wings has been variously interpreted since the last century. Formerly some claimed that it was a likeness of George Rapp; others that it was an angel.[15] The first suggestion is very unlikely. Rapp had a truly patriarchal look about him. Prior to emigration, he grew a long beard, which he maintained for the rest of his life. Rapp would likewise not have supported his image being combined with

---

[10]Arndt, *Rapp's Harmony Society*, 107f.

[11]Stotz refers to the "hands" as a bowtie. Charles Morse Stotz, *The Early Architecture of Western Pennsylvania: A Record of Building before 1860 Based Upon the Western Pennsylvania Architectural Survey, a Project of the Pittsburgh Chapter of the American Institute of Architects*, intro. Fiske Kimball. (Pittsburgh: University of Pittsburgh Press, 1995), 193.

[12]Lewis, "Harmonist Architecture," 70.

[13]Stotz, *Architecture*, 193.

[14]Although approximately twenty other Harmonists were listed as stone masons in the 1830s, Frederick was the only Harmonist to be designated an "architect" in the census rolls. This fact points to the prominent role Frederick Rapp had within the Society as architectural planner and designer (not just craftsman). Lewis, "Harmonist Architecture," 53 and 80, Footnote 12. Cf. Viktor Rauscher, "Des Separatisten G. Rapp Leben und Treiben," *Theologische Studien aus Württemberg* 6 (1885): 297. Although there is no conclusive documentary evidence to state with certainty that Frederick Rapp planned or executed the Sophia lintel, there is a relative degree of probability that he at least planned it.

[15]"Harmony. Commemorating the Centennial of the Borough of Harmony, Pennsylvania, 1838-1938," Harmony, Pa.: [s.n.], 1938, 12.

wings, the symbol of semi-divinity. The most common and preferred interpretation today is that the figure represents Sophia and not a mere angel.[16]

Figure 3
Sophia Lintel, Harmony Pennsylvania

The suggestion that the figure is a mere angel rather than the female personification of Wisdom from the Old Testament canonical and apocryphal Wisdom literature is to be rejected for the following reasons. First, Sophia could be and was depicted in Christian art, particularly in the Russian

---

[16]The pamphlet published for the centennial of the Harmony Borough stated that "[a]lmost positive proof is now available that it is a representative of the 'Virgin Sophia.'" "Harmony, 1838-1938," 12. The proof that is offered is two-fold. First, the pamphlet states that the most common representation or symbol of Sophia corresponds to the stone lintel in Harmony - a head with wings. Second, the Harmonist hymnbooks reveal the devotion of this radical Pietist group to the female personification of Wisdom, Sophia. The pamphlet is absolutely correct about the second point. Sophia was depicted as an angel by the Greek and Russian Orthodox churches, but not in all traditions. For instance, Barbara Walker, *A Women's Dictionary of Symbols and Sacred Objects* (San Francisco: Harper, 1988), 205f, states that the most common representation of Sophia is a triumphant dove (dove with outspread wings).

and Greek Orthodox Churches, as an angel-like figure with wings.[17] Therefore, the wings that frame the face need not automatically indicate an angel and not Sophia. Second, both Gottfried Arnold's *Das Geheimnis der göttlichen Sophia* (*The Secret of the divine Sophia*) and Boehme referred to the angelic or (semi-)divine nature of Sophia. Arnold's volume was definitively known and used by both Rapp and the Harmonists as will be demonstrated below.[18] Arnold and Boehme were almost certainly the source for the Harmonist depiction of Sophia as an angel, rather than the Russian Orthodox tradition. Third, a Harmonist hymn addressed Sophia as "you [my] angel," who gives "angelic joys" (*Engel-Freuden*) to her followers.[19] Harmonists thus equated Sophia with an angel at least by the New Harmony era. Fourth, the Harmonists did not have a developed angelology. They upheld the orthodox Christian belief in the existence of angels, although Rapp only infrequently mentioned them in his sermons. When mentioned, it was most often a reference to the angelic, hermaphroditic nature (*Geistleib*) that believers strive to attain in the present dispensation, but would only fully be achieved in the eschatological kingdom. Angels per se, unlike the figure Sophia, did not play a significant role in Harmonist religious beliefs. Fifth, the simple dissenting style of architecture that the Harmonists used was inconsistent with the use of angels as religious symbols. We have already noted that the churches at their settlements were devoid of statues and symbolic

---

[17]Around 1400 a tradition arose in the Russian Orthodox Church to depict Sophia or Wisdom as a winged angel. In 1553, Metropolitan Makarius of Russia (1542-1563) defended two types of "winged Christ angels" against claims of heresy--Sophia (understood christologically to be the Word of God) and the "angel of good counsel." A. Ammann, "Darstellung und Deutung der Sophia im vorpetrinischen Russland," *Orientalia Christiana Periodica* 4, nos. 1-2 (1938): 120-156, here 134-143. The most famous example of the former is the Novrogod icon, found in the Cathedral of Hagia Sophia in that city, which depicted Sophia as a glowing red angel, crowned and clothed in royal vestments with prominent wings folded at her side. Thomas Schipflinger, *Sophia-Maria. A Holistic View of Creation*, trans. James Morgante (York Beach, Maine: Samuel Weiser, 1998), 281. The second type, the angel of good counsel (Isa 9:6) was portrayed in some Russian icons not as a full angel but as a (red) head with wings, that is, similarly to the Harmony stone lintel. The ducal house of Württemberg had marriage ties to the family of the czars of Russia in the eighteenth and nineteenth centuries. Hans-Martin Maurer, "Das Haus Württemberg und Rußland," *Zeitschrift für württembergische Landesgeschichte* 48 (1989): 201-222. It is therefore possible that Russian depictions of Sophia as an angel became known in the southwest corner of Germany in that era.

[18]Gottfried Arnold, *Das Geheimnis der göttlichen Sophia*, introduction by Walter Nigg (Stuttgart-Bad Cannstatt: F. Frommann, 1963). A head with wings figure is depicted at the bottom of the register of chapters after page 188 in this volume. Although the figure is not specifically identified with Sophia, its placement there is suggestive thereof.

[19]*Harmonisches Gesangbuch* (Allentown, Pa.: Heinrich Ebner, 1820), #369, 284 and *Harmonisches Gesangbuch* (Oekonomie, Pa.: Harmony Society Publications, 1827), #362, 284, Verses 1 and 5.

ornamentation. The one exception (the golden rose) reflected a distinctive radical Pietist (rather than established) church belief. In a parallel fashion, the angelic figure on the house in Harmony portrayed the radical Pietist doctrine of Sophia, a doctrine celebrated by the Harmonists frequently in sermon and song. The evidence thus supports interpreting the figure on the keystone as Sophia and not an angel.

Background to Sophialogy

The figure of Wisdom or Sophia makes her appearance in the Wisdom tradition of the canonical and apocryphal Old Testament. In the canonical Scriptures, she briefly appears in Job 28, a "Hymn to Wisdom" without any formal attempt at personification.[20] In Proverbs 1-9, however, she "raises her voice" in three main passages: 1:20-33, 8:1-36 and 9:1-6. Although much of Proverbs 1 echoes the Hebrew prophets, in this chapter the message is put into the mouth of Wisdom/Sophia. "Elsewhere it is Yahweh who will be sought but not found (Mic 3:4; Isa 1:15), to whom people will cry out but not be heard (Jer 11:11, 14), but now this has become the province of Sophia (Prov 1:28)."[21] Proverbs 8 includes a hymn describing Wisdom's role in the creation of the world, likewise something that the Hebrew Scriptures otherwise attribute to Yahweh and the New Testament to Christ, the Word of God. Verses 22-23 have been variously interpreted throughout the ages to mean that Sophia or Wisdom was a created being, the first-born of creation, or an eternal being that God possessed or acquired at the beginning.[22] Whether equiprimordial with God as a divine attribute or personified being, or subordinate to Him, Sophia according to Proverbs 8 was present when God "set the heavens in place" and when he "marked out the foundations of the earth," she was the "craftsman at his side" (Prov 8:27-30). In Proverbs 9, Sophia is the gracious hostess who has prepared her table with rich foods. She calls to bypassers, inviting them to eat her food. "Leave your simple ways and you will live; walk in the way of understanding" (Prov 9:6), she exhorts them. In the non-canonical Wisdom of Jesus ben Sirach (Sirach), Sophia likewise is an agent of creation. The "most innovative" aspect of his portrayal of the female figure, however, is her identification with Israel's Torah in Sir 24:13.[23] The Wisdom of Solomon is an apocryphal work, penned at the beginning of the Christian era, which reflects

---

[20] Martin Scott, *Sophia and the Johannine Jesus* (Sheffield: Sheffield Academic Press, 1992), 50.

[21] Scott, *Sophia*, 50-51.

[22] The Hebrew verb, קָנָה, in verse 22 is difficult and has been translated as "begat," "created", "possessed" or "acquired." Cf. Scott, *Sophia*, 51, n. 3 and Greg Edward Manship, "Feminist Sophialogy. A Philosophical and Theological Analysis of Feminist Sophialogy and Sophia-Christology: An Evangelical Response" (M.A. thesis, Trinity Evangelical Divinity School, 1994), 39f.

[23] Scott, *Sophia*, 54.

Alexandrian philosophy. In it the "figure of Sophia reaches her pinnacle . . . being at once the one who creates, saves, and reveals."[24]

Orthodox Lutheran theologians of the sixteenth to early eighteenth centuries most commonly upheld the view that Sophia in Proverbs 1 to 9 was to be directly equated with Christ the Wisdom of God (Col 2:3) and the Word of God (John 1:3). This interpretation extended back to the early church fathers, Clement of Alexandria and Athanasius, who in their battle with Arianism maintained that Wisdom in Proverbs was Christ, eternally begotten and of the same nature as the Father.[25] Luther's translation of Prov 8:22 supported this view–Wisdom/Sophia was "had" (*gehabt*) or "possessed" from the beginning. A century after Luther, orthodox theologians Abraham Calov and Johannes Olearius adamantly declared that Wisdom in Proverbs 8 was none other than the Christ, begotten from all eternity.[26] Later conservative Lutheran theologians of the eighteenth century were more willing to equate Sophia with a (quasi-personified) divine attribute of wisdom or a mere poetic/heuristic device (i.e. a non-being), instead of or alongside the equation with Christ.[27] Seldom would she be viewed as a hypostasis or true independent being. [28]

Some churchly and radical Pietists in the seventeenth and eighteenth centuries, however, reacted to the deadness of piety and theology in the established Lutheran and Reformed churches by turning to the older mystical traditions of Sophialogy as mediated by both the canonical and noncanonical Scriptures. Jacob Boehme, J. G. Gichtel, Gottfried Arnold and Jane Leade in the seventeenth century, Jung-Stilling, Michael Hahn and George Rapp in the eighteenth century discovered enriching spiritual fruit through

---

[24]Ibid., 55.

[25]Ammann, "Darstellung und Deutung der Sophia," 120-121.

[26]Abraham Calov, *Biblia testam. veteris illustrata* (Frankfurt: Balthasar Christoph Wust, 1672). Johannes Olearius, *Biblischer Erklärung. Dritter Theil* (Leipzig: Johann Christoph Tarnoven, 1679), 812. Cf. Johann Georg Starke, *Kurzgefaßter Auszug der grundlichsten und nutzbarsten Auslegungen über alle Bücher Altes Testaments*, Theil 4 (Leipzig: Bernhard Christoph Breitkopf, 1750).

[27]Sophia as divine attribute and Christ: Johann Augustin Dittelmair, *Die Heilige Schrift des Alten und Neuen Testaments. Siebenter Theil* (Leipzig: Bernhard Christoph Breitkopf, 1756), 19, 47-48 and 121. Sophia as divine attribute: Georg Friedrich Seiler, *Das größre biblische Erbauungsbuch*. Theil 4 (Erlangen: Bibelanstalt, 1791), 22-23, 60. Sophia as poetic device and Christ: Joseph Friedrich Shelling, *Summarien oder gründliche Auslegung der Schriften alten Testaments. Dritter Band, welcher die Bücher: Esra, Nehemia, Esther, Hiob, die Sprüche und den Prediger enthält zu öffentlicher Kirchenandacht in dem Königreich Württemberg, auch zum erbaulichen Hausgebrauch ausgefertigt* (Stuttgart: Königl. Hof- und Kanzlei-Buchdruckerei der Gebrüder Mäntler, 1810), 347-348, 398-399. Sophia as poetic device: August Dächsel, *Das Alte Testament, Band 2*. 3d ed. (Leipzig: A. Deichert, 1890), 458.

[28]The author is using the typology of Manship, *Feminist Sophialogy*, 66f and 139f.

their practice of Sophia veneration.[29] They did not hesitate to view Sophia as more than a personified divine attribute. To most of them, she was a true divine being, albeit not outside or independent of the Christian Trinity.

Harmonist Sophialogy

Sophialogy or the doctrine of Sophia was taught in Rapp's pastoral letters and sermons and sung about in Sophia-inspired Harmonist hymns. Prior to emigration Rapp wrote pastoral letters to his disciples in Württemberg (1793-1802), thirty-seven of which were preserved in copies made by his followers. Of these only two mention Sophia - one develops the Sophia doctrine with some detail and the other is a brief aside. Rapp, as will be shown, generally equated Sophia with the Holy Spirit, rather than with Christ, as earlier orthodox theologians did. In his sermons he referred much more frequently to the third person of the Trinity than to the female personification of wisdom. Nevertheless, reference to Sophia is found often enough in Rapp's sermons to establish the main outlines of his Sophialogical teaching. A relatively large number of Harmonist-composed as well as borrowed Sophia hymns are extant in the Harmony Society's manuscript and printed hymnbooks - *Eine kleine Sammlung* (1824), *Feurige Kohlen* (1826), and the 1820 and 1827 *Gesangbücher*. To this corpus, some of approximately 150 related hymns to the personified female figure Harmonie[30] and others extolling Solomon's Beloved may be added, since both of these female figures were at times in the Harmonist literature clearly equated with Wisdom.[31] Although Rapp was somewhat more restrained in his praise of Sophia than his followers and frequently preferred to utilize orthodox Trinitarian expressions, he nevertheless upheld the doctrine of Sophia. Judging by the frequency of Sophia, Harmonie, and Song of Solomon hymns in their hymnbooks, one must conclude that this form of mystical spirituality was meaningful and significant to the average Harmonist.

Rapp on more than one occasion noted that the doctrine of Sophia was not newly created by his generation. Rather the "prophets" [Solomon, Sirach], "holy fathers" [medieval mystics] and "friends of God" [Proto-Pietists and Pietists such as Boehme, Gottfried Arnold, etc.] from former days had understood the secret of Sophia, which however remained hidden to less

---

[29]Ruth Albrecht, "'Der einzige Weg zur Erkenntnis Gottes' – Die Sophia-Theologie Gottfried Arnolds und Jakob Böhmes," in *Auf den Spuren der Weisheit*, ed. Verena Wodtke (Freiburg: Herder, 1991), 102-117, here 102-103.

[30]The author spells the personified female figure "Harmonie," that is, with the German orthography, to distinguish it from normal usages of the term "harmony."

[31]Example: Harmonie is creator of world, as is Sophia, although she makes creation more complete: "O! Harmonie aus dem geistl: Wesen, u deiner eigenen Matere, daraus du anfängl: ein korpus, u in einen Leib, Leibhaftig gemacht worden. Darin das wahre vermögen der göttl: kraft in dir lebt, der ersten obersten geb: daraus die ganze Schöpfung vollständiger gemacht wird." MG-437/Box 22/Folder 82B/D-29.

enlightened souls.³² It was wise that they concealed this "best and most secret" mystery of union (*Lust*) with Sophia. Only those in this and former ages who could eavesdrop on the "heavenly conversation of the Holy Spirit," as by implication Rapp and the Harmonists could, could grasp this secret.³³

What were the secrets of Sophia that Rapp and the Harmonists treasured? Like other radical Pietists, Rapp held that Sophia was not merely a personified divine attribute; rather she was an uncreated being and therefore pre-existent and divine (albeit not separated from the Trinity).³⁴ This divine aspect of her person was depicted on the stone Sophia lintel at Harmony, Pennsylvania by the inclusion of wings with seven feathers on each side – seven being the sign of fullness and perfection that is often used in conjunction with deity.³⁵ Sophia assisted in the creation of the world by being the "life and movement of the divine Spirit." The female personification of Wisdom, who is likewise the Spirit in this passage, was the "prime material" out of which Adam and all of creation was made.³⁶ This suggests not creation *ex nihilo*, but creation from pre-existent, divine but chaotic and unordered matter (cf. Gen 1:2: "the earth was without form and void"). Another Rapp sermon spoke of the fellowship of God and Sophia that took place in the creation of the world, a fellowship between male and female principles.

> She [Sophia] created all things in fellowship with the great God. And this is what is meant, when it says: "Let there be light, and there was light." "Let there be light," signifies the rule of the Father. "And there was light" the office of the Mother. One sees therefore in this all, that the Queen [Sophia] is the mediatrix, by which all things come down from above and ascend from below.³⁷

---

³²MG-185/1-5004/Box 15/Folder 6/Q-44. It is no accident that Arnold's work on Sophia was called "The Secret of the divine Sophia."

³³"ja ihr h: Propheten, u ihr Freunde Gottes, wir lernen von euch; ihr habt das beste u geheimste von dieser lust mit Sophia weißlich verschwiegen, u auf die himmlische unterredung deß h: G: beybehalten: u also muß auch jezo noch das wichtige geheimniß deß Herrn unter denen bleiben, die es besizen u Erkennen." MG-185/1-5004/Box 15/Folder 5/N-143.

³⁴MG-185/Box 15/Folder 4/D-14.

³⁵Alva William Steffler, *Symbols of the Christian Faith* (Grand Rapids: Eerdmans, 2002), 134. Sophia built a house with seven pillars in Prov 9:1.

³⁶"u ist doch in Ihr verborgen das leben u bewegen deß göttl: Geistes, deßen der sie zusammen getrieben, neml: was die oberste himmel u die unterste der Elementarische [Symbol = Erde], u ist alles die prima Materia die simple Einfache Jungf:[rau] ... Daraus gemacht ward der erste M:[ensch] in seiner Figur. Also wirckt der G: noch alle dinge.." MG-437/Box 22/Folder 02B/C-6.

³⁷"sie hat im gemeinsch: mit dem grosen Gott alles geschaffen. u dieses ist es, wan es heißt Es werde Licht, u es ward Licht! Es werde Licht bedeutet die Herrschaft des Vatters! u es ward Licht gehet auf das amt der Mutter. man siehet also hieraus in allem, daß diese König:[in] die Mittlerin sey, bey einen jedem von oben herab, u von unten hinauf." MG-185/1-5004/Box 15/Folder 6/R-97.

The Father was the active (masculine) force, whose verbal *Fiat* brought the world into existence, though not without the corresponding reactive or passive (feminine) force of Sophia.

Rapp was careful not to depict Sophia as a fourth divine being independent of the Godhead. In several of his sermons he made abundantly clear that Sophia was to be equated with the Spirit of Jesus, that is, the Holy Spirit.

> Now we are well aware that the Spirit of Jesus and Wisdom are not two, rather one indivisible Being, who through divine activity constantly reveals itself in the church (*Gemeine*). Through this [revelation] the heavenly Sophia is always nearer and more known to the church, as a peculiar divine being. It [the divine being] is itself of course one with the Godhead, without whom also nothing is made or created, but nevertheless as the passive (*leydente*), feminine part, the fruit and progenerative matter (*Gebärungsstoff*), which is made known and visible in the church by its own divine character. But the church nevertheless attributes all the characteristics, activities and signs to the Holy Spirit, as does the New Testament.[38]

According to Rapp, it was appropriate to equate Sophia with the Holy Spirit, as the New Testament does, since the two "names are completely in one and indivisible."[39] The Holy Spirit however is the active (masculine) principle of this *one* divine Being, and Sophia the feminine, passive and progenerative principle. Creation occurred when the Holy Spirit "worked" upon the passive, receptive "material" of Sophia to bring about life.[40]

This close identification between the Holy Spirit and Sophia resulted in some of the offices of the Spirit being attributed to the female personified Being. Sanctification of believers, a role normally assigned to the Holy Spirit, was in some cases accredited to Sophia. Through the motherly role of Sophia, the believer experienced the necessary nurturing and correction necessary to bring him/her to maturity in Christ. "Sophia is known to the congregation under the image of the Holy Spirit in her capacity as an honorable, serious, loving mother, whose [duty] is to subdue, break and punish the degenerate nature, until within us a deferential obedience is

---

[38] MG-185/Box 15/Folder 4/L-32. This passage is lifted virtually verbatim from Gottfried Arnold, *Sophia*, Cap V, §3-6, 35-36. The differences between Rapp's sermon and Arnold will be discussed below. Cf. MG-185/1-5004/Box 15/Folder 5/N-143.

[39] MG-185/Box 15/Folder 4/L-32: "Weil die nahmens alle vollkommen in Eins, u unzertrennl: alle in Eins laufen u bleiben."

[40] MG-185/Box 15/Folder 4/L-32. MG-185/Box 15/Folder 5/C-33 likewise defines the "Spirit of Jesus as masculine" and the Church/soul/Sophia as "reactive or passive".

reached."[41] One Rapp sermon claimed that Wisdom as the Spirit of Jesus helps to protect believers through her own glory.[42]

Although most Harmonist sermons stressed the close association between Sophia and the Holy Spirit, at least one sermon as well as several hymns in the 1827 hymnbook links her with the person and work of Christ. After equating the Queen [Sophia] with the "Jerusalem that is above" (Gal 4:26), and the turtledove from the Song of Solomon (female images), Rapp switched metaphors and, in spite of the female pronoun, associated Sophia with Christ, the Messiah:

> *She* is the beginning of creation, to whom God has given the dominion over all things. *She* is called the dwelling of the Almighty God, as well as the countenance of the Lord, the Word or the speech of God. *The Queen* is hinted at through the word "I" and is the Lord himself, who appeared to Abraham, the Prince of Israel, who is greater than the angels, the Messiah, the son of Joseph.[43]

Sophia, in this case, was given roles and functions that the New Testament assigns to Christ alone (dominion over all things, the Word of God, the Lord). This switch of images is not as illogical as it appears at first sight. The Holy Spirit is the Spirit of Jesus, and Sophia is the feminine, passive aspect of the Holy Spirit. Therefore, she is likewise in one sense the feminine aspect of Christ, the Lord, the Word of God, the Messiah, the son of Joseph.

The first two verses of the hymn, "Der Weisheit holder Perlen-Schatz," which was included in both the 1820 and 1827 Harmonist *Gesangbücher*, were written by Gottfried Arnold and the remaining three by an unnamed Harmonist.[44] The fact that the complete hymn was included in both hymnbooks argues for its popularity among Harmony Society members. In the first two (Arnold) verses, Sophia is the pearl-bejeweled treasure whom true believers are exhorted to embrace. In the Harmonist addition, however, starting with verse three, the focus abruptly changes to choosing Jesus and consecrating one's entire life to him. Although there is no clear equation of

---

[41]"Sophia der Gem: bekannt wird unter dem Bild deß h: G. in der Eigensch: einer Ehrwürdigen, u ernstl: Liebreichen Mutter! die an der ausgearteten Natur zu bändigen brechen, u bestraffen hat. Biß in uns der Ehrerbietige gehorsam erreicht ist." MG-185/1-5004/Box 15/Folder 6/R-138.

[42]"Weish: jezt als der G: Jesu wird mich selber auch helfen bewahren in ihrer Herrlichk:." MG-185/1-5004/Box 15/Folder 5/N-143.

[43]"Die ist der anfang der Schöpfung, deren Gott die Herrsch: über alles gegeben, sie heißt die wohnung deß allm:[ächtigen] Gottes, wie auch das angesicht deß Herrn, u das Wort, oder die rede Gottes. Die König: wird angeditten durch das Wort Ich! u ist der Herr selbst, der dem Abrah: erschienen ist, der Fürst der Isral: der gröser ist als die Eng: der Mesias, der Sohn Josephs. . ." MG-185/1-5004/Box 15/Folder 6/R-97.

[44]1827 *Gesangbuch*, #72, 57 and 1820 *Gesangbuch*, #271, 204. Cf. Gottfried Arnold, *Neue Göttliche Liebes-Funcken und Ausbrechende Liebes-Flammen in fortgesetzten Beschreibungen der grossen Liebe Gottes in Christo Jesu*, published in Arnold, *Sophia*, #12, 246.

Sophia to Christ, the juxtaposition of the two figures is suggestive. Likewise, another hymn in the 1827 hymnbook, "Sophia, du weißt mein Leiden," abruptly switches from the joys of loving Sophia (verses 1 and 2), to desire for the bridegroom (verse 4). At the end of the hymn, the bridegroom is identified as "my heart's (play-)companion, my trusted Jesus."[45] Once again, the link between Sophia and Christ is less well-defined than the clear association between Sophia and the Holy Spirit. When talk was of union with Sophia, however, the conceptual jump to union with Christ the Bridegroom, the lover of the church and the individual soul, was but a small one.[46]

For the Harmonists, like Gottfried Arnold before them, Sophia appeared in the guise both of a bride in general as well as of Solomon's Beloved in the biblical book, *Song of Solomon*. Solomon's garden was often described in Rapp's sermons in millennial terms, as blooming, "young and fresh," "flowing with nectar" and "filled with pleasing scents." Here Sophia as Sulamith (Solomon's bride) wandered with her train of followers (sisters). The banner of love is not just over her but "is called, love over all of us" (cf. Song Sol 2:4).[47] The marriage union with Sophia, described often in somewhat erotic terms, was used as a metaphor of the mystical union with Christ. It was described in concrete, realistic terms as "eating, drinking, clothing oneself" and "possessing" Sophia/Christ with "hot passion" in the "deepest ground of the soul."[48] The result of this union was the experience of great joy. "Love pervades me with life, leading to complete recovery. Thus you are my greatest treasure. For the love spark divinizes me through and through (*durchgötterst mich*) with your hot glow."[49] One was enabled to participate in the divine nature, a fulfillment of the promise in 2 Pet 1:4, which the Harmonists and other churchly and radical Pietists literally sought.[50]

We saw above that although Sophia as mother was loving, she was not afraid to correct, that is, to practice "tough love." It was only after she had accomplished her pedagogical goal with the individual (obedience) that she altered her strict demeanor (*Gestalt*) for the charming, gracious one of a

---

[45]1827 *Gesangbuch*, #396, 309. The term אָמוֹן "skilled workman" in Prov 8:30 is translated in the Berleburg Bible as a playmate, *Schoos-Kind*, who plays before his countenance at all times, rather than a craftsman.

[46]"u. so ist mir Sophia zum Gemahl erkohren: u [ich] hab zugleich den Mann den Herrn, der soll mir alles seyn." MG-185/Box 15/Folder 5/O-2.

[47]MG-185/1-5004/Box 15/Folder 6/R-145. Cf. MG-185/1-5004/Box 15/Folder 6/Q-44.

[48]"So ist es mehr als wahr, daß ich den, den meiner Seele liebt Eigne, denn in tiefsten Grund der Seel, Eß, trinck u Zieh ich dich in mich mit hiziger Brunst." MG-185/Box 15/Folder 5/O-2.

[49]"die Liebe durchdringt mich durch leben; zum völligen genesen. So bist du mein höchster Schatz. Denn das liebes Funke durchgötterst mich mit deiner heißen Gluth." MG-185/Box 15/Folder 5/O-2.

[50]"durch die Widergeb: 2 in Eins, der Göttl: Natur theilhaftig sind." MG-185/1-5004/Box 15/Folder 5/N-138.

virgin.⁵¹ Sophia as mother was not just strict but also nurturing. One Harmonist hymn described Sophia as the "one who had raised me," who "had gently and affectionately nursed me," whose "heart carried my weight." ⁵² Sophia in her mother role wiped away tears, gave strength, comforted and instructed those who felt poor, small and alone. She led like a guardian angel (*Schutzgott*) with her "mother hands."⁵³ Another hymn boldly referred to Sophia as the "Mother Godhead," who lives in the glory of the Father.⁵⁴

Not just bride and mother, Sophia was also depicted in Harmonist sermons and songs as a "very pure and chaste" virgin.⁵⁵ Those who desired to follow her path must likewise avoid the fleshly and sexual temptations of "Delilah," which proved the downfall of the biblical Samson (Judges 16). Therefore, a Harmonist hymn expressed the prayer: "Let no Delilah creep her way into my heart!"⁵⁶ Only those who "surrender themselves completely to the discipline of the Holy Spirit," who "value nothing higher in this world" than striving to recover the "lost image of God," and who freely "choose the path of self-annihilation" (*Vernichtigung* – Tersteegian emphasis), only such ones will experience the joys of Virgin Sophia.⁵⁷

To the Harmonists, Sophia was an androgynous virgin. This aspect of her character was depicted on the Harmony Sophia lintel by the androgynous nature of the face with feminine hair plaiting. Sophia combined within her essence or being both the female and male natures, not just feminine or masculine characteristics. "This bride (*Gemahlin*) is also male (*männlich*), in two [natures]," stated Rapp in a sermon.⁵⁸ She was the virgin that Adam lost in Paradise, when he lusted after a conjugal partner such as the animals

---

⁵¹"Biß in uns der Ehrerbietige gehorsam erreicht ist. Als dann verwechselt sie ihre Ernsthafte gestalt, mit einer anmuthigen u nimmt uns auf als ein Weib der Jungfrausch: . . . " MG-185/1-5004/Box 15/Folder 6/R-138. Cf. MG-185/Box 15/Folder 5/E-45.

⁵²"So hat sie mich auferzogen, zärtlich hat sie mich gesäugt; ja, ihr Herz war mir gewogen."

⁵³1827 *Gesangbuch*: "Sophia, wann die Liebes-Hände," # 343, 268; "Die Weisheit ist mein bester Rath," #92, 71 (from Ephrata hymnbook); "Sophia, Theure, Holde, deren Anblick," # 342, 267.

⁵⁴"Sinkend in die Ohnmacht schwebend, werd ich Sophia geweiht, daß der Mutter Gottheit lebe, in des Vaters Herrlichkeit." 1827 *Gesangbuch*, #411, 321.

⁵⁵"sehr rein u keuschen Sophia." MG-185/1-5004/Box 15/Folder 5/N-138.

⁵⁶"Laß keine Delila sich in mein Herz einschleichen," 1827 *Gesangbuch*, #397, 310. Cf. ibid., #290, 237, which is a hymn from Gottfried Arnold, *Poetische Lob- und Liebes Sprüche*, #63, 74.

⁵⁷MG-185/1-5004/Box 15/Folder 5/N-95. "Wer nun der Zucht deß h: G: ganz ergibt, u nichts höhers in der Welt als seyn verlohrnes Eigenthum das Ebenb:[ild] Gottes Ehret, u mit [Symbol – Herzen] sinn u Seel sich gänzl: die volle freyl: zu seiner vernichtig:[ung] erwählet: der wird sich gewiß ganz getrost mit dem G: Jesu gemeinschafl: an die Arbeit wagen; der Sophia der er dient wird ihm kein Glück versagen..."

⁵⁸ MG-185/1-5004/Box 15/Folder 6/R-138.

had.⁵⁹ Sophia was the "pure element" that was separated from Adam's being, when Eve was formed from the rib taken from his side. "For the pure element is now after the Fall [taken] from us and [put] once again in Sophia, the highest glory in the image of God, and to recover that [image], it must be sought by us, even as the being [must be sought], from which man was originally made by God."⁶⁰ We have seen above, that Sophia was the being from which Adam, the first man was made. She was the androgynous being, which must be sought by man.

The reward for following the path of self-denial was finding Sophia and assuming the same form of androgynous corporality that Sophia embodied. This corporality was the *Geistleib* (spiritual or resurrection body). It combined within itself opposing dualities–God and man, male and female, spirit and physical body. Though Rapp referred to this as a "spiritual" body, it possessed the same form of true physicality that would be found in the millennial kingdom. This *Geistleib* was to be sought in this present age, although it would not be fully assumed by the individual until the *eschaton*, when the circle would be completed and the renewed humanity would reflect again the corporality that Adam had before the Fall. Rapp affirmed:

> Therefore, I will not let you [Sophia/Christ] out of the hand of my faith, until I have gone through death and been completed to blessing, and have been filled with the God-humanity (*Gottmenschheit*), that I may be like you, formed in Spirit and a new body, that the end through free will may attain again the beginning.⁶¹

Another reward for self-denial was achieving the pearl or pearl-crown of Sophia. This reward was likewise preserved in heaven for the faithful believers who persevered to the end. In a sermon, Rapp rhetorically asked Sophia to give him the pearl or pearl-crown now. She replied:

> O no, I want to hold my pearl along with the jewelry in safekeeping, said Sophia, but I will dwell, remain, rule in you, as if it were my kingdom of heaven. Don't be afraid. You will as a matter of fact experience how it will become your own. But [now] my countenance will watch and protect even the precious pearl within you. But the beautiful pearl crown, which you have indeed already seen, I have put aside for you as your full reward, until that time

---

⁵⁹"diese Jungf: ist eben dajenige, was Ad:[am] im Parad:[eis] verlohren hatte." MG-185/1-5004/Box 15/Folder 6/R-138.

⁶⁰"den das reine Element ist uns nun nach dem Fall wieder in der Sophia die höch-glorie im Ebenb: Gottes; u das wieder zu erlangen, muß von uns nichts anders gesucht werden als eben ein solches Wesen, woraus der M: anfängl: von Gott gemacht worden." MG-185/1-5004/Box 15/Folder 5/N-116.

⁶¹"Drum laß ich dich nicht aus der Hand meines glaubens, biß ich durch allen Tod zur Seegen vollendet bin, u mit der Gottmenschh:[eit] erfüllt: daß ich wie du, im Geist u neuen Leib ausgebildet bin: u das Ende den Anfang, durch das Frey w:[illen] wider erlangt hab." MG-185/Box 15/Folder 5/O-2. Cf. MG-185/1-5004/Box 15/Folder 6/R-81.

when bejeweled and completely pure you stand before me, then you may go, you may go into the wedding celebration.⁶²

In the Gottfried Arnold hymn "Der Weisheit holder Perlen-Schatz," and in a Sophia hymn borrowed from the Ephrata Cloister, Sophia herself was the "pearl of great price," which a wise man would give up all to possess (Matt 13:46).⁶³ Interestingly, although the Harmony stone lintel does not depict Sophia as crowned with a pearl crown, Greek and Russian icons often depicted her crowned as an empress.

This overview of Harmonist Sophialogy is in keeping with the depiction of Sophia on the keystone of the stone lintel in Harmony, Pennsylvania. The figure there is depicted as divine and perfect (wings with seven feathers). The figure is feminine (plaited hair) reflecting the Harmonist conception of Sophia as the feminine aspect of the Holy Spirit, as a mother and bride. She is also an androgynous virgin (androgynous face). The figure on the stone lintel is dominated by the largeness of the head in proportion to the body. In fact there is no body per se, but only a robe with miniscule hands that are proportionate to the robe but by no means to the head. The head is the seat of understanding and wisdom. It is therefore appropriate that Sophia as the Wisdom of God should have an overly large head.

Sources of Harmonist Sophialogy

It is not the aim to establish all the sources from which Rapp and the Harmonists drew their doctrine. That being said, it is possible to ascertain that Rapp and the Harmonists relied heavily on Gottfried Arnold for their Sophialogy and that they were likewise significantly influenced by Jacob Boehme.⁶⁴ Rapp and the Harmonists were well acquainted with the writings of Gottfried Arnold. The 1829 list of books owned by the Harmony Society contains two of his church historical works, *Erstes Marterthum* and *Kirchen u. Ketzer Historie*.⁶⁵ A comparison of Arnold's two collections of So-

---

⁶²"O, nein, ich will behalten, spricht Sophia, mein Perl: samt dem Schmuck in verwahrung, will aber in dir wohnen, bleiben, walten, als wär es mein himmelr: Hab nicht bang. Du solt es in der That erfahren, wie es dein Eigen seyn: doch soll mein Angesicht dich beobachten u hüten selbst in dir die Edle Perl: nun die schöne Perlen Crone, die du zwar schon hast erblickt, hab ich dir zum vollen Lohne, beygelegt biß du geschmückt, u ganz rein vor mir wirst stehen, dan gehst, gehst du zur Hochzeit ein." MG-437/Box 22/Folder 82B/C-25.

⁶³1827 *Gesangbuch*, #72, 57 (Arnold hymn) and #352, 279 "Perl aller keusch verliebten Seelen" (from Ephrata Cloister).

⁶⁴The Harmonists borrowed forty-three hymns from the hymnbook of the Ephrata house fathers and included them in their 1827 *Gesangbuch*. However, few of these were Sophia hymns and therefore the influence of Conrad Beissel and Ephrata was insignificant for Harmonist Sophialogy.

⁶⁵Karl J. R. Arndt, *George Rapp's Successors and Material Heirs 1847- 1916* (Teaneck, N.J.: Fairleigh Dickinson University Press, 1971), #107 and # 157, 414-428.

phia poems (*Lob- und Liebes-Sprüche* and *Göttliche Liebes-Funken*) with the Harmonist hymnbooks revealed that three of Arnold's Sophia hymns were included in the 1820 Harmonist hymnbook, and fourteen were in the 1827 expanded edition (see Appendix B). The borrowing of these Arnold hymns had not been previously discovered by scholars.[66] Rather, an Arnold poem, which was copied verbatim after one of Rapp's early pastoral letters (1791), was claimed by Karl Arndt in *George Rapp's Separatists* to be an anonymous Harmonist poem.[67] This borrowing of Arnold hymns took place in spite of the fact that Arnold's collections of Sophia poems included in the 1700 edition of his *Secret of the Divine Sophia* were not listed as belonging to the Harmonist library in 1829. This proves that others books were owned by the Harmony Society in addition to those on the 1829 list.

The Harmony Society by at least the New Harmony era (1820 onward) was divided into small groups called companies by gender, age and marital status. In the New Harmony era, the male and female companies wrote paraphrases and poems based on various passages of the Song of Solomon, in which they frequently equated Solomon's Beloved with Sophia.[68] These writings, which are preserved in a number of manuscript hymnbooks, reflect the spirituality of the average Harmonist. We have already seen that Rapp equated Sophia with Solomon's Beloved in some of his sermons. According to Tanner, this linking of Sophia to the Song of Solomon was the unique and innovative contribution of Arnold, whose teaching about Sophia otherwise was dependent on Boehme and Gichtel.[69] This same link between the female figures was also evidenced among the Harmonists.

Further, the Harmonist practice of writing poems to Sophia based on texts from the Song of Solomon paralleled Arnold's *Lob- und Liebes-Sprüche*, in which the latter did exactly that. Not only did the Harmonists follow Arnold's example in writing paraphrases or poems to Biblical texts from the Song of Solomon. In approximately half (thirteen of twenty-seven) of these group compositions to Sophia in one manuscript hymnbook, the female or male companies ended with a verse quoted verbatim from an Arnold hymn

---

[66]Wetzel in his chapter on Harmonist hymnody in *Frontier Musicians* (p. 37-70) did much work on establishing some of the sources of hymns in their hymnbooks (e.g. Ephrata hymnbooks and Rondorff's *Silberne Trompeten*), but he did not discover the borrowing from Arnold. Richard D. Wetzel, *Frontier Musicians on the Connoquenessing, Wabash, and Ohio: A History of the Music and Musicians of George Rapp's Harmony Society, 1805-1906* (Athens, Ohio: Ohio University Press, 1976).

[67]Arndt, *Doc. Hist. 1803-1815*, 245f. The poem "Komm Tauben Gatte" is found in Arnold, *Lob und Liebes-Sprüche*, #64, 77f.

[68]MS Hymnbook pM 10.3, 274f. (Franzin Companie); 285f (Steiger Companie); 300f (Alt Hörnles Companie); 304f (Conrad Feucht Companie).

[69]"Nur, daß er sie [das Hohelied] stellenweise mit Sophia zusammenbringt, ist das Besondere an seinen Versen, die im übrigen kaum über das hinausgehen, was ändere Fromme des 17. Jahrhunderts aus dem Hohelied heraus- oder in es hineindichteten." Fritz Tanner, *Die Ehe im Pietismus* (Zurich: Zwingli Verlag, 1952), 41. See footnote 75.

to Sophia. This further supports the significant influence of Gottfried Arnold's Sophia doctrine both on Rapp and the Harmonists.[70]

The greatest proof of influence was the verbatim utilization of large portions of Cap. IV and V of Arnold's *Secret of the Divine Sophia* by Rapp in one of his undated sermons (see Appendix C). As evidenced below, Rapp lifted verbatim or nearly verbatim key sentences from these two chapters, while leaving behind some of Arnold's lesser important lines. This Rapp sermon caught the author's attention because it was stylistically more cogent and precise than Rapp's normal rambling style. A parallel reading of Arnold's *Sophia* explained the reason why. Apparently Rapp felt that the rendering by Arnold more clearly and concisely expressed his own beliefs, better than he could state them in his own words.

Similarities between Rapp's Sophialogy and that of Arnold include the following: (1) Sophia is equated with the Beloved in the Song of Solomon, a distinctive element in Arnold likewise found in Rapp's sermons; (2) Sophia is described as virgin, bride and mother. In Ch. VI, §4 Arnold affirmed that the "divine Wisdom is introduced in the Scripture in the image of a woman, virgin, bride, mother, nurse, instructor, etc." These same roles for Sophia were found among the Harmonists; (3) Similar to Arnold, Rapp was more concerned with the personal relationship between the soul/*Gemeine* and Sophia than in solving questions of cosmogony; (4) Arnold supported his Sophia doctrine with biblical citations and quotes from the church fathers. Rapp likewise attempted to develop his Sophialogy on the bedrock of Scripture (though not the church fathers).

In spite of the fact that Rapp utilized Arnold's *Sophia*, he also significantly changed the latter's emphases in more than one place. One very important difference is that Rapp primarily equated Sophia with the third person of the Trinity, the Holy Spirit, rather than with Christ, with whom Arnold and the majority of Sophia-devotees associated her. Rapp omitted from his sermon (underlined above) the phrase found in *Sophia*, Ch. IV, §14: "He [Christ] is called Wisdom." Later Arnold in Ch. V, §6 attributed "all characteristics, activities and signs of Wisdom to *the Son of God* and his Spirit." Rapp omitted the phrase "Son of God" and added that *the church and the New Testament* attributed "all characteristics, activities and signs *to the Holy Spirit*" (underlined above). This is a significant difference since it is quite uncommon and contrary to the traditional orthodox Lutheran interpretation. Although Arnold allowed on occasion that Sophia could be identified with all three persons of the Trinity, his primary focus was to uphold the link be-

---

[70]MS Hymnbook pM 10.3 includes quotations from the following Arnold Hymns: *Lob u. Liebes-Sprüche* # 10, 12, 18, 20, 25, 34, 40, 45, 50, 51 and 61 and *Neue Göttliche Liebes-Funcken* #114 and 116. Only LLS #10 was later included in the 1820 and 1827 hymnbooks.

tween Sophia and the Word of God.[71] Likewise Boehme and Gichtel maintained the close identification between Sophia and Christ.[72]

Another difference between Rapp's and Arnold's Sophialogy is that Rapp consistently stressed the relationship of Sophia to the congregation (*Gemeine*) rather than to the individual soul, which is Arnold's focus.[73] Twice in this short sermon, Rapp replaced "in the soul" and "in man" with "in the congregation" (underlined above). Three other times Rapp emphasized that Sophia was "revealed in the congregation" through her divine activity. In the same passages in Arnold's *Sophia*, the author did not state where she was revealed but implied that it was in the individual soul. This emphasis on a visible church by Rapp reflected his "Anabaptist" ecclesiology, which stood in sharp contrast to Arnold's mystical-spiritualist stance. Finally, one other significant difference was that Rapp incorporated the concept of Sophia being the passive, feminine aspect of the Holy Spirit. This concept was not to be found in Arnold. A similar conception was found, however, in the writings of Jacob Boehme.

Therefore, the second primary source of Rapp's Sophia doctrine is to be found in the writings of Jacob Boehme. As noted above, Arnold was likewise dependent on Boehme, besides others.[74] Rapp's utilization of Arnold, there-

---

[71]Arnold, *Sophia*, Ch. IV, §9, 11, 14 and Ch. V, §13, 38. Cf. Albrecht, "Sophia Theologie," 106. Cf. Erich Seeberg, *Gottfried Arnold. Die Wissenschaft und die Mystik seiner Zeit* (Darmstadt: Wissenschaftliche Buchgesellschaft, 1964), 25-27: In Arnold's "last and most moderate book", the *Theologia experimentalis*, the author, although retaining Boehme's androgynous concepts, was "geneigt, Sophia mit Christus gleichzusetzen" (27). This is in keeping with the early church fathers. "Nach 1 Kor. 1, 24 und 30 und nach dem Zeugnis vieler Väter ist Christus die Weisheit..." (25).

[72]Tanner, *Ehe*, 31 (Gichtel) and Albrecht, "Sophia Theologie," 113. Radical Pietist J. E. Petersen, however, linked Sophia with the Holy Spirit. Martin H. Jung, "Johanna Eleonora Petersen," in *The Pietist Theologians*, ed. Carter Lindberg (Malden, Mass.: Blackwell, 2005), 147-160, here 156-157.

[73]Cf. Büchsel: "Es geht im 'Gottesdienst' allein um die Vereinigung mit Gott, zu der wohl Stille und Einsamkeit, nicht aber Gemeinschaft mit anderen Menschen nötig ist. Daraus folgt von selbst, daß 'aller äusserlicher Gottesdienst indifferent und unnöthig sey.'" Jürgen Büchsel, *Gottfried Arnold. Sein Verständnis von Kirche und Wiedergeburt* (Witten: Luther Verlag, 1970), 112.

[74]Benz finds the sources of Arnold's Sophialogy in Jacob Boehme, Gichtel, English Philadelphians and in the German mysticism of Seuse. Ernst Benz, "Gottfried Arnold's 'Geheimnis der göttlichen Sophia' und seine Stellung in der christlichen Sophienlehre," *Jahrbuch der Hessischen Kirchen Geschichtlichen Vereinigung* 18 (1967): 51-82, here 53. Peter Erb reminds us that "Arnold's *Das Geheimnis der göttlichen Sophia*... is not a Boehmist treatise despite the several motifs therein which Arnold borrowed from the Goerlitz shoemaker." "Verbal proximities and similar motifs and images" have all too often been viewed "as marks of influence and/or directives in interpretation." Peter C. Erb, "Gerhard Tersteegen, Christopher Saur, and Pennsylvania Sectarians," *Brethren Life and Thought* 20 (Summer 1975): 153-157, here 155.

fore, was an indirect appropriation of Boehmist thought. The Harmonists were not just indirectly influenced by Boehme. Even prior to emigration, the group around Rapp read and digested the works of Boehme first-hand. It is therefore not surprising that a number of Boehmist emphases were found in the cosmological aspects of the Harmonist leader's Sophialogy. The concept of Sophia as the "pure element" separated from Adam at the Fall has its roots in the Adam *mythos* of Jakob Boehme. Likewise, the concept of Sophia as the "movement" (*Bewegung*) within the Trinity can be credited to Boehme's account.[75] Rapp's reference to Sophia as the "prime material" or "progenerative matter" from which all of creation was made is reminiscent of certain statements of Boehme in his *Threefold Life of Man* and in his *Second Apologie to Balthasar Tilken*. In these works he stated: "Sophia is the mother of all being, the matrix (womb) in which the heavens, stars, elements, earth and all things that live and move are contained as in a single picture."[76] Further: "She gives birth, but she is not the divine principle . . . rather she is the mother, in which the Father works."[77] Likewise, Sophia "could not give birth unless the Spirit of God works in her."[78] In several Rapp sermons and in Boehme, Sophia is "worked upon" either by the Holy Spirit alone or by all three persons of the Godhead: Father, *Fiat* [Word of God or Son] and the Holy Spirit. Finally, in both Boehme and in Rapp, Sophia is the "corporality of the Holy Spirit." She "makes known and visible" that which she gives birth.[79]

Striving for Sanctification: The Labyrinth and Grotto

Mystical or theosophical knowledge was communicated by the Sophia lintel. A striving for sanctification, the concern for righteous, celibate, "harmonious" living was reinforced upon the members of the Society by two elements of the Harmonist material culture—the labyrinth and the grotto.

---

[75]Cf. Tanner, *Ehe*, 13.

[76]Jacob Boehme, *De Triplici Vita Hominis, oder vom Dreyfachen Leben des Menschen*, vol. 3, *Sämtliche Schriften*, ed. Will-Erich Peuckert (Stuttgart: Frommanns, 1960), ch. 11, §13, 201. Translated by Thomas Schipflinger in "Sophia bei J. Boehme," *Una Sancta* 41/3 (1986): 195-210, here 205. Cf. MG-437/Box 22/Folder 82B/C-6 and MG-185/Box 15/Folder 4/L-32.

[77]Jacob Boehme, *Schutzschriften wider Balthasar Tilken*, vol. 5, *Sämtliche Schriften*, ed. Will-Erich Peuckert (Stuttgart: Frommanns, 1960), II, §65, 119. Cf. MG-185/1-5004/Box 15/Folder 6/R-97 and MG-185/1-5004/Box 15/Folder 5/N-143.

[78]Boehme, *Tilken*, II, §67, 119.

[79]*Triplica vita*, ch. 5, §50, 90: "Dann Sie [die Weisheit Gottes] ist des Geistes Wesenheit, welche der Geist Gottes an sich führet, als ein Kleid, mit welchem Er sich offenbaret, sonst würde seine Gestalt nicht erkant, denn Sie ist des Geistes Leiblichkeit: Und da Sie doch nicht ein cörperlich begreiflich Wesen ist gleich uns Menschen, aber doch wesentlich und sichtig ist; und aber der Geist nicht wesentlich ist. " Cf. MG-185/Box 15/Folder 4/L-32.

Harmonist Labyrinths

The labyrinths established at each of the Harmonist settlements were a curiosity to visitors.[80] For such an elegant garden structure to be found on the frontier in Pennsylvania and Indiana was a continuing cause of amazement and therefore remarked upon in a number of travel journals and reports. Melish's account (1811) described the Harmony labyrinth as being formed of hedge rows and flowers. William Owen's diary (1824) likewise attested to the fact that the New Harmony labyrinth was formed of "foliage and flowers."[81] Later in life, Robert Dale Owen described the labyrinth based on his father's (Robert Owen, purchaser of New Harmony) recollections:

> [W]hat was called "The Labyrinth," [was] a pleasure-ground laid out near the village with some taste, and intended – so my father was told – as an emblematic representation of the life these colonists had chosen. It contained small groves and gardens, with numerous circuitous walks enclosed by high beech hedges and bordered with flowering shrubbery, but arranged with such intricacy, that, without some Daedalus to furnish a clue, one might wander for hours and fail to reach a building erected in the center.[82]

Later Harmonist John Duss referred to the labyrinth at Economy as planted with "wild plum, red berry and seedling pear."[83] These descriptions make clear that the Harmonist labyrinths were formed from hedge rows of bushes, trees and flowering shrubs. Most descriptions underscored the difficulty of finding one's way.[84]

---

[80]Examples of general scholarly studies of labyrinths include: Jürgen Hohmuth, ed. *Labyrinthe & Irrgärten* (München: Frederking & Thaler Verlag, 2003), Patrick Conty, *The Genesis and Geometry of the Labyrinth: Architecture, Hidden Language, Myths, and Rituals* (Rochester, Vt.: Inner Traditions, 2002), Horst Dieter Rauh, *Im Labyrinth der Geschichte. Die Sinnfrage von der Aufklärung zu Nietzsche* (München: Wilhelm Fink Verlag, 1990), and the older work by William Henry Matthew, *Mazes and Labyrinths: A General Account of Their History and Developments* (London: Longmans, 1922, 1970). A journal dedicated exclusively to the study of mazes and labyrinths, *Caerdroia*, was established in England in 1980.

[81]Karl J. R. Arndt, *Economy on the Ohio, 1826-1834. George Rapp's Third Harmony. A Documentary History* (Worcester, Mass.: Harmony Society Press, 1984), 352.

[82]Robert Dale Owen, *Threading My Way: An Autobiography* (New York: Augustus M. Kelley, 1967/1874), 242-243.

[83] John Samuel Duss, *The Harmonists: A Personal History* (Harrisburg: Pennsylvania Book Service, 1943), 219.

[84]Cf. William Faux' description of the New Harmony labyrinth: ". . . in a large pleasure garden is a curious labyrinth, out of which none but those who formed it, or are well acquainted with it, can find their way." Arndt, *Rapp's Harmony Society*, 277.

Figure 4
Reconstructed Labyrinth, New Harmony Indiana

The Harmonists consistently referred to these as labyrinths. In the past the terms "labyrinth" and "maze" were generally synonymous and used interchangeably. Today, however, the distinction between a labyrinth and maze is more carefully maintained. A labyrinth is unicursal, that is, there is only one path that leads to the middle. Although the walker of the labyrinth in the journey to the center successively approaches and retreats from the middle before arriving at the goal, he can see the goal and there is never any doubt that he will find the way. A maze on the other hand is multicursal, full of paths, intersections, and dead ends. The paths are usually hemmed by high hedges or walls, making the path to the center a challenging affair.[85] According to this distinction, the Harmonist labyrinths were actually hedge mazes. The Harmony Society archives contain three hand drawn plans for labyrinths, possibly one for each settlement.[86] Each of these plans depicts a hedge maze with multiple paths and a circular space for the grotto in the center. In this chapter the Harmonist designation of "labyrinth" will be used, rather than maze.

Most descriptions referred to the Harmonist labyrinths as pleasure gardens where the Harmonists could walk the paths in their leisure and enjoy

---

[85]Laishley, "Harmonist Labyrinths," 9.
[86]Ibid., 13f. assigns a labyrinth plan to each of the settlements. Since they are not labeled, this assignment is not verified.

the beauty and diversion they provided. George Rapp apparently enjoyed sitting in the labyrinth in his free time. His diary entry for May 4, 1823 included the note that he spent that Sunday afternoon reading Klopstock (a *Sturm und Drang* author) in the labyrinth.[87] Despite its use by the community as a pleasure garden, the labyrinth was built at each location as a testimony in hedge to key religious beliefs of the Society. This fact was apparent even to English-speaking visitors such as Melish and the Owens.

Harmonist Interpretation of the Labyrinth

Most scholars rely exclusively on the testimony of Melish and Robert Dale Owen for their interpretation of the religious significance of Harmonist labyrinths. Melish stated that the labyrinth was emblematical of "the difficulty of arriving at Harmony."[88] R. D. Owen's report included a similar statement – the labyrinth was "emblematical of the life these colonists had chosen" and "the difficulties of attaining a state of peace and social harmony."[89] Karl Arndt and Ross Lockridge echoed these traveler's descriptions in their interpretations of the labyrinths.[90] As noted above, the Melish report is undoubtedly reliable as it was given for correction to Frederick Rapp. The Harmonists, however, were quite secretive about their religious beliefs to outsiders. Therefore, for a true and full picture of their understanding of the religious significance of the labyrinth, it is necessary to go to Rapp's sermons, the German original of the later translated *Thoughts on the Destiny of Man* (1824) and Harmonist hymns. These sources were written exclusively for members of the group without an apologetic purpose. The "difficulty of achieving Harmony" was but one aspect of its religious significance. Rapp's sermons and Harmonist hymnody indicate that the labyrinth was likewise symbolic of the crooked paths of the world, full of temptation, sin and false knowledge. On yet another level the labyrinth was an allegory of the striving for sanctification in the Christian life.

Rapp used the labyrinth image on a number of occasions in his sermons. This is not surprising considering that they constructed labyrinths at each of their three settlements. Due to these references the researcher is not left

---

[87] Arndt, *Rapp's Harmony Society*, 247.
[88] Arndt, *Doc. Hist. 1803-1815*, 457.
[89] Owen, *Threading My Way*, 242-243.
[90] Arndt, *Rapp's Harmony Society*, 252. Ross F. Lockridge, *The Labyrinth of New Harmony Indiana* (New Harmony, Ind.: New Harmony Memorial Commission, 1941), 11 adds that the labyrinth likely symbolized Harmonist belief in an imminent millennium. Laishley, "Harmonist Labyrinths," 15 espouses a very inclusive interpretation of their significance. In her understanding, the Harmonist labyrinths are symbolic of "... the idea of harmony, the existence of paradise, the journey to paradise, the travails of such a journey, the transformation of the self, the union of opposites into one whole, the unwavering goal, that the spiritual nature is difficult to attain, and rebirth into spiritual perfection." Little primary source evidence is given for these claims.

in the dark regarding a Harmonist interpretation of the labyrinth. One undated sermon expanded in some detail upon the labyrinth image:

> Human life is a great labyrinth though not without a plan, a wilderness where weeds grow among the flowers, a garden which tempts with its forbidden fruits. Reason appears to have tested all forms of religion and all have collapsed without foundation, but they all desire a simple, mildly strict and comforting religion, which they have found in the church (*Gemeine*). In it God's Word must eternally remain the light and truth.[91]

Although Rapp referred in the first phrase to human life as a great labyrinth, the context shows that he was actually speaking of the labyrinth of the world in which the individual human was tempted. The image of temptation used in the sermon is reminiscent of Adam's temptation in the Garden of Eden. In both there is a "garden which tempts with its forbidden fruits." The Harmonists had adopted the Boehmist conception of the dual fall of Adam, the first fall being his sexual lust for a partner with whom to copulate, such as the animals had, and the second the desire to gain wisdom and be like God. This dual view of the fall provided the backdrop for Rapp's statement. The labyrinth then was an image of the snares of the secular world where "weeds grow among the flowers" and where the individual soul was tempted firstly with sexual and other fleshly lusts (forbidden fruits). The second source of temptation mentioned in this text is from reason and natural religion (desire for wisdom). Although reason in this Enlightenment era appeared to have annihilated all forms of religion, the simple religion of Jesus according to Rapp continued to be sought and found in the *Gemeine* among true believers. In contrast to natural Enlightenment religion with its critical view of Scripture, this religion was unashamedly based on the Word of God and must eternally remain true to it.

It is important to remember that the Rappite movement arose during the late blooming of Pietism, the "Neo-Pietism" of the late eighteenth century. Unlike the earlier Pietists (to circa 1750), who reacted and responded to the "deadness" of Lutheran Orthodoxy, the later Pietists in Württemberg reacted to the in breaking of Enlightenment theology in the Lutheran church. In the original German version of his *Thoughts on the Destiny of Man*, Rapp once again associated the labyrinth with the Enlightenment. Here he contrasted the "harmonious people" (Harmonists), who climb the heights to their goal, with worldly folk, who follow the "crooked snake path of world-famous arts [and sciences] and the false Enlightenment" (*dem krummen Schlangenweg der weltberuhmten Kunst und falsche Aufklärung*

---

[91]"Ja das M[ensch]liche Leben ist ein groses labyrinth doch nicht ohne Plan: eine wiltniß, wo unkraut unter den blumen wächst, ein garten der mit verbottenen Früchten versucht. Die Vernunft scheint alle Formen der relig[ion] versucht zu haben, u alle fielen ohne Grund zusammen, aber sie sehnten sich zuletzt nach einer Einfachen mildstreng[en] u Tröstend[en] relig:[ion] welche sie gefunden in der Gem[eine]. Darin muß Gottes Wort ewig Licht u Wahrh:[eit] bleiben." MG-185/1-5004/Box 15/Folder 5/ N-5.

folgen).⁹² Frederick Rapp's English translation of this text, "the *labyrinth* of the artificial philosophy of the world," smoothed the radicalism of the German original. George Rapp spoke of a "false Enlightenment" and not merely an "artificial philosophy." The German makes clear that false Enlightenment thought was in his estimation a labyrinthine path, a dead end that did not lead to God. The *Schlangenweg*, translated in the English with "labyrinth" and therefore in this case a legitimate synonym, was not merely a serpentine path that twisted back and forth. The term also contained an allusion to that serpent Satan, who had deceived our first parents in the garden.

It should be noted that Rapp was rejecting a false Enlightenment. Rapp and the Harmonists were enamored with and employed the newest scientific inventions of the industrial revolution. They upheld what they considered to be the right use of reason and were advanced in their pedagogy. In his *Thoughts on the Destiny of Man*, Rapp was writing a philosophical treatise. What they rejected was an Enlightenment characterized by a critical view of Scripture and an anti-Christian bias. This is also seen in other statements against a false Enlightenment found in another Rapp sermon and in other passages of his *Thoughts*.⁹³

The same terminology (*krummen Schlangenweg*) and images are found in Rapp's 1842 Harmony Fest sermon. Once again he contrasted the Harmonists with those caught in the labyrinth, the "crooked snake path." The former were a youthful generation, among the few who could wander the heights, because they had left behind the impediments of the "crooked snake path."⁹⁴ In another sermon, the Harmonists were those who had persevered and not become weary in the "labyrinthine entanglements" (*labyrenthesche Gewirr*).⁹⁵ This thought was reflected in a Harmonist composed

---

⁹²George Rapp, *Gedanken über die Bestimmungen des Menschen besonders in Hinsicht der gegenwärtigen Zeit* (Harmony, Ind.: [s.n.], 1824), 15. Cf. idem, *Thoughts on the Destiny of Man particularly with Reference to the Present Times* (Harmony, Ind.: s.n., 1824), 16.

⁹³Rapp rejected the anti-Christian Enlightenment of Voltaire, Rousseau etc. in the sermon MG-437/ Box 22/ Folder 82B/ Gr E-7. Rapp, *Thoughts*, 14: "The erroneous doctrines and nonsense propagated against the Christian religion and its founder ... [in] the present age ... [by] skeptics and despisers of the Bible." Cf. Ibid., 21, 37 etc. Nevertheless, Rapp spoke positively of the proper use of reason, "when every discovery and invention by the manifold arts and sciences are put together, and become a thoroughly combined Whole, where the mental capacities of all nations, and all the useful inventions of man meet and flow together in our time." Ibid., 55.

⁹⁴"Aber nun was fürchtet das Jung geschlecht jezt das in solchen neuen schauplaz auflebt u sich gewöhnt haben an die Engen Fußwege u Steilhöhen, auf denen wenige wandl:[en] können. aber diese höhen sind es, die da der Gem:[eine] streben zum Gipfel weil die von den krummen Schlangenwegen häut u. hinterniße zurückgelassen u. dafür wie ein junges geschlecht in diesen Einfalt neu auflebt." MG-437/Box 22/Folder 82B/A-22.

⁹⁵MG-185/1-5004/Box 15/Folder 6/ P-151.

poem/song: "Life on the cliffs does not tire you, nor does the view of labyrinthine entanglements."[96] Rapp in yet another sermon reminded his followers that the "labyrinth of abuses and wrong turns" was not endless. Rather there existed a "pure return path," on which the Harmonist could and should strive to achieve the true goal.[97] Union with the spirit of Harmonie, envisioned here as a female personified figure, enabled the Harmonists to escape the "irregular course paths."[98] All of these examples indicate that the labyrinth image for the Harmonists was essentially a negative concept for the entanglements and temptations of this world.[99] These entanglements could be physical lusts and sins. They could also be in the form of intellectual, false philosophies or religions, which espoused a weakened view of the Christian Scriptures. In any case one's aim was to escape from the labyrinth of a depraved world.

The reverse side of escaping from the entanglements of the labyrinth was reaching the freedom of the heights.[100] This theme was found parallel to the labyrinth theme in a number of the same texts. In the passage from Rapp's *Thoughts* and the 1842 Harmony Fest sermon quoted above, the Harmonists were encouraged metaphorically as pilgrims to pick up their hiking sticks and attempt to scale the heights.

> O harmonious folk! to whom neither the narrow footpath, nor the steep heights are too dreadful, upon which however few can wander but must re-

---

[96]"Nicht ermüdet dich das klippenvolle Leben, noch der Blick labyrinthischen Gewirren." *Eine kleine Sammlung Harmonischer Lieder als die erste Probe der anfangenden Druckerey anzusehen* (Harmonie, Ind.: Harmony Society Publications, 1824), 23.

[97]MG-185/1-5004/Box 15/Folder 5/ N-57.

[98]"H:[armonie] . . . ohne dich giengen wir den ungeregelten grausen Gang:[en]." MG-185/Box 15/Folder 5/C-23.

[99]Only one Harmonist text that the author discovered viewed the labyrinth in a positive fashion, a poem/hymn in *Feurige Kohlen der aufsteigenden Liebesflammen im Lustspiel der Weisheit* (Oekonomie, Pa.: Harmony Society Publications, 1826), #11: "Heb dich empor über die Ketten der Gewalten, in das weite Labyrenth der freyen und reichen Flur, durch welche die freye Geister wandeln, zum Licht der heiligen Unsterblichkeit."

[100]The dual concepts of the "labyrinth of the world" and escaping to paradise through Christ are found in Jan Comenius' *The Labyrinth of the World und the Paradise of the Heart* (1623). Comenius was a pedagogue and bishop of the Bohemian Brethren. There is no evidence to show that Rapp was aware of this work. There was, however, a long-standing "Western tradition [that] generally represents the labyrinth as a world that holds us captive, with Ariadne's thread being the symbol of liberation." Conty, *Genesis and Geometry*, 6. Of this Rapp must have been aware. This conception of the labyrinth of the world was replaced in the Enlightenment era with the labyrinth as a symbol for the "complexity of experience" for those seeking knowledge. Cf. Rauh, *Im Labyrinth der Geschichte*.

main behind. You climb the heights and your striving permeates all things through and through, until you reach the peak.[101]

The *Gemeine* was enabled to strive steadfastly toward the peak, having first left the "crooked snake path" behind.[102] The concept of exerting oneself, of striving was present in both passages. The pilgrim theme reflected above is likewise found in a number of Harmonist composed poems/hymns in their 1827 hymnbook. These hymns make clear that the path of the pilgrim was an allegory of the Christian life, the path of faith (*Glaubens-Lauf*).[103] This conception of the Christian life as a pilgrimage was likely influenced by their knowledge of John Bunyan's *Pilgrim's Progress*, which was listed as belonging to their library in 1829.[104] Thus, one escaped the labyrinth by becoming a pilgrim, by striving for sanctification in this life and for the heavenly home (or millennium) in the next age.

In at least one sermon the goal of their striving was the literal Jerusalem, the Promised Land, where the millennial kingdom would be established on earth.

> We stride with unconstrained [steps] directly toward that Spring day, toward the scene of the golden era ... Earnestly the *Gemeine* surges toward her goal of completion ... Your stride [is] to this higher path, the Orient (*Morgenland*), toward that location your homesickness is straining ... to the Promised Land.[105]

To travel this path one must first have had escaped the entanglements of the labyrinth (*labyrenthesche Gewirr*). The new or heavenly Jerusalem was depicted as the center of some medieval church labyrinths, in some seventeenth and eighteenth century drawings, as well as the goal of Christian in the *Pilgrim's Progress*.[106] For the Harmonists in the 1830s to 1840s the goal was the literal Jerusalem, however, and not a metaphorical or heavenly goal.

The third aspect of the Harmonist interpretation of the labyrinth and the one reported by Melish and the Owens was that the labyrinth signified the "difficulty of achieving Harmony." Harmony, chosen as the name for their Society, signified both the goal and, in a reduced sense, the everyday expe-

---

[101] Rapp, *Gedanken*, 15.

[102] MG-437/Box 22/Folder 82B/A-22.

[103] 1827 *Gesangbuch*, #111, 87. Cf. ibid., #67, 53-54, #113, 89, #180, 141, #239, 188.

[104] 1829 List of German books #355 – John Kangans Reise nach der Ewigkeit is a transcription mistake. Kangan should read Bunyan. Arndt, *George Rapp's Successors*, 428. In 1817 six copies of Bunyan's *Pilgrim's Progress* were ordered from a Philadelphia bookseller, Fran. David Brown. Melvin Miller, "Education in the Harmony Society, 1805-1905" (Ph.D. diss., University of Pittsburgh, 1972), 316. There is also evidence that some of Rapp's Separatists owned this work in Germany. LKA A 26 Nr. 473, 2 – Question 61.

[105] MG-185/1-5004/Box 15/Folder 6/ P-151.

[106] Laishley, "Harmonist Labyrinths," 17-18.

rience of this communal group. The bond of unity, friendship and love was renewed each year at the Harmony Fest on the anniversary of the founding of their Society. Numerous hymns written for these celebrations affirmed both the reality and yet the difficulties of maintaining the spirit of brotherhood and the bond of love. Walking the labyrinth provided Harmonists with a physical reminder of the importance of laying aside strife and pressing on toward the goal of true harmony.

Harmonist Grottoes

The religious interpretation of the labyrinth was underscored by the presence of a small, odd building in the center of each of their labyrinths. This building, called a grotto by the Harmonists, was described by a number of visitors. Melish in 1811 referred to the grotto at Harmony as a temple, which was "rough in the exterior, showing that, at a distance, it has no allurements; but it is smooth and beautiful within, to show the beauty of harmony when once attained."[107] The New Harmony grotto was described in William Hall's journal: "[T]hey have also . . . a beautiful Pleasure Garden with a Labyrinth & rude Summer House in the Center very rough & unsightly without but smooth & clean within."[108] At Economy, there was a grotto in the center of the labyrinth as well as a second one in George Rapp's garden. The latter, which is the only Harmonist grotto still extant, was described in some detail by an English Member of Parliament, James S. Buckingham in 1840:

> At one quarter of the garden, Mr. Rapp pointed to a circular building of rustic masonry, composed of very large unhewn stones, rudely piled on each other, and covered with a sloping roof of straw-thatch, with rough bark door and portals, resembling the buildings called hermitages, often found in English grounds. On entering the interior, however, the visitor is pleasingly surprised to find an ornamented circular-room, with wrought ceiling, and ornamented panels; and in the center of the whole, a well-executed female statue, meant as the personification of Harmony, holding a lyre, and presiding as the genius of the place. Around the walls of the interior were several inscriptions; one of which was, "The Traveler's Disappointment," meaning to express the surprise intended to be occasioned by the finding this statue and these ornaments within so rough an exterior; and another was "Harmony, founded by George and Frederick Rapp, Feb. 15, 1805.[109]

---

[107]Arndt, *Doc. Hist. 1803-1815*, 457.
[108]Karl J. R. Arndt, *A Documentary History of the Indiana Decade of the Harmony Society, 1820-1824*, vol. 2 (Indianapolis: Indiana Historical Society, 1978), 249.
[109]Karl J. R. Arndt, *George Rapp's Years of Glory. Economy on the Ohio, 1834-1847. George Rapp's Third Harmony. A Documentary History* (New York: Peter Lang, 1987), 473.

Figure 5
Grotto, Economy, Pennsylvania

These descriptions reveal that all of the Harmonist grottoes, which Buckingham correctly identified as hermitages and not as grottoes at all,[110] had one unifying characteristic: They were all formed with a rustic, rough exterior of unhewn stones, bark and thatch with a surprisingly smooth and beautiful interior. This contrast between the rough exterior and the beauti-

---

[110]According to C. L. Stieglitz' *Encyklopädie der bürgerlichen Baukunst* (Leipzig: [s.n.], 1792-1798), 545 a grotto is a garden building that imitates a natural cave, often as an entrance to an underground space. A hermitage on the other hand is a rustic hut formed of crude materials, reminiscent of the dwellings of early hermits. Though the Harmonist grottoes were hermitages, the beautiful interiors were unique and out of character for this class of garden structure. De Cunzo, "Rapp's Garden," 110-111. Cf. Charles Morse Stotz, "Threshold of the Golden Kingdom. The Village of Economy and Its Restoration," *Winterthur Portfolio* 8 (1971): 122-169, here 155.

ful interior was not accidental, but intended as Buckingham put it to surprise the visitor to the grotto. It was an intentional statement in their material culture, which was repeated in the grottoes at all three settlements. Melish correctly noted that the grotto had "emblematical" or symbolic religious significance. On both a corporate and individual level, it reflected the Harmonist understanding of the nature of their Society and of the individual Christian.[111] Melish noted that, on the outside, the grotto as a symbol of Harmony displayed few "allurements" to recommend itself, although it was beautiful within. This corresponds to the Harmonist understanding of its own Society. The Harmonists were well aware that their communal group, consisting of seven or eight hundred inhabitants at its peak, was small and unimpressive by worldly standards. Rapp reminded them and their neighbors, however, in his *Thoughts on the Destiny of Man*, that although their Society was small, it nevertheless could have great influence. "Small is often the source from which a large stream flows, and the more extensive its course, the greater its increase. Evolution and progress result from acquirements that proceed from small to great."[112] Their community was serving as leaven with which to ferment the whole of society. Although their communal system "for a higher social life" was at present "grossly and artfully derided," yet it could "never be mocked away." "Plain truth will be self-evident, a little leaven will ferment the whole dough; this is done by the fundamental rules of Harmony."[113] Although the Harmony *Gemeine* appeared to the outside world as a small rough hut (grotto), Rapp reminded them that they were in the process of becoming a magnificent temple of God.[114] In the imminent millennial kingdom they would serve as a kingdom of priests in the house of their God.[115] The grotto in the middle of the labyrinth reminded the Harmonists that appearances were deceptive.

What was corporately true for the Society as a whole was equally true for the individual Harmonist. Their physical bodies were rough, unsightly husks in comparison to the divine treasure that was hidden in the ground of their souls. A Rapp sermon reminded them:

---

[111]De Cunzo, "Rapp's Garden," 111, is correct in noting that the purpose of the grotto in Rapp's garden was different than those in the center of the labyrinths. The former had a representative character for visitors, as indicated by the inscriptions in English rather than in German.
[112]Rapp, *Thoughts*, 7.
[113]Ibid., 11.
[114]MG-185/Box 15/Folder 5/O-2.
[115]MG-185/1-5004/Box 15/Folder 5/O-122. MG-437/Box 22/Folder 82B/A-22. *Eine kleine Sammlung*, #11.

Within yourself you have caught sight of something divine. . . . I have found within myself the greatest treasure. . . . Thus it is more than true, that I lay hold of him [Christ], who loves my soul, for in the deepest ground of the soul, I eat, drink and draw you [Christ] into myself with heated ardor. . . . Thus the image of Jesus Christ is imprinted substantially within me. Love permeates me with life, completely healing me. You [Christ] are my greatest treasure. For the spark of love divinizes me with your hot glow. Therefore I will not let you out of the hand of my faith, until having gone through death I am made complete in blessing and am filled with the God-humanity, to be like you, formed in Spirit and a new body.[116]

Figure 6
Grotto Interior, Economy Pennsylvania

Participation in the divine nature was the result of union with Christ. Though begun in this life, being made complete and like Christ in body and spirit would only be fully realized in the next life. The grotto reminded the Harmonists of the high nobility of man's soul when it was permeated with God and his love. They carried a "pearl of great price" hidden within their unsightly bosoms. Freedom from the sin and temptations of the world and a striving for sanctification (labyrinth) were made possible when Christians

---

[116]MG-185, Box 15, Folder 5, O-2. Cf. MG-185, Box 15, Folder 6, P-218: "Temple of God, the body of Christ" hidden with a "body of death."

lived in unity and had the image of Christ implanted within their souls (grotto interior).

Millennial Beliefs: The Golden Rose Lintel

It has already been noted that the simple dissenting style of architecture adopted by the Harmonists afforded little place for religious symbolism in their material culture. For this reason the decorative use of the "golden rose" in one or more instances is that much more pronounced. Besides the "golden rose" stone lintel, which will be discussed presently, roses or "golden roses" were found on a variety of objects. The earliest was the tombstone of Johannes Rapp, the only biological son of George Rapp, who died during the Harmony era in 1812.[117] Adorning the upper portion of the tombstone are two fully bloomed and open roses on leafed stems. Four further open roses embellish the four corners of the stone. Flatirons used at Economy were likewise decorated with a raised rose ornament.[118] The beautifully plastered ceiling of the Grotto in the Economy garden has at its center what has been interpreted as the "Golden Rose of Harmony, the symbol of the Society" surrounded by twelve acanthus leaves.[119] Although the roses on the tombstone and flatirons may or may not represent the golden rose, the grotto decoration almost certainly does.

The most important example of the golden rose symbol was found on the stone lintel above the north door of the second, brick church at New Harmony.[120] This door, unlike the earlier Sophia doorway, evidenced the further assimilation by the Harmonists of the American Georgian architectural style.[121] The rugged and heavy stone porticoes reflective of their indigenous German classical heritage were replaced by this time with an ele-

---

[117]Johannes Rapp's is the only tombstone in all three Harmonist cemeteries, since the normal custom was to be buried in unmarked graves. Cf. Arndt, *Doc. Hist. 1803-1815*, 537-538. Stotz in "Threshold of the Golden Kingdom," 142-143 identifies the rose on Johannes Rapp's tombstone as the first use of the golden rose symbol by the Society.

[118]Ibid., 142.

[119]*Grotto at Old Economy*, 6. Donald Pitzer claims that the Harmonists placed the "golden rose" symbol on many of their products, which were sold not just to buyers in the United States, but also in France, Germany and England. Donald E. Pitzer and Josephine M. Elliott. *New Harmony's First Utopians, 1814-1024*, 2d ed. (Historic New Harmony: University of Southern Indiana, 2002), 235. Cf. *Grotto at Old Economy*, 6. However, the author was unable to find evidence of the "golden rose" trademark in the Harmony Society archives.

[120]The "door of promise" and golden rose lintel became the north door of the public school, when the church was dismantled in 1874. Since the razing of the school in 1988, the stone lintel has been in storage. Pitzer, *New Harmony's First Utopians*, 284.

[121]Lewis, "Harmonist Architecture," 70.

gant Georgian scheme. Half columns supported a pediment above which was found a triangular stone lintel under a shallow roof. In the center under the peak of the portico was an oval formed of leaves and buds with an open rose at the bottom. In the center of the oval a single stemmed rose was found, along with the Bible reference, Micah 4, verse 8. On either side of the oval was the year of the construction of the church, 1822. The rose, oval and date were originally painted in bright colors, a striking contrast to the white columns.

Figure 7
Golden Rose Lintel, New Harmony Indiana

The inclusion of the Bible text Mic 4:8 on the stone lintel provides incontrovertible proof that this is not any rose, but the golden rose symbol. Students of the English or Hebrew Bibles will wonder at the association between Mic 4:8 and the golden rose, for their versions do not contain this allusion. Luther's 1545 German translation of the Bible, however, interjects the phrase "your golden rose" (*deine güldene Rose*) into this verse, a phrase not found in the Hebrew original and therefore not in other translations, including later revisions of the Luther Bible.[122] This phrase was likewise

---

[122]This phrase was no longer included in the 1922 Luther Bible. Karl J. R. Arndt, "Luther's Golden Rose at New Harmony, Indiana," *Concordia Historical Institute Quarterly* 49 (Fall 1976): 112-122, here 121-122, n. 5.

eliminated by the publishers of the Berleburg Bible in their revision of the Luther text (published from 1726 to 1742). Although the Berleburg Bible was well-loved by the Harmonists, the Luther rendering of Micah 4:8 had so captured their imagination that the golden rose was emblazoned above their church door at New Harmony.

Luther's inclusion of "your golden rose" in Mic 4:8 did not significantly change the meaning of the text.[123] With or without the phrase, the meaning of the verse is that, in spite of the hopeless present, Israel and Jerusalem would be restored to their former greatness. Christians inherited this unfulfilled promise and some expected its fulfillment at the culmination of the age in the millennium or "New Jerusalem" (Rev 21 and 22). This promise of restoration was strengthened by Luther's poetic addition of the golden rose image. The "golden rose" was a sacred object of pure gold blessed and bestowed by popes from at least 1050 onward on Catholic regents in recognition of their achievements and loyalty to the Vicar in Rome.[124] "Luther injects the poetic *golden Rose* in his translation of Micah 4:8, as if to say: 'You presently weak and insignificant locality Eder [Jerusalem], you are going to be awarded that most coveted prize of Christendom, the Golden Rose.'"[125] You, Jerusalem, will once again experience untold greatness.

The golden rose image was appropriated and explicated by the eighteenth-century Separatist and radical Pietist, Christoph Schütz.[126] Schütz's work, *Die Güldene Rose*, published in 1731, was well-known by Rapp and his followers from the earliest days of their Separatist movement in Württemberg.[127] A leading member of the group, Christian Hörnle, testified to the

---

[123]"Und du thurm Eder/ eine Feste der Tochter Zion/ Es wird deine güldene Rose kommen/ die vorige Herrschafft/ das Königreich der tochter Zion." Arndt, "Luther's Golden Rose," 112, 115.

[124]P. M. J. Rock, "Golden Rose," in *Catholic Encyclopedia*, vol. 6, ed. Charles G. Herbermann, et al. (New York: Robert Appleton, 1909), 629-630.

[125]Arndt, "Luther's Golden Rose," 115. Arndt discusses in his article the personal significance of the Golden Rose to Luther. The golden rose was offered to Frederick the Wise in effect as a bribe to deliver up Luther to Rome.

[126]Christoph Schütz (1689-1750) was the sixth child of a well-established family in Umstadt. Grutschnig-Kieser's examination of the church records in Umstadt revealed that contrary to the previously held scholarly opinion, C. Schütz was not related to Johann Jacob Schütz, the early radical Pietist who was a member of Spener's conventicle in Frankfurt. C. Schütz by 1725 had separated from the Lutheran church and formed a private conventicle. He had close contact with the Inspired church; his conflict with J. F. Rock resulted in his never becoming a member of that group. Besides *Die Güldene Rose*, Schütz wrote a number of works in which his theological views were elaborated. He had contact with alchemistically oriented circles, and published an edition of von Welling's *Opus mago-cabbalisticum et theosophicum*. Konstanze Grutschnig-Kieser, *Der "Geistliche Würtz-Kräuter und Blumen-Garten" des Christoph Schütz. Ein radikalpietistisches "Universal-Gesang-Buch"* (Göttingen: Vandenhoeck & Ruprecht, 2006), 181-202.

[127]Christoph Schütz, *Die Güldene Rose oder ein Zeugnis der Wahrheit von der uns nun so nahe bevorstehenden Güldenen Zeit des tausendjährigen und ewigen Reichs*

Württemberg church authorities on three occasions in 1787 that Schütz's *Güldene Rose* was one of their key texts. When asked on June 5, 1787, which books were used in their private meetings, Hörnle responded that besides the Luther Bible, the *Berleburg Bible*, the works of Jacob Boehme, and Schütz' *Güldene Rose* were read.[128] The Lutheran church consistory summary of the 1787 interrogations of Rapp's Separatists (April 28, 1790) likewise underscored the importance of *Die Güldene Rose* for the developing group.[129]

Schütz' works were not only circulated among radical Pietists in Württemberg at the end of the eighteenth century, but as early as 1725, his hymnal *Geistliches Harpffen-Spiel* reached Germantown, Pennsylvania and made its rounds through the communication network of the German-speaking churches.[130] Schütz himself donated, among other books, copies of his own works, which were distributed by middlemen (including the well-known printer Christoph Sauer) to needy Pennsylvania Germans.[131] In 1809 a third edition of *Die Güldene Rose* was published and distributed in Germany and Pennsylvania.[132] The [partial] list of German books owned by the Harmonists in 1829 includes Schütz' *Göttliche Liebes-Triumpf* and possibly *Die Güldene Rose*.[133] Due to the continuing significance of *Die Güldene Rose* into the nineteenth century on both sides of the Atlantic and among the Harmonists, it is not surprising that they adopted this symbol to adorn the New Harmony church. To my knowledge, Schütz's *Die Güldene Rose* is likewise the only explication of this symbol from a churchly or radical Pietist

---

Jesu Christi und der damit verbundenen Wiederbringung aller Dinge (2 vols. 3d ed. [S.l.]: [s.n.], 1809).

[128]Karl J. R. Arndt, *George Rapp's Separatists, 1700-1803. A Documentary History* (Worcester, Mass.: Harmony Society Press, 1980), 116. Cf p.85 and 91. The Sendschreiben von der Wiederbringung aller Dinge is part three of *Die Güldene Rose*.

[129]Arndt, *Doc. Hist. 1700-1803*, 167.

[130]Hörnle made clear in his testimony that radical Pietist books were lent and borrowed within the communication network. He, however, had bought a copy of *Die Güldene Rose* from a woman in Wurmberg. Grutschnig-Kieser builds on Schrader's work, and outlines the distribution of Schütz's works through the radical Pietist communication network. Grutschnig-Kieser, *Geistliche Würtz-Garten*, 264f, here 266 and 274.

[131]Ibid., 268f.

[132]Example of the continuing significance of this work: Bishop Johannes Seybert of the German Methodist church owned a personal copy of the 1809 *Die Güldene Rose* (collection of Garrett Theological Seminary). His mother was a Harmonist, and he visited Economy on more than one occasion.

[133]Item #95 in the 1829 list, *Das Geheimnis der Gottseeligkeit*, could refer to *Die Güldene Rose*, since a work by Schütz with this name was published with *Die Güldene Rose* in both the 1731 and 1809 editions (see footnote 128 above). The "author" given in the 1829 list, J. Ganz, is incorrect–no man named Ganz wrote a book with that title. Arndt, *George Rapp's Successors*, 418-419.

standpoint.[134] It is therefore to Schütz' *Die Güldene Rose* as well as to Harmonist hymnody that we must turn to understand the meaning of the golden rose symbol for the Harmonists.

Schütz' *Die Güldene Rose* is the first part of three sections included in both the 1731 and 1809 editions. Immediately below the title of part one is printed Luther's 1545 rendering of Mic 4:8 and then Isa 35:1-2: "the desert... will bloom like the lily." *Die Güldene Rose* consists of a twenty-verse song about the "magnificent millennial kingdom of Jesus Christ" followed by approximately fifty pages of verse-by-verse explanations of the song's doctrinal content. Schütz did not leave his readers in doubt as to what he considered the "golden rose" to be.[135] In the prologue to his work, he stated:

> Regarding the main title of this little work, so report to the truth-loving reader that I did not give and ascribe to this little work such a splendid title without a good reason. For within it there is not only a clear witness to the future golden and delightfully blooming era, which the prophet Micah also with explicit words calls a *golden Rose*, 4:8, but also still a further witness to the noble power and virtue of Jesus Christ as the most beautiful rose of Sharon and lily of the valley, Song of Sol 2:1.... [W]ho reveals and imparts himself to all those of a humble and contrite spirit and revives makes and preserves them green and in bloom with the new life of the Spirit.[136]

For Schütz, the golden rose was primarily associated with the future millennial kingdom. It was both the chronological era, that "golden and delightfully blooming era" which Micah in Luther's 1545 rendering explicitly named a golden rose, and the millennial kingdom itself. In verse 19 of the

---

[134]The Christian concept of the golden era had a long tradition extending back to late antiquity. This tradition was revived among others by the French chiliast, Guillaume Postel in *La Doctrine du siecle dore* (Paris, 1553) and by Oetinger *Die güldene Zeit* (Frankfurt/Leipzig, 1759). Reinhard Breymayer, "Ein radikaler Pietist im Umkreis des jungen Goethe: Der Frankfurter Konzertdirektor Johann Daniel Müller alias Elias/Elias Artista (1716 bis nach 1785)," *Pietismus und Neuzeit* 9 (1983): 180-237, here 191-192.

[135]Breymayer's claim that the title of Schütz's *Die Güldene Rose* can only be understood against the background of the rose symbol found within alchemistical and Rosicrucian circles does not coincide with explicit statements made by Schütz within the work itself, and therefore is to be rejected. Breymayer, "Ein radikaler Pietist," 191. Cf. Grutschnig-Kieser, *Geistliches Würtz-Garten*, 197, n. 102.

[136]"Was den Haupt Titel dieses Werkleins betrift, so berichte den Wahrheitliebenden Leser, daß ich diesem Werklein solchen schönen Titel nicht ohne guten Grund gegeben und beygelegt habe, denn weil darinnen nicht nur ein klares Zeugniß von der zukünftigen güldenen und lieblich blühenden Zeit, welche auch der Prophet Micha mit ausdrücklichen Worten eine *güldene Rose* nennet, cap. 4,8, sondern auch noch ein weiteres Zeugniß von der edlen Kraft und Tugend Jesu Christi, als der allerschönste Blume zu Saron und Rose im Thal, Cant. 2,1, wie sich dieselbe... allen gedemüthigten und zerschlagenen Geistern offenbaren und mittheilen, und sie erquicken, und im neuen Geistes-Leben grünend und blühend machen wird, u. Erhalten ist." Schütz, *Die Güldene Rose*, 10.

song, Schütz lauded those who reached "such golden era."[137] He likewise noted that the Lord would establish his kingdom (the golden rose) physically on the earth (verse 5). The full number of Jews would be converted to Christ and enter into God's kingdom (verse 6). Great numbers from all nations would join with the people of Israel to serve the Lord (verse 9). No one would make war anymore; rather Solomon [Christ] would rule from his throne in peace (verse 12).[138] The "magnificent and peace-loving kingdom of Christ and Israel," that is, the golden rose, would flourish for one thousand years.[139] Schütz ended the song with the words: "Come then, you golden rose," a prayer that the imminent millennial kingdom would soon appear. The green and blooming spring and summertime [millennium] was vastly better than the present bare and bitter autumn.[140] The prologue to *Die Güldene Rose* makes clear that the golden rose symbol primarily alluded to the millennial kingdom. The concept was broad enough, however, to refer as well to Christ as the Rose of Sharon and to true believers, in whom the life of the Spirit resulted in their being "green and blooming." The explanation for verse fifteen spoke of Christ as the true vine and the tree of life, who blooms and produces fruit within believers. In the coming era the remnant of Israel would bloom like a rose.[141]

Very early in the history of the Harmony Society (January 1806) George Rapp wrote a hymn, "Kinder seyd nun alle munter," in which the golden rose image was included. "Soon there will be better times," the Harmonist leader wrote. "Zion, there you will be prepared, where your Friend [Christ] himself will pasture you... For now your *golden rose* blooms... and in the fields of Sharon white and red lilies bloom."[142] In this hymn the golden rose refers to the imminent millennial kingdom to be established on earth. In an undated sermon, Rapp presented an interpretation of the golden rose, which followed closely that of Christoph Schütz. Rapp claimed that the "beautiful golden rose" was a blossom that God, "according to the mystery of his holy will and the depths of the richness of his wisdom" had plucked from Eden and by means of the Holy Spirit planted in the present world.[143] This paradisiacal flower would become the "city of God" (the physical millennium on earth). Its "king [Christ] would be installed by God on his holy Zion, and from there his rule would extend to all lands." Physical [Jews] and spiritual Israel [Gentile believers] were "ordained" to blossom as the "mira-

---

[137]Ibid., 68.
[138]Ibid., 12-16.
[139]Ibid., 64-65.
[140]Ibid., 69.
[141]Ibid., 65.

[142]Arndt, *Doc. Hist. 1700-1803*, 151. This Rapp hymn was included in the 1820 and 1827 hymnbooks. It was written by George Rapp to encourage his community after the petition submitted to Thomas Jefferson to purchase government land was ultimately defeated by one vote in Congress. Arndt, *Rapp's Harmony Society*, 83-90.

[143]MG-185/1-5004/Box 15/Folder 6/P-114.

culous golden [rose] bush" in the millennial kingdom, a re-creation of the "most holy primeval world" (*heiligste Urwelt*) of Eden.[144]

As noted above, Schütz associated the rose of Sharon (Song Sol 2:1) and the lily blooming in the wilderness (Isa 35:1-2) with the golden rose. These images were likewise found in Rapp's sermons in connection with the millennial age. A Rapp sermon declared that the time for the inbreaking of the millennium was imminent. The wilderness of the old earth (Isa 35) would soon be renewed into a new Eden, a new paradise, in which the rose of Sharon and the lily of the valley would spring forth with the most beautiful blooms.[145] A Harmonist hymn in the 1827 hymnbook, "Der Lilien-Zweig," proclaimed that the time was near in which Christ the bridegroom would appear. Therefore, the lily-branch, a sign of the end had appeared.[146] Another hymn used the image of a completely opened bloom (such as the golden rose was depicted) as sign that the time had come for Zion to enter into its glory.[147]

The Harmonists equated the golden rose not just with the millennial kingdom. Like Schütz before them, who extended the symbol to include true believers, the Harmonists equated the golden rose symbol with the truest of believers, their own group. Rapp claimed in a sermon that the "congregation [of true believers] (*Gemeine*) grows throughout the whole world as a golden rose." Although the golden rose bush produced "flower after flower, one flower alone blooms – its name is Harmony." "Its leaves are inscribed with the words of the Kingdom of God ... and the names of the consecrated of God and his anointed one [Christ]."[148] Although Rapp allowed that other regenerated Christians were a part of the golden rose, the Harmonists were so in special measure. A song written to celebrate the anniversary of the founding of the Harmony Society reflects this fact:

> Harmony, you golden rose blossom,
> today we consecrate ourselves for the brethren fest,
> where true love glows like fire
> there your house of God is solidly built.[149]

This hymn was written before the erection of the golden rose lintel in 1822, since it was included in the 1820 hymnbook. Its inclusion in the revised 1827 *Gesangbuch* evidenced its continued popularity among the Harmonists.

Rapp's Separatist movement became aware of Schütz's use and interpretation of the golden rose early in their history (prior to emigration). Before 1820 the Harmonists had begun to equate their Society with the golden

---

[144] MG-185/1-5004/Box 15/Folder 6/P-114. Cf. MG-185/ Box 15/ Folder 4/ H-5.
[145] MG-185/1-5004/Box 15/Folder 6/R-145.
[146] 1827 *Gesangbuch*, #69, 55.
[147] Ibid., #71, 56.
[148] MG-185/1-5004/Box 15/Folder 6/P-114. Cf. MG-185/ Box 15/ Folder 4/ H-5.
[149] 1827 *Gesangbuch*, #164, 130 and 1820 *Gesangbuch*, #291, 220.

rose symbol, as the song quoted above indicates. The golden rose lintel on their second church in New Harmony proclaimed in stone that they themselves were uniquely chosen to be the golden rose as they anxiously anticipated the imminent establishment of the millennial kingdom on earth. The ceiling of the grotto in the Economy garden (plastered in 1831), which was meant to depict physically the Harmony Society, included a stylized golden rose in a prominent position, the center of the ceiling. These examples within their material culture gave physical testimony of the importance of this religious symbol. Although the Harmonists were largely dependent upon Schütz's interpretation of the golden rose, they extended the concept by equating the symbol with their own group.

7
Learning in the School of the Holy Spirit (1830-1847)

George Rapp remained a "learner" throughout his life. Although Rapp had been a craftsman-farmer in Württemberg, not a member of the so-called educated classes, and had only an elementary school education (to age fourteen), the autodidactic Separatist and later Harmonist leader voraciously consumed a steady diet of theological, philosophical and religious devotional books.[1] Rapp was a student of the Bible. Not just the Bible itself, but Scriptural commentaries, particularly on the Book of Revelation and the Old Testament prophetical books, were read and consulted for his own edification and for sermon preparation. Further, the Harmonist leader insured that the communal society placed a high value on education. The Articles of Association, which formed the Harmony Society in 1805, guaranteed that members would receive the "necessary instruction in church and school which is needful and requisite for temporal and eternal felicity."[2] In his philosophical treatise, *Thoughts on the Destiny of Man*, Rapp exclaimed, "Can this great work [the Harmony Society] be accomplished without the increase of knowledge? Surely not --Hence the arts, the sciences and every

---

[1]The 1829 list of some of the German books owned by the Harmony Society provides insight into the books that Rapp and the Harmonists had access to and read. This list is transcribed in Karl J. R. Arndt, *George Rapp's Successors and Material Heirs 1847- 1916* (Teaneck, N.J.: Fairleigh Dickinson University Press, 1971), 414-428. It was noted in chapter two that books were the means of transmitting (*Leitmedium*) radical Pietist thought in Württemberg.

[2]Karl J. R. Arndt, *Harmony on the Connoquenessing, 1803-1815. A Documentary History* (Worcester, Mass.: Harmony Society Press, 1980), 83. English translation found in idem, *George Rapp's Harmony Society 1785-1847*, rev. ed. (Teaneck, N.J.: Fairleigh Dickinson University Press, 1972), 74.

kind of learning are necessary, in proportion as they operate for the common good."³ For "[w]hat is a man if he knows not how to make use of his physical & intellectual powers? It is certain that we must learn how to use and employ them."⁴ To accomplish this end, the Harmony Society, unlike most communal societies formed on American soil, provided elementary school education for boys and girls aged six to fourteen, followed by apprenticeships in trades and domestic skills for the youth, and planned educational and cultural opportunities (music instruction, evening English classes) for the adults.⁵ Ongoing learning was facilitated by "one of the most extensive libraries" to be found on the frontier.⁶ The Harmony Society kept abreast of political and cultural trends by subscribing to a large number of both German and English newspapers and periodicals.⁷

The Harmonist emphasis on education made it natural for Rapp to employ a "learning" motif to describe growth in the Christian life. In numerous sermons Rapp described progressive sanctification as the result of "learning in the school of the Holy Spirit." This phrase was not unique to the Harmonist leader. Rather it was utilized by two of Rapp's favorite authors—Gottfried Arnold and Gerhard Tersteegen.⁸ Rapp latched onto the phrase and used it frequently. In an 1842 Harmony Fest sermon, he exclaimed how wonderful it was that the Harmony church had arrived at a "place of work and learning" after "fleeing into the wilderness" of America.⁹ Their group first had been "purified" in the "preschool of the world" (*Vorschule der Welt*).¹⁰ Over time they had been trained "by learning in the school of the Holy Spirit" to "understand the divine economy" and to "feel and enjoy now in the present a sweet foretaste of kingdom of God."¹¹ Rapp likened the

---

³George Rapp, *Thoughts on the Destiny of Man Particularly with Reference to the Present Times* (Harmony, Ind.: [s.n.], 1824), 4-5.

⁴Rapp, *Thoughts*, 22.

⁵Donald E. Pitzer, "Progressive Education in Harmonist New Harmony: 1814-1824," *Contemporary Education* 58, no. 2 (Winter 1987): 67-74, here 67. Pitzer notes that only ca. 15% of the 600 communal groups formed in the United States from colonial times to 1965 established formal educational programs. Ibid., 73, note 7.

⁶Pitzer, "Education," 72.

⁷See Melvin Miller, "Education in the Harmony Society, 1805-1905" (Ph.D. diss., University of Pittsburgh, 1972), appendix D, 323-325 for a list of periodicals to which the Harmony Society subscribed.

⁸Gottfried Arnold, *Die erste Liebe, das ist, Wahre Abbildung der ersten Christen*, 5th ed. (Leipzig: Samuel Benjamin Walthern, 1732), 15: Die ersten Christen "hatten gelernet, und *in der Schule des Heil. Geistes* würcklich erfahren . . . " Gerhard Tersteegen, *Geistliche Reden*, ed. Albert Löschhorn and Winfried Zeller (Göttingen: Vandenhoeck & Ruprecht, 1979), 35: "Wir müssen zuerst das A.B.C. lernen, ehe wir lesen wollen. Eben also müssen wir auch *in der Schule des heiligen Geistes* erst Kinder abgeben, ehe wir zum männlichen Alter gelangen und Väter vorstellen können."

⁹MG-437/Box 22/Folder 82B/A-22.
¹⁰MG 185/ Box 15/ Folder 4/L-25.
¹¹MG-437/ Box 22/ Folder 82B/ B-60.

"school of the Holy Spirit" with earthly schools. In both, there was "great preciseness, little praise and much incentive for progress."[12] He proclaimed to his audience: "You have never seen a wise person, who has not learned in the school of the Holy Spirit."[13]

The Harmony Society was a learning community which promoted the attainment of both secular and spiritual knowledge. One primary means for the Harmonists to spiritually "learn in the school of the Holy Spirit" was through careful attention to George Rapp's sermons. Twice on Sundays and on Wednesday evenings members of the Harmony Society had opportunity to listen to their spiritual leader preach. In this chapter as well as in the following two, the discussion of Rapp's theology will be based on his extant sermons. In chapter seven, first the extent, dating and nature of Rapp's sermons will be discussed. Then it will be proposed that two trajectories were present in Rapp's mature theology as evidenced in his late sermons (ca. 1830-1847)—a biblical-eschatological and a mystical-spiritual trajectory. Finally, three aspects of the biblical-eschatological trajectory found in Rapp's theology will be unpacked: core Reformation doctrines, churchly Pietist emphases, and elements of an "Anabaptist" ecclesiology.

George Rapp's Sermons

George Rapp's sermons have been quoted already numerous times in this volume. At this juncture, the beginning of three chapters in which his sermons will be systematically dissected for their theological content, it is appropriate to examine the extent, dating and nature of these primary sources. A large number of Rapp sermons are extant. They fall into three categories—Rapp's own sermon notes, sermons which a listener transcribed, and summaries of sermons which Rapp himself wrote down. Approximately 1680 of Rapp's sermon notes have been catalogued at the Harmony Society archives.[14] A small number of sermon notes have not been catalogued as they were found as place markers, for instance, within the Berleburg Bible. These sermon notes were just that, notes written in Rapp's own hand from which he preached. The sermon notes were densely written in miniscule handwriting on two sides of one piece of paper generally the size of a four inch by five inch index card, that is, small enough to tuck into his pocket. The inclusion of a Bible text or title on the top of one side of most sheets indicates that the majority of sermons (approximately three-quarters) consisted of only one two-sided sheet of paper. The author was able to locate the sermon notes that corresponded to a transcribed Rapp

---

[12] MG-185/1-5004/Box 15/Folder 6/P-238.
[13] MG-185, 1-5004, Box 15, Folder 6, Q-72.
[14] MG-185, Box 15, Folder 4, Groups A-M (125 Sermon sheets); MG-185, Box 15, Folder 5, Groups A-E (318); MG-185, Box 15, Folder 5, Groups N and O (280); MG-185, Box 15, Folder 6, Group P (283); MG-185, Box 15, Folder 6, Groups Q, R, S and T (393); MG-437 Box 22, Folder 82B, Groups A-E (282).

sermon in the 1838 sermon book for February 14, 1838.[15] Interestingly Rapp's small sheet of notes included all the chief ideas and same terminology as the three, full-sized pages of transcription by a listener. The transcription did include one long excursus (on King David), of which no mention was found in the sermon notes. This supports the contention that Rapp's sermon notes usually consisted of only one, two-sided page. It proved impossible for the author to correlate correctly the sermon notes in the less frequent case where more than one page was involved. The sermon notes were not full manuscripts, rather they included the key ideas which Rapp wanted to communicate. Although Rapp used extensive abbreviations and symbols to shorten the text, the sermon notes for the most part were written in full sentences and thus are still completely comprehensible.[16]

The 1838 sermon book includes 170 Rapp sermons preached from December 25, 1837 to December 30, 1838. Rapp regularly preached three times a week (Sunday morning, Sunday afternoon and Wednesday evening). The extra mid-week holiday sermons and one "company" message brings the total to 170 sermons, a stately number for the then eighty year old patriarch to prepare and preach in one year (he also taught and/or attended several company meetings each week). These sermons were not Rapp's manuscripts but were transcribed in another hand by a listener in a large, 500 page leather-bound volume. This volume is unique in that it is the only complete volume of its kind, and because it includes all messages for one year. All but four of the sermons in the 1838 sermon book listed the Bible text upon which the sermon was based. A tabulation of these Bible texts reveals the frequency with which individual Bible books formed the basis for sermons (see Appendix D).

An examination of this table reveals that Rapp preached from thirty-six different canonical books of the Bible in the one year period. Isaiah with thirty-three sermons was preached upon the most, closely followed by the book of Psalms (26). Third place was tied by the New Testament books of Revelation and the Gospel of John. Noteworthy is that two Old Testament apocryphal works, the Wisdom of Solomon and Jesus Sirach, were mined for their Sophialogical content as was the Song of Solomon with six sermons. Hebrews, Romans, Colossians and Ephesians were the favored New Testament epistles.

Besides the 1838 sermon book, two other smaller collections of transcribed sermons exist. A Wednesday night sermon from November 1834 (seven pages) appears to be in the same hand as the 1838 sermon book.[17]

---

[15]Compare MG 185, Box 15, Folder 4, L-9 (Rapp's sermon notes) with 1838 Sermon Book in MG-185, Box 1-4997, #8, Folder 2B (transcription of listener).

[16]The abbreviations were logical. Examples are Gl: for *Glauben*, Gem: for *Gemeine*, h: G: for *Heiliger Geist*, Herrlk: for *Herrlichkeit* etc. Rapp made use of common symbols for the four elements (earth, air, fire and water), for the sun, moon, heart, salt etc.

[17]MG-185/Microfilm Roll #316/General File/Scripture Book.

Three Easter Sunday sermons from 1837 (morning, afternoon and evening) and from April 9, 1837 appear to be one portion of a bound book. These sermons claimed to preserve "something from the sermon" preached by Father Rapp that Easter Sunday.[18] It likewise listed some of the hymns sung. The sermons in this small collection were in a different hand than the 1838 sermon book. Finally, George Rapp himself on two different occasions provided summaries of sermons in his own hand for the benefit of the "beloved brother Romaly" (Romelius Langenbacher), who was out of town representing the Harmony Society as its business manager. During the Easter season of 1839 Romelius was in New Orleans. Rapp wrote down that which he considered to be "the most striking sentences" from ten sermons preached between March 20 and March 31, 1839.[19] Likewise Rapp wrote in his own hand summaries of eleven sermons delivered between October 27, 1844 and November 20, 1844. Although not specifically addressed to Langenbacher as the 1839 Easter sermons were, a parenthetical insertion in the text ("Ach, Romaly, meditate on this sentence thoroughly") indicates that it was likewise prepared by Rapp for Romelius Langenbacher.[20]

The earliest extant sermon transcribed by a listener was dated November 1834. Other transcribed sermons were from 1837, 1838, 1839 and 1844, that is, from the last decade of Rapp's life (d. 1847). The vast majority of Rapp's sermon notes were undated. Those that bore a date frequently also included an abbreviation indicating that the sermon was preached at a Christian or Harmonist-specific holiday.[21] The earliest dated sermon note was ascribed (in Rapp's handwriting) to August 25, 1829, and was probably a Harvest Fest sermon.[22] Therefore, although most sermon notes were undated, it is not unlikely that the vast majority of them were from the Economy decades and date from circa 1830 until Rapp's death in 1847. This presupposes that undated sermons were roughly contemporary to the dated sermons, a fact that cannot be proven but which appears logical. If Rapp on an average preached 100 to 150 sermons a year, the number of extant sermon note sheets (1680) would suffice for ten to fifteen years, that is, roughly for the period in question. It is possible that Rapp or the Harmonists either did not save sermons until the last decade and a half of the patriarch's life, or that these were discarded prior to moving either to New Harmony or

---

[18]MG-437/1-5005/Box16/Folder 1. The fact that the last page of this small sewn pamphlet ends in the middle of a sentence suggests that it was but one portion of a larger bound collection of sermons (for the entire year 1837?).

[19]MG-185, 1-4997, Box #8, Folder 2. Cf. Thermometer Book 1839, MG 185 General File/Microfilm Roll # 309 for locations and dates when Langenbacher was away from the Harmony Society.

[20]MG-437/Box 22/ Folder 83.

[21]Examples are HF for Harmony Fest, LM for *Liebes Mahl* (love feast), and Ost: for *Ostern* (Easter).

[22]MG-185/Box 15/Folder 4/C-4. Although not labeled as such, the dating (the Harvest Fest was celebrated in late July or August) and topic (first fruits) indicate that this was presumably a Harvest Feast sermon.

Economy. The latter option is not unlikely since the amount of primary source documentation for the first two settlements is vastly smaller than for the Economy era. Perhaps the community, recognizing the advanced age of their spiritual leader, requested in the late 1820s that Rapp preserve all future sermons. At this same time, listeners began to write down some of his messages while they were being preached.

It has already been noted that approximately three-quarters of Rapp's sermon notes and virtually all of the transcribed sermons listed a Bible text upon which the sermon was based. Nevertheless, in many cases the connection between the biblical passage and the sermon is obtuse at best. Few of Rapp's sermons reveal a clear structure. Although a sermon might begin with an exposition of one topic, not infrequently Rapp switched midstream to another pet topic—self-denial or the mission of the Harmony Society in the *eschaton*, for instance. Furthermore, since so many of the sermons were mere notes and not full manuscripts, doctrinal topics, which the patriarch likely elaborated in his oral presentations, were written down briefly and cursorily. These characteristics make Rapp's sermons challenging to utilize and even more so to systematize. One sermon might discuss a number of themes and topics. Therefore, in order to elucidate to some degree Rapp's theology, it is usually necessary for the researcher to piece together bits and pieces from a large number of sermons.

Two Trajectories in Rapp's Theology

Rapp's theology as culled from his sermons was similar to that of many radical Pietists—eclectic. His sermons reveal that a number of divergent influences helped to shape his theology. These divergent influences can be grouped into two broad categories or trajectories.[23] The first trajectory was biblical and eschatological. It reflected core Reformation doctrine and key emphases found in Lutheran churchly Pietism and "Anabaptist" ecclesiology. Thus this trajectory reflected the Lutheran heritage and churchly Pietist roots of Johann Georg Rapp, a heritage that was staunchly biblical and theologically conservative. Although Rapp's millennialism contradicted Article 17 of the Augsburg Confession, it was based upon a literal, biblicist interpretation of key Scripture passages and was espoused by numerous promi-

---

[23]The inspiration for this approach to Rapp's theology was the masterly biography of Hochmann von Hochenau by Renkewitz, in which the latter explicated two *Grundkräfte* or *Gedankengruppen* in the theology of Hochmann, a biblical-salvation historical-eschatological and a mystical-spiritual group of ideas. It is not surprising that the theology of other radical Pietists besides Hochmann (such as Rapp) reflected both Lutheran and Lutheran Pietist roots as well as distinctive radical Pietist emphases (mystical-spiritualism). Thus, this approach has a more general application than to merely Hochmann alone. Heinz Renkewitz, *Hochmann von Hochenau (1620-1721)* (Witten: Luther-Verlag, 1969), 361-382.

nent churchly Pietists, as well as Puritans and others.[24] Rapp's admiration for the primitive Jerusalem church, which led to his adoption of certain aspects of an "Anabaptist" ecclesiology, was likewise rooted in a literal, biblicist approach to Scripture. Therefore, this ecclesiology, although sectarian in the neutral sense, logically belongs to the biblical-eschatological trajectory. These aspects of Rapp's theology will be discussed in chapters seven (Reformation roots, churchly Pietist emphases and "Anabaptist" ecclesiology) and nine (eschatology).

A second trajectory co-existed within Rapp's theology. This trajectory did not espouse a literal and biblicist approach to Scripture. Rather it was characterized by a return to a medieval Scriptural hermeneutic, which upheld that deeper spiritual, mystical or allegorical senses were present in Scripture alongside the literal, historical meaning. To ignore these spiritual meanings within the biblical record was to remain content with the "dead letter" rather than the "spirit" of the passage. This trajectory gave priority to the inner Word of God imparted by the Holy Spirit over the external biblical Word. True Christianity was inward and spiritual. Therefore, the outward forms and sacraments of the Church were rejected in favor of a spiritualist ecclesiology. The mystical union with God (Christ in us) was more important than forensic justification (Christ for us). The regress to a spiritual-mystical-allegorical hermeneutic paved the way for reception of theosophical and cosmological speculation, cabbalism and alchemistical conceptions within Rapp's theology. These elements will be explored in chapter eight. Because Rapp made no attempt to systematize his theology, these two trajectories intersected only at times. Often they co-existed parallel to one another.

Both of these trajectories within Rapp's theology have already been encountered in earlier chapters of this volume. The biblical-eschatological trajectory was reflected in Rapp's espousal of core Reformation doctrines in his pastoral letters dating from the Württemberg era: justification by faith and the rejection of Pelagianism, of good works as the basis for salvation (chapter 3). The Easter and love feast liturgies of the Harmony Society upheld the centrality of Christ's atoning sacrifice (chapter 5). Churchly Pietist influence was found in Rapp's treatment of the doctrine of regeneration in his pastoral letters (chapter 3). Rapp as a Neo-Pietist adopted a decidedly anti-Enlightenment stance. In his sermons and *Thoughts on the Destiny of Man* he clearly rejected Neologism and Enlightenment theology in favor of a high view of the authority and reliability of Scripture (chapter 2). The anti-Enlightenment stance was likewise echoed in Rapp's references to the laby-

---

[24]Article 17 (translation from the German original): "Likewise rejected are some Jewish teachings, which have also appeared in the present, that before the resurrection of the dead saints and righteous people alone will possess a secular kingdom . . ." *The Book of Concord. The Confessions of the Evangelical Lutheran Church*, ed. Robert Kolb und Timothy J. Wengert, trans. Charles Arand et. al. (Minneapolis: Fortress Press, 2000), 50.

rinth within the material culture of the Harmony Society (chapter 6). Rapp's eschatological views of the Sunwoman and of the imminence of End were discussed in chapter four; the eschatological meaning and significance of the golden rose in chapter six. The mystical-spiritual trajectory was most clearly evidenced in the quietistic mysticism (chapter 3) and Sophialogy of Rapp and the Harmonists (chapter 6).

The intersection between the two trajectories was likewise encountered at three junctures in earlier chapters. First, in chapter two the dynamic tension between a primitivist ecclesiology (based on a biblicist approach to Scripture) and a spiritualist ecclesiology was discovered. The development from a primarily spiritualist to a primitivist-biblicist ecclesiology will be examined later in this chapter under "Anabaptist ecclesiology." Second, the discussion of Tersteegian, quietistic mysticism (chapter 3) revealed that this form of spirituality included core Reformation doctrine (justification by faith, rejection of salvation by works) and Pietist emphases (doctrine of regeneration). It thus reflected aspects of the biblical-eschatological trajectory as well as elements from mystical-spiritualism (the medieval mystical heritage of Tauler, Meister Eckhardt and French and Spanish Quietists). Third, the theological rationale of Rapp's doctrine of celibacy (chapter 5) included aspects from both trajectories: Boehmist cosmogony and a biblicist interpretation of 1 Cor 7 and Rev 14.

Core Reformation Doctrines

The Lutheran Church in seventeenth and eighteenth-century Germany was not a theologically monolithic structure. Although Lutheran theology was and is based upon the Augsburg Confession and the other creeds and articles included in the Book of Concord (1580), the interpretation of these documents was not static. Rather the Lutheran confessions "entered the stream of tradition" as a dynamic and "living influence."[25] Lutheran theologians in the generations following Luther were not in agreement on all fine points of theology. Interpretations of even the central doctrine of justification by faith were not monolithic. When expositing this doctrine, theologians advocated primarily either an anthropocentric focus (Melanchthon), a theocentric focus (Andreas Osiander) or one in which both aspects were emphasized (Johann Gerhard).[26] After (and to a certain extent during) the confessional wars of the sixteenth and seventeenth centuries, the German Lutheran Church set its pegs broad enough to tolerate within its tent some pastors and theologians who supported disputed (primarily mystical-spiritual or chiliastic) views. In 1697 Gottfried Arnold radically separated from the Lutheran Church after penning the polemical "Burial hymn for

---

[25]Wilhelm Maurer, *Historical Commentary on the Augsburg Confession*, trans. H. George Anderson (Philadelphia: Fortress Press, 1986), 3.

[26]Martin Schmidt, "Spener's Wiedergeburtslehre," in *Wiedergeburt und Neuer Mensch* by Martin Schmidt (Witten: Luther Verlag, 1969), 169-194, here 182.

Babel" (*Babels Grablied*). He later published two theologically controversial works: the *Secret of the Divine Sophia* and the *Ketzer-Geschichte* in 1700. Nevertheless, the supposedly confirmed celibate married in 1701 and promptly *was offered* and accepted the Lutheran court pastorate in the city of Allstedt. In Württemberg, Johann Albrecht Bengel adopted and published chiliastic views in his commentary on Revelation (1740) and in *Ordo Temporum* (1741) that were rejected in the "anathemas" attached to Article 17 of the Augsburg Confession. Yet, Bengel was generally considered to be "orthodox" and he remained faithful to the Lutheran Church throughout his life. Bengel's disciple, Friedrich Christoph Oetinger (1702-1782), served as pastor and special superintendent in Württemberg, although he combined Swedenborgian, Boehmist, cabbalistic and alchemistical conceptions in his theological writings. In the second half of the eighteenth century Neologism and Enlightenment theology flourished in Germany, despite their rejection of traditional interpretations of the Book of Concord. It is thus apparent that it is impossible to speak of a unified Lutheran theology in the seventeenth and eighteenth centuries. It is, however, possible to speak of core Reformation doctrines, that is, traditional interpretations of key doctrines present in the Augsburg and Heidelberg Confessions and in the Reformed and Lutheran Churches in the first generations after the Reformation. In this section it will be demonstrated that George Rapp advocated the following core Reformation doctrines: the authority of Scripture, an orthodox understanding of the Trinity, the centrality of Christ's atoning sacrifice, and justification by faith through grace. Although these doctrines were found in both the Reformed and Lutheran confessions, primary emphasis will be upon the Lutheran creeds, since George Rapp and his disciples were raised in that confession.

Scripture

The Lutheran Formula of Concord, written in 1577, clearly expressed the Reformation *sola Scriptura* principle: "We believe, teach, and confess that the only rule and guiding principle according to which all teachings and teachers alike are to be evaluated and judged are the prophetic and apostolic writings of the Old and New Testaments alone . . ."[27] Furthermore, the Lutheran (and Reformed) confessions upheld the veracity (and verbal inspiration) of Scripture. "God's Word cannot deceive." It is "not false or deceitful."[28] George Rapp remained true to the high view of Scripture that the Reformers affirmed. He believed that the Old and New Testaments were God's revealed Word, the "book of God's revelation [given] through the prophets and apostles." They were "divine writings," and "the words of Je-

---

[27] *Book of Concord*, Formula of Concord, Epitome, §1, 486.
[28] *Book of Concord*, Large Catechism, Baptism, 464 and Formula of Concord, Art. 7, §5, 505.

sus Christ."²⁹ Therefore, "it is not enough to view [the Bible] as a learned book. One must above all things believe that it was given by God through the agency of the prophets and apostles."³⁰

Since the Scriptures were God's divine revelation, "God's truth shines forth" from this "wondrous book (*Wunder schrift*)."³¹ The veracity of God's Word extended even to those passages which modern, "enlightened" men rejected as "unbelievable." With regard to the tablets of stone that Moses received on Mt. Sinai, Rapp proclaimed:

> We do not doubt that [the finger of] God himself wrote on the tablets. For if God desires, he can have human hands and feet . . . It is irrelevant whether the finger of the divine will engraved the letters, or whether angels wrote it with their godly fingers . . . We proclaim that not only the tablets of the Law but the entire holy Scripture was written with the Finger of God.³²

Rapp thus upheld the verbal inerrancy and divine origin of Scripture. One further example of an "unbelievable" text was the battle between the Archangel Michael and the Dragon in Revelation 12. Rapp declared:

> One of the most horrible and *most unbelievable* things in the holy Scripture is the battle between Michael and the Dragon. But because many, particularly scholars, recognize that if this [passage] is true then their teaching is false, therefore they prefer to consider Revelation a fable and a Jewish letter. How much more venerable is it for those who believe the testimony [of Scripture]! For what a great word is this that a voice from heaven pronounced to the church: The devil, who accused you, has been cast down.³³

Rapp recognized that faith was necessary to believe those aspects of the divine Word which appeared contrary to human reason. In contrast to the Neologians and Enlightenment theologians, Rapp the Neo-Pietist upheld a high view of Scripture.

Rapp maintained that the Scriptures were given to man for instruction and teaching in temporal and spiritual things.³⁴ Just as earthly bread was needed for the physical body, so the Word of God was essential as spiritual nourishment for the soul. Rapp exhorted his listeners to be more concerned with "heavenly bread" than its earthly counterpart.³⁵ "Eating means appropriation, and you may appropriate whatever word you desire, as long as it is from Jesus and is found in the Bible. . . . For the sake of our spiritual health, we should consume much Word of God."³⁶ Since the Bible was a

---

²⁹MG-185/1-5004/Box 15/Folder 6/P-45 and Q-20.

³⁰"so ists nicht genug als es für ein gelehrtes Buch anzusehen, man muß vor allen Ding: den glauben haben, daß es von Gott gegeben sey, durch das mittel seiner Proph: u Apo: ." MG-185/1-5004/Box 15/Folder 6/P-84.

³¹MG-185/1-5004/Box 15/Folder 6/P-84.

³²MG-185/1-5004/Box 15/Folder 5/E-13.

³³MG- 185/1-5004/Box 15/Folder 6/R-40.

³⁴MG-185/1-5004/Box 15/Folder 6/P-45.

³⁵MG-185/1-5004/Box 15/Folder 6/P-178

³⁶MG-185, 1-4997, Box #8, Folder 2. March 20, 1839.

"deep sea," "continuous, thorough study or meditation" was necessary to mine the riches of its truth. Study of the Bible was the "greatest science," since it was closely associated with "knowledge of the infinitely great God."[37] Knowledge of the Most High and spiritual growth were the reasons for immersion in the Word of God.

Trinity

George Rapp and the Harmonists were staunch Trinitarians. Unlike contemporary "enlightened" thinkers (Deists) and sectarians (Shakers), who rejected orthodox formulations of the Trinity, members of the Harmony Society throughout their existence upheld Article 1 of the Augsburg Confession: "It is with one accord taught and held . . . that there is one divine essence which is named God and truly is God. But there are three persons in the same one essence, equally powerful, equally eternal: God the Father, God the Son and God the Holy Spirit."[38] Admittedly, the Harmonists at times employed mystical, cabbalistic and Boehmist conceptions, that is, nonorthodox language to describe the Godhead, as will be shown in chapter eight. Nevertheless, a bedrock of orthodox Trinitarian belief undergirded their theological understanding of the Deity. This bedrock was reflected in a number of Rapp's sermons.

According to Rapp, "the doctrine of the holy Trinity is expounded most purely and forcibly in the Rev 1:4. There the churches are greeted: (1) from him who is, who was and who is coming; (2) likewise especially from the seven spirits of God, who are, were and shall be; and (3) particularly also from Jesus Christ."[39] These three persons of the Trinity--Father, Word of God and Holy Spirit--are not three gods but one being.[40] Jesus Christ was not a merely an exemplary man as some "enlightened" theologians proclaimed, but fully and truly the second person of the Godhead.[41] "Therefore, God is in Christ a person, but not another God," he stated.[42] Rapp utilized the language of Col 1:15-19 in one sermon. "The Messiah . . . is the image of the great God. . . . In fellowship with the great God he has created all things. . . . The Father has given to him [Christ] authority over all."[43] The Holy Spirit was equally divine. Rapp described the third person of the Trinity as "the

---

[37] MG-185/1-5004/Box 15/Folder 6/Q-71.

[38] *Book of Concord*, Augsburg Confession, Art. 1 (Translation of German original), 36.

[39] MG-437/Box 22/Folder 82B/D-85. MG-185, 1-5004, Box 15, Folder 6, P-268. This statement reflects both orthodox and cabbalistic doctrine.

[40] "Diese 3 sind ein einiger:. " MG-185, 1-5004, Box 15, Folder 6, P-268.

[41] MG-185, 1-5004, Box 15, Folder 6, Q-54.

[42] "So ist Gott in Christo eine Person aber nicht ein anderer Gott." MG-185, 1-5004, Box 15, Folder 6, Q-72.

[43] MG-185/1-5004/Box 15/Folder 6/R-97.

uncreated, independent, divine Spirit, who has his origin exclusively from himself as the eternal God. This eternal Spirit has his nature from God."[44]

While residing at New Harmony, Indiana (1814-1824), the Harmonists came into contact with Shakers living at a nearby settlement (West Union) on the Busseron Creek. The two groups established and maintained friendly relations with one another for the next decades. The Shakers' desire to unite with the Harmonists[45] was prevented, however, for theological reasons, most notably concerning the role of Mother Ann Lee, the authority of Scripture, and the deity of Christ.[46] The Harmonists expressed most clearly their belief in the divine nature of Christ in response to what they considered to be the lesser and "anti-Christian" views of the Shakers. Although written in 1865, eighteen years after the death of Rapp, these statements are relevant, since the second document notes that their then deceased founder likewise believed thus. Furthermore, these statements corroborate with passages from Rapp's sermons. On May 11, 1865 Romelius Langenbacher wrote to the Shaker, H. L. Eales, that some Shaker statements recently published in newspapers "about our Lord Jesus Christ [were] derogatory to his divine character." Such sentiments were "anti-Christian, quite unbecoming to his followers."[47] These published Shaker declarations revealed that a basis for fellowship between the two groups no longer existed. An undated response to the Shakers, presumably prepared shortly thereafter in 1865, elaborated the Harmonist position.

> Our love and veneration for Jesus Christ, the visible Representative of the invisible father, in whom the father is seen, and with whom he is one, to whom is given all power in heaven and on earth, who did no sin and in whose mouth was found no guile, who is the only mediator between God and man, in whom dwelleth all the fullness of the Godhead bodily, our love and veneration for him and his holy word are unlimited and inexpressible. So that we fully subscribe to the motto of a former good Society, which is: "Jesus is God." ... We might have shared [the Shaker view about Christ] ... had it not been our great fortune to be specially protected through the grace of God and the humble but penetrating and sharp-seeing spirit of the *founder of our Society* and the leading members of the same before and since his death, who always distrusted and rejected anything which did not glorify and exalt God in Jesus Christ.[48]

---

[44]MG-185/1-5004/Box 15/Folder 5/E-13.

[45]See letter from George Rapp to Frederick Rapp, June 22, 1816. Karl J. R. Arndt, *A Documentary History of the Indiana Decade of the Harmony Society, 1814-1819* (Indianapolis: Indiana Historical Society, 1975), 226-230, especially 228.

[46]Cf. Letters from Harmony Society, 1848-1878, CO 25, May 11, 1865 and MG-437/Box 22/Folder 113. Letter to Shakers.

[47]Letters from Harmony Society, 1848-1878, CO 25, May 11, 1865.

[48]MG-437/Box 22/Folder 113. Letter to Shakers. Although unsigned, it may have been written by Jacob Henrici, the spiritual leader and trustee after Rapp's death. A modern penciled notation claims that the letter is in Henrici's handwriting. The author was unable to confirm this.

This later statement declared that Rapp throughout his lifetime was diligent in protecting and upholding the doctrine of the deity of Christ.

Atonement of Christ

George Rapp adamantly rejected the conclusions of so-called "enlightened" theologians, who claimed that "Jesus was but a good man," and that "Christ's work of redemption was merely allegorical," since man was saved from sin by living morally. Rapp argued in one sermon that such an approach denigrated the centrality of Christ's atoning sacrifice for the sins of mankind, and thus "completely annihilates the Christian religion at its foundation."[49] As a convinced Neo-Pietist, Rapp took a strong stance against such liberal theological trends. He firmly maintained the core Reformation conviction of the overriding importance of Christ's substitutionary atonement. Like Melanchthon, who penned the *Apology of the Augsburg Confession* (1531), Rapp held that the death of Christ accomplished satisfaction not only for the guilt of original sin, but also for all sins and for eternal death. In "note-like" fashion, Rapp stated that:

> [Christ was the] Savior of the world ... who tasted death for us ... He accomplished within himself redemption. ... He conquered the curse [of sin]. ... The ignominy of Christ, which he suffered in his members accomplished victory and glory ... Death and hell were vanquished by the obedience and humility of the Son. While he was experiencing forsakenness on the cross, he struggled for the sake of our depravity ... and completed the work. "It is accomplished." And then he died.[50]

Forgiveness of sins required prior retribution to appease the justice of God. Rapp claimed that "some [falsely] believe that they will be saved merely by the mercy of God without the ransom of Christ ... although truly in him guilty humanity was punished."[51] In his passion and death, "the Son of God carried the weight of the wrath of God."[52] Although man, due to his transgressions, "deserved death and the eternal fire of divine justice," Christ instead "bore the entire divine justice and accomplished [salvation]."[53] Christ who "knew no sin" was "made sin" for man. "He was slaughtered just as the innocent, pure animals" were in the Old Testament. Jesus Christ provided the final "expiation" and the "satisfaction" (*Genugtuung*) for sins, to which the Old Testament sacrificial system could only point. He suffered in

---

[49] MG-437/ Box 22/ Folder 82B/ Gr E-7.
[50] MG-185, 1-5004, Box 15, Folder 6, P-100. Cf. *Book of Concord*, Apology, Art. 12, 211; Apology, Art. 24, 261; and Augsburg Confession, Art. 24, 68-69.
[51] MG-185, 1-5004, Box 15, Folder 6, Q-54.
[52] MG-185, 1-5004, Box 15, Folder 6, P-268. Cf. MG-185, 1-5004, Box 15, Folder 5, A-58.
[53] MG-185, 1-5004, Box 15, Folder 5, N-129. Cf. MG-185, 1-5004, Box 15, Folder 6, P-100.

our stead (*stellvertretend*) and was the "valid, acceptable sacrifice to expunge the Adamic guilt ... with the intention that we would become *in him* the righteousness that avails before God."[54] Jesus was the "kindly annihilator of sin" (*freundlichen Sünden-Tilger*), the "Mediator, whose merit and suffering" enabled mankind to live a transformed life.[55] Within the "miracle of the atoning work [of Christ] all contradictory concepts come together ... justice, grace, payment, gift, wrath, love, guilt, innocence, forgiveness, death and healing."[56]

Justification by Faith

The doctrine of justification by faith was not an innovation introduced by the Reformers of the sixteenth century. Its biblical foundation was well established, primarily in the Pauline corpus of the New Testament. The doctrine was then developed by Augustine in late antiquity in response to the prevailing Pelagian controversy. Later during the Middle Ages it was extensively discussed. In spite of this background, it is accurate to state that the doctrine of justification by faith was viewed by the sixteenth-century Reformers in a new and innovative fashion and elevated in importance to the core doctrine of the Christian faith.[57] The Reformed understanding of justification differed from that advocated in Lutheranism due to the federal theology espoused by the former after the early 1560s, as well as their focus on unconditional predestination and limited atonement.[58] Nevertheless, a broad basis of agreement existed between the Reformed and Lutheran confessions with regard to this doctrine as developed between 1530 and 1700. According to Alister McGrath, both confessions: (1) defined justification "as the forensic declaration that the believer is righteous, rather than the process by which he is made righteous" (change in *status* rather than *nature*); (2) clearly distinguished between justification and sanctification or regeneration; and (3) understood "justifying righteousness ... as the alien righteousness of Christ, external to man and imputed to him, rather than a righteousness which is inherent to him."[59] Against this backdrop, Rapp's statements in his sermons concerning justification will be examined.

---

[54]MG-185, 1-5004, Box 15, Folder 5, N-129.
[55]MG-185, 1-5004, Box 15, Folder 6, Q-54.
[56]Ibid.
[57]Alister McGrath, *Justification by Faith* (Grand Rapids: Academie Books, 1988), 7 and 47.
[58]Alister McGrath, *Iustitia Dei. A History of the Christian Doctrine of Justification*, vol. 2 *From 1500 to the Present Day* (Cambridge: Cambridge University Press, 1986), 50. The predestination of the elect was unconditional in early Lutheran writings as well. Georg Kraus, "Predestination," in *Dictionary of the Reformation*, ed. Klaus Ganzer and Bruno Steimer, trans. Brian McNeil (New York: Crossroad, 2002), 253-254.
[59]McGrath, *Iustitia Dei*, vol. 2, 2.

George Rapp used the term *zurechnen* (to reckon or credit to one's account) to describe God's external action by which he declares the sinner to be righteous.

> To reckon means in the holy Scripture to consider future things as already present. Because the works of God are great and require long periods of time to be accomplished, we would never be completed without reckoning. On the other hand, God uses the method that he did with Abraham. God already reckoned to him his faith when he first believed ("Therefore your seed shall be") as if he [Abraham] had already completed his course. . . . God is willing to reckon to his believers that which they should first become . . . He reckons them to be crucified, dead and risen with Christ. For the righteousness *of God* is reckoned [to us], because it is never completely in our power [to achieve] but remains in God. . . . In such a manner the righteousness of God is bestowed upon us, 2 Cor 5:21.[60]

This passage from one of Rapp's undated sermons unites two core ideas. First, the act of justification in which the righteousness of God is reckoned to the account of the believer is performed by God alone. God is the one who does the reckoning, and that which is reckoned is his own righteousness. An alien righteousness, that is, God's righteousness, is bestowed upon man. When God looks upon man, he sees Christ, crucified, died and risen. It is outside of man's ability and power to achieve justifying righteousness. Therefore, "we become *in him* [Christ] the righteousness that avails before God."[61]

On the other hand, the righteousness that is accredited to the believer's account *should* little by little become an actual reality. "God is willing to reckon to his believers" in the present "that which they should become" in the future. Although man can never achieve justifying righteousness through his own efforts, according to Rapp he can and should strive to transform the imputed and alien righteousness of Christ into a living reality. Alien righteousness ought to become inherent righteousness within man. Rapp recognized, however, that this often remained unrealized, *in spe* but not *in re*. The transformation of alien righteousness into a present reality belonged not within the realm of justification per se, rather within regeneration and sanctification.[62] Rapp clearly distinguished between the two theological concepts. Justification referred to the reckoning of the righteousness of God to the believer, an external act of God. Regeneration, on the other hand, was the subjective and "inward appropriation" of justification, resulting in "the transformation of the will toward God."[63] Through conversion and regeneration, man became a new creation (2 Cor 5:17) with a transformed will able to bring forth works suitable to salvation.

---

[60]MG- 185, 1-5004, Box 15, Folder 5, O-70.
[61]MG-185, 1-5004, Box 15, Folder 5, N-129.
[62]Cf. *Book of Concord*, Apology, Art. 4, §72, 133.
[63]MG- 185, 1-5004, Box 15, Folder 5, O-70.

The atoning sacrifice of Christ "brought satisfaction before God and is adequate and sufficient to save us (*uns seelig zu machen*)" when appropriated "*by faith.*"[64] Rapp made abundantly clear to his listeners that righteousness was not earned by good works or the moralism so prevalent among Enlightenment theologians. Rather, salvation and "forgiveness of sins was a great, royal gift of the Lord," which was received by faith.[65]

> He who desires to be righteous through moralism—this is questionable. An eternal battle will remain within him. . . . What kind of gospel did Paul preach? An inward one, in which is revealed the righteousness that avails before God, which proceeds from faith to faith. We do not have a righteousness that is from the law or from moralism, rather it is reckoned by God on account of faith.[66]

Justification was received by faith as a gift of God's grace. Rapp defined grace as "voluntary loving-kindness, the free inclination to remit and to give without expecting anything in return. Grace is contrary to the law and works, Rom 6:14. Where gifts are freely distributed, there grace is revealed."[67]

In conclusion, it is clear that Rapp's doctrine of justification faithfully reflected core Reformation doctrine. Like the sixteenth-century Reformers, Rapp distinguished between justification and sanctification. Justification referred to the reckoning of the alien righteousness of Christ to believers. Unlike many proponents of Lutheran orthodoxy, however, Rapp, along with other churchly and radical Pietists, strongly emphasized the necessity of regeneration and personal piety. Therefore, even Rapp sermons that discussed justification quickly proceeded to the subjective appropriation of that doctrine in the life of the believer—increasing Christ-likeness. Thus, Rapp implied that alien and imputed righteousness must become inherent righteousness through the process of regeneration and sanctification. This implication reflected Rapp's Pietist background, rather than the understanding of justification found within Lutheran orthodoxy.[68]

Churchly Pietist Emphases

Not only did the Harmonist leader uphold core Reformation doctrine (a high view of Scripture, orthodox formulations of the Trinity and the deity of Christ, and a Protestant understanding of the atonement and justification by faith). The biblical-eschatological trajectory of George Rapp's theology likewise reflected several typically churchly Pietist emphases, most notably, a Pietist understanding of the doctrine of regeneration and its theological

---

[64]MG-185, 1-5004, Box 15, Folder 5, A-58.
[65]MG- 185, 1-5004, Box 15, Folder 5, O-70.
[66]MG-185, 1-5004, Box 15, Folder 6, Q-54.
[67]MG-185, 1-5004, Box 15, Folder 6, Q-136.
[68]See McGrath, *Iustitia Dei*, 51-53 for differences between Lutheran Orthodox and Pietist conceptions of justification.

implications— the freedom of the will, the necessity of good works for salvation, and perfectionism. Furthermore, churchly (and radical) Pietists appropriated Luther's doctrine of the priesthood of all believers and applied it practically in daily life. Not just pastors, but laymen were given the freedom to read, interpret and teach the Bible in Pietist conventicle meetings. These topics are referred to as *Pietist* emphases since they *characterize* this seventeenth and eighteenth century reform movement, although some were likewise discussed or advocated to a lesser degree within the contemporary Lutheran and Reformed confessions. These emphases characterize *churchly* rather than radical Pietist thought. Typical, distinctive radical (as opposed to churchly) Pietist doctrine belongs almost exclusively within the mystical-spiritual trajectory. References to the views of Philipp Jakob Spener, the founder of Lutheran churchly Pietism in Germany, will be included as a foil against which Rapp's theology might best be understood.

Regeneration

Philipp Jakob Spener transferred the doctrine of justification by faith from the locus of central importance it held within Lutheran orthodoxy. The Pietist founder did not eliminate the biblical concept. Rather, he subsumed justification under the broader concept of regeneration (*Wiedergeburt*), which was the Pietist leader's primary concern.[69] Spener, unlike Rapp and other radical Pietists, did not reject the Lutheran concept of baptismal regeneration.[70] Nevertheless, Spener argued that but few Christians actually remained in the grace of regeneration received at baptism. Most Christians baptized as infants required a "second regeneration."[71] He likewise complained that the *Apology of the Augsburg Confession* falsely interpreted regeneration as justification, whereas he (and Luther) correctly defined it as the creation by God of a new nature within man.[72] Spener was convinced

---

[69]Spener's three stages of *Wiedergeburt* were the awakening of faith, *justification* and the creation of the new nature. Erhard Peshke, "Spener's Wiedergeburtslehre und ihr Verhältnis zu Franckes Lehre von der Bekehrung," in *Traditio—Krisis—Renovatio aus theologischer Sicht*, ed. Bernd Jaspert and Rudolf Mohr (Marburg: Elwert, 1976), 206-224, here 213f. Cf. Schmidt, "Spener's Wiedergeburtslehre," 171-173. McGrath notes that the "emphasis upon the necessity of regeneration [within Pietism] led to the assertion of the priority of regeneration over justification—a tendency already evident within Lutheran Orthodoxy . . ." McGrath, *Iustitia Dei*, 53. In contrast to Schmidt and Peshke, Emanuel Hirsch argued that Spener's goal was to make justification a practical and living reality for the individual. Emanuel Hirsch, *Geschichte der neuern evangelischen Theologie*, vol. 2 (Gütersloh: Bertelsmann, 1951), 140. See Peshke, "Spener's Wiedergeburtslehre," 206-207 for historiography concerning Spener and regeneration.

[70]Cf. *Book of Concord*, Apology, Art. 2, 36, 117.

[71]Peschke, "Spener's Wiedergeburtslehre," 212.

[72]Ibid., 213. Cf. *Book of Concord*, Apology, Art. 4, §72, 132: "And because 'to be justified' means that *out of unrighteous people righteous people are made or*

that the present despicable state of Christianity was due to the general ignorance among the masses of the crucial doctrines of salvation, particularly regeneration.[73] Not surprisingly, Spener's emphasis on regeneration was appropriated by the Pietist movement. "[T]he image of spiritual re-birth (*Wieder-Geburt*) as the requirement for a true relationship with God [became and] is the central expression of Pietist self-understanding."[74]

When it came to the doctrine of regeneration, George Rapp was a thoroughly convinced Pietist. Like Spener and Luther before him, Rapp defined regeneration using the biological and biblical terms associated with physical birth and spiritual rebirth. Regeneration was the process by which "the *new man* is created in us. This happens through the indwelling of the Holy Spirit. He [the Spirit] is the one who forms anew the *new creation*. . . . The Holy Spirit enters the soul and takes possession of it, in order to bring about the great work of regeneration (*Wiedergeburt*) there."[75] Rapp used two biblical images when speaking of regeneration: the creation of the *new man* to replace the old man (*alter Mensch*) crucified with Christ (Rom 6:1f), and the *new creature* or creation (2 Cor 5:17). According to the Harmonist leader, the "old man is slothful, rude, impure, dark, destructive, weak and lacking in power." Through the "washing of regeneration" he becomes a new creature who exhibits the opposite characteristics.[76] The center of the new man or creature was his will. Through regeneration, man's will was renewed, transformed and aligned with the will of God, thus enabling him/her to live a life pleasing to the Lord.[77]

Like Spener, Rapp used the term *Wiedergeburt* broadly to connote the entire process of man coming to saving faith, as well as narrowly for the creation of the new nature within man. In a number of Rapp's sermons, the Harmonist leader outlined one or more of the steps to salvation, an *ordo salutis*. These steps progressed from awareness of sin to awakening of faith, conversion, justification, and regeneration. Rapp described the process of gaining awareness of sin in several ways. In one sermon, he stated that the "first step of conversion" was to "resist sinful inclinations" and to "learn what God's will is." Rapp made perfectly clear that this step "did not destroy

---

regenerated, it also means that they are pronounced or regarded as righteous." Other passages in which the concepts of regeneration and justification are virtually synonymous are Apology, Art. 4, §67-68, 131 and §161, 145f.

[73]Schmidt, "Spener's Wiedergeburtslehre," 171.

[74]Markus Matthias, "Bekehrung und Wiedergeburt," in *Geschichte des Pietismus*, vol. 4, *Glaubenswelt und Lebenswelten*, ed. Hartmut Lehmann (Göttingen: Vandenhoeck & Ruprecht, 1995), 49-79, here 49.

[75]"u daß der neue M: in uns erschaffen wird, geschieht durch die jnwohnung deß h: G: selbst. Er ist es der die neue Creatur neu bildet. Den wenn die Zeit gekomken ist, daß der h: G: in die Seele eingehen will u selber besiz nimmt das grose werck der widergeb: allda zu verrichten..." MG-185, 1-5004, Box 15, Folder 6, P-65.

[76]MG-185, 1-5004, Box 15, Folder 5, O-37.

[77]MG-185, 1-5004, Box 15, Folder 5, O-70.

the root [of sin] within us."[78] Nor did it crucify the old man or sin nature. The purpose of this step was to come to the experiential realization that one is incapable of achieving good works on one's own. "This first work [of the Holy Spirit] was so that the soul forsakes its own abilities . . . and experiences how great and difficult the imprisonment of sin is."[79] All of man's efforts to fulfill God's law were no more than "cutting off the branches of an evil tree." The tree remains evil in its core in spite of man's best pruning efforts.

This period of gaining awareness of sin was characterized by severe psycho-spiritual anguish and unrest in the soul. Because of man's sinful deeds, his soul was troubled by a guilty conscience and he lacked peace. Rapp described this as experiencing the fire of God's wrath and disfavor. "The sinner senses that this fire consumes and condemns. And yet he finds no means to comfort himself and to salve his conscience save through Jesus Christ."[80] This experience of "spiritual death" had a cleansing and curative effect for some. The "purifying torture" (*läuterungs quaal*) of God's wrath broke the self-will and soured and dulled "the lusts and pleasures of this earthly life." Man became "troubled by his sins and seeks salvation."[81] Through the working of the Holy Spirit, the soul became "shocked" by its own depravity, so that it "takes ahold of itself and denies itself."[82] This first step toward conversion, which normally involved psycho-spiritual anguish, was reminiscent of the *Busskampf* (repentance struggle) propagated by August Hermann Francke and Halle Pietism.[83] It was likewise similar to Rapp's own extended conversion experience, in which he first attempted to become "pious through his own works," only to realize fully the futility of man's efforts and that "salvation was in Christ alone."[84]

The second step in Rapp's *ordo salutis* was the awakening of faith through the Word of God and the Holy Spirit. At the "proper time" (*zur bestimmten Zeit*), when "the soul had been adequately fatigued" by its "torture," the love of Jesus Christ "appears to the soul through the Word and the Holy Spirit."[85] Whereas the awareness of sin involved experiencing God's wrath, the awakening of faith came through Christ's love. The "living Word of God," the Scriptures, were so deep "that no one may learn them through hearing or reading" alone. The "Spirit of promise" must open the Bible for

---

[78]MG-185, 1-5004, Box 15, Folder 6, P-65.
[79]Ibid.
[80]MG-185, 1-5004, Box 15, Folder 6, P-268.
[81]MG-185, 1-5004, Box 15, Folder 5, N-62.
[82]MG-185, 1-5004, Box 15, Folder 6, Q-72.
[83] See Peschke, "Spener's Wiedergeburtslehre," 220-224 and Matthias, "Bekehrung und Wiedergeburt," 60-65.
[84]Karl J. R. Arndt, *George Rapp's Separatists, 1700-1803. A Documentary History* (Worcester, Mass.: Harmony Society Press, 1980), 71. See chapter two above, Conversion of Johann Georg Rapp.
[85]MG-185, 1-5004, Box 15, Folder 6, P-268.

the seeking soul.[86] Therefore, one must "ask God that he might lend to us the true understanding of his Word, and the grace to carry out his commands."[87] Once again, Rapp stressed that this step, as "necessary as this beginning was . . . was nevertheless inadequate to put to death the old man."[88] It did however accomplish that "through the Holy Spirit a higher desire [was] awakened, which yields a higher, greater happiness" than the sins of the world.[89] The "character of saving faith" (*seeligmachenden Glauben*), awakened by the Holy Spirit within the soul of the seeker, was found in its "desire for God and for union with him."[90]

The third step in Rapp's *ordo salutis* was conversion itself. Rapp described the act of conversion with terminology reminiscent of Tersteegen's quietistic emphasis (*Abkehr* and self-denial), which was also found in Spener:

> The turning away (*Abkehr*) from ourselves and the return (*Wiederkehr*) of our will to God is conversion (*Bekehrung*). Through this action of our will we deny ourselves. We entrust ourselves to God and give back to him that which belongs to him, which is our very selves. Therefore our Savior demands from us that we should deny ourselves and all things, Matt 16 and Lk 14. If we then make this firm decision, then Jesus Christ receives us as his possession by virtue of this consent to his command and the voluntary gift [of ourselves] to him.[91]

Rapp defined conversion as the turning away from self and the turning toward or retuning to God. Turning from self of necessity required the new believer to submit to Christ's clear commands in the Gospels (Matt 16:24f; Lk 14:26-27) and deny him or herself. Without prior turning from self it

---

[86] MG-185, 1-5004, Box 15, Folder 6, Q-72.
[87] MG-185, 1-5004, Box 15, Folder 6, P-66.
[88] Ibid.
[89] MG-185, 1-5004, Box 15, Folder 5, N-62.
[90] Ibid.
[91] "Aber die Abkehr von uns selbst, u die widerkehr deß willens zu Gott heißt bekehrung u durch diese handl: unsers willens verläugnen wir uns selbst. Wir überlassen uns, und geben Gott wider, was Ihm gehört, welches wir selber sind. Darum fodert unser Heiland wider von uns, daß wir uns selbst, u allen dinge verläugnen sollen Math 16 u Luc 14. Faßen wir uns nun diesen vesten Entschluß, so nimmt Jes: Chr: uns in kraft dieser Einwilligung in seyn gebot , u freywillige schenkung an Ihn, uns für seyn Eigenth: an." MG-185, 1-5004, Box 15, Folder 6, P-66. See chapter three for a discussion of Tersteegen's quietism. For Spener's use of the language of *Abkehr von der Welt* see Peschke, "Spener's Wiedergeburtslehre," 218. There is no evidence that Rapp read Spener's works, although he likely absorbed some of his views through attendance at churchly Pietist conventicles prior to separation from the Lutheran Church. The concept of *Abkehr* with regard to regeneration was almost certainly received through Rapp's reading of Tersteegen's revival sermons, *Geistliche Brosamen*, which frequently dealt with this topic. The Harmonists owned at least two copies of this volume in 1829. Arndt, *Rapp's Successors*, 420, #136.

was impossible to turn toward God. The Harmonist leader rejected any notion of "easy believism" or "decisionism." Conversion was a serious affair that required that the "old nature or man" be crucified (Rom 6:6).

Rapp's teaching on conversion likewise stressed the central role of man's volition. According to Rapp, the will was the "active power" (*Thätige Kraft*) and "rudder" of the soul.[92] It was created by God and given freedom of choice. Nevertheless, since the Fall man's will had been corrupted and incapable of true freedom—it could not avoid sin and choose the good.[93] Like Spener and Luther before him, Rapp believed that man of his own accord had no natural capacity for faith. As shown above, the awakening of faith in Rapp's theology was a work of God through the Scriptures and the Holy Spirit.[94] Man could not initiate faith, but man could resist and obstruct God's grace in salvation. In other words, Rapp believed that God's grace was resistible in contrast to a Reformed understanding.[95] According to the sermon quoted above, conversion was an "action of our will." Man chose to entrust himself to God and to "make this firm decision" after faith had been awakened through God's initiative. At times Rapp spoke of conversion as the decision to "accept Jesus Christ as Savior," in other instances as "submission to the Holy Spirit."[96] In either case, Rapp stressed man's free will and ability either to respond or not respond to the prompting of the Holy Spirit for salvation. He thus taught a form of synergism or cooperation of man in conversion that was likewise found in the writings of Spener.[97] Faith was understood to be active rather than passive in conversion, since man must respond to and work with the Holy Spirit. Nevertheless, through his own efforts he was incapable of effecting salvation or any good thing. Like

---

[92] MG-185, 1-5004, Box 15, Folder 6, R-61 and MG-185, 1-5004, Box 15, Folder 5, N-99.

[93] MG-185, 1-5004, Box 15, Folder 6, P-100.

[94] MG-185, 1-5004, Box 15, Folder 6, P-268, ibid., Q-72 and ibid., Folder 5, N-62. This was taught by Spener and found in the Augsburg Confession. Stein, "Spener," 90. *Book of Concord*, Augsburg Confession, Art. 18, 50: "However without the grace, help and operation of the Holy Spirit a human being cannot become pleasing to God, fear or believe in God with the whole heart, or expel innate evil lusts from the heart. Instead this happens through the Holy Spirit, who is given through the Word of God."

[95] Rapp likewise held that it was possible to lose one's salvation. "Wieder diesem Staub haben wir, als wieder unsern ErbFeind lebens lang zu kämpfen, u das ewige Licht Christum anzuruffen, damit die ewige Finsterniß nicht das regiment bekomme, u uns zu Kinder deß Todes u der Hölle mache: . . . so haben wir zu wachen, u wieder deren Einflüsse zu streiten, daß wir nicht unser ewiges Erbtheil verliehren." MG-185, 1-5004, Box 15, Folder 6, Q-27.

[96] MG-437/ Box 22/ Folder 82B/C-3 and MG-185, 1-5004, Box 15, Folder 5, A-58 (accepting Christ as Savior). MG-185, 1-5004, Box 15, Folder 6, P-268 (submission to the Holy Spirit).

[97] MG-185, 1-5004, Box 15, Folder 6, R-207. Cf. Peschke, "Spener's Wiedergeburtslehre," 211.

the founder of Pietism, Rapp was careful to avoid, on one hand, the pitfalls of Pelagianism, and on the other, the determinism of Reformed formulations of predestination. The Harmonist leader's understanding of free will was thus closer to that advocated in the Lutheran Book of Concord than to that in Reformed theology.[98]

Like Spener, Rapp considered justification to be one stage within the broader concept of regeneration. Justification occurred at the point of conversion, when man turned from self-will to God. At that juncture, "through faith man was clothed with the merit of Jesus Christ."[99] Justification was the external act of God in which instantly during conversion the alien righteousness of Christ was imputed to the believer. In contrast, the final stage of Rapp's *ordo salutis*, regeneration in the narrow sense, was not an outward declaration but an inward transformation wrought by the Holy Spirit.[100] At conversion, the Holy Spirit took up residence within the believer. "The new man [or nature] that is created in us occurs through the indwelling of the Holy Spirit himself."[101] Just as in the first stages of the *ordo salutis* the old nature was crucified, so in the process of regeneration, the new nature was risen from the dead and given resurrection power to fulfill (at least imperfectly) the commands of God. In regeneration:

> He [God] imparts to us the divine power with which the Savior overcame trials and temptations. It occurs through the appropriation of his merit that we are victorious and through suffering able to put to death the old man. Through this merit of Jesus Christ . . . he has purchased for us the grace that the new man might be formed in us.[102]

"After the healing death of our self[-will], what a resurrection of the divine is there in us!" Rapp proclaimed.[103]

Implications of the Pietist Doctrine of Regeneration

George Rapp's theology reflected the Pietist critique of the antinomian tendencies potentially inherent in *sola fide*. According to Spener, the reason Luther emphasized justification by faith alone and faith more than works was as a corrective to the Pelagian tendencies within the contemporary Roman Catholic Church. In contrast, the church-historical context for Spener's generation was entirely different. Spener claimed that many Lutherans at the end of the seventeenth century gave little thought to holy living, be-

---

[98]One point of difference was concerning the activity or passivity of justifying faith. Lutheran Valentin Löscher rejected the Pietist assertion of activity of faith by appealing to Luther's insistence on the passivity of justifying faith. McGrath, *Iustitia Dei*, 51-52.

[99]MG-185, 1-5004, Box 15, Folder 5, N-62.
[100]MG-185, 1-5004, Box 15, Folder 5, O-70.
[101]MG-185, 1-5004, Box 15, Folder 6, P-65.
[102]MG-437/ Box 22/ Folder 82B/C-3.
[103]MG-185, 1-5004, Box 15, Folder 6, R-207.

ing content with verbal assent to the doctrines of the Augsburg Confession. To counteract this trend, the Pietist reform movement shifted the theological focus from justification to regeneration and sanctification, although most Pietists continued to uphold a forensic understanding of the former.[104] Like Spener, Rapp insisted that true, saving faith and works always occurred together.

> Is faith a living, energetic, active, powerful thing! ... Then it is impossible that it should not continuously produce good works. The believer does not ask whether he should do good works, for before man asks he has already done them and is always doing them. So it is impossible to separate faith from works ... God himself becomes the inner disposition in us by the power of Jesus Christ's merit alone through the working of the Holy Spirit. It is as if Christ's merit were our merits ... We become righteous apart from our merits. ... For faith united with works is living and therefore justifying.[105]

Although good works were the natural outgrowth and accompaniment of justifying faith, they were not the basis for salvation and acceptance by God, which was found in the merits of Jesus Christ alone. Nevertheless, "salvation without sanctification is impossible ... This is what the converted person does. He makes amends where he can. The rest is the work of the Savior, which his Spirit accomplishes in us."[106] Rapp's approach to faith and works avoided Pelagianism--he insisted that salvation was grounded in the merits of Christ's atoning sacrifice and not in human works. Man was saved by grace through faith and regenerated so that he/she might walk in newness of life.

A second implication of the Pietist doctrine of regeneration was perfectionism. In regeneration man became a completely new creature. The old man of sin was annihilated, replaced by a new nature, which was able, at least potentially, to conquer and root out sin. This conviction was first outlined within Pietist circles by Spener in his published sermons on regeneration (*Der hochwichtige Articul von der Wiedergeburt*).[107] Striving for perfection was later adopted by members of the Pietist movement. Ernst Stoeffler lists perfectionism as a subcategory of religious idealism, one of four basic

---

[104]Peschke, "Spener's Wiedergeburtslehre," 216. Cf. Matthias, "Bekehrung und Wiedergeburt," 50-53 and McGrath, *Iustitia Dei*, 53.

[105]MG-185, 1-5004, Box 15, Folder 5, O-36. This emphasis on faith and works is found in Spener's writings, who cited Luther's Prologue to Romans. Peschke, "Spener's Wiedergeburtslehre," 215.

[106]MG-185, 1-5004, Box 15, Folder 5, A-58.

[107]The clearest statement supporting perfectionism was found in *Hochwichtige Articul*, 836-837: "Also weil die sünde unser gröstes elend ist / so ist hingegen diese gerechtigkeit / die wir in Christo haben ... unser gröstes gut / das uns von solchen grössesten übel der sünden befreyet: denn es werden nach art zu reden der schrifft / die sünde gantz weggenommen / daß es vor Gott seye als wäre sie nie gewesen." Quoted in Schmidt, "Spener's Wiedergeburtslehre," 177, note 25.

characteristics of historic Pietism.[108] Like other Pietists, George Rapp believed that the biblical concept of perfection (Mt 5:48: "Be perfect as your Father is perfect") should be taken seriously. Although perfection in this life remained elusive, it was nevertheless an "impossible possibility."[109]

According to the Harmonist leader, the free will of man was sanctified through the renewal brought about in regeneration.[110] In a sermon on 1 John 3:9 ("He who is born of God does not sin"), Rapp explained the verse in the following manner:

> He [the Apostle John] is saying that whoever has a sanctified will knows from experience that even in the frequent temptations, to which man is exposed from without, immediately an inward impulse resists the temptation and prevents it from taking root. So it now occurs with the sanctified person in whom God dwells through faith, just as it even more so already occurred with the man Christ--according to his [God's] promise, the sanctified man cannot sin.[111]

Regenerated man no longer had a "corrupted will" (*verderbten Willen*). Rather he possessed an "illuminated will" able to "perform the powerful deeds of righteousness. For whoever clings in love to God in the person of Jesus Christ gradually loses the desire and ability to sin."[112] The ability to perform righteous deeds was not due to man's inherent goodness. Rather "Christ strengthens the fulfillment of perfection within us, the freedom from sin."[113] "In the death of Jesus lies the power to slay the sin within us."[114] Rapp affirmed that man must cooperate with God in the annihilation of sin. "We condemn the sin in our flesh through the grace of Christ until it is po-

---

[108]F. Ernst Stoeffler, *The Rise of Evangelical Pietism* (Leiden: E. J. Brill, 1965), 16-17.

[109]This term was used by Stein of Spener's view of perfection. K. James Stein, "Philipp Jakob Spener (1636-1705)," in *The Pietist Theologians. An Introduction to Theology in the Seventeenth and Eighteenth Centuries*, ed. Carter Lindberg (Malden, Mass.: Blackwell, 2005), 84-99, here 93.

[110]Cf. *Book of Concord*, Formula of Concord, Art 2, §60 and §63, 555-556, which likewise speaks of the renewal of will after conversion/regeneration.

[111]"1 Jn 3.9. Wer aus Gott geboren ist, thut nicht Sünde. Er will damit sagen, wer einen Geheiligten Willen hat, der wird aus der Erfahrung wißen, daß bey den Häuffigen versuchung: deren wir ausgesetzt sind, sich dem reiz von außen, so gleich ein jnnerer gegenstand wider sezt, u das wurzlen verhindert; wie es nun hier mit dem geheiligten M: geschieht in welchem Gott durch den Gl: wohnt, nach seiner verheißung daß er nicht sündig: kan so geschah es um so mehr mit dem M: Christus." MG-185/1-5004/Box 15/Folder 6/P-72.

[112]"Den wir haben einen verklärten Willen u üben kräftige Thaten der gerechtigk: Den wer Gott in der Person Jes: Christi mit Liebe anhängt, allmähl: Lust u Fähigkeit verliert zum sündigen." MG-185, 1-5004, Box 15, Folder 6, Q-54 and MG-185, 1-5004, Box 15, Folder 6, P-100.

[113]MG-185/1-5004/Box 15/Folder 6/P-78.

[114]"im Tode jesu ligt die Kraft zur Tödung der sünde auch in uns." MG-185, 1-5004, Box 15, Folder 5, N-99.

werless. Through this we establish the beginning and the completion of freedom from sin."[115] The most effective way to defeat the sin in one's life was to submit willingly to trials and suffering, another Tersteegian emphasis.[116]

Despite the possibility and promise of perfection, the struggle against sin was long and difficult. Man was still enclosed in the bonds of the world of sensual pleasures (*Sinnenwelt*).[117] Furthermore, man was hindered by his earthly, sin nature. Rapp referred to this as "dust" (*Staub*), a reference to the Genesis account where man was formed from the dust of the earth (Gen 2:7).

> We have to fight our life long against this dust and against our Ancient Foe. We have to call on Christ, the eternal light, in order that the eternal darkness does not gain control . . . Even if we immediately gain victory over the emotions, lusts and desires dwelling in our dust, we may not completely triumph over these, because original sin . . . still moves within us and desires to act, 2 Cor 12:7. This always causes a new battle in us and this will continue until the end of our life.[118]

According to Rapp, man's sin nature continued to raise its ugly head even in regenerated man. This fact, along with the wiles of the devil ("our Ancient Foe") and the enticements of this world, made perfection an elusive goal. Every time man examined his spiritual state, he became convinced of his own sinfulness and lack of perfection. Therefore, Rapp encouraged his imperfect listeners to turn to the Bible. For "faith gains courage in the Word of God" to continue to strive for perfection.[119]

Priesthood of all Believers

George Rapp and the Harmony Society not only strongly believed in the priesthood of all believers, but they put their belief into practice. Philipp Jakob Spener in his programmatic call for church reform, *Pia Desideria* (1675), underscored Luther's conviction that "not only the preacher, but all Christians have been made priests by their Savior, been anointed with the Holy Spirit and been appointed to perform priestly functions." Therefore, Christians were entitled and obliged to "teach, discipline, warn, convert, [and] edify" their fellow believers.[120] Luther first proposed the concept of lay responsibility in spiritual affairs. But it took Spener and the Pietist

---

[115]"so verdammen wir aus Christi gnad die Sunde im Fl: biß zur unmacht u begründen dardurch den anfang u die vollendung die freyh: der sünde." MG-185/1-5004/Box 15/Folder 6/P-72.
[116]MG-185, 1-5004, Box 15, Folder 6, P-100.
[117]MG-185/1-5004/Box 15/Folder 6/P-72.
[118]MG-185, 1-5004, Box 15, Folder 6, Q-27.
[119]MG-185/1-5004/Box 15/Folder 6/P-238.
[120]Philipp Jacob Spener, *Pia Desideria. Umkehr in die Zukunft. Reformprogramm des Pietismus*, rev. Erich Beyreuther, 5th ed. (Giessen: Brunnen, 1995), 56-57.

movement to transform theory into practice. In his remarks to a group of young Harmonists at the Harmony Fest, 1829, Rapp extolled the appropriateness and benefits of group Bible discussions, a practice that he said extended back to the beginnings of the Iptingen Separatist conventicle in circa 1788:

> When we first gathered together as a *Gemeinschaft* in 1788 or so we would have discussions after our religious services in which each person who has something to say would say it. In God's garden there are many flowers and each are different and each beautiful and each person knows something that others do not. When someone has something good to say we listen and as a result we have the best advice on everything.[121]

Rapp affirmed that each person had an important contribution to make to the group. Without the active participation of each person, described as beautiful flowers in God's garden, the best and fullest advice would be lacking. Male and most likely female company leaders even led small-group Bible discussions within the Harmony Society.

This staunch conviction of the priesthood of all believers was reflected in some of Rapp's later sermons. After the formation of the Harmony Society, Rapp's concept of the priesthood of all believers was closely connected to their practice of communalism. In chapter five it was shown the Harmony Society attempted with its communal lifestyle to reinstitute the structure of the primitive Jerusalem church. According to a Rapp sermon, members of the Harmony Society were those who "feel and perceive the most intimate joy of unity," who have "become one heart and one soul" [allusion to Acts 4:32], and who have chosen the communal motto "what is mine is yours, and what is yours is mine."[122] These lay members have learned to put into practice the priesthood of all believers and to use their spiritual gifts to serve one another. Therefore:

> The strength of the strong is shield and refuge for the weak. The light of the illuminated is the guide for those needing light. Every gift is common. Its true owner does not rejoice over it [the gift] until others enjoy it with him ... So beautiful and great is the glory of the building, upon which the Spirit of Jesus truly works in the congregation. So great is the happiness and the purpose of the workers ... The fellowship of all gifts and strengths and sacrifice for others—this is happiness.[123]

The lay members were enabled to use their gifts for others because "the common Spirit works in all of us with the same power." Therefore, "we make decisions and share with one another teaching, sorrow and joy ... For the congregation is a trusting organ of fellowship for our innermost feelings."[124] The Rapp Separatist movement was a lay movement, which from

---

[121] Remarks by George Rapp, Feb. 15, 1829. (OEV, Daniel Reibel's file).
[122] MG-437/Box 22/Folder 82B/B-9.
[123] Ibid.
[124] MG-437/Box 22/Folder 82B/D-59.

its inception and throughout its later history as the Harmony Society put into practice the Pietist conviction of the priesthood of all believers.

"Anabaptist" Ecclesiology

In the discussion of the Lomersheimer and Ölbrunner declarations of faith in chapter two, it was demonstrated that Rapp's Separatists made the decisive move from a spiritualist ecclesiology to one which advocated a visible community of believers by 1790. In that year the Separatist movement had its first Eucharistic celebration with love feast and the first instance of rebaptism of adult believers by immersion in the Nagold River. In 1798-1799, the movement began to refer to itself as a visible believers' church (*Gemeine*). This development from a spiritualist to "Anabaptist" ecclesiology took place in Württemberg more than a decade before emigration, even though a fully-realized visible church was not yet an option. Later in the environment of religious freedom available on the American continent, the Harmony Society further developed their believers' church. In this chapter, further developments within the "Anabaptist" ecclesiology of the Harmony Society will be discussed. These developments include: (1) the Harmonist concept of a visible, gathered or believers' church; (2) the necessity of the outward ordinance of the Lord's Supper and the desirability of believers' baptism by immersion; (3) the necessity of separation from the world and, therefore, of the use of "shunning" or the ban.

The Harmonists also resembled Anabaptists theologically and outwardly in several other ways as well. Like Anabaptists, the Harmonists rejected any creed but the Bible. Christianity was the "religion of Jesus" and the "imitation of Christ," as it was in many Anabaptist groups.[125] From the beginning of their movement, Rapp's followers used typical Anabaptist arguments for their pacifist stance. Later, when Harmonist young men were drafted into the military in 1814 to defend the nearby city of Erie, Pennsylvania, they refused to serve. Rather the Harmony Society throughout its history paid fees to redeem their young men from military service.[126] While serving on the Indiana Constitutional Convention (1816), Frederick Rapp supported articles against compulsory military service.[127] Furthermore, Rapp's Separatists and the Harmony Society used primitivist arguments to support the practice of community of goods, just as some Anabaptist groups (Hutterites) did. Lastly, there was outward similarity between the Harmonists and many Anabaptist groups. At least in the early years of the Harmony Society, Harmonist wore uniform "plain" clothing, quite similar to that of the Amish

---

[125]Arndt, *Rapp's Harmony Society*, 75, 78, 84, and 98. Cf. James M. Stayer, "Täufer/Täuferische Gemeinschaften I," in *Theologische Realenzyklopädie*, vol. 32, ed. Gerhard Müller (Berlin: W. de Gruyter, 2001), 597-617, here 597.

[126]Arndt, *Rapp's Harmony Society*, 128 and 134.

[127]Ibid., 168.

and Hutterites.[128] The men likewise wore long beards without a moustache, as did men in many Anabaptists groups.[129] Documentary evidence does not allow us to determine whether Rapp's Separatists in Württemberg read Anabaptist literature or had personal contact with Anabaptists, for instance with those living on the Lerchenhof and Friedrichshof estates near Rapp's home town of Iptingen. After immigration to Pennsylvania, however, the Harmonists definitively developed acquaintances among the resident Mennonite population.

Believers' Church

The conviction of the necessity of a visible church of believers led the Rappites to develop a "Separatist church" in Württemberg prior to emigration. Only on American soil within the Harmony Society, however, did their believers' church come to full fruition. According to Rapp's later sermons, the church must be a *visible* community of regenerated persons or *true believers*.

> For the congregation (*Gemeine*) is the dwelling of the Trinity and God's temple. In the united souls and in the brethren, God, who is the Spirit, dwells and rules. This is the body of Christ and his Church (*Kirche*), the gathering of true comrades in faith (*Glaubens Genoßen*), who alone are to be found inwardly and *outwardly* in a congregation, since the persons from which it consists must be living members.[130]

Rapp stressed that the church was not just an inward or invisible entity. It was likewise an outward, physical congregation. On several occasions both prior to and after emigration, Rapp spoke of the outward physicality (*Leiblichkeit*) of the church. A visible community of saints, not an invisible

---

[128]Donald E. Pitzer and Josephine M. Elliott, *New Harmony's First Utopians, 1814-1824*, 2d ed. (Historic New Harmony, Ind.: University of Southern Indiana Press, 2002), 237. A Rapp sermon advocated moderation (plainness) in clothing, furniture and food. "Wen der M[ensch]: von einem jedem unüzen Wort rechensch: geben muß wird er nicht auch von überflüßigen kleider Mobilien Speisen u Getrank rechensch: geben müßen, der M: braucht wenig zu seinem unterhalt, alles andere ist sünde." MG-185, 1-5004, Box 15, Folder 5, O-83. After the Harmony Society began to produce silk, Harmonists began to wear self-manufactured silk clothing. Cf. Feb 1, 1844 letter from George Rapp to Ernst Brauns. Arndt, *Rapp's Harmony Society*, 593.

[129]The wearing of long beards was adopted by Separatist men in Iptingen by 1794, according to that year's annual church report. "Ihr, der hiesigen Separatisten äusserlicher Caracter besteht würklich darinnen, daß sie sich lassen bärte wachsen, die schon so lang sind, daß sie sich einen grauenhafften anblik geben." Arndt, *Doc. Hist. 1700-1803*, 258.

[130]"Den die Gem: ist ja eine Wohnung der 3heit, u Gottes Temp: den in den vereinigten Seel: u br: wohnet u regiert Gott, der den G: ist. Diß ist der Leib Christi u seine Kirche, als die versammlung der wahren Glaubens Genoßen, welche jnnerl: u äußerl: in einer Gem: allein zu suchen ist, weil die Personen woraus sie besteht lebendige Glieder seyn müßen." MG-185, 1-5004, Box 15, Folder 6, P-268.

church of the Spirit, was able to make God perceptible to the world.[131] The true church was likewise the dwelling of the Most High. To belong to the invisible and visible church, one must be a regenerated believer, a true comrade in faith, a living member of the body of Christ. Rapp stated the same conviction in another sermon: "Those who have the Spirit of Christ are members of the body of Christ in the congregation."[132] The obvious implication is that those who have not been regenerated and thus are not indwelt by the Holy Spirit are not members of the visible and invisible body of Christ. Rapp proposed a visible, gathered or believers' church.[133]

The primitivism reflected in the 1798 Lomersheimer Declaration remained a guiding principle within Rapp's Separatist movement and the Harmony Society. Not just the adoption of communalism, but all their ecclesial principles were "arranged according to the model of the first church after Acts of the Apostles in the 2d and 4th chapters."[134] According to a Rapp sermon, "in the first centuries Christianity blossomed."[135] Therefore, "the spiritual purpose of our brotherhood [Harmony Society], which [is] based upon the word of God, calls back to life original Christianity, which long ago became extinct in so-called Christendom."[136] The primitivist idealization of

---

[131] MG-185/1-5004/Box 15/Folder 6/R-97. Cf. Pastoral Letter #31, Collection #2, MG-185, 1-5005, Box 16, Folder 1.

[132] MG-185, 1-5004, Box 15, Folder 6, Q-68.

[133] Harris Franklin Rall first used the "gathered church/given church" distinction for the contrast between Methodist class meetings and the institutional Church of England. George Williams in 1991 argued that this distinction might be used to analyze other ecclesial bodies. The advantage of the gathered/given classification is both its flexibility and the avoidance of Troeltsch's term "sect" to denote Anabaptist groups. James Wm. McClendon, "The Believers Church in Theological Perspective," in *The Wisdom of the Cross*, ed. Stanley Hauerwas, Chris K. Huebner, Harry J. Huebner, and Mark Thiessen Nation (Grand Rapids: Eerdmans, 1999), 309-326, here 311-312. The concept of a believers' church emphasizes the necessity of a regenerated constituency. Its voluntary nature explicitly distinguishes itself from the "involuntarism" of pedobaptism and the confessions of the magisterial Reformation. Cf. The Dordrecht Confession of 1632: "We believe in and confess a visible Church of God, consisting of those who . . . have truly repented, and rightly believed; who are rightly baptized, united with God in heaven, and incorporated into the communion of saints on earth." Quoted in George Vandervelde, "Believers Church Ecclesiology as Ecumenical Challenge," in *The Believers Church: A Voluntary Church*, ed. William H. Brackney (Kitchener, Ont.: Pandora, 1998), 199-200.

[134] Letter by Frederick Rapp on March 7, 1822. Karl J. R. Arndt, *A Documentary History of the Indiana Decade of the Harmony Society, 1820-1824* (Indianapolis: Indiana Historical Society, 1978), 363. Cf. ibid, 465, 488-489, 512 and Karl J. R. Arndt, *George Rapp's Disciples, Pioneers and Heirs: A Register of the Harmonists in America*, ed. Donald E. Pitzer and Leigh Ann Chamness (Evansville, Ind.: University of Southern Indiana Press, 1994), 7.

[135] MG-185, 1-5004, Box 15, Folder 6, Q-18.

[136] Letter from George Rapp to Ernst Ludwig Brauns, February 1, 1844. Quoted in Arndt, *Rapp's Harmony Society*, 593.

the early church resulted in the adoption of communalism, the love feast accompanying the Eucharistic celebration, the rejection of infant baptism, believers' baptism, and the ban. This same desire to restore the primitive church was found in many of the Anabaptist groups.[137]

Lord's Supper

At the time of his separation from the Lutheran Church in Württemberg (1785), Rapp advocated a spiritualist view of the Eucharist—true participation of the Lord's Supper was inward and spiritual. Movement away from a purely spiritualist view of the Eucharist was evident in 1787. By 1790 members of Rapp's Separatist movement began to celebrate the Eucharist outwardly in a fashion modeled on the primitive Jerusalem church—prior confession, participation at a love feast (*agape*) followed by the Eucharistic celebration itself. This outward, physical understanding of the Lord's Supper was continued in the Harmony Society.

In his later sermons, the Harmonist leader underscored the legitimacy and necessity of physical, outward Communion. In the first place, the physical partaking of the bread and wine served to communicate God's presence to the senses. "But because the Lord is not perceived by our senses, we could not enjoy him except through the memorial, which the outward signs [bread and wine] convey and awaken within us. With these [outward signs] we celebrate his sacrificial death."[138] Furthermore, the celebration of an outward Eucharist was commanded by Christ for all generations until he visibly returns in his Second Advent.[139] Rapp's disciples rejected a spiritualist understanding of Communion in favor of an outward "Anabaptist" one.

Unlike Anabaptists, however, Rapp's followers did not espouse a Zwinglian, memorialist view of the Lord's Supper.[140] For Zwingli, the ontological barrier that existed between matter and spirit had the logical corollary that Christ could not be present in bread and wine.[141] While Lutherans (and

---

[137]Stayer, "Täufer I," *TRE*, 599.

[138]"Den weil der Herr für unsre Sinnen abwesend ist, so können wir ihn nicht genießen, als durch das Gedächtniß das die äußern Zeichen mit sich führen, das sie in uns erwecken, u womit wir seinen opfer Tod feyern." MG-185, 1-5004, Box 15, Folder 6, T-4.

[139]MG-185, 1-5004, Box 15, Folder 6, R-57.

[140]Finger, *Anabaptist Theology*, 186-197. Finger argues that all Anabaptists uphold a Zwinglian memorialist view of the Lord's Supper.

[141]Zwingli interpreted the words, "this is my body," in a metaphorical sense. He drew on the exegetical suggestions of the Dutch humanist, Cornelius Hoen, and interpreted the verb "to be" as "to be signified." Zwingli's dualistic understanding of human nature had as a corollary that "[s]piritual goods are communicated immediately to the human spirit by the action of God rather than mediately through physical objects," such as bread and wine. David C. Steinmetz, *Luther in Context* (Bloomington, Ind.: Indiana University Press, 1986), 74-76. Nevertheless, Christians feast on Christ spiritually and communally through the contemplation of faith. Ibid.,

Roman Catholics) would affirm that an ontological distinction existed, they believed that spirit could be "directly conveyed or expressed" through matter.[142] Therefore, for Luther, Christ was present with, under and in (real presence) the elements in the Eucharist.[143] Rapp did believe that the Lord's Supper was a commemorative feast, in which Christ's sacrificial death was remembered. "Here the sacrifice of Christ is brought into remembrance, as often as the holy meal is celebrated."[144] In the Lord's Supper "remembrance is renewed."[145] Nevertheless, Rapp espoused a more Lutheran understanding of the Eucharist. According to the Harmonist leader, when Christ spoke the words, "This is my body," he meant "his *own body*."[146] "Just as Christ the man is God, even so are the bread and wine Christ's body."[147] In this sermon, Rapp explained this concept with two analogies. Just as sunshine (spirit) unites itself with fruit (matter), so the man Christ (matter) is united with divinity (spirit), and bread and wine (matter) are Christ's body (spirit). Rapp was affirming that Christ was truly present in the Lord's Supper. In both of the elements, bread and wine, the "entire Christ" was to be found.[148] In fact, Rapp claimed that bread and wine became "a holy food in the very moment they are blessed and consecrated by a priest . . . or superintendent," that is, by Rapp himself. Then the elements "serve to communicate the Savior."[149] The Harmonist leader thus rejected a Zwinglian understanding in favor of real presence with the elements.

---

77. Cf. Jaroslav Pelikan, *Reformation of Church and Dogma (1300-1700)* (Chicago: University of Chicago Press, 1984), 193-196 and 201.

[142]Finger, *Anabaptist Theology*, 190. Cf. William R. Estep, Jr., "Contrasting Views of the Lord's Supper in the Reformation of the Sixteenth Century," in *The Lord's Supper. Believers Church Perspectives*, ed. Dale R. Stoffer (Waterloo, Ont.: Herald Press, 1997), 53-62.

[143]Luther retained the concept of real presence but rejected the theory of transubstantiation, which rested on the Aristotelian distinction between substance and attributes and which had been adopted by the Roman Catholic Church at the Fourth Lateran Council in 1215. "The real miracle of the eucharist is that Christ is present, not that the substance of bread and wine are absent. . . . Christ is present in the eucharist but so are the bread and wine in their full reality." Steinmetz, *Luther in Context*, 73-74.

[144]MG-185, 1-5004, Box 15, Folder 6, T-4. Cf. MG-185, 1-5004, Box 15, Folder 6, R-57.

[145]MG-185/ Box 15/ Folder 5/ Gr C-36. In this sermon, Rapp likewise stressed that the physical elements were incidental in comparison to faith. "When we do this [celebrate the Lord's Supper], we do not need teeth to bite with. Rather we break the bread with a desirous heart and complete faith."

[146]MG-185, 1-5004, Box 15, Folder 6, R-57.

[147]MG-185/ Box 15/ Folder 5/ Gr C-36.

[148]MG-185, 1-5004, Box 15, Folder 6, S-94.

[149]"fer:[ner] daß der Herr sich der Gem: Mittelbar durch ihren Vorsteher oder Priester mittheilen u mit ihr der Gem: Eins wird. Den es ist in dem Augenblick eine heilige Speise wo sie von Prie: gesegnet u gebenedezet ist, u zur mittheilung deß Heylands dienet." MG-185, 1-5004, Box 15, Folder 6, T-4.

Thomas Finger, in *A Contemporary Anabaptist Theology* (2004), notes that the Anabaptist/Zwinglian intellectual presupposition of an ontological barrier between spirit and matter was contradicted in actual Anabaptist Communion practice. Although a "crudely material" notion continued to be rejected, "Anabaptists very often affirmed Christ's presence through the Spirit," a view not greatly different from the Harmonist one.[150] Furthermore, a secondary Zwinglian theme, the congregation as Christ's earthly body, was at least as important as the memorial view in the Eucharistic teaching of the three branches of Anabaptism.[151] Christ was experienced communally through the breaking of the bread and drinking of wine. This aspect was likewise found in Rapp's love feast sermons. "For the bread [of the Lord's Supper] consolidated us all firmly into one body in the common spirit and presented us as an enduring, physical, visible entity, which you see with your eyes."[152]

Believers' Baptism

A dynamic tension between a spiritualist and an "Anabaptist" understanding of baptism developed during the early years of Rapp's Separatist movement. By 1787 infant baptism was rejected by Rapp as being inconsistent with biblical teaching. He argued that pedobaptism was wrongly confused with regeneration. Only if a person had repented and been converted did the waters of baptism have any use. In the first years of the Separatist movement, Rapp still clearly emphasized Spirit baptism rather than physical baptism.[153] By 1790, however, a decisive shift took place from a spiritualist understanding to a primitivist-biblicist one, influenced by Gottfried Arnold's depiction of early church practice. In that year the first rebaptism of a four of Rapp's followers took place by immersion in the Nagold River. Yet the Lomersheimer Declaration of 1788, signed and presumably written by Rapp, reluctantly allowed infant baptism, although it stated that believers' baptism was the practice of the early church and preferable.[154] Thus, although many of Rapp's followers moved to an "Anabaptist" understanding of baptism, some leeway was tolerated on this issue. This understanding appears to be contradicted by the annual Iptingen church report of 1804. This document, which was prepared and submitted by church authorities months after Rapp and hundreds of his most committed followers had immigrated to the United States, stated that the Separatists upheld a spiritualist understanding of baptism—that "outward baptism contributes nothing

---

[150] Finger, *Anabaptist Theology*, 197.
[151] Ibid., 188 and 196-197. Cf. Donald F. Durnbaugh, "Believers Church Perspectives on the Lord's Supper," in *The Lord's Supper. Believers Church Perspectives*, ed. Dale R. Stoffer (Waterloo, Ont.: Herald Press, 1997), 63-78, here 65.
[152] MG-185, 1-5004, Box 15, Folder 6, S-94.
[153] Arndt, *Doc. Hist. 1700-1803*, 108, 122, and 165-166.
[154] Ibid., 275.

to salvation," that "the inward baptism with the Holy Spirit in regeneration" was of central importance, and that "Bible passages that speak of water baptism actually refer to baptism of the Spirit."[155] Rapp would have agreed with the first two of these statements, but not with the third. The Harmonist leader from the 1790s onward advocated outward believers' baptism and not just Spirit baptism as the correct biblical pattern. Although this document might have reflected the opinions of remaining Separatists, it did not represent the view of Johann Georg Rapp and his most committed followers.

Several of Rapp's later sermons clearly espouse believers' baptism by immersion. This is not surprising, on one hand, since Rapp's convictions had developed in this direction by 1790. These later sermons merely indicate that his opinion concerning baptism had not changed since then. What is somewhat surprising, however, is that there appears to be no primary source evidence of baptisms performed in the Harmony Society other than these sermons. One might expect that one of the traveler's descriptions, letters to outsiders concerning their religion, or memorandum books maintained by members would have mentioned baptism celebrations, if they had taken place. There is no mention of young people being baptized in conjunction with joining the Harmony Society. Is this dearth of evidence an insurmountable problem? Perhaps not. In the first place, documentary evidence is spotty and scanty, particularly for the first three decades. These decades were the years when most baptisms would have taken place. After the 1832 secession of one-third of their membership, the Harmony Society quickly became an aged community, as few new members were admitted. Secondly, the Harmonists were reticent to share their religious views with outsiders. This could explain the fact that no travelers' accounts mentioned baptism, although some did mention the love feast. Third, the lack of confirming evidence could indicate that believers' baptism remained optional and therefore was practiced infrequently, particularly in later years. Nevertheless, the existence of several Rapp sermons that discuss believers' baptism

---

[155]"Die Wassertauffe, wenigstens die Kindertauffe, werde wohl bey ihnen hin furo gar unterbleiben, da man . . . die äußerliche Tauffe nichts zur Seeligkeit beytrage, ohne Tauffe das doch geworden wären, was sie seyen, die innerliche mit der Wiedergeburt verbundne Geistestauffe die Hauptsache bei den Christen sey, und die Stellen, die man von der Wassertauffe anführe, eigentlich von dißer Geistestauffe handeln." Ibid., 453. A reply of unnamed Württemberg theologians to a letter from Oct. 14, 1834 by an unnamed member of the Harmony Society (not Rapp, as the context makes clear) was published on March 5, 1835 in the Stuttgart *Christenbote*. The author was unable to locate the original letter that forms the basis of the response by the theologians. Their reply clearly implied that this member of the Harmony Society upheld a spiritualist view of baptism. Therefore, apparently not all members of the Harmony Society agreed with Rapp's stance of the necessity of outward baptism. The reply of the theologians is found in Arndt, *Doc. Hist. 1834-1847*, 76-88, here especially 83-84.

strongly suggests that immersion baptism occurred at least occasionally within the Harmony Society.

In his later sermons George Rapp stressed the legitimacy and desirability of outward baptism. He argued that the "hidden [spiritual] content" of baptism could only be understood by the congregation when the "concepts are made material, or become visible in time and space. For we only recognize the eternal Spirit in his manifold works."[156] Rapp made a similar argument with regard to the necessity of an outward Eucharist. Only through the human senses could the workings of the Holy Spirit be perceived—thus, the legitimacy and necessity of outward sacraments. The Harmonist leader made a clear distinction between outward, water baptism and inward baptism with the Holy Spirit and fire (allusion to Matt 3:11).[157] In one baptism sermon, Rapp explicated the difference between the two forms of baptism.

> But baptism itself as an immersion with water is cleansing or death-producing. It is the image of inner cleansing and of the death of our old nature, but at the same time effective through the power of Christ and the Holy Spirit to impart to us forgiveness of sins, to raise us up with God to the blessed covenant of a good conscience, and to cause us to participate in the resurrection to a new life ... when our desire grasps hold of the power offered to us. The fire baptism of the Holy Spirit is something else. This directly aims to effect a complete transformation, transfiguration and elevation of our nature and all its powers. For through water and fire or through water and Spirit all renewal of the creature takes place.... Jesus himself indicated and said that his baptism by John was a type of his suffering, death and resurrection. Therefore it is appropriate for us to fulfill all righteousness.... We then become participants with him, and we confess through baptism to faith, through him who is baptized with us.[158]

Water baptism was to be performed on believers by immersion. Immersion baptism reflected most clearly the image employed in Rom 6:3-4 of being buried and resurrected with Christ. It was a ritual, outward reenactment of the "cleansing," "death of the old nature," and "resurrection to a new life," which had previously occurred inwardly in the process of conversion and regeneration. Therefore, water baptism was only appropriate if the person had already been born again. In water baptism, the baptismal candidate became a participant in Christ's death and resurrection. The candidate obeyed a clear command of Christ ("fulfilled all righteousness"), and made an outward confession of inward faith. In contrast, the fire baptism of the Holy Spirit effected regeneration, the transformation of the old nature into a renewed one. The Harmonist leader taught that "a baptism not only

---

[156] MG-185, 1-5004, Box 15, Folder 6, P-211.
[157] Ibid., and MG-185, 1-5004, Box 15, Folder 6, P-233.
[158] MG-185, 1-5004, Box 15, Folder 6, P-211.

of water, but also of the Holy Spirit must take place within us."¹⁵⁹ Both were essential "for the renewal of the creature to take place."¹⁶⁰ Similar to many Anabaptists, Rapp advocated outward, believers' baptism by immersion.

Separation from the World and "Shunning"

In 1949, historian Robert Friedmann published the highly influential book *Mennonite Piety Through the Ages*. Friedmann's thesis that "Mennonite communities were best defined in terms of '"boundaries' and 'boundary maintenance'" was adopted by a subsequent generation of scholars. According to this view, "faithful Mennonite communities were separated from the fallen world by theological, ethical, and cultural boundaries. These boundaries, maintained through the exercise of church discipline, clearly identified the redeemed, gathered community living in faithful obedience to the precepts of Christ."¹⁶¹ Although all sects, not just Mennonites and other Anabaptists, maintain strict boundaries, the latter groups were distinct in the degree of separation from the world they maintained, and in their theological rationale for it. Church discipline for many Anabaptists was integrated into the sacramental life. Anabaptists expressed willingness to submit to and exercise discipline in their baptismal vow. Discipline was likewise practiced with regard to the Lord's Supper. These disciplinary practices were rooted conceptually in a sharp dualism between the world and the church, believers and non-believers, repentant and unrepentant persons. For Anabaptists, discipline and the ban were based on the precept of Jesus in Math 18:15-18. Its aim was salutary: to reform the excommunicated sinner, to frighten other believers from sin, and to maintain the purity of the church's witness to the world. Banning from the community was in historical Anabaptism "literally Christ's judgment to eternal condemnation."¹⁶²

Like Anabaptists, Rapp's Harmony Society also practiced strong "boundary maintenance." In a number of sermons, Rapp contrasted sharply the "kingdom of God" found within the Harmony congregation from the "kingdom of the world." The former was the Temple of God, a "kingdom of faith," and vastly different from the surrounding society.¹⁶³ According to Rapp:

---

¹⁵⁹"u deßweg: eine Taufe nicht nur deß [symbol = Wassers], sondern deß h. G: u deß [symbol = Feuers] in uns vorgehen müße." MG-185, 1-5004, Box 15, Folder 6, Q-72.

¹⁶⁰"Die Widergeb: geht jnwendig vor, aus [symbol = Wasser] u Geist u besteht in einer anneig: u umwandlung deß Willens zu Gott." MG-185, 1-5004, Box 15, Folder 5, O-70.

¹⁶¹John D. Roth, "Pietism and the Anabaptist Soul," in *The Dilemma of Anabaptist Piety*, ed. Stephen L. Longenecker (Bridgewater, Va.: Forum for Religious Studies, 1997), 17-33, here 23. Roth argues that Friedmann's thesis needs to be partially revised since Mennonite boundaries were never impermeable.

¹⁶²Finger, *Anabaptist Theology*, 208-212.

¹⁶³MG-437/Box 22/Folder 82B/B-9.

> The true members in the congregation withdraw in living faith ultimately from all creatures. . . . He does not need any rubbish except that which is allowed and permitted for us by the Holy Spirit in the holy Scriptures . . . He does not want anything that is not godly and useful for the kingdom of heaven . . . The congregation inquires so little [as possible] about the world. For, as much and often as the congregation must have contact with the world— that is a cross for it to bear. Therefore, the world considers us to be a monster and rubbish.[164]

The Harmony Society anathematized the world, and isolated its membership as much as possible from the surrounding culture. During Rapp's lifetime, a linguistic, cultural, and theological barrier was maintained from the surrounding "English" community. Children attended the Harmonist private school. Older members lived, worked and worshipped in the Harmonist settlement with little need or opportunity to become acquainted with the outside world.

In an 1822 letter to Edward Page of New York, Frederick Rapp described the Harmonist practice of church discipline:

> Whoever acts and lives contrary to the truth and commits sins or error is forbidden first by a brother or sister, chiefly however by our president, and is directed to improve himself, if he recognizes the error and promises to improve himself it is good, if not he is brought before the congregation and if he does not bear it anymore and does not want to improve he will no longer have a friend and cannot hold himself in the congregation but of his own accord goes away to the big world where his evil works are no longer punished.[165]

Like the Anabaptists, Rapp's Harmony Society attempted to put into practice the injunctions of Matthew 18. First, the wayward sinner was corrected by Rapp or another member. If he did not repent, he was brought before the congregation. If this attempt was unsuccessful, he was severed from the congregation and left to his own accord. Two phrases in this text are especially important. In the first place, a strong contrast is made between the congregation and the "big world where evil works go unpunished." Secondly, although the term "ban" or "shunning" (*meiden*) was not used to describe the process, in effect that it is what was described in the case of unrepentance. The unrepentant sinner would no longer be a part of the congregation, and would "no longer have a friend." That is, he or she would be shunned.

Harmonists used the same arguments that Anabaptists did to justify discipline and shunning—the need to cut off the putrefying flesh to maintain the health of the corporate body. Frederick Rapp wrote the following lines on February 18, 1808 concerning two families who had been severed or departed from the Harmony Society.

---

[164]MG-185, 1-5004, Box 15, Folder 6, P-234A.
[165]Arndt, *Rapp's Harmony Society*, 236.

And so the *Harmonie* will quickly cast out all filth in order that the body may be cleansed and purified of all foreign substance, and this is a good sign, although it gives offense to many. Whoever has been in the *Harmonie* and has left it again, be it for whatever cause it may, is not worthy of the Kingdom of God . . . and therefore such are persecutors and scorners of his name: therefore, hate such and have no sympathy with them, so that you will not be spotted by their false spirit, but rather damn such spirits, for they are worthy of it.[166]

Throughout its history, the Harmony Society shunned former members, who left of their own accord or due to church discipline. The Society reaped much criticism from outsiders due to their harsh conduct and banning of former Harmonists. From their perspective, however, shunning was theologically and practically necessary to maintain the purity of their Society. In their church discipline, in their emphasis on the necessity of a visible community of saints, and in their practice of believers' baptism and the Lord's Supper, the Harmonists reflected an "Anabaptist" ecclesiology. These aspects along with core Reformation doctrine and churchly Pietist emphases belong to the biblical-eschatological trajectory of George Rapp's theology.

---

[166]Ibid., 102. Cf. Balthasar Hubmaier's statement: "cut off the corrupt and stinking flesh together with the poisoned and unclean members, so that the entire body might not thereby be deformed, shamed and destroyed." Quoted in Finger, *Anabaptist Theology*, 211.

8

The Quest for "Deeper Knowledge" (1825-1847)

George Rapp and his original disciples grew to manhood in a tumultuous era of intellectual change that swept both Europe and the New World. Traditional interpretations of Scripture had been called into question a century earlier by Spinoza, George Herbert, John Toland, and the like.[1] German Protestantism attempted to respond to the theological implications of the rise of rationalism and modern scientific knowledge. Neologism and Enlightenment theology surrendered in the process key aspects of traditional doctrine. Lutheran orthodoxy, on the other hand, remained faithful to the Augsburg Confession. Nevertheless this conservative branch was entrenched for the most part in a scholastic approach to theology that appeared sterile and irrelevant to many in the pew. It was thus not surprising that some "radical" German Christians in the seventeenth and eighteenth centuries turned away from rationalism and Protestant orthodoxy and to mystical and theosophical traditions within both the Roman Catholic and Protestant confessions to meet their spiritual need for "deeper knowledge" and a numinous experience of God.

Rapp's Separatists and later the Harmony Society consistently sought to delve the depths of the Godhead and to ascertain the hidden mysteries of the revealed Word of God. Just two years after separation from the Lutheran Church in Württemberg, Rapp on May 18, 1787 proclaimed to the church authorities in Iptingen that although the local pastor might preach

---

[1]Baruch Spinoza (1632-1677) was a rationalist who laid a foundation for the rise of the Enlightenment and modern biblical criticism in the eighteenth century. George Herbert (1593-1633) is frequently referred to as the "father of English Deism." John Toland (1670-1722) in *Christianity not Mysterious* (1696) argued that there are no doctrines in the Bible inconsistent with reason.

well enough for others, the sermons "were not deep enough for him."[2] Fellow Iptingen Separatist, Johannes Hörnle, concurred: "What was preached [in the Iptingen church] was too light for him."[3] Not only were the sermons in the local Lutheran church lacking, in the Separatists' opinion, in spiritual substance and power. Rapp and his followers found even the theosophical-tinged writings of fellow radical Pietist Michael Hahn to be "not deep and mystical enough."[4] Later in the New Harmony era (1814-1824), George Rapp came to a similar conclusion with regard to the Shakers. According to the spiritual leader, the religion of "the *Harmonie* went much deeper" than that of the Shakers, although the latter (wrongly) were convinced that they had spiritually left the Harmony Society "far behind them."[5] The Harmony congregation believed that because they "knew God," they also possessed "the key with which to open the most secret rooms of wisdom," and to air "the great secret hidden in the book of divine truth."[6] The Godhead with its secrets dwelt bodily within the soul of the believer. Therefore, the regenerated person had direct access to mysteries hidden from the worldly wise.[7] This quest for deeper knowledge and numinous experience was thus a persistent focus among Rapp's followers. It co-existed parallel to more traditional, orthodox expressions of their Christianity.

In the preceding chapter, two trajectories of Rapp's mature theology found in his later sermons were introduced. A biblical-eschatological trajectory was reflected in the Harmonist leader's faithfulness to core Reformation doctrine (authority of Scripture, Trinity, doctrine of atonement and justification by faith), to churchly Pietist emphases (regeneration, perfectionism, priesthood of all believers), and to "Anabaptist" ecclesiology (visible church of saints, believers' baptism, church discipline). Two key aspects of a second, mystical-spiritual trajectory within Rapp's theology have already discussed at some length: Rapp's adoption of Tersteegen's brand of quietistic mysticism (chapter three), and the Sophialogical views of the Harmony Society (chapter six). In this chapter several other elements of the mystical-spiritual trajectory will be examined. Rapp believed that God intentionally imbedded within the biblical text a fuller meaning alongside the grammatical-historical sense intended by the human author. Therefore, in the first section of this chapter, the Harmonist leader's typological-

---

[2]Karl J. R. Arndt, *George Rapp's Separatists, 1700-1803. A Documentary History* (Worcester, Mass.: Harmony Society Press, 1980), 105.

[3]Arndt, *Doc. Hist. 1700-1803*, 91.

[4]Johann Michael Hahn, *Send-Briefe über einzelne Capitel aus dem alten und den vier Evangelisten und Antworten auf Fragen über Herzenserfahrungen, auf Verlangen an Freunde der Wahrheit geschrieben* (Tubingen: L.F. Fues, 1828), Part 1, 802.

[5]Letter of George Rapp to Frederick Rapp, June 22, 1816. Karl J. R. Arndt, *A Documentary History of the Indiana Decade of the Harmony Society, 1814-1819* (Indianapolis: Indiana Historical Society, 1975), 228-229.

[6]MG-185/1-5004/Box 15/Folder 5/N-116 and MG-185/1-5004/Box 15/Folder 6/R-21.

[7]MG-185, 1-5004, Box 15, Folder 6, R-42.

Christological and spiritual-allegorical interpretations of Scripture will be examined. In the preceding chapter, Rapp's orthodox conceptions of the Trinity were discussed. In a second section of this chapter his cabbalistic and theosophical descriptions of the Godhead will be unpacked. Section three depicts Rapp's understanding of the biblical account of creation and the fall, an understanding strongly influenced by Boehmist cosmogony and anthropology. Finally, in section four the author will discuss the short-lived practice of alchemy by key members of the Harmony Society, and the more persistent use of alchemistical language in Rapp's sermons to describe regeneration/sanctification and the formation of the resurrection body (*Geistleib*). The common denominator behind each section of this chapter is the striving of Rapp and the Harmony Society for deeper, arcane knowledge. The quietistic mysticism and Sophialogy of the Harmonists, which were previously discussed, reflected the desire for a numinous experience of God.

Allegorical Scriptural Hermeneutic

Allegory is a "principle of interpretation that treats the text as having a less-than-straight-forward meaning."[8] This approach when applied to Scripture is built upon the conviction that beneath the "obvious 'surface' meaning" or historical-literal sense (which, in some cases, might itself be a spiritual meaning) deeper meaning or meanings were intentionally hidden in the text by God for the edification of the spiritually astute.[9] In the Christian tradition the use of an allegorical hermeneutic of Scripture is most often associated with Origen and the Alexandrian school of biblical interpretation. The Western Church in the medieval period kept alive the central concerns of the Alexandrian school by adopting a fourfold sense of Scripture. In addition to the literal sense, an allegorical, tropological (moral), and anagogical (mystical or eschatological) sense were to be found in many passages of Scripture.[10]

Allegorical Interpretation in Historical Theological Context

In his first major exegetical work, his lectures on the Psalms (1513-1515), Luther began with the fourfold sense of Scripture, the *Quadriga*, common in the medieval period. Even in his early expositions, however, Luther was not particularly interested in two of the four senses, the allegorical and anagogical, although he resorted to allegory at times, not to estab-

---

[8] Andrew Louth, "Allegorical Interpretation," in *A Dictionary of Biblical Interpretation*, ed. R. J. Coggins and J. L. Houlden (Philadelphia: Trinity Press, 1990), 12-14, here 12.
[9] Ibid.
[10] Ibid., 13.

lish doctrine but rather to illustrate or embellish it.[11] Instead the Wittenberg Reformer focused his attention on the literal and tropological meanings.[12] In Luther's time the literal sense included "both the unfolding historical narrative (the literal-historical sense) and whatever typological meanings were foreshadowed in the story (the literal-prophetic sense)."[13] Later Luther abandoned the fourfold sense of Scripture, but he continued to value a tropological sense since it nurtured faith, and the christologically-oriented, prophetic sense. For Luther, the center of both the Old and New Testament Scriptures was Christ and "what drives Christ" (*was Christum treibet*). Despite his warning "beware of allegories," the Reformer from Wittenberg classified three sorts of allegory: those whose interpretations were found in Scripture itself and therefore binding; those established through other clear Scripture passages; and those based on man's opinions without a biblical basis.[14] While the first two categories of allegorical interpretation were legitimate in Luther's opinion, the final category was arbitrary and

---

[11] David C. Steinmetz, "Martin Luther," in *Dictionary of Biblical Interpretation*, ed. John H. Hayes (Nashville: Abingdon, 1994), 96-98, here 97. Luther stated in his lectures to the Psalms: "It is very difficult for me to break away from my habitual zeal for allegory. And yet I was aware that allegories were empty speculations and the froth, as it were, of the Holy Scriptures. It is the historical sense alone which supplies the true and sound doctrine." Quoted in Gerald Bray, *Biblical Interpretation-Past & Present* (Downers Grove, Ill.: InterVarsity, 1996), 198.

[12] Steinmetz, "Martin Luther," 97. For a discussion of Luther's biblical hermeneutic see: Jaroslav Pelikan, *Luther the Expositor. Introduction to the Reformer's Exegetical Writings* (St. Louis: Concordia, 1959), K. Hagen, "Luther, Martin (1483-1546)," in *Historical Handbook of Major Biblical Interpreters*, ed. Donald K. McKim (Downers Grove, Ill.: InterVarsity, 1998), 212-220; Steinmetz, "Martin Luther;" and, idem, "Hermeneutic and Old Testament Interpretation in Staupitz and the Young Martin Luther," *Archiv für Reformationsgeschichte* 70 (1979): 24-58.

[13] Steinmetz, "Martin Luther," 97. Richard A. Muller, in "Biblical Interpretation in the Era of the Reformation: A View form the Middle Ages," in *Biblical Interpretation in the Era of the Reformation*, ed. Richard A. Muller and John L. Thompson (Grand Rapids: Eerdmans, 1996), 3-22 discusses both continuity and discontinuity between medieval and Reformation exegesis. He notes that some usages of the fourfold sense in the medieval period emphasized allegory and trope (Gregory the Great) and others literal interpretation (Albert the Great and Thomas Aquinas), the latter evidencing considerable continuity with the Reformers. Furthermore, despite Luther and Calvin's focus on the literal meaning, "the underlying assumption that the meaning of the text is ultimately oriented to the belief, life, and future of the church contains significant affinities with the *quadriga*, the basic pattern of the so-called 'allegorical exegesis' of the Middle Ages." Ibid., 12.

[14] "'Beware of allegories' was the motto of many of his lectures to his students." Pelikan, *Luther the Expositor*, 89. Gerhard Ebeling in *Evangelische Evangelienauslegung* argued cogently for Luther's break with an allegorical interpretation. Pelikan, *Luther the Expositor*, 89.

speculative and therefore soundly rejected.[15] Both Martin Luther and John Calvin upheld and practiced a proper use of typology, which most scholars distinguish from an allegorical interpretation.[16] Whereas an allegorical interpretation of a Bible text had "no continuity with the historical intention of its writer ... typology argues for a continuity in God's plan such that the Old Testament is a true 'prefiguration'... of what God would do in the New Testament."[17]

Like Luther, Philipp Jakob Spener, the father of German Lutheran Pietism, recognized the legitimacy of a prudent use of allegory. An allegorical interpretation of Scripture could be spiritually enriching, but ought to be practiced only by those persons with the requisite understanding to apply afresh to the life of the believer that which occurred once in Scripture. To prevent abuse and speculation, Spener, like Luther before him, limited allegory to interpretations included in Scripture.[18] August Hermann Francke, a churchly Pietist disciple of Spener, was one of the most important exponents of Pietist biblical hermeneutics. He believed that historical-grammatical exegesis was the key to a deeper, *spiritual* understanding of the text. Like Luther, Francke claimed in *Christus, der Kern Heiliger Schrift* (1702) that Christ was the core (not the husk) of Scripture. Everything that was written in Scripture pointed directly to the Messiah.[19] He thus supported the use of typology.

Radical Pietists perpetuated the Christological interpretation of Scripture common to contemporary Lutherans and churchly Pietists. Unlike these groups, however, they insisted that the Word of God contained hidden, mystical secrets.[20] Besides the literal meaning, the Berleburg Bible, the most important radical Pietist Bible translation and commentary, claimed two other senses--a spiritual-moral sense and a secret-spiritual (*geheim*) sense. The latter was then further subdivided into a typological or salvation-historical sense, and a mystical sense concerning the spiritual states of the individual soul.[21] In the prologue to volume one of the Berleburg Bible,

---

[15]Beate Köster, *Die Luther Bibel im frühen Pietismus* (Bielefeld: Luther-Verlag, 1984), 44. Cf. Luther, *Lectures on Genesis*, 173: "The bare allegories, which stand in no relation to the account and do not illuminate it, should simply be disapproved as empty dreams. This is the kind that Origen and those who follow him employ." Quoted in Pelikan, *Luther the Expositor*, 28, n. 74.

[16]Stuart George Hall, "Typologie," in *Theologische Realenzyklopädie*, vol. 34, ed. Gerhard Müller (New York: W. de Gruyter, 2002), 208-224, here 215.

[17]Brian McNeil, "Typology," in *A Dictionary of Biblical Interpretation*, ed. R. J. Coggins and J. L. Houlden (Philadelphia: Trinity Press, 1990), 713-714, here 713.

[18]Köster, *Luther Bibel*, 44.

[19]Ibid., 91.

[20]Martin Brecht, "Die Berleburger Bibel. Hinweise zu ihrem Verständnis," in *Ausgewählte Aufsätze*, vol. 2, *Pietismus* (Stuttgart: Calwer Verlag, 1997), 369-408, here 389.

[21]"Daß also diese dreyfache Erklärung / des Buchstabens / des geistlichen und des geheimen Sinnes / gleichsam wie im Menschen so in heiligen Schrifft den Leib /

the authors of the commentary skillfully attempted to avert criticism by claiming that the Scriptural text had but one sense with manifold implications intended by the Holy Spirit. Like the Trinity, the individual biblical passage was both one and manifold.[22] Orthodox scholars were not fooled by this verbal maneuver. They recognized that in essence the Berleburg Bible upheld *multiple senses* of Scripture, and thus had regressed to a pre-Reformation, medieval hermeneutic.[23]

Rapp's Typological and Allegorical Interpretation of Scripture

George Rapp approached the biblical text with radical Pietist presuppositions and convictions. Similar to others in the radical wing of the Pietist movement, Rapp believed that the Bible contained secret, hidden layers of meaning. The Harmonist leader most commonly used forms of the term "deep" to describe the mysteries embedded in the Word of God. In one sermon he exuberantly extolled the depths of Scripture:

> The *depths* of the words of Jesus Christ extend through all the ages ... What wisdom, what *depths* do we now perceive in these divine Scriptures. What delicacy do we observe shimmering in it, what new savor for the truth, for the divine, may we draw from them. How great is the amazement, when man observes that neither the intelligent nor the wise can read or interpret it. Ra-

---

Seele und Geist derselben / ausmachen: ... Man verstehet aber hier durch den geistlichen Sinn den so-genannten Moral-Verstand / oder die Nutz-Anwendung der Schrifft / wie dadurch die Seele muß gebessert werden: durch den geheimen Sinn hergegen die innere Erkenntniß / die durch den Geist Gottes in der Seele gewircket wird ... Diese innere Erkenntniß ist die wahre Erkenntniß Gottes im Geist und in der Wahrheit / die Grund seyn muß von dem wahren Dienst und der wahren Anbehtung Gottes im Geist und in der Wahrheit / die Christus erfordert." Johann Heinrich Haug et al. *Die Heilige Schrift Altes und Neues Testaments, nach dem Grund-Text aufs Neue übersehen und übersetzet. Nebst einiger Erklärung des buchstäblichen Sinnes wie auch der fürnehmsten Fürbildern und Weissagungen von Christo und seinem Reich, und zugleich einigen Lehren, die auf den Zustand der Kirchen in unseren letzten Zeiten gerichtet sind,* vol. 1 (Berlenburg: [s.n.], 1726), Vorrede. Cf. Brecht, "Berleburger Bibel," 388 and Martin Brecht, "Die Bedeutung der Bibel im deutschen Pietismus," in *Geschichte des Pietismus,* vol. 4, *Glaubenswelt und Lebenswelten,* ed. Martin Brecht and Klaus Deppermann (Göttingen: Vandenhoeck & Ruprecht, 2004), 102-120, here 106-107.

[22]"Man weiß sich übrigens wol zu bescheiden / daß die H: Schrifft gleichwol keinen doppelten oder dreyfachen / sondern eigentlich allerdings nur einen Sinn habe ... Man glaubet aber daß ... die H. Schrifft ... auf einmal und mit einem Wort vieles ausspreche / das gleichwol in seiner gantzen Zusammenfassung ein Sinn bleibet / aber in verschiedener Eröffnung; und daß alles / was ein erleuchteter Mensch Gutes aus der Schrifft ziehen und hervorbringen mag / von dem H. Geist auch wircklich selbst intendiert sey. ... warum sollte Gott nicht mehr als einerley hinlegen können oder wollen?" Haug, *Berleburg Bibel*, vol. 1, Vorrede.

[23]Brecht, "Berleburger Bibel," 388-389.

ther simple and unlearned persons, who possess more the quality of a child than a scholar, understand the secrets of the holy Scriptures without difficulty as if they [the secrets] unravel themselves.[24]

The secrets of Scripture were hidden from the worldly-wise with their academic, rationalist approach to the Bible. Rapp affirmed here the churchly and radical Pietist conviction that only pious, regenerated believers could properly understand the plain meaning, let alone the divine mysteries concealed in the Bible.[25] Rapp employed the term "deep" or "depths" to indicate the spiritual core of the Scriptures that lay hidden beneath the literal, historical sense of the biblical text.

The "message of the Bible" was a "deep sea."[26] It contained both "flesh" or a literal, grammatical-historical sense and "spirit." The "spirit" of the Scriptural passage referred to the "innumerable metaphors, allegories, and mysteries" that were included in the text "by the counsel of the Holy Spirit."[27] All of Scripture was prophetic and embodied metaphors or allegories (*Gleichniße*), frequently multiple allegories at the same time and in the same passage. The Bible was "a library of metaphors (*Bilder*)" from which the congregation should extract "wisdom and understanding" through "continuous, deep study and contemplation."[28] Through practice, "true children of God" gradually became "accustomed to allegorical thinking" (*sinnbildliches dencken*) and progressed from the "visible elements" of Scripture, the literal sense, to "the mysteries of the Spirit."[29] Like the radical Pietist authors of the Berleberg Bible commentary, the Harmonist leader affirmed that Scripture had multiple senses. Rapp greatly valued the spiritual and allegorical senses. It was a poor man indeed who was satisfied with the "flesh" or "letter" of Scripture without the corresponding "spirit." Only by paying careful attention to the manifold senses of the Bible could one attain the ultimate goal—deep "knowledge of the eternal greatness of God."[30]

---

[24] MG-185/1-5004/Box 15/Folder 6/Q-20.
[25] "Wen du o M: Gottes Wort verstehen will, so ists nicht genug als es für ein gelehrtes Buch anzusehen, man muß vor allen Ding: den glauben haben, daß er von Gott gegeben sey, durch das mittel seiner Proph: u Apo: welche selber lernen mußten aus dem Was ihnen gegeben wurden, u es nicht für selbst werck ansehen, sondern den Einfalt Christi haben welche uns fähig macht zu empfang: u endl: muß man ohn unterlaß um den h: G: bitten daß er dir ein pförtner werde zu thür der offenb: u ihr siegel dir löse, dir den Heiland verklären, ferner must du ein treues reines [Symbol – Herz] haben Gott zu schauen, u seine Geheimniße erlang: . . . " MG-185/1-5004/Box 15/Folder 6/P-84. Cf. Markus Matthias, "Bekehrung und Wiedergeburt," in *Geschichte des Pietismus*, vol. 4, *Glaubenswelt und Lebenswelten*, ed. Hartmut Lehmann (Göttingen: Vandenhoeck & Ruprecht, 1995), 49-79, here 65-67 for a discussion of the Pietist *theologia regenitorum*.
[26] MG-185/1-5004/Box 15/Folder 6/Q-71.
[27] MG-185/1-5004/Box 15/Folder 5/E-13.
[28] MG-185/1-5004/Box 15/Folder 6/Q-71.
[29] MG-185/1-5004/Box 15/Folder 5/E-13.
[30] MG-185/1-5004/Box 15/Folder 6/Q-71.

Rapp and the Harmonists eagerly read the Berleburg Bible commentary. Several copies of the eight-volume set belonged to the Harmony Society library during Rapp's lifetime. It is therefore not surprising that the Harmonist leader appropriated categories of spiritual as opposed to literal interpretation, similar to those in the Berleburg Bible. Besides the moral and ethical application of the biblical passage, Rapp likewise divided the spiritual interpretation into two primary categories—a typological, usually Christological interpretation, and an allegorical interpretation concerning the spiritual state of the individual believer or congregation.

The Harmonist leader believed that "the central focus of Scripture, history, and of the entire existence of the world and humanity [was] the appearance of the Savior."[31] Because Christ was and would be the "one and all" throughout all eternity, it was not surprising that the Old Testament Scriptures frequently pointed to the Messiah. The most common spiritual interpretation employed by Rapp was a typological-Christological one. In this method of biblical interpretation, the type refers to a person, place, thing or event that foreshadows a future person or event. The type is a shadow or promise of an antitype, which is both greater than the type and clearer to understand.[32] According to Rapp, there were dozens of types of Christ in the Old Testament. He acknowledged in one sermon that:

> Christ was prefigured (*vorgebildet*) in many excellent men of the Old Testament and in just as many metaphors, forms and characters. For the holy men of the old covenant were physical types (*sinnliche Vorbilder*) for us, and those of the new covenant spiritual anti-types (*geistliche Nachbilder*) of our head [Jesus Christ].[33]

Joseph was a supreme type of Christ. Like the Messiah, Joseph was the beloved of his father. He suffered innocently at the hands of his brothers, was buried in the pit and arose again from it.[34] Jesus Christ was the "true Solomon," whose marriage with Sulamith, depicted in the Song of Solomon, prefigured the believers' union with Christ.[35] Joshua, the servant of Moses, foreshadowed Christ's role as a "servant of the eternal Father."[36] Adam, Abel, Seth, Abraham, Isaac, David, and many other Old Testament saints prefigured Christ the Messiah.[37] Not just persons, but things were types of Christ. In one Rapp sermon, the Harmonist leader interpreted the altar of burnt-offering as a type of Christ (Ex 27:1-8). The altar was filled with earth, which pointed to the humanity of Jesus. It was covered with pure

---

[31] MG-185/1-5004/Box 15/Folder 5/O-55.
[32] McNeil, "Typology," 713.
[33] MG-185/1-5004/Box 15/Folder 6/P-16.
[34] Ibid.
[35] MG-185/1-5004/Box 15/Folder 5/N-37.
[36] MG-185/1-5004/Box 15/Folder 6/P-145.
[37] MG-185/1-5004/Box 15/Folder 6/P-192; MG-185/1-5004/Box 15/Folder 6/Q-143; MG-185, 1-5004, Box 15, Folder 6, P-268; MG-185/1-5004/Box 15/Folder 5/O-12; and MG-185/1-5004/Box 15/Folder 5/O-55.

bronze, a symbol of his divinity. The sacrifices upon this altar foreshadowed Christ's atonement for the sins of the world.[38] Similarly the table of showbread, upon which the bread of presence was placed, pointed to Christ, the bread of life.[39] Furthermore, non-Christological types were found in the Old Testament.

> The prophet Elijah is proof that not only Christ, but also other persons and things of subsequent times were prefigured in the Old Testament, although they all are connected with him [Christ] as the central point of all prophecy. The prophet Malachi viewed Elijah as a future figure, but Christ clearly stated that John the Baptist was this future Elijah.[40]

Rapp's typological interpretation was primarily Christological and seldom extravagant or wildly speculative. It frequently fit within the acceptable boundaries for typology set by Luther and the other Reformers. Rapp remained in the mainstream with his typological-Christological interpretations of Scripture.

In contrast, the Harmonist leader's spiritual-allegorical interpretation wandered from the Reformation hermeneutical practice. Like the Berleburg Bible, Rapp employed a spiritual-allegorical hermeneutic, which applied biblical persons and things to the spiritual states of the individual soul. For example, Jacob was a figure of "sanctified humanity" and of the goodness inherent in man created in God's image. Esau, on the other hand, typified man living according to the sin nature, which all men inherit due to the fall of Adam. Every person born into this world struggled with these "twin" characteristics.[41] Rapp, however, replaced the individualistic focus in the Berleburg Bible with a corporate one. Although the spiritual states of the individual soul were addressed at times, more frequently allegorical interpretations were applied to the congregation (*Gemeine*). For example, the altar of incense, table of showbread, and golden lampstand within the tabernacle not only signified the three persons of the Trinity, but also the three chief duties of the church (not the individual)—prayer, good works and pure doctrine.[42] Esther was a type of the last, eschatological church.[43] Such spiritual-allegorical interpretations were more arbitrary and speculative than the previously cited typological and Christological interpretations, which had some support in the Old and New Testament tradition.[44] They lacked any historical continuity with the author's original intention.

---

[38]MG-185, 1-5004, Box 15, Folder 6, Q-102.
[39]MG-185/1-5004/Box 15/Folder 5/O-45.
[40]MG-185, 1-5004, Box 15, Folder 6, P-117.
[41]MG-185, 1-5004, Box 15, Folder 6, P-260.
[42]MG-185/1-5004/Box 15/Folder 5/O-45.
[43]MG-185/1-5004/Box 15/Folder 5/N-15.
[44]Cf. Hos 2:14f; 1 Cor 5:7; 10:1-11; 15:45-49; Rom 5:12f; Heb 7:11f; 8;5f; 9:23f and 1 Pet 3:21f.

Cabbalistic and Theosophical Descriptions of God and Man

The Cabbala is the traditional term used narrowly for a complex of Jewish esoteric and mystical teachings from the twelfth century onwards, and broadly for esoteric movements within Judaism from the end of the Second Temple period. The term "Cabbala" signifies "something handed down by tradition," thus reflecting a widely accepted notion within Judaism that the Cabbala was the esoteric portion of the Law given orally to Moses at Mount Sinai and then handed down from generation to generation. From its origin, cabbalism "embraced an esotericism closely akin to the spirit of Gnosticism, one which was not restricted to instruction in the mystical path but also included ideas on cosmology, angelology, and magic."[45] In the fifteenth century a form of cabbalism that harmonized cabbalistic notions with the Christian doctrines of the Trinity and the Incarnation developed among certain Christians of a mystical or theosophical persuasion. The renowned Florentine humanist, Giovanni Pico della Mirandola (1463-1494), is considered the father of this Christian school of cabbalism.[46] Mirandola in turn influenced the Swabian Hebraic scholar, Johannes Reuchlin (1455-1522), who published two Latin works on the subject, *De Verbo Mirifico* (1494) and *De Arte Cabalistica* (1517). Later Baron Knorr von Rosenroth (1636-1689) wrote in essence a commentary of the Jewish cabbalistic book *Zohar* entitled *Cabbala Denudata* (1675). This work was enthusiastically received in the early radical Pietist circle of Johann Jakob Schütz in Frankfurt, was admired by the founders of German Pietism, Philipp Jakob Spener and August Hermann Francke, and studied by the philosopher Leibniz.[47]

Christian Cabbalism and Württemberg Pietism

Christian cabbalism had a long tradition in Württemberg that extended back to its native son, Johannes Reuchlin. This tradition was directly received by the circle surrounding Princess Antonia of Württemberg (1613-1679), who had an elaborate, cabbalistic didactic painting (*Lehrtafel*) installed in the church in Bad Teinach.[48] In 1759 the Württemberg pastor and

---

[45]Gerschom Scholem, *Kabbalah* (New York: Meridian, 1974), 3-6, here 5.

[46]Ibid., 196-198. Mirandola was not the creator of Christian cabbalism, since the latter was found as early as the end of the thirteenth century among Jewish converts to Christianity.

[47]Ernst Benz, *Die Christliche Kabbala. Ein Stiefkind der Theologie* (Zurich: Rhein-Verlag, 1958), 16-24.

[48]Reuchlin's works were read by Princess Antonia and her circle. Antonia was the daughter of Württemberg Duke Johann Friedrich and the sister of the Duke Eberhard III, who reigned from 1633-1674. Otto Betz, "Kabbala Baptizata. Die jüdisch-christliche Kabbala und der Pietismus in Württemberg," *Pietismus und Neuzeit* 24 (1998): 130-159, here 131, n. 8 and 132. For a discussion of the *Lehrtafel* of Princess Antonia see Betz, "Kabbala Baptizata"; Hansmartin Decker-Hauff,

theologian, Friedrich Christoph Oetinger (1702-1782), was requested by Jakob Friedrich Klemm, his future son-in-law, to write an explanation of Princess Antonia's *Lehrtafel*. Oetinger's explanation of the painting (1763) spanned 430 pages, and included translations from the Jewish Cabbala (*Zohar*), a comparison of cabbalism with Zinzendorf's theology, Newtonian philosophy, Wolffian philosophy, Swedenborg's, Plouquet's and Cluver's systems.[49] Oetinger was uniquely qualified to provide a commentary of the *Lehrtafel*. During his theology studies at Tübingen (1722-1725), Oetinger came first into contact with cabbalistic doctrine. Later during a study tour to Frankfurt (1729-1730), he visited Jewish cabbalist, Koppel Hecht, who encouraged him to read Boehme to understand better the Cabbala. In the same year (1730), Oetinger studied at Halle the cabbalistic writings of Jizchak Lurija with an unnamed Jewish cabbalist. Oetinger continued to study and integrate this doctrine into his theology in the following decades. He thus became the chief proponent of Christian theosophy and cabbalism in Württemberg Pietism.[50] His writings, particularly his *Lehrtafel*, "contributed to the unique intellectual characteristics and theological development of Pietism in Württemberg."[51] Oetinger's cabbalistic notions directly influenced Württemberg pastor Philipp Matthäus Hahn, Michael Hahn, and others in the duchy.[52] George Rapp's mature sermons indicate that the Harmonist leader likewise belongs squarely in this line of influence. Like Boehme and especially Oetinger before him, Rapp appropriated cabbalistic notions, particularly the *Sephiroth* doctrine, in order to understand better and explain the Godhead.

Sources of Rapp's Cabbalistic Notions of God

George Rapp adopted virtually unchanged elements of Oetinger's Christian cabbalism. Oetinger's works were well-known and influential in Württemberg in the late eighteenth century. Fellow Württemberg radical Pietist, Michael Hahn, with whom Rapp shared many theological commonalities, likewise appropriated aspects of Oetinger's cabbalistic doctrine.[53]

"Prinzessin Antonia, Herzogin von Württemberg (1613-1679) und die Teinacher Lehrtafel," *Blätter für Württembergische Kirchengeschichte* 92 (1992): 89-96; and Benz, *Christliche Kabbala*, 39-45.

[49] Friedrich Christoph Oetinger, *Die Lehrtafel der Prinzessin Antonia*, ed. Reinhard Breymayer and Friedrich Häussermann, vol. 1 (New York: Walter de Gruyter, 1977).

[50] Benz, *Christliche Kabbala*, 7.

[51] "Oetingers Schriften und die von ihm hoch geschätzte kabbalistische Lehrtafel der Prinzessin Antonia haben die gedankliche Eigenart und theologische Entfaltung des Pietismus in Württemberg mitbestimmt." Betz, "Kabbala Baptizata," 132.

[52] Wilhelm August Schultze, "Friedrich Christoph Oetinger und die Kabbala," *Judaica* 4 (1948): 268-274.

[53] Hahn adopted from Oetinger the cabbalistic doctrine of *Zimzum*, the contraction and expansion of the Godhead in the act of creation. Schultze, "Oetinger und die Kabbala," 273.

There is no evidence of cabbalism in Rapp's early pastoral letters (1791-1802), written prior to emigration. In his later sermons (ca. 1830-1847), however, Rapp revealed intimate acquaintance with a number of Oetinger's published works.[54] In fact, the Harmonist leader imported verbatim into at least nine sermons long passages from Oetinger's cabbalistic writings without giving credit to the source—from the *Lehrtafel der Prinzessin Antonia* (excerpts found in six Rapp sermons), from Oetinger's 1758-1759 Weinsberger collection of sermons (one sermon), from his *Emblematic Lexicon* (one sermon), and from his collection of theosophical writings (one sermon).[55] It is very likely that Rapp imported texts from Oetinger in more than the nine sermons that were established definitively. Rapp's normal sermon style did not include Latinized words and advanced syntax. Inclusion of the latter was often a sign that Rapp, who did not attend Latin school, borrowed from a "more educated" source. A fair number of Rapp's cabbalistic sermons embodied such characteristics, and therefore were possibly lifted from an Oetinger text that the author was unable to locate.[56] Rapp did not import texts from Oetinger into his sermons completely unchanged. Rather, the Harmonist leader eliminated Hebrew and Latin terms and gave only the German equivalents, which Oetinger also supplied (see Appendix E).[57] Rapp's Christological focus and emphasis on the corporate *Gemeine* led him to make minor changes in Oetinger's text. Despite these changes, Rapp's cabbalist notions of the Godhead paralleled closely those of

---

[54]Interestingly, none of Oetinger's works are listed in the 1829 list of German books owned by the Harmony Society. This is once again evidence of the incompleteness of this list. It is possible that this list did not include works in Rapp's private possession.

[55]Rapp imported material from Oetinger's *Lehrtafel* in MG-185, 1-5004, Box 15, Folder 6, P-167, (*LT*, 227-228), MG-185, 1-5004, Box 15, Folder 6, P-139 (*LT*, 91, 93, 97), MG-437, Box 22, Folder 82B, Group B-45 (*LT*, 203), MG-185, 1-5004, Box 15, Folder 6, P-169 (*LT*, 102-103, 172), MG-185, Box 15, Folder 5, Group B-48 (*LT*, 93) and MG-185, 1-5004, Box 15, Folder 5, O-50 (*LT*, 132-134, 179), from Friedrich Christoph Oetinger, *Theosophische Schriften*, vol. 1 (Stuttgart: Steinkopf, 1858), 29 in MG-185, 1-5004, Box 15, Folder 5, N-112, from idem, *Biblisches und Emblematisches Wörterbuch* (Heilbronn: [s.n.], 1776), 224-227, MG-185, 1-5004, Box 15, Folder 6, P-156; and from idem, *Weinsberger Evangelienpredigten* (Metzingen: Ernst Franz Verlag, 1972), 319-320 in MG-185, 1-5004, Box 15, Folder 5, N-78.

[56]For example MG-185, 1-5004, Box 15, Folder 6, P-199 and MG-185, 1-5004, Box 15, Folder 5, B-10 both contained Latinized terms although the author was unable to find the source (if there was one) in Oetinger.

[57]In MG-185, 1-5004, Box 15, Folder 6, P-139 Rapp eliminated the Hebrew names for the *Sephiroth*, and the Latin terms *Actu purissimo endelechico* and *sensoria*. He changed "Wisdom" to Christ, the Word of God, and added "in the congregation" twice. In MG-185, 1-5004, Box 15, Folder 6, P-169, Rapp substituted for "Wisdom" in Oetinger once *Gemeine* and once *Schechina*. In MG-185, 1-5004, Box 15, Folder 5, O-50, Rapp replaced Oetinger's "Adam Kadmon" once with "Word of God" and once with *Urmensch*.

Friedrich Christoph Oetinger, as will be shown in the discussion of Rapp's sermons, which follows this section.

Oetinger's Christian cabbalism was dependent not only directly upon Jewish cabbalistic sources, but also on the writings of Jakob Boehme, whom he studied with renewed enthusiasm on the recommendation of Koppel Hecht. Boehme's works, particularly *Aurora* (1612) and *Three Principles of the Divine Essence* (1619), contained much that resembled the theosophy of the cabbalists.[58] Although his cabbalistic sources have not been definitively established, modern scholars are convinced that Boehme was intimately acquainted with cabbalism and employed it in this theosophical system.[59] His three principles and seven qualities or spirits of God properly understood are a reflection of cabbalistic doctrine. Consistently in his theological writings, Oetinger claimed that Boehme's Christian perspective was more influential on his cabbalistic teaching than the Cabbala itself.[60] It is tempting to take Oetinger's statements at face value and deemphasize direct Jewish cabbalistic sources of his theology. This would be a mistake. It can easily be argued that Oetinger's *Sephiroth* doctrine, both in terminology and content, was found in essence in the Jewish Cabbala of Jizchak Lurija and his disciple, Chajim Vital.[61] Furthermore, there are very significant differences between Oetinger's and Boehme's cabbalism. Trautwein notes the following differences between the two: 1) In contrast to Boehme, Oetinger stressed unity rather than duality within "God in his essence" (*Ungrund*). Therefore, "[a]lthough Oetinger may have adopted certain terms from Boehme in his doctrine of God, in his description of the *Ungrund*, the *En-Sof* of the Cabbala dominates." 2) The term that Oetinger employed for the *Sephiroth*, *Abglänze* (reflected splendor), stands in sharp contrast to Boehme's "qualities" or "source spirits." 3) Oetinger in his cabbalistic doctrine, unlike Boehme, stressed the teleological goal of permeation of matter with spirit (*Geistleib*).[62] Because George Rapp was directly influenced by Oetinger's cabba-

---

[58]Betz, "Kabbala Baptizata," 134.

[59]It is possible that Boehme was acquainted with Reuchlin's writings. Benz, *Christliche Kabbala*, 8 and 57-58, n. 2. Cf. Schultze, "Oetinger und die Kabbala," 269. Trautwein suggests that Boehme only received cabbalistic teaching orally. Joachim Trautwein, *Die Theosophie Michael Hahns und ihre Quellen* (Stuttgart: Calwer Verlag, 1969), 150, n. 31.

[60]Oetinger would usually reference Boehme rather than the Cabbala in his writings. The reason for this may be that Oetinger preferred that his readers turn to Boehme rather than directly to the Jewish Cabbala. Oetinger wrote a tract, *Aufmunternden Gründen zu Lesung der Schriften Jakob Boehmens* (1731) to encourage reading of Boehme. Martin Weyer-Menkhoff, *Christus, das Heil der Natur. Entstehung und Systematik der Theologie Friedrich Christoph Oetingers* (Göttingen: Vandenhoeck & Ruprecht, 1990), 171-172.

[61]Ibid., 171.

[62]Trautwein, *Theosophie Michael Hahns*, 129-130, n. 21. Cf. Sigrid Grossmann, *Friedrich Christoph Oetingers Gottesvorstellung. Versuch einer Analyse seiner Theologie* (Göttingen: Vandenhoeck & Ruprecht, 1979), 130-132 and 132, n. 111.

listic doctrine of God, and Oetinger was influenced by Boehme, Rapp was likewise indirectly influenced by Boehme. Nevertheless, Rapp consistently used Oetinger's *Sephiroth* terminology, rather than Boehme's "qualities." Rapp's cabbalistic and theosophical notions of the divine in his sermons reflected almost exclusively his reading of his fellow Württemberger Oetinger.

Rapp's Cabbalistic and Theosophical Notions of God

George Rapp's concept of the Godhead made a clear distinction between "God in his essence" and "God in his revelation," although the former was less frequently discussed than the latter.[63] In his sermons the Harmonist leader borrowed Oetinger's language from the *Lehrtafel* and other volumes to describe God's essential being. The two men's descriptions of "God in his essence" were akin to the Jewish cabbalistic notion of the *En-Sof*, the "Infinite." For both Rapp and Oetinger, "God [in his essence] is an unfathomable depth, who dwells within himself."[64] In his essential being, God was "infinite ... a boundless and incomprehensible sea of light (*Lichtmeer*)."[65] He was the "eternal one" and the "ancient of days" of Dan 7:13.[66] In Rapp's theology, "[t]he infinite essence [of God] is the Father, the *Ungrund* of the Godhead."[67] *Ungrund* is a Boehmist term, referring to "God in his absoluteness, separate from his revelation."[68] This term was occasionally used by Rapp (and Oetinger) to describe God's essential being, although *Wesen* (essence) was more commonly used by the Harmonist leader.[69]

Weyer-Menkhoff likewise lists important differences between Oetinger and Boehme: (1) Oetinger changed Boehme's "chemical" terminology (qualities) to "physical" terminology; (2) Oetinger inserted a teleological, goal-oriented motif into the *Sephiroth* doctrine, whereas Boehme's conception focused on the on-going struggle between qualities; and (3) Oetinger's conception of nature did not have the depths of God's eternal nature in view (Boehme), rather the creation of the visible world. Weyer-Menkhoff, *Christus, das Heil der Natur*, 169. In contrast, Friedrich Häussermann, "Theologia Emblematica. Kabbalistische und alchemistische Symbolik bei Fr. Chr. Oetinger und deren Analogien bei Jakob Boehme," *Blätter für württembergische Kirchengeschichte* 68/69 (1968-1969): 207-346, here 258 and 282 sees more continuity between Boehme's *Ungrund* and Oetinger's "God in himself" (the cabbalistic *En-Sof*) than subsequent scholars.

[63] Weyer-Menkhoff, *Christus, das Heil der Natur*, 150-151 and 151, n. 218.
[64] MG-185, 1-5004, Box 15, Folder 6, P-139. Cf. Oetinger, *Lehrtafel*, 93; Grossmann, *Oetingers Gottesvorstellung*, 130-132; Weyer-Menkhoff, *Christus, das Heil der Natur*, 150f.; and Scholem, *Kabbala*, 88-96 (*En-Sof*).
[65] MG-185, 1-5004, Box 15, Folder 5, B-10.
[66] Ibid.
[67] MG-185, 1-5004, Box 15, Folder 6, P-231.
[68] Jakob Böhme, *Glaube und Tat. Eine Auswahl aus dem Gesamtwerk*, ed. Eberhard Hermann Pältz (Marburg: Oekumenischer Verlag, 1976), 367.
[69] Cf. Oetinger, *Theosophische Schriften*, vol. 1, 133 and vol. 6, 125.

For both Rapp and Oetinger, "in the depths of the Godhead ... [wa]s the immoveable centerpoint."[70] In the ground and depths of his being, God was unchangeable and at rest. Although the absolute or essential God was in one sense at rest as a "motionless personal being" (*ein stillstehent Persöhnl: Wesen*), this rest was not a complete stillstand, but included "constant activity" (*beständigem wircken*). This constant activity was manifested in God's continuous revelation of himself.[71] According to Rapp, "God brings about from eternity to eternity his Word, as the revelation of the depths of God."[72] Oetinger (and, by extension, Rapp) thus rejected the static view of God proposed by adherents of Wolffian philosophy in favor of a dynamic view of the Godhead.[73] Life and self-movement, according to the Württemberg theologian and the Harmonist leader were the central characteristics of the divine.[74] God was the *actus purissimus*, and the "eternally begetting power."[75] Nowhere was the motion within the Godhead more clearly seen than in the *Sephiroth* doctrine.

It was only in the revelation of himself, in his glory, that God could be perceived by man and could enter into relationship with his creation. God in himself (*Gott in sich*) desired to communicate. Therefore, according to Rapp,

---

[70] MG-185, 1-5004, Box 15, Folder 6, P-117 and MG-185, 1-5004, Box 15, Folder 5, N-112. Cf. Friedrich Christoph Oetinger, *Die Theologie aus der Idee des Lebens abgeleitet*, ed. Julius Hamberger (Stuttgart: Steinkopf, 1852), §15, 110; Idem, *Lehrtafel*, 93; and Grossmann, *Oetingers Gottesvorstellung*, 132. This contrasts with the struggle between polar forces within Boehme's conception of the *Ungrund*.

[71] MG-185, 1-5004, Box 15, Folder 6, P-18. Cf. Grossmann, *Oetingers Gottesvorstellung*, 136, n. 142; and Oetinger, *Theologie aus der Idee des Lebens*, §15, 110: "Denn Gott ist lautere Thätigkeit (*Actus purissimus*)."

[72] MG-185, 1-5004, Box 15, Folder 6, P-18.

[73] Oetinger, *Wörterbuch*, 713: "Wenn man GOtt, wie Wolff, als eine stillstehende Kraft, sich alle mögliche Welten vorzustellen, betrachtet, so ist freilig dieser ... der Vernunft eine Thorheit, denn da ist in GOtt Bewegung, Ausgang aus sich, Offenbarung seiner innersten Einschrenkung Manifestatio sui." Oetinger, like some other contemporaries, tended to equate the philosophies of Wolff and Leibniz, and reject both. Grossmann, *Oetingers Gottesvorstellung*, 49.

[74] "Das ewige Leben und Selbst-Bewegung seyn die erste und höchste Ideen von GOtt. ... in Heil. Schrift geht überall das Leben voran. ... Die ewige Geburt GOttes aus dem verborgensten der Gottheit ins offenbahre ... kan nicht seyn ohne eine in sich selbst würckende Bewegung." Oetinger, *Lehrtafel*, 170. Cf. MG-185, 1-5004, Box 15, Folder 6, P-169.

[75] MG-185, 1-5004, Box 15, Folder 6, P-156. Rapp imported the text of this sermon (with only minimal changes) from Oetinger, *Wörterbuch*, 224-227. Oetinger based his dynamic concept of God on Acts 17:28, "In him we live and move and have out being," a favorite Bible text of Rapp, as well as on the "wheel of nature" of James 3:6, and the vision of the four wheels of Ezekiel 1 and 10. Weyer-Menkhoff, *Christus, das Heil der Natur*, 156. The author has not found evidence that Rapp used the latter two Bible texts to support the concept of movement within the Godhead. Weyer-Menkhoff, ibid., 150 notes that the Lutheran theologian Oetinger, on one hand, upheld the immutability of God, while undermining it on the other hand.

God as the *Urquelle* or original source "emanated and brought forth out of himself seven streams [from the sea of light]. These are the ten light sources," the *Sephiroth*.[76] The *Sephiroth* refer to God's manifestation of himself through successive emanations, which took place within the Godhead itself. Although strongly influenced by Neo-Platonic notions, in the Jewish Cabbala "emanation as an intermediate stage between God and creation [Neo-Platonism] was reassigned to the divine. . . . The hidden God in the aspect of the *En-Sof* and the God manifested in the emanation of *Sephiroth* are one and the same."[77] The ten stages of emanation were generally viewed as "no more than the various attributes of God or descriptions and epithets which can be applied to Him."[78] The diverse writings that made up the Jewish Cabbala, as well as Christian cabbalism, attempted (sometimes unsuccessfully) to avoid pantheistic notions of creation by stressing that the emanations took place within the Godhead.

In the cabbalism espoused by George Rapp and Oetinger, a distinctly Christian interpretation was assigned to the *Sephiroth*. The ten *Sephiroth* were divided into two groups. The upper three represented the Trinity, the lower seven were the seven-fold spirit of God. In one sermon Rapp stated clearly that "we also discern the Trinity in the *Sephiroth*."[79] The primary biblical support for this interpretation was Rev 1:4-5. The churches of Asia Minor were greeted "from him who is, and who was, and is to come," that is, from the triune God, and from the "seven spirits before the throne." According to Rapp: "The teaching concerning the seven spirits [was] the key to understanding the holy Scriptures. . . . This figure of light breaks forth from the *Ungrund* of eternity. He is God in his originality (*Ursprünglichkeit*), out of which one emanation (*Ausgang*) after another flow into the Trinity and the seven spirits."[80]

---

[76]MG-185, 1-5004, Box 15, Folder 5, B-10. The term *Sefira* (singular) and *Sephiroth* (plural) originated in the Jewish cabbalistic Book of Creation. The *Sephiroth* in this interpretation were ten archetypical numbers (derived from *safar*, to number). The etymology of *Sephiroth* in the twelfth century Book of Bahir was *sappir*, "sapphire". According to this etymology, the *Sephiroth* were *Abglänze Gottes* (reflections of God's splendor). Oetinger (and Rapp) appropriated this understanding of the *Sephiroth*. Grossmann, *Oetingers Gottesvorstellung*, 167-168. Both men used the terms *Abglänze, Ausgänge* or *Ausflüße* (reference to the *Mozaoth* of Mic 5:1), as well as *Sephiroth* to refer to the phenomenon. Cf. Oetinger, *Lehrtafel*, 86, 91, 205, and 248, and Rapp in MG-437, Box 22, Folder 82B, D-85; MG-185, 1-5004, Box 15, Folder 6, P-199; and MG-185, 1-5004, Box 15, Folder 5, N-78: "Dieser ausgänge Glänze u Lichter als die Sephiren Zählen."

[77]Scholem, *Kabbala*, 98.

[78]Ibid., 99.

[79]MG-185, 1-5004, Box 15, Folder 5, N-78. This statement is found in Friedrich Christoph Oetinger, *Sämtliche Schriften*, Abteilung I, *Predigten*, vol. 4 (Stuttgart: Steinkopf, 1977), 328.

[80]MG-437, Box 22, Folder 82B, D-85. Cf. Oetinger, *Lehrtafel*, 86; Benz, *Christliche Kabbala*, 40, and 51-52; and Häussermann, "Theologia Emblematica," 211. In MG-

Oetinger refrained from using the most widespread Jewish listing of the *Sephiroth* in favor of a secondary list, and it was this list that Rapp appropriated.[81] In the "first *Sephira* God appears as a crown or immeasurable periphery of the expansion of his innermost point (Ps 150:1)."[82] Unlike the Jewish Cabbala, Christian cabbalists such as Rapp and Oetinger equated the second *Sephira*, *chochmah*, with Jesus Christ, the second person of the Trinity. Rapp borrowed sentences from Oetinger to describe the begetting of Christ. "The Word, who was with God [John 1:1], is not limited, but just as God is, unlimited. . . . Therefore the primordial man (*Urmensch*) was not created as the Word, rather he issued forth from God, so that from the beginning he cannot be separated [from God]."[83]

In this passage, Rapp twice replaced the Jewish cabbalistic term for primordial man, Adam Kadmon, which Oetinger employed, once with "Word" and once with *Urmensch*. Rapp specifically identified the *Urmensch* in another sermon as Christ, "the only-begotten Son."[84] It should be noted that although Oetinger retained the term "Adam Kadmon," he infused it with a new Christological content. Adam Kadmon was no longer the Gnostic, mythical primordial man of Jewish cabbalism, rather he was Jesus Christ, the Word of God.[85] In his cabbalistic sermons, Rapp only briefly mentioned the third *Sephira*, understanding (*Bina*), which Christian cabbalists equated with the Holy Spirit, who revealed and made concrete the hidden wisdom of

---

185, 1-5004, Box 15, Folder 5, N-112, Rapp discussed the division of the ten *Sephiroth*: "Das ist Gott in der [3]heit, u ferner alle ausflüße der 7 geister. . . Die Haupt quelle sind 3, u 7 macht 10."

[81]Oetinger changed the fourth and fifth *Sephiroth* in the most widespread Jewish cabbalist listing (*Din* and *Chessed*) to secondary Jewish readings, which were roughly equivalent to one another: *Gebhura* and *Gedullah* (expansion-contraction) in the *Lehrtafel*, and *Größe* and *Stärke* in his *Wörterbuch*, 712. Grossmann, *Oetingers Gottesvorstellung*, 168-173 and 310. Rapp adopted Oetinger's lists in MG-185, 1-5004, Box 15, Folder 5, B-10 (*Größe-Stärke*) and MG-185, 1-5004, Box 15, Folder 6, P-139 (expansion-contraction).

[82]Oetinger's statement, *Lehrtafel*, 93 found in Rapp sermon, MG-185, 1-5004, Box 15, Folder 6, P-139.

[83]MG-185, 1-5004, Box 15, Folder 5, O-50. Cf. Oetinger, *Lehrtafel*, 133.

[84]MG-185, 1-5004, Box 15, Folder 6, P-199. Cf. MG-185, 1-5004, Box 15, Folder 6, P-264: The following cabbalististic notions correspond with the holy Scripture: "der Saphiren baum mit dem Lebens B: verglichen, die Sche[china] mit dem Wolken säule . . . u zuletzt der Ad: Kadmon als der Sohn Gottes."

[85]"Gleichwohl haben die Cabbalisten, weil sie *Christum im Fleisch* nicht gewußt, sich viel gewagt, das Geheimniß der Gottheit zu verstehen. . . . Sie haben eine originale Menschheit geglaubt, welche sie Adam Kadmon, den eingebohrnen Sohn, und welche Orpheus das eingebohrne Wort genennet, in welchem alle Arten und Geschlechte der Dinge verborgen gelegen. Sie haben geglaubet, daß Gott durch den Adam Kadmon oder durch die originale Menschheit alles geschaffen nach den Schrancken der 7 Sephirot oder nach den Lichtern der 10 Sephirot." Oetinger, *Lehrtafel*, 132. Ibid., 133 states that Adam Kadmon is the unlimited, uncreated, Word of God, inseparable from the Father, thus guarding against Arianism.

the second *Sephira*.⁸⁶ The lower seven *Sephiroth* were the seven-fold spirit. Rapp spent considerably more time discussing them: "The seven spirits are not only one individual spirit, otherwise the number seven would be unnecessary. They are clearly identified as seven in Zech 4: [2, 10]. But the seven are in one another, so that they flow into one at the point of exit and entrance."⁸⁷

It has already been noted that Boehme's seven qualities, also called nature or original spirits (*Naturgeister* or *Quellgeister*), although based on cabbalistic doctrine, were considerably different than Oetinger's and Rapp's *Sephiroth*.⁸⁸ Besides the obvious differences in terminology and order, Boehme's qualities lacked the teleological and eschatological focus found in Oetinger and Rapp, two theologians influenced by Bengel's eschatological system. Boehme's qualities were in constant strife, whereas for the men from Württemberg, there was a steady progression within the seven-fold spirit that culminated in the seventh spirit or tenth *Sephira*.⁸⁹ Rapp explained in one sermon that "the fullness of God, which flows from the Godhead, comes to its completion" in its teleological goal.⁹⁰ Furthermore:

> The *Sephiroth* are subordinated under one another. The lower ones are always dependent on those above and those above exert influence on those below them, so that all perfections issuing forth from the *Urmensch* [Christ] come together and physically and visibly appear in the kingdom of God, the church, as the lowest *Sephira*. . . . The lowest *Sephira* is also called the *Schechina*, whose name is derived from the highest original source (*Urquelle*) through various levels (*manicherley stuffen*), so that it [the lowest *Sephira*] is not separated from the *Urquelle*.⁹¹

The *telos* or goal of this progression within the *Sephiroth* was the lowest or tenth *Sephira* (*Malchuth*), also known as the church or kingdom of God. This *Sephira* embodied physically, materially and visibly the qualities or characteristics of the first six spirits. Oetinger used the terms "essence" and "substance" to express the distinction within the lower seven *Sephiroth*. The first six spirits of God were essences (*Essentiae*) or essential powers (*wesentliche Kräfte*), which flowed continuously into one another and ultimately into the seventh spirit, where all the essences became substantial in materiality (*Leiblichkeit*). For Oetinger, materiality permeated with spirit was the goal of all divine activity.⁹² Rapp adopted the distinction between es-

---

⁸⁶Grossmann, *Oetingers Gottesvorstellung*, 172.
⁸⁷MG-185, 1-5004, Box 15, Folder 5, O-115.
⁸⁸See Grossmann, *Oetingers Gottesvorstellung*, 310-311 for charts comparing Oetinger's *Sephiroth* and Boehme's qualities. Cf. footnote 60 and Trautwein, *Theosophie Michael Hahns*, 150-151, n. 32.
⁸⁹Weyer-Menkhoff, *Christus, das Heil der Natur*, 169.
⁹⁰MG-185, 1-5004, Box 15, Folder 6, P-156.
⁹¹MG-185, 1-5004, Box 15, Folder 5, N-35.
⁹² Friedrich Christoph Oetinger, *Swedenborgs irdische und himmlische Philosophie*, ed. Karl Chr. Eberhard Ehmann and intro. Erich Beyreuther (Stuttgart:

sences and substance from Oetinger, and also applied it to the seven-fold spirit.

> The church (*Gemeine*) possesses only God's eternal essence and all of his characteristics... all of which now in the church appear revealed and visible ... The church has its eternal root and original status from the Godhead alone.... For the church is that through which God reveals himself, is made visible, and leads all things that are in essence (*in Wesen*) into materiality (*Leiblichkeit*).[93]

In this sermon, Rapp made clear that God's essence, which flowed from him in the successive emanations in the *Sephiroth*, culminated within the lowest *Sephira*, the church, as the material expression of the essence of God.

The cabbalistic doctrine of Oetinger contributed to Rapp's high view of the status and role of the church in the present age and in the coming *eschaton*. The church as the tenth *Sephira* exhibited all the fullness of the Godhead. Rapp was convinced that "the end of all things is very near."[94] Like Oetinger, Rapp combined his cabbalistic notions with a teleological and eschatological goal—materiality permeated with spirit (*Leiblichkeit* or *Geistleiblichkeit*), the return of Christ, and the establishment of the millennium.

> Here is the key to the divine Cabbala... When the number 10 [reference to the tenth *Sephira*, the church] evolves into 1 and 0, then the Godhead comes, in the active, progressive transition to rest, to eternal calm, to Sabbath and to kingdom, in Jesus and the church (*Gemeine*). There the Godhead proceeds into a new, eternal epoch, a concealed status for men and angels.[95]

In the coming age, the church with the help of Christ and the Holy Spirit would fulfill the mandate given to Adam to "maintain and rule over all creation," and "to bear sons and daughters for God through the power of the Holy Spirit."[96]

Steinkopf, 1977), 352: "Die siebente [*Sephira*] macht, daß alle in einer unzerstörlichen Leiblichkeit beisammen bestehen, und diß heißt eigentlich Substanz, wenn ein geistliches Wesen seinen unzerstörlichen Leib durch die vollkommene Ordnung und Zusammenwirkung der sechs vorhergehenden Sephiren bekommt... Diese Leiblichkeit eine Vollkommenheit und keine Unvollkommenheit seie... Alsdann wird aus Essentiis eine Substanz." Similarly in Rapp: "Geist ist nicht ohne leibliches Wesen; leibliche unzerstörlichk: ist das Ende der Wercke Gottes. Sie ist im G; Gottes wesenl: u in Christo körperl: u gehet jezo aus leibl: u geistl: in die Gem: " MG-185, 1-5004, Box 15, Folder 6, P-117. Cf. Woyer-Menkhoff, *Christus, das Heil der Natur*, 175.

[93]MG-185, 1-5004, Box 15, Folder 5, O-108.
[94]MG-185, 1-5004, Box 15, Folder 5, N-112.
[95]MG-185, Box 15, Folder 5, Group B-48. The last two sentences are borrowed from Oetinger, *Lehrtafel*, 93.
[96]MG-185, 1-5004, Box 15, Folder 5, N-35 and MG-185, 1-5004, Box 15, Folder 6, P-13. This refers to the restoration of pre-Fall Adam's "magical propagation" within the eschatological church. See below the discussion of Rapp's theosophical views of Adam and the Fall.

The didactic painting commissioned by Princess Antonia included a depiction of the church, the tenth *Sephira*, as the Sunwoman of Revelation 12, which was then discussed in Oetinger's *Lehrtafel*.[97] This association between the church, the tenth *Sephira*, and the Sunwoman in the Wilderness was appropriated by Rapp as further support for the Harmony Society's sectarian self-understanding as the eschatological figure of Revelation 12. The key to the "divine Cabbala" was the "great mystery," the birth of Christ spiritually and physically as the male son of the Sunwoman in the last eschatological church.[98] This eschatological church was none other than the Harmony Society, which Rapp likewise depicted with the millennial image, the "blooming lily."

> *Harmonie*, you have the spirit to investigate the ten sources of light [the *Sephiroth*].... You carry the active powers of the universe within you.... Spirit of brotherhood, delve deeper into the shining source of the Word, and open within the *Gemeine* the deep interconnected thoughts of the universe, the laws of the new age and creation.... For to you has come that which was prophesied about you, the perfect one, for you are the blooming lily.... The kingdom of good becomes constantly greater and more glorious in the fellowship [the Harmony Society]. Your mustard seed becomes a great tree, so that peoples and nations might dwell beneath its branches, for that which grows has a small beginning.[99]

Although the Harmony Society appeared small and unpresuming, it would play a crucial role in the millennial kingdom as the true eschatological church. Like Oetinger, Rapp combined a Christian interpretation of cabbalism with a teleological and eschatological focus. Nevertheless, Rapp's utilization of cabbalistic doctrine to support the Society's sectarian convictions was without precedent in Oetinger's writings.

Despite this obvious difference, the main outlines of Rapp's *Sephiroth* doctrine were adopted virtually unchanged from the eighteenth-century Württemberg theologian.[100] Both taught an interpretation of Christian cabbalism that contrasted significantly from that espoused by Boehme. For the two men from Württemberg, the *Ungrund* of God paralleled the *En-Sof* of

---

[97] Oetinger, *Lehrtafel*, 86, 132-134
[98] MG-185/ Box 15/ Folder 5/ B-48.
[99] MG-185/Box 15/Folder 5/N-130.
[100] One other significant difference between Oetinger's and Rapp's cabbalistic doctrine was the hesitancy of the former to allow for male and female principles within the Godhead. Cf. Oetinger, *Lehrtafel*, 134: "Inzwischen, wenn man ... es mit reinem Verstande ansihet, so heißt es gar nichts von dem, was die Schwenkfelder sagen, daß Vater und Mutter in der Gottheit sey, die den Menschen Christum von Ewigkeit zeugen und gebähren, sondern es heißt nur so viel, daß Gott gegen seiner Gemeine alles, was zart und mütterlich kan genennet werden, so wohl exemplariter und enimenter als auch effective beweise.... O wie viel besser ist es, wenn man bey den Ausdrücken des *Symboli Apostolici* bleibet, als daß man solche Concepte annimmt und sich allzufrüh in das Braut-Bette legt, ehe man Recht darzu hat." Cf. Grossmann, *Oetingers Gottesvorstellung*, 292-297.

the Jewish Cabbala, not the doctrine of God found in Boehme's writings. There was rest rather than strife (Boehme) in the depths of the Godhead. God was best characterized by life and self-movement and by his desire to reveal himself (*manifestatio sui*). Both Oetinger and Rapp made a clear distinction between the upper three *Sephiroth* (Trinity) and the lower seven (the seven-fold spirit of God), and used cabbalistic rather than Boehmist terminology to describe them. Both reinterpreted the cabbalistic mythical, primordial man, Adam Kadmon, as Christ, the second person of the Trinity.

One final theosophical conception of God needs to be addressed—the existence of dual forces within the Godhead. The seventeenth-century theosophist from Görlitz, Jakob Boehme, in his attempt to solve the problem of good and evil in the world, "grounded both qualities in the Godhead itself."[101] To avoid the charge of Manichean dualism, Boehme conceived of God as a combination of both dynamic movement and form or essence. In this manner God "could contain evil as a moment or quality understood dynamically and yet could be called good because of his essence in which the polarities are balanced."[102] Although the opposing principles of love and wrath and fire and light were in equilibrium, it is significant that *both* were found within the Godhead in Boehme's theology. In chapter seven of his Genesis commentary, *Mysterium Magnum*, Boehme acknowledged that dualistic principles were found within God:

> God in Trinity is manifest in the fire and light: according to the property of the free lubet or divine property [he is manifest] as a great fiery flame of light and love; and according to the property of the dark fire-world [he is manifest] in a property wrathful and painful in its source; and yet he is the One.[103]

In contrast, Oetinger affirmed Luther's conviction that "[w]rath is truly the alien work of God which he takes up contrary to his nature, compelled to it by the wickedness of man."[104] According to the Württemberg theologian, love, not wrath, belonged to God's essential nature. Wrath was "not

---

[101] Arlene A. Miller, "The Theologies of Luther and Boehme in the Light of Their Genesis Commentaries," *Harvard Theological Review* 63 (1970): 261-303, here 283. Cf. H. Bornkamm, "Böhme," in *Die Religion in Geschichte und Gegenwart*, vol. 1, ed. Hans Frhr. v. Campenhausen, et. al. (Tübingen: Mohr, 1957): 1340-1342.

[102] Miller, "Theologies of Luther and Boehme," 283.

[103] Jacob Boehme, *Mysterium Magnum or an Exposition of the First Book of Moses called Genesis*, vol. 1, trans. John Sparrow (Kila, Mont.: Kessinger Publ. Co., 1990), ch. 7, §13, 37.

[104] Martin Luther, *Werke. Kritische Gesamtausgabe* (Weimar: H. Böhlau, 1883-), vol. 42, 356. Quoted and translated in Miller, "Theologies of Luther and Boehme," 285. Elisabeth Zinn views the different approaches to the problem of evil with the corollary of the presence or non-presence of wrath in God's nature as the most significant difference between Oetinger's and Boehme's theology. Grossmann, *Oetingers Gottesvorstellung*, 268, n. 1154.

something in God," that is, in his essence; rather it was provoked as a consequence of the fall of Lucifer.[105]

With regard to dual principles within God, George Rapp followed Oetinger's rather than Boehme's lead. Love not wrath was the essence of the divine. In one sermon, Rapp clearly reflected Oetinger's conception of wrath being provoked by the fall of Lucifer.

> No creature can endure God's holy primeval fire unless it is mitigated by light. For just as the night was not yet revealed in day and fire in light, so there was a time when only pure day and light existed, although the possibility of fire and of night laid hidden within light and day.... For the first revelation of God was in two principles, God in himself, and God in the world of light. That was the time, when fire and air were not yet separated. Eons passed away, and fire still dwelled in light. Creatures and beings were the recipients of the light and light receptacles, types of the revealed image of light. The activity of these beings was to allow God, the source of light, to work within them—that was their life. Their blessedness was the ribbon of light with which they fastened themselves to the Godhead, the central point of God's goodness, the mirror in which his light was reflected in full measure, in order that [they might] affect other beings. But the greatest receiver of light was Lucifer, the light-bearer, who bore the light image of God in his nature. For until that time God had not given fire any leeway (*keinen Raum geben*), rather he mitigated it with love.... Lucifer was chosen to communicate the pure reception of light. [Since Lucifer's fall] the opposite is now suffering, despair, death and darkness, the *results of the kindling of divine wrath*.[106]

In this passage, Rapp affirmed that from eternity past God's essence was only revealed in light and love. His primeval and *potential* fire was always mitigated by love and light. These were God's essential characteristics, which were then experienced by the angelic world, the recipients of light. It was only after the rebellion of Lucifer and his angels that divine wrath was kindled, resulting in suffering, death and darkness. Sinful humanity since the fall of Adam likewise has experienced that: "The fire of the pure love of God can tolerate no impurity. It produces unrest, suffering and pain in the soul in the form of wrath.... The sinner senses that this fire consumes and condemns, and discovers that there is no means to appease and quiet a guilty conscience except through Jesus Christ."[107] The wrath of God was kindled first by the rebellion of Lucifer and later by sinful man. It was a divine response to sin, not an aspect of God's essence, as it was in Boehme. Thus the prevailing historiographical notion that Boehme's influence on Rapp was most significant and all-encompassing is once again called into question.

---

[105]Grossmann, *Oetingers Gottesvorstellung*, 263. Cf. Friedrich Christoph Oetinger, *Herrenberger Evangelienpredigten* (Metzingen: Ernst Frank Verlag, 1987), 533-540 (sermon entitled, "Daß Gott lauter Liebe ohne Zorn sei").

[106]MG-185, 1-5004, Box 15, Folder 6, P-127.

[107]MG-185, 1-5004, Box 15, Folder 6, P-268.

Rapp's Theosophical View of Man and the Fall

George Rapp's cabbalistic views were adopted almost exclusively from Friedrich Christoph Oetinger. The Harmonist leader's anthropology and doctrine of the Fall, however, reflected the theosophical views of Jakob Boehme. Boehme's doctrine of Adam and the Fall was enormously influential on Western religious and intellectual history. In his Genesis commentary, *Mysterium Magnum*, and in other writings, Boehme reworked the Gnostic, Platonic, and cabbalistic *mythos* of an androgynous Adam to fit it into his Christian theosophical system.[108] Boehme's views, including his anthropology, were widely received in the following centuries by the English Behemists (John Pordage, Jane Leade), the German Philadelphians (authors of the Berleburg Bible) and other radical Pietists, and influenced scientists and philosophers such as Newton, Leibniz, Goethe and Schelling. The influence of Boehme in Württemberg Pietism was particularly far-reaching, and received new impulse in the mid to late eighteenth century through the writings of Friedrich Oetinger and Michael Hahn.[109] Rapp's anthropology and doctrine of the Fall closely paralleled Boehme's approach to the first three chapters of Genesis, as will be demonstrated below. It is known that Rapp and his followers owned and read Boehme's writings both prior to emigration and after the formation of the Harmony Society.[110] Therefore, although Boehmist notions were also found in Oetinger, Hahn,

---

[108]Ernst Benz, *Adam, der Mythus vom Urmenschen* (Munich: Barth Verlag, 1955), 16 and 31. The primordial man in Gnosticism was androgynous. This motif was appropriated by Philo, Gregory of Nyssa, and Maximus Confessor. The myth of the androgynous *Uradam* was prominent in Jewish cabbalism, in the Renaissance era primarily in the writings of Leone Ebreo (1460?-1525?). Eberhard H. Pältz, "Jacob Boehmes Hermeneutik, Geschichtsverständnis und Sozialethik," (Habilitation thesis, Schiller Universität, Jena, 1961), 105, n. 14. Cf. Andrew Weeks, *Boehme. An Intellectual Biography of the Seventeenth-Century Philosopher and Mystic* (Albany, NY: State University of New York Press, 1991), 114 notes that it is a "surprising step" that Boehme recast the "heretical myth of the first Adam," since there was little foundation of the myth in the Bible.

[109]Eberhard H. Pältz, "Böhme," in *Theologische Realenzyklopädie*, vol. 6, ed. Horst Robert Balz, et al. (New York: Walter de Gruyter, 1980), 748-754, here 751-752.

[110]Christian Hörnle told the visitation committee in Iptingen (February 21, 1787) that he owned the writings of Boehme. On May 18, 1787, Rapp reported to the church authorities that he had borrowed one volume of Boehme's works from Ehninger Hof. Karl J. R. Arndt, *George Rapp's Separatists. 1700-1803. A Documentary History* (Worcester, Mass.: Harmony Society Press, 1980), 85 and 106. The 1829 list of German books owned by the Harmony Society included Boehme's collected works (#69) and ten individual volumes (#118-127). Idem, *George Rapp's Successors and Material Heirs 1847- 1916* (Teaneck, N.J.: Fairleigh Dickinson University Press, 1971), 417-419.

and the Berleburg Bible, Rapp received them directly as well from Boehme's own writings.[111]

Three distinctive beliefs were central to Boehme's theosophical interpretation of Genesis 1 to 3—the androgynous nature of the "heavenly" Adam before the Fall (*Uradam*), the double Fall of Adam, and the application of the androgynous ideal to the Godhead.[112] George Rapp adopted all three of these beliefs. According to the Harmonist spiritual leader, "God created Adam as his most excellent creature." Luke the evangelist correctly named him a "son of God on account of his heritage."[113] Adam prior to the Fall did not possess a coarse, physical body. Rather at creation he was endowed with a heavenly, spiritual body akin to that of the angelic creatures.[114] This body required neither sleep nor food and therefore lacked eyelashes and digestive organs. Both genders were perfectly united in the heavenly Adam. Rapp explained that "[i]n the newly created man [Adam] . . . were both tinctures, the fiery one and the passive one, a man and a woman in one person."[115] In another sermon he clarified that the fiery tincture in *Uradam* was the male principle, "the urge to propagate," and that water was the passive, receptive and feminine principle.[116] Because Adam combined both male and female within his person, reproduction "took place by magical, holy propagation according to the manner and privilege of the Godhead."[117]

---

[111] See Benz, *Adam, Der Mythus vom Urmenschen*, 163-170 and 189-208 for an introduction to and primary source readings reflecting Oetinger's and Hahn's view of Adam and the Fall.

[112] Pältz, "Boehmes Hermeneutik," 101-119 uses these three elements to organize his discussion of Boehme's anthropology. Cf. Weeks, *Boehme*, 114-120 on the androgynous nature of Adam.

[113] MG-185, 1-5004, Box 15, Folder 6, R-69.

[114] "Adam war . . . eine Eng: gestalt." MG-185, Box 1-5004, Box 15, Folder 6, Q-39 Cf. Jakob Böhme, *Von der Menschwerdung Jesu Christi*, ed. Gerhard Wehr (Frankfurt: Insel Verlag, 1995), I, 3, §24, 62: "Denn des Adams reines Bildnis war . . . nach Gottes Geist, nach der Dreizahl, ein ganz züchtig Bild gleich den Engeln."

[115] MG-437/Box 22/Folder 82B/B-30.

[116] "So dann es war nur ein Mann und Weib in einer einzigen Person, denn Adam hatte feuer und Wasser in sich. Feuer war also der Trieb zur Zeugung, und das Wasser war das leydente oder Weibliche." 1838 Sermon Book, OEV, MG-437, Box 25, November 11, 1838, morning. Cf. Böhme, *Menschwerdung*, I, 3, §18, 59 and §23, 61-62: "Auch hatte er weder männliche noch weibliche Gestalt oder Form, denn er war beide und hatte beide Tincturen . . .", and I, 6, §6, 91: "in beiden Tinkturen des Feuers und Wassers."

[117] MG-185, Box 1-5004, Box 15, Folder 6, P-208. Cf. Böhme, *Menschwerdung*, I, 3, §18, 59 and §23, 61-62: "Auch hatte er weder männliche noch weibliche Gestalt oder Form, denn er war beide und hatte beide Tincturen . . ." Benz notes that "dieses Zeugen und Gebären nach dem Urbild des innertrinitarischen Vorgangs des Sohnes aus dem Vater gedacht ist: der gezeugte Sohn ist das Bild des Vaters, in dem er sich selbst erkennt und Gestalt, Form und Wesen wird. Ebenso vollzieht sich die Zeugung

He [Adam] was also a male virgin [an androgynous figure] and could through his own imagination grasp and love himself and, through the seven spirits, according to the eternal birth of the eternal Word, form and give birth to an image and essence such as he was and similar to God. By this manner, the entire human race would have been formed by God through these most holy means.[118]

"Bestial" reproductive organs had no place in Adam's spiritual body before the Fall. For a short period of time after his creation, Adam was a "pure and enlightened being, free from all fleshly and sensuous inclinations."[119]

Adam's fall from grace took place in Rapp's and Boehme's theology in two stages. The Harmonist leader attributed the first fall of Adam to sinful, sexual lust, rather than merely to self-will.[120] Although pre-Fall Adam was perfectly united with the heavenly virgin Sophia, he chose with his free will to "turn his lust" away from his heavenly bride and "toward earthly creatures."[121] "The first man . . . was aroused by bestial pleasures," and "overcome by the lust principle of this world. . . . He began to desire to reproduce as the animals did (*nach Thierischer Art fortzupflanzen*)."[122] This lust for the things of this world was nothing less than an adulterous betrayal of Sophia, who had no choice but to abandon Adam and the entire world.[123] To protect

---

und Gebärung des androgynen Urmenschen als Selbstabbildung." Ernst Benz, *Der vollkommene Mensch nach Jacob Boehme* (Stuttgart: Kohlhammer, 1937), 55.

[118]MG-437/Box 22/Folder 82B/B-30. Cf. Böhme, *Menschwerdung*, I, 5, §8, 77: "[D]enn so Adam hätte magisch geboren, so wäre das Paradies auf Erden geblieben." Cf. ibid., I, 5, §2, 73.

[119]MG-185, 1-5004, Box 15, Folder 6, R-69.

[120]Boehme generally emphasized self-will as the cause of the fall. Cf. Boehme, *Mysterium Magnum*, I, 18, §26-30, 127: "These forty days Adam . . . was tempted between three Principles. . . . This was the right *proba* of what the free will of the soul would do; whether it would remain in the divine harmony, or whether it would enter into the self-hood." The emphasis on sexual lust was more prominent in the writings of Boehme's disciple and editor, Johann Georg Gichtel (1638-1710). Johann Georg Gichtel, *Eine kurze Eröffnung und Anweisung der dreyen Principien und Welten im Menschen* (Berlin: Ringmacher, 1779), 2, § 41, 23: "Und das ist nun eigentlich Adams Fall: Er wolte nicht mehr mit der himmlischen Jungfrauen sich vermehren, und in ihrem Gehorsam gehen, sondern, wie alle Thiere, ein Weiblein haben, und der irdischen Frucht und Lust im Leibe genießen." Cf. Fritz Tanner, *Die Ehe im Pietismus* (Zurich: Zwingli Verlag, 1952), 21-22. Gichtel's *Theosophische Sendschreiben* and *Drei Prinzipien* were owned by the Harmony Society in 1829. Arndt, *Rapp's Successors*, 419. Nevertheless, the desire for bestial propagation as cause for the fall was found to a lesser degree in Boehme. Boehme, *Mysterium Magnum*, I, 19, §25, 135: "Adam in his perfection . . . did amuse himself on (or imagine after) the beasts, and introduced himself into bestial lust, to eat and generate according as the beasts do."

[121]MG-185, 1-5004, Box 15, Folder 5, N-103.

[122]MG-185, Box 1-5004, Box 15, Folder 6, P-239 and MG-185, 1-5004, Box 15, Folder 6, Q-39.

[123]MG-185, 1-5004, Box 15, Folder 5, N-103.

him from even greater errors, God in his grace allowed Adam, who before this required no rest, to fall into a deep sleep.[124] This sleep was a "sign of Adam's weakness," that he had been overcome by the powers of this world.[125] "He sank into a deep sleep and in this very hour his heavenly body became flesh and blood, his powerful strength became limbs.... In his sleep Adam became a different image. Prior he was an angelic figure, now a bestial man."[126]

Not only did Adam lose Sophia and surrender his angelic body in the deep sleep. Eve was created by "being taken from his body."[127] For Rapp and Boehme, the first woman was the feminine half of androgynous Adam, and was taken from Adam's essence, not just his flesh. Prior to her formation into flesh and blood in the deep sleep, "this portion or matrix was suspended in the life powers of Adam."[128] Thus the first fall of Adam was a fall from a heavenly body to an earthly one and from perfect androgynous unity into the duality of the two genders. The second fall of Adam in Rapp's and Boehme's theology corresponded to the biblical account in Genesis 3. Adam was tempted in his pride to be like God. The first pair ate of the forbidden fruit, and they were cursed with pain, suffering and death.

Boehme's application of the androgynous ideal to the Godhead was particularly offensive to contemporary Lutheran Orthodox scholars.[129] On one hand, Boehme's doctrine of God polarized the two genders—maleness being found in the Godhead itself and the female principle in the heavenly Sophia. On the other hand, Boehme argued in his theosophical writings that Christ, the second Adam, reestablished in his person the lost androgynous unity of the first Adam.[130] On the cross, Sophia entered into Christ's body, thus creating the possibility for regenerated believers to achieve the union

---

[124] MG-185, Box 1-5004, Box 15, Folder 6, P-208. Cf. Pältz, "Boehmes Hermeneutik," 106.

[125] MG-185, 1-5004, Box 15, Folder 5, N-103. Cf. Boehme, *Mysterium Magnum*, I, 19, §4, 129: "Even then he forthwith sank down into a swoon into sleep, viz. into an inability, which signifieth the death: for the image of God, which is immutable, doth not sleep."

[126] MG-185, Box 1-5004, Box 15, Folder 6, Q-39.

[127] Ibid.

[128] MG-185, 1-5004, Box 15, Folder 5, N-141. Cf. Boehme, *Mysterium Magnum*, I, 19, §2, 129: "For we find that the woman was taken and formed in the Fiat out of Adam's essence, both in body and soul."

[129] Abraham Calov (1612-1686), the leader of orthodoxy in Wittenberg expressed this sentiment vehemently in his work, "Antiboehmius." Benz, *Adam, der Mythus*, 297, n. 4.

[130] Boehme, *Mysterium Magnum*, II, 56, §20, 621: Christ became man "so that the masculine and feminine principle might be quite changed into one image again; as Adam was before his Eve, when he was neither man nor woman, but a masculine virgin."

of both genders.[131] George Rapp in his Sophialogical doctrine cherished the feminine principle within the divine. Like Boehme, he occasionally taught that Christ achieved an androgynous nature. "Jesus Christ introduced the masculine part again into the body of the virgin woman, so that the two once again became a single image and being. The male characteristics prevail of course, but they are mitigated and moderated by the light force of the woman."[132] "Christ did not marry in this world, for he was destined to become the second Adam and to acquire again the chaste Sophia."[133] Unlike Boehme, Rapp did not specify how or when Christ became androgynous. He implied however, that it took place at the Incarnation. Although Rapp adopted the main outlines of Boehme's anthropology and doctrine of the Fall, he did not slavishly follow the Görlitz theosophist in every detail.

Alchemistical Practice and Language

The practice of alchemy had a long and checkered history, which extended back to ancient Egypt and Greece. In the ninth century, Islamic practitioners coined the current term *al-kimiya* (alchemy) to refer to the transmutation of base metals into gold through an involved, pyrotechnical process. Alchemists earnestly endeavored to develop both the correct transformative process and a secret substance to effect the transmutation of base metals into precious ones, a substance usually referred to as the philosophers' stone (*lapis philosophorum*). In addition, they sought to produce an elixir promoting health, long life or immortality.[134]

The historic roots of alchemy were decidedly religious in nature. In ancient Egypt, gold was the metal of the gods and a symbol for life after death. Medieval Islamic mystics used alchemistical terminology to describe the spiritual transformation of the soul from iron to gold.[135] By the early modern period a distinction was generally made between speculative, theosophical or religious alchemy describing the spiritual progression of the soul, and a praxis-oriented, medicinal-pharmaceutical or metallurgical branch that later formed the foundation of modern chemistry.[136] Following these distinctions, contemporary scholars generally divide alchemy into three different schools: transmutation alchemy, which aimed to produce gold from base metals; medicinal alchemy, which sought to explain pathological

---

[131]Boehme, *Mysterium Magnum*, I, 19, §7, 130: "And when Christ on the cross had again accomplished this redemption of our virgin-like image from the divided sex of male and female, and tinctured it with his heavenly blood in the divine love, he said, *It is finished*."

[132]MG-185, 1-5004, Box 15, Folder 5, D-11.

[133]1838 Sermon Book. OEV, MG-437, Box 25, Nov. 11, 1838 morning.

[134]Sven S. Hartman, "Alchemie I," in *Theologische Realenzyklopädie*, vol. 2 (Berlin: De Gruyter, 1978), 195-199.

[135]Hartman, "Alchemie I," 196-197.

[136]Joachim Telle, "Alchemie II," in *Theologische Realenzyklopädie*, vol. 2 (Berlin: De Gruyter, 1978), 199-227, here 199.

processes and develop therapeutic remedies; and spiritual alchemy, which employed alchemistical terminology to describe spiritual transformation from a base to a nobler plane.[137]

Alchemy and Pietism

Interest in spiritual or theological alchemy was widespread within both the churchly and radical branches of German Pietism.[138] Pietists drew upon the tradition of spiritual alchemy that developed in the early modern era. Theophrast von Hohenheim, called Paracelsus (1493-1541), a theologically (self)-trained physician, greatly influenced both theological and medicinal alchemy and was eagerly read by medical and religious reformers, including Pietists.[139] Later, Paracelsus' disciple, Heinrich Khunrath, used alchemistical terminology to describe spiritual renewal. The soul was re-melted *(Umschmelzung)* and purified from all impurities in the act of regeneration. Christ himself was the philosophers' stone that effected this transmutation.[140] According to his own admission, Jakob Boehme was not a practicing alchemist.[141] Rather, he utilized the alchemistical transmutation process as a religious symbol. In chapter seven of *De Signatura rerum*, Boehme developed in great detail the alchemistical analogy between Christ's atoning work and man's transformation from a sin nature to a regenerated state and ultimately from a physical body to a resurrection body. Christ was not

---

[137]Christa Habrich, "Alchemie und Chemie in der pietistischen Tradition," in *Goethe und der Pietismus*, ed. Hans-Georg Kemper and Hans Schneider (Tübingen: Niemeyer, 2001), 45-77, here 47-50. A. Köberle, however, posits four branches of alchemy: (1) alchemy as nature philosophy; (2) transmutation of substances; (3) psychic development stages; and (4) spiritual transformation through mystical practices. Konstanze Grutschnig-Kieser, *Der "Geistliche Würtz-Kräuter und Blumen-Garten" des Christoph Schütz. Ein radikalpietistisches "Universal-Gesang-Buch"* (Göttingen: Vandenhoeck & Ruprecht, 2006), 219, n. 201.

[138]Grutschnig-Kieser, *Geistliche Würtz-Garten*, 220.

[139]Renate Wilson, *Pious Traders in Medicine. A German Pharmaceutical Network in Eighteenth-Century North America* (University Park, Pa.: Pennsylvania State University, 2000), 49-52 notes the connection between medical and religious reforms. The Pietist academic physicians at Halle were medical reformers, who built upon the traditions of medical alchemy. W. R. Ward, *Early Evangelicalism. A Global Intellectual History 1670-1789*. Cambridge: Cambridge University Press, 2006, 11-12 likewise points to the influence of Paracelsus on Arndt and Francke.

[140]Habrich, "Alchemie und Chemie," 48-50.

[141]"Es ist aber nicht meine Meinung, den Menschen in unverstandene, unnütze Kunst, darzu er nicht von Gott beruffen noch begabet, einzuführen, *weil ich sie auch selbsten nicht in der Praxi führe noch treibe*, sondern nur die Möglichkeit aller Dinge, nebenst der besten Praxi der neuen Wiedergeburt anmelde, und den von Gott darzu begabten zu den äusseren Dinge Anleitung gebe." Jacob Böhme, *De signatura rerum, oder Von der Geburt und Bezeichnung aller Wesen*, in *Sämtliche Schriften*, vol. 6, ed. Will-Erich Peuckert (Stuttgart: Frommanns, 1957), Vorrede, §5, 2-3.

only the true philosophers' stone, but in his incarnation and resurrection he served as the prototype for man's transmutation.[142]

Most churchly and some radical Pietists (such as the physician Johann Samuel Carl and Tersteegen) rejected active laboratory work in favor of the metaphorical use of alchemistical terminology for spiritual processes. A smaller group of radical Pietists in Homburg, Hanau, Offenbach and Frankfurt, members of the Inspired Church, as well as some churchly Pietists (Johann Arndt, F. C. Oetinger, P. M. Hahn) in the seventeenth and eighteenth centuries, were not content with metaphorical usage but likewise engaged in alchemistical experiments.[143] It is important to note that although Enlightenment thought had begun to drive a wedge between scientific and religious knowledge, this trend was not yet fully developed.[144] Seventeenth and eighteenth century Pietists, who engaged in alchemy, often justified their practice by pointing to the correlation between the two books of revelation: the Bible (special revelation) and the book of nature (general revelation or natural theology).[145] They argued that the book of nature (*liber naturae*) as the second source of divine revelation was essential for a full and correct interpretation of Scripture. In their view, alchemy was not separated from theology, but united to it. Alchemistical-chemical processes could and did shed light on man's understanding of the Bible.[146] For example, Oetinger claimed that alchemy was the "science of the high priests' Urim and Thummin" (Ex 28:30), and necessary "to understand every last notion in Holy Scripture." No philosopher should write without having first practiced alc-

---

[142]Pältz, "Boehmes Hermeneutik," 310. Ward, *Early Evangelicalism*, 12 claims that Luther saw "alchemy as a metaphor of the resurrection."

[143]Habrich, "Alchemie und Chemie," 58-73. Johann Arndt's *Wahres Christentum* was enormously influential on the rise of Pietism. Arndt supported both a philosophical and medicinal form of alchemy in his own laboratory work. In a letter to Johann Gerhard (Feb. 19, 1607) he wrote: "Abgesehen von meinen nicht profanen Arbeiten verwende ich noch einige Zeit und einiges Nachdenken auf die spagyrische Kunst (oder Alchemie): ich arbeite an der Schmelzung und Auflösung des Goldes, für Philosophie und Medizin gleich bedeutsam, denn hierin ist die ganze Summe der Medizin und der Edelsteinwissenschaft verborgen." Quoted in Pältz, "Boehmes Hermeneutik," 312, n. 11.

[144]Richard L. Bushman in *Joseph Smith and the Beginnings of Mormonism* (Urbana, Ill.: University of Illinois Press, 1984), 79 notes that in rural America "[m]any Christians hoped for a return of primitive Christianity's divine gifts, and water witching, stone gazing, treasure hunting, and spiritualism went on despite the scorn of newspaper editors, ministers, and physicians who spoke for Enlightenment values..."

[145]The concept of the book of nature was found in Clement of Alexandria, Origen, and Augustine, in the orthodox Lutheran Johann Gerhard, and in proto-Pietists Johann Arndt (book four of *Wahres Christentum*) and Jacob Boehme. Pältz, "Boehmes Hermeneutik," 294. Cf. Telle, "Alchemie II," 209.

[146]Martin Brecht, "Der württembergische Pietismus," in *Geschichte des Pietismus*, vol. 2, *Der Pietismus im achtzehnten Jahrhundert*, ed. Martin Brecht and Klaus Deppermann (Göttingen: Vandenhoeck & Ruprecht, 1995), 275.

hemy.¹⁴⁷ Philipp Matthäus Hahn, a Lutheran churchly Pietist pastor in Württemberg (1739-1790) and a disciple of Oetinger, justified his alchemistical experiments by asserting that through them he "learned to discern nature *in order to understand Scripture* [my emphasis]."¹⁴⁸

Nevertheless, Hahn, like many Pietists, was inwardly conflicted by his alchemy practice. On one hand, he rationalized that gold produced through his experiments could be used to further the kingdom of God. Yet in the same paragraph Hahn admitted that if successful in gold-production, he "could no longer teach and understand the path of suffering."¹⁴⁹ Radical Pietist Christoph Schütz (1689-1750) had laboratory experience, maintained contact with practicing alchemists, and included an appendix of rare "chemical" manuscripts to his edition of Georg von Welling's *Opus magocabbalisticum et theosophicum*. Although he allowed for a proper use of alchemistical experiments, he nevertheless warned his readers against charlatans and "would-be gold-makers." Man's relationship to God, not laboratory work, ought to be the primary concern. Therefore, in the prologue to Welling's *Opus*, Schütz urged: "We heartily wish that all people would seek and find God rather than gold. But because we know that every man willingly seeks and studies something, therefore we consider it permissible in proper moderation to pursue this noble art [alchemy]."¹⁵⁰

Johann Samuel Carl (1676-1757), a radical Pietist physician in Berleburg as well as in other locations, dabbled in alchemy early in life. Later, even after discontinuing such practice, Carl admitted that he and his students frequently struggled against temptations to return to the "magical arts" (*Zauber Kunst*) and his "alchemy addiction" (*Alchymie-Sucht*).¹⁵¹ Not only did practicing alchemists of the Pietist persuasion recognize its potential spiritual dangers and struggle at times with guilty consciences. Oetinger's parishioners during his Weinsberger pastorate claimed that they could not receive the Eucharist from their pastor's hands, since he had soiled them with alchemistical experiments.¹⁵² In Pietist circles in the seventeenth and eighteenth centuries an ongoing "religious war" was waged over the role of

---

¹⁴⁷Oetinger, *Lehrtafel*, 205.

¹⁴⁸ Martin Brecht and Rudolf F. Paulus, *Philipp Matthäus Hahn. Die Kornwestheimer Tagebücher 1772-1777* (Berlin: Walter De Gruyter, 1979), 445. Oetinger, the mentor of P. M. Hahn, likewise used this rationalization. Cf. Betz, "Kabbala Baptizata," 140.

¹⁴⁹"Den 7. [August], Sonntag [1774]. Fiel mir ein, ob nicht Gott mir die Kunst geben könte, Gold zu machen, oder sonst ein Glück, daß ich eher könte hin- und herreißen und den Wachsthum seines Reichs befördern. Aber wir könten alsdann den Leydensweg nicht mehr lehren und verstehen. Wir wären selbst nicht, was wir andere lehrten. Ich sehe also nicht, wie es möglich sey." Brecht, *Hahn's Kornwestheimer Tagebücher*, 269.

¹⁵⁰Quoted in German in Grutschnig-Kieser, *Geistliche Würtz-Garten*, 220. This is the same Christoph Schütz who authored the *Güldene Rose*.

¹⁵¹Habrich, "Alchemie und Chemie," 65.

¹⁵²Schulze, "Oetinger und die Kabbala," 272.

spiritual alchemy and active alchemistical laboratory work among "true children of God."[153]

Alchemistical Experiments and the Harmony Society

Documentary evidence for alchemistical activity in the Harmony Society is limited to several key individuals and a narrow window of time during the early Economy era (1825-1832). The first reference to alchemy is found in the travel journal of the German economist, Friedrich List, describing his visit to Economy in November 1825. In the account he mentioned that "the physician . . . does a great deal of chemistry."[154] List did not specify which Harmonist physician he had in mind--Christoph Müller or Wilhelm Schmidt. A letter from Wilhelm Schmidt to Frederick Rapp on January 30, 1827 strongly suggests that it was Schmidt and that it was not merely chemistry, but alchemy that he was engaged in. In this letter Schmidt reported to the Harmony Society business manager, who was away from Economy, the reasons for his lack of success in his current alchemistical endeavor. The "fig leaves and animal skins" of the chemical elements were not completely removed, that is, the elements were not adequately purified. The proportion of ingredients was incorrect, and Satan the enemy had caused the fire to be too hot. In this letter Schmidt personified and theologized the inert chemical substances. The ingredients would soon "repent of their sins in tears" and become black (one step in the alchemistical process). Through the addition of the oil of grace the mixture would put on white clothing like the martyrs beneath the altar (Rev 6:9-11). Whitening was a further step in the alchemistical process. The sun of righteousness would shine upon the material, original sin would be destroyed and the material would arise as a (golden) scepter out of the fire. The production of gold was the goal of the process. Schmidt intended to correct his mistakes and repeat the experiment in several days. Meanwhile he suggested that Frederick obtain the alchemistical volume, *Aurea Catena Homeri*, the Golden Chain of Homer.[155]

On February 10, 1827 Schmidt reported to Frederick on the unsatisfactory state of his laboratory progress. The previous day a fiery explosion had occurred during his experiment, which seriously burned his arm and re-

---

[153]Habrich, "Alchemie und Chemie," 73.

[154]Karl J. R. Arndt, *Harmony on the Wabash in Transition, 1824-1826. A Documentary History* (Worcester, Mass.: Harmony Society Press, 1982), 688. Karl Arndt apparently assumed that Christoph Müller was the physician to which List referred. Karl J. R. Arndt, *George Rapp's Harmony Society 1785-1847*, rev. ed. (Teaneck, N.J.: Fairleigh Dickinson University Press, 1972), 500-501.

[155]Karl J. R. Arndt, *Economy on the Ohio, 1826-1834. George Rapp's Third Harmony. A Documentary History* (Worchester, Mass.: Harmony Society Press, 1984), 105-106. The influential *Golden Chain of Homer*, written or edited by Anton Josef Kirchweger, was published in Frankfurt and Leipzig in four German editions in 1723, 1728, 1738 and 1757. A Latin version was published in Frankfurt in 1762, and further German editions followed.

sulted in the loss of his carefully purified ingredients. Despite the accident, Schmidt did not intend to discontinue his alchemistical activity. Several lines at the end of this letter are especially significant for dating George and Frederick Rapp's alchemistical activity. Schmidt reported that *"Father* has also begun to work. He has had two of the furnaces in *your* laboratory altered, because he could not produce a strong enough fire. [Eusebius] Böhm and Hildegard [Mutschler] are his helpers."[156] This text indicates that after the move to Economy in 1825 but no later than January 1827, Frederick Rapp had his own laboratory in which to perform alchemistical experiments. Father George Rapp had begun just recently in early 1827 to participate in the "great work." George Rapp's choice of the young, pretty, and probably seductive Hildegard Mutschler as one of his laboratory assistants led to serious recriminations from his adopted son Frederick. On September 29, 1829 Frederick strongly voiced his objections in a letter to the then seventy-one year old founder of the Society:

> But when you took the girl [Hildegard Mutschler] fully as an assistant in your laboratory work--that was more to me than anything else that had preceded it. I know surely that alone on that account the great work could not succeed and was not to succeed for she was too far removed from the wisdom which performs this work. Even if her hands had not touched it (which they often did), her unclean breath would have spoiled it, since the heavenly forces of light on her account could not have come near. As soon as I became aware of that I did not want to have any more to do with the work and no longer asked about it, even though it had always been my favorite occupation. So with sadness I had to give up my hopes.[157]

It was believed that only pure souls could successfully produce the philosophers' stone or gold from base metals. Therefore, since the "unclean" Hildegard was involved, in Frederick's opinion Rapp's experiments were doomed to failure. Her involvement so spoiled Frederick's enjoyment of his "favorite occupation" (alchemy) that sometime after February 1827 ("as soon as I became aware of it") he discontinued his alchemistical activity. It is possible that Frederick resumed transmutation alchemy at an unknown date after laboratory assistant Hildegard Mutschler ran away from the Harmony Society with Conrad Feucht (June 1829) in order to get married, although no documentary evidence exists to support this conjecture. If so, Frederick did not resume alchemistical activity until after late September 1829 when he wrote to the elder Rapp objecting to Hildegard's involvement.[158] There is no documentary or physical evidence of laboratory-based

---

[156]Arndt, *Doc. Hist. 1826-1834*, 117. Fritz, "'Viele fromme Seelen und Querköpfe,'" 183 claims that Rapp's practice of alchemy was influenced by Oetinger or Moritz Siegfried von Leiningen. It is not possible to limit the influence to these two men.

[157]Arndt, *Doc. Hist. 1826-1834*, 405 (Arndt's translation with minor corrections).

[158]The married couple was readmitted before 1832. They disregarded the celibate lifestyle and produced three children, at least two while living in the

alchemy in the Harmony and New Harmony eras (1804-1824). Frederick's involvement in the "great work" lasted but a few years (from ca. 1825-1827 and possibly from 1829-1832). He died soon thereafter on June 24, 1834.

Presumably George Rapp continued to practice transmutation alchemy until approximately 1832. There were two key alchemistical works in the Harmony Society library during Rapp's lifetime—the collected works of Paracelsus (*Opera*, Strasburg 1603) and Rapp's personally signed copy of Georg von Welling's *Opus mago-cabbalisticum et theosophicum*.[159] The importance of transmutation alchemy to Rapp is evidenced in one undated sermon. In it he rhetorically posed the question of whether transmutation was possible.

> The big question is, can this art [alchemy] be elevated up to nature and enter into the innermost part of the workshop, and eavesdrop on the secret workshop? Can it [the art of alchemy] grasp the simple principles of creation? Answer—yes, man can penetrate into the innermost realms of nature, can study its secret ways and make use of its principles *to bring forth new creations* (*um neue schaffungen hervor zu bringen*). This art is the most exalted of all arts. It is unknown to the common man.[160]

It is significant that Rapp used the term "secret workshop" or "laboratory" (*geheime Werckstat*) as the locus where this "art" took place. Rapp declared that not only could some enlightened men understand the principles of nature but actually use these principles to transmute materials from one state to another, "to bring forth new creations." Although this sermon is undated, its content corresponds well to the narrow time frame (ca. 1827-1832) when Rapp actively practiced alchemy.[161] The statements in this

---

Harmony Society— Tirza (b. May 19, 1830), Benjamin (b. July 31, 1834), and Heinrich (b. June 14, 1837).

[159]Welling's *Opus* was bought by Rapp prior to emigration, since he marked "Iptingen" on the inside cover. Versluis notes that there were marginal notations (which he was unable to read) in Rapp's copy of Welling's work. Arthur Versluis, "Western Esotericism and the Harmony Society." http://www.esoteric.msu.edu/Versluis.html. [Accessed October 15, 2006], 37. The author has carefully examined all notations in Rapp's copy of the volume in the Harmony Society archives. The notations do not refer to transmutation alchemy as Versluis suggests. Most are home medicinal recipes (use of fried onions for cough, p. 8, recipes for a sweat-producing potion and for camphor, back cover) or other recipes (for linen, back cover). One recipe (after p. 00) is either medicinal or possibly alchemistical (tincture formed of red *Weingeist* and *spiritalis salmiac*), but it is not in Rapp's handwriting. A marginal note on page 198 states that "potabile gold" serves as a medicine (*dienet zur arzney*), which it did in this era. See Wilson, *Pious Traders*, 72-77 for the medicinal usage and sale of potabile gold by Halle Pietists. One long marginal notation uses alchemistical terminology for spiritual transformation (p. 64) in a spiritual alchemy fashion.

[160]MG-185/1-5004/Box 15/Folder 6/P-267.

[161]Of course, it is impossible to state with certitude that the sermon was written at this time.

sermon must be balanced, however, by those in a second undated sermon. Here the Harmonist leader cautioned his hearers of the spiritual dangers inherent in hermetic activity and encouraged his listeners to draw spiritual nourishment entirely from the Word of God.

> He who merely devotes himself to the secret arts as a mystic, so that he only flutters in circles without having his eyes firmly set on the central point [Christ] . . . the mysticism of such a person belongs to the wrong side, for it is death. Such people do not want to enter the supernatural world through humble supplication and petition. Rather they desire to conjure it [the supernatural world] into the natural world for their own enjoyment. In sum, faith, patience, doing one's duty, and silence . . . this is the mysticism that honors man and makes him happy until he enters into the kingdom of God. It can be practiced by everyone. . . . I want to have something for my immortal soul, namely the Word of God. . . .The *Gemeine* will never lack complete spiritual nourishment from the Word of God, from which we draw food for the heart, love, which is the bond of perfection.[162]

In a manner reminiscent of Christoph Schütz's prologue to Welling's *Opus*, Rapp did not categorically reject the "secret arts," but warned that they ought not to become the Christian's central focus. This must always be Christ and the Word of God.

In September 1831 the German charlatan Count Leon and his retinue arrived at Economy. The major schism that the bogus Count caused within the Harmony Society in 1832 will be discussed in chapter nine. What is significant in this context is the role that alchemy played in the ensuing conflict. Maximilian Ludwig Proli, alias Count Leon, was both a high level Mason and a practicing alchemist. Prior to arriving in the United States, Count Leon had achieved a reputation in Germany as a gold-boiler (*Goldbrüher*).[163] Soon after arriving at Economy, he had a laboratory built for his alchemistical experiments. Leon's claim to possess the philosophers' stone contributed much to his appeal to disgruntled Harmonists during his six-month residence in the community. Frederick Rapp in a public statement a year after the schism (April, 1833) listed the reasons that some Harmonists seceded with Proli: "Proli . . . promised them [the Harmonists who seceded with him] good days, that is a good life without work, by claiming that he could see God face to face, that he had been anointed by God himself, was the Holy Spirit, *he could make gold*, and all the treasures of the earth were known to him."[164]

Similarly in a letter to Johannes and Michael Bengel, George Rapp claimed that Count Leon's "promise to produce for the secessionists much gold" was a motivating factor for those "evil" Harmonists for whom the

---

[162] MG-185/1-5004/Box 15/Folder 5/N-119.
[163] Arndt, *Doc. Hist. 1826-1834*, 472.
[164] Ibid., 879 (Arndt's translation).

"path of conversion was too narrow and restrictive."[165] In such letters and public statements, both George and Frederick Rapp pointed derisively to Count Leon's bombastic claims and alchemistical attempts to produce gold.[166] There is no further documentary evidence of alchemistical activity in the Harmony Society after 1832. Alchemist Wilhelm Schmidt, a leader of the secessionists, was no longer present in the Society. Frederick Rapp, who died shortly thereafter, may or may not have resumed alchemistical experiments after 1829. Count Leon's laboratory was destroyed by the seceding Harmonists and never rebuilt.[167] After the debacle with Count Leon in 1832, George Rapp distanced himself publicly and presumably privately from active alchemistical laboratory work. In conclusion, transmutation alchemy was short-lived within the Harmony Society. It was practiced by several key persons (Wilhelm Schmidt, Frederick and George Rapp), but only for a relatively brief period of time in the early Economy era (ca. 1825-1832). Spiritual alchemy, the use of alchemistical terminology for spiritual processes, was much more persistent within the Harmony Society, as will be shown in the subsequent section.

Spiritual Alchemy and the Harmony Society

In the 1834 letter from George Rapp to Johannes and Michael Bengel referenced above, Rapp distanced himself from gold-seeking, transmutation alchemy. In this same letter, however, he used spiritual-alchemistical language to describe sanctification and religious transformation. The rebellion and schism that the Harmony Society had recently experienced served "to *distill* [them] upward to a higher spiritual life."[168] Furthermore, the "Spirit of Jesus" would wondrously bring them to a "higher plane" by transmuting them into the spiritual body (*Geistleib*) originally possessed by Adam.[169]

---

[165] Karl J. R. Arndt, *George Rapp's Years of Glory. Economy on the Ohio, 1834-1847. George Rapp's Third Harmony. A Documentary History* (New York: Peter Lang, 1987), 41.

[166] Cf. G. W. Featherstonhaugh's report of his visit to Economy, which likewise mentioned Count Leon's claims to be able to make gold as one motivation for secession. (Featherstonhaugh would have received this information from the Rapps and other faithful Harmonists.) Arndt, *Doc. Hist. 1834-1847*, 119.

[167] Jacob Bauer charged Johann Andre Zickwolf, a member of Count Leon's retinue, for labor and materials for Leon's alchemistical laboratory, which the seceding members had destroyed. Arndt, *Doc. Hist. 1826-1834*, 775.

[168] Distillation was part of the alchemistical process. The number of steps included in the alchemistical process varied. They included some or all of the following: calcination, solution, separation, distillation, descension, conjunction, putrefaction, coagulation, cibation, sublimation, fermentation, exaltation, fixation, ceration, multiplication and projection. Telle, "Alchemie II," 202.

[169] "so gehören also alle Schicksale, die wir durch geloffen und mit verwebt waren, sind weiter nichts, als Entwickelungen zu einem geistigen höhern Leben hinauf distilirt zu werden, welches aber freilich immer nur eine kleinere Zahl ausmacht, die die breite Landstrasse verlassen und den schmalen Fusspfad der

This text combined the two aspects for which Rapp used alchemistical terminology—for regeneration/sanctification and for the transmutation of the physical body into a spiritual, resurrection body in the *eschaton*. The use of alchemistical language for regeneration, sanctification, and exaltation to the *Geistleib* was not original to Rapp, but found in Boehme and Boehme-enthusiasts such as Gichtel and Gottfried Arnold.[170]

George Rapp used alchemistical language to describe regeneration and growth in sanctification in a number of his mature sermons. According to the Harmonist spiritual leader, man carried a treasure within his soul, a spark of God himself. This treasure could be compared with the "finest potable gold" (*aurum potabile*), an alchemistical tincture of ground gold dissolved in water or wine.[171] This "proper and true potable gold" was man's "pure, virginal self," which, unlike its physical equivalent, "cost nothing," although it was of supreme value. It was produced through "crushing and dissolution."[172] Similarly, gold ore was tested and purified repeatedly in the fires of the forge. These alchemistical fires of purification were utilized as a religious metaphor for the annihilation of the self-will (*Vernichtigung*), one aspect of Rapp's theology of regeneration and sanctification that reflected Tersteegen's influence. According to Rapp, when "gold is tried in the fire, all impurities fall away.... This points to the true and voluntary spiritual rebirth, or the complete death and voluntary annihilation [of self-will], which is the solitary goal."[173] All "foreign elements" or impurities were consumed in the fire. "He who endures this [purification] trial" experiences that the "divine is united with the natural," the "new humanity" is regenerated and made complete "like flowing, tinctured gold, poured out" of the crucible.[174]

Nachfolge Christi freiwillig wählen. Und sollte es nicht so seyn, da der Geist Jesu uns eben so wunderbar zu einer hohern Bildung in das geistleibliche Haus des ursprunglichen Lebens zu einer höhern Stufe bereiten will. . . " Arndt, *Doc. Hist. 1834-1847*, 40.

[170] See Boehme, *De Signatura rerum*, for alchemistical terminology for regeneration (7, §53, 70, and 7, §35, 65), the transformation of God's wrath to love by Christ (7, §24-25, 62-63), and transmutation of physical to resurrection body (5, §8, 44; 5, §11, 44; 5, §14, 44-45; and 7, §50, 69). Cf. Gichtel, *Theosophia Practica*, 24f and 575f (transmutation to *Geistleib*), referenced in Habrich, "Alchemie und Chemie," 56, n. 55 and 56; and G. Arnold, *Divine Sophia*, 97 and 107 (regeneration/sanctification), 151f (*Geistleib*), referenced in Habrich, "Alchemie und Chemie," 57, n. 60-62. Cf. Douglas H. Shantz, "The Origin of Pietist Notions of New Birth and New Man. Alchemy and Alchemists in Gottfried Arnold and Johann Heinrich Reitz," in *The Pietist Impulse in Christianity*, eds. Christian T. Collins Winn, et al. (Eugene, Org.: Pickwick Publications, 2011), 29-41, here 30 argues for the influence of alchemy, Rosicrucianism and hermeticism on Pietist notions of new birth.

[171] MG-185/1-5004/Box 15/Folder 6/Q-79. Cf. Wilson, *Pious Traders*, 72.

[172] MG-185/1-5004/Box 15/Folder 6/R-121.

[173] MG-185/1-5004/Box 15/Folder 6/R-56. Cf. MG-185/1-5004/Box 15/Folder 6/R-131.

[174] MG-437/Box 22/Folder 82B/B-26.

Furthermore: "The *Gemeine* has the wonderful [philosophers'] stone that turns base metals into gold. . . . Therefore we allow the Holy Spirit to rule within us, [even when] during the purification process . . . faults are revealed, from which we thought we had already been freed."[175] The crucial secret ingredient that alchemists sought, the philosophers' stone, was possessed by the true church. It was employed by the Holy Spirit in the purification process to turn sinful men (base metals) into righteous, regenerated ones (gold).

Another alchemistical process was used by Rapp to describe the Christian's laying aside of sin—separation (*scheiden*). According to Rapp, the Harmony Society as the true church had the "key to the secret art of separation, by virtue of which curse can be separated again from victory, and evil can be brought into good."[176] The separation from sin was but an early step toward sanctification. A later alchemistical step was *tingieren* or dyeing. This step aimed to achieve the stabile, red-gold color that alchemists sought as evidence that base metals had actually been changed into gold.[177] For the Harmonist leader, being tinctured to red-gold was a metaphor for spiritual perfection, which must be earnestly sought after by the Christian.

> In order to achieve the completely perfect status of ripeness and maturity, we must first be dyed or tinctured (*gefärbet oder tingiert*) to perfection . . . He [sic] must intend and give effort not only to be purified, but to be tinctured so highly that he becomes seven times more beautiful, redder and more powerful.[178]

Once again, Rapp used alchemistical terminology as an analogy for growth in sanctification.

George Rapp used alchemistical language most frequently to describe the transmutation of the physical body into the resurrection body in the *eschaton*. Like Friedrich Oetinger before him, Rapp argued that physicality or materiality (*Leiblichkeit*) was not inimical to spirit. The founder of the Harmony Society paraphrased his fellow Württemberger Oetinger when he stated, "Spirit is not without a physical essence. Physical indestructibility is the end of the works of God."[179] Rapp conceded that scholars might view the

---

[175] MG-185/1-5004/Box 15/Folder 5/C-9.
[176] MG-185/1-5004/Box 15/Folder 6/Q-42.
[177] Hans-Werner Schütt, *Auf der Suche nach dem Stein der Weisen. Die Geschichte der Alchemie* (Munich: Beck, 2000), 54-55, 495.
[178] MG-185/1-5004/Box 15/Folder 6/R-21.
[179] MG-185, 1-5004, Box 15, Folder 6, P-117. Cf. Oetinger, *Irrd. u himml. Philos.*, ed. 1855, 350: "Leiblichkeit ist nicht eine Unvollkommenheit, sondern eine Vollkommenheit." Ibid., *Theologie aus der Idee des Lebens*, §16, 111, n. 3: "Ebenso ist die Leiblichkeit nothwendiges Correlat der Geistigkeit." "Leiblichkeit ist das Ende aller Wege Gottes." Benz, *Christliche Kabbala*, 51. See Weyer-Menkhoff, *Christus, das Heil der Natur*, 175-176 and 205-212 for a discussion of materiality (*Leiblichkeit*) in Oetinger's theology. Weyer-Menkhoff notes that J. A. Bengel's concrete, realistic, and

concept of the spiritual body (*Geistleib*) to be "too material or crude."[180] But "those who read the holy Scriptures like a child and without prejudice see on the first reading that... the blessed in the kingdom of God are to be seen in nothing but living, spiritual, corporeal forms.... All things live in the kingdom of God physically (*leiblich*)."[181] For the "spiritual body (*Geistleib*) was the highest culmination of the works of God."[182] Therefore, "we seek a corporeality made from the highest purified element, a living gold, which is compared with God."[183]

The resurrection body was a renewal of Adam's spiritual body before the Fall. Rapp stated in a mature sermon: "Instead of this earthly, fleeting, impure body... which is incapable of seeing God... the body of the new humanity is a heavenly, imperishable, pure body, capable of seeing God face to face.... From such Adam's body had been formed."[184] The *Geistleib* in Rapp's theology was formed of both spirit and transformed or renewed physical matter. The resurrection body resembled Adam's body before the Fall in that it combined not just spirit and matter, but another set of opposites--both genders into one androgynous being. "The elect will be like the angels... namely... neither man nor woman, for the angels have another nature."[185] In one sermon Rapp used distinctively alchemistical language to depict the androgynous nature of the resurrection body. Regenerated humanity would "be placed again in the desirable state, which they had in the original creation." They would be "transformed into a true double being (*ein wahres Doppel Wesen*)... as man and woman."

> Therefore, the body that has seen death is alive again, and has become clear, white and glowing, and is brought into [the state] of a double being, which is the image of God in man and woman, the white and red lily, or the white woman and the red man... Then when the sun and moon are brought into one body, the sun or gold, for us red and of a fiery nature, reconciles with the soul and the nature of the moon... the pure nature, white and shiny like silver.[186]

---

material conception of time, space and salvation-history was one source of Oetinger's materialism. Ibid., 208.

[180]Oetinger rejected the materialist theory of the eternality and exclusivity of material. On the other hand, Oetinger affirmed "Scriptural materialism" that viewed physicality positively as a gift of God, and not as an evil to be overcome. Weyer-Menkhoff, *Christus, das Heil der Natur*, 205-206.

[181]MG-185, 1-5004, Box 15, Folder 5, N-88.
[182]MG-185, 1-5004, Box 15, Folder 5, A-42.
[183]MG-185/Box 15/Folder 5/E-45.
[184]MG-185, 1-5004, Box 15, Folder 6, P-68.
[185]MG-185, 1-5004, Box 15, Folder 5, N-88.
[186]MG-185, 1-5004, Box 15, Folder 6, R-139.

Polar opposites such as sun (male) and moon (female), gold (male) and silver (female), and red (male) and white (female) denoted the two genders within the hermaphrodite in alchemistical writings.[187]

A third set of opposites joined spirit-matter and male-female within the spiritual body—God and man.

> Thus it was fitting for the Godhead to unite itself with the pure, undefiled, sinless and perfect humanity. For just as Christ was from all eternity according to his Godhead, but according to his humanity born in the fullness of time, without any blemish or defect, an upright and perfect man, so also all within the church, who achieve the image of God, namely an indivisible God-man being (*Gott Menschlichen Wesens*), carry within themselves in their soul both God and man, God and a body ... Therefore, we are *with Christ*, according to his perfection as a God-man. We are *with him* as members [of his body], *with him* purified through his salutary tincture, at the same time united *with him*. *With him* we are made and perfected into a pure spiritual body (*Geistleib*) through the Holy Spirit. Just as Jesus Christ, the transfigured king of the kingdom of God is God and man in one person, so also we reach and achieve perfection, and at the same time are one *with him* and reach an indissoluble physicality *with him*.[188]

Rapp declared that the resurrection body of the believer combined within itself human and divine elements, God and man. Nevertheless, the Harmonist spiritual leader was careful to avoid a pantheistic notion of regenerated humanity. Man did not become God. The union of God and man in the *Geistleib* was only possible due to the essential union of the believer with Christ. Seven times in this short passage Rapp included the phrases "with Christ" or "with him." On account of this essential union, the believer's resurrection body would reflect Christ's own transfigured body, which included human and divine elements.

Rapp used decidedly alchemistical language to describe the transmutation from a physical to a spiritual body. "You seek the quintessence, your pure virgin, which is whiter than snow. This whitening comes about through cooking, when saltwater coagulates and hardens or is made in the union of the *Geistleib*."[189] Two steps in the alchemistical process are included in this sentence as part of the transmutation process to the resurrection body—whitening through cooking, and coagulation. Quintessence, or fifth essence, was employed in Rapp's theology as a rough synonym for the *Geistleib*. In the process of transformation from a physical to a spiritual body, man dies to the old "heavy physical nature" and "instead receives and possesses the fifth essence [quintessence], from the nature of the spirit, the fine pure essence drawn from the four elements."[190] The four elements--

---

[187]Schütt, *Stein der Weisen*, 373-378.
[188]MG-185, 1-5004, Box 15, Folder 6, R-122. Cf. MG-185, 1-5004, Box 15, Folder 5, N-108.
[189]MG-185/1-5004/Box 15/Folder 5/N-26.
[190]MG-185, 1-5004, Box 15, Folder 5, R-91.

earth, air, fire and water--pass away and in their place a fifth element, the quintessence, appears as a white vaporous substance.[191]

> You receive a subtle substance . . . of a very fine body, which is the quintessence, a pure virgin whiter than snow. Thus the inward [nature] becomes so clear, pure and spiritual and ascends in the heights as in the air in the form of a white fog. From this the first man was created, and here it is named the virginal milk.[192]

The quintessence was the true spiritual essence of the resurrection body. Rapp described its formation by reference to alchemistical processes. In the sermon quoted at the beginning of this paragraph, two steps of the alchemistical process were used metaphorically. The same sermon continued to describe the transmutation to the resurrection body through several other stages of the alchemistical procedure--*separation* of the pure from the impure, *dissolution, conjunction* of spiritual with physical, *sublimation*, and *ascension* (exaltation) of the pure material.[193] In a second sermon Rapp claimed that the "pure essence [quintessence] of our virginal inheritance" was "*extracted*" form the "corrupt elements" of the old nature. The "crude . . . parts were *separated* and the subtle, fine ones were *united* with the powers

---

[191] Rapp's description of the *Geistleib* as a white vaporous fog contrasts with Boehme's crystalline character. "Diese gute Kraft des tödtlichen Leibes sol in schöner / durchsichtiger crystallinischer / materialischer Eigenschaft / in geistlichem Fleische und Blute wiederkommen und ewigen Leben. Wie dan auch die gute Kraft der Erden / da dan die Erde wird auch crystallinisch sezn / und das Göttliche Licht wird in allem Wesen leuchten." Boehme, *Gespräch vom übersinnlichen Leben*, ch. 46, 1698. Quoted in Ernst Benz, *Der vollkommene Mensch nach Jacob Boehme* (Stuttgart: Kohlhammer, 1937), 122. Benz notes that Boehme's crystalline resurrection body deviated from the orthodox view of the resurrection body as a "Wiedererneuerung des verstorbenen Fleishes-Leibes." Ibid., 123.

[192] MG-185, 1-5004, Box 15, Folder 5, N-126. The concept of quintessence is found in alchemy. Schütt, *Stein der Weisen*, 357. It is likewise found in Boehme, *De Signatur rerum*, 7, §48-49, 69: "so aß der innere Mercurius (verstehet menschliche Eigenschaft) im Geschmack des Göttlichen Worts wieder von Gottes Wesen, und die vier elementische Eigenschaften assen von der Nacht Eigenschaft, alsolange bis der menschliche Mercurius sein Leben emporschwang, und *die vier Elementa in Eins transmutirete*, und das leben den Tod tingirete, welches am Creutze geschah. Da gingen die vier Eigenschaften von Ihme, das ist, Er starb der Zeit, als der Nacht ab, als den 4 Elementen, und stund auf *dem reinen Element* [=quintessence], und lebte der Ewigkeit." Cf. Gottfried Arnold, *Das Geheimnis der göttlichen Sophia*, intro. Walter Nigg (Stuttgart-Bad Cannstatt: F. Frommann, 1963), 151-152: "Denn dieses ist nichts anders als ein solch lauteres geistlich wesen oder quint-essenz von den kräfften der zukünfftigen welt / welche den gantzen neuen menschen munter / lebendig und activ machet / alle angst und kümmernüß außtreibet /die sinnen erfreuet / alle kräffte erfrischet." For Arnold, the quintessence is the life force within new humanity, whereas in Boehme (and Rapp) the focus is on the pure spiritual essence formerly found within the four elements but now distilled into a spiritual body.

[193] MG-185/1-5004/Box 15/Folder 5/N-26.

from above and *coagulated* in the oven, and in patience *ripened* and *set.*"[194] Spiritual alchemistical metaphors and language were employed by George Rapp to describe the spiritual transformation that took place in regeneration and sanctification as well as for the transmutation of the physical body into the resurrection body.

The quest for deeper knowledge by George Rapp and the Harmony Society led them to seek multiple, spiritual or allegorical meanings in the Scriptural text. The founder of the Harmony Society drew upon Friedrich Christoph Oetinger's Christianized cabbalistic interpretations to enrich his understanding of the Godhead. Boehme's theosophical depiction of the creation and Fall of Adam, which was adopted by the Harmonists as well as by the majority of radical Pietists, formed the basis of their anthropology and cosmogony. Finally, the quest for deeper knowledge led several key Harmonists to practice transmutation alchemy for a brief period. The use of alchemistical terminology for spiritual transformation was more persistent within the Harmony Society. These beliefs and practices have one element in common—all reflected a fascination with deeper, arcane knowledge. All belonged to the spiritual-mystical trajectory of Rapp's mature theology.

---

[194]MG-185/1-5004/Box 15/Folder 5/N-116.

9
Yearning for the Eschaton
(1824-1847)

By March of 1824 the Harmony Society decided to move from their second settlement, New Harmony, located on the Wabash River in Indiana. Already in the preceding year, business manager Frederick Rapp had been diligently searching for a new location for the seven-hundred-member communal society. By early April of 1824 Frederick was convinced that he had found the ideal plot of ground—land between Legionville and Sewickly Creek, Pennsylvania, directly on the Ohio River twenty miles northwest of Pittsburgh. Shortly thereafter, the land was purchased and the Harmony Society made plans to move themselves and their manufacturing operations to the new location in Pennsylvania.[1] For this purpose a steam-boat, the Ploughboy, was rented (May 24-June 6, 1824) to ferry the first contingent of Harmonists, under the leadership of George Rapp, down the Wabash and up the Ohio River to the new settlement. A second steamboat, the William Penn, was constructed specifically for the Harmony Society and used to transport the remaining goods and persons from New Harmony in the spring of 1825.[2]

Unlike the first two settlements which bore the name "Harmony," the third Harmonist settlement received the name "Economy." For the Harmonists this nomenclature was not chosen to reflect their orderly business affairs. Rather the term in Harmonist sources, besides being used as a proper name for the new town, referred both to the ordered chain of salvation-historical, eschatological events, the divine economy, as well as to their present form of communal living which would be continued in the millen-

---

[1]Karl J. R. Arndt, *George Rapp's Harmony Society 1785-1847*, rev. ed. (Teaneck, N.J.: Fairleigh Dickinson University Press, 1972), 287f.
[2]Arndt, *Rapp's Harmony Society*, 315f.

nium.³ The spiritual rather than secular sense of the proper name was underscored by the addition of the adjective "divine" to Economy in a number of Harmonist sources. George Rapp in a talk given to the young people during the 1829 Harmony Fest stated, "Almost all of you have heard the call [to become members of the Harmony Society] since we have moved here to the *divine Oekonomie*."⁴ In an undated sermon, the Harmonist leader enthusiastically praised the way of life within the communal society, "How serious and cohesive is this divine Economy!"⁵ Furthermore, in a November 1824 letter to his adopted son Frederick, Rapp proclaimed that the "true and divine human form" which had already appeared in the *Harmonie*, had sprouted more fully in the "godlike Economy" (*gottähnliche oeconomie*).⁶

The German term *Haushaltung*, referring to well managed affairs or housekeeping, is the equivalent of the Latin term *oeconomia*. Rapp on at least two occasions clearly equated the two terms "economy" and (God's) "housekeeping."⁷ Since he generally avoided Latinized terms in his sermons, the term *Haushaltung* or *Gottes Haushaltung* predominated over *Oekonomie*, when the latter was not used as a proper name for their third settlement. The correct sense is best maintained by translating *Haushaltung* with "economy" rather than "housekeeping," which has a different connotation in English. Rapp's synonymous usage of the two terms underscores the appropriateness of such translation. Martin Brecht notes that the terms "economy" and "divine economy" were widely and variously used as theological slogans in eighteenth-century German Pietist circles.⁸ The best

---

³The second half of Arndt's statement that "In naming their third settlement 'Ekonomie', however, they were thinking of a divine economy, a city in which God would dwell among men, a city in which perfection in all things was to be attained," is inadequate and does not take into account references in Rapp's sermons. Arndt, *Rapp's Harmony Society*, 308. Arndt is incorrect when he states that "the term 'Economy' also reflected their increasing concern with industry in their new location." Karl J. R. Arndt, "George Rapp's Harmony Society" in *America's Communal Utopias*, ed. Donald E. Pitzer (Chapel Hill, N.C.: University of North Carolina Press, 1997), 57-87, here 74. The term was chosen for its religious connotation. The term "divine economy" was used with reference to their communal life-style in George Rapp, *Thoughts on the Destiny of Man Particularly with Reference to the Present Times* (Harmony, Ind.: [s.n.], 1824), 63-64. Interestingly, this treatise was written in New Harmony just months before resettlement to Economy.
⁴Remarks by George Rapp, Feb. 15, 1829. OEV, Daniel Reibel's file.
⁵MG-185/1-5004/Box 15/Folder 5/O-10.
⁶Karl J. R. Arndt, *Harmony on the Wabash in Transition, 1824-1826. A Documentary History* (Worcester, Mass.: Harmony Society Press, 1982), 260.
⁷Shaker Questions, #8, MG-437/Box22/Folder 113: "die oeconomie der Haußhaltung Gottes." Cf. MG-185/1-5004/Box 15/Folder 6/R-79: "oecono:[mie] u Haußhaltung."
⁸Martin Brecht, "Johann Albrecht Bengels Theologie der Schrift," *Zeitschrift für Theologie und Kirche* 64 (1967): 99-120, here 112-113. Brecht notes that Pierre Poiret, J. W. Petersen, Joh. Chr. Pfaff, Joachim Lange, Joh. Heinrich May, and J. A. Bengel all used this concept in their written works.

known proponent of the *oeconomia divina*, however, was the Württemberg theologian, Johann Albrecht Bengel (1687-1752).

> His [Bengel's] salvation history was based on the idea of an *oeconomia divina*, God's housekeeping, which was constituted by a firm plan for the world, worked out chronologically from the beginning to the end. This scheme was deduced from the Bible ... [I]t conferred an understanding of the dealings of God with man, not only in the past; it revealed the future, not to gratify idle curiosity, but to enable man better to walk in God's ways.[9]

Some of Rapp's sermons reflected Bengel's conception of the divine economy as an ordered, salvation-historical and chronological scheme of God's dealings with mankind.[10] Rapp's usage of the term, however, focused not on God's past activity but on imminent eschatological events. George Rapp was convinced that members of the Harmony Society were uniquely "able to understand the divine economy" (*die göttliche Haußhaltung*) since they had been "trained in the school of the Holy Spirit."[11] Knowledge of this divine economy had already begun to sprout within the Harmony congregation in the "beautiful ... plans for the future" that would come to fruition in the millennial kingdom, at the "promised day of the Lord."[12] Nevertheless, "deeper research to penetrate into the secrets of the kingdom of God, [to gain] accurate knowledge of the order and economy (*haußhaltung*) of the kingdom of God" ought continuously to be pursued.[13] Rapp thus emphasized the eschatological nature of the divine economy and the unique ability of the Harmony Society to understand God's plan for the end times.

In other instances, the Harmonist spiritual leader employed the term *Haushaltung* to refer to the communal form of government that existed in the present dispensation within the Harmony Society and that would be

---

[9] W. R. Ward, *Early Evangelicalism. A Global Intellectual History 1670-1789* (Cambridge: Cambridge University Press, 2006), 117. Cf. Brecht, "Bengels Theologie der Schrift," 112-116, for a good discussion of the *oeconomia divina* in Bengel's theology, and Johann Albrecht Bengel, *Erklärte Offenbarung Johannis: oder vielmehr Jesu Christ: aus dem revidirten Grund-Text übersetzt durch die prophetischen Zahlen ausgeschlossen und allen, die auf das Werk und Wort des Herrn achten, und dem, was vor der Thür ist, würdiglich entgegen zu kommen begehren, vor Augen geleget* (Stuttgart: Fr. Brodhag, 1834), §45, 112: "Mehr angeregte Progression gibt endlich das wahre Weltalter mit seinen historischen und prophetischen Zeitläufen ... wodurch die Wahrheit der ganzen heiligen Schrift alten und neuen Testaments, insonderheit aber auch der Offenbarung ausbündig bestärket, und die darinn begriffene wunderschöne *göttliche Oeconomie* aufgeschlossen wird ... zur Betrachtung alles göttlichen Thuns, wie es sich durch alle Weltzeiten erstrecket." Bengel, ibid., 135-136, declared that the Book of Revelation spoke "von der Stiftung und dem Ziel der *göttlichen Oeconomie*."

[10] In MG-185/1-5004/Box 15/Folder 5/O-61 Rapp used the term *Ekonomie* for stages of salvation history.

[11] MG-437/ Box 22/ Folder 82B/ Gr. B-60.

[12] MG-185/1-5004/Box 15/Folder 5/O-10.

[13] MG-437/Box 22/Folder 82B/B-56.

universally practiced in the millennial kingdom.[14] In one sermon Rapp made a distinction between the "old economy of this world" (*alten Haußhaltung dieser Welt*) outside of the Harmony Society and the "new economy in the kingdom of peace," the millennium.[15] In the latter the apostolic model of community of goods (Acts 2-4) would form the economic basis for deep-seated, inner-personal unity.

> Creation knows nothing nobler than hearts and lives that have become one [Acts 2 and 4], that are united for a common goal, hands and souls voluntarily and indissolubly clasped together. . . . This is the beautiful *economy* (*Haußhaltung*) . . . [when] many are joined to one another, when the feeling of common blessedness is ordered by the Word of the Holy Spirit. The government of the kingdom of God is composed of this happy family.[16]

It is not unlikely that Rapp adopted the name "Economy" for the third Harmonist settlement from his reading of Bengel's salvation-historical and eschatological writings.[17] Even if this should be the case, the Harmonist spiritual leader gave his own distinctive twist to Bengel's concept of the *oeconomia divina* by emphasizing eschatological events almost exclusively and by including the notion of a communal form of government in the millennium.

It was most significant that the Harmony Society at this juncture of its historical development chose the eschatologically-tinged name "Economy" for its third settlement. Whereas the proper name "Harmony" reflected the Society's commitment to apostolic unity and community of goods, the name "Economy" in Harmonist sources combined the notion of communalism with a strongly eschatological focus. In the 1820s the eschatological yearnings of the Harmonists reached a fever pitch. According to Rapp's later calculation, Christ would return visibly to establish his millennial kingdom on earth in 1829. Later this date was changed to 1836, Bengel's reckoned date for the beginning of the millennium, still later to circa 1850. Thus the last decades of George Rapp's life (d. 1847) were characterized by an ongoing heightened expectation of the imminent inauguration of the end-time events prophesied in the Book of Revelation. The Harmonists believed that their tenure in the wilderness as the Sunwoman would soon be over. Short-

---

[14] F. C. Oetinger likewise argued in *Güldene Zeit*, 30, that the apostolic model of community of goods would be practiced within the millennial kingdom. Friedhelm Groth, *Die "Wiederbringung aller Dinge" im württembergischen Pietismus* (Göttingen: Vandenheock & Ruprecht, 1984), 115. The author has demonstrated in chapter eight that Rapp was well acquainted with Oetinger's writings.

[15] MG 185/ Box 15/ Folder 4/L-10.

[16] MG-437/Box 22/Folder 82B/D-62.

[17] The Harmony Society in 1829 owned at least two copies of Bengel's *Welt-alter*. Rapp quoted from Bengel's commentary on Revelation, *Erklärte Offenbarung*. Karl J. R. Arndt, *George Rapp's Successors and Material Heirs 1847- 1916* (Teaneck, N.J.: Fairleigh Dickinson University Press, 1971), 418.

ly they would reign with Christ on earth as priests in his millennial kingdom.

In chapter seven, the concept of two trajectories within George Rapp's mature theology as reflected in his sermons was introduced. A biblical-eschatological trajectory was revealed in the Harmonist leader's faithfulness to core Reformation doctrine, to churchly Pietist emphases, and to "Anabaptist" ecclesiology. A mystical-spiritual trajectory was discovered in the Society's quietistic mysticism and Sophiological beliefs, as well as in its theosophical cosmogony and anthropology, Rapp's use of cabbalistic notions to describe God, and of spiritual alchemistical language for the processes of regeneration and sanctification. In this chapter the later eschatological beliefs of the Harmony Society will be examined. These beliefs properly fit almost entirely within the biblical-eschatological trajectory, as they were based on a literal, biblicist, premillennial interpretation of the Book of Revelation and of the Old and New Testament prophets. Nevertheless, in one aspect of their eschatology, the belief in the renewal of the earth and mankind to its pristine pre-Fall state in the *eschaton* (which included androgyny), Boehmist theosophical notions or the mystical-spiritual trajectory were likewise evidenced.

In this chapter, the history of the Harmony Society in the Economy era until Rapp's death (1824-1847) will first be briefly depicted. Then the eschatological presuppositions and approach of George Rapp and the Harmony Society will be compared and contrasted with other key Württemberg Pietists. It will be shown that although Rapp was clearly influenced by the eschatological tradition within Württemberg Pietism, he nevertheless rejected key aspects of that tradition in favor of his own original interpretation. In the third section, Rapp's order of eschatological events will be outlined and elaborated. The sectarian-inspired glorification of their community and the key role assigned to the Harmony Society in the *eschaton* will be discussed. The universalistic concept of the restoration of all things, so prominent in Württemberg Pietism, will likewise be unpacked.

History of the Harmony Society in the Economy Era (1824-1847)

The reasons for the transfer of the Harmony Society from its location on the Wabash River in Indiana to Pennsylvania were not clearly delineated in contemporary primary source documents. Two letters written by George Rapp immediately after moving to Economy in June 1824, however, provide some insight into this question. On June 7, Rapp wrote to the remaining Harmonists in Indiana that the new settlement was "one of the healthiest places in all of America."[18] This fact was important since New Harmony's swampy location on the Wabash River bred malaria and other disease and

---

[18]Arndt, *Doc. Hist. 1824-1826*, 31.

contributed significantly to the high mortality rate during the New Harmony decade (1814-1824). The German obituary of George Rapp, printed shortly after his death on August 7, 1847, likewise stated that the Society returned to Pennsylvania "because of health issues" (*um der Gesundheit willen*).[19] On both June 7 and June 19, 1824 the elder Rapp underscored the spiritual benefits of the move to Pennsylvania. The challenges of the move and resettlement would serve to wean the Harmonists from their mother's milk and teach them to digest stronger (spiritual) food (Heb 5:12-13).[20] The Harmony Society, like Abraham, had been commanded (by God) to "leave your present abode, leave your fatherland . . . and continue the pilgrimage with good courage."[21] "Whoever, therefore, seriously desires the kingdom of heaven, let such a one leave to the sensuous Lot . . . the fat valley of Sodom, but you who are homesick hurry toward the Promised Land that you may take possession of it with the sons of Abraham."[22]

In addition to these reasons, several other practical considerations certainly influenced the decision to transfer their Society to Economy, Pennsylvania. The Harmony Society did not receive the large influx of emigrants that they had expected during the great migration from Württemberg (1816-1820), and therefore needed less land than they possessed in Indiana. Relationships with their "English" neighbors were somewhat strained on the western frontier, making the return to the bi-cultural (German-English) state of Pennsylvania that much more appealing. Unlike Economy, New Harmony was isolated from the eastern markets where many Harmonist products were sold.[23] In January 1825 the village of New Harmony was sold to the Scottish social reformer, Robert Owen, who established a short-lived communal society there.

Within a short period of time the hard-working German immigrants had erected a flourishing village on the banks of the Ohio River. Approximately one hundred fifty neat brick homes were built on wide streets for family or surrogate family units. The church, love feast hall, and the large imposing Rapp house with formal gardens and a labyrinth behind formed the center

---

[19]Karl J. R. Arndt, *George Rapp's Years of Glory. Economy on the Ohio, 1834-1847. George Rapp's Third Harmony. A Documentary History* (New York: Peter Lang, 1987), 1074.

[20]Arndt, *Doc. Hist. 1824-1826*, 30-31, 42. Arndt states that Rapp justified the move "by quoting scripture . . . [that] it was time for the Sunwoman of Revelation to again flee into the wilderness." The author has found no appeal to the Sunwoman motif in the primary sources as justification for the move. Arndt, "Rapp's Harmony Society," 73.

[21]Ibid., 42-44.

[22]Ibid., 42-43. The term "homesickness" (*Heimweh*) is an allusion to Jung-Stilling's novel, *Das Heimweh*, in which the main character is homesick for the future millennial kingdom. Five copies of this novel were owned by the Harmony Society. Karl J. R. Arndt, *A Documentary History of the Indiana Decade of the Harmony Society, 1814-1819* (Indianapolis: Indiana Historical Society, 1975), 261.

[23]Arndt, "Rapp's Harmony Society," 73.

of the community. The Society produced wool and cotton yarn and cloth as well as flour in a four-story woolen mill and a five- story flour and cotton mill equipped with the latest steam-driven machinery. George Rapp's granddaughter Gertrude oversaw the silk industry of the Harmony Society, which was inaugurated in 1826. By 1831 the Society had become one of the leading producers of silk in the United States.[24] In 1839 and 1844 Harmonist silk won the gold prize at the New York exhibition of silk manufacturers.[25] Besides textiles, the Society produced hats, shoes, whiskey and wine, which were shipped as far south as New Orleans and as far north as Boston. Not only did Economy become an economic showplace in mid-nineteenth century America. The Society further developed its cultural activities during the Economy era. A professional Pittsburgh musician, W. C. Peters, was hired in 1827 to give musical instruction to all willing Harmonists. With Peters' input and Christoph Müller's direction the Harmony orchestra began to perform increasingly sophisticated symphonic pieces by world renowned composers in concerts attended by their own community and outside guests. Likewise during the early Economy era the Harmony Society established a well-stocked museum of natural history that was open to the public.[26]

Conflict within the Harmony Society increased sharply during the first decades at Economy. In 1827 a revised constitution was submitted to the membership for ratification. The six articles of the new document paralleled exactly those of the original 1805 Articles of Association, albeit in firmer and more legally binding terminology. One phrase in the prologue, however, was new. It stated that "the Community ... formed by George Rapp and many others ... [was] faithfully derived from the sacred Scriptures, [and] include[s] the *Government of the Patriarchal Age* [my emphasis], united to the Community of Property, adopted in the days of the Apostles."[27] With this statement George Rapp, as the patriarch and leader of the Society, claimed more power for himself than he had previously. Opposition to these articles mounted and some members withdrew rather than sign them. After 1826, the Society became embroiled more frequently and virulently than previously in lawsuits with disgruntled former members.[28] While still in Germany and during the early years of the Harmony Society's existence, Rapp preached an imminent return of Christ without setting any specific dates.[29] According to a contemporary account (1833) by a newly-withdrawn member, Jonathan Wagner, tension began to arise within the community in the New Harmony era when Christ failed to return to inaugu-

---

[24]Arndt, *Rapp's Harmony Society*, 392-394 and 579f.
[25]Arndt, *Doc. Hist. 1834-1847*, 411, 713 and 801.
[26]Arndt, "Rapp's Harmony Society," 74.
[27]Translated and quoted in Arndt, *Rapp's Harmony Society*, 355.
[28]Arndt, "Rapp's Harmony Society," 75.
[29]This topic will be discussed more thoroughly in the section on eschatological presuppositions.

rate the millennial kingdom as expected. Rapp's preaching and predictive abilities were called into question by some younger Harmonists. To quell the rising discontent and to refocus attention on the imminent end, the elder Rapp, according to Wagner, calculated circa 1820 that the return of Christ would occur on Sept. 15, 1829.[30] During this period of tension particularly the young people became disillusioned with their spiritual leader and questioned the Society's discouragement of the marital relationship and the not-so-subtle social pressure exerted on members to adopt a celibate lifestyle.[31] Rapp's preferential treatment of his erstwhile laboratory assistant, Hildegard Mutschler, after she ran away to get married was resented by the community.[32]

September 15, 1829 came and went uneventfully, resulting in deep disappointment for Rapp and the Harmonists. A few days later, on Sept. 24, however, their despair was turned to joy.[33] An elaborately sealed letter arrived at Economy from Bernhard Mueller, the illegitimate son of Baron Dalberg of Aschaffenburg, Germany. Mueller, who referred to himself as Count Leon, Proli or the Lion of Judah, had sent in 1829 letters to numerous monarchs and ecclesiastical leaders in Europe, calling the faithful to depart from Europe, which was doomed for destruction, and to gather in America. He likewise sent a letter to the Harmony Society at that time and received an enthusiastic reply and invitation to come to Economy. On October 18, 1831 Count Leon arrived with a retinue of forty persons at the Harmonist settlement and was welcomed warmly. Within a short time, however, con-

---

[30]Wagner's depiction of the Harmony Society is negatively biased and must be employed critically. Nevertheless, his recounting of Rapp's eschatological views and miscalculation is at least partially confirmed by other sources. Wagner gives a fuller description than is found in any other primary source for this topic. Jonathan Wagner, *Geschichte u. Verhältnisse der Harmoniegesellschaft* (Vaihingen an der Enz: Deininger, 1833), 9.

[31]Ibid. Cf. Arndt, "Rapp's Harmony Society," 76.

[32]The resentment over this issue was particularly noted in the minutes of the anti-Rapp group during the secession (Feb. 13, 1832). Karl J. R. Arndt, *Economy on the Ohio, 1826-1834. George Rapp's Third Harmony. A Documentary History* (Worchester, Mass.: Harmony Society Press, 1984), 702-703.

[33]George Rapp described this change of emotion in his reply on Oct. 29, 1829 to Count Leon's letter the previous month. "Und gerade in dieser dunklen Nacht habt ihr uns überrascht durch euer Schreiben, welches die Finsterniß zertheilte, so daß wir den schönen Morgenstern am Kirchenhimmel wieder glänzen und den Herrn in den Wolken des Himmels, nemlich in Gesellschaften verbrüderter Seelen kommen sehen ... Ihr könnt kaum denken, was euer Schreiben als es in der Versammlung verlesen wurde, für einen Eindruck in den Seelen, und Herzen der Heimweh kranken machte. Alles lebt hier in denen Aussichten der Aufschließung des Reichs Jesu Christi aufs neue auf, die mehrsten weinten vor Freuden über die Erbarmungen des Herrn, *unsre Zeitrechnung der 3 1/2 Zeiten des Weibs in der Wüste, lief zu Ende in der Mitte Sept. dieses Jahrs und am 24ten nemlichen Monats,* erhielten wir euren Brief welcher den Tag ankündet, ja, ja, wenn der Winter ausgeschneyet tritt der schöne Sommer ein." Arndt, *Doc. Hist. 1826-1834*, 443.

flict arose between the bogus count and the Harmonist leader. The count's bombastic claims to be the reincarnated Messiah and his rejection of celibacy did not sit well with confirmed Rappites, but was enthusiastically received by less convinced Harmonists. On January 28, 1832, a document crafted by representatives of the 175 seceders deposed George and Frederick Rapp from leadership and declared the count their temporary head.[34] The pro-Rappite contingent, consisting of two-thirds of the membership, countered with a statement expressing full confidence in their Society's leadership. In March 1832, the seceders left Economy and established a short-lived communal experiment named the New Philadelphia Society at nearby Philippsburg (today Monaca), Pennsylvania.[35]

Shortly after the schism, Frederick Rapp died at the age of fifty-nine on June 24, 1834. With the passing of Frederick, George Rapp assumed both spiritual and secular leadership of the Society, albeit with the help of a business manager. The community after 1832 was a smaller, purged group of approximately 450 Rapp loyalists. Following the schism, new members were no longer accepted, the only exceptions being the children and a few close relatives of current members. In 1836, Article VI of the Articles of Association, which provided for the return of property to departing members, was eliminated from the document. Although the Harmony Society would continue to exist until 1905, the 1832 schism clearly "marked the beginning of the end" for the rapidly aging celibate community.[36]

Rapp's Eschatological Presuppositions and Approach

Before outlining Rapp's interpretation of the Book of Revelation, it is expedient to examine the Harmonist leader's presuppositions that influenced his approach to the last book of the Bible. George Rapp's presuppositions will be compared and contrasted with members of the "Württemberg eschatological tradition." This tradition built on the exegetical commentaries and writings of Johann Albrecht Bengel (1687-1752), who in turn was influenced by the eschatological hope of the founder of churchly branch of German Lutheran Pietism, Philipp Jacob Spener.[37] Bengel's importance in the realm of eschatological interpretation did not lie in his complex chronological and eschatological reckoning per se, which has not been adopted *wholesale* by any theologians after the dawn of the nineteenth century. Rather the importance of his interpretation was that it avoided some of the pitfalls and extremes of the "false chiliasm" that was rejected by Article 17 of the Augs-

---

[34]Ibid., 675-683.
[35]See Arndt, *Rapp's Harmony Society*, 449-499, for a detailed description of the 1832 schism.
[36]Arndt, "Rapp's Harmony Society," 78.
[37]See Groth, *Wiederbringung*, 70f. for the influence of Spener on Bengel.

burg Confession.[38] Bengel, like Spener before him, made chiliasm acceptable in Lutheran churchly Pietist circles in eighteenth-century Württemberg.[39] Furthermore, the Württemberg theologian spawned a devoted school of disciples in the duchy (and beyond), who either adopted his approach to the last book of the Bible wholesale or were influenced by it. Scholars speak of two groups of Bengel's disciples, a conservative wing that adopted their mentor's teachings virtually unchanged, and a more "creative" wing that appropriated other influences and further developed Bengel's teachings.[40] Both wings were part of the "Württemberg eschatological tradition," which in this volume refers to those pastors and theologians who adopted either a conservative or looser, Bengelian-influenced approach to the book of Revelation. The advantage of the term "Württemberg eschatological tradition" as opposed to "Bengel and his disciples" is that it focuses specifically on distinctive, Bengelian-influenced, eschatological beliefs among churchly and radical Pietists in the duchy. George Rapp was well acquainted with Bengel's eschatological system. The Harmony Society owned two copies of Bengel's *Welt-Alter* in 1829. The Harmonist leader likewise had access to his *Erklärte Offenbarung*, since he borrowed passages from this commentary on Revelation in at least two sermons.[41] Rapp belonged to that second "more creative" group of Württemberg Pietists, who were influenced by the Bengelian eschatological tradition, yet adapted or changed many of its central tenets.

---

[38]Bengel, *Erklärte Offenbarung*, Beschluß Stück IV, 676.

[39]Spener's eschatological "hopes for better times for the church" was deemed non-heretical in the 1694 Pietist edict in Württemberg. In this edict, Article 17 of the Augsburg Confession was (re)interpreted to reject "radical chiliasm," but not the milder Spenerian form. The way was thus paved in the duchy for Bengel's more radical eschatology. Groth, *Wiederbringung*, 52.

[40]The German literature does not use the term "Württemberg eschatological tradition." Rather it speaks of the Bengel and his disciples (*Schüler*). See Gerhard Schäfer, *Zu Erbauen und zu Erhalten das rechte Heil der Kirche. Eine Geschichte der evangelischen Landeskirche in Württemberg* (Stuttgart: Steinkopf, 1984), 156-159; and Martin Brecht, "Der württembergische Pietismus," in *Geschichte des Pietismus*, vol. 2, *Der Pietismus im achtzehnten Jahrhundert*, ed. Martin Brecht and Klaus Deppermann (Göttingen: Vandenhoeck & Ruprecht, 1995), 225-295, here 259-285. Groth, *Wiederbringung*, 89; Brecht, "Der württembergische Pietismus," 259-285; and Gottfried Mälzer, *Johann Albrecht Bengel. Leben und Werk* (Stuttgart: Calwer Verlag, 1979), 373 speak of two wings of Bengel's disciples. Members of the conservative wing include Philipp Burk, P. F. Hiller, J. F. Reuß, J. C. Storr, and Israel Hartmann. F. C. Oetinger, P. M. Hahn, J. L. Fricker, K. F. Hartmann, Michael Hahn, and J. J. Friedrich belonged to the second wing, as did George Rapp.

[41]See footnote 17 above. Rapp gave credit to Bengel in MG-437/Box 22/Folder 82B/A-3 (taken from *Erklärte Offenbarung*, 616-617), but not in MG-185/1-5004/Box 15/Folder 6/R-39 (ibid., 612-618).

Progressive Revelation

Like Johann Albrecht Bengel before him, Rapp was convinced that God's revelation was progressive and successive.[42] In a sermon on Col 1:25-26, the Harmonist leader explained that the Apostle Paul had been commissioned to preach the mystery that had been hidden from past generations, but now was revealed to the church—that Jews and Gentiles were united under the headship of Christ.[43] According to Rapp, Paul understood more of the divine mystery than did the Old Testament prophets before him. However, "God ordered and desired that the greatest mystery would be saved until the very latest time."[44] This mystery was not comprehended by the apostle to the Gentiles. It was revealed first to Christ and finally, in the form of the Book of Revelation, to the Harmony congregation. Just as the New Testament was the "key" to the Old Testament, so the Book of Revelation was the "key" to the New Testament.[45] Revelation was the "third perfect testament" in the Bible and "a gift from the hand of God."[46] It was "the only [Bible] book which was written due to God's emphatic command, and was dictated by him."[47] It contained vitally important information about imminent eschatological events--Christ as Lamb, angels, state of the righteous dead, Satan and his angels, heaven, the kingdom of God on earth, death, hell, the lake of fire, and the last judgment.[48] Rapp followed closely in Bengel's eschatological footsteps when he stressed the crucial importance of the Book of Revelation.

Literal Biblical Hermeneutic

Like Bengel and his disciple Oetinger, Rapp rejected an inappropriate "spiritualization" of the biblical concepts found in the Book of Revelation through a "false mysticism" or "rationalism." The former eradicated the historical nature of the book through "endless allegorizing and types." The latter sought merely to uncover the spiritual message hidden beneath the crude Judaic language.[49] In contrast, Rapp's approach to Revelation can best

---

[42]Groth, Wiederbringung, 66.
[43]MG-185/1-5004/Box 15/Folder 5/O-55.
[44]MG-185/1-5004/Box 15/Folder 6/R-79.
[45]Groth, Wiederbringung, 65. Cf. Bengel, Erklärte Offenbarung, 41-42: "Also ist die Offenbarung ... so beschaffen, daß wir, sie zu verstehen, andere Propheten nicht nöthig haben, sondern vielmehr vermittelst der Offenbarung andere Propheten verstehen lernen müssen. Es führet ... seinen Schlüssel bei sich."
[46]MG-185/1-5004/Box 15/Folder 6/Q-138 and MG-185/1-5004/Box 15/Folder 6/R-79.
[47]MG-185/1-5004/Box 15/Folder 6/R-146. This sentiment is likewise found in Bengel, Erklärte Offenbarung, 132.
[48]MG-185/1-5004/Box 15/Folder 6/R-146. Cf. Bengel, Erklärte Offenbarung, 136.
[49]1834 Vorwort by W. Hoffmann to Bengel's Erklärte Offenbarung, VI.

be described as literal and biblicist. That is, he believed in the literal, historical fulfillment of the events depicted, often in symbolic and apocalyptic language, in Revelation as well as in Old and New Testament prophecy. Rapp did not uphold a "spiritualizing" or allegorical hermeneutic of these texts, corresponding to the mystical-spiritual trajectory likewise found in his theology. His literal hermeneutic reflected the biblical-eschatological trajectory. It was rooted in a strongly-held conviction of the inerrancy of Scripture. It was applied by Bengel, Bengel's disciples and Rapp, not just to propositional statements found within the prophetic and apocalyptic works, but to biblical numbers and chronology as well.[50]

George Rapp applied a literal biblical hermeneutic to the Old and New Testament prophecies concerning Israel. He taught that those prophecies concerning Israel's conversion and return to the land of Palestine would be fulfilled literally prior to and during the millennium.[51] God's plan for the Jewish people was not set aside or eradicated through the development of the New Testament people of God, the church. Rapp distinguished clearly between "physical" Israel (the Jewish people) and "spiritual" Israel (the church). According to the Harmonist leader, during the millennium both of these entities, that is:

> Physical and spiritual Israel would form God's nation state in the Jewish ancestral land. . . . But the Jews who dwell in the land and in Jerusalem are no longer Jews with regard to their religion, but Christians, although Jewish with regard to their national background. For the Jewish temple with its ceremonies can never again be revived. The religion of Jesus has supplanted this typological shadow. On Mount Moriah then nothing other than a Christian church can be erected. . . . For the old has passed away . . . and physical Israel has been transformed into spiritual Israel.[52]

Although he clearly distinguished between the two peoples, Rapp made clear that the Jewish people in the millennium were Christ-followers, Christians with regard to their religion, though Jews with regard to their nationality. On Mount Moriah a Christian church, not a Jewish temple, would be erected. Old Testament sacrifices would not be reinstituted in the millennium, since Christ had paid already the ultimate sacrifice for sins. Rapp's

---

[50]Stephen Holthaus, "Prämillenniarismus in Deutschland. Historische Anmerkungen zur Eschatologie der Erweckten im 19. und 20. Jahrhundert," *Pietismus und Neuzeit* 20 (1994): 191-211, here 208.

[51]This topic will be discussed in more detail under "Immigration to Palestine" below.

[52]MG-185/1-5004/Box 15/Folder 6/R-23. Cf. MG-437 / Box 22/ Folder 82B/ Gr D-20. The first pastor of Korntal, Johann Jakob Friedrich, in *Glaubens- und Hoffnung-Blick des Volks Gottes in der anti-christlichen Zeit aus den göttlichen Weissagungen gezogen* ([s.l.]: [s.n.], 1801), 34-37, argued that the Old Testament sacrifices would be renewed in the millennium, although they would not take away sin, but only reveal God's wrath in response to sin.

approach to Old and New Testament prophecies concerning Israel was influenced by the later eschatological tradition of Württemberg Pietism.

Biblical Numerology and Chronology

A literal hermeneutic was applied to the numbers and chronological references in Revelation and the Old Testament prophets. Johann Albrecht Bengel believed that God had revealed to him in 1724 the exegetical key to unlock the chronological references in the Book of Revelation.[53] The Württemberg theologian was convinced that the number 666 in Rev 13:18 referred to natural years, which he correlated with the high point of the Roman papacy beginning in the reign of Gregory VII.[54] From this fixed point, the time when the beast from the sea (Rev 13:1) reached its full strength, Bengel erected his chronological system that extended backward and forward in time. A second key element of his chronological scheme was Bengel's equation of the 666 *natural* years with the forty-two *prophetic* months of Rev 13:5. A prophetic month in his reckoning was thus equivalent to 15 6/7 natural years (666 divided by 42). The number 666 served thus as the boundary between natural or common time and prophetic time.[55] A complex system based on these two key numbers permitted the Württemberg theologian to correlate virtually all the eschatological events of Revelation with either past profane or church history or with datable future events such as the onset of the millennium in 1836. It should be remembered that the use of biblical numbers to erect an elaborate chronology neither originated nor died with Bengel, but was pursued by many biblical literalists in the last three centuries.[56]

George Rapp approached the numbers and chronological references in the book of Revelation in a fashion remarkably similar to that of Bengel. The similarity between the two men's approach to the text was nowhere more evident than in the following Rapp sermon.

---

[53]Bengel, *Erklärte Offenbarung*, Preface to first edition, §II, XIV.

[54]Bengel, *Erklärte Offenbarung*, 433: "Das päbstliche Königreich hat Hildebrand oder Gregor VII aufgerichtet. Unter allen römischen Bischöfen kommt mit Gregor VII keiner, sonderlich vor ihm in Betrachtung... die Aehnlichkeit des hildebrandischen Pabstthums mit der Beschreibung des Thiers in der Weissagung." Cf. Groth, *Wiederbringung*, 68. Johann Heinrich Jung-Stilling, in *Erster Nachtrag zur Siegesgeschichte der Christlichen Religion in einer gemeinnützigen Erklärung der Offenbarung Johannis* (Nürnberg: Raw, 1805), 61-62 adapted Bengel's system, stating that in 1170, the reign of Pope Alexander III, the beast from the sea reached its full power. When 666 is added to 1170, the year of the dawn of the millennium, 1836, is achieved. This is thus an adaption of the Bengelian system.

[55]Groth, *Wiederbringung*, 68 and 290, n. 42.

[56]J. J. Zimmermann anticipated the return of Christ in 1693. After Bengel, Jung-Stilling (1836), the Adventists (1843), Frederick Franson (1897), Henry Grattan Guinness (1917), William Blackstone (1916-1934) and Hal Lindsey (1980s) all set dates for the return of Christ. Holthaus, "Prämillenniarismus in Deutschland," 211.

The beast with the seven heads and ten horns, which John saw come out of the sea, was the Roman papacy as it reached its peak 600 years ago. John saw another beast with two horns like a lamb, Rev 13:11, arise from the earth. It took its beginning in 1776 and ended in 1836. For the number 666 should be understood as prophetic days. Each week consists of seven common days, that is, six workdays and one Sabbath. For all things proceed through the number seven. . . . God has taken away from Satan his Sabbaths, and only allowed him the six workdays. Therefore the number 666 no longer consists in the number seven, rather in the number six. If one multiplies the number 666 with its six workdays, one arrives at 3996 days . . . or eleven years minus nineteen days. For the 1260 days, [Rev] 12:6 and the three and a half times of the [Sun]woman have one meaning. Both numbers refer to the flight of the Sunwoman.[57]

This is the only instance that the author has discovered where Rapp adopted a historicist interpretation of a text within Revelation 4-22. Like Bengel, he interpreted the beast arising from the sea as the Roman papacy at the height of its power 600 years ago.[58] However, unlike Bengel, who argued that the beast from the *earth* arose in the distant past, Rapp placed this creature/person in the immediate past, namely from 1776 to 1836, the latter being Bengel's date for the onset of the first of two millennia.[59] Instead of understanding 666 as natural years as his prominent predecessor had, Rapp construed them to be "prophetic days." The number seven, indicating the Sabbath, was the number of perfection, and therefore taken from Satan, to whom remained only the six workdays and 666. Like Bengel before him, Rapp engaged in eschatological mathematics when he multiplied 666 with the six workdays. The meaning of the resulting number, eleven years minus nineteen days, remains unclear. For both Rapp and the Württemberg theologian the numbers 666 and the forty-two months of Rev 13:5 (equal to the 1260 days and the three and half times of the Sunwoman in the wilderness) were the crux of their eschatological reckoning.[60] These key numbers, however, were used quite differently by the two men. In contrast to Bengel, one of Rapp's concerns was to equate the Sunwoman of Revelation 12 with his own Society and to discover the eschatological timeline in reference to her. Rapp's occasional attempts to demonstrate the biblical basis of the Harmony Society as the Sunwoman in the wilderness was a dis-

---

[57]MG-185/ Box 15/ Folder 5/ Group C-15. Cf. Bengel, *Erklärte Offenbarung*, 422-445.

[58]The dating is closer to Jung-Stilling's adaptation of Bengel's approach, that is ca. 1200, and not during the era of Gregory VII. See footnote 54 above.

[59]Bengel taught that "das andere Thier aus der Erden [ist] diejenige Macht, welche die Lehre von des Pabsts Gewalt am eigentlichsten, wiewohl aus eigenem Interesse unterhält. Ob und was die Dominikaner-, Franziskaner- und Jesuiten-Orden, die Inquisition sc. dazu beitragen, ist noch nicht zu erachten." Bengel, *Erklärte Offenbarung*, 458.

[60]Rapp also developed other eschatological reckoning schemes. See his scheme to arrive at 1836 below.

tinctly sectarian endeavor that was absent in the Württemberg churchly Pietist eschatological tradition. Rapp thus altered for his own purposes Bengel's key discovery of the correlation of the 666 natural years with the forty-two prophetic months of Revelation 13. Despite this change, both men's approach to biblical numbers and chronology remained remarkably similar.

Dating the Return of Christ

Bengel's eschatological system included dating the time of the inauguration of the millennium in the year 1836. While still in Württemberg and in the first decade and a half of the Harmony Society's existence, George Rapp, unlike Bengel, refrained from setting a date for the return of Christ. Rather he stressed the imminence of Christ's return in a number of pastoral letters written prior to emigration. In one such letter dated Sept. 12, 1798, Rapp declared that "the [remaining] time is very short and everything proves and testifies to the imminent coming of our Lord Jesus."[61] A similar stance was adopted during the early years of the Harmony Society. George wrote a letter to Frederick Rapp on March 25, 1810, "My waiting for the new era becomes ever stronger.... I think that the grapevine has budded," a sure sign of the "near return of Christ."[62] Frederick penned a similar sentiment. "[T]he signs of the times pointed out to us by the scripture let us apprehend sufficiently, that the coming of the Lord is not far off."[63] Rapp stressed imminence because, according to the earlier Knittlingen Report of the interrogation of the Separatist leader from March to May 1803, that is, before emigration, "no one [of his group] did or was able to set a specific date [for the return of Christ]."[64] Later however, this stress on imminence was replaced with specific dating for Christ's return. Harmonist Jonathan Wagner's 1833 account of the Society's history, written shortly after he departed from Economy during the 1832 schism, reported:

> After the *Harmonie* had existed for approximately fifteen years [circa 1820] . . . many young people began to doubt the teaching and preaching of their superintendent [Rapp], for he had already announced the end of the world for a long time without it appearing.... He solemnly declared his earlier predictions once again, yes, he even swore that his congregation, was "the woman clothed with the sun, who had fled into the wilderness where she would be

---

[61]MG-185, 1-5005, Box 16, Folder 1, #24. Cf. Pastoral Letter from Feb. 3, 1799, MG-437, Box 25, #15: "daran kan wohl merken, daß das Ende nahe [ist]. " MG-185, 1-5005, Box 16, Folder 1, #20.

[62]Karl J. R. Arndt, *Harmony on the Connoquenessing, 1803-1815. A Documentary History* (Worcester, Mass.: Harmony Society Press, 1980), 380-381.

[63]Letter from Frederick Rapp to Samuel Worchester, Dec. 19, 1822. Karl J. R. Arndt, *A Documentary History of the Indiana Decade of the Harmony Society, 1820-1824* (Indianapolis: Indiana Historical Society, 1978), 512.

[64]Karl J. R. Arndt, *George Rapp's Separatists, 1700-1803. A Documentary History* (Worcester, Mass.: Harmony Society Press, 1980), 351.

nourished for a time and two times" . . . a space of time of twenty-four and a half years, which began with their first Harmony Fest on February 14 [sic], 1805.[65]

Much of Wagner's account is biased and must be used cautiously. This statement, however, not only rings true, but the dating of mid-September 1829 for the return of Christ is confirmed in George Rapp's response written in October 1829 to Count Leon's letter. "Our time reckoning of the three and half times of the woman in the wilderness came to an end in the middle of September of this year," the Harmonist leader wrote.[66] This time reckoning was arrived at by multiplying the three and half times of Rev 12:14 by seven, the number of perfection, thus arriving at twenty-four and a half years from the date of the establishment of the Harmony Society as the Sunwoman in the wilderness on February 15, 1805. Once again, the number seven and the three and a half times or forty-two prophetic months (see above) were crucial to Rapp's eschatological reckoning.

Wagner likewise provides valuable insight into Rapp's resolution of the quandary that arose when Christ did not personally and visibly return in 1829.

> Up to this time Rapp always had preached the personal return of Jesus Christ, but now he alleged, that Jesus Christ first would come in spirit and even had come in the letter received [written on behalf of Count Leon by his adjutant, Johann Georg Göntgen], which announced the arrival of so many believers, who desired to join them. But afterward, when all the good people were gathered together and God's judgments upon Europe and particularly upon Germany and France were completed, the second coming of Christ would occur in 1836, when he would come down personally from heaven on a white horse [allusion to Rev 19:11].[67]

Rapp thus solved the problem of Christ's apparent non-appearance in 1829 by claiming that the Messiah had indeed returned at the proper time, but *in spirit* with the arrival on Sept. 24, 1829 of the letter written on behalf of Count Leon. Christ would then return visibly in 1836. Wagner's account is confirmed by statements in several of Rapp's sermons.

> The hidden God has taken up residence in the *Gemeine* as Savior, but after a certain amount of growth, he will reveal himself in glory. This glory and

---

[65] Wagner, *Geschichte der Harmoniegesellschaft*, 9.
[66] Arndt, *Doc. Hist. 1826-1834*, 443.
[67] Wagner, *Geschichte der Harmoniegesellschaft*, 17. Michael Kannenberg, in "Der württembergische Erweckungspietismus als millenarischer Kommunikationsraum," *Blätter für württembergische Kirchengeschichte* 112 (2012): 145-155 discusses ways that Württemberg Pietists dealt with the disappointmant of 1836: Verinnerlichung, Verkirchlichung, Offentlichkeitsarbeit, Umwandlung des Zeitsbewusstseins, Individualisierung, Quietismus, Nationalisierung, Leistungsstufen, Domestizierung und Moralisierung. Cf. Ibid., *Verschleierte Uhrtafeln. Endzeiterwartungen im württembergischen Pietismus zwischen 1818 und 1848*. (Göttingen: Vandenhoeck & Ruprecht, 2007), 315-336.

power will soon also reveal itself *visibly* . . . The one who is coming stands now at the gates of the world. He is coming in his *third coming* in great power to judge and to *visibly erect his kingdom*.⁶⁸

Rapp thus distinguished between Christ's second invisible coming (in 1829) as the Messiah "hidden" within the church and his *third visible* coming when he would establish his millennial kingdom and judge the nations. In the early 1830s, the Harmonist leader anticipated Christ's visible, third coming to occur in 1836, Bengel's date for the onset of the first millennia (though not for the return of Christ). "All things concur that in the year 1836 an important epoch will occur. The light has dawned in the innermost, in the sanctuary . . . In the outer world all things order themselves according to the secret time reckoning."⁶⁹

Later in the sermon Rapp explained how he arrived at the year 1836 for the visible return of Christ. His "secret time reckoning" involved multiplying thirty-six (the length of one side of the New Jerusalem in Rev 21:17) by fifty (the year of jubilee, a symbol of the millennium) and adding it to the date of the death of Christ.⁷⁰ One thus arrived roughly at 1836. After 1836 came and went, Rapp no longer set specific dates for the return of Christ. He never wavered, however, in his belief in the near return of Christ. James S. Buckingham, a visitor to Economy in April 1840, reported that Rapp continued to be "a firm believer in the millennium, or the second coming of the Messiah . . . [and] that he believed their [sic] accomplishment would take place before the year 1850; in which case he [Rapp] might be alive to see it."⁷¹ After 1836 Rapp kept the eschatological expectation alive through preaching the necessity of the Harmony Society to migrate to Palestine to meet Christ at his coming. This preaching resulted in "a very lively revival of religion" in the years 1844-1845, which Rapp interpreted as "a sure sign of the nearness of the long hoped for event."⁷²

Contemporary-Futurist Approach

Unlike Bengel and his followers, Rapp did not believe that large portions of Revelation 8-14 could be correlated with past church and profane histo-

---

⁶⁸MG-185/ Box 15/ Folder 5/E-18. Cf. MG-185/1-5004/Box 15/ Folder 5/ O-107.

⁶⁹MG-185/ Box 15/ Folder 5/ Group E-51. Interestingly, the year 1836 is crossed through on the original manuscript. The undated sermon was written with all probability prior to 1836. Most likely after 1836 someone crossed through the year given in the text.

⁷⁰The length of one side of the New Jerusalem was actually 144 cubits. MG-185/ Box 15/ Folder 5/ Group E-51. Cf. MG-185/1-5004/Box 15/Folder 5/ Group O-14, and MG-185/ Box 15/ Folder 5/ Group A-63.

⁷¹Arndt, *Doc. Hist. 1834-1847*, 475.

⁷²Ibid., 1073.

ry. Rapp proposed a contemporary-futurist approach to Revelation 4-22.[73] The events portrayed in those chapters had either been fulfilled in the immediate past, were being fulfilled in the present, or would come to past in the imminent future. For example, in Rapp's eschatological system, Emperor Franz Joseph II began to eat the flesh of the whore Babylon (Rev 17:16) through his secularization efforts in the immediate past (circa 1783).[74] The first bowl of wrath in Rev 16 was poured out at the time of the French Revolution (1789 to ca. 1790), the fifth bowl during the Vienna Congress (1814-1815).[75] The sojourn of the Sunwoman in the wilderness (Rev 12:6) was taking place in the present within the Harmony Society. The secession of the one-third of the membership during the 1832 schism was a contemporary fulfillment of Rev 12:4 in which the dragon Satan swept away with his tail a third of the stars that crowned the Sunwoman.[76] Christ would return visibly and personally in the imminent future to establish his kingdom on earth. The comparison of contemporary events and those in the immediate past with the Book of Revelation was a well-established practice among Württemberg Pietists.[77]

Premillennial Interpretation

The Harmonist leader's premillennial interpretation of the last book of the Bible contrasted with J. A. Bengel's postmillennialism. All premillennial interpretations state that the Second Coming of Christ is a future event that will occur *prior* (hence *pre*millennialism) to Christ's reign over or on the earth for one thousand years. The millennium is followed by the general resurrection, the great throne judgment and the inauguration of the new heavens and the new earth. This interpretation is based on a literal or natural (as opposed to spiritual or allegorical) reading of Revelation 20-22 and is distinguished from amillennial and postmillennial interpretations.[78]

---

[73]This approach to eschatology was discussed in some length with regard to the Sunwoman of Revelation 12 in chapter four of this dissertation.

[74]Arndt, *Doc. Hist. 1700-1803*, 282. Cf. Pastoral Letter #30, Viehmayer Collection, MG-185, 1-5005, Box 16, Folder 1.

[75]Rapp's exposition of the seven bowls of wrath (1824), USI, MSS #311/Box 36/Folder 6.

[76]Arndt, *Doc. Hist. 1826-1834*, 658. Cf. MG-185/1-5004/Box 15/Folder 6/R-26.

[77]J. J. Friedrich, the first pastor of Korntal, held "newspaper meetings" in which current events were compared with the book of Revelation. Württemberg Pietist Christian Armbruster in *Die sieben letzten Posaunen* (1814) made specific connections between the tumultuous events surrounding the French Revolution and the trumpet judgments in John's Apocalypse. Michael Hahn likewise compared current events with Revelation. Joachim Trautwein, *Die Theosophie Michael Hahns und ihre Quellen* (Stuttgart: Calwer Verlag, 1969), 211-213.

[78]Robert G. Clouse, *The Meaning of the Millennium. Four Views* (Downers Grove, Ill.: InterVarsity Press, 1977) is a helpful guide to understanding millennial interpretations. Walvoord divides premilleniel interpretations into three types: (1)

Rapp's premillennial stance stood in sharp contrast to Bengel's di-chiliasm and postmillennialism. Bengel and his most devoted early disciples believed that two successive millenniums were to be found in Revelation 20.[79] In this scheme, verses one to three depicted the first thousand-year millennium in which Satan was bound. This millennium would begin in 1836 and end in 2836. At the beginning of the second millennium (Rev 20:4-6), which would follow immediately upon the first, Satan would be released for a "short time," equal to 111 1/9 years in Bengel's reckoning. Those raised in the first resurrection would reign with Christ in heaven during the second millennium. Only after the end of the second millennium in 3836 would Christ return to judge the world and initiate the new heavens and new earth.[80] Since Christ returns *after* the millennium in this scheme, Bengel was a *post*millennialist. Later disciples of Bengel in Württemberg (and beyond) rejected his concept of a double millennium. They held that the binding of Satan and the millennium occurred synchronically. For these later disciples 1836 became the decisive year in which Christ would descend from heaven to establish the millennium on earth—a premillennialist and mono-

---

"Premillennarians of the historical school . . . interpret Rev 6-19 as largely fulfilled in history but hold that chapter 20 and following are future;" (2) Premillennial Covenant theologians (e.g. George Ladd) emphasize the "soteriological character of the millennium" and "subordinate . . . the political character of the kingdom and the prominence of the nation Israel;" and (3) Dispensational premillennialism considers "the millennium . . . a period in which Christ will literally reign on earth as its supreme political leader and that many promises of the Old Testament relating to a kingdom on earth in which Israel will be prominent and Gentiles will be blessed will have complete and literal fulfillment." John F. Walvoord, *The Revelation of Jesus Christ* (Chicago: Moody Press, 1966), 283-284. Holthaus, "Prämillenniarismus in Deutschland," 194-195, divides German premillennialism into two groups: historic and futuristic.

[79] The following disciples of Bengel held to the double millennium: Christoph Karl Ludwig von Pfeil (1712-1784), P. M. Hahn (1739-1790) in his early but not later works, and F. C. Oetinger. Jung argues that Oetinger rejected Bengel's di-chiliasm. Martin Jung, "1836 – Wiederkunft Christi oder Beginn des Tausendjährigen Reichs? Zur Eschatologie Johann Albrecht Bengels und seine Schüler," *Pietismus und Neuzeit* 23 (1997): 131-151, here 141f. Groth, on the other hand, states that Oetinger followed his mentor and upheld di-chiliasm. Groth, *Wiederbringung*, 109-118. The author was unable to obtain a copy of Oetinger's *Güldene Zeit* to check Jung's arguments. In Friedrich Christoph Oetinger, *Die Theologie aus der Idee des Lebens*, ed. Julius Hamberger (Stuttgart: Steinkopf, 1852), 402-403, however, Oetinger clearly taught Bengel's double millennium.

[80] See Groth, *Wiederbringung*, 70-77; Ulrich Gäbler, "Geschichte, Gegenwart, Zukunft," in *Geschichte des Pietismus*, vol. 4, *Glaubenswelt und Lebenswelten*, ed. Hartmut Lehmann (Göttingen: Vandenhoeck & Ruprecht, 1995): 19-48, here 33-36; and Jung, "1836 – Wiederkunft Christi?" for discussions of Bengel's di-chiliasm and postmillennialism. In his article, Jung corrects much contemporary confusion concerning the dating of the return of Christ in Bengel's system.

chiliastic view.[81] It is in this later eschatological tradition in Württemberg, in which Bengel's views were revered yet freely adapted, that George Rapp belongs.

Optimistic Eschatology

Unlike twentieth century premillennialists, who tend to emphasize the gloominess and evilness of the period preceding the return of Christ, Rapp had a generally optimistic view of this era. Such optimism is normally consistent with a postmillennialist and not a premillennialist stance. In Rapp's *Thoughts on the Destiny of Man*, which was self-published by the Harmony Society in 1824 shortly before their move to Economy, this optimism was stated most clearly. The purpose of this ninety-page treatise was to provide an apology for the religious and communal structure of the Harmony Society. Rapp concluded the treatise with a second aim, an "ardent hope" that: "This sublime, predestinated [sic] system of *Brotherly Union & Social Harmony* will ere long be universally established, for the restoration of the golden age, the dignity of the human character, and the happiness of man."[82]

In Rapp's estimation, there had been "great improvement of mankind" since the time of the early church. "Persecutions no longer impede our progress; from these horrid consequences of gross barbarism, the present generation is entirely and happily free."[83] The "rights of man [were] firmly established" by the constitution of the United States.[84] The "arts and sciences" had greatly advanced in the present century.[85] Newly-discovered, "useful inventions" were true "contributions to genuine freedom."[86] The "cause of truth has taken root," the "understanding of man [was] becoming gradually enlightened," there was a "great diffusion of light in our time."[87] Christianity was being "revived & propagated . . . in many parts of the world," all signs of the improvement of humanity.[88] Granted, Rapp argued

---

[81]These views were held by the later P. M. Hahn, Michael Hahn and Johann Jakob Friedrich (1759-1827), the first pastor at Korntal. The latter's work, *Glaubens- und Hoffnungsblicke*, was owned by the Harmony Society, as were the collected writings of Michael Hahn. Jung, "1836 – Wiederkunft Christi?" 146-147. See Johann Heinrich Jung-Stilling, *Erster Nachtrag zur Siegesgeschichte der Christlichen Religion in einer gemeinnützigen Erklärung der Offenbarung Johannis* (Nürnberg: Raw, 1805), 65-74 for his arguments against Bengel's double millennium. Jung-Stilling was not from Württemberg, but he loosely based his Revelation commentary on Bengel's eschatological scheme. The *Erster Nachtrag* volume and Jung-Stilling's Revelation commentary were owned by the Harmony Society.

[82]Rapp, *Thoughts*, 95-96.
[83]Ibid., 73.
[84]Ibid.
[85]Ibid., 80.
[86]Ibid., 55-56 and 63.
[87]Ibid., 20 and 54
[88]Ibid., 20.

that the example provided by the Harmony Society was central to both the present and future melioration of the "whole human race."[89] But the fact remains that, according to Rapp, "progression," "improvement" and "melioration" were occurring increasingly in the present penultimate age—an optimistic view generally believed to be inconsistent with premillennialism. It should be noted that an optimistic eschatology was prevalent in Pietist circles. Philipp Jakob Spener's eschatological "hope for better times for the church" (*Hoffnung besserer Zeiten für die Kirche*) was decidedly optimistic (and postmillennial).[90] Spener's confident eschatological hope was adopted both by the postmillennialist Bengel and by the premillennialist J. W. Petersen.[91] Like the radical Pietist Petersen, Rapp combined an optimistic view of the period preceding Christ's return with a premillennial interpretation of Revelation 20.

It is thus evident that the Harmonist leader's eschatological presuppositions and approach to the book of Revelation were influenced in a number of ways by Bengel and others within the "Württemberg eschatological tradition"—in the importance of the book of Revelation, a literal and biblicist hermeneutic of this apocalyptic work, the dating of the return of Christ, the importance of the year 1836, eschatological reckoning schemes which incorporated 666 and the 42 prophetic months, and an optimistic view of the period before the return of Christ. Despite these noteworthy influences, George Rapp's eschatology was not merely a rehash of other Württemberg Pietists at the dawn of the nineteenth century. Rather it was an original blend of chiliastic beliefs, which incorporated insights from the Württemberg eschatological tradition and combined them with his own sectarian concerns and contemporary-futurist and premillennial interpretations.

The Progression of Eschatological Events in Rapp's Theology

George Rapp employed a literal, biblicist hermeneutic when exegeting the Book of Revelation. This interpretation of the New Testament apocalyptic work was both contemporary-futurist and premillennial. In this section details of the Harmonist leader's later eschatology will be unpacked, particularly the progression and interpretation of the eschatological events depicted in the Book of Revelation. It will be shown that George Rapp espoused a form of modern premillennialism that anticipated that the Old Testament prophecies of Israel's conversion and return to the land of Pales-

---

[89]Ibid., 71.

[90]See Groth, *Wiederbringung*, 35-38, and Gäbler, "Geschichte, Gegenwart, Zukunft," 23-25, for a description of Spener's eschatology. Rapp likewise combined an optimistic hope for "better times" with eschatology in Rapp, *Thoughts*, 31, 33, 42 and 52.

[91]Groth, in *Wiederbringung*, 38-51, demonstrates the influence of Spener on Petersen; the same volume, 70 shows his influence on Bengel.

tine would be literally fulfilled prior to and during the millennium. The conversion of large numbers of Jews to Christ would result in the formation of a united Jewish-Gentile church in the last days. The Harmony Society congregation would constitute a key portion of the saints that rise again in the first resurrection and reign physically with Christ on earth during the millennium. They would serve within the Melchizedekan priesthood and rule and teach the nations. Rapp's premillennialism was influenced by the later eschatological tradition of Württemberg Pietism. Rapp contributed much that was original to the blend, however, particularly his unique correlation of contemporary events with Revelation, his stress on the physical reign of Christ and his saints on earth (not in heaven), and his decidedly sectarian focus.

Trumpet and Bowl Judgments

Rapp's progression of eschatological events began with the onset of the trumpet and bowl judgments in the immediate past, in the present or in the near future. In 1824, shortly before or after moving to Economy, the Harmonist leader taught his community extensively about these judgments. Romelius Langenbacher took copious notes on this teaching in a notebook that has been preserved. In the charts below, the content of this teaching has been correlated with the biblical text, and for the bowl judgments, with Jung-Stilling's Revelation commentary, *Die Siegesgeschichte* (1799).

An examination of the tables in Appendix F reveals several significant points. In the first place, despite the fact that George Rapp and his disciples had immigrated to the United States twenty years previously the Harmonist leader nevertheless looked to European events rather than to American t ones when seeking to correlate the "signs of the times" with the Book of Revelation. All of the specific historical referents given in Rapp's exposition took place in Europe or in the Middle East (the Turkish Ottoman Empire) and not on the American continent. Similarly, in a letter from George to Frederick Rapp contemporary to his Revelation messages (October 10, 1824), the elder Rapp related current events in Spain, France, Portugal, Prussia, Austria, Germany and Greece to Revelation, but not events in the United States.[92] This is true despite the fact that the Harmony Society re-

---

[92]"Es geht sehr viel merckwirdiges vor, es ist nicht ganz so still wie du es meynst; in *Spanien* ist es wieder laut genug die *Fransshoßen* haben bey Tariff ihren anführer u vielle leuthe verlohren durch die Consistucialisten, u in andern gegenden ist es dasselbe, so gar in *Madrid* sind ziml. *Franzs.* umgekommen, u in *Portugal* ists auch Misserrabel genug, *Preusen* zieht eine arme zusammen von 80,000 M. um *Östreich* den Gewalt zu zeigen wegen *Mainz* u selben prov: Die *Griechen* scheint es müssen ohne alle Gnade doch noch ausgerottet werden, wan nicht bald ein anders Hilfsmittel erscheint, *Der Heil. Bund* fahrt fort zu untergraben alle Mauern u Wäale darhinter die Freyheit sich aufhält ... Esaias davon sagt: ein anders Zeichen welches mich immer mehr aufmerksamer macht, daß sich so *viel geselschaften* bilden überall

ceived numerous American newspapers and Rapp and his followers were interested in American politics and current affairs. How can this be explained?

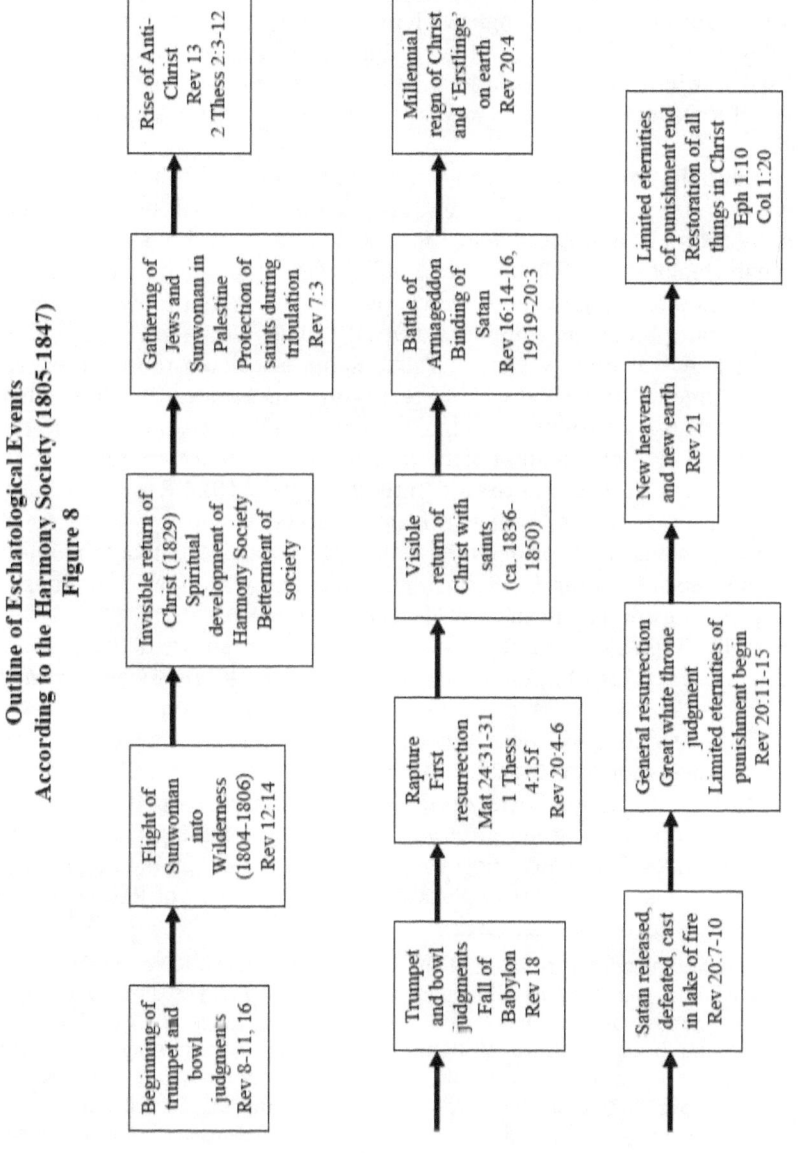

Outline of Eschatological Events According to the Harmony Society (1805-1847)
Figure 8

unter allen Fächer, u das Wort deß Herrn so schon in Erfüllung geht." Arndt, *Doc. Hist. 1824-1826*, 208.

Unlike some members of his Society, George Rapp did not speak or read English. Due to this fact, he remained influenced primarily by German-language books and German theological trends throughout his forty odd years in the "American wilderness." The vast majority of books purchased by the Harmony Society during Rapp's lifetime were works in German by German authors. A few English (John Bunyan, Thomas Bromiley, Jane Leade) and French authors (Pierre Poiret, French Quietists) were purchased, but in German translations. Seen in this light, the correlation of the Book of Revelation with European and not American events is understandable.

Second, Rapp's Neo-Pietist rejection of Enlightenment theology came to the fore in trumpets three, four and five and in the fourth bowl judgment. The initiators of Enlightenment thought, Voltaire and Rousseau, and the German Neologians Edelmann and Semler were mentioned by name. Rapp likewise pointed to positive spiritual signs in the Age of Enlightenment—the Berleburg Bible, the works of Gottfried Arnold, Kant and Fichte, and the establishment of Bible societies. Third, Rapp associated the trumpet and bowl judgments primarily with contemporaneous events or with events in the immediate past—with the reign of Louis XV of France, the (French) revolution, the rise of Enlightenment thought, the Vienna Congress and the wars between Turkey and Greece. Interestingly, in 1824 Rapp anticipated that in the near future "believers from all sects" would immigrate to the "American wilderness" prior to the return of Christ, presumably to join the Harmony Society. After 1836, however, Palestine was viewed by Rapp as the correct location to await their Messiah.

Finally, Rapp's exposition of the bowl judgments shows dependence on Johann Heinrich Jung-Stilling's Revelation commentary, *Die Siegesgeschichte* (1799), and on his 220 page addendum to the commentary, *Erster Nachtrag* (1805). Jung-Stilling was not a Württemberger, but his interpretation of the book of Revelation was significantly influenced by Bengel's eschatological system.[93] The Harmony Society during Rapp's lifetime owned twenty-nine individual copies of fifteen different titles by Jung-Stilling, including five copies of his eschatological novel *Das Heimweh*, one copy of the *Siegesgeschichte* and one of the *Erster Nachtrag*.[94] A comparison of Rapp's exposi-

---

[93]Jung-Stilling's interpretation of the trumpet judgments, for example, was an historicist one, that was both dependent on Bengel and yet differed from his renowned predecessor in many details. Nevertheless, Jung-Stilling (1740-1817) accepted the basic structure of Bengel's chronological reckoning (the latter's interpretation of an hour, day, month and year). "Die Worte . . . 'die Stunde, Tag, Monat und Jahr' . . . stärkender treffen sie zu, wenn eine Stunde, Tag, Monath und Jahr *nach Bengels prophetischer Zeitrechnung* berechnet werden . . . [gives Bengel's correlation of these time periods] Es ist zum Erstaunen, wie genau auch hier wieder zutrifft." Jung-Stilling, *Siegesgeschichte*, 244-245. Cf. Bengel, *Erklärte Offenbarung*, 319-321, for his explanation of the hour, day, month and year.

[94]The other Stilling works owned by the Harmony Society are *Geister Kunde* (1 copy), *Grauer Mann* (3), *Menschen Freund* (3), *Gesammelte Schriften* (1), *Gedichte* (1),

tion of the bowls of wrath and Jung-Stilling's *Siegesgeschichte* reveals that in five of the seven judgments Rapp followed Jung-Stilling's interpretation. In some cases the exact same terminology was used, although we do not have Rapp's original manuscript but rather Romelius Langenbacher's extensive notes of the Harmonist leader's teaching on the trumpet and bowl judgments. For example, both Jung-Stilling and Rapp used the distinctive term *Revolutions-Geschwür* (the cancer of revolution) to describe the result of the first bowl of wrath. In his exposition of the fourth bowl, Rapp appropriated conceptions and language that more closely followed Jung-Stilling's *Erster Nachtrag* rather than the *Siegesgeschichte*. In both Jesus Christ was the "sun of the spirit world," and Enlightenment theology was in view.[95] Verbatim borrowing from Jung-Stilling's *Nachtrag* is found in another Rapp sermon as well.[96] In his exposition of the trumpet judgments, however, Rapp did not follow Jung-Stilling's historicist approach, which associated the judgments with profane and church historical events in the distant past. Nevertheless, the Harmonist leader appropriated Jung-Stilling's interpretation of the sun, moon and stars (fourth trumpet) as denoting religion, morals and spiritual teachers.[97] Thus once again, Rapp both depended on Jung-Stilling, and departed from him to suit his purposes.

Immigration to Palestine

The next two major eschatological events in Rapp's scheme, the flight of the Sunwoman and the invisible return of Christ, have already been discussed in chapter four and earlier in this chapter, respectively (see table 6). The subsequent event on the Harmonist leader's timetable of the end times was the return of the Jews to their ancestral homeland. In his 1824 explanation of the bowls of wrath and in at least one sermon, Rapp alleged that the sixth bowl of wrath poured out on the Euphrates River (Rev 16:12-16) would lead to the downfall of the Turkish Ottoman Empire, which controlled Palestine in that era, and open the way for full-scale emigration of the Jews to the land of Palestine.[98]

Theobald (1), *Antwort über Catholicismus und Protestantismus* (1), *Biblische Erzählungen* (3), *Kleine Schriften* (1), *Taschenkalender* (5), *Florentin von Fahlendom* (1), and *Lebenslauf* (1). Arndt, *Rapp's Successors*, 426, idem, *Doc. Hist. 1814-1819*, 261, and idem, *Doc. Hist. 1820-1824*, 440.

[95]Jung-Stilling, *Nachtrag*, 200. Rapp also drew on the anti-Enlightenment language in ibid., 189f.

[96]In MG-185/1-5004/Box 15/Folder 6/P-4 Rapp borrowed verbatim from Jung-Stilling, *Nachtrag*, 76-80.

[97]Jung-Stilling, *Siegesgeschichte*, 225-226. Bengel interprets the sun as Caesar, the moon as the Roman senate and the stars as military commanders. Bengel, *Erklärte Offenbarung*, 306.

[98]"u nun ist die Zeit nahe da sie [Geschlechter der Israeliten] in der 6 Zorn Schale alle zusammen bringen wolle: da wird der Erzhirte mit ihnen ein Band der liebe mit ihnen aus machen, als eine Einge Heerde seines Schaafsstalls verEinigt werden ... so

The Lord will send his messengers and angels, who will gather his honored people, the Israelites, from all four corners of the earth, and bring them to their land in order to unite the 124 [sic – 144?] thousand with the new church body of the prepared *Gemeine*, and to form an entirety under the headship of Jesus. There [in Palestine] little by little many thousand more will join the others. . . . Moreover the Lord says, all of this cannot occur until Israel is already in her fatherland, Math 24:34-35.[99]

Rapp admitted that it seemed "unbelievable" that the Israelites, that "stubborn, stiff-necked people," would be "converted to Christ, and yet it will happen. . . . For the gathering and conversion of all of Israel and Judah was promised clearly in many ways by all the prophets and specifically sworn to by Jehovah."[100] Rapp expected that the Old Testament prophecies concerning the people of Israel would be literally fulfilled. God's plan for the Jewish people was not set aside or eradicated through the development of the New Testament people of God, the church.

Simultaneous to the Jewish return, the Sunwoman in the American wilderness, the Harmony Society, would likewise immigrate to Palestine. Rapp came to the conviction that the Sunwoman must emigrate from the United States to Palestine relatively late in his life. Shortly before their emigration from Württemberg in 1804-1807, the Separatist leader and his followers had identified the proper location of the "wilderness" in Revelation 12:6 to be in America.[101] In his 1824 exposition on the bowl judgments, George Rapp still fully anticipated that his Society would remain on American soil until the return of Christ. Shortly before the Second Coming, true believers ("brethren") from "all sects" or confessions would join the Harmonists in the American wilderness. Later, however, the Harmonist leader readjusted his eschatological scheme. Rapp, who regularly purchased German journals, newspapers and books, was certainly informed of the ongoing theological debate over the correct location of the "wilderness" in his former homeland from ca. 1800-1820. Three locations in particular came into question for radical Pietist emigrants during the famine years in Württemberg in 1816-1817--America, Russia or Palestine. Southern Russia was supported by Jung-Stilling and favored by many Separatists. It was farther east and closer to Palestine than Germany, making it an ideal interim location until emigration to the former became possible.[102] J. J. Friedrich, the first pastor at Korn-

---

wird ein durchbrecher vor ihnen den weg öfnen, u alle hinternißen wegräumen als ihr führer vor ihnen her . . . u sie werden durchbrechen, durch alles was sie aufhalten will." MG-185/1-5004/Box 15/Folder 6/Q-105.

[99]MG-185/1-5004/Box 15/Folder 5/O-79.

[100]MG-185/1-5004/Box 15/Folder 6 /P-138.

[101]See immigration songs in Arndt, *Doc. Hist. 1700-1803*, 442-449.

[102]Although older, Leibbrandt's volume provides a very good discussion of the emigration from Württemberg to Russia during and following the famine of 1816-1817. Georg Leibbrandt, *Die Auswanderung aus Schwaben nach Rußland 1816-1823* (Stuttgart: Ausland und Heimat Verlag, 1928). Newer works include Renate Föll, *Sehnsucht nach Jerusalem: Zur Ostwanderung schwäbischer Pietisten* (Tübingen:

tal, argued in *Glaubens- und Hoffnungsblicke* (1801) that "true believers" should wait until political changes opened immigration to the homeland of their Savior.[103] Michael Hahn was hesitant to state which location was correct. Rather he encouraged his followers to wait and only immigrate to Russia if it proved possible to flee from there to the ultimate "wilderness" of Palestine. America was a less attractive option for Hahn as well as for Jung-Stilling, due to the dangers of falling prey to prosperity and materialism on that continent.[104] This theological discussion probably led Rapp to come later to believe that Palestine was the ultimate destination for the Harmonists.

Presumably after Christ did not visibly return as expected in 1836, Rapp readjusted his eschatological scheme. It is not unlikely that he desired to refocus and intensify the frustrated eschatological hope of the Harmonists and to bring it once again to a fever pitch. Even after the non-appearance of Christ in 1836, Rapp continued to anticipate and preach the imminent return of Christ. One new element was added, however. The Harmony Society as the Sunwoman in the wilderness would join the Jewish people in their journey to Palestine before the return of Christ. The first dated sermon that the author found to espouse such a view was from February 11, 1838, that is, shortly after 1836. In April 1840 an English visitor to Economy, James S. Buckingham, reported that Rapp "had strong hopes . . . of being able to remove, with all his community to Palestine, when the unequivocal signs of the immediate advent of the Messiah should show the hour to be near at hand."[105] The Old Testament "patriarchal area of the Orient," that is Palestine, was "the proper and elect land of God . . . for you, O Harmony," Rapp proclaimed.[106] "In the location where Christ had his fellowship [of apos-

---

Tübinger Vereinigung für Volkskunde, 2002), and Andreas Groß, *Missionare und Kolonisten. Die Basler und Hermannsburger Mission in Georgien am Beispiel der Kolonie Katharinenfeld 1818-1870* (Hamburg: LIT, 1998).

[103]Friedrich, *Glaubens und Hoffnungsblicke*, 160-161: "Wann aber die Zeit da ist, daß das Volk Israel in sein altes Vaterland zurückkehren soll . . . Zu dem Ende muß eine große wichtige Veränderung mit dem türkischen Reiche, und mit dem Volke Israel, bald vorgehen. Sobald aber Israel die Erlaubniß hat, ins Land Kanaan zurück zu kehren: sobald werden auch die wahren Kinder Gottes, das Weib in der Wüste, der Israel Gottes, sich an jene anschließen, und mit ihnen ins Land Israel ziehen." Friedrich identified the Sunwoman with all true believers and not the Harmony Society.

[104] Hartmut Lehmann, "Endzeiterwartung und Auswanderung: Der württembergische Pietist Johann Michael Hahn und Amerika," in *Alte und Neue Welt in wechselseitiger Sicht. Studien zu den transatlantischen Beziehungen im 19. und 20. Jahrhundert*, ed. Hartmut Lehmann (Göttingen: Vandenhoeck & Ruprecht, 1995), 185- 204, here 191-196.

[104]See immigration songs in Arndt, *Doc. Hist. 1700-1803*, 442-449

[105]Arndt, *Doc. Hist. 1834-1847*, 475.

[106]MG-437/ Box 22/ Folder 82B/ Gr. B-60.

tles], there the elect will be gathered."[107] For the Harmonists "may not await the return of Christ in America."[108]

Rapp was well aware that emigration to Palestine would involve great effort and sacrifice on the part of the rapidly aging celibate community. Therefore, he encouraged his community to accept the challenge and prepare themselves inwardly to emigrate.

> Just as Rachel said to Jacob, "Come, let us go into our land," so it will be also soon true for us.... The Holy Spirit now says, "Come, let us go into our land." Ephraim [Christ] will soon arrive, for whom we are waiting.... One does not read that old Jacob left any of his family behind. Let us hope that the *Gemeine* at the end does not lose more people.[109]

The Harmonist leader sincerely hoped that all would accept the call to emigrate, and that the Society would not lose members over this issue as they had recently lost so many in the 1832 schism. He reminded his followers that they should not seek a "permanent abode" here on earth, but always:

> Hold the staff of faith in their hands, and always to be ready in every way, to enter [the land] according to the will of God and to follow his call with no regrets for places, houses and comforts.... So the Lord will bring us, his congregation (*Gemeine*), to a safe place ... to receive Jesus Christ at his Coming.[110]

To enable a quick exodus to Palestine (and to ensure economic security), George Rapp collected by 1845 half a million dollars in gold and silver currency, an incredible sum in that age.[111] He concealed the money in a vaulted space that is still accessible under his bedroom at Economy. Furthermore, from 1841 until Rapp's death in 1847, 1731 barrels of roasted wheat, 100 barrels of corn meal and 208 of rye meal were held in readiness to enable a sudden eastward departure of the community.[112]

The Harmonist leader clearly had changed his view of where the Harmony Society should meet Christ at his coming. In a number of sermons, however, Rapp was careful to state that immigration to the United States had not been an eschatological miscalculation, but rather a divinely ordained first step in their pilgrimage.

> For this purpose, North America was chosen, because the northern air hardens people more than they could be hardened in the warm hothouse of the east and south.... They received there [in America] an arena in which the

---

[107] MG-185/1-5004/Box 15/Folder 5 /O-119.
[108] 1838 Sermon, Oct. 14, 1838, Book MG-185/Box 1-4997/Box # 8/ Folder 20
[109] 1838 Sermon Book, Feb. 11, 1838, MG-185/Box 1-4997/Box # 8/ Folder 20.
[110] MG-185/1-5004/Box 15/Folder 6 /Q-73.
[111] Arndt, "Harmony Society," 79.
[112] MG-185/Microfilm roll #168, Memorandum of flour roasted for expected pilgrimage to Holy Land, 1841-1850.

congregation (*Gemeine*) has worked, suffered, waited and been hardened very greatly.[113]

The Harmonists, members of the Sunwoman, had spent their youthful years in the "wilderness" of America. The cold northern climate allowed them to achieve the necessary endurance and strength to resist the lusts of the flesh and thus grow to spiritual manhood.[114] Celibacy would have been impossible to achieve in Palestine, according to Rapp. Nevertheless, Palestine was their ultimate goal. Although the fields there were currently arid and empty, they would soon bring harvests for a better humanity, which would renew the earth.[115] The Harmonists in the last decade of Rapp's life were "homesick" to reach the higher country of Palestine.[116]

Rapture, First Resurrection and Return of Christ

Rapp's 1824 exposition of the trumpet and bowl judgments depicted them as being fulfilled predominantly in the immediate past or present. A comparison with his other sermons, however, reveals that Rapp likewise believed that there would be a sudden, final and cataclysmic fulfillment of the trumpet and bowl judgments after the rise of the Anti-Christ and immediately before the return of Christ. In one sermon Rapp declared that "the trumpets, woes and bowls of wrath belong to the Day of the Lord," the final judgment that would occur at Christ's return.[117] "Soon after the pouring out of the bowls of wrath, he himself [Christ] will immediately come."[118] Unlike the beginnings of the trumpet and bowl judgments, which were milder and stretched out over time, their final fulfillment would be similar to the plagues in Egypt before the Exodus of God's people—sudden, concentrated, devastating.[119] "The bowls of wrath will follow quickly on the heels of one another. The more terrible they are, the shorter they will last."[120]

Rapp was apparently somewhat uncertain as to whether there would be a pre-tribulation or post-tribulation rapture, that is, whether the Sunwoman and other true believers would experience the final tribulation on

---

[113]"Darzu war das nordische America ersehen, weil die Nord luft die M: mehr härtet, als sie im warmen Triebhauße osts, u Süds gehärtet werd[en] konnten. . . . erhielt sich auf einen schauplaz da sie nöthig war, worauf die gem: jezt so viel gewirckt, gelitten, gedultet, u gehärtet." MG-437, Box 22, Folder 82B, D-17.

[114]"Denn unsere Jungl:[ings] Jahre sind jezt in der Wüsten zum Mans alter durch viel übungen gereift. Da Nordländische räucre härte hat der gem: dauer u stärke in den anfällen geg: l:[lust] roher Tapferk: den weicherin Morg[en]länder weit voran kommt." MG-185, 1-5004, Box 15, Folder 6, P-129.

[115]Ibid.

[116]MG-185, 1-5004, Box 15, Folder 6, P-151. Here again Rapp borrowed from Jung-Stilling the term "homesickness" (*Heimweh*) for eschatological yearning.

[117]MG-185/1-5004/Box 15/Folder 6/P-28.

[118]MG-185/1-5004/Box 15/Folder 6/R-106.

[119]Ibid.

[120]MG-185/1-5004/Box 15/Folder 6/P-272.

earth before being caught up into heaven to meet Jesus. In one sermon he stated: "The people of God will not experience the smallest portion of the plagues of the bowls of wrath, just as Israel did not in the land of Goshen. For presumably the church of Christ is still in the wilderness."[121] In this passage the Harmonist leader qualified his statement that the church would be in the wilderness during the tribulation with the word "presumably" (*vermuthlich*). Yet in other sermons, George Rapp clearly proclaimed that believers would be present on earth during the tribulation. "The Lord would preserve us, his *Gemeine*, in a secure location" in Palestine "until the terrible judgments announced in Revelation 18" were completed, he preached.[122] In another sermon Rapp asserted that prior to the final outpouring of the bowl judgments, the Sunwoman, "the church of Jesus Christ," would be gathered by the "eagle" of Revelation 12:14 to a "corner of the wilderness" in Palestine, where she would "remain during the tribulation."[123] However in at least one sermon, George Rapp hinted possibly at a pre-tribulation rapture. "It will be a portion of the joy of the blessed, that they will look down from above on these judgments, which are described by Jesus, the prophets and Revelation. . . . They will also rejoice in heaven . . . that the great prostitute [Rev 18] has been judged."[124]

Whether or not Rapp was advocating a pre-tribulation rapture is dependent on the exact meaning of the term "blessed" (*Seeligen*)—previously deceased believers or previously raptured believers. One thing is very clear in Rapp's thinking—if the Sunwoman and other true believers were still on earth during the tribulation, they would not experience its wrath, but be preserved in a safe place (*einen sichern Ort*).

Immediately prior to Christ's return, the "members of the Sunwoman . . . will meet him [Christ] in the air. We will be lifted up, and united with the multitude that comes with him, and accompany them." Rapp in this sermon was describing the rapture, in which believers still alive at the return of Christ would be caught up into heaven to meet their Savior (1 Thess 4:15-17). Simultaneous to the rapture, in the process of being lifted up into heaven, their "mortal bodies would be changed and transformed into visible immortal bodies."[125] They would lay aside their mortal "husk" (*Hülle*) and put on a resurrection body, a *Geistleib*. Rapp believed that some members of

---

[121] MG-185/1-5004/Box 15/Folder 5/N-46.

[122] MG-185/1-5004/Box 15/Folder 6 /Q-73. Cf. MG-185/1-5004/Box 15/Folder 5 /O-119.

[123] MG-185/1-5004/Box 15/Folder 5/O-79. Cf. MG-185/1-5004/Box 15/Folder 5 /O-119. The contexts of these sermons make clear that Rapp had the wilderness in Palestine in view. Friedrich likewise believed that the Sunwoman would be preserved from the tribulation in Palestine. Friedrich, *Hoffnungsblicke*, 18-19.

[124] MG-185/1-5004/Box 15/Folder 5/C-13. Cf. MG-185/1-5004/Box 15/Folder 6/P-272: "Wärend ach u Weh auf [Symbol = Erde] ist, u die entsezlichsten plag: über die auf dieser Welt noch lebenden M: kommen: wird im Himmel jubel seyn, ach die Gerechten werden sich freuen."

[125] MG-185/Box 22/Folder 82B/A-6. Cf. MG-185/1-5004/Box 15/Folder 5/N-50.

the Harmony Society, the Sunwoman of Revelation 12, would be alive at the imminent return of Christ. They would form an important part of the multitude experiencing the first resurrection (Rev 20:4-6). The Harmonist leader taught that:

> Not all pious people will have a share in the millennial kingdom. Some pious people must wait until the Day of Judgment, when they likewise will receive their reward. Only those who personally have fought for the cause of the kingdom of God, and sacrificed their own interests and lives for the common spirit (*Gemein Geist*) will participate in the universal world monarchy [the millennium].[126]

The Harmony Society as the Sunwoman was uniquely qualified to participate in the first resurrection as *Erstlinge*, firstlings or first fruits.[127] They had been "completely purified, refined, and preserved" during "more than forty years in the refuge of the wilderness." This made them eligible to be included in the fold of the "last martyrs and confessors of Jesus, who refused to worship the beast and his image," an allusion to Rev 20:4.[128] Despite his decidedly sectarian leanings, George Rapp always allowed that other believers would likewise participate in the first resurrection and the millennium. The Sunwoman would be joined in those eschatological events by living and deceased saints, who had reached a "state of perfection" that

---

[126] MG-185/1-5004/Box 15/Folder 6/P-280. Cf. "So bald aber Christus wider auf [Symbol – Erde] kommt, also bald geschiehet die erste auferstehd: C: 20. Die andern Toden, aber ob sie auch fromm gelebt hätten, ruhen fort in ihrem Kammern biß zur 2 aufersteh: in Jüngsten Tage: nach dem grosen Sabath: Thesal: 4.15." OEV, uncatalogued Rapp sermon found in vol. 5, *Berleburg Bible*, p. 10-11.

[127] *Erstlinge* in Rapp's understanding were all "children of the first resurrection," which included both Harmonists and other saints. MG-437/ Box 22/ Folder 82B/ Gr. D-9. Cf. MG-185/ Box 15/ Folder 5/ Group C-31, and MG-185/ Box 15/ Folder 5/ Group A-63. Michael Hahn likewise used the concept of *Erstlinge* for participants in the first resurrection, and particularly for the Sunwoman. "Wer zur Braut Jesu gehört, muß zur ersten Auferstehung gelangt seyn, wenn Er kommt, Hochzeit zu halten. Und diese Auferstehung *der Erstlinge* des Herrn ... Michael Hahn, *Briefe und Lieder über die zweite Epistel Pauli an die Korinther, die Episteln an die Epheser, Kolosser, Philipper und Thessalonicher und die zweite und dritte Epistel Johannis* (Stuttgart: Hahnsche Gemeinschaft, 1938), Phil., 80. "Zu derselben Zeit werden viele edle, ausgeborene Kinder Gottes vor dem Wider- oder Antichristen geflohen seyn nach Jerusalem ... Diese Fliehenden ... sind das fliehende Weib, welches Off. 12. beschrieben ist. Dieses Weib, aus vollendeten Seelen bestehend, gehört als die sichtbare Gemeine der Heiligen, als *Erstling* der Herrlichkeit Jesu, zu den Auferstandenen, die mit Jesus kommen." Ibid., *Briefe von der ersten Offenbarung Gottes durch die ganze Schöpfung bis an das Ziel aller Dinge, oder das System seiner Gedanken* (Tübingen: L. F. Fues, 1839), 483.

[128] OEV, uncatalogued Rapp sermon found in vol. 5, *Berleburg Bible*, p. 10-11. Rapp declared elsewhere that the self-denial practiced by the Harmony Society was a form of martyrdom. "Wir sind erst vollens durch das jnnere Matherth: der selbst verläugn: u der Erleuchtung in gedult reif geworden." MG-185/1-5004/Box 15/Folder 5/O-10.

entitled them "to help erect the kingdom of God."[129] This united, resurrected or raptured "cloud of the righteous" (*Wolken der Gerechten*) would accompany Christ personally to earth to establish the millennial kingdom.[130]

Millennium

After Christ had defeated his enemies at the Battle of Armageddon (Rev 16: 14-16; 19:19-21), Satan would be bound and thrown into the abyss. Then Christ would establish his reign on earth for one thousand literal years (Rev 20:1-7). According to Rapp, evidence for a literal millennial kingdom was found not just in Revelation 20, but in prophetic passages throughout the Old and New Testaments.[131] When preaching on the millennium, George Rapp emphasized frequently and repeatedly in the same sermon that Christ's millennial kingdom was "on earth." He argued against an overly spiritualized interpretation and in favor of a literal hermeneutic.

> How is it possible to confuse the Second Coming with the great, world-wide Day of Judgment? How can the earth be allowed to completely dissolve and disappear, and the Kingdom of God be displaced merely into heaven? ... Can something be destroyed that God himself has created? Only sin will be destroyed ... but the world remains.... The bliss of this [earthly] kingdom surpasses even the blessedness of heaven.[132]

Rapp's frequent emphasis on the earthly millennium served to distinguish his teaching from Bengel and other Württemberg Pietists such as Michael Hahn, who generally viewed the location of the saints and Christ during the millennium to be in the "upper regions of the air," in heaven.[133] For the Harmonist leader Christ himself would reign among his saints in the earthly millennial kingdom.

> At the seventh great Sabbath [millennium] Christ the Messiah will be recognized and held sacred by the children of Israel. Then the great glory of the thousand year kingdom of Christ and his church here on earth will occur ... Christ Jesus will dwell visibly, personally and in great glory among them, and will be their God.[134]

The seventh Sabbath referred to the frequently held eschatological notion among German Pietists (as well as others) that the world would last 7000 years--six workdays of one thousand years each, and a seventh thou-

---

[129] MG-185/1-5004/Box 15/Folder 6/P-48.
[130] MG-185/1-5004/Box 15/Folder 5/N-75.
[131] "Dieses reich ist gegenstand unzähl: verheißungen deß alten u neuen Test:. " MG-185/1-5004/Box 15/Folder 6/P-280. Cf. "In allen Theil: der Hl Schrift findet sich ... das Taus: Jährige reich die Erfüllung der verheißung: u weissagung: deß alten u neuen Test: ist." MG-185/1-5004/Box 15/Folder 5/O-57.
[132] MG-185/1-5004/Box 15/Folder 5/O-48.
[133] Trautwein, *Theosophie Hahns*, 215. Cf. Bengel, *Erklärte Offenbarung*, 585.
[134] MG-437/Box 22/Folder 82B/B-35.

sand year period, the millennium or Sabbath.[135] During this era Christ himself, not a representative from the house of David, would visibly and personally dwell among them and rule over them.[136]

At the onset of the millennium the earth would be renewed to the paradisiacal state that it enjoyed before the Fall of Adam. According to the Harmonist leader, the millennium was not just the "day of rest for the world" but also:

> The day of the restoration of mankind and the world to the way it was in the first creation. It is also a completion of the work of redemption. Heaven and earth will be renewed to the state they had before the sin of Adam. . . . All that was contaminated by sin will be cleansed and brought back to its original state.[137]

It would be a "kingdom of peace" and a golden age.[138] "A rejuvenated people of the Lord will appear and be revived in the new Spring in the garden of God, in the beautiful, lovely and young creation."[139] The concept within Rapp's eschatology of a return to a paradisiacal, pre-Fall state reflected Boehmist theosophical notions. The Harmonist patriarch was careful to distinguish between the millennium and the new heavens and the new earth of Revelation 21-22. "Before the complete transformation of heaven and earth, there is yet an earthly kingdom of God in the interim, where a

---

[135]Rapp correctly referred to the seven ages of man as an "old Israelite teaching." "So viel ist nun gewiß daß eine uralte Geschichte eine Welt Woche annimmt, auch daß das schicksal der Gem: Christi auf Erd: nach der ofb: Joh: in 7 Zeiten beschlossen ist. . . . Denn Petrus bestätigt die Israelitische lehre, die deß Haußes Eli lang vor Christi geb: wornach die Welt biß zum reich Gottes auf [Symbol – Erde] 6000 Jahr währen soll. d. ist 6 Wercktage biß zum Sabath: nach dem wird in der Gem: vollzogen der befehl die Welt zum Canaan zu machen, d: ist zum R: Gottes. MG-185/1-5004/Box 15/Folder 6/Q-52. Rapp borrowed Jung-Stilling's listing of the seven ages of man, *Nachtrag*, 76-80, in MG-185/1-5004/Box 15/Folder 6/P-4. Cf. MG-185/1-5004/Box 15/Folder 6/P-58, and MG-185/1-5004/Box 15/Folder 5/O-63. This conception was also found in Michael Hahn, albeit with some minor variations. Trautwein, *Theosophie Hahns*, 210. Luther, Melanchthon et al. reckoned the earth would exist for 6000 years until the seventh day-age, the Day of Judgment and not the millennium, appeared on the scene. Ibid., 214, n. 84 and Eberhard H. Pältz, "Jacob Boehmes Hermeneutik, Geschichtsverständnis und Sozialethik" (Habilitation thesis, Schiller Universität, Jena, 1961), 506-509.

[136]Friedrich, *Glaubens und Hoffnungshlicke*, 25, stated that most likely a descendant of David, not Christ himself, would rule on Mt. Zion during the millennium. "Und, da es nicht wahrscheinlich ist, daß Christus sichbarlich auf dem Thron Davids zu Jerusalem regieren werde, so wird ein Nachkömmling aus Davids Familie als König oder vielmehr als Stadthalter Christi daselbst auf dem Thron Davids sitzen und regieren."

[137]MG-185/1-5004/Box 15/Folder 6/P-274. Cf. MG-185/1-5004/Box 15/Folder 5/O-97, MG-185/1-5004/Box 15/Folder 5/N-50.

[138]MG-185/1-5004/Box 15/Folder 6/R-23.

[139]MG-185/1-5004/Box 15/Folder 5/O-10.

paradisiacal but not yet completed transfigured nature is found."[140] Although paradisiacal, the millennium would pale in comparison to the new heavens and the new earth, into which the millennial kingdom would dissolve after the great white throne judgment.[141]

Faithful Harmonists and other *Erstlinge* from the first resurrection would be rewarded for their devoted service to Christ by participation in the millennial kingdom. "This is the kingdom which is promised as a reward for those who have proven themselves. It outweighs all the suffering of this world," Rapp declared.[142] "The day of rest at the end of the world [the millennium] will be . . . a time of rest from all completed work, furthermore, a time of reward for those who have lived for Jesus Christ."[143] All those who had practiced "self-denial," who had been "sanctified through and through," and who had "proven themselves to be the most excellent fighters for the cause of Christ" would be "entrusted with the honor of ruling" with Jesus in the millennium.[144] They would serve as "resurrected priests of God and Jesus Christ . . . according to the order of Melchizedek."[145]

Members of the Melchizedekan priesthood would have a special and important role in the millennial kingdom.[146] Like Melchizedek, king of Salem and priest of the Most High (Gen 14:18-20; Heb 7), members of this order would have both royal and priestly authority. Priests according to the order of Melchizedek would "rule with Christ on thrones" during the millennium.[147] They would not only rule, but spiritually judge the nations as well.

> In the Old Testament . . . the high priest in Israel was at the same time the highest secular ruler. . . . And he, who is intimately connected to God, likewise possesses the necessary characteristics to be the highest judge and ruler. Only he understands the divine will, and can at any moment assure himself of the truthfulness of a matter. Such a priestly judge cannot be deceived—truth and falsehood lay exposed before him.[148]

---

[140]MG-185/1-5004/Box 15/Folder 6/R-23.

[141]"Aber was das reich deß Herrn betrifft wird auf unserer [Symbol – Erde] seyn. . . . Es wird als ein ungemein herrliches reich beschrieben; seine dauer wird ewig genannd, u zwar in der Ewigk: ofb: Joh: auf Taus: Jahr bestimmt. u wann diese um sind, so geht dieses in ein ewiges noch herrlicheres reich über." MG-185/Box 22/Folder 82B/A-6.

[142]MG-185/1-5004/Box 15/Folder 5/O-48.

[143]MG-185/1-5004/Box 15/Folder 6/P-274.

[144]MG-185/1-5004/Box 15/Folder 6/P-280.

[145]Ibid. Cf. MG-185/1-5004/Box 15/Folder 5/O-57.

[146]The concept of the Melchizedekan priesthood was prominent in the theology of radical Pietist Hochmann von Hochenau. See Heinz Renkewitz, *Hochmann von Hochenau (1620-1721)* (Witten: Luther-Verlag, 1969), 94-100, for a description of the Melchizedekan priesthood in Hochenau's writings.

[147]MG-437/Box 22/Folder 82B/B-42.

[148]MG-185/Box 1-5004/# 15/ Folder 5/N-20.

Melchizedekan priests would have open access to the "most secret chamber" of the Temple, the Holy of Holies, in the millennium.[149] The offering they would bring into this most sacred place would not be a physical sacrifice. Rather they would "cut off the sensuous from the authentic within the congregation, and sacrifice all crudeness."[150] In Rapp's estimation, Melchizedekan priests must be celibate.

> They should lay aside all sensuousness, and not seek a marriage partner, who is attached and used to the freedom of the sensual world. Rather [he should be] a virgin from God's lineage of the house of Israel, who has not been contaminated by a foreign love, who is a chaste, lovely virgin according to the image of God.[151]

Members of the Harmony Society were uniquely prepared to serve as Melchizedekan priests in the millennial kingdom, since they had faithfully and heroically achieved a celibate lifestyle in the present dispensation.

A sectarian-inspired glorification of their own Society is particularly evident in a number of Harmony Fest sermons preached in the last decade of the patriarch's life. In them Rapp accentuated in extravagant language the unique role of faithful Harmonists in preparation of and within the imminent millennial kingdom. "You *Harmonie* [female personification of their Society] prepare the work of the end times... You yourself are a world of wonders... You sense within yourself the existence of a higher eternal being."[152]

According to Rapp, the Harmony Society revealed in the present dispensation the proper plan for life within the millennial kingdom.

> The Harmony Society manifests in its presence an exceptional development of the powers of a united spirit. Through these powers the temple of God is erected again, the eternal sanctuary is made ready... The [proper] order of the kingdom of God is also ours.... Later when the last church gives birth as the mother to the nations, she fills the sphere of the earth with sanctified persons, and is the proper owner of an unfading inheritance, just as we have believed.[153]

Within the Harmony Society "lay the goal and qualification to erect the entire economy (*Haußhaltung*) of the kingdom of God."[154] It had been chosen to "order earthly and heavenly things, which the progression of times

---

[149]MG-185/Box 1-5004/# 15/ Folder 5, N-90.

[150]MG-437/ Box 22/ Folder 83/ Hymn #3.

[151]MG-185/Box 1-5004/# 15/ Folder 5, N-90. Both Hochmann from Hochenau and Gichtel believed that members of the Melchizedekan priesthood must be celibate. Renkewitz, *Hochmann von Hochenau*, 96; and Erich Seeberg, *Gottfried Arnold. Die Wissenschaft und die Mystik seiner Zeit* (Darmstadt: Wissenschaftliche Buchgesellschaft, 1964), 28.

[152]OEV, Library Box 26, Harmony Fest 1839.

[153]1840 Harmony Fest sermon. MG-437/Box 22/Folder 82B/A-22. Transcribed in Arndt, *Doc. Hist. 1834-1847*, 443-445.

[154]Undated Harmony Fest sermon. MG-437/Box 22/Folder 82B/D-75.

will bring to completion."¹⁵⁵ "For the Harmony Society is the axis around which everything turns . . . for we envelop all things."¹⁵⁶ Despite these extravagant claims preached most boldly on the anniversaries of the founding of their Society, Rapp nevertheless consistently affirmed that non-Harmonist believers would be saved from damnation and other *Erstlinge* would participate in the millennial kingdom.

Restoration of All Things

At the end of the millennium, the second or general resurrection of remaining pious souls and of all evil individuals would occur. All men would appear before the great white throne of God and be judged for their deeds. Those whose names were not written in the book of life would be cast into the lake of fire (Rev 20:11-16). Rapp believed that: "All creatures will be subjected to the judgment of Christ . . . The sheep will be put to the right of Christ and the goats [to the left] [Matt 25:32-33], namely they will remain and be pointed toward the source in which they had lived."¹⁵⁷

In this sermon Rapp affirmed that after the great throne judgment a so-called "double outcome" (*doppelter Ausgang*) would occur.¹⁵⁸ This doctrine was supported by Article 17 of the Augsburg Confession, which stated that after judgment men and angels would either experience eternal blessedness in heaven or eternal torment in hell.¹⁵⁹ Rapp did defend the earnestness and seriousness of judgment for sins. But like Johann Albrecht Bengel, Friedrich Christoph Oetinger, Michael Hahn and other prominent representatives of Württemberg churchly and radical Pietism, George Rapp believed in a form of universalism that was referred to as the "restoration of all things" (*Wiederbringung aller Dinge*).¹⁶⁰ This doctrine was based on an interpretation of certain New Testament passages, as well as an understanding of the Hebrew word for eternal, *olam*, that stressed its limited, rather than unending

---

¹⁵⁵Undated Harmony Fest sermon. MG-185/Box 15/Folder 5/C-23.
¹⁵⁶1842 Harmony Fest sermon. MG-437/Box 22/Folder 82B/A-22.
¹⁵⁷MG-185/1-5004/Box 15/Folder 6/R-51.
¹⁵⁸Groth, *Wiederbringung*, 11-13.
¹⁵⁹"It is also taught that our Lord Jesus Christ will return on the Last Day to judge, to raise the dead, to give eternal life and eternal joy to those who believe and are elect, but to condemn the ungodly and the devils to hell and eternal punishment." *The Book of Concord. The Confessions of the Evangelical Lutheran Church*, ed. Robert Kolb und Timothy J. Wengert, trans. Charles Arand et al. (Minneapolis: Fortress Press, 2000), Augsburg Confession, Art. 17, 50.
¹⁶⁰The definitive work on this topic is Groth, *Wiederbringung*. The exact designation *Wiederbringung aller Dinge* or *apokatastasis panton* (avpokata,sewj pa,ntwn) is found only in Acts 3:21. The concept of the *Wiederbringung* was not just found in Württemberg Pietism, but in the theology of other earlier radical Pietists such as Jane Leade, J. W. Petersen and Christoph Schütz, as well as incipiently in P. J. Spener. Groth, *Wiederbringung*, 35-51.

character.[161] Supporters of the restoration of all things argued that God's judgment on sin should by no means be robbed of its seriousness. The purpose of judgment, however, was not punitive but curative and aimed at rehabilitation. The eons of judgment were limited and not unending eternities. Therefore, after a very long but limited time period, God's eternal goal of restoring all of creation to its original state and purpose would be accomplished. All persons and angels, even Satan, would ultimately *willingly* submit to Christ's authority.[162] The doctrine of the restoration of all things in Württemberg Pietism differed from the later universalism found within Protestant theological liberalism. Unlike the latter, the doctrine of the *Wiederbringung* was based on a high view of Scripture and biblical exegesis, although it resulted in a non-orthodox formulation.

George Rapp was clearly influenced by the biblically-argued universalism so widespread in Pietist circles in Württemberg. The 1804 annual church report in his hometown of Iptingen noted that members of Rapp's Separatist movement prior to emigration believed in a *Wiederbringung aller Dinge* and that even the devil and his angels would eventually reach blessedness.[163] This eschatological hope never dimmed within the Harmony Society during Rapp's lifetime. According to the Harmonist leader, the "restoration of mankind and of all things was the foundation of all religion."[164] Like other proponents of the *Wiederbringung*, Rapp also alleged that judgment was curative and not punitive. In the fires of purification all of man's coarse works would be consumed.[165] The "rottenness" (*Verdorbenheit*) within him would "be removed."[166] For the "Lord turns all punishment and torment into good and uses it for a solitary purpose."[167] The purpose of judgment for Rapp was none other than to bring healing to sin-enslaved beings. "The judgment of the world serves to redeem" those in need, Rapp declared.[168] The aim and goal was the rehabilitation of sinners, and not retribution.

Like Bengel, Rapp based his argument for the restoration of all things on the meaning or meanings of the word "eternal." In his sermons he proclaimed that God alone was eternal in the absolute sense of the term.

> It is proven that, compared with the absolute eternity of God, no evil can persist equally eternal to God. For if it [evil] was only subjugated but not ab-

---

[161]Key New Testament support was found in Rom 5:10 and 18, Rom 11:32, 1 Cor 15:21f, Eph 1:9f, Phil 2:10, Col 1:15 and 20, Rev 5:13 and 20:13f. The exegesis of *olam* formed the crux of Bengel's argument for the *Wiederbringung*. Groth, *Wiederbringung*, 79-81.
[162]Groth, *Wiederbringung*, 43-45.
[163]Arndt, *Doc. Hist. 1700-1803*, 453.
[164]MG-185/1-5004/Box 15/Folder 5/A-68.
[165]MG-185/1-5004/Box 15/Folder 6/R-51.
[166]MG-185/1-5004/Box 15/Folder 6/P-90.
[167]MG-185/1-5004/Box 15/Folder 6/P-101.
[168]MG 185/ Box 15/ Folder 5/ Group E-33.

rogated, what good would it do us.... In this the eternal victory of good or of God consists, that all creatures that have fallen away from God return to him. ... For we believe that in the long eternity, no evil can persist equally eternal to God.[169]

Since absolute eternity was to be found in God alone, neither sin nor punishment for sin was unending. Although the essence of God's character was love and mercy, he was also the "righteous one."[170] Due to his righteousness God would punish, but not force his creatures to love and submit to him against their own free will.[171] As a result "damnation," though not eternal in the absolute sense, needed to be "incredibly long" and consist of "unimaginable eternities."[172] This punishment or "damnation" was "called eternal because it lies outside man's conception of time. Therefore its end cannot be comprehended by us or by any creature. It can only be understood in comparison to the endlessness of God."[173] If the length of punishment was long (but not unending) for sinful man, it was that much longer for Satan and his angels. Nevertheless eventually even Satan would "willingly lie down at the feet of Christ."[174] Rapp's argument for the *Wiederbringung* was grounded in the meanings of the word eternal, just as it was for Bengel, although Rapp, who knew no Hebrew, understandably did not argue from the meaning of the Hebrew word *olam* as did his prominent predecessor.

The goal of the *Wiederbringung* was to restore mankind and all things to their original paradisiacal and pristine state.[175] This was God's eternal purpose and decree (*rathschluß Gottes*), which would and could not be frustrated by the rebellion of man and demons.[176] For this reason Christ came into the world, to destroy the works of Satan, to tear down the very gates of hell.[177] Ultimately God would put all things in *willing* subjection under Chr-

---

[169]MG-185/1-5004/Box 15/Folder 6/P-234B.

[170]MG-185/1-5004/Box 15/Folder 6/Q-8 and MG-185/1-5004/Box 15/Folder 6/P-90.

[171]Rapp emphasized strongly the free will of man and angels in the midst of their restoration to God in MG-185/1-5004/Box 15/Folder 6/Q-8, MG-185/1-5004/Box 15/Folder 6/R-78, MG-437/ Box 22/ Folder 82B/ Group B-42, and MG-185/1-5004/Box 15/Folder 6/P-175.

[172] MG-185/1-5004/Box 15/Folder 6/P-234B and MG-185/1-5004/Box 15/Folder 6/Q-8.

[173]MG-185/1-5004/Box 15/Folder 6/Q-8.

[174]MG 185/ Box 15/ Folder 4/ Group L-25. Cf. MG 185/ Box 15/ Folder 4/ Group L-10, MG 185/ Box 15/ Folder 5/ Group E-33 and 1838 Sermon Book MG-437 Box 25, Kürze Säze aus Privat Versammlungen: "Unsre Grundsäze sind, nicht nur der größte Sünder, sondern auch der Satan kommt noch heraus, aus seiner Höll, ud. zu seiner Haabe u. Erbtheil."

[175]MG-185/1-5004/Box 15/Folder 5/A-68. Cf. MG-185/1-5004/Box 15/Folder 6/R-78.

[176]MG-185/1-5004/Box 15/Folder 6/R-78 and MG-185/1-5004/Box 15/Folder 6/P-175.

[177]MG 185/ Box 15/ Folder 4/ Group L-25.

ist's feet (1 Cor 15:27). Then all creatures would praise God wholeheartedly and voluntarily (Rev 6:13), and God would be "all in all" (Eph 1:23; 1 Cor 15:28).[178] At an undeterminable time after the beginning of the new heavens and the new earth, the limited eternities of punishment and the work of restoration would be completed, and the kingdom would be turned over to God (1 Cor 15:24).

George Rapp and his Harmony Society yearned fervently for the return of Christ and the inauguration of his millennial kingdom. This eschatological hope was present from the very beginnings of Rapp's Separatist movement in Württemberg. Nevertheless, eschatological expectation reached a fever pitch after the move to Economy in 1824-1825, as the time drew closer to the anticipated return of Christ, first in 1829, then in 1836 and finally circa 1850. The Harmonist leader never wavered in his ardent anticipation of the onset of the end times. He fully expected to live to lead his community eastward to Palestine to meet Christ at his Coming. Rapp's eschatology, like that of others within the "Württemberg eschatological tradition," was characterized by optimism, a literal biblical hermeneutic that extended to numbers and chronological references, a contemporary-futurist approach, and a premillennial interpretation of Revelation 20. Like Bengel, Oetinger and Michael Hahn, Rapp espoused a form of universalism called the restoration of all things. Rapp's eschatology included a decidedly sectarian emphasis. The Harmony Society as the Sunwoman in the wilderness would help establish the millennial kingdom and serve within it as priests according to the order of Melchizedek.

---

[178]MG-437/ Box 22/ Folder 82B/ Group B-42. Cf. MG-437/ Box 22/ Folder 82B/ Group B-19 and MG-437 / Box 22/ Folder 82B/ Gr D-20.

10
Conclusion

In July 1847, the health of George Rapp, the eighty-nine year old founder of the Harmony Society, began to fail. The aging patriarch soon became bedridden and was unable to attend worship on July 11, 18 and 25. On August 1, 1847, however, Rapp gathered enough strength to address his community for the last time through the open window of his bedroom to the congregation gathered in the garden outside. Numerous hand-written copies of the seven main points of Father Rapp's last address to his followers are extant in the Harmony Society archives. In this last message the Harmonist spiritual leader first encouraged his disciples to "be patient in suffering" and to trust that they like gold would "be preserved in the fire of tribulation." "All their intentions should be subjected to the will of God." The "fire" of their "warm heart religion" must never be extinguished, but "combined with the Word of God, if their faith was to grow." They should faithfully "strive in the fight against the world of the senses and of darkness." Rapp ended his sermon with an adapted Aaronic blessing (Num 6:24-26): "The Lord bless you and keep you *in the communal spirit* from now until eternity."[1]

Rapp's condition deteriorated rapidly and on August 7, 1847 the community was given opportunity to bid adieu to their "teacher, father and friend."[2] Rapp's final words, recorded during the last night of his life by one of the elders present, were fully in keeping with his life-long conviction of Christ's imminent return. The memorandum by the eyewitness reported:

---

[1] Karl J. R. Arndt, *George Rapp's Years of Glory. Economy on the Ohio, 1834-1847. George Rapp's Third Harmony. A Documentary History* (New York: Peter Lang, 1987), 1072.

[2] Karl J. R. Arndt, *George Rapp's Harmony Society 1785-1847,* rev. ed. (Teaneck, N.J.: Fairleigh Dickinson University Press, 1972), 600.

> His [Rapp's] strong faith in the literal fulfillment of the promises concerning the personal coming of Jesus Christ, and the gathering of the whole of Israel . . . remained unshaken to his last moments, as was shown by his last words, when he felt the strong grip of the hand of approaching death, saying: "If I did not so fully believe, that the Lord has designed me to place our Society before his presence in the land of Canaan, I would consider this my last."[3]

At one o'clock in the afternoon on August 7, 1847 George Rapp, founder and patriarch of the Harmony Society, quietly died. Three days later he was buried according to Harmonist custom in an unmarked grave under apple trees in the cemetery at Economy. For the occasion Jacob Henrici, who would become the new spiritual leader of the Harmony Society, delivered a moving sermon that inspired the grieving community to "renew the holy bond of brotherhood" that knit their hearts and lives together.[4] Thus the legacy of George Rapp continued until the dissolution of the Harmony Society in 1905.

Father Rapp's last address and deathbed confession formed the last will and testament of the founding father of the communal group. These words summarized in brief form some of the key religious convictions upon which the Harmony Society was founded. They corresponded in most points to the seven main principles of the Harmony Society formulated in February, 1838.[5] In his final address Rapp reiterated the necessity of patient suffering in the fires of purification. Suffering and absolute submission to the will of God were requisite for growth in sanctification and constituted Tersteegian emphases adopted by the Harmonist leader. Rapp's Pietist background was reflected in the exhortation to combine "warm heart religion" with faithful adherence to the Word of God. Furthermore, Harmonists should fight bravely against the world of the senses and of evil powers. This statement promoted, in shorthand form, both an ascetic, celibate lifestyle and progressive sanctification. In the Aaronic blessing, the dying patriarch prayed that the Society would be preserved in the "communal spirit" until the end of time, thus highlighting the on-going necessity of abolition of private property in favor of economic community of goods. Finally, on his deathbed, Rapp testified to his unwavering belief in the literal fulfillment of biblical prophecies concerning the personal return of Christ, the ingathering of Israel, and the imminent inauguration of the millennium.

---

[3]Arndt, *Doc. Hist. 1834-1847*, 1073.
[4]Arndt, *Rapp's Harmony Society*, 600.
[5] "Die Hauptgrundsäze der Harmonie Gesellschaft sind, 1tens Güttergemeinschafft. 2tens Enthaltsamkeit. u. 3tens Priesterthum. Das sind di 3 Wichtigste. Ferner, 4tens die Ehre Gottes ud. das Wohl des Menschen beföderm. . . . 5ten Alle Rückstündige Leiden vollends nachbringen. 6tens der alte Mensch muss mit seine Werke untergehen. 7tens Sich auf die Zukunft des Herrn Jesu zubereiten."
Arndt, *Doc. Hist. 1834-1847*, 327.

Conclusion   337

The last address and final words of George Rapp illustrate several central contentions found in this volume. First, George Rapp, and the Separatist movement and Harmony Society that he founded, actively adopted key religious elements from a relatively wide variety of orthodox Lutheran and churchly and radical Pietist sources. These elements were not appropriated passively, thoughtlessly, or unchanged. Rather they were often adapted and united by Rapp into his own unique and original blend of theological beliefs. Rapp's mature theology, reflected in his sermons preached in the last two decades of his life (ca. 1830-1847), was characterized by two divergent categories of influence, what has been labeled the biblical-eschatological and mystical-spiritual trajectories. Second, due to the manifold sources that helped shape his theology, an interpretation of Rapp's beliefs that overemphasizes Boehmist influence is inadequate. The Harmony Society's defining beliefs were not found exclusively or primarily in the cosmogony and anthropology of Jakob Boehme, which, not surprisingly, were not included in the final address. Rather other distinctive emphases of radical and churchly Pietism, namely, millennialism, primitivistic communalism, quietistic mysticism and a focus on growth in sanctification were much more central to Rapp's theology. Third, an interpretation that neglects the religious and historical background of Harmonist beliefs in Württemberg radical and churchly Pietism likewise misses the mark. Finally, Rapp's Separatist movement, and particularly the Harmony Society that he founded, had a distinctively sectarian self-understanding. The concluding remarks in this chapter will be organized around the four contentions above.

Biblical-Eschatological and Mystical-Spiritual Trajectories

Rapp's theology as culled from his mature sermons embodied two broad categories or trajectories of divergent influences. The biblical-eschatological trajectory reflected the Lutheran heritage and churchly Pietist roots of Johann Georg Rapp, a heritage that was staunchly biblical and theologically conservative. It was based upon a literal, biblicist interpretation of Scripture. A second trajectory co-existed within Rapp's theology. Rather than a literal, biblicist interpretation of the Bible, this trajectory was characterized by a return to a medieval hermeneutic, which upheld that deeper spiritual, mystical or allegorical senses were present in Scripture alongside the literal, historical meaning. The regress to an allegorical hermeneutic paved the way for reception of theosophical, cabbalistic and alchemistical conceptions within Rapp's theology. These two trajectories co-existed at times parallel to one another, since Rapp made little attempt to systematize his theology. For example, Rapp's theology included both orthodox Trinitarian formulations and the non-orthodox *Sephiroth* doctrine of Oetinger. On the other hand, both trajectories intersected occasionally. For example, the Tersteegian quietistic mysticism that Rapp and his disciples appropriated combined aspects of the biblical-eschatological trajectory (justification by faith, rejection of salvation by works) as well as elements from mystical-spiritualism (the medieval mystical heritage of Tauler, Meister Eckhart and the French and Spanish Quietists).

George Rapp was a voracious reader of theological and religious works, some of which directly influenced his theology. The issue of influence or dependency is a complicated one. In this volume influence or dependency is only claimed when: (1) Rapp borrowed verbatim from another source (e.g., Gottfried Arnold, Oetinger, Bengel, and Jung-Stilling), or; (2) Rapp paraphrased concepts from another author, and clear evidence exists that Rapp or the Harmony Society owned the volume in question (e.g. Tersteegen, Boehme, Gichtel, Christoph Schütz). The influence of other theologians upon Rapp's theology is found both within the biblical-eschatological and mystical-spiritual trajectories.

George Rapp's theology and that of his disciples evidenced significant areas of continuity with the Lutheran heritage from which they had sprung. They believed that the Scriptures were God's divine revelation, verbally inspired and entirely truthful, the sole basis for faith and practice. They advocated orthodox formulations of the Trinity. Christ was fully and truly the second person of the Godhead, not merely an exemplary man as some "enlightened" theologians proclaimed. Rapp firmly maintained the core Reformation conviction of the central importance of Christ's substitutionary atonement for the sins of mankind and of justification by faith. In the act of justification the alien righteousness of God was reckoned to the account of the believer, who was declared righteous apart from works. Justification was received by faith as a gift of God's grace. These aspects of Harmonist doctrine show continuity with the Lutheran background of the membership, specifically with core Reformation doctrine. Nearly twenty-five years ago, Hans Schneider in a historiographical survey of research on radical Pietism noted that the roots of radical Pietism in the Reformation churchly tradition have been largely ignored. Instead scholarship has focused on establishing the heterodox elements of the movement.[6] The focus on aspects of continuity between the Lutheran heritage and the religious beliefs of the Harmony Society in this volume thus provides a helpful corrective to existing scholarship.

Johann Georg Rapp experienced a lengthy process of conversion (1780-1782) while attending churchly Pietist conventicles in his homeland of Württemberg. Rapp's roots were in churchly Pietism prior to the radicalization of his beliefs and separation from the Lutheran church in 1785. Several aspects of George Rapp's mature theology reflect typical churchly Pietist doctrine that was likewise frequently found among radical Pietists. Like Spener and other members of the Pietist movement, Rapp elevated the doctrine of regeneration to a place of prominence within his theology. The term

---

[6]Hans Schneider, "Der radikale Pietismus in der neueren Forschung," *Pietismus und Neuzeit* 8 (1983): 15-42 and 9 (1984): 117-151, here 141.

Wiedergeburt (regeneration) was used broadly to connote the entire process of man coming to saving faith and narrowly for the creation of a new nature within man. In his sermons Rapp outlined the steps to salvation, an *ordo salutis* that included the awareness of sin, awakening of faith, conversion, justification, and regeneration. One step in the *ordo salutis*, the awareness of sin, was reminiscent of the psycho-spiritual anguish of the repentance struggle (*Busskampf*) common to Halle Pietism. Like other Pietists, Rapp stressed the necessity of active rather than passive faith in salvation, the necessity of human cooperation and response to the promptings of the Holy Spirit (synergism) in conversion. Salvation was grounded in the merits of Christ's atoning sacrifice. Nevertheless, good works and growth in sanctification were the natural and necessary outgrowth and accompaniment of justifying faith, although not the basis for acceptance by God. Perfection in this life, although elusive, remained an "impossible possibility" for believers. The later Neo-Pietist movement, to which Rapp belonged, took Luther's and particularly Spener's teaching on the priesthood of all believers seriously. Rapp and other laymen taught the Bible and led Separatist conventicles while still in Württemberg. Within the Harmony Society both men and women led company meetings, wrote hymns that were published, and were encouraged to use their spiritual gifts. This aspect illustrates the continuity between the churchly and radical wings of the Pietist movement.

A third aspect of the biblical-eschatological trajectory is what has been referred to as an "Anabaptist" ecclesiology. George Rapp's Separatists and later the Harmony Society, like the Schwarzenau Brethren before them, made a decisive move by 1790 from the spiritualist ecclesiology common within radical Pietism to one that advocated a visible community of believers. The port of entry for this "Anabaptist" ecclesiology is unclear. Rapp and his disciples may have had personal or literary contact with Anabaptists, since some Mennonites lived near to Rapp's hometown of Iptingen in the eighteenth century. Rapp's reading of the New Testament in conjunction with Gottfried Arnold's historical works certainly contributed to the adoption of similar convictions as those reached by the Schwarzenau Brethren. These convictions included the necessity of a visible community of believers, an outward Eucharistic celebration modeled on the primitive Jerusalem church (prior confession, love feast followed by Eucharist), and optional believers' baptism by immersion. Although scholars have long been aware that Rapp's disciples rejected pedobaptism while still in Württemberg, the general assumption has been that Rapp's Separatists and the Harmony Society espoused a spiritualist concept of inward baptism with the Holy Spirit without outward water baptism. An early act of re-baptism by immersion (1790) of a four of Rapp's followers in the Nagold River in Württemberg and the discovery of several later baptism sermons by Rapp has challenged this assumption. Immersion believers' baptism occurred at the very least optionally and occasionally within Rapp's Separatist movement and the Harmony Society. Furthermore, the Harmony Society employed similar arguments to support their pacifist stance and the practice of shunning that other Anabaptist groups used. The explication of the "Anabaptist" ecclesiology adopted by Rapp and his followers is an original contribution.

In chapter nine, the later eschatological beliefs of the Harmony Society were unpacked, which likewise belong to the biblical-eschatological trajectory. Rapp's eschatology was based on a literal biblical hermeneutic of Old and New Testament prophecies and a contemporary-futurist approach to the Book of Revelation. Rapp followed Bengel and the "Württemberg eschatological tradition" when he applied this literal hermeneutic not only to propositional statements, but to biblical numbers and chronological references. In Germany and during the early years of the Harmony Society, Rapp preached an imminent return of Christ without setting a specific date for the event. After 1820, however, the Harmonist spiritual leader, like Bengel before him, used eschatological reckoning schemes to predict the return of Christ. He calculated that the return of Christ would occur mid-September, 1829. Rapp solved the quandary that arose by Christ's non-appearance at that time by claiming that the Messiah had indeed returned, but in spirit and invisibly. He would return visibly in 1836, Bengel's date for the onset of the millennium. After 1836, the Harmonist leader no longer set specific dates. He kept the eschatological hope alive by preaching the necessity for his community to immigrate to Palestine to meet Christ at his Second Coming. Rapp's eschatology, despite its premillennialist stance, was decidedly optimistic.

Rapp believed that the Old Testament prophecies concerning the Jewish people would be literally fulfilled. The Jews would be converted to Christ and together with the true eschatological church, the Sunwoman of Revelation 12, gathered in the land of Palestine. There they would be preserved during the final tribulation, the bowl and trumpet judgments. Members of the Sunwoman (the Harmony Society) and other true believers would be caught up into heaven to meet Christ. They would return to earth with their Savior in resurrection bodies to help establish the thousand-year reign of Christ, centered upon Jerusalem. At the end of the millennium, the general resurrection and great white throne judgment would occur. Rapp defended the earnestness and seriousness of the ensuing judgment of sins. But like Johann Albrecht Bengel, Friedrich Christoph Oetinger, Michael Hahn, and other prominent representatives of Württemberg churchly and radical Pietism, George Rapp believed in a form of universalism that was referred to as the "restoration of all things" (*Wiederbringung aller Dinge*). Supporters of the restoration of all things argued that the eons of judgment for men, angels, and even Satan were limited and not unending eternities. Ultimately, God's eternal goal of restoring all of creation to its original state and purpose would be accomplished. All things would be put under Christ's feet and God would be "all in all" (Eph 1:23; 1 Cor 15:28). Rapp's eschatology was dependent on Jung-Stilling, Christoph Schütz, and Bengel and his disciples (the "Württemberg eschatological tradition"). It nevertheless included much that was original (correlation of contemporary events with Revelation, physical reign of Christ on earth—not in heaven, sectarian understanding of the Harmony Society as the Sunwoman and the "golden rose"). Details of Rapp's eschatology have been largely unknown to scholars, since Rapp's sermons have not been utilized prior to this time.

The desire for "deeper knowledge" and a numinous experience of God was reflected in the mystical-spiritual trajectory within Rapp's mature theology. In his later sermons, George Rapp employed at times a spiritual hermeneutic of Scripture. The most common spiritual interpretation utilized by the Harmonist leader was a typological-Christological approach. According to Rapp, there were dozens of types of Christ in the Old Testament—both persons (e.g., Solomon, Joseph, David) and things (e.g., altar of burnt-offering). Whereas Rapp's typological approach usually remained within the acceptable boundaries for typology set by Luther and the other Reformers, his spiritual-allegorical interpretation departed from the Reformation hermeneutical practice. Rapp's application of biblical persons and things to the spiritual states of the individual soul or corporate body lacked continuity with the literal-historical sense of Scripture. This latter approach was popularized within the radical Pietist movement by the Berleburg Bible commentary which George Rapp and other members of his Society owned and used.

The Jewish cabbalistic doctrine of the *Sephiroth* or ten emanations or light sources within the Godhead was adapted by Christian cabbalists to harmonize with the doctrines of the Trinity and the Incarnation. In addition to his orthodox formulations of the Trinity, George Rapp adopted aspects of the Christian cabbalism of Friedrich Christoph Oetinger to explain the triune God. In Oetinger's and Rapp's scheme, the upper three *Sephiroth* represented the Trinity, the lower seven the seven-fold spirit of God (Rev 1:4-5). For both of these men from Württemberg, there was steady, dynamic movement and progression within the Godhead as the *Sephiroth* that culminated in the teleological goal, the tenth *Sephira*, the church or kingdom of God. Rapp depended strongly upon Oetinger's cabbalistic notions of the Godhead, not those of Jakob Boehme. In one other aspect of his theology proper, Rapp followed Oetinger's lead rather than Boehme's. Both men from Württemberg denied that dualistic principles (fire-light, love-wrath) co-existed within God's essential being. These aspects of Rapp's theology were explicated exclusively in his later sermons and not in his pastoral letters from the Württemberg era. Rapp's appropriation of Oetinger's *Sephiroth* doctrine was unknown until this volume.

In contrast to the later-appropriated *Sephiroth* doctrine, Rapp absorbed much of Gerhard Tersteegen's Reformed, pietistically-informed, quietistic mysticism early in his spiritual journey, probably at the time of his separation from the Lutheran Church in 1785. Tersteegen's form of spirituality was popular among churchly and radical Pietists in Württemberg in the last half of the eighteenth century. Members of Rapp's Separatist movement owned copies of Tersteegen's hymnbook, *Geistliches Blumen-Gärtlein*, while still on German soil. This hymnbook was used to meet the musical and worship needs of the Harmony Society in the early years, until the latter produced its own hymnbooks in 1820 and 1827. In his early pastoral letters written in Württemberg as well as in his mature sermons, Rapp utilized a mystical, quietistic concept popularized in Pietist circles by Tersteegen to describe the action of turning away from the world and self-will—annihilation (*Vernichtigung*). The annihilation of the self-will in the process of regeneration and sanctification resulted in the human personality being enabled to react with *Gelassenheit* (passive resignation) to the vagaries of everyday life. The path to the mystical union with God was of necessity lined with pain and suffering. These experiences of spiritual darkness aided in the process of turning away (*Abkehr*) from self and the world in order to enter into (*Einkehr*) deep communion with God. In his early pastoral letters, Rapp described the mystical union as "sinking into God himself" in the ground of the soul and as "beholding the Godhead." These emphases show dependence not only on Tersteegen, but on Johannes Tauler as well, whom Rapp's Separatists read while still in Württemberg. In Rapp's mature sermons as well as in Harmonist hymnody produced from 1820 onward, the earlier, Tersteegian-influenced concept of the mystical union was replaced almost entirely with union with Sophia/Christ. Some of Rapp's pastoral letters have been published in Arndt's volumes of documentary history. Nevertheless, the influence of Tersteegen's quietistic mysticism on Rapp's theology has not been noticed in scholarly treatments of the Harmony Society to date.

A further element of Rapp's theology that belonged to the mystical-spiritual trajectory was the doctrine of Sophia or Sophialogy. George Rapp and the Harmonists relied heavily on Gottfried Arnold and to a lesser degree on Jakob Boehme for their Sophia doctrine. Rapp believed that Sophia or Wisdom (Prov 1-9) was not merely a personified divine attribute, but an eternal, pre-existent and divine (female) being inseparably bound to the Trinity. Like Arnold, Rapp in his veneration of Sophia equated her with the Beloved in the Song of Solomon. She was the female principle within the Godhead, the bride with whom the soul sought to be united, the mother who nurtured and corrected, and the androgynous virgin who demanded chastity from her followers. Sophia was the pure element that was removed from the androgynous Adam when he lusted after a conjugal partner. Rapp's Sophialogy differed from Arnold's in several key elements. Unlike Arnold, Rapp primarily equated Sophia with the Holy Spirit rather than with Christ, with whom Arnold and the majority of Sophia-devotees associated her. For Rapp, Sophia was the feminine, passive and progenerative principle within the Holy Spirit. Creation occurred when the active, masculine principle of the Holy Spirit "worked" upon the passive, receptive "material" of Sophia to bring about life. These male and female principles were both found within the *one* divine being of the Holy Spirit. This last aspect reflected Boehmist influence. Research on Rapp and the Harmonists has consistently noted the prominence of their Sophialogy and the influence of Boehme upon it. An original contribution of this study is documented evidence of Arnold's influence.

The chief area of Boehmist influence in Rapp's theology was found in his cosmogony and anthropology. Three distinctive beliefs were central to Boehme's theosophical interpretation of Genesis 1 to 3, all of which were adopted by Rapp. First, Adam before the Fall had a heavenly and androgynous body. Because Adam combined both male and female within his person, reproduction could take place as God had originally intended it, by "magical, holy propagation." Second, Adam's fall from grace took place in two stages. The first fall occurred when Adam turned his desire from his heavenly bride Sophia and desired to reproduce as the animals did. To protect Adam from even greater errors, God allowed Adam to fall into a deep sleep. During this sleep his heavenly body became an earthly one and Sophia departed from the first man. Adam's perfect androgynous unity was transformed into the duality of the two genders when Eve was taken from his essence. Finally, the androgynous ideal was applied to the Godhead. Boehme and Rapp polarized the two genders within the Godhead, maleness being found in God himself, and the female principle in the heavenly Sophia. They likewise argued that Christ, the second Adam, reestablished in his person the lost androgynous unity of the first Adam. One final aspect of the mystical-spiritual trajectory in Rapp's mature theology was the use of spiritual alchemistical language to describe growth in sanctification and the transformation of the imperfect, physical body into a resurrection body (*Geistleib*) in the *eschaton*.

This summary of Rapp's teachings within the biblical-eschatological and mystical-spiritual trajectories reveals the *apparent* disparate nature of his theology. Theologically conservative and orthodox Christian beliefs coexisted with mystical-spiritual elements rejected by the Lutheran and Reformed confessions as incompatible with Scripture and orthodox creedal formulations. Yet Rapp's theology was not a mere collection of eclectic and disparate elements gathered undigested from a broad range of orthodox and heterodox theologians. Rather it was erected upon a bedrock of orthodox Christian beliefs reflecting the Lutheran heritage and churchly Pietist background from which he had sprung—a high view of Scripture, orthodox formulations of the Trinity, Christ's atonement, justification by faith, regeneration, priesthood of all believers, and millennialism. The mystical-spiritual elements within his theology would not have been viewed by Rapp and the Harmonists as inconsistent with Scripture. As Neo-Pietists, they adamantly opposed the secularization and rationalization of theology by the German Neologians and other enlightened theologians in favor of a high view of Scripture. Elements within the mystical-spiritual trajectory reflected the desire of Rapp and his followers for heart-felt religion, a numinous experience of God, and deeper knowledge of the revealed Word of God. Seen in this light, the theology of George Rapp and his disciples had its own internal logic--it was not a mere collection of disparate and eclectic elements.

Boehmist Influence

The summary of the biblical-eschatological and mystical-spiritual trajectories in the section above reveals that Rapp's theology, although original in its own right, was impacted by a myriad of sources. Rapp's Lutheran heritage in Württemberg exerted a formative influence on his religious beliefs. In addition, certain doctrines in Rapp's theology were directly or indirectly impacted by theologians of the churchly and radical Pietist movements in Germany, namely, by Gottfried Arnold, Johann Albrecht Bengel, Philipp Jakob Spener, Christoph Schütz, Johann Heinrich Jung-Stilling, Gerhard Tersteegen, Friedrich Christoph Oetinger, Johann Georg Gichtel, and Jakob Boehme. Due to these numerous sources of influence, the overemphasis on Boehmism that many scholars of radical Pietism have proposed is inaccurate and inadequate for the theology of George Rapp and the Harmony Society. The danger of overemphasizing Boehmism on Rapp's Separatist movement and the Harmony Society (or on other radical Pietist groups) is that other important sources of influence tend to fade into the background, resulting in a skewed interpretation.

Much of Boehme's complex theosophical system was not adopted by George Rapp. Boehme's central teaching on the three principles did not find its place in Rapp's theology. Boehme's dialectical approach of dualism or polar opposites within God's essential being (love-wrath) was rejected by the Harmonist leader. The wrath of God was kindled as a divine response to the rebellion of man and angels—it was not an aspect of God's nature in Rapp's estimation. Rapp appropriated Oetinger's cabbalistic language of the *Sephiroth*, rather than the seven qualities or nature or original spirits so crucial to Boehme's system. Distinctive Boehmist language (*Tinctur, Ungrund, Fiat, Spiritus Mundi*) was only sparingly used by Rapp. Furthermore, key aspects of Rapp's theology were not found in Boehme. Boehme was not a chiliast. He rejected the concept of a literal earthly millennium. His eschatological hope centered on the imminent dawning of the *eschaton*, which he understood to be the Last Judgment and the new heavens and new earth, without a prior millennium. This contrasts with the strong premillennial stance of Rapp and the Harmony Society.

Boehmist influence within Rapp's theology was limited almost exclusively to cosmogony, anthropology, and Sophialogy. Creation occurred when the active, masculine force of the Holy Spirit worked upon the passive, feminine, progenerative material of Sophia. The Gnostic *mythos* of the androgynous pre-Fall Adam was central to Rapp's anthropology and had broad implications. Incarnate Christ, the second Adam, was viewed as having or obtaining an androgynous nature when Sophia united with the Godman at the incarnation or on the cross. The restoration of the image of God in man was understood to include androgyny. The resurrection body (*Geistleib*) would unite both genders in one person. Arguments for celibacy included (among other reasons) the necessity to return to the perfect state before the Fall, when "holy, magical procreation" was intended, not bestial copulation. Even the millennium was described as a return to the paradisiacal, Edenic state. Boehmist influence significantly impacted Rapp's cosmogony, anthropology and Sophialogy. Yet these doctrines surfaced in Rapp's sermons considerably less frequently than issues related to sanctification.[7] A Tersteegian emphasis on self-denial and submission to the will of God was much more central to Rapp's theology.

The question of Rapp's originality is an important one, given the many documented influences upon his theology. When it came to the appropriation of theological conceptions from other sources, Rapp was an active agent and not a passive recipient. He read broadly but critically. The Harmonist leader picked and chose those elements that corresponded to his own reading of Scripture. Rapp quoted verbatim from Arnold's *Divine Sophia*, Harmonists tacked Arnold verses to the end of company compositions, and the Harmony Society published fourteen Arnold hymns to Sophia in their 1827 hymnbook—clear evidence of Arnold's influence on their Sophialogy. Yet Rapp was not afraid to change Arnold's equation of Sophia with Christ to identification with the Holy Spirit, since the latter, in his opinion, was taught in the New Testament. Furthermore, Rapp replaced Arnold's spiritualist-ecclesial emphasis on the relationship of Sophia to the individual soul with her relationship to a visible community of believers, the *Gemeine*. This reflected Rapp's early rejection of the spiritualist ecclesiology so common among radical Pietists in favor of an "Anabaptist" ecclesiology. Despite Rapp's extensive borrowing from Oetinger's doctrine of the *Sephiroth*, the Harmonist leader had qualms about using the Jewish cabbalistic term for primordial man, Adam Kadmon, found in Oetinger's writings. Rather he replaced the term with Jesus Christ, the Word of God. Furthermore, Rapp's eschatological beliefs evidenced both continuity with the "Württemberg eschatological tradition" and discontinuity. Rapp's exposition of the bowl judgments in 1824, on one hand, drew directly from Jung-Stilling's writings in five out of seven cases. Yet Rapp did not hesitate to change the interpretation of his prominent contemporary when he saw fit. In contrast to many Württemberg Pietists (Bengel, Michael Hahn), Rapp insisted that the thousand-year reign of Christ would take place on this earth, not in the heavenly realms. Although Rapp drew upon contemporary theological trends within churchly and radical Pietism in Germany, he formed his own

---

[7]The author has not tabulated the topics of all 1680 sermon notes and of the 170 sermons in the 1838 sermon book. This statement is based on impressions won through extensive reading of Rapp's sermons. It is supported by a tabulation of topics taught in company meetings (based on the summary statements). 55% of the company meetings discussed topics related to sanctification. The next highest category was eschatology with 14%. The fall of Adam and anthropology was the topic in only 10% of the meetings. Alice T. Ott, "Community in 'Companies': The Conventicles of George Rapp's Harmony Society compared to those in Württemberg Pietism and the *Brüderunität*," in *Pietism and Community in Europe and North America, 1650-1850*, ed. Jonathan Strom (Leiden: Brill, 2010), 249-277.

distinct blend of beliefs, thus evidencing both continuity with the past and discontinuity.

Importance of the German Religious and Historical Background

Sociologist Bryan Wilson has labeled the Harmony Society an introversionist sect. By that he means that the Harmonists insulated themselves from the surrounding culture physically, socially, and linguistically. Wilson's analysis is not accurate across the board. The Harmonists influenced the American historical context in a number of significant ways. They contributed to the settling of the Western frontier by founding three flourishing towns. The successful example of the Harmony Society stimulated the formation of other communal settlements in the United States. The Harmony Society's financial prowess encouraged local economic growth. Key Harmonists provided valuable public service, most notably on the Constitutional Committee of the State of Indiana. By exercising their right to vote, the Harmony Society brought influence to bear on local politics. All of these activities are inconsistent with an entirely introversionist sect.

Wilson's introversionist label is largely accurate, however, in the realm of Harmonist religious beliefs during Rapp's lifetime. George Rapp never learned to read or speak more than rudimentary English, although he lived on the American continent for forty-three years. The Harmony Society purchased both German and English primers, spellers, and textbooks for use in their elementary school.[8] But theological works (purchased most likely primarily for George Rapp) were almost exclusively in the German language. There is evidence that Rapp borrowed verbatim from Gottfried Arnold, F. C. Oetinger, Bengel, and Jung-Stilling and indirectly from a number of other German writers. Yet there is no documentary evidence that Rapp was acquainted with English and American religious writers, except for a few authors (Jane Leade, Thomas Bromiley, John Bunyan) in German translation. Although Rapp was interested in religious issues and probably informed of American theological trends, no hard evidence that Rapp's theology was influenced by these trends was discovered. The 1807 revival within the Harmony Society may or may not have been influenced by revivals taking place among the German and English-speaking population in Pennsylvania. In his 1824 exposition of the bowl judgments twenty years after emigration, Rapp equated eschatological events in Revelation with contemporary occurrences in Europe, not the United States. The plan to migrate to Palestine to meet Christ at his Second Coming reflected interaction with a theological debate taking place in Württemberg. The only Anglo-American religious group that Rapp and the Harmony Society were known to have

---

[8] Melvin Miller, "Education in the Harmony Society, 1805-1905" (Ph.D. diss., University of Pittsburgh, 1972), 316-319.

interacted with on a significant level were the Shakers. Rapp (1816) and later Romelius Langenbacher and Jacob Henrici (1865) examined the religious beliefs of this communal society and found them wanting. The Harmony Society during George Rapp's lifetime was oriented theologically toward Germany. It was introversionist with regard to its religious beliefs.

Therefore, to understand properly Harmonist religious beliefs, the German religious and historical background is of key importance. The practice of alchemy and Rapp's authoritarian, patriarchal style of leadership are most understandable when set against the religious and historical context in Württemberg Pietism. Rapp's theology was formed for the most part prior to emigration. Two aspects of his theology were adopted or intensified after arrival on American soil. Oetinger's cabbalistic doctrine of the *Sephiroth* was found only in Rapp's mature sermons. Mystical union with Sophia was incipiently present in Germany, but intensified after emigration. Both of these aspects of Rapp's theology were appropriated through the reading of German (Oetinger, Arnold, Boehme) and not Anglo-American authors.

Sectarian Spirit

In the neutral, sociological sense, a sect is a group that has broken off from the established church. Rapp's Separatist movement arose in response to the perceived spiritual deadness of the Lutheran Church in Württemberg. Like Boehme and other radical Pietists before them, Rapp and his followers heaped aspersions upon the Lutheran church. The church was "Babel," and deserving of God's imminent judgment. Lutheran pastors were hypocritical and ignorant of the deeper meaning of the Bible. It was an abomination that the Eucharist was distributed to those who were not born again. Members of Rapp's Separatist movement had experienced the new birth and, therefore, were "true children of God." This self-understanding promoted a sense of spiritual elitism and an incipient sectarian spirit.

Several years before Rapp's disciples immigrated to the United States, they began to view their Separatist movement as the true eschatological church, the Sunwoman in the wilderness. This self-understanding was never revised during Rapp's lifetime. Rather, in the atmosphere of religious toleration found on the American continent, Rapp and his followers increasingly considered their own group to occupy a favored, crucial role both in the present dispensation and in Christ's millennial kingdom. They had discovered the key to interpret properly the Book of Revelation. Unlike the lukewarm Christians around them, the Harmony Society was putting into practice in the penultimate age God's plan for the millennium—celibate living, oneness of heart and mind, community of goods, self-denial, and submission to the will of God. Unlike some sects, Rapp and the Harmony Society always allowed that salvation was possible for those outside their group. Nevertheless, the Harmony Society exhibited a sectarian spirit. It believed it was privileged above others as the "golden rose" and the Sunwoman in the wilderness. In a later sermon, George Rapp, founder and patriarch of the Harmony Society, reminded members of the Sunwoman, his beloved community:

> For this reason the Sunwoman lives in the wilderness. The wilderness is the proper location. There she worships inwardly and outwardly in spirit and in truth, and quietly waits. There she is properly nourished with the bread of life.... In the wilderness it is said of her: "those that wait upon the Lord will daily renew their strength." The congregation of the Sunwoman has separated itself from others. Gradually it is formed and purified.[9]

Members of the Harmony Society had separated themselves from lukewarm Christianity and formed a visible community of believers in the American wilderness. There they had grown in sanctification as they patiently awaited the imminent return of Christ.

---

[9] MG-185/1-5004/Box 15/Folder 6/R-26.

Appendix A

Manuscript Collections of George Rapp's Pastoral Letters

#	Composition Book (Arndt) MG-437, Box 25	#	Viehmeyer Collection MG-185, 1-5005, Box 16, Folder 1, #1 (Microfilm Roll 324)	#	Collection # 2 MG-185, 1-5005, Box 16, Folder 1, #2
1	Feb 26, 1793	1	Feb 26, 1793	23	Sept 26, 1793
2	1791[1]	2	1791	5	No date
3	Oct 10, 1794	3	d:[en] ... date unreadable	29	Oct 10, 1794
4	No date	4	No date	10	No date
5	Mar 20, 1796	5	March 20, 1796	11	No date
6	Feb or Seb [=Sept] 11, 1796	18	11te 7tr [Sept] 1796	17	Sept 11, 1796
7	1797	6	1797		-----
8	1797	7	1797		-----
9	No date	8	No date	7	No date
10	No date	9	No date	21	No date
11	No date	10	No date	14	No date
12	Jan 28, 1800	11	Jan 28, 1800	15	Jan 28, 1800
13	No date	12	No date	9	No date
14	Feb or Seb[=Sept] 28, 1798	13	28. 7te [Sept] 1798		-----
15	Feb or Seb [=Sept] 3, 1799	14	3. 7te [Sept.] 1799	18	Sept 3, 1799
16	1800	15	1800		-----
17	Jan 27, 1800	16	Jan 27, 1800		-----
18	Aug 13, 1802		-----		-----
		17	No date	3	No date
		19	No date	24	No date
		20	No date	8	No date
		21	No date	16	No date
		22	Feb 12, 1798	13	Feb 12, 1798
		23	9ten 8br [Oct] 1799	2	Oct 9, 1799
		24	12te 9br [Nov] 1798	28	Nov 12, 1798
		25	Jan 6, 1802	12	Jan 6, 1802

---

[1]Arndt incorrectly dated this letter 1794. The composition book and MF 324 clearly assign the date 1791. Once again he was probably swayed by the (incorrect) statement at the beginning of the composition book that the letters were written between 1793 and 1802.

		26	Sept 8, 1801	26	Sept 8, 1801
		27	July 26, 1801	19	July 26, 1801
		28	No date	20	No date
		29	May 1?, 1799	4	May 13, 1799
		30	No date	25	End of letter missing
				1	Oct 16, 1794
				6	April 12, 1798
				22	No date
				27	Oct 24, 1795
				30	No date
				31	No date/incomplete letter

Appendix B

Poems by Gottfried Arnold Included in the 1820 and 1827 *Gesangbücher*

Abbreviations:
Arnold, *Lob und Liebes-Sprüche* (LLS)
Arnold, *Neue Göttliche Liebes-Funcken* (NGLF)
1820 *Gesangbuch* (1820 GB)
1827 *Gesangbuch* (1827 GB)

Arnold Poem	1820 GB	1827 GB	Comparison
Der Weisheit holder Perlen-Schatz liegt (NGLF, #12, p. 246)	#271, p. 204	#72, p. 57	Exactly same as NGLF; GB adds 3 verses
Ihr Salem's Töchter hört (LLS, #10, p. 7)	#341, p. 262	#232, p. 182	Very minor changes; GB adds 2 lines
Nachdem der grosse Streit (LLS, #86, p. 111)	#343, p. 263	#287, p. 226	Very minor changes; GB omits 2 lines
Ich weiß nicht wie mir ist (LLS, #49, p. 67)		#216, p. 171	GB omits vv. 7-13
Die Vernunft mag noch so sehr (LLS, #44, p. 44)		#90, p. 70	Exactly same as LLS
Ihr Zions-Töchter, die ihr nicht (LLS, #41, p. 40)		#237, p. 186	GB omits v. 13
Nichts, gar nichts auf dieser Erden (LLS, #8, p. 6)		#290, p. 229	Exactly same as LLS
Nun weiß ich Gottes Lob (LLS, #63, p. 74)		#290, p. 237	GB omits v. 8
O Königin, du Crone der Jungfrauen (LLS, #74, p. 95)		#330, p. 259	GB omits v. 6
O sanftes leiden, edle Ruh, darinn mein (LLS, #54, p. 60)		#334, p. 261	Exactly same as LLS
So bald das Leben Jesu sich in mir (LLS, #32, p. 31)		#387, p. 303	Exactly same as LLS
Strenger Winter, fleuch von hinnen (LLS, #26, p. 23)		#404, p. 316	Exactly same as LLS
Sulamith, versüßte Wonne (LLS, #100, p. 145)		#405, p. 316	GB omits vv. 8, 9 and 11

Wie, wenn die dunkle Wolke deckt der heitren (LLS, #31), p. 29		#459, p. 358	Exactly same as LLS

Appendix C

Comparison of Rapp Sermon and Arnold's Divine Sophia

Rapp Sophia Sermon (complete text) MG-185/Box 15/Folder 4/ L-32	Gottfried Arnold's *Das Geheimnis der göttlichen Sophia*	Chapter-§-Page
In der h: Schrift hat Christus manicherley nahmen, wodurch man die Geheim: der göttl: Economi, oder verordnung erkennen mag: Er heißt erstl: das Wort weil er aus dem Munde Gottes ausgegangen u. der Vatter nichts ohne das Wort gemacht hat, u. jezt uns die Geheimn: deß himmelr: durch den G: u Wort verkünd:	Der Christus wird auff vielerley art benennet, wodurch man die Geheimnisse der Göttlichen oeconomien oder verordnungen erkennen mag. Er heißt das wort, weil er eigentlich aus dem Munde Gottes ausgegangen, und weil der Vater nichts ohne ihn gemacht und befohlen hat. <u>Er wird die Weisheit genennet, weil er aus deß Vatters Herzen kam,</u> und uns die geheimnisse in dem himmlischen verkündigt hat.	Ch. IV, §14, 33-34
Die Weisheit welche der Vatter gezeuget hat, wird am bequemsten seyn Wort genannt, weil der Vatter am eigenlichsten dardurch bekannt wird.	Die Weisheit welche Gott der Vatter gezeuget hat, wird am bequemsten sein Wort genennet, weil durch dieselbe der Vater nach den allergeheimsten kennzeichen bekannt wird.	Ch. IV, §15, 34.
Nun ist uns wohl bewußt daß, der G: Jesu u der Weish: nichts 2 sondern ein unzertrennlichs Wesen, welches sich durch göttl: Wirckung stätig <u>in der gem:</u> offenbaret. Durch diß wird <u>der Gem:</u> die himml: Sophia jmmer näher u bekannt, als ein sonderbares göttliches Wesen.	Sie erkennet auch dabey, daß der Geist Jesu und der Geist der Weisheit nicht zwey unterschiedene Geister seyn, sondern ein einiger Geist und ein unzertrennliches Wesen, welches sich in ihr durch Göttliche würckungen bey einfältigem gehorsam stätig offenbahre.	Ch. V, §3, 35.
welches zwar an sich selbst mit der Gotth: eins ist, auch ohne sie nichts wircken oder schaffen, aber dennoch ... unter seinem Eigenenem	welches zwar an sich selbst mit der ewigen Gottheit eins, auch ohne und derselben nimmermehr nichts würcket oder schaffet, dennoch aber	Ch. V, §5, 35.

Göttlichem Charachter sich <u>in der Gem</u>: kund u sichbar macht	unter seinem eigenen Göttlichen Characher kund machet	
Da aber <u>die Gem</u>: dennoch alle Eigensch: Wirckung:[en] u kenzeichen <u>dem h: G</u>: als <u>neu Test</u>: zuschrieben. Weil die nahmens alle vollkommen in Eins, u unzertrennl: alle in Eins laufen u bleiben	Da ist es zwar vergönnet, alle eigenschafften, würckungen und kennzeichen der Weisheit <u>dem Sohn Gottes</u> und seinem Geist zuzuschreiben: weil sie alle vollkommen in eines und unzertrennlich seyn und bleiben.	Ch. V, §6, 35-36.
So ergreifet uns <u>der h: G</u>: in der Materi deß leydenten theils, als in der Sophia noch genauer, u bringet ihr läuterendes, u scharfreinigend:[es] [Symbol – Feuer] in die Seele u machet den neuen Tempelbau deß Kraft leibes der Gem: aus der M:heit Jesu welcher <u>in der Gem</u>: nach aller geburts schmerzen u Wehen vollens aus; so sezt der h: G: seyn [Symbol – Feuer] u Heerd mitten ein, so wächst das neue leben zu dessen grosen u vollendetem reifen Geist der Gem: jnnerlich u äußerl:	So dann ergreiffet uns <u>Sophia</u> gleichsam noch genauer, und bringet ihr läuterendes und scharfreinigendes Feuer in die Seele, machet den geistlichen Tempelbau des neuen Krafftleibes auß der menschheit Jesu, welcher <u>in der Seele</u> nach allen geburts-schmerzen und wehen im fleisch kommen war vollends auß, setzet ihr feuer und heerd mitten drein und machet anstalt zur wesentlichen niederkunfft des H. Geistes, und zu dessen grossen und vollendenden reiche im Geist des Menschen.	Ch. V, §7, 36.
Da tritt den der h: G: im Wort der verheißung <u>der Gem</u>: jmmer näher, u salbet u durchdringet die [Symbol – Herzen], u verbeßert, verfeinert alles, was sich unterwirft, u begnadigt seyn will; u stärket das schwache mit seinem [Symbol – Feuer] u Licht, so daß endl: die Gem: in ihrem Gemüthe angezündet, gleichsam eine [Symbol – Feuer] burg, einen [Symbol – Feuer] brennend: Busch, u gar das allerheiligste eröfnet siehet; darinnen Gottes nahmen Jehova Jesus! geistl: u. leibl: da wohnet, u sich <u>die Gem</u>: insgesamt zum vollkommenem Sieg rüstet, u. wesentl: hervor thut den lezten kampf zu behaupten mit Christo, u allen heiligen.	Da tritt denn der H. Geist der verheissung, welches eben der Geist der Weisheit und der Geist Jesu ist näher zu, und salbet und durchdringet die an ihr selbst noch zarte und überwindliche neue Menschheit, und stärcket sie also mit seinem feuer und Licht, daß die Seele mit ihren gemüths-Augen gleichsam eine feurige Burg, einen brennenden Busch, und das allerheiligste in sich selbst erblicket, darinnen Gottes name Jehovah Jesus im Geist wohnet, und sich zum vollkommenen sieg wesentlich hervor thut.	Ch. V, §8, 36.

Appendix D

Bible Texts Given for Sermons Transcribed in 1838 Sermon Book

Bible Book	Sermons	Bible Book	Sermons
Genesis	5	Matthew	3
Exodus	3	Luke	1
Leviticus	1	John	10
Numbers	1	Acts	2
Deuteronomy	2	Romans	8
2 Samuel	1	1 Corinthians	1
Esther	1	2 Corinthians	3
Psalm	26	Ephesians	5
Proverbs	2	Colossians	6
Ecclesiastes	1	2 Thessalonians	1
Song of Solomon	6	Hebrews	8
Isaiah	33	1 Peter	4
Jeremiah	3	2 Peter	1
Ezekiel	2	1 John	3
Daniel	2	Jude	1
Hosea	1	Revelation	10
Joel	1		
Micah	1	Wisdom of Solomon	2
Zechariah	4	Jesus Sirach	2
Malachi	3		

Appendix E

Comparison of Rapp Sermon and Oetinger's *Lehrtafel*

Rapp Sermon - MG-185, 1-5004, Box 15, Folder 6, P-139	Oetinger, *Lehrtafel* (1977 edition)	Page, Lines
Es will manchem fremd vorkommen, daß 10 ausflüße Gottes seyn sollen, aber die h: Sch: sagt ja von einer Fülle Gottes, also von etwas das durch viele ausgänge, oder ausflüsse erfült wird. Micha am 1 spricht deutl: daß Christus nach seiner Gottheit nicht einen, sondern mehrern ausgänge habe von ewigk:	Will es dem natürlichen Menschen fremd vor kommen, daß zehen Ausflüsse Gottes seyn sollen, so bedenke er, daß die Heil. Schrift von einer Fülle Gottes rede, also von etwas, das durch viele Ausgänge oder Ausflüsse Gottes erfüllt wird … In Micha c. 5 stehet deutlich, daß Christus nach seiner Gottheit nicht nur einen, sondern mehrere Ausgänge, »Mozaot«, habe von Ewigkeit.	91, 36-39 and 41-42
wie man sich die 10 ausgänge Gottes vorstellen soll	Wie man sich die Lehren von den zehen Ausgängen Gottes einfältig vorstellen solle?	93, 4-5
Gott ist aber die unergründl: tiefe, der in sich selbst wohnt, dieser will sich dem geschöpf mittheil:	GOtt ist die unergründliche Tieffe, der AEn Soph, der oben an der Tafel stehet, der in sich selbst wohnt, dieser will sich den Geschöpffen mittheilen.	93, 6-7
durch die erste tritt Gott als eine Crone in die unermeßliche peripherie in Christo u der Gem: Der ausbreitung seines jnnersten P: Ps 150:1.	Durch die erste tritt Gott als eine Crone oder unermeßliche Peripherie der Ausbreitung seines innersten Puncts (Ps. 150,1)	93, 10-11
Die 2. als das Wort beschauet er er sich in sich selbst.	Durch die andern: als die Weißheit beschauet Er sich in sich selbst, chochmah.	93, 12
Durch die 3 gibt er die unterscheidung in sich selbst hervor. u der H: G: unterscheidet die verborgenheiten der Weish: durch die 2 in 3. u durch diese in 7. u noch weiter biß in die Gem:	Durch die dritte gibt er die Unterscheidung der vorweltlichen Original-Ideen in sich selbst hervor. Die Weißheit spielt Gott vor, und Gott bestätiget seinen Vorsatz (Prov. 8); der h. Geist unterscheidet die Verborgenheiten der Weißheit durch zwey in drey und durch diese in sieben und noch weiter	93, 13-16

	ins unendliche (Hiob 11,6): Binah.	
Durch die 4 breitet er seine kräfte aus, in sich selbst Ps 50. Lobet ihn in der ausbreitung seiner kraft.	Durch die vierte, Gedulah, breitet er seine Kräften aus in sich selbst (Ps. 150, 1: Lobet ihn in der Ausbreitung seiner Kraft).	93, 17-19
u in der 5 verfaßt er sie wider zusammen daß wir ihn in seinen kräften loben.	Durch die fünfte, Gebhurah, intendirt und verfaßt Er sie wieder zusammen, daß wir ihn in seinem[!] Gebhurot, »Kräften«, loben (Ps. 150,1).	93, 18-20
In der 6 sezt er die widrigk: in aus dem streit, in die lieblichste schönh: wie der Ps: sagt, Lob u Zierde ist vor ihm, u schönh: ist in seinem Heiligth: Ps 96:6.	Durch die sechste, Tiphaeraet, setzt Er die Extension und Intension aus dem Streit in die lieblichste Schönheit, wie der Psalmist singt: hod vehadar lephanav, Lob und Zierde ist vor Ihm, und Schönheit ist in seinem Heiligthum (Ps. 96,6).	93, 20-22
Aber in der 7 gehen also die wirckenden kräfte u ausgänge so lang froet, biß alles in der Gem: zur ruhe kommt.	Durch die siebende, Naezach ... So gehen also Gottes würckende Kräften und Ausgänge solang fort, biß sie zur Ruhe kommen.	93, 23, 26- 27
Herrlk: ist das Grundw: deß neuen Test: u ist die 8, Herrlk: u geht noch höher u näher zur voller Leiblk: dahin lauft zulezt alles hinaus.	Durch die achte, Hod »Herrlichkeit«, geht es näher zur Ruhe. Herrlichkeit ist das Grund-Wort Neuen Testaments	93, 29-30
Durch die 9 bekommt alles seinen bestand, alles was daurend, u bestandhaltend ist, hat da seine wurzel. Ein fels ist Gott, darum ist seyn werck vollkommen.	Durch die neunte, Jesod, bekommt alles seinem Verstand. Alle sensoria, alle reflexive Kräften, die Unvergänglichkeit der Seele, alles, was daurend und bestand-haltend ist, hat da seine Wurtzel. Ein Fels ist Gott, darum ist sein Werck vollkommen.	93, 32-34
Durch die 10 kommt die Gottheit zur ewigen faßung, zum Sabath,zum Königr: in dem Herrn aller Herren u der Gem: in Christo: Da begibt sich die Gotth: in einen neuen,von ewigen Zeiten verschwigenen Stand, für die M: u Engel.	Durch die zehende, Malkut, kommt die Gottheit aus dem Actu purissimo endelechico, d. i. würckend fortschreitenden Übergang, zur Ruhe, zur ewigen Fassung, zum Sabbat, zum Königreich, und das ist in Adonai, in dem Herrn aller Herrn, Christo, da begibt sich die Gottheit in einen neuen von ewigen Zeiten verschwigenen Stand für die Menschen und Engel.	93, 35-39
Die 3heit ist überall offenb:	Die Dreyheit ist höchst	94, 7-8

aber die 7benheit ist eine dopelte wohnung der 3heit, vereinigt in die Einh:	intellectual. Die Siebenheit ist eine doppelte Wohnung der Dreyhelt, vereinigt in die Einheit;	
Seelig ist der erfährt, was das heißt wir wollen zu ihm kommen u wohnung bey ihn machen.	Seelig ist, der erfährt: Wir wollen zu Ihm kommen und Wohnung m Ihm machen.	94, 11-12

Appendix F

Rapp's Interpretation of the Trumpet Judgments (1824)

	Verse	Biblical Text	Past or Contemporary Fulfillment[1]
1	Rev 8:7	Hail and fire burns up third of earth	Decline in morals through luxurious and sensuous living during reign of Louis XV of France (1710-1774)
2	Rev 8:8-9	Mountain falls into sea; destroys third of fish and ships	Import of foreign and luxurious goods (not stated from where to where) Violence and war at sea
3	Rev 8:10-11	Star falls on third of rivers, which become bitter	Naturalistic religion of Voltaire and Rousseau
4	Rev 8:12-13	Third of heavenly bodies are darkened	Sun (religion), moon (morals), stars (teachers) are darkened through Neologians Edelmann and Semler; Positive light of Berleburg Bible
5	Rev 9:1-12	Locusts torture those without seal	Positive signs of spiritual life seen in Gottfried Arnold, Kant, and Fichte despite Enlightenment religion
6	Rev 9:13-21	Angels at Euphrates destroy third of mankind by plagues	Contemporary wars between Turkish Empire and Greece begin to open path for emigration to Palestine; Establishment of Bible societies
7	Rev 11:15	Kingdom of God is established	Brethren leave all sects and emigrate to American wilderness

---

[1]This chart and the one below are based on notes recorded in the notebook of Romelius Langenbacher. The author was unable to locate the actual notebook in the Harmony Society archives. She found Karl Arndt's transcription of the text, and photocopy of the original in the University of Southern Indiana archives, Evansville, Indiana. USI/ MSS #311/ Box 36/ Folder 6. Romelius mentioned in a letter to his brother and fellow Harmonist, Johannes Langenbacher, on Oct. 22, 1824, that he was taking notes on Rapp's teaching for the benefit of Johannes. This letter provides the *terminus ad quem* (Oct. 1824) for the exposition on the bowl judgments. "The time and the judgments of God are hurrying and it is proved that the 6th vial of wrath is being poured out, as you will hear, for I have each time written up for you the most important points, which space here does not permit me to write." Arndt, *Doc. Hist. 1820-1824*, 126.

Rapp's Interpretation of the Bowl Judgments (1824)

Bowl	Biblical Text	Contemporary Fulfillment in Rapp	Jung-Stilling, *Siegesgeschichte*[2]	
1 Rev 16:2	Sores on those with mark of beast	Cancer of revolution and insatiable hunger for freedom	Cancer of revolution French Revolution (386-388)	same
2 Rev 16:3	Sea turns to blood; creatures in sea die	Stoppage of shipping trade	Stoppage of shipping trade (388-390)	same
3 Rev 16:4-7	Rivers turn to blood	Import of foreign goods (not stated from where to where) and luxury leads to poverty	Enlightenment theology (390-392) Reign of Terror Christian martyrs	different
4 Rev 16:8-9	Sun scorches people with fire	Enlightenment theologians	Enlightenment theology (*Nachtrag*, 200-204)	same
5 Rev 16:10-11	Kingdom of beast plunged into darkness; men curse God because of troubles	Vienna Congress (1814-1815) Luxurious lifestyle of ruling class, who curse God	Rebellion and revolution (394-395)	different
6 Rev 16:12-16	Euphrates river dried up; kings of earth gather for Armageddon	Present/future unrest in Turkish empire Opens way for emigration to Palestine	Revolution in Turkish empire Opens way for emigration to Palestine (395-398)	same
7 Rev 16:17-21	Great earthquake with lightening, thunder and hailstones	Revolutions Future actual earthquake Past earthquakes in Spain and Naples	Revolutions Future actual earthquake Past earthquake in Calabria (402-403)	same

[2]USI/ MSS #311/ Box 36/ Folder 6. Cf. Johann Heinrich Jung-Stilling, Die Siegesgeschichte der Christlichen Religion in einer gemeinnützigen Erklärung der Offenbarung Johannis (Nürnberg: [s.n.], 1799), 386-403.

Bibliography

Primary Sources (Archival)

Articles of Association (1805-1824). OEV, MG-185, C-001.
Book of Women's Clothing, 1821-1827. OEV, MG-185, Microfilm Roll #216.
Exposition on the Seven Bowls of Wrath, 1824. USI, MSS #311, Box 36, Folder 6.
Family Book 2W, 1819-1826. OEV, MG-185, Microfilm Roll #215.
George Rapp's Hymns. OEV, MG-437, Box 22, Folder 83, Hymns #1-14.
Harmony Fest Hymns and Sermons. OEV, Library Box 26.
Letters from Harmony Society, 1848-1878. OEV, Correspondence Book (CO) 25.
Love Feast Records. OEV, MG-185, Microfilm Roll #316, General File.
Manuscript Hymnbooks. OEV, pM 4.7, pM 10.1, pM 10.3, pM 12.2, pM 12.3.
Manuscript Sermons. OEV, MG-185/1-5004/Box 15/Folders 4, 5 and 6. OEV, MG-437/Box 22/Folder 82B.
Memorandum Book, 1827-1828. OEV, MG-185, C-0133.
Memorandum of Flour roasted for expected Pilgrimage to Holy Land, 1841-1850. OEV, MG-185, Microfilm roll #168.
Notes from Bible Discussion (March, 1832). USI, MSS # 311, Box 46, Folder 14.
Pastoral Letters. OEV, MG-185, 1-5005, Box 16, Folder 1, Viehmayer Collection and Collection #2. MG-437, Box 25.
Remarks by George Rapp, Feb. 15, 1829. OEV, Daniel Reibel's file.
Shaker Questions and Answers. OEV, MG-437, Box 22, Folder 113.
Thermometer Books. OEV, MG-185, General File, 1-4994, Box C-0002.
Uncatalogued Rapp Sermon. OEV, *Berleburg Bible*, vol. 5, p. 10-11.
Wallrath Weingärtner's 1832 map of New Harmony. OEV, MG-185, Maps and Land drafts, 06.72.17.84.
1832 Easter celebration. USI, MSS #311, Box 46, Folder 14.
1838 Sermon Book. OEV, MG-437, Box 25 and MG-185/Box 1-4997/Box # 8/ Folder 20.

Primary Sources (Printed)

Christian Armbruster, *Die sieben letzten Posaunen oder Wehen, wann sie anfangen und aufhören und von den 70 Danielischen Wochen und 42 prophetischen Monaten.* Ulm: [s.n.], 1814.

Arndt, Karl J. R. *A Documentary History of the Indiana Decade of the Harmony Society, 1814-1819.* Indianapolis: Indiana Historical Society, 1975.

_____. *A Documentary History of the Indiana Decade of the Harmony Society, 1820-1824.* Indianapolis: Indiana Historical Society, 1978.

_____. *Economy on the Ohio, 1826-1834. George Rapp's Third Harmony. A Documentary History.* Worcester, Mass.: Harmony Society Press, 1984.

_____. *George Rapp's Separatists, 1700-1803. A Documentary History.* Worcester, Mass.: Harmony Society Press, 1980.

_____. *George Rapp's Years of Glory. Economy on the Ohio, 1834-1847. George Rapp's Third Harmony. A Documentary History.* New York: Peter Lang, 1987.

_____. *Harmony on the Connoquenessing, 1803-1815. A Documentary History.* Worcester, Mass.: Harmony Society Press, 1980.

_____. *Harmony on the Wabash in Transition, 1824-1826. A Documentary History.* Worcester, Mass.: Harmony Society Press, 1982.

Arnold, Gottfried. *Das Geheimnis der göttlichen Sophia.* Introduction by Walter Nigg. Stuttgart-Bad Cannstatt: F. Frommann, 1963.

_____. *Die erste Liebe, das ist, Wahre Abbildung der ersten Christen : nach ihrem lebendigen Glauben und heiligen Leben, aus der ältesten und bewährtesten Kirchen-Scribenten eigenen Zeugnissen, Exempeln und Reden, nach der Wahrheit der ersten einigen christlichen Religion, allen Liebhabern der historischen Wahrheit, und sonderlich der Antiquität, als in einer nützlichen Kirchen-Historie, treulich und unparteyisch entworfen : worinnen zugleich des Hn. William Cave Erstes Christenthum nach Nothdurft erläutert wird.* 5th. ed. Leipzig: Samuel Benjamin Walthern, 1732.

_____. *Unpartheyische Kirchen- und Ketzer-Historie vom Anfang des Neuen Testaments bis auf das Jahr 1688.* Hildesheim: Georg Olms, 1967.

Bengel, Johann Albrecht. *Erklärte Offenbarung Johannis: oder vielmehr Jesu Christ: aus dem revidirten Grund-Text übersetzt durch die prophetischen Zahlen ausgeschlossen und allen, die auf das Werk und Wort des Herrn achten, und dem, was vor der Thür ist, würdiglich entgegen zu kommen begehren, vor Augen geleget.* Stuttgart: Fr. Brodhag, 1834.

_____. *Sechzig erbauliche Reden über die Offenbarung Johannis oder vielmehr Jesu Christi, sammt eine Nachlese gleichen Inhalts.* 3d ed. Stuttgart: [s.n.], 1835.

Bernhard, Duke of Saxe-Weimar Eisenach. *Travels through North America during the Years 1825 and 1826.* 2 vols. Philadelphia: Carey, Lea and Carey, 1828.

Boehme, Jacob. *De signatura rerum, oder Von der Geburt und Bezeichnung aller Wesen.* Vol. 6. *Sämtliche Schriften.* Edited by Will-Erich Peuckert. Stuttgart: Frommanns, 1957.

_____. *De Triplici Vita Hominis, oder vom Dreyfachen Leben des Menschen.* Vol. 3. *Sämtliche Schriften.* Edited by Will-Erich Peuckert. Stuttgart: Frommanns, 1960.

_____. *Glaube und Tat. Eine Auswahl aus dem Gesamtwerk.* Edited by Eberhard Hermann Pältz. Marburg: Oekumenischer Verlag, 1976.

_____. *Informatorium Novissimorum oder Unterricht von den Letzten Zeiten an Paul Kaym in zwei Theilen.* [s.l.]: [s.n.], 1730.

_____. *Mysterium Magnum: Or an Exposition of the First Book of Moses Called Genesis.* Translated by John Sparrow. Kila, Mont.: Kessinger, 1990.

_____. *Schutzschriften wider Balthasar Tilken.* Vol. 5. *Sämtliche Schriften.* Edited by Will-Erich Peuckert. Stuttgart: Frommanns, 1960.

_____. *The Aurora.* Translated by John Sparrow. Edited by Charles J. Barker and D. S. Hehner. London: J. M. Watkins, 1960.

_____. *The Signature of All Things: And Other Writings.* Edited by Clifford Bax. London: James Clarke, 1969.

_____. *The Way to Christ.* Translated and with an Introduction by Peter Erb. New York: Paulist Press, 1978.

_____. *Von der Menschwerdung Jesu Christi.* Edited by Gerhard Wehr. Frankfurt: Insel Verlag, 1995.

Brecht, Martin and Rudolf F. Paulus, eds. *Philipp Matthäus Hahn. Die Echterdinger Tagebücher 1780-1790.* Berlin: Walter De Gruyter, 1983.

_____. *Philipp Matthäus Hahn. Die Kornwestheimer Tagebücher, 1772-1777.* Berlin: Walter De Gruyter, 1979.

Bromme, Traugott. *Nord-Amerika Bewohner, Schönheiten und Naturschätze.* Stuttgart: J. Scheible, 1839.

Büchsel, Jürgen. *Gottfried Arnolds Weg von 1696 bis 1705. Sein Briefwechsel mit Tobias Pfanner und weitere Quellentexte.* Halle: Verlag der Franckesche Stiftungen, 2011.

Calov, Abraham. *Biblia testam. veteris illustrate.* Frankfurt: Balthasar Christoph Wust, 1672.

Cuming, Fortescue. *Sketches of a Tour to the Western Country.* Pittsburgh: Cramer, Spear and Eichbaum, 1810.

Dittelmair, Johann Augustin. *Die Heilige Schrift des Alten und Neuen Testaments.* Siebenter Theil. Leipzig: Bernhard Christoph Breitkopf, 1756.

Doctrinal Standards of the Christian Reformed Church Consisting of the Belgic Confession, the Heidelberg Confession and the Canons of Dort. Grand Rapids: Christian Reformed Church, 1962.

Eine kleine Sammlung Harmonischer Lieder als die erste Probe der anfangenden Druckerey anzusehen. Harmonie, Ind: Harmony Society Publications, 1824.

Erb, Peter C. *Pietists: Selected Writings.* New York: Paulist Press, 1983.

Evangelische Deutsche Original-Bibel von 1741: Hebräischer und Griechischer Original-Text mit der Deutschen Originalübersetzung Martin Luther. 2 vols. Berlin: Eva Berndt, 1986.

Feurige Kohlen der aufsteigenden Liebesflammen im Lustspiel der Weisheit. Oekonomie, Pa.: Harmony Society Publications, 1826.

Flattich, Johann Friedrich. *Briefe.* Edited by Hermann Ehmer and Christoph Duncker. Stuttgart: Calwer Verlag, 1997.

Friedrich, Johann Jakob. *Glaubens- und Hoffnung-Blick des Volks Gottes in der anti-christlichen Zeit aus den göttlichen Weissagungen gezogen.* [s.l.]: [s.n.], 1801.

Gichtel, Johann Georg. *Eine kurze Eröffnung und Anweisung der dreyen Principien und Welten im Menschen.* Berlin: Ringmacher, 1779.

Hahn, Johann Michael. *Briefe über die Apostel-Geschichte, den Brief an die Galater und Judä; Briefe und Lieder über die Epistel Petri und Jakobi.* Tübingen : L.F. Fues, 1820.

———. *Briefe und Lieder über die heilige Offenbarung Jesu Christi.* Tübingen: L.F. Fues, 1820.

———. *Briefe und Lieder über die zweite Epistel Pauli an die Korinther, die Episteln an die Epheser, Kolosser, Philipper und Thessalonicher und die zweite und dritte Epistel Johannis.* Stuttgart: Hahnsche Gemeinschaft, 1938.

———. *Briefe von der ersten Offenbarung Gottes durch die ganze Schöpfung bis an das Ziel aller Dinge, oder das System seiner Gedanken.* Tübingen: L. F. Fues, 1839.

———. *Send-Briefe über einzelne Capitel aus dem alten und den vier Evangelisten und Antworten auf Fragen über Herzenserfahrungen, auf Verlangen an Freunde der Wahrheit geschrieben.* Tubingen: L.F. Fues, 1828.

———. *Send-Briefe über einzelne Capitel aus dem alten und neuen Testament und Antworten auf Fragen über Herzenserfahrungen. Nebst einem Anhang von Briefen über das Hohe Lied Salomo und einigen Liedern.* Tubingen: L.F. Fues, 1830.

Harmonisches Gesangbuch. Oekonomie, Pa.: Harmony Society Publications, 1827.

Harmonisches Gesangbuch. Allentown, Pa.: Heinrich Ebner, 1820.

Haug, Johann Heinrich, et al. *Die Heilige Schrift Altes und Neues Testaments, nach dem Grund-Text aufs Neue übersehen und übersetzet. Nebst einiger Erklärung des buchstäblichen Sinnes wie auch der fürnehmsten Fürbildern und Weissagungen von Christo und seinem Reich, und zugleich einigen Lehren, die auf den Zustand der Kirchen in unseren letzten Zeiten gerichtet sind.* 8 vols. Berlenburg: [s.n.], 1726-1742.

Horch, Heinrich. *Mystische und profetische Bibel, Das ist die gantze Heil. Schrifft, Altes und Neues Testasmants, auffs neue nach dem Grund verbessert, Sampt Erklärung der fürnemsten Sinnbilder und Weissagungen, Sonderlich des H. Lieds Salomons und der Offenbarung J. C. wie auch denen fürnehmsten Lehren, bevoraus die sich in diese letzen Zeiten schicken.* Marburg: Joh. Kürtzner, 1712.

Jung-Stilling, Johann Heinrich. *Das Heimweh. Vollständige, ungekürzte Ausgabe nach der Erstausgabe von 1794-1796.* Edited and introduced by Martina Maria Sam. Dornach, Switzerland: Verlag am Goetheanum, 1994.

_____. *Die Siegesgeschichte der Christlichen Religion in einer gemeinnützigen Erklärung der Offenbarung Johannis.* Nürnberg: [s.n.], 1799.

_____. *Erster Nachtrag zur Siegesgeschichte der Christlichen Religion in einer gemeinnützigen Erklärung der Offenbarung Johannis.* Nürnberg: Raw, 1805.

Kelpius, Johannes. *The Diarium of Magister Johannes Kelpius.* Annotations by Julius Friedrich Sachse. Vol. 27. *Narrative and Critical History.* Lancaster, Pa.: Pennsylvania-German Society, 1917.

Leade, Jane. *Revelations of Revelations* (1683) http://www.passtheword.org/Jane-Lead/revelatn.html [accessed November 15, 2006].

_____. *Sixty Propositions* (1697). http://www.passtheword.org/Jane-Lead/60-propositions.html [accessed November 15, 2006].

Luther, Martin. *Werke. Kritische Gesamtausgabe.* Weimar: H. Böhlau, 1883-.

Markworth, Hermann.

_____. "Die Rappischen Kolonien." *Beilage zur Sonntagsmorgen.* Cincinnati: Heinrich Haacke & Co, July 16, 1882.

Melish, John. *Travels through the United States of America.* Philadelphia: T&G Palmer, 1812.

Oetinger, Friedrich Christoph. *Biblisches und Emblematisches Wörterbuch* (Heilbronn: [s.n.], 1776.

_____. *Die Lehrtafel der Prinzessin Antonia.* Edited by Reinhard Breymayer and Friedrich Häussermann. Vols. 1 and 2. New York: Walter de Gruyter, 1977.

———. *Die Theologie aus der Idee des Lebens*. Edited by Julius Hamberger. Stuttgart: Steinkopf, 1852.

———. *Herrenberger Evangelienpredigten*. Metzingen: Ernst Frank Verlag, 1987.

———. *Sämtliche Schriften*. Abteilung 1. *Predigten*. Vol. 4. Stuttgart: Steinkopf, 1977.

———. *Swedenborgs irdische und himmlische Philosophie*. Edited by Karl Chr. Eberhard Ehmann and introduced by Erich Beyreuther. Stuttgart: Steinkopf, 1977.

———. *Theosophische Schriften*. Vols. 1 and 6. Stuttgart: Steinkopf, 1858.

———. *Weinsberger Evangelienpredigten*. Metzingen: Ernst Franz Verlag, 1972.

Olearius, Johannes. *Biblischer Erklärung. Dritter Theil.* Leipzig: Johann Christoph Tarnoven, 1679.

Owen, Robert Dale. *Threading My Way. An Autobiography*. New York: A. M. Kelley, 1874.

Petersen, Johann Wilhelm. *Das Geheimniß des in der letzten Zeit gebährenden Apocalyptischen Weibes, Mit welchen eine Neue Kirchen-Zeit angehet, und welches das Grosse Zeichen im Himmel ist, das bisher von den wenigsten erkannt, itzo aber durch den aufschliessenden Geiste Gottes aus den Schrifften der Propheten und Apostel, und absonderlich aus der Heil. Offenbarung am XII c. nach dem wahrhafftigen Sinn eröffnet ist*. Frankfurt: Samuel Heyl and Joh. Gottfried Liebezeit, 1708.

Rapp, George. *Gedanken über die Bestimmungen des Menschen besonders in Hinsicht der gegenwärtigen Zeit* Harmony, Ind.: [s.n.], 1824.

———. *Thoughts on the Destiny of Man Particularly with Reference to the Present Times*. Harmony, Ind.: [s.n.], 1824.

Shelling, Joseph Friedrich. *Summarien oder gründliche Auslegung der Schriften alten Testaments. Dritter Band, welcher die Bücher: Esra, Nehemia, Esther, Hiob, die Sprüche und den Prediger enthält zu öffentlicher Kirchenandacht in dem Königreich Württemberg, auch zum erbaulichen Hausgebrauch ausgefertigt.* Stuttgart: Königl. Hof- und Kanzlei-Buchdruckerei der Gebrüder Mäntler, 1810.

Schneider, Hans, ed. *Gottfried Arnold. Die Erste Liebe.* Leipzig: Evangelische Verlagsanstalt, 2002.

Schütz, Christoph. *Güldene Rose, oder ein Zeugniss der Wahrheit von der uns nun so nahe bevorstehenden Güldenen Zeit des tausendjährigen und ewigen Reichs Jesu Christi und der damit verbundenen Wiederbringung aller Dinge.* 2 vols. 3d ed. [s.l.]: [s.n.], 1809.

Seiler, Georg Friedrich. *Das größre biblische Erbauungsbuch*. Theil 4. Erlangen: Bibelanstalt, 1791.

Spener, Philipp Jacob. *Pia Desideria. Umkehr in die Zukunft. Reformprogramm des Pietismus.* Revised by Erich Beyreuther. 5th ed. Giessen: Brunnen, 1995.

Starke, Johann Georg. *Kurzgefaßter Auszug der grundlichsten und nutzbarsten Auslegungen über alle Bücher Altes Testaments.* Theil 4. Leipzig: Bernhard Christoph Breitkopf, 1750.

Stieglitz C. L. *Encyklopädie der bürgerlichen Baukunst.* Leipzig: [s.n.], 1792-1798.

Tersteegen, Gerhard. *Geistliches Blumengärtlein inniger Seelen nebst der Frommen Lotterie.* Stuttgart: Steinkopf, 1868.

_____. *Geistliche Reden.* Edited by Albert Löschhorn and Winfried Zeller. Göttingen: Vandenhoeck & Ruprecht, 1979.

The Book of Concord. The Confessions of the Evangelical Lutheran Church. Edited by Robert Kolb und Timothy J. Wengert. Translated by Charles Arand et. al. Minneapolis: Fortress Press, 2000.

Wagner, Jonathan. *Geschichte u. Verhältnisse der Harmoniegesellschaft.* Vaihingen an der Enz: Deininger, 1833.

Williams, Aaron. *The Harmony Society, at Economy, Penn'a.* Pittsburgh: W. S. Haven, 1866.

Zimmermann, Johann Jacob. *Muthmaßliche Zeit-Bestimmung gewiß gewärtiger, beedes Göttlicher Gerichten uber das Europeische Babel und Anti-Christenthum ietzigen Seculi, als auch hierauff erfolgenden Herrlichen Auffgangs des Reichs Christi auf Erden, So Aus Veranlassung bißheriger Cometen Erschein- und Beschreibungen Jedoch nicht bloßhin nach Astrologischen Sätzen sondern vielmehr nach heiliger Schrifft Anleitung ausgearbeitet Ambrosius Sehmann, von Caminiez.* Frankfurt: [s.n.], 1684.

_____. "Untersuchung eines Bedenkens, ob die Evangelischen Kirche mit Recht babel sey und antichristlich zu schelten und davon auszugehen seye? Sonderlich wegen der Symbolischen Bücher." In *Theologische Bedencken.* Vol. 1. Edited by Philipp Jakob Spener. Halle: Waysenhaus, 1712, 341-352.

Secondary Sources:

Ahlstrom, Sydney E. *A Religious History of the American People.* New Haven: Yale University Press, 1972.

Albrecht, Ruth "'Der einzige Weg zur Erkenntnis Gottes' – Die Sophia-Theologie Gottfried Arnolds und Jakob Böhmes. " In *Auf den Spuren der Weisheit,* ed. Verena Wodtke, 102-117. Freiburg: Herder, 1991.

Ammann, A. "Darstellung und Deutung der Sophia im vorpetrinischen Russland." *Orientalia Christiana Periodica* 4, nos. 1-2 (1938): 120-156.

Arndt, Karl J. R. *George Rapp's Disciples, Pioneers and Heirs: A Register of the Harmonists in America.* Edited by Donald E. Pitzer and Leigh Ann Chamness. Evansville, Ind.: University of Southern Indiana Press, 1994.

―――――. "George Rapp's Harmony Society." In *America's Communal Utopias*, ed. Donald E. Pitzer, 57-87. Chapel Hill, N.C.: University of North Carolina Press, 1997.

―――――. *George Rapp's Harmony Society 1785-1847.* Rev. ed. Teaneck, N.J.: Fairleigh Dickinson University Press, 1972.

―――――. *George Rapp's Successors and Material Heirs 1847- 1916.* Teaneck, N.J.: Fairleigh Dickinson University Press, 1971.

―――――. "Herder and the Harmony Society." *Germanic* Review 16, no. 2 (April 1941): 108-113.

―――――. "Luther's Golden Rose at New Harmony, Indiana." *Concordia Historical Institute Quarterly* 49 (Fall 1976): 112-122.

Bach, Jeff. "Der Pazifismus und die Schwarzenauer Neutäufer." In *Der radikale Pietismus. Perspectiven der Forschung.* Edited by Wolfgang Breul, Marcus Meier and Lothar Vogel. Göttingen: Vandenhoeck & Ruprecht, 2010, 229-236.

―――――. *Voices of the Turtledoves: The Sacred World of Ephrata.* University Park, Pa.: Pennsylvania State University Press, 2003.

Benrath, Gustav Adolf. "Die Erweckung innerhalb der deutschen Landeskirchen, 1815-1888." In *Geschichte des Pietismus.* Vol. 3. *Der Pietismus im neunzehnten und zwanzigsten Jahrhundert*, ed. Ulrich Gäbler, 150-271. Göttingen: Vandenhoeck & Ruprecht, 2000.

―――――. "Tersteegen's Begriff der Mystik und der mystischen Theologie." In *Der radikale Pietismus. Perspectiven der Forschung.* Edited by Wolfgang Breul, Marcus Meier and Lothar Vogel. Göttingen: Vandenhoeck & Ruprecht, 2010, 303-325.

Benz, Ernst. *Adam, der Mythus vom Urmenschen.* Munich: Barth Verlag, 1955.

―――――. *Der vollkommene Mensch nach Jacob Boehme.* Stuttgart: Kohlhammer, 1937.

―――――. *Die Christliche Kabbala. Ein Stiefkind der Theologie.* Zurich: Rhein-Verlag, 1958.

―――――. "Gottfried Arnold's 'Geheimnis der göttlichen Sophia' und seine Stellung in der christlichen Sophienlehre." *Jahrbuch der Hessischen Kirchen Geschichtlichen Vereinigung* 18 (1967): 51-82.

Bernet, Claus. *'Gebaute Apokalypse.' Die Utopie des himmlischen Jerusalem in der frühen Neuzeit.* Mainz: Verlag Philipp von Zabern, 2007.

Betz, Otto. "Kabbala Baptizata. Die jüdisch-christliche Kabbala und der Pietismus in Württemberg." *Pietismus und Neuzeit* 24 (1998): 130-159.

Bister, Ulrich. "Gerhard Tersteegen – Die Rezeption seiner Schriften in Nordamerika und sein dortiger Freundeskreis." In *Gerhard Tersteegen – Evangelischer Mystik inmitten der Aufklärung*. Edited by Manfred Kock and Jürgen Thiesbonenkamp. Cologne: Rheinland Verlag, 1997, 123-134.

Bjorndalen, Anders Jorgen. "Allegory." In *A Dictionary of Biblical Interpretation*, ed. R. J. Coggins and J. L. Houlden, 14-16. Philadelphia: Trinity Press, 1990.

Bonomi, Patricia. *Under the Cope of Heaven: Religion, Society and Politics in Colonial America*. New York: Oxford University Press, 1986.

Bornkamm, H. "Böhme." In *Die Religion in Geschichte und Gegenwart*. Vol. 1, ed. Hans Frhr. v. Campenhausen, Erich Dinkler, Gerhard Gloege, Knud E. Logstrup, and Kurt Galling, 1340-1342. Tübingen: Mohr, 1957.

Bratt, James D. "A New Narrative for American Religious History?" *Fides et Historia* 23 (1991): 19-30.

Brecht, Martin. *Ausgewählte Aufsätze*, Vol. 2: *Pietismus*. Stuttgart: Calwer Verlag, 1997.

_____. "Chiliasmus in Württemberg in 17. Jahrhundert." *Pietismus und Neuzeit* 14 (1988): 25-49.

_____. "Das Aufkommen der neuen Frömmigkeitsbewegung in Deutschland." In *Geschichte des Pietismus*. Vol. 2. *Das 17. und frühe 18. Jahrhundert*, ed. Martin Brecht, 113-203. Göttingen: Vandenhoeck & Ruprecht, 1993.

_____. "Der radikale Pietismus – die Problematik einer historischen Kategorie." In *Der radikale Pietismus. Perspectiven der Forschung*. Edited by Wolfgang Breul, Marcus Meier and Lothar Vogel. Göttingen: Vandenhoeck & Ruprecht, 2010, 11-18.

_____. "Der Spätpietismus—ein vergessenes oder vernachlässigtes Kapitel der protestantischen Kirchengeschichte." *Pietismus und Neuzeit* 10 (1984): 124-151.

_____. "Der württembergische Pietismus." In *Geschichte des Pietismus*. Vol. 2. *Der Pietismus im achtzehnten Jahrhundert*, ed. Martin Brecht and Klaus Deppermann, 225-295. Göttingen: Vandenhoeck & Ruprecht, 1995.

_____. "Die Bedeutung der Bibel im deutschen Pietismus." In *Geschichte des Pietismus*. Vol. 4. *Glaubenswelt und Lebenswelten*, ed. Martin Brecht and Klaus Deppermann, 102-120. Göttingen: Vandenhoeck & Ruprecht, 2004.

_____. "Die Berleburger Bibel. Hinweise zu ihrem Verständnis." In *Ausgewählte Aufsätze*. Vol. 2. *Pietismus*, 369-408. Stuttgart: Calwer Verlag, 1997.

_____. "Einleitung." In *Geschichte des Pietismus*. Vol. 1. *Der Pietismus vom siebzehnten bis zum frühen achtzehnten Jahrhundert*, ed. Martin Brecht, 1-10. Göttingen: Vandenhoeck & Ruprecht, 1995.

_____. "Johann Albrecht Bengels Theologie der Schrift," *Zeitschrift für Theologie und Kirche* 64 (1967): 99-120.

_____. "Philipp Matthäus Hahn und der Pietismus im mittlerem Neckarraum." *Blätter für württembergische Kirchengeschichte* 77 (1977): 101-131.

Breul, Wolfgang and Christian Soboth, eds. *"Der Herr wird seine Herrlichkeit an uns offenbahren." Liebe, Ehe und Sexualität im Pietismus.* Halle: Verlag der Franckeschen Stiftung, 2011.

Breul, Wolfgang, Marcus Meier and Lothar Vogel, eds. *Der radikale Pietismus. Perspectiven der Forschung.* Göttingen: Vandenhoeck & Ruprecht, 2010.

Breul, Wolfgang. *"Ehe und Sexualität im radikalen Pietismus."* In *Der radikale Pietismus. Perspectiven der Forschung.* Edited by Wolfgang Breul, Marcus Meier and Lothar Vogel. Göttingen: Vandenhoeck & Ruprecht, 2010, 403-418.

Breymayer, Reinhard. "Ein radikaler Pietist im Umkreis des jungen Goethe: Der Frankfurter Konzertdirektor Johann Daniel Müller alias Elias/Elias Artista (1716 bis nach 1785)." *Pietismus und Neuzeit* 9 (1983): 180-237.

Büchsel, Jürgen. *Gottfried Arnold. Sein Verständnis von Kirche und Wiedergeburt.* Witten: Luther Verlag, 1970.

Bunners, Christian. "Gerhard Tersteegen's Lieder im Gesangbuch. Ein Rezeptionsgeschichtlicher Beitrag." In *Gerhard Tersteegen – Evangelischer Mystik inmitten der Aufklärung*, ed. Manfred Kock and Jürgen Thiesbonenkamp, 77-100. Cologne: Rheinland Verlag, 1997.

Bushman, Richard L. *Joseph Smith and the Beginnings of Mormonism.* Urbana, Ill.: University of Illinois Press, 1984.

Butler, Jon. "The Future of American Religious History: Prospectus, Agenda, Transatlantic *Problematique*." *William and Mary Quarterly*, 3d ser., 42 (1985): 167-183.

_____. "The Spiritual Importance of the Eighteenth Century." In *In Search of Peace and Prosperity. New German Settlements in Eighteenth-Century Europe and America*, ed. Hartmut Lehmann, Hermann Wellenreuther and Renate Wilson, 101-114. University Park, Pa.: Pennsylvania State University Press, 2000.

Clasen, Claus-Peter. *Die Wiedertaüfer im Herzogtum Württemberg und in benachbarten Herrschaften. Ausbreitung, Geisteswelt und Soziologie.* Stuttgart: W. Kohlhammer Verlag, 1965.

Claus, W. *Württembergische Väter. Von Brastberger bis Dann. Bilder aus dem christlichen Leben Württemberg.* Vol. 2. Stuttgart/Calw: Verlag der Vereinssbuchhandlung, 1905.

Cleveland, Catherine C. *The Great Revival in the West 1797-1805.* Gloucester, Mass.: Peter Smith, 1959.

Clouse, Robert G. *The Meaning of the Millennium. Four Views.* Downers Grove, Ill.: InterVarsity Press, 1977.

Coclanis, Peter A. "Atlantic World or Atlantic/World?" *William and Mary Quarterly,* 3d ser., 63 (October 2006): 725-742.

Cohen, Charles L. "The Post-Puritan Paradigm of Early American Religious History." *William and Mary Quarterly,* 3d ser., 54 (October 1997): 695-722.

Conty, Patrick. *The Genesis and Geometry of the Labyrinth: Architecture, Hidden language, Myths, and Rituals.* Rochester, Vt.: Inner Traditions, 2002.

Crawford, Michael J. *Seasons of Grace. Colonial New England's Revival Tradition in Its British Context.* New York: Oxford University Press, 1991.

Dächsel, August. *Das Alte Testament.* Band 2. 3d ed. Leipzig: A. Deichert, 1890.

Decker-Hauff, Hansmartin. "Prinzessin Antonia, Herzogin von Württemberg (1613-1679) und die Teinacher Lehrtafel." *Blätter für Württembergische Kirchengeschichte* 92 (1992): 89-96.

De Cunzo, Lu Ann, Therese O'Malley, Michael J. Lewis, George E. Thomas, and Christa Wilmanns-Wells. "Father Rapp's Garden at Economy: Harmony Society Culture in Microcosm." In *Landscape Archaeology: Reading and Interpreting the American historical Landscape,* ed. Rebecca Yamin and Karen Bescherer Metheny, 91-117. Knoxville: University of Tennessee Press, 1996.

Deppermann, Andreas. *Johann Jakob Schütz und die Anfänge des Pietismus.* Tübingen: Mohr Siebeck, 2002.

Dietrich, Christian and Ferdinand Brockes. *Die Privat-Erbauungsgemeinschaften innerhalb der evangelischen Kirchen Deutschlands.* Stuttgart: Buchhandlung des Deutschen Philadelphiavereins, 1903.

Durnbaugh, Donald F. "Believers Church Perspectives on the Lord's Supper." In *The Lord's Supper. Believers Church Perspectives,* ed. Dale R. Stoffer, 63-78. Waterloo, Ont.: Herald Press, 1997.

―――. "Radikaler Pietismus als Grundlage deutsch-amerikanischer kommunaler Siedlungen." *Pietismus und Neuzeit* 16 (1990): 112-131.

Durnbaugh, Hedwig T. "Ephrata, Amana, Harmonie: Drei christliche kommunistische Gemeinschaften in Amerika. Beispiele kirchlicher Identität im Kirchenlied." *Bulletin der Internationalen Arbeitsgemeinschaft für Hymnologie* 24 (1996): 203-218.

Duss, John Samuel. *The Harmonists: A Personal History.* Harrisburg: Pennsylvania Book Service, 1943.

Ehmer, Hermann. "Blumhardt und die Christentumsgesellschaft." *Blätter für württembergische Kirchengeschichte*, 106 (2006): 13-26.

———. "Der ausgewanderte Pietismus: Pietistische Gemeinschaftsprojekte in Nordamerika." In *Das Echo Halles: Kulturelle Wirkungen des Pietismus*, ed. Rainer Lächele, 315-357. Tübingen: Bibliotheca Academica, 2001.

———. "Johann Georg Rapp (1757-1847)." In *Kirchengeschichte Württembergs in Porträts: Pietismus und Erweckungsbewegung*, 219-243. Holzgerlingen: Hänssler Verlag, 2001.

———. "Württemberg." In *Theologische Realenzyklopädie.* Vol. 36, ed. Gerhard Müller, 343-368. New York: W. de Gruyter, 2004.

Ehmer, Hermann, Heinrich Frommer, Rainer Jooß and Jörg Thierfelder, eds. *Gott und die Welt in Württemberg.* Stuttgart: Calwer, 2000.

Eißner, Daniel. "Zum Verhältnis religiöser Autonomieerklärung und sozialer Erfahrungen pietistischer Laien, vornehmlich der Handwerker." In *"Aus Gottes Wort und eigner Erfahrung gezieget." Erfahrung – Glauben, Erkennen und Gestalten im Pietismus.* Edited by Christian Soboth and Udo Sträter. Halle: Verlag der Franckeschen Stiftung, 2012: 209-223.

Eller, David B. "The Recovery of the Love Feast in German Pietism." In *Confessionalism and Pietism. Religious Reform in Early Modern Europe.* Edited by Fred van Lieburg. Mainz: Verlag Philipp von Zabern, 2006: 11-30.

Ensign, Chauncey David. "Radical German Pietism (c. 1675- c. 1760)." Ph.D. diss., Boston University, 1955.

Erb, Peter C. "Gerhard Tersteegen, Christopher Saur, and Pennsylvania Sectarians." *Brethren Life and Thought* 20 (Summer 1975): 153-157.

Estep, William R. Jr. "Contrasting Views of the Lord's Supper in the Reformation of the Sixteenth Century." In *The Lord's Supper. Believers Church Perspectives*, ed. Dale R. Stoffer, 53-62. Waterloo, Ont.: Herald Press, 1997.

Findeisen, Hans-Volkmar. "Pietismus in Fellbach 1750-1820 zwischen sozialem Protest und bürgerlicher Anpassung." Ph.D. diss., University of Tübingen, 1985.

Finger, Thomas N. *A Contemporary Anabaptist Theology.* Downer's Grove, Ill.: Inter-Varsity Press, 2004.

Föll, Renate. *Sehnsucht nach Jerusalem: Zur Ostwanderung schwäbisher Pietisten.* Tübingen: Tübinger Vereinigung für Volkskunde, 2002.

Franz, Hermann. "Joseph II." In *Catholic Encyclopedia*, Vol. 8, ed. Charles G. Herbermann, Edward A. Pace, Conde B. Pallen, Thomas J. Shahan, and John J. Wynne, 508-511. New York: Appleton, 1910.

Frei, Hans. *The Eclipse of the Biblical Narrative.* New Haven: Yale University Press, 1974.

Fritz, Eberhard. "Christian Gottlob Pregizer und die 'Pregizianer.' Zur Genese einer pietischen Gruppierung im frühen 19. Jahrhundert." In *Tradition und Fortschritt. Württembergische Kirchengeschichte im Wandel.* Edited by Norbert Haag et al. Epfendorf/Neckar: Bibliotheca Academica, 2008: 239-268.

_____. "Das Ende des langen 18. Jahrhunderts. Erfahrungen des frühen Pietismus als Voraussetzung für die Selbstorganization und Institutionalisierung des württembergischen Pietismus im frühen 19. Jahrhundert." In *"Aus Gottes Wort und eigner Erfahrung gezieget." Erfahrung – Glauben, Erkennen und Gestalten im Pietismus.* Edited by Christian Soboth and Udo Sträter. Halle: Verlag der Franckeschen Stiftung, 2012: 879-892.

_____. "Die Kirche im Dorf. Studien und Beobachtungen zur kirchlichen Situation in der ländlichen Gemeinde des Herzogtums Württemberg." *Zeitschrift für Württembergische Landesgeschichte* 52 (1993): 155-178.

_____. "Die Konsolidierung des württembergischen Pietismus im frühen 19. Jahrhundert. Eine Befragung von 1821 als als Dokument einer Übergangszeit." *Blätter für württembergische Kirchengeschichte,* 108-109 (2008-2009): 363-392.

_____. "Entstehung von pietistischen Privatversammlungen und Widerstand gegen die Liturgie von 1809." *Blätter für württembergische Kirchengeschichte* 91 (1991): 173-188.

_____. "Johann Christoph Blumhardt und die Anhänger des Johann Georg Rapp in Iptingen." *Blätter für Württembergische Kirchengeschichte,* 106 (2006): 27-37.

_____. "Johann Georg Rapp (1757-1847) und die Separatisten in Iptingen. Mit einer Edition der relevanten Iptinger Kirchenkonventsprotokolle." *Blätter für Württembergische Kirchengeschichte* 95 (1995): 129-203.

_____. "Kirch seye eben ein steinen Hauß, Gott wohne nicht darinn. Verhörprotokolle als Quellen zur Geschichte des radikalem Pietismus in Württemberg." *Blätter für württembergische Kirchengeschichte* 102 (2002): 69-108.

_____. "Pietismus in Württemberg. Zum Stand der Forschung." *Blätter für württembergische Kirchengeschichte,* 112 (2012): 31-43.

_____. *Radikaler Pietismus in Württemberg: Religiöse Ideale im Konflikt mit gesellschaftlichen Realitäten.* Epfendorf: Bibliotheca Academica, 2003.

_____. "Schweizerisch-württembergische Verbindungen im radikalen Pietismus. Indizien für frühe kulturelle Beziehungen zwischen beiden Ländern?" In *Gegen den Strom. Der radikale Pietismus im schweizerischen und internationalen Beziehungsfeld.* Edited by J. Jürgen Seidel. Zürich: Dreamis, 2012: 225-238.

———. "Urchristliches Ideal und Staatsraison: Württembergische Separatistinnen und Separatisten im Zeitalter Napoleans." *Zeitschrift für Württembergische Landesgeschichte* 59 (2000): 71-98.

———. "'Viele fromme Seelen und Querköpfe.' Der Ihinger Hof im Besitz der Familie von Leiningen als Ort der Kommunikation zwischen Pietisten und Separatisten im 18.Jahrhundert." *Blätter für Württembergische Kirchengeschichte* 111 (2011): 161-189.

Fritz, Friedrich. "Die Wiedertäufer und der württembergische Pietismus." *Blätter für württembergische Kirchengeschichte* 43 (1939): 81-109.

———. "Johann Jakob Friederich. Ein Kapitel vom Glauben an einer Bergungsort und an das Tausendjähriges Reich." *Blätter für württembergische Kirchengeschichte* 41 (1937): 140-197.

———. "Konventikel in Württemberg von der Reformationszeit bis zum Edikt von 1743." *Blätter für württembergische Kirchengeschichte* 50 (1950): 65-121.

Gäbler, Ulrich. "Geschichte, Gegenwart, Zukunft." In *Geschichte des Pietismus.* Vol. 4. *Glaubenswelt und Lebenswelten*, ed. Hartmut Lehmann, 19-48. Göttingen: Vandenhoeck & Ruprecht, 1995.

Games, Alison. "Beyond the Atlantic: English Globetrotters and Transoceanic Connections." *William and Mary Quarterly*, 3d ser., 63 (October 2006): 675-742.

Gestrich, Andreas. "Ehe, Familie, Kinder im Pietismus. Der 'gezähmte Teufel.'" In *Geschichte des Pietismus.* Vol. 4. *Glaubenswelt und Lebenswelten*, ed. Hartmut Lehmann, 498-521. Göttingen: Vandenhoeck & Ruprecht, 1995.

Goertz, Hans-Jürgen. *Religiöse Bewegungen in der Frühen Neuzeit.* Vol. 20. *Enzyklopädie Deutscher Geschichte*. Munich: R. Oldenbourg, 1993.

Grabbe, Hans-Jürgen, ed. *Halle Pietism, Colonial North America, and the Young United States.* Kempten: Franz Steiner Verlag, 2008.

Groß, Andreas. *Missionare und Kolonisten. Die Basler und Hermannsburger Mission in Georgien am Beispiel der Kolonie Katharinenfeld 1818-1870.* Hamburg: LIT, 1998.

Grossmann, Sigrid. *Friedrich Christoph Oetingers Gottesvorstellung. Versuch einer Analyse seiner Theologie.* Göttingen: Vandenhoeck & Ruprecht, 1979.

Groth, Friedhelm. *Die "Wiederbringung aller Dinge" im württembergischen Pietismus.* Göttingen: Vandenheock & Ruprecht, 1984.

Grutschnig-Kieser, Konstanze. *Der "Geistliche Würtz-Kräuter und Blumen-Garten" des Christoph Schütz. Ein radikalpietistisches "Universal-Gesang-Buch."* Göttingen: Vandenhoeck & Ruprecht, 2006.

Gutekunst, Eberhard. "Das Pietistenrescript von 1743," *Blätter für Württembergische Kirchengeschichte* 94 (1994): 9-26.

Haag, Norbert. "Bücher auf dem Lande. Zum Genese des Ulmer Pietismus." *Blätter für württembergische Kirchengeschichte* 89 (1989): 48-98.

Habrich, Christa. "Alchemie und Chemie in der pietistischen Tradition." In *Goethe und der Pietismus*, ed. Hans-Georg Kemper and Hans Schneider, 45-77. Tübingen: Niemeyer, 2001.

Hall, Stuart George. "Typologie." In *Theologische Realenzyklopädie*. Vol. 34, ed. Gerhard Müller, 208-224. New York : W. de Gruyter, 2002.

"Harmony. Commemorating the Centennial of the Borough of Harmony, Pennsylvania, 1838-1938." [Pamphlet]. Harmony, Pa.: [s.n.], 1938.

Hartman, Sven S. "Alchemie I." In *Theologische Realenzyklopädie*. Vol. 2, ed. Gerhard Krause and Gerhard Müller, 195-199. Berlin: W. de Gruyter, 1978.

Häussermann, Friedrich. "Theologia Emblematica. Kabbalistische und alchemistische Symbolik bei Fr. Chr. Oetinger und deren Analogien bei Jakob Boehme." *Blätter für württembergische Kirchengeschichte* 68/69 (1968-1969): 207-346.

Hermelink, Heinrich. *Geschichte der evangelischen Kirche in Württemberg von der Reformation bis zur Gegenwart.* Stuttgart/Tübingen: Rainer Wunderlich Verlag, 1949.

Hippel, Wolfgang von. *Auswanderung aus Südwestdeutschland: Studien zur württembergischen Auswanderung und Auswanderungspolitik im 18. und 19. Jahrhundert.* Stuttgart: Klett-Cotta, 1984.

Hirsch, Emanuel. *Geschichte der neuern evangelischen Theologie*. Vol. 2. Gütersloh: C. Bertelsmann, 1951.

Hohmuth, Jürgen, ed. *Labyrinthe & Irrgärten*. München: Frederking & Thaler Verlag, 2003.

Holthaus, Stephen. "Prämillenniarismus in Deutschland. Historische Anmerkungen zur Eschatologie der Erweckten im 19. und 20. Jahrhundert." *Pietismus und Neuzeit* 20 (1994): 191-211.

Holtz, Sabine. *Theologie und Alltag. Lehre und Leben in den Predigten der Tübinger Theologen 1550-1750.* Tübingen: J.C. Mohr, 1993.

Hudson, Winthrop S. *Religion in America*. 2d ed. New York: Scribner's Sons, 1973.

Hughes, Richard T. *The American Quest for the Primitive Church.* Urbana, Ill.: University of Illinois Press, 1988.

Hughes, Richard T., and Crawford Leonard Allen. *Illusions of Innocence: Protestant Primitivism in America, 1630-1875.* Chicago: University of Chicago Press, 1988.

Hutchinson, William R. "From Unity to Multiplicity: American Religion(s) as a Concern for the Historian." *Amerikastudien* 38 (1993): 343-350.

Jakubowski-Tiessen, Manfred. "Eigenkultur und Traditionsbildung." In *Geschichte des Pietismus*. Vol. 4. *Glaubenswelt und Lebenswelten*, ed. Hartmut Lehmann, 195-210. Göttingen: Vandenhoeck & Ruprecht, 1995.

Janzen, Wolfram. "Gerhard Tersteegen." In *Biographisch-Bibliographisches Kirchenlexikon Online*, Band XI (1996) Spalten 674-695. http://www.bautz.de/bbkl. [Accessed December 14, 2006].

Jung, Martin H. "1836 – Wiederkunft Christi oder Beginn des Tausendjährigen Reichs? Zur Eschatologie Johann Albrecht Bengels und seine Schüler." *Pietismus und Neuzeit* 23 (1997): 131-151.

———. "Johanna Eleonora Petersen." In *The Pietist Theologians*, ed. Carter Lindberg, 147-160. Malden, Mass.: Blackwell, 2005.

———. *Nachfolger, Visionärinnen, Kirchenkritiker. Theologie- und frömmigkeits-geschichtliche Studien zum Pietismus*. Leipzig: Evangelische Verlagsanstalt, 2003.

Kannenberg, Michael. "Erweckte Erinnerungsorte. Eine millenarische Topographie des württembergischen Pietismus." *Blätter für württembergische Kirchengeschichte*, 111 (2011): 193-203.

———. "Der württembergische Erweckungspietismus als millenarischer Kommunikationsraum." *Blätter für württembergische Kirchengeschichte*, 112 (2012): 145-155.

———. *Verschleierte Uhrtafeln. Endzeiterwartungen im württembergischen Pietismus zwischen 1818 und 1848*. Göttingen: Vandenhoeck & Ruprecht, 2007.

Klein, Wassilios. "Propheten/Prophetie." In *Theologische Realenzyklopädie*. Vol. 27, ed. Gerhard Müller, 473-476. New York: Walter de Gruyter, 1997.

Köster, Beate. *Die Luther Bibel im frühen Pietismus*. Bielefeld: Luther-Verlag, 1984.

Kraus, Georg. "Predestination." In *Dictionary of the Reformation*, ed. Klaus Ganzer and Bruno Steimer, trans. Brian McNeil, 253-254. New York: Crossroad, 2002.

Kroh, Andreas. *Die Wiederentdeckung des Heidelberger Katechismus nach Sturm und Drang des radikalen Pietismus. Ein Beitrag zur Geschichte der reformierte Kirche in Wittgenstein*. Rödingen: ß-Verlag, 2011.

Laishley, Lilan. "The Harmonist Labyrinths." *Caerdroia* 32 (2001): 8-20.

Langen, August. *Der Wortschatz des Deutschen Pietismus*. 2d ed. Tübingen: Max Niemeyer, 1968.

Lashlee, Ernest L. "Johannes Kelpius and His Woman in the Wilderness. A Chapter in the History of Colonial Pennsylvania Religious Thought." In

Glaube Geist Geschichte. Festschrift für Ernst Benz, 327-338. Leiden: Brill, 1967.

Lauchert, Friedrich. "Pietism." In *The Catholic Encyclopedia*. Vol. 12, ed. Charles G. Herbermann, Edward A. Pace, Conde B. Pallen, Thomas J. Shahan, and John J. Wynne, 80-82. New York: Appleton, 1911.

Lehmann, Hartmut. "Der politische Widerstand gegen die Einführung des neuen Gesangsbuches von 1791 in Württemberg." *Blätter für Württembergische Kirchengeschichte* 66-67 (1966-67): 247-263.

———. "Endzeiterwartung und Auswanderung: Der württembergische Pietist Johann Michael Hahn und Amerika." In *Alte und Neue Welt in wechselseitiger Sicht. Studien zu der transatlantischen Beziehungen im 19. und 20. Jahrhundert*, ed. Hartmut Lehmann, 185-204. Göttingen: Vandenhoeck & Ruprecht, 1995.

———. "Four Competing Concepts for the Study of Religious Reform Movements, including Pietism, in Early Modern Europe and North America." In *Confessionalism and Pietism. Religious Reform in Early Modern Europe*. Edited by Fred van Lieburg. Mainz: Verlag Philipp von Zabern, 2006: 313-322.

———. "Neupietismus und Säkularisierung. Beobachtungen zum sozialen Umfeld und politischen Hintergrund von Erweckungsbewegung und Gemeinschaftsbewegung." *Pietismus und Neuzeit* 15 (1989): 40-58.

———. "Pietism in the World of Transatlantic Religious Revivals." In *Pietism in Germany and North America 1680-1820*. Edited by Jonathan Strom, Hartmut Lehmann and James Van Horn Melton. Burlington, VT.: Ashgate, 2009: 13-21.

———. *Pietismus und weltliche Ordnung in Württemberg vom 17. bis zum 20. Jahrhundert*. Stuttgart: W. Kohlhammer, 1969.

———. "Pietistic Millenarianism in Late Eighteenth-Century Germany." In *The Transformation of Political Culture. England and Germany in the Late Eighteenth Century*, ed. Eckhart Hellmuth, 327-338. London:German Historical Institute, 1990.

Leibbrandt, Georg. *Die Auswanderung aus Schwaben nach Rußland 1816-1823*. Stuttgart: Ausland und Heimat Verlag, 1928.

Leube, Hans. *Die Reformidee in der Deutschen Lutherischen Kirche zur Zeit der Orthodoxie*. Leipzig: Dörffling & Francke, 1924.

Lewis, Michael J. "Harmonist Architecture: Its Sources and Meaning." Paper presented at the Fifteenth Annual Historic Communal Studies Conference, Winston-Salem, North Carolina, Oct. 6-9, 1988, 51-84.

Littell, Franklin H. "Radical Pietism in American History." In *Continental Pietism and Early American Christianity*, ed. F. Ernest Stoeffler, 164-183. Grand Rapids, Mich.: Eerdmans, 1976.

Lockridge, Ross F. *The Labyrinth of New Harmony Indiana.* New Harmony, Ind.: New Harmony Memorial Commission, 1941.

Longenecker, Stephen L. *Piety and Tolerance. Pennsylvania German Religion, 1700-1850.* Metuchen, N.J.: Scarecrow Press, 1994.

Louth, Andrew. "Allegorical Interpretation." In *A Dictionary of Biblical Interpretation*, ed. R. J. Coggins and J. L. Houlden, 12-14. Philadelphia: Trinity Press, 1990.

Ludewig, Hansgünter. *Gebet und Gotteserfahrung bei Gerhard Tersteegen.* Göttingen: Vandenhoeck & Ruprecht, 1986.

Mälzer, Gottfried. *Johann Albrecht Bengel. Leben und Werk.* Stuttgart: Calwer Verlag, 1979.

Manship, Greg Edward. "Feminist Sophialogy. A Philosophical and Theological Analysis of Feminist Sophialogy and Sophia-Christology: An Evangelical Response." M.A. thesis, Trinity Evangelical Divinity School, 1994.

Martin, Ann Smart. "Material Things and Cultural Meanings: Notes on the Study of Early American Material Culture." *William and Mary Journal*, 3d ser., 53, no. 1 (Jan. 1996): 5-12.

Matthew, William Henry. *Mazes and Labyrinths: A General account of Their History and Developments.* London: Longmans, 1922.

Matthias, Markus. "Bekehrung und Wiedergeburt." In *Geschichte des Pietismus.* Vol. 4. *Glaubenswelt und Lebenswelten*, ed. Hartmut Lehmann, 49-79. Göttingen: Vandenhoeck & Ruprecht, 1995).

Maurer, Hans-Martin. "Das Haus Württemberg und Rußland." *Zeitschrift für württembergische Landesgeschichte* 48 (1989): 201-222.

Maurer, Wilhelm. *Historical Commentary on the Augsburg Confession.* Translated by H. George Anderson. Philadelphia: Fortress Press, 1986.

McClendon, James Wm. "The Believers Church in Theological Perspective." In *The Wisdom of the Cross*, ed. Stanley Hauerwas, Chris K. Huebner, Harry J. Huebner and Mark Thiessen Nation, 309-326. Grand Rapids: Eerdmans, 1999.

McGrath, Alister. *Iustitia Dei. A History of the Christian Doctrine of Justification.* Vol. 2. *From 1500 to the Present Day.* Cambridge: Cambridge University Press, 1986.

———. *Justification by Faith.* Grand Rapids: Academie Books, 1988.

McNeil, Brian. "Typology." In *A Dictionary of Biblical Interpretation*, ed. R. J. Coggins and J. L. Houlden, 713-714. Philadelphia: Trinity Press, 1990.

Meier, Marcus. *Die Schwarzenauer Neutäufer. Genese einer Gemeindebildung zwischen Pietismus und Täufertum.* Göttingen: Vandenhoeck & Ruprecht, 2008.

Miller, Arlene A. "The Theologies of Luther and Boehme in the Light of their Genesis Commentaries." *Harvard Theological Review* 63 (1970): 261-303.

Miller, Melvin. "Education in the Harmony Society, 1805-1905." Ph.D. diss., University of Pittsburgh, 1972.

Mirbt, Carl. "Pietism." In *The New Schaff-Herzog Encyclopedia of Religious Knowledge*. Vol. 9, ed. Samuel Macauley Jackson and George William Gilmore, 53-67. Grand Rapids, Mich.: Baker, 1951.

Moore, R. Lawrence. *Religious Outsiders and the Making of Americans*. New York: Oxford University Press, 1986.

Muller, Richard A. "Biblical Interpretation in the Era of the Reformation: A View from the Middle Ages." In *Biblical Interpretation in the Era of the Reformation*, ed. Richard A. Muller and John L. Thompson, 3-22. Grand Rapids: Eerdmans, 1996.

Muncy, Raymond Lee. *Sex and Marriage in Utopian Communities: 19th Century America*. Bloomington, Ind.: Indiana University Press, 1973.

Murray, Iain H. *Revival and Revivalism. The making and Marring of American Evangelicalism 1750-1858*. Edinburgh: Banner of Truth, 1994.

Narr, Dieter. "Berührung von Aufklärung und Pietismus in Württemberg des 18. Jahrhunderts." *Blätter für württembergische Kirchengeschichte* 66/67 (1966-1967): 264-277.

Noll, Mark. "Pietism." In *Evangelical Dictionary of Theology*. 2d ed., ed. Walter A. Elwell, 855-858. Grand Rapids, Mich.: Baker, 2001.

Nordhoff, Charles. *The Communistic Societies of the United States*. New York: Hilary House, 1875.

Oliver, W. H. *Prophets and Millennialists. The Uses of Biblical Prophecy in England from the 1790s to the 1840s*. Auckland: Auckland University Press, 1978.

O'Brien, Susan. "A Transatlantic Community of Saints. The Great Awakening and the First Evangelical Network, 1735-1755." *American Historical Review* 91 (1986): 811-832.

Oehler, K. Eberhard. "Michael Hahn und seine Lieder." *Blätter für württembergische Kirchengeschichte* 108/109 (2008-2009): 427-436.

O'Malley, J. Steven. *Early German-American Evangelicalism: Pietist Sources on Discipleship and Sanctification*. Lanham, Md.: Scarecrow Press, 1995.

_____. *John Seybert and the Evangelical Heritage*. Lexington, Ky.: Emeth Press, 2008.

_____. "Pietistic Influence on John Wesley: Wesley and Gerhard Tersteegen." *Wesleyan Theological Journal* 31 (Fall, 1996): 48-70.

_____. "The Influence of Gerhard Tersteegen in the Documents of Early German-American Evangelicalism." In *Pietism, Revivalism and Moderni-*

ty, 1650-1850. Edited by Fred van Lieburg. Newcastle upon Tyne: Cambridge Scholars Publishing, 2008, 232-255.

Ott, Alice T. "Community in 'Companies:' The Conventicles of George Rapp's Harmony Society compared to those in Württemberg Pietism and the Brüderunität." In *Pietism and Community in Europe and North America, 1650-1850*. Edited by Jonathan Strom. Leiden: Brill, 2010, 249-277.

―――――. "Singing to the Lord a New Song: Hymnody and Liturgy in George Rapp's Harmony Society, 1805-1847." In *The Pietist Impulse in Christianity*. Edited by Christian T. Collins Winn, et al. Eugene, Org.: Pickwick Publications, 2011, 233-244.

Pace, Edward A. "Quietism." In *The Catholic Encyclopedia*. Vol. 12, ed. Charles G. Herbermann, Edward A. Pace, Conde B. Pallen, Thomas J.Shahan, and John J. Wynne, 608-610. New York: Appleton, 1911.

Pältz, Eberhard H. "Böhme." In *Theologische Realenzyklopädie*. Vol. 6, ed. Gerhard Krause and Gerhard Müller, 748-754. New York: Walter de Gruyter, 1980).

―――――. "Jacob Boehmes Hermeneutik, Geschichtsverständnis und Sozialethik." Habilitation thesis, Schiller Universität, Jena, 1961.

Pelikan, Jaroslav. *Luther the Expositor. Introduction to the Reformer's Exegetical Writings*. St. Louis: Concordia, 1959.

―――――. *Reformation of Church and Dogma (1300-1700)*. Chicago: University of Chicago Press, 1984.

Peshke, Erhard. "Spener's Wiedergeburtslehre und ihr Verhältnis zu Franckes Lehre von der Bekehrung." In *Traditio—Krisis—Renovatio aus theologischer Sicht*, ed. Bernd Jaspert and Rudolf Mohr, 206-224. Marburg: Elwert, 1976.

Pitzer, Donald E. "Progressive Education in Harmonist New Harmony: 1814-1824." *Contemporary Education* 58, no. 2 (Winter 1987): 67-74.

Pitzer, Donald E., and Josephine M. Elliott. *New Harmony's First Utopians, 1814-1824*. 2d ed. Historic New Harmony, Ind.: University of Southern Indiana Press, 2002.

Popkin, Beate. "Der Kirchenkonvent in Württemberg." *Blätter für württembergische Kirchengeschichte* 96 (1996): 98-118.

Rauh, Horst Dieter. *Im Labyrinth der Geschichte. Die Sinnfrage von der Aufklärung zu Nietzsche*. München: Wilhelm Fink Verlag, 1990.

Rauscher, Viktor. "Des Separatisten G. Rapp Leben und Treiben." *Theologische Studien aus Württemberg* 6 (1885): 253-313.

Renkewitz, Heinz. *Hochmann von Hochenau (1620-1721)*. Witten: Luther-Verlag, 1969.

Reventlow, Henning Graf, Walter Sparn,and John Woodbridge, eds., *Historische Kritik und biblischer Kanon in der deutschen Aufklärung*. Wiesbaden: Harrossowitz, 1988.

Rock, P. M. J. "Golden Rose." In *Catholic Encyclopedia*, Vol. 6. Edited by Charles G. Herbermann, Edward A. Pace, Conde B. Pallen, Thomas J. Shahan, and John J. Wynne, 629-630. New York: Robert Appleton, 1909.

Roeber, A. Gregg. "Creating Order with Two Orders of Creation." In *Halle Pietism, Colonial North America, and the Young United States*. Edited by Hans-Jürgen Grabbe. Kempten: Franz Steiner Verlag, 2008: 289-308.

_____. "Der Pietismus in Nordamerika im 18. Jahrhundert." In *Geschichte des Pietismus*. Vol. 2. *Der Pietismus im achtzehnten Jahrhundert*, ed. Martin Brecht and Klaus Deppermann. Gottingen: Vandenhoeck & Rupprecht, 1995: 666-699.

_____. "The Problem of the Eighteenth Century in Transatlantic Religious History." In *In Search of Peace and Prosperity. New German Settlements in Eighteenth-Century Europe and America*, ed. Hartmut Lehmann, Hermann Wellenreuther and Renate Wilson, 115-138. University Park, Penn.: Pennsylvania State University Press, 2000.

Roth, John D. "Pietism and the Anabaptist Soul." In *The Dilemma of Anabaptist Piety*, ed. Stephen L. Longenecker, 17-33. Bridgewater, Va.: Forum for Religious Studies, 1997.

Runyon, Theodore. "German Pietism, Wesley, and English and American Protestantism." In *Halle Pietism, Colonial North America, and the Young United States*. Edited by Hans-Jürgen Grabbe. Kempten: Franz Steiner Verlag, 2008: 135-145.

Sauer, Paul. "Not und Armut in den Dörfern des Mittleren Neckarraumes in vorindustriellen Zeit." *Zeitschrift für württembergische Landesgeschichte* 41 (1982): 131-149.

Schaab, Meinrad, Hansmartin Schwarzmaier, and Michael Klein. *Handbuch der Baden-Württembergischen Geschichte*. Vol. 2. *Die Territorien im Alten Reich*. Stuttgart: Klett-Cotta, 1995.

Schad, Petra. *Buchbesitz im Herzogtum Württemberg im 18. Jahrhundert am Beispiel der Amtsstadt Wildberg und des Dorfes Bissingen/Enz*. Stuttgart: Thorbecke Verlag, 2002.

Schäfer, Gerhard. *Zu erbauen und zu erhalten das rechte Heil der Kirche: Eine Geschichte der Evangelischen Landeskirche in Württemberg*. Stuttgart: J. F. Steinkopf, 1984.

_____. "Zum württembergischen Gesangbuch vom Jahr 1791." *Zeitschrift für württembergische Landesgeschichte* 41 (1982): 400-413.

Schempp, Hermann. *Gemeinschaftssiedlungen auf religiöser und weltanschaulicher Grundlage*. Tübingen: Mohr, 1969.

Schipflinger, Thomas. "Sophia bei J. Boehme." *Una Sancta* 41, no. 3 (1986): 195-210.

_____. *Sophia-Maria. A Holistic View of Creation*. Translated by James Morgante. York Beach, Maine: Samuel Weiser, 1998.

Schlereth, Thomas J. "Material Culture Studies and Social History Research." *Journal of Social History* 16 (1983): 111-143.

Schmidt, Martin. "Das Frühchristentum in der evangelisch-lutherischen Überlieferung für das Verständnis und die Autorität der altkirchlichen Tradition." *Oecumenica* 6 (1971-1972): 88-110.

———. "Spener's Wiedergeburtslehre." In *Wiedergeburt und Neuer Mensch* by Martin Schmidt. Witten: Luther Verlag, 1969.

Schmidt, Martin, ed. *Der Pietismus als Theologische Erscheinung*. Vol. 2. *Gesammelte Studien zur Geschichte des Pietismus*. Edited by Kurt Aland. Göttingen: Vandenhoeck & Ruprecht, 1984.

Schnabel-Schüle, Helga. "Calvinistische Kirchenzucht in Württemberg? Zur Theorie und Praxis der württembergischen Kirchenkonvente." *Zeitschrift für württembergische Landesgeschichte* 52 (1993): 169-223.

Schneider, Hans. "Der radikaler Pietismus im 17. Jahrhundert." In *Geschichte des Pietismus*. Vol. 1, ed. Martin Brecht, 391-439. Göttingen : Vandenhoeck & Ruprecht, 1990.

———. "Der radikale Pietismus im 18. Jahrhundert." In *Geschichte des Pietismus*. Vol. 2, *Der Pietismus im achtzehnten Jahrhundert*, ed. Martin Brecht and Klaus Deppermann, 107-197. Gottingen: Vandenhoeck & Rupprecht, 1995.

———. "Der radikale Pietismus in der neueren Forschung." *Pietismus und Neuzeit* 8 (1983): 15-42 and 9 (1984): 117-151.

———. "The Attitude of Pietists toward Anabaptism." In *The Dilemma of Anabaptist Piety*, ed. Stephen L. Longenecker, 47-55. Bridgewater, Va.: Forum for Religious Studies, 1997.

———. "Ruckblick und Ausblick." In *Der radikale Pietismus. Perspectiven der Forschung*. Edited by Wolfgang Breul, Marcus Meier and Lothar Vogel. Göttingen: Vandenhoeck & Ruprecht, 2010, 451-467.

———. "Understanding the Church—Issues of Pietist Ecclesiology." In *Pietism and Community in Europe and North America, 1650-1850*. Edited by Jonathan Strom. Leiden: Brill, 2010, 15-35.

Scholem, Gerschom. *Kabbalah*. New York: Meridian, 1974.

Schultze, Wilhelm August. "Friedrich Christoph Oetinger und die Kabbala." *Judaica* 4 (1948): 268-274.

Schütt, Hans-Werner. *Auf der Suche nach dem Stein der Weisen. Die Geschichte der Alchemie*. Munich: Beck, 2000.

Schwarzmaier, Hansmartin, Hans Fenske, Bernhard Kirchgässner, Paul Sauer, Meinrad Schaab, and Michael Klein. *Handbuch der Baden-Württembergischen Geschichte*. Vol. 3. *Vom Ende des Alten Reiches bis zum Ende der Monarchien*. Stuttgart: Klett-Cotta, 1992.

Schwartz, Hillel. *The French Prophets. The History of a Millenarian Group in Eighteenth-Century England.* Berkeley, Calif.: University of California Press, 1980.

Scott, Martin. *Sophia and the Johannine Jesus.* Sheffield: Sheffield Academic Press, 1992.

Seagle, Gladys Inez. "The Rappist Revolt against Lutheranism, 1804-1904." Ph.D. diss., New York University, 1963.

Seastoltz, R. Kevin. *A Sense of the Sacred: Theological Foundations of Sacred Architecture and Art.* New York: Continuum, 2005.

Seeberg, Erich. *Gottfried Arnold. Die Wissenschaft und die Mystik seiner Zeit.* Darmstadt: Wissenschaftliche Buchgesellschaft, 1964.

Shantz, Douglas H. *An Introduction to German Pietism. Protestant Renewal at the Dawn of Modern Europe.* Baltimore, MD: Johns Hopkins University Press, 2013.

_____. "The Origin of Pietist Notions of New Birth and New Man. Alchemy and Alchemists in Gottfried Arnold and Johann Heinrich Reitz." In *The Pietist Impulse in Christianity.* Edited by Christian T. Collins Winn, et al. Eugene, Org.: Pickwick Publications, 2011, 29-41.

Sheppard, Gerald T., and William E. Herbrechtsmeier. "Prophecy." In *Encyclopedia of Religion*, 2d ed., ed. Lindsay Jones, 7423-7429. Detroit: Thomson Gale, 2005.

Sick, Walter Alfred. *Die Conventikel des Separatismus in Baden.* Schönau-Schwarzwald: A. Müller, 1936.

Stayer, James M. "Täufer/Täuferische Gemeinschaften I." In *Theologische Realenzyklopädie.* Vol. 32, ed. Gerhard Müller, 597-617. Berlin: W. de Gruyter, 2001.

Steffler, Alva William. *Symbols of the Christian Faith.* Grand Rapids: Eerdmans, 2002.

Stein, K. James. "Philipp Jakob Spener (1636-1705)." In *The Pietist Theologians. An Introduction to Theology in the Seventeenth and Eighteenth Centuries*, ed. Carter Lindberg, 84-99. Malden, Mass.: Blackwell, 2005).

Stein, Stephen J. "Some Thoughts on Pietism in American Religious History." In *Pietism in Germany and North America 1680-1820.* Edited by Jonathan Strom, Hartmut Lehmann and James Van Horn Melton. Burlington, VT.: Ashgate, 2009: 23-32.

Steinmetz, David C. "Hermeneutic and Old Testament Interpretation in Staupitz and the Young Martin Luther." *Archiv für Reformationsgeschichte* 70 (1979): 24-58.

_____. "Martin Luther." In *Dictionary of Biblical Interpretation*, ed. John H. Hayes, 96-98. Nashville: Abingdon, 1994.

_____. *Luther in Context.* Bloomington, Ind.: Indiana University Press, 1986.

Stoeffler, F. Ernst, ed. *Continental Pietism and Early American Christianity.* Grand Rapids, Mich.: Eerdmans, 1976.

_____. *German Pietism during the Eighteenth Century.* Leiden: E. J. Brill, 1973.

_____. *Mysticism in the Devotional Literature of Colonial Pennsylvania.* Allentown, Pa.: Pennsylvania German Folklore Society, 1949.

_____. *The Rise of Evangelical Pietism.* Leiden: E. J. Brill, 1965.

Stoffer, Dale R. "Anabaptized Pietism: The Schwarzenau Brethren." In *The Dilemma of Anabaptist Piety*, ed. Stephen L. Longenecker, 35-45. Bridgewater, Va.: Forum for Religious Studies, 1997.

Stotz, Charles Morse. *The Early Architecture of Western Pennsylvania: A Record of Building Before 1860 Based upon the Western Pennsylvania Architectural Survey, a Project of the Pittsburgh Chapter of the American Institute of Architects.* Introduction by Fiske Kimball. Pittsburgh: University of Pittsburgh Press, 1995.

_____. "Threshold of the Golden Kingdom. The Village of Economy and Its Restoration." *Winterthur Portfolio* 8 (2001): 122-169.

Strom, Jonathan, Hartmut Lehmann and James Van Horn Melton, eds. *Pietism in Germany and North America 1680-1820.* Burlington, VT.: Ashgate, 2009.

Sutton, Robert P. *Communal Utopias and the American Experience: Religious Communities, 1732-2000.* Westport: Praeger, 2003.

Tanner, Fritz. *Die Ehe im Pietismus.* Zurich: Zwingli Verlag, 1952.

Telle, Joachim. "Alchemie II." In *Theologische Realenzyklopädie.* Vol. 2, ed. Gerhard Krause and Gerhard Müller, 199-227. Berlin: W. de Gruyter, 1978.

"The Grotto at Old Economy." [Pamphlet]. Ambridge, Pa.: Harmony Press, 1959.

Tholuck, Friedrich August Gotttreu. *Vorgeschichte des Rationalismus.* Vol. 2. *Das kirchliche Leben des siebzehnten Jahrhunderts bis in die Anfänge der Aufklärung.* Berlin, Wiegandt und Grieben, 1861.

Thurman, Lawrence. "An American Alchemist." *Rosicrucian Digest* 32 (March 1954): 101.

Trautwein, Joachim. *Die Theosophie Michael Hahns und ihre Quellen.* Stuttgart: Calwer Verlag, 1969.

Van Andel, Cornelis Pieter. "Gerhard Tersteegen." In *Orthodoxie und Pietismus*, ed. Martin Greschat, 331-346. Stuttgart: Kohlhammer, 1982.

Vandervelde, George. "Believers Church Ecclesiology as Ecumenical Challenge." In *The Believers Church: A Voluntary Church*, ed. William H. Brackney. Kitchener, Ont.: Pandora, 1998.

Versluis, Arthur. "Western Esotericism and the Harmony Society." http://www.esoteric.msu.edu/Versluis.html. [Accessed October 15, 2006].

Von Schlachta, Astrid. "Anabaptism, Pietism and Modernity: Relationships, Changes, Paths." In *Pietism, Revivalism and Modernity, 1650-1850*. Edited by Fred van Lieburg. Newcastle upon Tyne: Cambridge Scholars Publishing, 2008, 1-22.

Vosa, Aira. "Die Ehe bei Jakob Böhme und Johann Georg Gichtel." In *"Der Herr wird seine Herrlichkeit an uns offenbahren." Liebe, Ehe und Sexualität im Pietismus*. Edited by Wolfgang Breul and Christian Soboth. Halle: Verlag der Franckeschen Stiftung, 2011: 81-88.

Wallmann, Johannes. *Der Pietismus*. Göttingen: Vandenhoeck & Ruprecht, 1990.

———. "Frömmigkeit und Gebet." In *Geschichte des Pietismus*. Vol. 4. *Glaubenswelt und Lebenswelten*, ed. Hartmut Lehmann, 80-101. Göttingen: Vandenhoeck & Ruprecht, 1995.

———. "Kirchlicher und radikaler Pietismus. Zu einer kirchengeschichtlichen Grundunterscheidung." In *Der radikale Pietismus. Perspectiven der Forschung*. Edited by Wolfgang Breul, Marcus Meier and Lothar Vogel. Göttingen: Vandenhoeck & Ruprecht, 2010, 19-43.

———. *Philipp Jakob Spener und die Anfänge des Pietismus*. 2d exp. ed. Tübingen: Mohr, 1986.

———. "Pietismus – ein Epochenbegriff oder ein typologischer Begriff?" *Pietismus und Neuzeit* 30 (2004): 191-224.

———. "Pietismus und Orthodoxie: Überlegungen und Fragen zur Pietismusforschung." In *Geist und Geschichte der Reformation*, ed. Hanns Rückett. Berlin: de Gruyter, 1966.

Walker, Barbara. *A Women's Dictionary of Symbols and Sacred Objects*. San Francisco: Harper, 1988.

Walvoord, John F. *The Revelation of Jesus Christ*. Chicago: Moody Press, 1966.

Ward, W. R. *Christianity under the Ancien Regime 1648-1789*. Cambridge: Cambridge University Press, 1999.

———. *Early Evangelicalism. A Global Intellectual History 1670-1789*. Cambridge: Cambridge University Press, 2006.

———. *The Protestant Evangelical Awakening*. Cambridge: Cambridge University Press, 1992.

Weeks, Andrew. *Boehme. An Intellectual Biography of the Seventeenth-Century Philosopher and Mystic*. Albany, NY: State University of New York Press, 1991.

Weigelt, Horst. "Der Pietismus im Überrgang vom 18. zum 19. Jahrhundert." In *Geschichte des Pietismus*. Vol. 2. *Der Pietismus im achtzehnten*

Jahrhundert, ed. Martin Brecht and Klaus Deppermann, 701-754. Göttingen: Vandenhoeck & Ruprecht, 1995.

Wellenreuther, Hermann. "Die atlantische Welt des 18. Jahrhunderts. Überlegungen zur Bedeutung des Atlantiks für die Welt der Frommen im Britischen Weltreich." In *Transatlantische Religionsgeschichte. 18. bis 20. Jahrhundert*, ed. Hartmut Lehmann, 9-30. Göttingen: Wallstein, 2006.

Werbick, Jürgen. "Penance, Sacrament." In *Dictionary of the Reformation*, ed. Klaus Ganzer and Bruno Steimer, trans. Brian McNeil, 239. New York: Crossroad, 2002.

Wessel, Carola. "The Impact of Halle pietism on North America as Reflected in German-Language Broadsides." In *Halle Pietism, Colonial North America, and the Young United States*. Edited by Hans-Jürgen Grabbe. Kempten: Franz Steiner Verlag, 2008: 161- 177.

Wetzel, Richard D. *Frontier Musicians on the Connoquenessing, Wabash, and Ohio: A History of the Music and Musicians of George Rapp's Harmony Society, 1805-1906.* Athens, Ohio: Ohio University Press, 1976.

_____. "The Hymnody of George Rapp's Harmony Society." *The Hymn* 23, no. 1 (Jan. 1972): 19-29.

Weyer-Menkhoff, Martin. *Christus, das Heil der Natur. Entstehung und Systematik der Theologie Friedrich Christoph Oetingers.* Göttingen: Vandenhoeck & Ruprecht, 1990.

Williamson, Beth. *Christian Art: A Very Short Introduction.* New York: Oxford University Press, 2004.

Wilson, Bryan, ed. *Patterns of Sectarianism: Organisation and Ideology in Social and Religious Movements.* London: Heinemann, 1967.

Wilson, Bryan. "An Analysis of Sect Development," in *Patterns of Sectarianism: Organisation and Ideology in Social and Religious Movements*, ed. B. R. Wilson, 22-45. London: Heinemann, 1967.

_____. *The Social Dimensions of Sectarianism: Sects and New Religious Movements in Contemporary Society.* Oxford: Clarendon Press, 1990.

Wilson, Ellen Judy. "Aufklärung." In *Encyclopedia of the Enlightenment*, ed. Peter Hanns Reill, 22-23. New York: Facts on File, 1996.

_____. "Pietism." In *Encyclopedia of the Enlightenment*, ed. Peter Hanns Reill, 328. New York: Facts on File, 1996.

Wilson, Peter H. *War, State and Society in Württemberg, 1677-1793.* Cambridge: Cambridge University Press, 1995.

Wilson, Renate. *Pious Traders in Medicine. A German Pharmaceutical Network in Eighteenth-Century North America.* University Park, Pa.: Pennsylvania State University, 2000.

Winn, Christian T. Collins, et al. eds. *The Pietist Impulse in Christianity*. Eugene, Org.: Pickwick Publications, 2011.

Zwink, Eberhard, and Joachim Trautwein. "Geistliche Gedichte und Gesänge für die nach Osten eilenden Zioniden, 1817." *Blätter für württembergische Kirchengeschichte* 94 (1994): 47-90.

www.ingramcontent.com/pod-product-compliance
Lightning Source LLC
Chambersburg PA
CBHW031542300426
44111CB00006BA/141

The Asbury Theological Seminary Series in Pietist/Wesleyan Studies

This volume is published in collaboration with the Center for the Study of World Christian Revitalization Movements, a cooperative initiative of Asbury Theological Seminary faculty. Building on the work of the previous Wesleyan/Holiness Studies Center at the Seminary, the Center provides a focus for research in the Wesleyan Holiness and other related Christian renewal movements, including Pietism and Pentecostal movements, which have had a world impact. The research seeks to develop analytical models of these movements, including their biblical and theological assessment. Using an interdisciplinary approach, the Center bridges relevant discourses in several areas in order to gain insights for effective Christian mission globally. It recognizes the need for conducting research that combines insights from the history of evangelical renewal and revival movements with anthropological and religious studies literature on revitalization movements. It also networks with similar or related research and study centers around the world, in addition to sponsoring its own research projects.

In this title, Professor Alice Ott effectively challenges the consensus of extant interpretations of one of the leading figures in radical Pietism millennial communities in early nineteenth century American history, George Rapp and the Harmony/New Harmony Society. She convincingly engages a breadth of primary and secondary sources to demonstrate that his theology and ministry was based in a wide reading of radical and churchly Pietist literature, rather than being predominantly influenced by a single source, Jacob Boehme. This south German (Wuerttemberg)-originated transatlantic community found its new world home in Harmony, Pennsylvania, and then shifted for a decade to New Harmony, Indiana, before returning to its Pennsylvania base. Ott demonstrates that the literature produced by Rapp and his associates represents a multi-faceted engagement of a spectrum of theological, ethical, and ecclesial issues, set in an eschatological context. Its impact on its culture is also featured. Appropriate to this series, her study represents an empathetic yet critical examination of a key nineteenth century revitalization movement in American religious history, whose enduring legacy has now at last been brought to light.

J. Steven O'Malley
General Editor
The Asbury Theological Seminary Series in Christian Revitalization Studies